THE ARTWORK CAUGHT BY THE TAIL

OCTOBER Books

George Baker, Yve-Alain Bois, Benjamin H. D. Buchloh, Leah Dickerman, Hal Foster, Denis Hollier, Rosalind Krauss, Annette Michelson, Mignon Nixon, Malcolm Turvey, editors

Broodthaers, edited by Benjamin H. D. Buchloh

AIDS: Cultural Analysis/Cultural Activism, edited by Douglas Crimp

Aberrations: An Essay on the Legend of Forms, by Jurgis Baltrušaitis

Against Architecture: The Writings of Georges Bataille, by Denis Hollier

Painting as Model, by Yve-Alain Bois

The Destruction of Tilted Arc: Documents, edited by Clara Weyergraf-Serra and Martha Buskirk

The Woman in Question, edited by Parveen Adams and Elizabeth Cowie

Techniques of the Observer: On Vision and Modernity in the Nineteenth Century, by Jonathan Crary

The Subjectivity Effect in Western Literary Tradition: Essays toward the Release of Shakespeare's Will, by Joel Fineman

Looking Awry: An Introduction to Jacques Lacan through Popular Culture, by Slavoj Žižek

Cinema, Censorship, and the State: The Writings of Nagisa Oshima, by Nagisa Oshima

The Optical Unconscious, by Rosalind E. Krauss

Gesture and Speech, by André Leroi-Gourhan

Compulsive Beauty, by Hal Foster

Continuous Project Altered Daily: The Writings of Robert Morris, by Robert Morris

Read My Desire: Lacan against the Historicists, by Joan Copjec

Fast Cars, Clean Bodies: Decolonization and the Reordering of French Culture, by Kristin Ross

Kant after Duchamp, by Thierry de Duve

The Duchamp Effect, edited by Martha Buskirk and Mignon Nixon

The Artwork Caught by the Tail

Francis Picabia and Dada in Paris

George Baker

An OCTOBER Book

The MIT Press
Cambridge, Massachusetts
London, England

First MIT Press paperback edition, 2010

This book was set in Bembo by Graphic Composition, Inc.

Library of Congress Cataloging-in-Publication Data

Baker, George (George Thomas), 1970–.
The artwork caught by the tail : Francis Picabia and Dada in Paris / George Baker.
    p.   cm.
Includes bibliographical references and index.
ISBN 978-0-262-02618-5 (hardcover : alk. paper), 978-0-262-51486-6 (pb)
1. Dadaism—France—Paris. 2. Avant-garde (Aesthetics)—France—Paris—History—
20th century. 3. Picabia, Francis, 1879–1953. I. Title.

NX456.5.D3B34   2007
709.04′062—dc22

                                                                    2006036058

For my family

An eel, held by the tail, is not yet caught.

—Latin proverb

Contents

ACKNOWLEDGMENTS

It has been ten years since I first began to research and write this book. This is a long time. I sometimes find it hard to remember who I was when the writing began, or, indeed, why it began at all. However, in recent years, I often considered my work on this book entirely too hasty. I have fantasized that perhaps I should hold on to the book for just a little longer, or that I might never publish it at all. By this I meant not just to cover up its inevitable faults and weaknesses, but somehow to ensure that the work it involved, and the love it encompassed, would not end. The book had become a way of generating love, and also, debts beyond measure. Publishing it at least represents an opportunity to acknowledge some of these debts.

One origin of this book that I can remember lies with my dissertation. It would have been inconceivable without the unique space provided by Columbia University in the 1990s for the study of modernism, modernity, and the avant-garde. First and foremost, I thank my co-advisors at that time, Rosalind E. Krauss and Benjamin H. D. Buchloh. The immense challenge of their work and their intellectual generosity has been indispensable to my own formation as an art historian, a critic, and a writer. Of course working with the two of them together was a reasonably impossible task, given the chasm that separates their views and approaches to the avant-garde. No situation could have been better for a project, like this one, that deals with Dada.

My work on Dada, however, had its origins even earlier in a project undertaken while I was a Helena Rubinstein Fellow in the Independent Study Program of the Whitney Museum of American Art. I am particularly grateful to both

Jonathan Crary and Hal Foster, with whom I worked while attending the ISP, for the direction they provided at a crucial moment, and for the reconfigured visions of art history they both advocated. Interactions with Ron Clark and Mary Kelly were indispensable to the productivity of this moment for me.

But the origins of this project probably lie much further back in time. I thus need to thank several mentors who pushed me at the earliest stages toward my current work on the avant-garde and contemporary art. For the example of her teaching and her manner of inhabiting the field, few art historians have been more important to me than Linda Nochlin. Both Jonathan Weinberg and Maud Lavin introduced me to the study of Dada—one wants to say initiated me into it—and their example made working on modernism seem an important task in the present. More recently, Kaja Silverman has become, first, the interlocutor found in the darkness when one least expects it, and then, a close friend. Her lessons and her laughter have transformed this book.

My work was made possible by a series of fellowships and grants. A blissful period of research in France was facilitated by a Georges Lurcy Fellowship in 1997–1998; the initial writing was completed while I was the recipient of a Chester Dale Fellowship from the Center for Advanced Study in the Visual Arts in 1998–1999, and a Whiting Foundation Fellowship in 1999–2000. More recently, summer travel grants such as the Grant Family Foundation Research Fellowship and the Greenwood Fund from SUNY Purchase allowed for the dissertation to be extended into a book, a process brought to completion by another blissful return to France in 2003–2004 as the recipient of a postdoctoral fellowship from the Getty Research Institute.

In my editor at MIT Press, Roger Conover, this book has had on its side one of the great supporters today of the study of the avant-garde, and a connoisseur of Dada. To Marc Lowenthal, Assistant Editor at the Press, I also owe thanks for his regular prodding, and for sharing his intimate knowledge of Picabia's writings when this was needed most. The manuscript and my writing were much improved by the labors of Judy Feldmann. It was a pleasure to work again with Yasuyo Iguchi, to whom I am indebted for the beautiful cover and book design.

My work on Picabia was facilitated on all levels by the generosity of the Comité Picabia. I am grateful to the artist's widow, Olga Picabia, for granting me full access to Picabia's archives before her death in 2002. Beverley Calté and Jana Peltier provided images, advice, and enthusiastic support. I also thank Patrick Bailly-Cowell, Picabia's grandson, for image assistance from his collection and for reminiscences. Despite the often polemical rhetoric of my text—this is a book concerned with Dada after all—I am deeply indebted to prior scholars of Picabia's work, especially Michel Sanouillet, William Camfield, and Arnauld Pierre (who helped me illustrate here the sources for Picabia's images that he has discovered).

This text would have remained unpublished, however, without the aid of my indefatigable research assistant, Mika Yoshitake. She put aside her own important work on the Japanese neo-avant-garde for far too long to help bring this book to completion. The institutions and individuals who aided Mika and myself along the way are too numerous to list in full. I thank especially the staff of the Bibliothèque Littéraire Jacques Doucet, the Avery and MOMA Libraries, and the curator's library at the Centre Georges Pompidou. Enrique Juncosa, Head of the Curatorial Department of the Instituto Valenciano de Arte Moderno, Gérard Audinet of the Musée d'art moderne de la ville de Paris, and Julio Sims of the Getty Research Institute assisted in various ways. For advice and generosity with images and reproduction rights, I am indebted to Francis M. Naumann, Barbara Buhler Lynes of the Georgia O'Keeffe Museum, Laurie Klein of the Beinecke Rare Book and Manuscript Library, Magnus Malmros from the Moderna Museet, Joanna Cook and The Menil Collection, and Constance af Trolle of the Dansmuseet in Stockholm.

Parts of this book have been presented to my students at SUNY Purchase and now at UCLA, as well as to audiences at UC Berkeley, UC San Diego, Yale University, the Frick Collection, the Drawing Center, Princeton University, and in a bar on La Cienega called Mandrake. The responses I received on these occasions were invaluable, and often surprising. I am grateful to Leah Dickerman and the Center for Advanced Study in the Visual Arts for their invitation to take part in the "Dada Seminars," prior to Leah's recent retrospective of Dada at the National Gallery. Over the course of two years, our discussions proved the study of

Dada to be in a moment of utter transition, a condition that then spread (alarmingly) to this book. From this context, I thank especially T. J. Demos, Helen Molesworth, David Joselit, and Brigid Doherty. David and Brigid kept the dialogue alive by traveling to my seminar at UCLA to share further research on Duchamp and on Berlin Dada.

There have been two institutional homes for this book in recent years. One has been the magazine *OCTOBER* and the conversations with my fellow editors, most of whom I have already thanked here in their other capacities in my life and work. I need to extend special gratitude to Yve-Alain Bois, and also to Denis Hollier, who was a reader of this project in its earliest stages and a valuable skeptic in the face of all my attempts to relate Dada to Bataille.

The other home was found again when least expected, and far from this book's origins, namely, the Department of Art History at UCLA. Fully aware that such an atmosphere is not the norm, I almost feel that it should be unlawful for an academic environment to be so supportive and so fun. For their wisdom and welcome, I thank especially Miwon Kwon, Steven Nelson, Saloni Mathur, Hui-Shu Lee, and Aamir Mufti. David Ziegler and Susan Rosenfeld from the Visual Resource Collection provided last-minute support with images.

The first reader of early versions of most of the chapters that follow was Rachel Haidu. Her enthusiasm and critiques touched me, and I surely benefited from her bilingual abilities in French. I thank as well for their ideas and aid Rhea Anastas, Carlos Basualdo, Eric de Bruyn, Mark Godfrey, Christina Kiaer, Branden Joseph, Richard Meyer, Fido Rodenbeck, Felicity Scott, Margaret Sundell, and Kathryn Tuma. I reserve special thanks for Tom McDonough and Aruna D'Souza, my former colleague at Purchase, for the intensity of their dialogue.

Carl Ghazarossian provided consistent support and lessons in all things French. Not least, along with Lionel Chevalier, he also opened his home to me, just blocks away from Picabia's own, as a base for my research in Paris. It is ridiculous even to try to thank Ken Storer, the friend of a lifetime, who not only brought me to Carl, but also has fueled specific intellectual ambitions of mine since childhood, and recently helped me to settle—and thus to complete this project—in Los Angeles.

And in terms of the direction of my thinking on the avant-garde, I cannot begin to measure the importance of the challenge presented by the work and by my dialogue with a number of contemporary artists, including Knut Åsdam, Doug Ashford, Tom Burr, Gerard Byrne, James Coleman, Ann Burke Daly, Nancy Davenport, Tacita Dean, Eshrat Erfanian, Andrea Fraser, Pierre Huyghe, Gareth James and the collective Scorched Earth, Laura Larsen, Louise Lawler, Zoe Leonard, Simon Leung, Sharon Lockhart, Anthony McCall, Allan McCollum, Mike Minelli, Christian Philipp Müller, Nils Norman, Sarah Pierce, Andrea Robbins and Max Becher, Liisa Roberts, Jason Simon, Jim Welling, and Robert Whitman. Although he is no longer with us to receive my thanks, Leon Golub long ago advised and encouraged me, when I was just beginning to write about art. He made many things possible. All taught me invaluable lessons. If what we learn about dialogism is true, their voices and concerns are present in this text in ways beyond my calculation. But they are also there by calculation, for in reality, this book was written for them all.

The book is dedicated to my family, to my father and mother, George and Adrienne Baker, and my brother and sister, Thomas and Nicole Baker, who supported me in every possible way. Any words of gratitude that I could write here would betray the enormity of their contribution. And so I refuse to do so. Let it just be said that if a thinking of the gift informs much of what follows, it is a lesson that I did not learn in books.

Finally, I must thank Silvia DiPierdomenico. Here I find myself again without words. I could point to the example that her own work as a writer has been for me. I could point to her doubt and her joy. Only she will know how deeply the events of our life together have touched my writing and my ideas in this book. They almost brought them to a halt. "L'operazione dell'angoscia è riuscita." She will recognize these words. But she was always this book's greatest distraction, and for that, I thank her most of all.

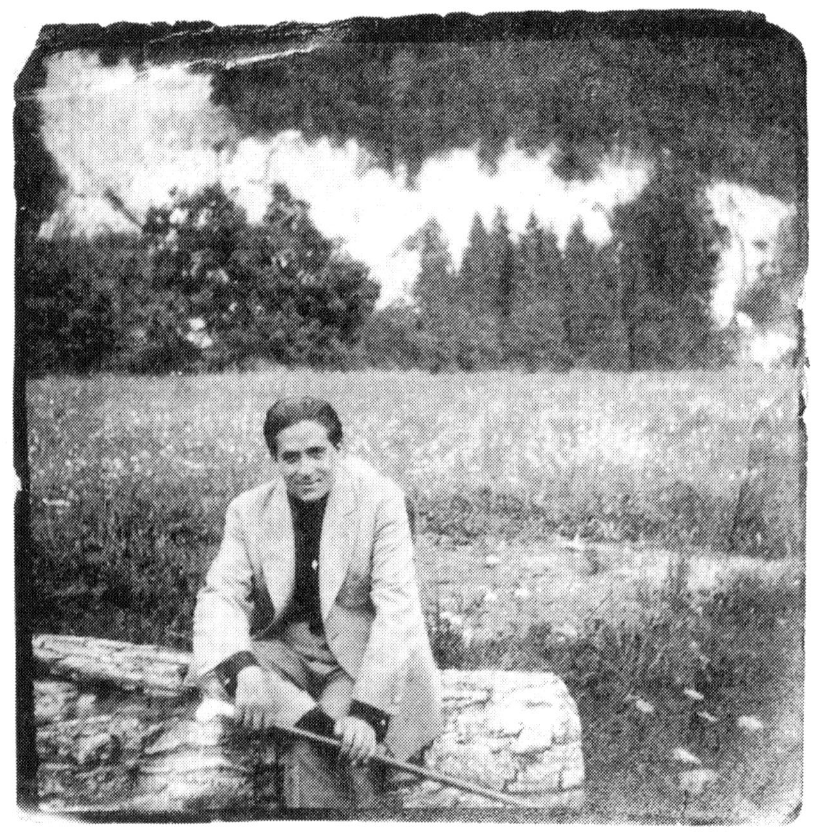

Francis Picabia in the Jura, c. 1912. Photograph. Collection Patrick Bailly-Cowell.

MIT Press books may be purchased at special quantity discounts for business or sales promotional use. For information, please email special_sales@mitpress.mit.edu or write to Special Sales Department, The MIT Press, 55 Hayward Street, Cambridge, MA 02142.

This book was set in Bembo by Graphic Composition, Inc., and was printed and bound in the United States of America.

Library of Congress Cataloging-in-Publication Data

Baker, George (George Thomas), 1970–.
The artwork caught by the tail : Francis Picabia and Dada in Paris / George Baker.
    p.   cm.
Includes bibliographical references and index.
ISBN 978-0-262-02618-5 (hardcover : alk. paper)
1. Dadaism—France—Paris. 2. Avant-garde (Aesthetics)—France—Paris—History—
20th century. 3. Picabia, Francis, 1879–1953. I. Title.

NX456.5.D3B34   2007
709.04′062—dc22

                                                     2006036058

10 9 8 7 6 5 4 3 2 1

Universal Prostitution

You will find on every page this simple word: Farewell.

—*Philippe Soupault,* Proverbe *no. 2 (March 1920)*

Zone.—It was not the first time they had traveled together, which had occurred the summer before the fall of 1912 when, by all accounts after one too many cocktails with Claude Debussy, Francis Picabia and Guillaume Apollinaire took to one of the painter's automobiles and drove the long road from Paris to Boulogne and then continued on to England by boat. That spontaneous trip was meant to reunite the painter and the poet with Gabrielle Buffet, Picabia's wife, on her summer vacation in England, but the voyage became difficult owing to the poet's drunken boast that he spoke English turning out to be not quite true. No one on the boat understood him and he later admitted to Picabia that his dialect in fact was "ancient Irish." After five days they returned, and, as the painter recalled years later, thanks to his friend's extraordinary memory, the poet knew English by that point just as well as he did—which was a joke, for, despite several later voyages to America, he too hardly spoke a word of it. As they returned from this country where neither painter nor poet understood the language, and where, it seemed to them, the claim to speak a vanquished and ancient tongue could sow the seeds of greatest confusion, as they watched the signs pass by in unfamiliar cadences, they discussed abstract art. They called it, in the patois of the French avant-garde of that all-important year of 1912, "pure painting," by which they meant a painting that broke with any reference to the outside world of physical appearance—a world that in 1912 was growing ever darker anyway, ever more crepuscular, although it must be admitted that they may have seen things differently, mistaking the impending gloom for morning's light. It must also be admitted that they saw things differently when it came to abstraction, as the poet fresh from spouting Old Irish at the English violently repudiated the most modern of pictorial possibilities as "inhuman," as entirely "unintelligible." Each time the Picabias tried to recall this conversation, which took place en route to Paris in Boulogne over a dinner meant to wash away the memory of their English repasts, it seemed that their friend was taking the side of the Cubists, whether the "realism of the object" espoused by the newly consolidated academic Cubists, or the infamous hostility to abstraction that would always be the creed of the poet's great friend, Pablo Picasso, just then himself barely free of the haze of the near-abstract hermetic phase, as it is called, of Cubist painting. Apollinaire's testimony, however, is as confusing as that hermetic fog from which, although it was not yet entirely clear to them, all that was most vital in the avant-garde culture of the twentieth century would emerge. *More than anything,* Apollinaire concluded, in a book on Cubism begun in that same summer of 1912 and finished immediately upon the friends' return from England, *artists are men who want to become inhuman.* Who can say whether the poet shared this thought with his friends? Or whether he even meant this equally confusing statement as praise? For no one knows whether the half-hearted Nietzscheanism of the phrase was penned before the midsummer dinner in Boulogne, coloring the vagueness of the poet's remarks, or only in its aftermath, when, having sensed the irreversible tide carrying not only artists but all of Europe toward the "unintelligible," the poet offered up his thought as something like a slogan for the epoch.

Even then, far from Boulogne in the beer halls of Bavaria, a twenty-five-year-old friend of both painter and poet had taken the prophetic phrase as his own without, surely, having heard a word of it. Although it is entirely possible instead that Apollinaire's maxim came into being only in the wake of experiencing the most recent work of Marcel Duchamp, completed in that summer of 1912 during a short-lived exile in the city of Munich. After spending the months from late June until early October in and around this southern German capital, for reasons that were never made entirely clear to anyone except himself, although perhaps the reasons for this voyage were known to him least of all, the young artist returned to Paris with two major new paintings, *The Bride* and *The Passage from the Virgin to the Bride,* the first of which he presented to Picabia as a gift. His friend was impressed by these entirely modest canvases, so much smaller than his own and, as it were, expressly made for traveling, canvases in which the older man understood the younger's solution to the Cubist dilemma. Gone indeed were the imploded landscapes and desiccated still-lifes of Cubism; gone, as well, Picabia noted, any reference to a world where singular or self-contained objects could be said to exist at all. In their place the painter saw before his eyes a series of irregular facets forever leaching into one another, not one of whose shapes matched that of any other. He saw a noisome stew of earth tones in an infinite array of transitions, from clay to burnt ocher to umber, from butter cream to raw sienna and back to yellow, a collection of chocolates both light and dark, the whole highlighted in unhealthy nets of feeble green, or sunk into a deep but quiet ash, before subsiding into the profound blackness of the surround. He saw the Cubist obsession with *passage,* as it was called in French, borrowed and elaborated from Paul Cézanne's paintings in which each object exerts an effect on everything that surrounds it, each brushstroke forms a continuum that annihilates separate viewers, spaces, things—he saw this *passage* become finally the sole basis of painting, an activity now understood not as a mimetic recording of a world that preexists it, like a memory or a monument, but as perpetual transition, the very model of endless transformation. And yet at the same time he saw this *passage* literalized as if it were a joke, made over into an actual passage, considered as a voyage between states—"the passage," as his friend inscribed one work, "from the virgin to the bride." Whenever Picabia tried to picture this scene, which he did so often that it seemed as if he were compelled, he found himself dwelling instead on Apollinaire's maxim, and, conversely, whenever he attempted to recall that phrase, he saw Duchamp's work, so completely did the visions of poet and artist complement one another, so totally had painting become in these works an art of "becoming," even of a "becoming inhuman," as the poet's words summoned up from the otherwise abstract field of the Munich paintings a passage not only from virgin to bride, but a journey from body to machine, evoking a melancholic but shifting landscape of limbs and viscera, gears and pistons and connecting rods, diagrammatic vectors and utilitarian dotted lines. And it is because of the fact that journeys of course can never really be remembered—despite the fact that an entire industry now called tourism has arisen to deny this fact, and an army of travelers covers the globe with an endless snapping of cameras as if to freeze their every movement for posterity—it is precisely because that which perpetually changes can never really be recalled, and even memories themselves are constantly evolving and transforming themselves from one moment to the next, that upon his return to Paris, the young Marcel Duchamp immediately abandoned the art of memories.

The artist was thus free to accept the invitation that arrived when, scarcely ten days after his return to the French capital, Picabia suggested departing once more on a trip in the company of Apollinaire. This trip too was meant to reunite the friends with Gabrielle, now on a harvest vacation with her mother at their ancestral home in the faraway mountains of the Jura. And as today when traveling between distant countries one flies under cover of darkness, perhaps in order to avoid an inevitable sense of dislocation, or perhaps with the hope of escaping the voyage altogether in the mists of sleep, the three men climbed as always into Picabia's automobile for what became a nighttime drive that quickly obliterated any trace of the autumn foliage that had descended little by little that October, like the spread of a bloody wound, across the entirety of the French countryside. Memory is divided on the character of this murky trip to the borderlands of France, where, according to some, the friends were greeted by a landscape ever more desolate as they wound their route from Paris, and where, as they climbed up and up into the Alps in search of the tiny village of Etival—a town that even today counts only a few hundreds of people among its population—the night gave way to drenching sheets of impenetrable rain, causing Picabia to lose his way from time to time along washed-out mountain roads made almost impassable to his motored vehicle. Picabia, however, remembered things differently. He remembered, above all, the eternally light spirit of Apollinaire who hailed the immense night through which they traveled by never ceasing to sing a childlike song of his own invention, and which, so Picabia claimed, was full of references to primitives and to machines, like a nursery rhyme for the then-quickly-fading infancy of the modern world. Behind this memory one suspects in reality another event of that same year of 1912 when, just before the beginning of its fateful summer, Picabia accompanied both Duchamp and Apollinaire to the theater to witness a startling production of Raymond Roussel's *Impressions of Africa*. But if Apollinaire did in all truth greet the miserable night with song, his chant then was already a memory, a reminder among the friends of a momentous occasion, even a pact suggesting that Roussel's voyage was now their own, as they continued to speed by automobile through the endless night. The young Marcel began to think this way, as even before they reached their destination, the voyage in Picabia's car suggested to him a grand project, something to replace the abandoned activity of painting, a Rousselian fantasy based on the "idea of a colony" with several characters, "five nudes, one the chief," who "form a tribe." These "five nudes" with one at the lead were literally inspired by Picabia's automobile, like a graft or a translation, with the machine's five tires—*cinques pneus*—rhyming in French with the word for nude or *nu,* the fifth wheel that is the spare positioned, as was the custom in those early days of travel by automobile, on high. Here were the "five nudes, one the chief," who, like the endless rotation of Picabia's tires through the night, gave birth to the idea of a work of art that would no longer *represent* but *embody* motion and transformation, and gave birth literally within Duchamp's imaginings to another character, the "headlight child," for whom the artist invented an enigmatic string of descriptions which no one has fathomed to this day. The headlight child could be a "comet," the artist averred, "which would have its tail in front." It was the "divine blossoming of this machine-mother." It was like "the primitive's Jesus," and it "will have to be *radiant with glory.*" It was a kind of vector, imagined by Duchamp as a line, meeting in battle another "infinite"—or rather, he concluded, "indefinite"—path in the endless Jura-Paris road. Such were the thoughts of the young Marcel as the older painter's car lamps cut a narrow swath through the black pitch before them, picking out here and there the wayward road, but touching or connecting with nothing, ever reaching and ever hurrying on in front of the three friends toward their distant goal. It seemed as if their trip might never end. Only much later, after the artists' safe arrival in Etival, perhaps even after their return to Paris, did the young Marcel take pen to paper and place his imaginings of the dark voyage into words. Now he could volatize, allowing memory to sweep along the relentless muddy path. His first title was grand: *The chief of the 5 nudes extends little by little his power over the Jura–Paris road*. He found this too "ambivalent." The title was changed: *The chief of the 5 nudes increases little by little his power over the Jura–Paris road*. In the languorous sprawl of the words, slowly churning, the artist named an artwork that even then was not done changing shape, a work of art that, or so it seemed, would never put a halt to its variation, but that was baptized, eventually—and more economically, it comes as a surprise to realize—*The Bride Stripped Bare by Her Bachelors, Even*.

Arrival in Etival, in the vague borderland that the French call the "Zone," heralded a period of country pleasures somehow outside of time, with forest walks and excessive feasting on delicacies such as wild morels, fresh cream, the first autumn game, and earthy local wines. But Gabrielle remembered one night above all others. She remembered the group huddled together against the sudden chill of the evening air, a fire of fragrant pine logs sending its far-flung emissaries dancing along the inadequately polished beams of their farmhouse parlor's ceiling, with Apollinaire's Italianate profile emerging out of the darkness in high relief and, as it were, floating upon the air, a beacon in the shadows. It was a night of recited poetry, one of which struck the assembled friends as more revelatory than its companions, opening up to them, as it did, a string of childhood memories that the poet otherwise never allowed himself to mention. But this poem too began with the automobile, and with modernity in all its forms, as the poet now invented a seemingly inexhaustible list of slogans for the epoch.

You are tired at last of this old world

O shepherd Eiffel Tower the flock of bridges bleats at the morning

You have had enough of life in this Greek and Roman antiquity

Even the automobiles here seem to be ancient

The poet's voice gained speed in the darkness, gathering up all his listeners as if in readiness for another voyage. The "You" to whom his first line was addressed began to shift, even to travel as it seemed to Picabia, from self to other and back again, covering greater distances than their minds were at first prepared to follow.

You alone in all Europe are not antique O Christian faith
The most modern European is you Pope Pius X
And you whom the windows look down at shame prevents you
From entering a church and confessing this morning
You read prospectuses catalogues and posters which shout aloud
Here is poetry this morning and for prose there are the newspapers

If Gabrielle was moved emotionally by the poet's subsequent confession of his memories, an entire panorama of the shame and melancholy of childhood and the bitter aftertaste of its dispersal, Picabia sensed another motion that evening in his friend's insistent cataloging of restless pronouns, as well as a host of other verbal shape-shifters, so to speak, pushing the poem's connections forward as if its metaphors were no longer frozen evocations, but were in danger at any moment of becoming real. *Voilà la poésie ce matin,* the poet read, and the painter discerned amid the piles of adverts and posters, beyond the nonsynchronous modernity mistaken by the poet for antiquity with all its heralds and its augurs, a repeated performance of equally vertiginous leaps through space and time, a movement that only certain words could signal, the platform for so many immediate voyages, so many dusty memories hurtling through the years to return and present their humble treasures at his feet. The painter began to feel dizzy in the face of the incessant connectives, the relentless lurching: *Tu. Vous. Voilà. Te voici.*

Here is the young street and you are once again a little child . . .

Here you are in Marseilles amid the watermelons

Here you are in Coblenz at the Hotel of the Giant

Here you are in Rome sitting under a Japanese medlar tree

Here you are in Amsterdam with a girl you find pretty and who is
   ugly . . .

You are in Paris at the *juge d'instruction*
Like a criminal you are placed under arrest
You have made sorrowful and happy trips
Before noticing that the world lies and grows old
You suffered from love at twenty and thirty
I have lived like a fool and wasted my time
You no longer dare look at your hands and at every moment I
   want to burst out sobbing
For you for her I love for everything that has frightened you

As the reading eventually gave way to stunned silence, Picabia's vertigo was complete. It seemed to the painter that he stood at the edge of an abyss. Only Gabrielle's mother dared to break the mute spell that embraced them all, like a blanket against the cold. But what do you call it? the old woman asked. The poet hemmed and he hawed, the poem was declared unfinished, nameless, an anonymous proposition for the moment like its labile string of "you's" and "I's." And then he turned, inspired, the flames glinting softly across his features and softly glinting, like a field bathed in an other-worldly orange light, the last stragglers from the innumerable rays of sunshine by which we are bombarded every day, and he announced: I will call it "Zone." The title was site-specific. It signaled a place outside of modernity, created by modernity. It named a place of the outside, a limit, a borderland. The name was an interregnum, pointing to a place in between—but in between what, of course, is the question that the poet's listeners asked themselves. It was a question that the older painter never tired of answering, as something like Dada began that night for Francis Picabia, in the sap-scented shadows, caught between and along the imaginings of the Jura–Paris Road and of "Zone." "Adieu, adieu," the poet concluded, in his newborn work's penultimate verse.[1] Farewell, farewell.

This is not a book on Dada.—I have often imagined that the best, if not the only way to introduce a book on Dada is to open with a statement of that which the book *will not* be. And so: This will not be a book on Dada. While it looks closely at the Dada work of Francis Picabia from the end of the First World War to the beginnings of Surrealism in 1924, it is also not exactly a monograph on Picabia. Art history has already been blessed with at least two of these, and a catalogue raisonné is on the way. Instead of seeing all of Picabia's oeuvre as cut from a single cloth—from his early Postimpressionism to his Orphism to his Dada years to his later art historical pastiches and realist paintings based on photography—this book argues passionately for the singularity of Picabia's Dada strategies.[2] But it also argues for the specificity of tactics that emerged only *after* the war, at the start of Dada in Paris, thus splitting Picabia's Dada work in two.

Although art history has long considered the so-called mechanomorphs and object-portraits that Picabia produced during the war, and mostly in New York, as central to Dada's canon, this book will not be an account of these works (at least not primarily). This may seem perverse: the artist himself publicly stated that these works and years were constitutive of Dada, and spent most of the time-period covered in this book trying to distance himself from the official life of the movement, while embodying it through dissidence nonetheless.[3] But this moment, the immediate aftermath of the war, has remained problematic for modernist art history. It is a lost period for the avant-garde, an interregnum, no longer the heroic years of Dada (in New York) but not yet the shibboleth that became French Surrealism; and supposedly witnessing the withering of the utopic claims of a once triumphant Cubism for the eclectic or reactionary "return to order" of antimodernist neo-classicism. When named at all, the years just prior to 1924 have been called a formless *époque flou;* the shattered avant-garde of the time has remained indistinct as well, a *mouvement flou.* Marginal in every sense, these years marked, ironically, the apex of Picabia's influence within the historical avant-garde, the years when it could convincingly be argued that this otherwise marginal actor within the grand narratives of modernism was in fact the most important cultural figure of the day.

A marginal period, a marginal figure, a blind-spot for art history: It is the argument of this book that from this half-forgotten, not-yet-congealed historical moment can emerge a rereading of the terms of Dada, a revision of its central practices. More: From this nebulous blind-spot, from the margins and the borderlands of the interregnum, a reversal can be achieved, a shifting of Picabia from the margins of modernism to its center, as well as a revision of the actions and the progression of the avant-garde in general and of its supposedly central formal or critical paradigms.

An anti-monograph on a marginal figure in the moment of the *mouvement flou,* the moment of the dissolution of Dada: this book's counterintuitive writhings, I promise you, do not end here. Instead of attempting to chart Picabia's course through the years in question, a complete and total narrative of his role within Dada in Paris, this book isolates a representative series of Dada "activities"—as we once pointed to a "Surrealist activity," or, later, a "Structuralist activity"—case studies for a collection of Dada practices that art history has not yet recognized. Following the line of Picabia's critical strategies at this historical moment, and presented chronologically (to an extent), the case studies are organized by chapter around recognized mediums or newly established strategies of modernist work: "Dada Drawing," "Dada Painting," "Dada Photography," "Dada Abstraction," "Dada Cinema," and "Dada Montage." The reader will eventually discover that one of the case studies—namely photography—doesn't concern itself with Picabia at all, focusing instead on a specific reaction to Picabia's work by the artist Man Ray. In almost all the chapters, Picabia amounts to but one of several key figures.

The monograph falls here again and, to make matters potentially worse, the reader should also immediately perceive that in its stead there seems to be little internal coherence to the Dada "categories" that my case studies set out to trace, or, perhaps, "invent." There are mediums—drawing, painting, photography, cinema—but not all of them. Where does "abstraction" fit in, and what of "montage"—genres, perhaps, or tactics, maybe? And if mediums are enumerated, the missing ones seem crucial—where is sculpture?—and, linked to this question, the genres also seem incomplete—if this is a book on Dada, where is the readymade?[4]

The answer to this last question might be: everywhere and nowhere, as, on the one hand, this is not a book "on" Dada, and yet, on the other, it is a book that sees the readymade as a much larger cultural phenomenon than just a crucial Dada invention of Marcel Duchamp. The readymade becomes here (it became for Picabia) almost a "theoretical object," to paraphrase Rosalind Krauss in a different domain, perhaps even *the* theoretical object of the avant-garde, a modality by means of which the various artistic mediums and modernist genres could be ruptured, surely, but also reformed, potentially recast. Conceived as a tool less of destruction than of reinvention, the Dada readymade becomes a form of interrelation, a mediating force, and, of course, we have always known that the readymade's strategies of appropriation were a Dada form of the relational, even a manner of dialogue.

Consequently, and here rupturing the monograph structure perhaps definitively, dialogue and conversations of every sort structure this book throughout. If I begin with an origin story about a voyage between friends, a voyage to the land of the between, this book will continue to trace—instead of the development of a single artist's oeuvre—the dialogue between Picabia and Duchamp, as well as between Duchamp and Picabia. It will listen to the dialogue of Man Ray with them both. Apollinaire will drop out, a tragic casualty of the times, but the book will take seriously the dialogue between painters and poets, between Picabia and Tristan Tzara, Picabia and Louis Aragon, Picabia and André Breton. It will focus on works of art that are, in the literal sense of the term, "dialogic," given over to the voices and expressions of a collectivity instead of a single author. It will turn, in its climactic chapter, to a notion of the work of art as nothing but dialogue, collaboration, in this case in a ballet and film "by" Picabia called *Relâche* and *Entr'acte,* involving dialogues between Picabia and composer Erik Satie, between Picabia and filmmaker René Clair, and many others besides.

Or, conversely, the book will undercut this utopia of dialogue to trace the *pas-de-deux* of rivalry, a consequence and corollary of casting the work of art as a space *between* the self and other. And if dialogue emerges here as a Dada form, one that art history has had trouble narrating, it is also something this book will attempt to trace *between forms*. We will see that one of Picabia's recurrent strategies during the years of Paris Dada was to create his work in significant, even structural, pairs. But the Dada dialogue between forms can be taken much further: As opposed to the separation sought by modernism in its quest for medium-specificity, this book will isolate an opposite strategy, which will not in fact reside in medium-specificity's utter collapse (one of the normative narratives of the readymade). It will instead involve a strategy that art history has not yet been able to envision, something like medium "conversation," the sharing or interaction of forms. Finally, and perhaps most disturbing to some of my readers (it has proven so for many thanked in my acknowledgments), this book will end with an actual "dialogue" (called here for tradition's sake an epilogue), as the book attempts at its conclusion, however incoherently, to remake its own art historical form in the guise of the Dada work it brings to light, to be recast by the readymade in turn.

But, finally, one might say that this book's attention to the relational or the dialogic, its recasting of the Dada readymade as a form of recasting, emerges from its methodological orientation. For to conceive of the readymade as a "theoretical object" dedicated to the recasting of other forms—the altered practices of Dada Painting, Dada Drawing, Dada Photography, and so on—is to echo that primary form of recasting in modernity, which is, of course, capital: the incessant force of recoding that belongs to the monetary and to exchange. The revision of Paris Dada that follows relies deeply on a—Marxist and structuralist—notion of *exchange* as a unifying concept within the social field. I turn for one of the most compelling analyses of this "unifying concept" to the work of literary critic and philosopher Jean-Joseph Goux. With Goux's theorization of what he calls "symbolic economies," we witness an extension of Karl Marx's critique of the value form, the phenomenon of money, and the structure of commodity exchange to almost every corner of human endeavor: the exchange of subjects (according to the law of the Father), the exchange of objects of desire (by the dictates of the Phallus), and the exchange of signs (subsumed to the rule of Language).

While I prefer to allow the lineaments of my use (and abuse) of the notion of symbolic economies to emerge within the text itself, my reading of Paris Dada proceeds by tracing the inception of a shifting set of strategies that could, first, potentially rupture a given symbolic economy, a mad attempt to seize directly upon the "general equivalents" that Goux allows us to perceive as ruling these economies themselves (Father, Phallus, Language, Money). And, as a corollary to this drive, later chapters then attempt to imagine a different set of Dada strategies, more "optimistic" or utopic perhaps, that do not simply rupture a hegemonic symbolic order, but attempt to create alternate symbolic economies on the other side of this order's dissolution, or to release quite "ancient" or repressed ones, loosening forgotten forms of symbolic exchange.

In a sense, this methodological concern with exchange is itself a methodology of the between. It is, in fact, offered as a kind of "third term" that might mediate—or rather, transgress—a definitive split within recent art historical studies of the avant-garde, a kind of insurmountable wall, or a dualism, involving two models of avant-garde critique. On the one hand, the vision is of the avant-garde as opening up a critique of art's institutions (context, frame, distribution, social definition): here lie the claims made for the radical break signaled by Marcel Duchamp and the Dada readymade, or by Russian Constructivism and Soviet Productivism with their dissolution of the bourgeois category of art. On the other hand is the retrospective claim that the avant-garde achieved a thoroughgoing critique of representation (a refashioning of the subject and sign): here Surrealism comes to the fore as the crux of the historical avant-garde. Marx versus Freud, you could somewhat crudely say, or so it surely seemed to a young art history student left surveying the scorched earth produced in the wake of the battles in the 1970s and 1980s of the "new art history." In contrast to those heady years, we have surely entered another interregnum. But perhaps this too can now become a boon.

The model of a symbolic economy holds the potential to mediate this split, articulating the concerns of both institution and representation, object and subject, frame and discourse, the social and the formal. In the time period of Dada in Paris, to discuss such an "economic" model leads inevitably to a serious anachronism, for its strategies bring Dada close to the later (dissident Surrealist) concerns of Georges Bataille. It was Bataille for whom the economic—and its rupture—first became a major critical paradigm within the cultural field, in his notions of a "sacrificial economy," or later, a "restricted" versus a "general economy." But this "anachronism" instead should be taken as an attempt at an archaeology, from Goux and post-Structuralism back to the broader concerns of Bataille, and from there even further (and broader perhaps again) to the initiation of these concepts in earlier formations of the French avant-garde. Thus Picabia and Bataille emerge as strangely linked figures in this book, both dissident and dissonant in relation to the avant-garde that coalesced around André Breton.

But we might extend this archaeology yet further back again. For to narrate the strategies of the historical avant-garde as a kind of work upon symbolic economies is to prioritize, ultimately, neither the readymade (in the first instance) nor Productivism, and surely not Surrealism, but rather the semiotic understanding of art that we now realize was achieved, first, by Cubism.[5] Rather than Productivist or Surrealist, a model of the avant-garde as working on symbolic economies would reconnect with Cubism. However, if such is the case, Dada represents a vast expansion of the semiotic labor undertaken by Cubist art, with such semiosis no longer bracketed but, in the wake of the First World War, attached to (and attacking) its social and psychic bases. Significant alterations to the semiotics of Cubism would have to be imagined (and this book is just the beginning of such imagining, in fact a call for this imagining to occur): a shift from a concern with stable semiotic *structure,* for one, to a labile enactment of *process*; or a turn from the work of art reinvented through an analogy with language to its dissolution by locating semiosis in a much more general field, one that undoes such logocentrism. In other words, the narrative that this book elaborates can be seen as a kind of contextualization, embedding at least one strain of Dada within the Cubist avant-garde from which it emerged. The narrative is one of Cubism *radicalized,* taken to the *root*: precisely the kind of force we have been told was utterly missing in the formless *époque flou.*

My first chapter ("*Le saint des saints*") opens with a lost work by Picabia and a massive departure from the earlier New York mechanomorphs: a drawing in the form of a hole that was entitled *La jeune fille,* a work distributed in magazine form at the most important of the initial public Dada manifestations in Paris in 1920. This (until recently) forgotten work is in fact a companion piece to a well-known "drawing" by Picabia entitled *La Sainte-Vierge*; the two pieces form an opposed pair that represent a Dada dismantling of the very activity of drawing or the graphic. Contextualized in relationship to the theatrical manifestations of Dada in 1920, as well as to Dada's assault on the language of Cubism, Picabia's pair articulates a conception of drawing best described by Bataille's notion of transgression or a "sacrificial economy," where drawing would be founded upon that which it "lacks." This dismantling then itself becomes foundational, for Picabia and for my book, determining each of his subsequent projects and my chapters, with drawing (the loss of drawing) at the basis of all things, fueling a potlatch of further losses, instead of laying the cornerstone of art.

The second chapter ("The Artwork Caught by the Tail") presents an interpretation of Picabia's 1921 anti-masterpiece, *L'oeil cacodylate,* offering a reading of the work in terms of Picabia's dialogue with Marcel Duchamp and the practice of the readymade, registered in Picabia's invention of categories of objects that he branded "Dada Drawing" and "Dada Painting," which consisted of specially selected examples of the two artists' work. These objects seize upon all of the major signifiers that Goux has called general equivalents, and the Dada assault upon and use of these signifiers allows the practice of the readymade to be reconceived in analogy to Bataille's later notion of expenditure. A third chapter ("Keep Smiling") departs from the focus upon both Picabia and Paris Dada to examine Man Ray's response in 1921 to Picabia's invented "mediums," when the American artist entitled a specific photograph published in *New York Dada* a "Dadaphoto." As opposed to the rupture of symbolic economies and of general equivalency that was posed by Picabia's categories, this chapter will test the thesis that the "Dada Photograph" explored a repressed symbolic economy of infinite visual equivalencies.

In the fourth chapter ("*Prolem sine matre creatam*"), I expand this notion of nongeneral equivalency, returning to Europe in order to reconstruct and interpret Picabia's massive but long-ignored 1922 exhibition in Barcelona, where Picabia resurrected the mechanomorph in a form that registered the shifts in his practice since the initiation of Paris Dada. These new mechanomorphs—though based on copies of photographs and diagrams—teetered impossibly on the verge of abstraction, approximating the forms of Kasimir Malevich's Suprematism or El Lissitzky's Constructivist abstractions, and yet Picabia's works submitted the "productive" concerns of modernist abstraction to unproductive ends, indeed to an excessive visual experience of blind spots and loss. Chapter 5 examines Picabia's turn toward cinema in 1923–24 and the Dada film *Entr'acte,* analyzing how the Dada play with symbolic economies works within the structure of this film, but also beyond it: this cinematic turn allowed Picabia to bring to a climax a drive to work between modernist mediums, and in excess of their limits, in a manner much more radical than previous understandings of "assemblage" or "intermedia" would have us believe. And here I will break with the convention of introductions, and return to saying what this book will not do. I will say nothing here of my epilogue or conclusion, except to admit that it is hardly a conclusion at all.

Here is Dada.—With Apollinaire occupied with his soldiering in the First World War, and Duchamp occupied with slowly collecting and then nailing his newly invented readymades to the studio floor, or hanging them from the ceiling, working in secret on *The Bride Stripped Bare by Her Bachelors, Even,* the public announcement of what we now recognize as the start of Dada was left to Picabia. In 1915, having escaped war-torn Europe to settle briefly in New York, Picabia filled the pages of the new magazine *291,* a publication headed by Marius de Zayas, with such announcements

In fact, he filled the magazine's pages with cries, heralds, proclamations. *Ici, c'est ici Stieglitz*: Here is Stieglitz, appended to a mechanical drawing of a (broken) camera.[6] *Voilà Haviland*: Here is Haviland, clinging to schematic copy of an image of an electrical lamp—to which Picabia added, *La poésie est comme lui,* poetry is like him. *De Zayas! De Zayas!,* another drawing cried out—in imitation of the ancient *Thalassa! Thalassa!,* "the sea, the sea!"—following a diagrammatic plan for an enigmatic machine with lines speeding out in all directions.

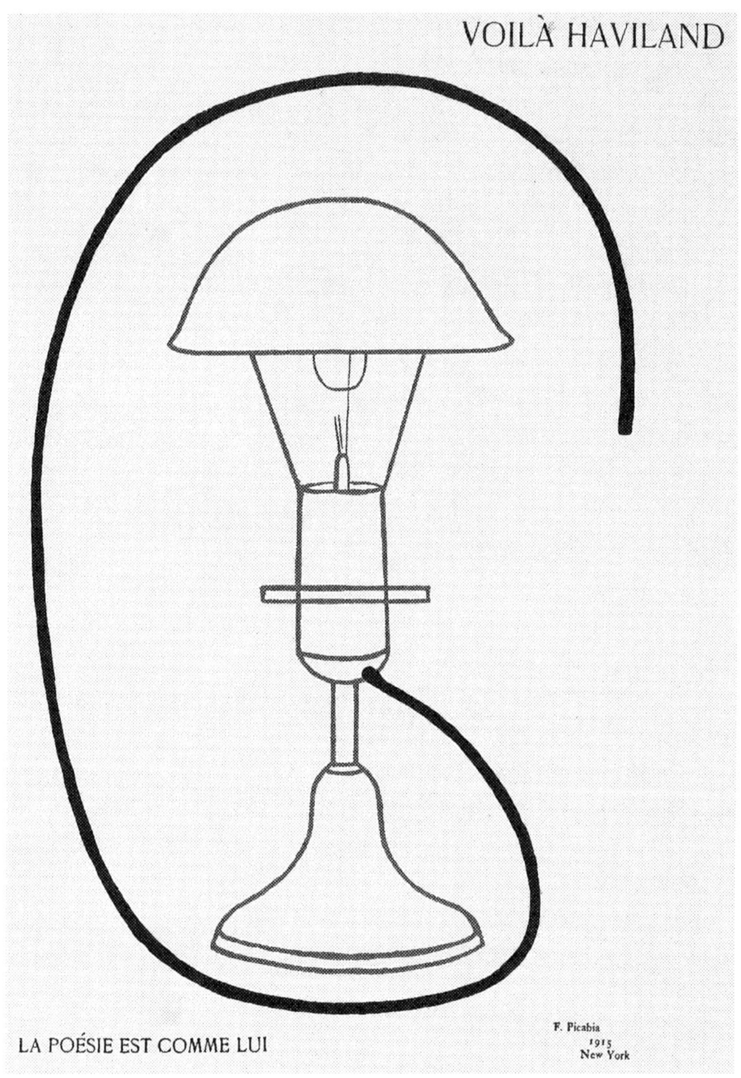

Francis Picabia, *Voilà Haviland,* 1915. Published in *291* 5–6 (July–August 1915). Research Library, The Getty Research Institute, Los Angeles. © 2005 Artists Rights Society (ARS), New York/ADAGP, Paris/Estate of Francis Picabia.

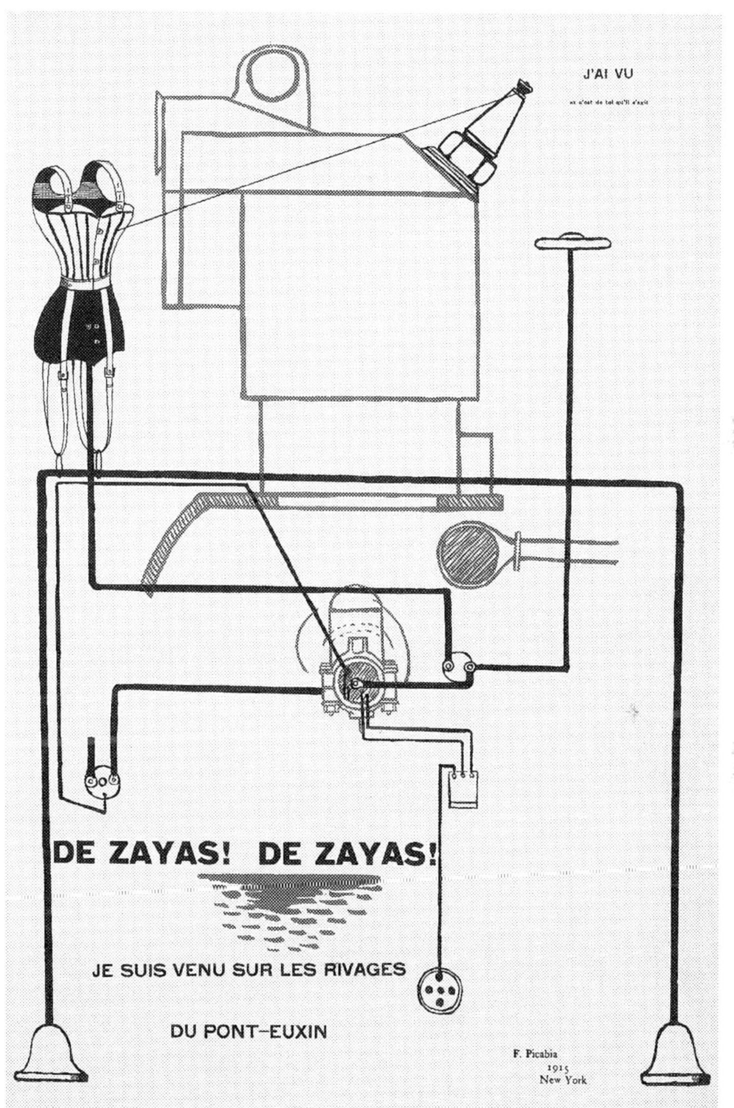

Francis Picabia, *De Zayas! De Zayas!,* 1915. Published in *291* 5–6 (July–August 1915). Research Library, The Getty Research Institute, Los Angeles. © 2005 Artists Rights Society (ARS), New York/ADAGP, Paris/Estate of Francis Picabia.

The thematics of Picabia's first mechanomorphs announce the secret project of Duchamp's *Bride Stripped Bare,* the latter's anonymous bachelor machines now erupting in Picabia's version across the pages of the print media and as a negotiation of so many relations between friends—private speech made public. In form too the mechanomorphs share Duchamp's concerns, from the appropriated commodity objects of the first readymades to the technique of mechanical drawing that replaced traditional painterly craft in the *Large Glass.*

And they emerge from the same semiotic landscape as well. As Rosalind Krauss has demonstrated, Duchamp's *Large Glass* and the readymades that accompanied it were a recoding of art in terms of the kind of sign that a photograph embodies, namely, what Charles Sanders Peirce called an "index." As opposed to iconic signs, where reference is motivated by resemblance, or symbolic signs (like most written language), where the relation of sign to referent is arbitrary, an indexical sign is physically *caused* by the thing to which it refers, like a shadow cast by the setting sun, or a fingerprint left behind at the scene of a crime, or a sneeze erupting from a freshly caught cold.[7] A collection of imprints, molds, and impressions, Duchamp's *Glass* involved a vast accumulation of indexical marks, as if the entire panoply of the work was to be analogized to the physical capture of a photograph. As a work on glass, Duchamp's project also opened itself to the *hic et nunc* of its situation, pressing itself tight against the world out of which it emerges. And so too would physical connection come to occupy Picabia, as the mechanomorphs prioritized a form of drawing based on the trace, given over to the copy, hitching iconic resemblance (in an admittedly hybrid manner) to the "here and now" of indexical causation.

But Picabia rushed ahead of Duchamp's inventions by attaching words to his indexical drawings. Still entranced by the poetic innovations of "Zone," Picabia's supplements were of a specific kind. The mechanomorphs were a veritable catalog of those rare words that qualify as indexical forms of language, long before Duchamp's last painting, *Tu m',* in 1918—the empty pronouns, the "shifters" and deictics, whose meaning is completely void until determined by the context of their pronouncement: *Je, lui, moi, toi, ici, voilà.* But these words also force a radicalization of the semiotic reading of Dada, for like "Zone," their effects exceed the context of the here and now. Like Picabia's appropriated objects pushing up against the work's framing edge (*Stieglitz*), or "thrusting" into the hull of another machinic form (the self-portrait in the series, *Le saint des saints*), or offering up so many protrusions—like the elongated tip of a sparkplug or the end of a spiraling electrical wire—simply begging to be plugged in to another object that is not yet shown, the mechanomorphs' inscriptions placed the representation in motion. For their shifters were in fact the enactment of so many virtual voyages, their deictics like lines pointing toward unseen shores, vectors leading beyond the objects we perceive.

In the image "of" Marius de Zayas, and in a mechanomorph from a later issue of *291* entitled *Voilà Elle* that Picabia placed in dialogue with a calligrammatic poem by de Zayas, such mobility came to be embodied in a form of representation that not only copied schematic or diagrammatic machine parts, but gathered these fragments into a new assembly that itself must be described as a *diagram*. Here the index as physical causation, a connection between sign and referent, immediately accelerates into an almost abstract concern with semiotic connection and linkage. Such is the manner in which David Joselit has recently described the semiotics of the diagram, announcing Picabia's and Duchamp's play with the diagrammatic to be a third key Dada tactic alongside the long-recognized Dada strategies of the readymade and photomontage.

As opposed to Cubist semiotics, whose effect Joselit calls "implosive" as "objects collapse under their own mounting semiotic obscurity," the Dada diagram is "expansive," a matter of "vectors and relations" that do not return to a post-Cubist mimetic or representational image, even of the machine, but instead present a mode of linkage characteristic of such technology. "The diagram," Joselit writes, "reconnects the disconnected fragments of representation invented by cubism." This reconnection hardly amounts to a "return to coherence," but instead exists as a further liberation of the transformational energies of Cubist semiotics, now become a labile semiosis. The result is "a free play of polymorphous linkages," a boundless "connectivity between discrete elements." The diagram, for Joselit, emphasizes a "pure relationality *between* things," producing

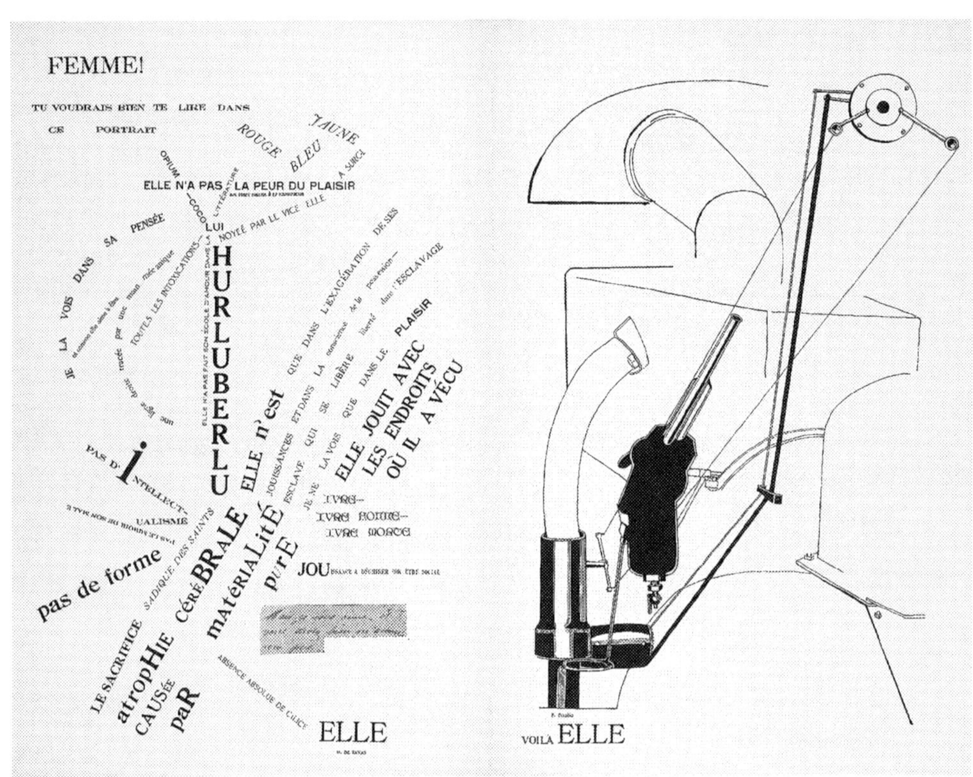

Marius de Zayas, *Elle (She),* and Francis Picabia, *Voilà Elle (Here She Is),* 1915. Two-page spread from *291* 9 (November 1915). Research Library, The Getty Research Institute, Los Angeles. © 2005 Artists Rights Society (ARS), New York/ADAGP, Paris/Estate of Francis Picabia.

"an interstitial space," a space forever *between,* one thing on the way to becoming another: the work of art as a semiological waystation or pivot.[8]

From this (semiotic) perspective, Picabia's hanging of the entire series of the mechanomorphs under the aegis of a reference to Ovid's *Metamorphoses* makes perfect sense. For what seems to be Picabia's first mechanomorphic drawing, produced just prior to the *291* series, was a loose conglomeration of disjunctive iconic fragments sutured by mobile vectors that the artist entitled *Fille née sans mère (Girl Born without a Mother).* If this transitional work still breathes the air of the nostalgic elegies of Picabia's Orphism, recalling like a fading memory Picabia's prior memorial *I See Again in Memory My Dear Udnie,* that latter work itself was already a memory, a "seeing again," a translation of Duchamp's gift to the artist of the 1912 painting *The Bride.* But this chain of memories was also a chain of transformations, and Picabia's title for *Fille née sans mère* acknowledges this by simply appropriating a line attributed to Ovid's tale of shifting shape and endless change.[9]

The mechanomorphs, as Dada diagrams, were not then poorly named. They were a modern imagining of metamorphosis, the radicalization of semiotic transformation now become a force of linkage between things, a mobile assemblage of relations and vectors, a momentous breakdown of form as stable and everlasting. In addition to being the most diagrammatic of the *291* series, *De Zayas! De Zayas!* was the most Ovidian as well, its inscriptions making up an entire congeries of classical references. *J'ai vu, Je suis venu*: an updating of "I came, I saw, I conquered." But the work's transformation of the exclamation "The sea! The sea!" into a friend's last name, and the qualification of "I came" to the full statement "I have come to the shores of Pont-Euxin," now admit of a deep identification on Picabia's part with Ovid. For "Pontus Euxinus" was Latin for the Black Sea, the site of Ovid's banishment.[10] And form enters a kind of exile here as well, as Dada begins with another kind of voyage, a scene of seemingly aimless wanderings, displacements, vectors.

Universal Prostitution.—From this vantage point, where Dada representation seems to provide an echo of mythic equivalence and "divine" transformation, a place where indeed even the "automobiles appear to be ancient," the central

Dada strategy of the readymade begins to look quite different as well. To put this somewhat crudely: Picabia has been compared negatively to Duchamp in most art historical narratives of the avant-garde, a fellow-traveler who plagiarized or stole ideas (no matter that this was the very logic of the readymade), and who, perhaps worse, pictorialized Duchamp's invention, using the readymade not to negate the medium of painting, but to remain firmly within the conventions of that medium, if perhaps only to empty them all the more effectively.

Such is the reading of Picabia as parodist. His was the more conservative option, we are meant to understand: the path of appropriation and pastiche, the path that led to a lifetime of painting as a kind of paroxysm of the copy, of excessive, endless reiteration, as opposed to the monklike abstention from painting of Duchamp. But this may be a false opposition, and the two artists surely never saw their activities as entirely contradictory. They instead saw them as in dialogue. Indeed, Picabia's mechanomorphs might be seen as an *expansion* of the readymade's semiotic logic, rather than its diminution. Thus understood, the readymade becomes a much less stable affair than the objects now embalmed in the museums it supposedly exceeded, and Picabia's "pictorializing" of the strategy, a recasting of representation in its wake, the potentially more radical option.

For Picabia seemed immediately to intuit that the readymade was hardly a *thing,* but instead a kind of symbolic *force,* one that was intensely labile and thus hostile to the static forms of art. Rather than a challenge to art that would simply replace painting and sculpture with mass-produced objects drawn from the world of the commodity, the readymade for Picabia carried along with it the nomadic existence of those commodities within modernity, their deeper logic as tokens of abstract exchange—in fact, their inherent transmutability from concrete *things* into fluid *money.* As enacted in the Dada diagrams that Picabia flung like so many feckless coins into the fountain of the circulating media, the readymade responded not to the commodity as an object, but to its existence as a form of exchange, a tool of circulation, a temporary pitstop on the endless racetrack of money.

We sense this engagement with monetary circulation in the mechanomorphs' transformational model, an endless performance of one thing becoming another, one thing linked to another, one relation after another. We sense it in the mechanomorph's relay of word and image, language and vision, with one kind of sign emerging from or becoming connected to another. We sense it in all the mechanomorphs that, although composed of frozen, indexical traces, nevertheless imaged forth so many mechanical gears, "turning quickly" as they were sometimes inscribed in words by Picabia, the emblem of a kind of circulation that could be conceived as economic in the broadest sense of the term, a relentless symbolic voyage like Picabia's tires spinning through the infinite night. We sense it in the thematic of promiscuity that the mechanomorphs began to explore, as when another circulatory wheel on the cover of the first issue of Picabia's Dada journal *391* was entitled *Novia,* a "girlfriend" who, we are told—in another inscription— is open to the "first occupant," an emblem-of-circulation as symbolic whore. But the larger emblematic explored with such promiscuity was money or capital's endless promiscuity of form, the readymade as a never-ending semiotic voyage.

Thus, as Jean-Joseph Goux, citing Marx, describes the existence of money as currency, the "general equivalent" in its role as a medium of circulation, the semiotic logic of the Dada diagram is revealed:

> "Gold [Marx writes], in so far as it performs the function of coin or in so far as it continually circulates, actually forms only a *connecting link* between the metamorphoses of commodities." What functions in the symbolic representation is not materialized value but only connection, linkage, relation. The symbolic order of currency is that of *pure* concatenation . . . in that the circulation process in the world of commodities takes shape as "a link not only of one endless chain of metamorphoses, but of many such chains." In this world of circulation, monetary forms are fleetingly articulated, strung together, but not arrested in the form of use-value. . . . Extended circulation thus makes viable . . . a *purely* symbolic order. . . .[11]

Picabia deploys the readymade as an enactment of this "pure" symbolic order. By the close of the First World War, however, the diagrammatic space invented by Picabia's mechanomorphs had reached its culmination. As often occurs at such

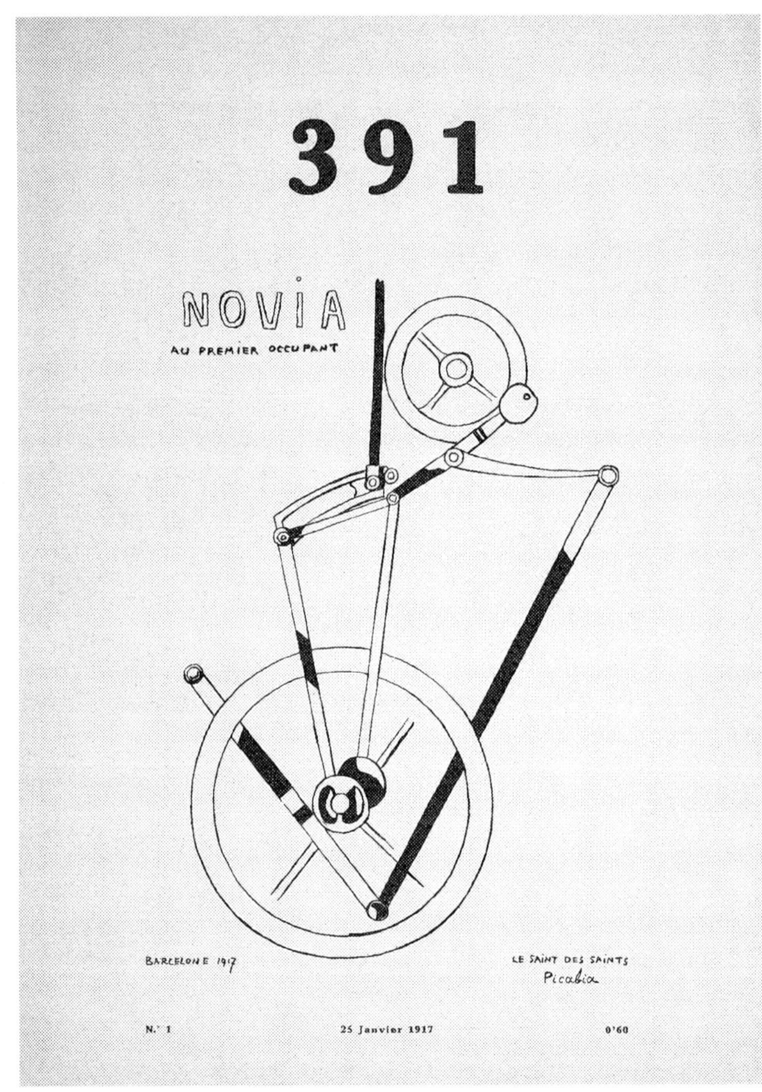

Francis Picabia, *Novia (Girlfriend),* 1917. Cover of *391* 1 (25 January 1917). Research Library, The Getty Research Institute, Los Angeles. © 2005 Artists Rights Society (ARS), New York/ADAGP, Paris/Estate of Francis Picabia.

liminal moments, during periods of transition and decay, Picabia comes to name the monetary strategy of the readymade explicitly only at this point. This is the period that witnesses Picabia entering metallic gold and silver paints into his oeuvre, if not for the first time, then with increased urgency; the glint of such pigments, for example in *Child Carburetor* (1919), seems not so much an announcement of the sheen of kitsch, but the (perhaps linked) glow of the money form, the readymade as general equivalent.[12] And this is also the moment that sees Picabia naming one of these paintings embellished with the metallic shine of money *Universal Prostitution,* after a phrase perhaps first popularized by Karl Marx, its circuitous vectors blazing a round-trip pathway of gold and silver paint.[13]

The strategy of Dada at its inception was the strategy of "universal prostitution," the strategy of a pure symbolic order, of endless concatenation. It was an attempt to exacerbate on every level the labile force of exchange and monetary circulation, to seize upon that which cannot be seized: the readymade or commodity as immaterial money, abstract currency, pure symbolic flow. It was an attempt to take currency to a place it had never been, to abstractions it could barely, in those years, imagine (the imaginations of the monetary in our own time are another matter entirely). But *Universal Prostitution* was also an end, a plateau, or, at least, a transition. If its melancholic embodiment of symbolic exchange seems to shift the monetary metaphor into realms more blatantly erotic or sexual, the painting might be read as a moment wherein Dada begins to discover in money itself the key to the symbolic more generally. The "pure" symbolic order of monetary exchange offers entry into the larger processes of symbolization. It offers the very model of the symbolic, and thus provides entry into symbolic economies entirely other than the one that belongs to the capitalist world, to the heart-rending economy of commodities.

This universal symbolic prostitution, however, also seemed immediately to open up a new strategy for Dada and for Picabia. Rather than exacerbate the commodity's circulatory power, intensifying and radicalizing it, a logical corollary instead arises. One could immediately begin to imagine the rupture of circulation, the gumming up of the free flow of exchange: a challenge to the endless

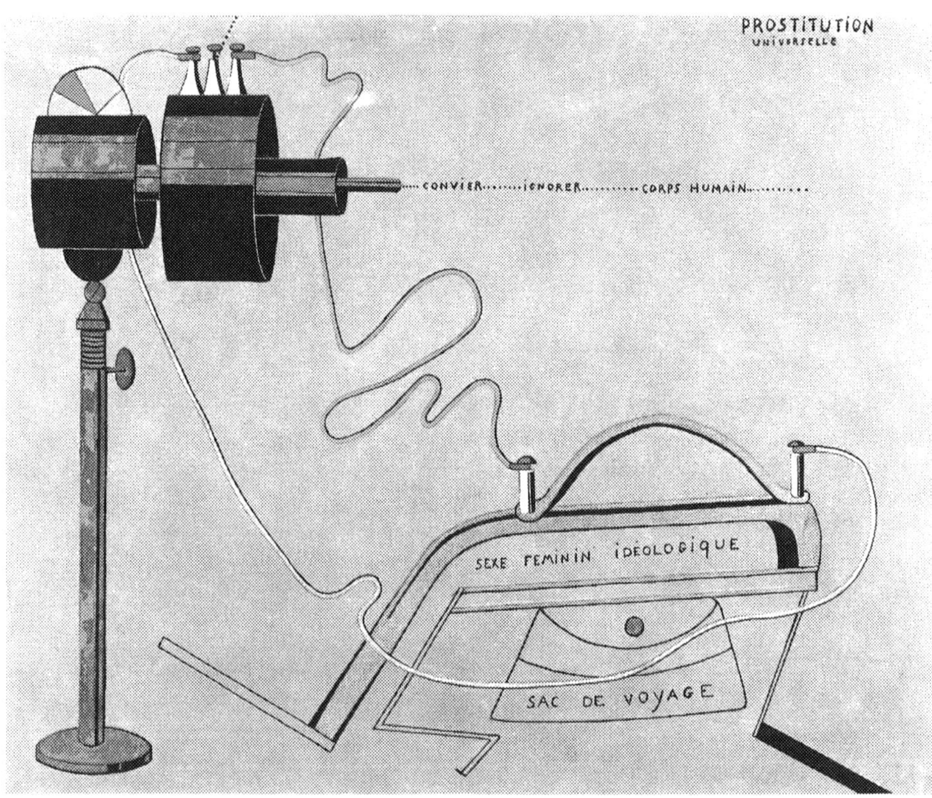

Francis Picabia, *Universal Prostitution,* 1918–19. Ink, tempera, and metallic paint on board, 74.5 × 94.3 cm (29 3/8 × 37 1/8″). Yale University Art Gallery, Gift of Collection Société Anonyme. © Artists Rights Society (ARS), New York/ADAGP, Paris/Estate of Francis Picabia.

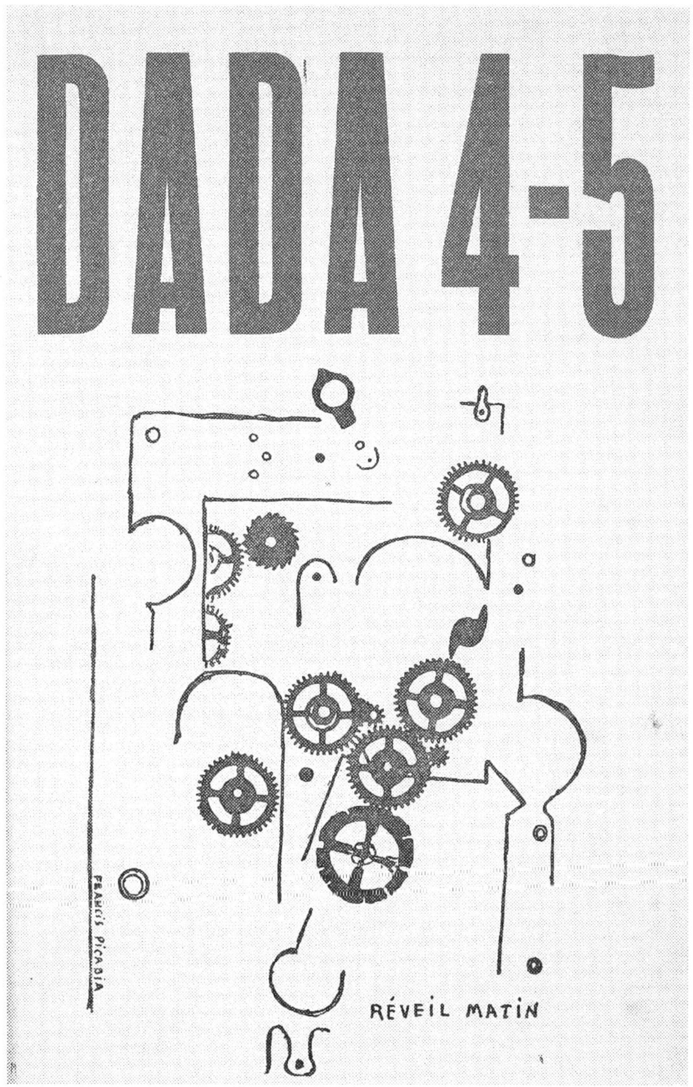

Francis Picabia, *Alarm Clock,* 1919. Title page of *Dada 4–5,* May 15, 1919.
Research Library, The Getty Research Institute, Los Angeles. © 2005 Artists
Rights Society (ARS), New York/ADAGP, Paris/Estate of Francis Picabia.

drift of the Dada diagram. And it is in this way that I understand the very different proclamation that Picabia offered up in another public media space in 1919, another magazine, just as the events of Paris Dada were about to unfold.

The world of the *291* object-portraits was already beginning to slip into the distant past. Now in Zurich, and having begun a dialogue with Tristan Tzara, Picabia entered the media space of the Zurich Dadaists with a "mechanomorphic" drawing published on the title page of Tzara's magazine *Dada*. Entitled *Reveil Matin* or "Alarm Clock," the drawing was a wake-up call. For here was the first—but surely not the last—of what we might begin to call Picabia's "destroyed diagrams." It was an image of a machine taken apart. Vectors disappear. Relations and links dissolve. An instrument of measurement, a standard—in this case a clock—falls to pieces. The gears no longer intimate circulation, but freeze stock still, the innards of the eviscerated machine dipped in ink and imprinted one after the other in a random distribution across the magazine cover, the shattered frame of the clock traced here and there as well, the circular insides of the gears peppered like buckshot across the page.

It is the first sign in Picabia's Dada work of an engagement with what we might call "de-monetarization," a tactic that no longer accelerates exchange but challenges its very basis, and thus challenges the smooth workings of symbolization itself. It is the first sign of the readymade as a monetary phenomenon turning around on itself, biting its own tail. It is the first sign of a new project for Picabia, one that will be worked out and expanded in all the subsequent events of Dada in Paris. The story of this sudden shift in tactics is the one that will occupy me in the remainder of this book.

Voilà.—Dada began with a *voilà*. It began with a magic trick. As in "Zone," the exclamation announced a connection, between word and image, between person and thing, between representation and the real. It allowed a connection to the outside. Dada traversed the relation between.

And so it began with a *voilà*. And so too does this book.

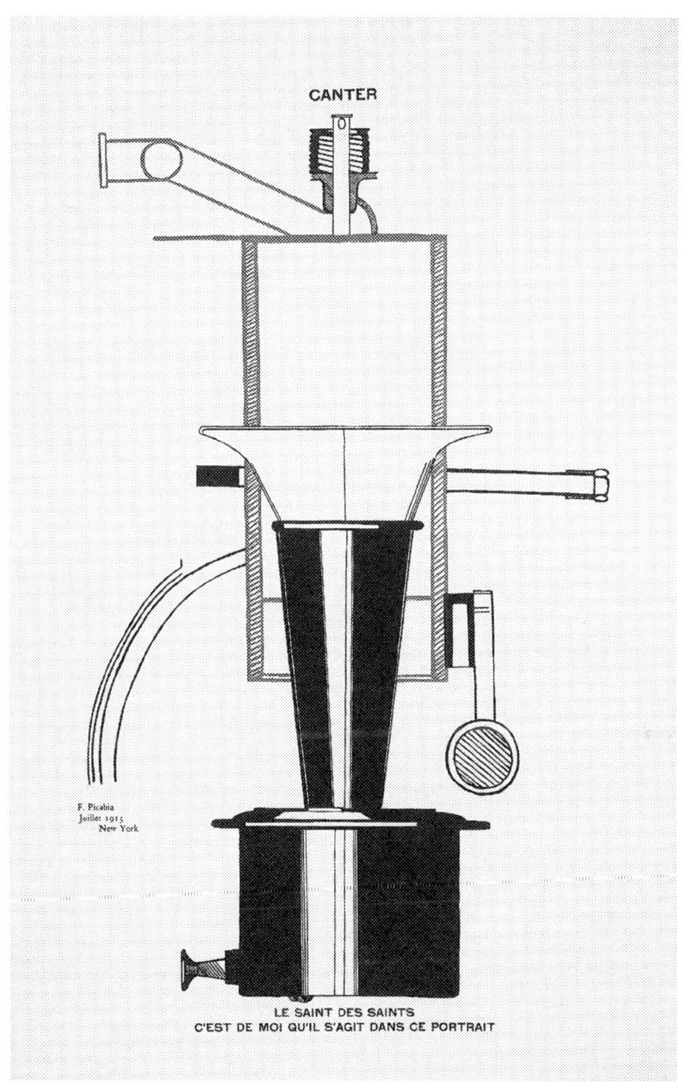

Francis Picabia, *Le saint des saints,* 1915. Published in *291* 5–6 (July–August 1915). Research Library, The Getty Research Institute, Los Angeles. © 2005 Artists Rights Society (ARS), New York/ADAGP, Paris/Estate of Francis Picabia.

Le saint des saints: Dada Drawing

Comme ceux de la Providence certains dessins sont impénétrables.

—*Francis Picabia, Dada street slogan, 1920*[1]

Here is an image of Picabia. For that is what he tells us, calling out from the surface of this purgative of an image, a representation that consists at least in part of a copied diagram of a car horn, rendered with graphic inscriptions so dry that almost none of the tell-tale wavering of the human hand can be seen, its lines so many testaments to the actions of tracing, or straightedge, or compass.

"This portrait is about me," he claims, collapsing the genre of the portrait with a mechanical object floating in an empty space without context, a stunning marriage of the impersonality of the drawing's production to the lack of personality to which the portrait can now attest. But Picabia is not finished. "*Le saint des saints,*" he inscribes it: the saint of saints, the holy of holies, "this portrait is about me."

It was an important phrase for Picabia, one that would reappear in various guises, emerging two years later, for example, with his signature on the image *Novia* that he used for the cover of the very first issue of his Dada magazine *391*. The art historians tell us that, just like the diagrammatic car horn, the phrase amounts to an example of artistic creation as appropriation, as copying, the language lifted straight from the "pink pages" of the *Petit Larousse Illustré* that defined various Latin phrases for the benefit of French schoolchildren.[2] The artist often mined these dictionary pages as a source for his inscriptions. *Sanctum sanctorum,* the holy of holies: this was a phrase provided to Picabia by the stratified order that language attains in the dictionary (for every word, a single meaning, or at the most, a quantified list). But it was also a common enough pun in the New York Dada milieu in which Picabia was a central figure. *Le saint des saints*: spoken, the phrase in French is formed through alliteration, a form of auditory doubling, of repetition, not unlike the word Dada itself. Spoken, the phrase begins to multiply homophones, and therefore multiply meanings, with a ferocity worthy of Mallarmé, as the "*saint*" of saint wheels off in French into the "*sain*" of healthy, or the "*sein*" of breast, as the original "*des saints*"—of saints—slips into the "*dessein*" of design or plan, or the "*dessin*" of drawing.

Marcel Duchamp liked this pun. Moving it away from the dictionary, he returned Picabia's found phrase to either the church or to the school, transforming it several years later into something like a chant or a parodic French grammar lesson that he called the "Litany of the Saints." In Duchamp's hands, the puns were multiplied, as the artist played again with the confusion between saints and breasts (*seins*), or between designs (*desseins*) and drawings (*dessins*), but also between rising up (*debout*) and going deep into something (*du bout*), between feeling (*sentir*) and meaning (*sens*). Largely untranslatable, Duchamp's version went like this:

> Litanie des saints
> Je crois qu'elle sent du bout des seins.
> Tais-toi, tu sens du bout des seins.
> Pourquoi sens-tu du bout des seins?
> Je veux sentir du bout des seins.[3]

Closer to home, Marius de Zayas, collaborating with Picabia in 1915, had already incorporated the pun into his poem "Elle" or "She," mentioning there "the sadistic sacrifice of the saints" (*le sacrifice sadique des saints*).[4] But again, this last phrase evokes the sadistic sacrifice of drawing, an increasingly familiar play on words redoubled by Picabia's graphic echo of de Zayas's poem on its facing page, a drawing Picabia entitled *Voilà elle* (*Here She Is*). It was a schoolboy pun, unable to keep the saints away from the breasts, entangling the sacred with desire, relating all of this somehow to drawing. It was a pun that made the high a function of the low, and vice versa. *Le saint des saints*: the saint of saints, the breast of breasts, the healthy drawing, the holy drawing. *Le saint des saints*: the holy of holies, the singular, the exceptional, slipping somehow through this alliterative, auditory doubling into the realm of the multiple. It was more than a catchword for Picabia's 1915 self-portrait. It was more, even, than an allegorical motto for the artist's identity. It was something like a slogan, a banner that announced Picabia's Dada work.

In April 1920, Picabia exhibited *Le saint des saints* in a one-man show organized as part of the initial onslaught of Dada in Paris.[5] The slogan was returning at a moment that had nothing to do with coincidence. It was as if Picabia were announcing a program, the program of Dada in Paris, a project that emerged from the artist's New York drawings called "mechanomorphs" only to exceed them. For at the very same moment as the exhibition of this now five-year-old self-portrait, Picabia produced a new drawing, perhaps his most notorious. It was a drawing whose title literalized one of the meanings of his earlier slogan, taking *le saint des saints* as *le saint dessin,* the "holy drawing." I am referring to Picabia's *La Sainte-Vierge* or *The Blessed Virgin,* published at the height of the introduction of Dada to Paris, in March of 1920, in the twelfth issue of Picabia's magazine *391*.

La Sainte-Vierge consists of an accumulation of splashes, or better, violent drippings of ink on a white sheet of paper. It thus seems to have very little to do with Picabia's earlier mechanomorphic images, given over as the latter are to the impersonal artistic language of mechanical drawing, and to the readymade condition of the copy. However, *La Sainte-Vierge* does take its place alongside a host of other Dada experiments with chance procedures, its technique every bit as impersonal—as violent toward authorship—as Picabia's earlier appropriated images.

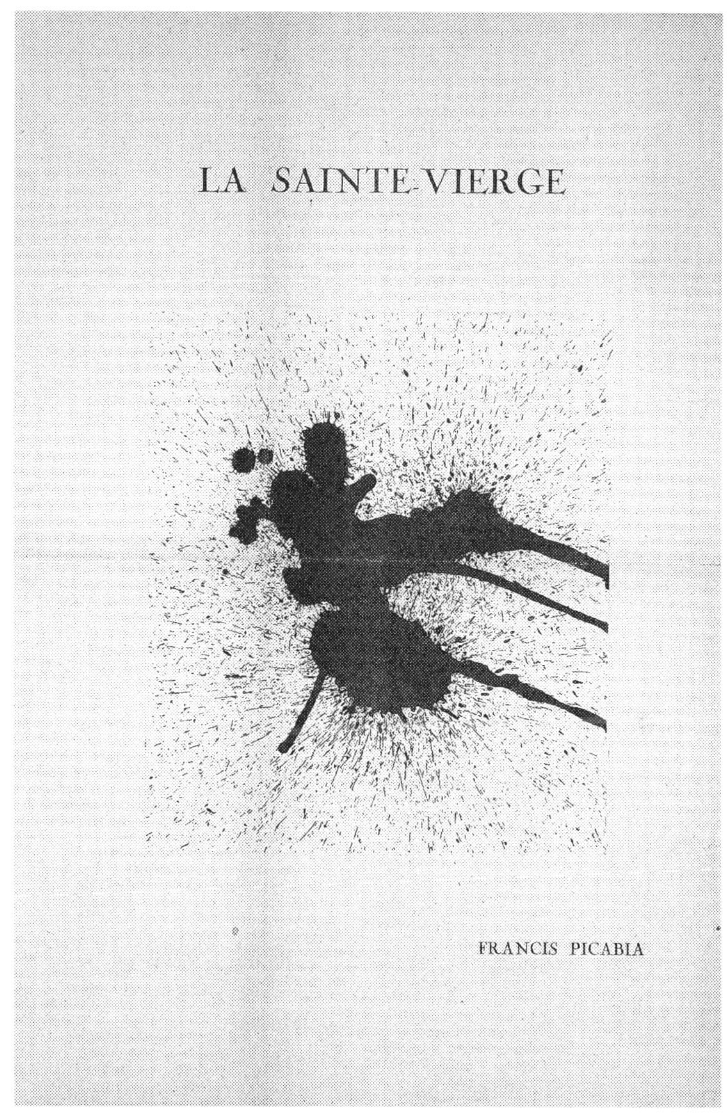

Francis Picabia, *La Sainte-Vierge (The Blessed Virgin)*, 1920. Published in *391* 12 (March 1920), p. 3. Research Library, The Getty Research Institute, Los Angeles. © 2005 Artists Rights Society (ARS), New York/ADAGP, Paris/Estate of Francis Picabia.

And what were these precedents? Obviously, Marcel Duchamp's and Jean Arp's experiments with chance were all-important to Picabia, who had just at this moment returned from Switzerland, where Arp's collages constructed "according to the laws of chance" were a revelation. Duchamp's work, no matter how secretive, was always something of which Picabia was intimately aware; we will see again and again that the artist would never cease developing the implications, for drawing, of Duchamp's *Three Standard Stoppages,* three meter-long "lines" of string dropped from the height of one meter and deformed by gravity and by chance. But the art historians see other connections here beyond a shared Dada mode of production. They see direct allusions on Picabia's part to Duchamp's favored themes, setting off *La Sainte-Vierge* as yet another "answer" by Picabia to Duchamp's activities, in an endless dialogue that, strangely, only ever seems in these narratives to go in one direction. There is the reference to the "virgin" of Picabia's title, the perennial theme of Duchamp's cubism, but there is, too—or so says the art historian—a direct play on the "sexual shots" produced by chance in Duchamp's most important image of a virgin, *The Bride Stripped Bare by Her Bachelors, Even (The Large Glass).* In the *Large Glass,* these "shots" were Duchamp's way of "connecting" the disparate, ever divided zones of the Bride and her Bachelors; as if emerging from the part of the Bachelors' zone called by Duchamp the "oculist witnesses," a series of paint-dipped matches were fired by the artist from a miniature toy cannon at the region of the Bride directly above. At each point where the shots splattered the *Glass,* Duchamp then drilled a series of identical holes through the work.[6]

But Duchamp is not the master referent for Picabia, nor for his drawing; other precedents abound, precedents that open up a larger Dada concern with drawing to which Picabia would now turn. More to the point, indeed, would be Picabia's relationship to a little-known image by Man Ray from 1915, a precedent that thus dates from roughly the same moment as Picabia's second sojourn to New York and his production of the *291* object-portrait series to which *Le saint des saints* belongs. In his own magazine, the scatological *Ridgefield Gazook,* Man Ray published an image on its last page that he entitled *Art Motes.* In a magazine whose contributions—or so the masthead barked—would be received "in

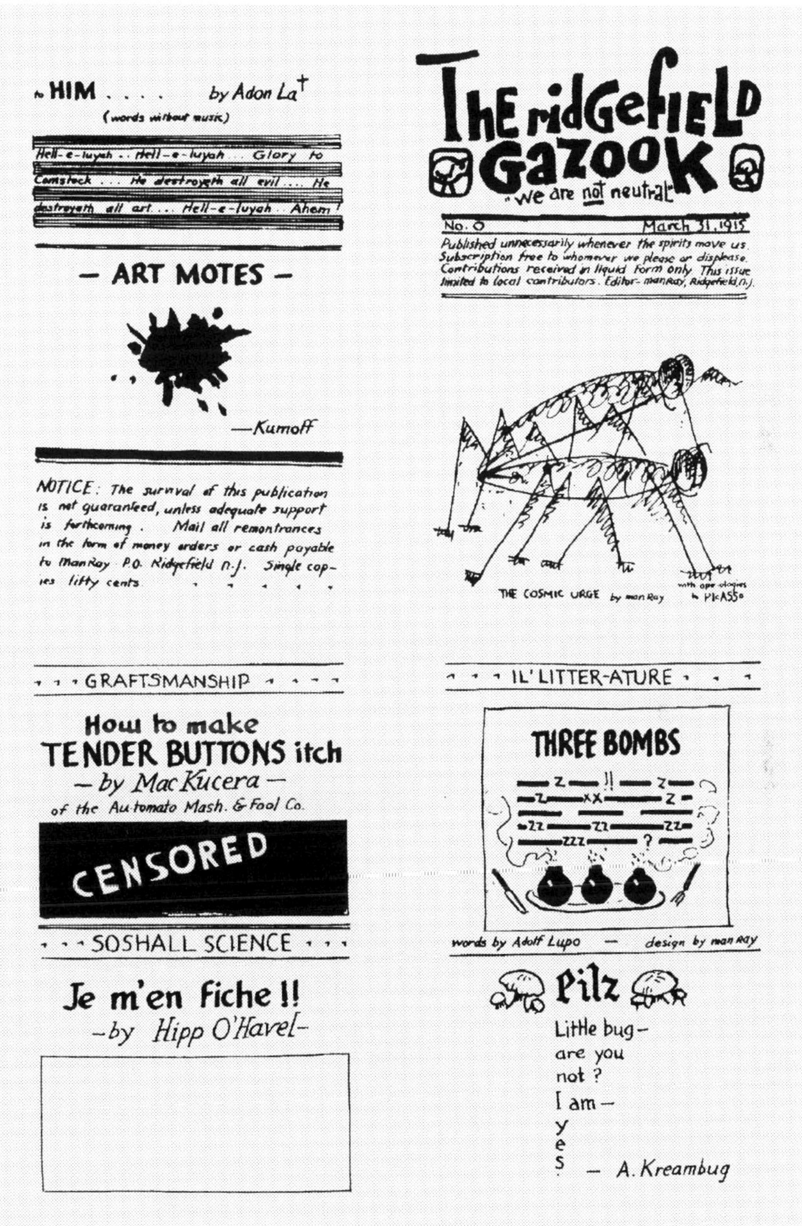

Man Ray, *The Ridgefield Gazook* 0 (March 31, 1915). © 2005 Artists Rights Society (ARS), New York/ADAGP, Paris/Man Ray Trust.

liquid form only," *Art Motes* concluded what was a series of decidedly sexual, parodic forays into the current idioms of the poetic and visual avant-garde. Prefiguring Picabia's action in *391,* Man Ray's work consisted of a simulated version of an ink splash. Signed with the Russian-sounding name "Kumoff," *Art Motes* seemed to tie together all the divergent stakes of the various parodies in *The Ridgefield Gazook*: the connection of drawing—modernist drawing—to a sexual thematics (as the first syllable of the signature "Kumoff" punctuates the orgasmic conclusion that *Art Motes* seems to draw); the turn—throughout the magazine, throughout Dada, and throughout Man Ray's later experiments in poetry—to procedures of erasure and deletion (as, again, the signature "Kumoff" splits into two English cognates, "come off," enacting in words the visual processes that Man Ray had just put into play); and the new importance of the interrelationship of the verbal and the visual in Dada works of art.[7] The "motes" of the image's title refers literally to a small particle or speck, and thus to the image before us, but Man Ray could also be invoking the French word *mots,* or "words" (he produced *The Ridgefield Gazook* in collaboration with his French-speaking wife, Adon Lacroix).[8] Typical of Picabia's procedures during and after his Dada years, we can thus see *La Sainte-Vierge* not only as another Dada image formed through chance, but as an appropriation of sorts with little claim to originality. And given how Picabia would articulate the implications of this drawing, such a seeming paradox was neither a fortuitous combination nor an insignificant artistic feat.

But key differences do exist between *Art Motes* and *La Sainte-Vierge*; the appropriation may not be original, but it is not a true copy. It could not be, and this, in fact, may be the drawing's point. Unlike *Art Motes, La Sainte-Vierge,* of course, is no simulation; it is a real ink splash, and thus an enactment more of a process than an image. Dropped from a certain height, ink performs here as it is able: it splatters, forming a myriad of shooting marks; it drips, slipping away now toward the bottom of the image, now toward its right side; it bleeds, leeching into the paper as it coagulates. Bleeding is the right word here, for it captures the sense that a certain amount of violence went into the production of this image. Or at least a certain amount of force. The ink provides an index of that force with every splatter and spray, just as it registers the other procedures of the making of *La*

Sainte-Vierge: the ink's fall through gravity from a certain height onto a horizontal field, or the sheer excessive quantity of the stuff that Picabia must have employed, visible in the rivulets of ink making their way in a surprisingly ordered march out of the pictorial field. We are left with the mess—we are left, that is, with a mistake, with an accident embraced as artistic creation. A glob. A spill. "Pas de forme," clamored de Zayas in another line from his poem "Elle," describing the female object of his verse. And yet, of course, refusing to describe at the same time. *Pas de forme.* No form. That seems about right.

But it does have a form, counters the art historian. Look, one could say, *La Sainte-Vierge* even reads, just a little bit, like a body: a minimal, if not squashed, head; a monstrous arm; two drips for legs. This is no Dada pun, no play on words able to evade meaning through the device of rhyme, or homophone, or alliteration. This is a drawing. As such, *La Sainte-Vierge* remains a fixed representation, no matter how "incontinent," and the art historians consequently respond that it must have a fixed meaning, a referent in the world to which it points. If a body can be seen in it, perhaps one can see other things besides.

In the face of such an interpretive mission, *La Sainte-Vierge* has become something like the Rorschach image of modernist art history, an art history still dragging along its apparatus of iconography and stylistic analysis, transforming Picabia's work into a site for the practice of art history as an endless proliferation of sheer projection. The ink splash, says one, "unmodified by aesthetic considerations," is the Blessed Virgin. Or perhaps, the art historian continues, the besmirched white page is the Virgin—for this is Dada, after all, and this image is blasphemous. But that is too general, counters another, for surely we are looking at the contravention of the Immaculate Conception, at the literal blood-letting of the Virgin's defloration by God. It stands for bodily secretions altogether, claims another, and we are told, in a spiraling chain, that *La Sainte-Vierge* represents the blood of defilement; the blood sacrificed by soldiers in World War I; a parodic bleeding heart; a milky twist on the Christian iconography of the Virgin offering her breast to the infant Jesus; a semen stain; a "black" virgin, like the one worshiped by prostitutes at Chartres; a silhouette; a reference to the annual "white sales" at Parisian department stores; even the oil stain left after a mechanic (Picabia?) has finished working on his signature "machine drawings."[9]

So much for what one could call the attempt to construct an "iconography" of Dada. Art history seems to have forgotten that Dada was not entirely interested in discovering the meaning of works of art. Meaninglessness was its goal. Iconography, even "hidden" or secret meanings, were surely invoked by many Dada works. But usually this was done in the spirit of travesty, a devastating annihilation of the apparatus of meaning that had always supported the traditional work of art. Perhaps the time has come for the deployment of another interpretive model. And indeed we could start with the simple suggestion that Picabia's *La Sainte-Vierge* is not an image "of" anything at all.

On this point, the Dadaists would agree with us. Already in 1921, the poet Louis Aragon had been forced to come to Picabia's defense in this matter:

> In the domain of the inimitable, Picabia, a painter . . . allows ink to fall on a white page, and the ink sprawls, it spurts: unique spatters that no one could ever copy. "But anyone could do that!": How not to see the weakness of this complaint? . . . The moment that the hand tilts bottle over paper, what a beacon in the night of mankind! If, under his ink stain, Picabia writes: "La Sainte-Vierge," he explains an accident [*il définit un hasard*].
>
> Immediately, taking the name for the meaning, an illustrated magazine, *Les Hommes du jour,* under the title "Two Schools," reproduced this image next to the Virgin by Ingres. This contempt rather faithfully reflects the magnificence of the criticism of our time: one can hardly judge a thing except by analogy, or through punning.[10]

The work of art could be understood only through metaphor, substitution, analogy: this for that, this is like that. For Aragon, by contrast, *La Sainte-Vierge* wasn't *like* anything (in other words, it was not mimetic). It entailed an operation. It performed a (paradoxical) task. It had a job: to produce an *inimitable* work of art, an image literally unable to be manually copied. One could never pastiche *La Sainte-Vierge*; divorced from the hand of the artist and thus purged of any traces of what we might call "style," one could only follow Picabia's procedure, producing another *Sainte-Vierge,* itself inimitable in turn. Picabia would do this. Aragon too, it seems, would do this, playing along with Picabia's gesture in a series of ink stains preserved by Picabia in his personal scrapbooks.[11] And the poet would still remind us of the result nine years later in his seminal essay on collage aesthetics, "La peinture au défi," claiming that "Undoubtedly when Picabia spoke of the ink spot he had signed, he did not fail to attract attention to the *inimitable* quality of such splashings. He congratulated himself that his ink spot could not be copied as well as a Renoir."[12] We should consider why such a claim, such an interpretation, surfaces as an integral part of the most important essay on the aesthetics of collage produced during the modernist era. But such indeed was the horizon of expectation through which Picabia's fellow Dadaists understood his drawing. And it was this lesson of the drawing that the Dadaists repeatedly threw in the face of the public in the wake of Picabia's action.

Listen, for example, to Tristan Tzara, gleefully teasing us in his completely false advertisement for Picabia's Dada "treatise" *Jésus-Christ Rastaquouère (Jesus Christ, Playboy),* an advertisement published later that year, in the fall of 1920, in *391*: "At Povolozky's. 5 Francs. 1000 special editions and a single one on ordinary paper. There is a special printing on soft, transparent paper so that one may trace La Sainte-Vierge."[13] With the language of poetry replaced by the language of advertisement, Tzara gives us a list of lies, the last one the most egregious—for it is an action whose impossibility we have already noted.

But is that all? Was there nothing else? Does Picabia's image stand alone?

Singular, unrepeatable, Picabia's drawing seems to fly in the face of the rationalization of drawing, in the face of the reduction of drawing to the principle of exchange, to which French modernism had turned by 1920. Think of all the dreams

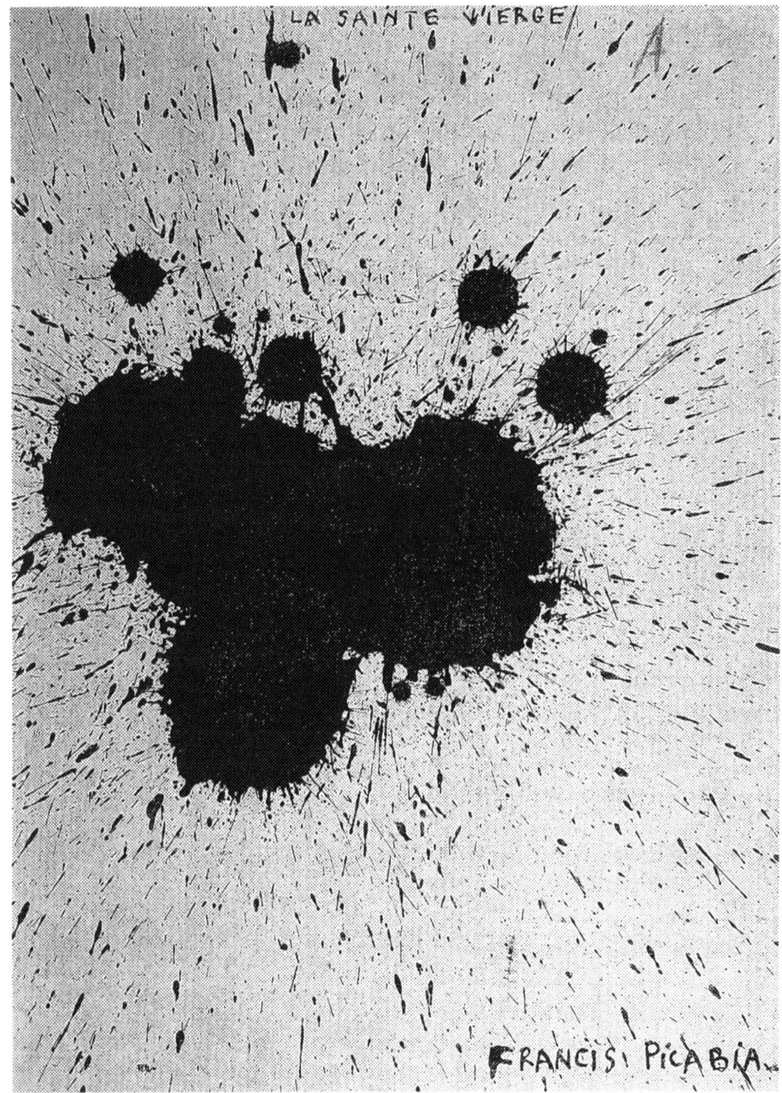

Francis Picabia, *La Sainte-Vierge II,* c. 1920. Bibliothèque Littéraire Jacques Doucet, Paris. © 2005 Artists Rights Society (ARS), New York/ADAGP, Paris/Estate of Francis Picabia.

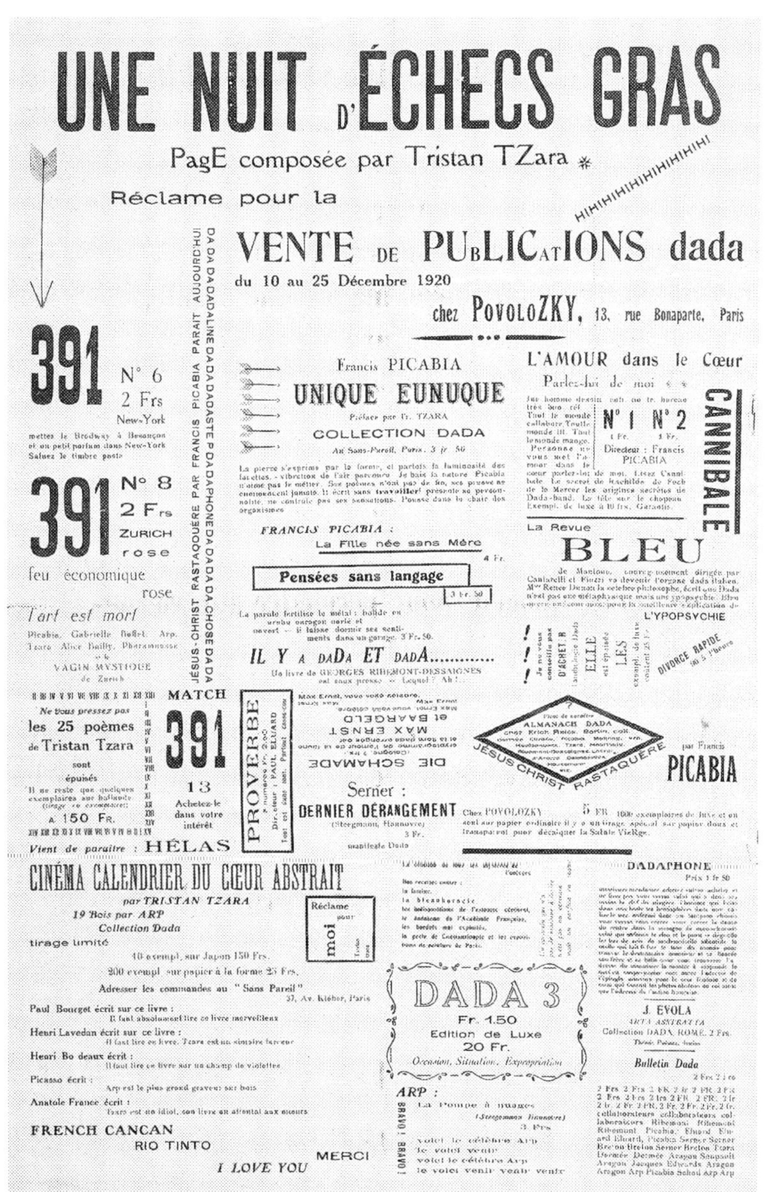

Tristan Tzara, "Une Nuit d'Échecs Gras," 1920. Published in *391* 14 (November 1920), p. 4. Research Library, The Getty Research Institute, Los Angeles.

of the Section d'Or cubists, of the dawning realization that their discoveries had opened onto the potential mass production of paintings, a position Albert Gleizes would take, for example, by 1920. Think too of the entrance onto the artistic scene of the Purists, and of their strident call for the representation of what they called *objets types* to standardize the painted object, the use of "regulating lines" to standardize compositional arrangements, and the parallel standardization of canvas size, producing an aggressive equalization that would lead to Le Corbusier's call for every home to have a "library of paintings" that could be shuffled through a given domestic space at will. But Picabia's demonstration would also seem to work against the defining principle of his own Dada images, images formed since the early 1910s through the readymade appropriation of mechanical drawings and photographs—formed, that is, precisely through copying. *La Sainte-Vierge* thus becomes, in this view, a sort of sensational exception within Picabia's production, the singular transgression that only serves to prove the rule.[14]

But is that all? Was there nothing else? Was *La Sainte-Vierge* alone?

Although all of the art historical work on Dada has missed this fact, the answer to these questions must be returned as an emphatic "No." An operational analysis of Picabia's drawing does not have to stop here; and it need not leave *La Sainte-Vierge* in the isolation to which the iconographical studies and art history at large have confined it. In fact Picabia did not leave *La Sainte-Vierge* in isolation. The work was exceptional—it was a work whose very principle was the exception—but it was not singular. *La Sainte-Vierge* was to be but one-half of a larger demonstration, a larger operation. For Picabia produced with it a companion piece, a double, a sister project.

In stark contrast to the messy accidents of *La Sainte-Vierge,* this long-ignored drawing consisted simply of a perfectly formed circle. Far from referring to the Blessed Virgin, this drawing was called, more expansively, but with the same Dadaist nudge and wink, *La jeune fille (The Young Girl).* One version of it sat,

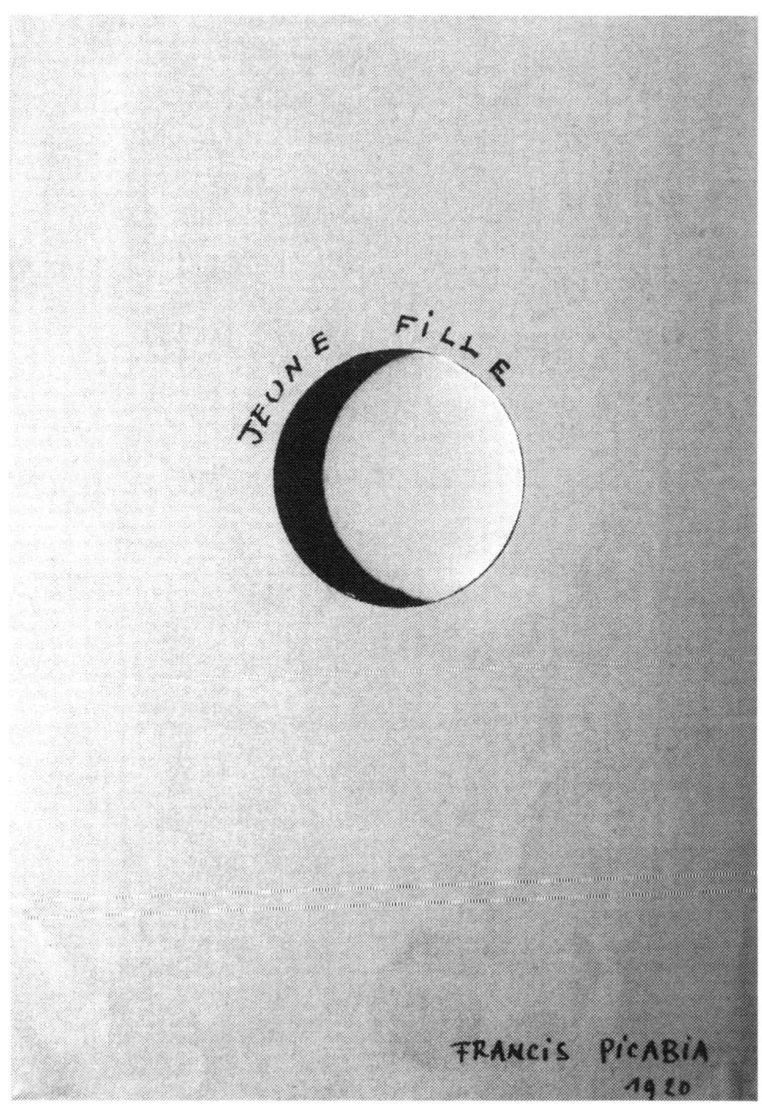

Francis Picabia, *Jeune fille (Young Girl),* 1920. Ink on paper with circle cut out, 28 × 22.3 cm (11 × 8³⁄₄″). Collection Paul Destribats, Paris. © 2005 Artists Rights Society (ARS), New York/ADAGP, Paris/Estate of Francis Picabia.

unnoticed and unexhibited, for decades among the papers and possessions of Tristan Tzara, and was only recently unearthed by art historians interested in the turn toward geometric abstraction that Picabia's work would later take. This the art historians call the "original" version of the drawing, or perhaps its "maquette"— a claim that must be challenged—for Picabia reproduced *La jeune fille* in a Dada magazine just as he did *La Sainte-Vierge,* using, in fact, basically the same format and layout for both drawings. Picabia did this during the same great Dada season of 1920, the opening salvo of Dada in Paris, in a short-lived but crucial and singularly forgotten magazine edited by the poet Paul Éluard called *Proverbe,* in its fourth issue, in April, just weeks—perhaps days—after the publication of *La Sainte-Vierge* in *391.*[15]

But perhaps there was no delay at all. All the facts point to an explicit connection between the two works; the sleuth work of the art historian points as well to the absolute contemporaneity of their production. The facts are as follows: We know, through the work of Dada scholar Michel Sanouillet, that the March 1920 issue of *391* that contained *La Sainte-Vierge* was probably not available until quite late in the month. Sanouillet notices that it responds to a riposte in Éluard's *Proverbe 3,* which was dated 1 April 1920, but was probably available to Picabia around March 25.[16] That would put the publication, or at least the distribution, of the March issue of *391* at around the date on which we know it was actually distributed: at the Dada manifestation that took place in Paris at the Maison de l'Oeuvre on March 27. *La Sainte-Vierge,* as well as the entire issue of *391* in which it was contained—an issue that carried on its cover a version of Duchamp's infamous parody of the Mona Lisa, *L.H.O.O.Q.*—was meant to perform as yet another element in the total assault of this key Dada demonstration, a manifesto in the form of an image as stark as any of the verbal essays that the Dadaists read upon the stage that day. Now, as *Proverbe* 3 was dated "1 April 1920," and *Proverbe* 5 was labeled "1 May 1920," the fourth issue with *La jeune fille* floats dateless within this general time frame, with the art historian guessing, logically, that it must have been produced in between the two issues, sometime early in the month of April.

But the Dadaists were not known for their logic, nor for their blind faith in the telos of chronology. Dateless, the fourth issue of *Proverbe* emerged as an

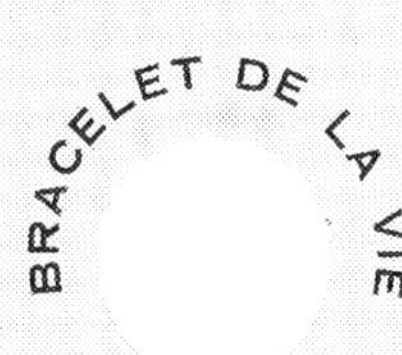

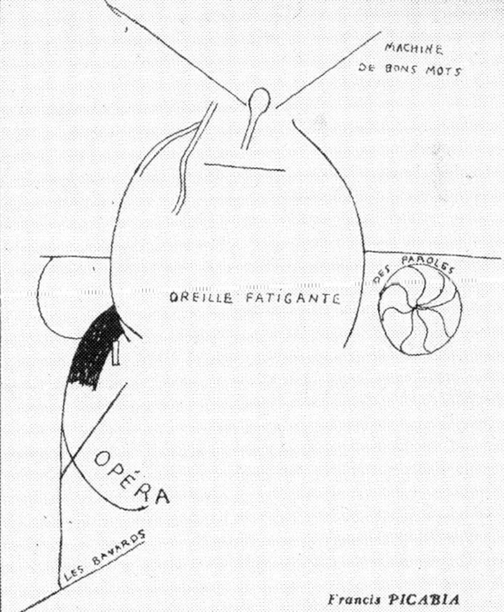

**NUMÉRO SPÉCIAL
D'ART & DE POÉSIE**

Adresser tout ce qui concerne
PROVERBE à M. PAUL ELUARD
3, rue Ordener, PARIS (XVIIIe)

PROVERBE
FEUILLE MENSUELLE

ÉCHANTILLON GRATUIT

Abonnements :

Edition ordinaire : 5 fr. par an

Edition de luxe : 15 fr. par an

(Tirage à 15 exemplaires)

Exemplaire No

LA JEUNE FILLE

FRANCIS PICABIA

ENTRE VOLEURS

Mais le jeu de l'archet
                sur les trois bougies allumées
magnétise le coffre aux jetons…
                Un gagnant
puis vient une ballade en lambeaux
Le baladin est mort
                au bout de sa chanson

Céline ARNAULD.

ÉCRIRE ENCORE

Tous les mots tournent et se pincent l'oreille vite
A l'affût on mâchonne une herbe trop amère
Ce qu'on cherchait on le trouve au porte-manteau
Le couvert d'argent écrit l'excuse de ma visite
La lampe offusque enfin la fausse gloire du jour

Paul DERMÉE.

Pour lire les **22** manifestes

DADA

abonnez-vous à

LITTÉRATURE

revue mensuelle
37, Avenue Kléber (XVIe)
Abonnements : 18 francs par an

(chanté)

Hee ! que disions-nous ? que disions-nous ?
Nous avons perdu la mémoire.
Hoo ! que faisions-nous ? que faisions-nous ?
Nous avons perdu la mémoire.

Paul ELUARD.

DÉRAILLEMENT

machiniste d'ombres boréales connues
l'effigie de l'empereur nous envoie des flèches
                ou des instruments de pêche
les archanges ont aussi des besoins scandaleux
souvenir collectif et parasiste la fontaine dans
                la boîte
marchands de projections scarabées cabrés et
                crabes
entre le taureau et le serpent il y a le lys
                hiver tuyau et l'emballage.

Tristan TZARA.

Il n'y a pas de main-d'œuvre et il n'y en
aura plus de main-d'œuvre.

Avec DADA, tous les jours, rendez-vous n'importe où.

DÉTOUR PAR LE CIEL

enfant trame un désespoir de perles
s'inspire des boîtes qu'il a reçues pour sa communion
se pose le problème de la naissance sous forme d'une jolie
                équation en do
barricade sa fenêtre de ses cils
joue avec la prière de sa petite sœur qui est plus argentée
                que la sienne
endure les mauvais traitements
de 2 à 3
se multiplie à la façon des microbes de son livre notamment
par scissiparité celui qui se sépare de lui a des ailes
il pense aux belles karyokinèses
pendant la messe
1919

André BRETON.

UNE

Une tristesse de mauvais temps, les
ébats bondissants de la fumée et du
vent, un ciel gris prêt à la pluie,
on dit que la musique perd le sentiment.

Cette douce
Cette belle,
Assise de couleurs,
Tranquille
Et, surveillant le ciel,
Négligeant la chaleur

Paul ELUARD.

THÉOPHILE

Dieu en habit caporal dit à Dieu en habit berlingot
Qui
Les jambes en chapeau perles disent au ventre perroquet
Il y a un certain nombre de choses
Dieu en veste à pellicules à Dieu en harpe moisie
Je n'ai jamais vu Nu

G. RIBEMONT-DESSAIGNES.

GÉNUFLEXION

Océan mon cœur et ma vie
ne sont rien près de vous Marie
c'est la mort que déjà j'oublie

abbé Philippe SOUPAULT.

Paul Éluard, ed., *Proverbe* 4 (Special Issue on Art and Poetry), n.d. (March 27, 1920). Beinecke Rare Book and Manuscript Library, Yale University. © 2005 Artists Rights Society (ARS), New York/ ADAGP, Paris/Estate of Francis Picabia exceptional case in Éluard's journal, a self-proclaimed "special issue on art and poetry" existing in relation to the regular numbers as a kind of issue *hors série*. It was, as Sanouillet admits, "distributed free at various Dada manifestations," its purpose being, supposedly, to "attract subscribers" to the journal. Its format, too, differed from the regular numbers of *Proverbe,* with their minimal booklike folding, for the fourth issue appeared as a one-sided broadsheet ready for distribution, less a book than a poster or a handbill. And since the next major Paris Dada manifestation after the Maison de l'Oeuvre was not until the Festival Dada on May 26, a full two months later, one has to imagine the occasion of this distribution, this advertisement for *Proverbe,* as none other than March 27, upon the evening of the Maison de l'Oeuvre demonstration, in the company of Picabia's *391* and *La Sainte-Vierge.* One has to imagine, that is, the simultaneous production and distribution of *La Sainte-Vierge* and *La jeune fille,* and the presentation, on Picabia's part, of an absolutely intentional pair.

But there was only silence, you see. Deafening silence.

It was a silence that wiped the historical record clean. We are lucky, in a sense. Perhaps we should even be grateful. For the proof of this pairing need not rely on the vague testimony of publication dates and demonstrations, on the imperfect reconstruction of a disposable history long since lost. Whether *La jeune fille* was present at the Maison de l'Oeuvre or not, Picabia's pairing of the two works produced an utter failure to signify, engendering a silence unbroken by the critical fury of the time or the art historical worship of today, catapulting one drawing to cultural infamy and the other to the critical oblivion of the unexamined archive. The proof of this pairing, then, will not be a matter for history, for the careful parsing of dates and times, but rather a matter for theory, and for the thorough analysis of the testimony given by form.[17]

And it is form that remains the most unusual thing about Picabia's *La jeune fille,* a form that the printed version in *Proverbe* makes clear far exceeds the contrast provided to *La Sainte-Vierge* by any understanding of its companion piece as a reassertion of an interest in abstract geometry. This would be a contrast, merely, of hard-edged, geometric shape and biomorphic splash, an opposition well within the traditional purview of the art historical analysis of style, even considering the strange coincidence of both drawings' production by the same artist, and thus the cancellation of the singular attachment of artist and style upon which such analysis depends. *La jeune fille,* however, emerges as much more exceptional than this, standing out, in fact, as perhaps the most extraordinary moment in the entire run of Éluard's ill-fated journal (there would only be six issues, and one short year of existence). What makes the drawing remarkable is this: When Picabia reproduced *La jeune fille* within the context of Éluard's magazine, the drawing was published, not simply as a geometric shape, but as a literal hole cut through the surface of the single broadsheet that made up that issue of the journal.[18]

A literal hole—one can see through *La jeune fille,* but it also takes on an object status, and one can touch it, piercing its surface with both hand and eye. *Prière de toucher.* To consider this as the companion piece to *La Sainte-Vierge*—to take seriously their twinned layouts, their simultaneous presentation in the Dada magazines, their linked titles, their shared purpose to be distributed in large numbers at the major Dada manifestations—is to notice what no art historians have noticed since the moment of the two drawings' manifesto-like presentation. On the level of form, a project has been announced, and that project takes shape around a deceptively simple, but exceedingly clear, understanding of the relation of a medium to form.

For in these two works, Picabia performs an incredibly precise operation upon the traditional structure, definition, and logic of the medium of drawing itself. If, for example, the Dadaists celebrated *La Sainte Vierge* for its inability to be copied, for its inimitable nature, that was of course because Picabia's ink splashes—considered in relation to drawing—provided a way to draw an image without recourse to line, forming no recognizable shape, escaping through a transgressive gesture drawing's traditional task of defining contour. One cannot trace that which bounds no shape or forms no contour, and *La Sainte-Vierge* provides us with everything but the form that depends on line: a glob, a spill, a drip, a run, a bleed, and a thousand miniature splatters adding up to nothing within the realm

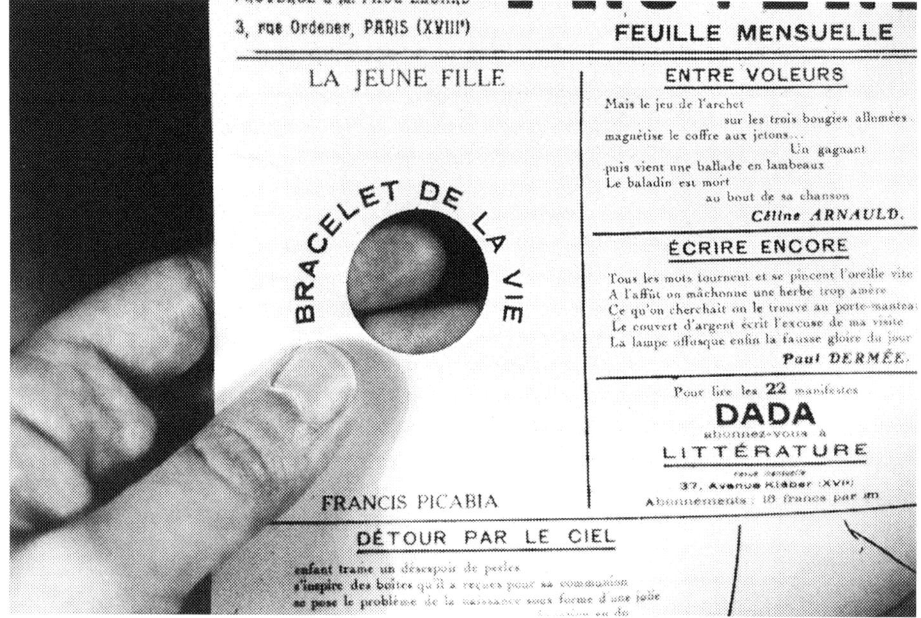

Francis Picabia, *La jeune fille (The Young Girl),* from *Proverbe* 4, 1920. Photographed by author. © 2005 Artists Rights Society (ARS), New York/ADAGP, Paris/Estate of Francis Picabia.

of form, and to an impossible task for the hand to copy. But at the same moment, Picabia presents *La jeune fille,* a drawing that—in a manner exceeding that of any drawing previous to it—must be described as being *all* contour, to the point of defining drawing as a cut, and this cut as a loss.

And the consequences of this conceptual pairing only begin to multiply. On the one hand, we are faced with a drawing that attempts to obliterate its ground, perhaps to desublimate it, producing a quite literal, almost sadistic, opacification (*La Sainte-Vierge*). On the other, we face a rather different kind of obliteration of the ground (*La jeune fille*), a drawing that so reverses figure/ground relations that its ground becomes a figure against the space of the world—or perhaps better, its ground becomes a frame for a figure now readable as literally transparent. It is in this sense—that the drawing would be less a framed, self-contained entity than a frame itself providing a view of life around it—that one can read the inscription that Picabia placed around the hole in Éluard's magazine ("the bracelet of life"), and indeed the notion of transparency would become crucial to Picabia's later artistic career. Its literal enactment was the subject of another celebrated Dada work—the painting *Danse de Saint-Guy (St. Vitus' Dance)* exhibited in 1922. Picabia's literalness is typical, but biting: he recasts modernist hermeticism as an obliterating stain, modernist structural transparency as a work through which one can see.

And what we see is another image of Picabia. In the spring of 1922, the avant-garde journal *The Little Review* dedicated a special issue to Picabia. There, accompanying his essay "Anticoq," Picabia published a photograph of himself holding up *Danse de Saint-Guy,* fresh from its scandal-causing entry to the Salon des Indépendants of that same year. Here is Picabia in pin-stripes and bow-tie, hair greased and shining, a smile on his face that, for once, radiates neither bemusement, nor mischief, nor the excess of Dada mockery. It seems a knowing smile, a smile of self-control; a smile dedicated, perhaps, to the future. Posed behind *Danse de Saint-Guy*'s taut strings and randomly distributed phrases on paper labels, it seems the smile of someone who knows a secret.

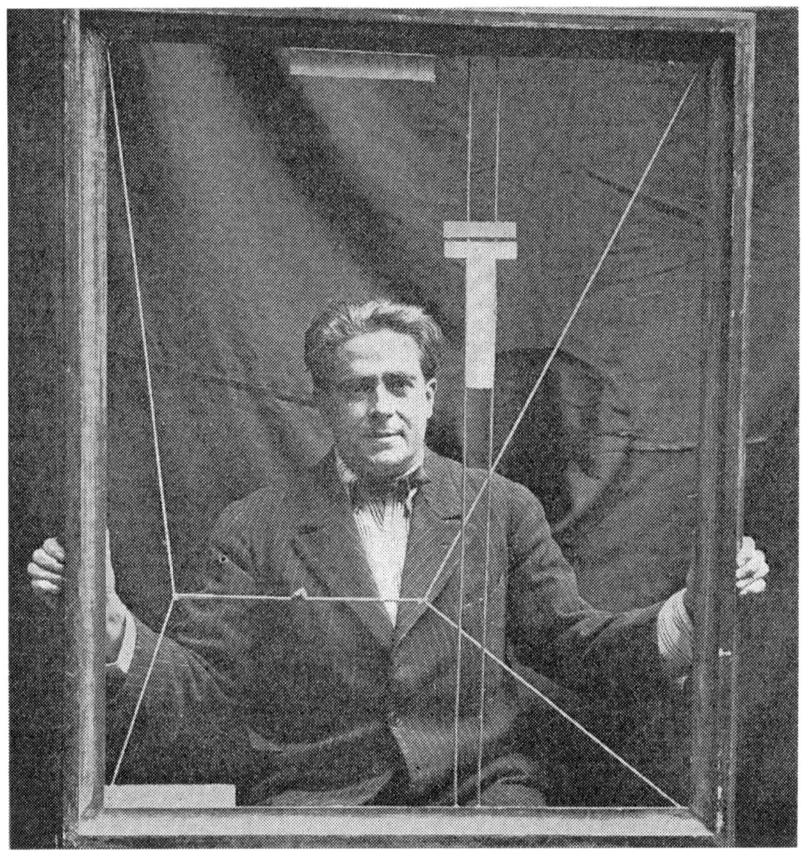

Anonymous [Man Ray?], *Francis Picabia with Danse de Saint-Guy (St. Vitus' Dance),* from *The Little Review,* special issue on Picabia, vol. 8, no. 2, Spring 1922. Research Library, The Getty Research Institute, Los Angeles.

For the photograph, like so much else in Picabia's work, was a copy. Who could have known this in 1922, except for Man Ray, perhaps—did he make this photograph of Picabia, as he did so many others? Who else could have done it?— or Marcel Duchamp, certainly. It had been Man Ray, in fact, who had produced—as he did so many others—the photograph of Duchamp to which Picabia now returned. In it, we see Duchamp, arms outstretched and gripping the frame of his semicircular *Glider,* a well-known preparatory work among many for Duchamp's *Large Glass.* We see, that is, Duchamp through the glass surface of his *Glider,* announcing the centrality of transparency to the project upon which, by 1913, he had embarked. Gripping the frame of *Danse de Saint-Guy,* Picabia seconds this announcement.

It would become one of the tenets of his aesthetic. He would continue to proclaim it until the end of his life, in his works and paintings, but also, for instance, in an interview with Georges Charbonnier published in the 1950s shortly after Picabia's death. By that time, *Danse de Saint-Guy* had been rechristened *Tabac-Rat (Rat Tobacco),* its strings tightened and rearranged, its labels altered, but its demonstration basically unchanged. We should listen to this interview:

> G.C.—At your Galerie Drouin exhibition, there was a painting that intrigued the visitors very much. This painting consisted of a frame. And only a frame. Without a canvas. Within the frame were stretched four strings.
>
> F.P.—This painting was made to be hung in a room, in a gallery . . .
>
> G.C.—Hung against a wall?
>
> F.P.—Ah! No. Hung from the ceiling! The painting must remain "transparent." The strings accompany the movement of anything that passes beyond the frame and constitute a painting. Thus one can only hang this painting far from the wall, outside the reach of the wall that would only obstruct it. The painting divides space into volumes.[19]

Motion and transparency were crucial components of the conceptual ground of *Danse de Saint-Guy.* But it seems as if we are getting ahead of ourselves. I promise

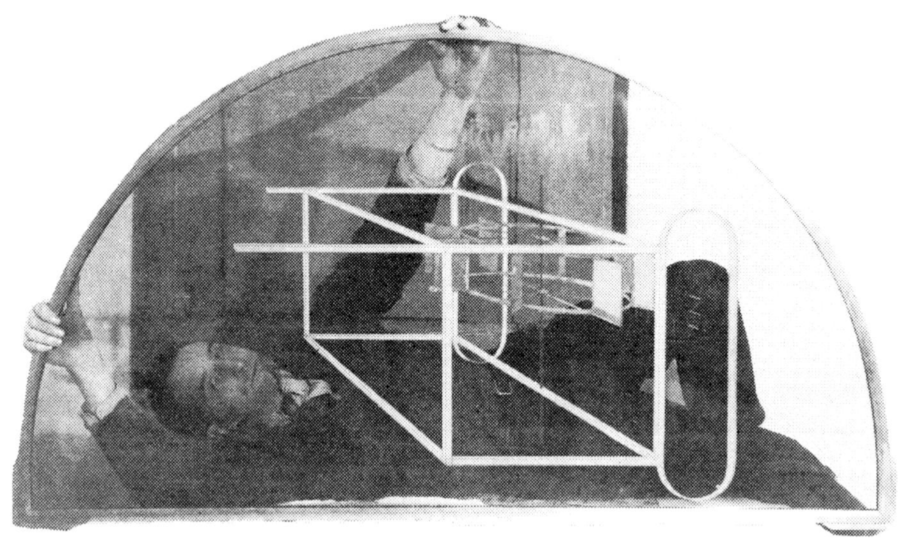

Man Ray, *Marcel Duchamp with Glider,* 1917. Gelatin silver print, arched, 8.6 × 15.4 cm ($3^3/_8 × 6^1/_{16}''$). The J. Paul Getty Museum, Los Angeles. © 2005 Artists Rights Society (ARS), New York/ADAGP, Paris/Man Ray Trust.

that we are not. We will come, eventually, to Picabia's investment in transparency as a kind of anti-type to modernist transparency, in fact the defining principle of Picabia's insistent practice of pastiche or the copy. We will come, more directly, to the events of 1922, and to the motivation that would bring Picabia to return to *Danse de Saint-Guy,* to thrust it into a different public space, into the space of a Salon. I did say return. We know that it was, in fact, a return on Picabia's part, even a recycling of sorts. For in some form at least, *Danse de Saint-Guy* already existed in 1920. It dates from precisely the same moment as *La jeune fille,* and from the moment of the birth of Dada in Paris. It actually preceded *La jeune fille,* by just a little, and the two works must be thought together.

We know this from a letter, dated 15 February 1920, sent by André Breton to Picabia. I apologize for the minute details, for the mundane quality of the evidence, but this story must be told. It is crucial to the matter at hand, and the details have been forgotten, as neglected as *La jeune fille* itself. The letter tells us much. From the period when Breton and Picabia were still new to each other, it is characteristic of the sometimes seductive, sometimes pleading tone the younger poet took with the older artist in his attempt to cement a friendship that would never quite take. First, the seduction: In mid-February, Breton had just received a manuscript of Picabia's, a text for a manifesto called "Dada Philosopher" that Picabia dedicated to the poet in a characteristic gesture of friendship. Breton was not unmoved. "What always amazes me about you," Breton wrote, "is precisely the opposite of how you were always described to me, that is, your rare ability to love. I told a friend, rather clumsily, that your books have been written in the language of love." Now, the pleading: "This letter is ridiculous," Breton admits. "I have reread 'Dada Philosopher' so often that I am impregnated by its melancholy." This was by way of segue to the true subject of the letter, a potential misunderstanding over a work by Picabia that Breton calls a *tableau en cordes*—a painting made of rope.

> I remember that one evening, while contemplating the painting
> made out of rope that is in the antechamber at the rue Émile-Augier
> [the apartment of Germaine Everling, where Picabia lived], I laughed

a lot without really knowing why. You seemed surprised. However, I assure you that I am rather disposed to take things too seriously. I was and still am afraid that you took this for incomprehension on my part. Which makes me sad. How to explain this event. I would behave similarly before *DADA Philosopher*; it is, after all, nothing else but a sign of your power.[20]

We may wonder how well Breton actually could have understood this "painting," given his perspective in 1920, and how little he actually knew Picabia's previous work; how little, still, he could have known the work of Duchamp and the events of New York Dada. (Laughter, after all, may not be a sign of incomprehension, but it is its own form of not understanding, of the sovereign power that Dada typically sought in an object that leeches away the firm ground of meaning itself.) Perhaps Breton understood the work in the way that Louis Aragon later would, as a violent negation of the "luxury" of painting, and an embrace of the ephemeral in art—a work that would not last, that would incorporate chance and the temporal—that would, in fact, constantly change or even disappear.[21] In this, he would not have been wrong, not really. And it seems that Picabia and Breton must have come to some agreement over the work, some sort of mutual understanding. For the importance of *Danse de Saint-Guy* only became more pronounced as the first great Dada season of 1920 progressed. The *tableau en cordes* would not sit idly in Picabia's apartment, only to be displayed, publicly, for the first time at the Salon des Indépendants in 1922. It was shown, in some form, for the first time in March of 1920. It was present at the Dada manifestation at the Maison de l'Oeuvre.

I have been calling the Dada season of 1920 "great." Of course, it was nothing of the kind. Dada, in Paris at least, was a colossal failure. The first season of 1920 was "great" simply in comparison to what would come after, to the insistent accumulation of defections, of internal strife, of public debacles, of false starts. Optimistically—ironically?—the Dadaists saved the term "great" for the planned events of 1921, the self-proclaimed *grande Saison Dada*. No matter. They would be sounding the death knell soon enough. But, as we all know, Dada embraced this failure. Failure was its life-blood, its raison d'être. Hence its dedication to self-immolation. (Consider the eulogy of Picabia's friend, Georges Ribemont-Dessaignes: "Dada was finished. . . . it had understood that it could work only toward its own ruin. It was aware of its bankruptcy and did not fight it. For bankruptcy was its sign.")[22]

I like to think of several moments of the 1920 Paris Dada season as defining its paradoxical "greatness," as defining, that is, the coiled energies that fueled Dada's inevitable failure.[23] Key among them would be the climactic moment of the very first public manifestation of the Dadaists in Paris, the Premier Vendredi de Littérature that was staged on January 23 in a popular cinema on the rue St.-Martin. It took time for the Dadaists to find their voice; their first manifestation took the form, simply, of an aggressive poetry reading, with a display of modern paintings besides. But by the end of this event, it was time to present to an unsuspecting public the already notorious Tristan Tzara, who had recently arrived in Paris and had been, for the most part, hiding in Picabia's apartment. Tzara strode onto the stage. He began to read, but not, as had been promised, from his poetry. He read, instead, a recent political speech by the royalist Léon Daudet that had been printed in the Parisian newspapers. No one heard a word of it. For at the precise moment that his discourse began, Breton and Aragon, waiting in the wings, took their cue and began to ring electric bells that completely drowned out every word of Tzara's performance.[24] Politics and the newspapers replaced poetry, at least for a moment. But they would not be given free rein. They would not be allowed to register. Their language was canceled, inaudible, unavailable, an absence registered before the hall of outraged spectators. The spectators would be trained to do the canceling themselves in time. At the crossroads of politics and art, Dada created a void, a resounding noise, a hideous, incomprehensible buzz. It was a first "great" moment of Dadaist negation.

My second moment has been largely forgotten: February would find the Dadaists, or at least four of them—Tzara, Aragon, Breton, and Ribemont-Dessaignes—traveling to the outskirts of Paris, to the rue de Puteaux, to a deconsecrated church, Saint-Antoine de Padoue, where they presented their ideas before the Club du faubourg, a descendant of the old Revolutionary clubs. I told you it would take time for the Dadaists to find their voice. (Although perhaps this move by the Dadaists was not as odd or eccentric as it seems, but merely neglected and underestimated; listen, for instance, to the following declamation by Aragon: "Following a custom that was dear to some of us, we took up the comparison of our intellectual situation and that of the French Revolution. It had to do with preparing and suddenly declaring the Terror. Everything occurred as if, with the Revolution happening, we were at its head. And in addition we had decided not to wait for '93, but the Terror right away: in '89."[25] The insistent comparison of Breton to Robespierre should tell us much.) At the Club du faubourg, on February 7, they read manifestos instead of poems, manifestos that had been presented just two nights earlier within the frame of the Salon des Indépendants at the Grand Palais. They came to the Club du faubourg, however, seeking escape from the rarefied atmosphere of the artistic milieu; they came, in fact, seeking workers. They had been ill informed. Greeted, to their amazement, by an audience of up to one thousand people, the Dadaists quickly realized that this mass mostly excluded the working class, and that they were in a room full of intellectuals and of politicians of various stripes. There were many socialists, who seemed eager to attack the Dadaists. But there were anarchists there too, and the comedy of misunderstandings of this evening saw the debate devolve into a vigorous conflict between the socialists and the anarchists, with the anarchists putting up a brisk defense of the four men and siding with the Dadaists against socialism. The Dadaists quickly put an end to any hopes for an alliance. But politics had raised its head again, pulling Paris Dada back into its orbit, the very last thing we would expect from the received wisdom on the life of this movement.[26]

A third moment: The Dadaists finally confront the workers. After the Club du faubourg, the next Dada manifestation did not take place until 19 February, at an anarchist-leaning institution called the Université populaire du faubourg Saint-Antoine. Here, the Dadaists promised a Borgesian list of discourses on such topics as "Dada locomotion, life and skating; Dada pastry, architecture, and morals; Dada chemistry, tattooing, finance, and typewriters." What they delivered were more manifestos, read this time to a mostly working-class audience. Picabia's "Dada Philosopher" was read. So too Tzara's "Mr. Antipyrine's Manifesto." Expecting uproar in the hall, baiting the audience with their transgressions, the Dadaists were greeted only with mild surprise. With curiosity. Hands went up around the hall; the proletarians were asking questions, demanding additional commentaries, even explanations. The evening proved an utter debacle, with the Dadaists missing their target again, falling into the immense chasm that separated their intentions from their audience's response, their aggressive monologue from the vagaries of dialogue.

These would be lessons learned. The divorce between the Dadaist assault—what they liked to call their "revolt"—and the traditional language of politics would be slow in coming, slower than we have been led to believe, but in the end the divorce was total, one of the crucial outcomes of the great Dada season of 1920. And if I raise the specter of that divorce here, it is only because this must be seen as one of the potential contexts surrounding Picabia's move to create an artwork that is a hole, that is as much a void and an absence as Tzara's "political" speech at the Premier Vendredi de Littérature. This was at least part of the situation surrounding Picabia's move to position drawing between what we could call the stain and the cut, between the two extreme options of *La Sainte-Vierge* and *La jeune fille.*

Other contexts exist. By the time of the Maison de l'Oeuvre demonstration on 27 March, the Dadaists had found their voice, and, consequently, their form. This is the form with which we are familiar. No longer the avant-garde poetry reading, or a declamation before a political audience, the Dada manifestation would take the form of cabaret, returning to its Zurich origins, shrouding itself in spectacle, in theater, and in all the trappings of the variety show. There would be plays, and music, and manifestos, and dance, and various entertainments. Politics still entered the fray, but now only under the sign of parody. As, for example, in Picabia's "Cannibal Dada Manifesto," read by Breton before the audience at the Maison de l'Oeuvre with a musical accompaniment like a great patriotic oration:

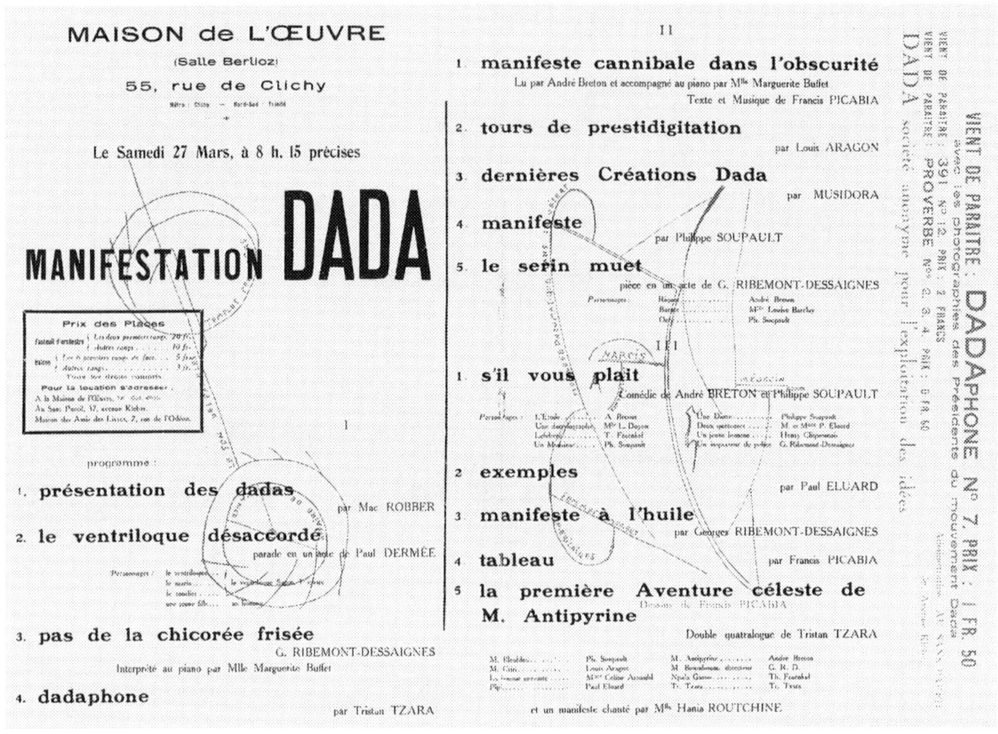

Program for the Dada Manifestation at the Maison de l'Oeuvre, March 27, 1920. Beinecke Rare Book and Manuscript Library, Yale University.

Stand up—you are all accused. The orator can only speak to you if you are standing up.

Stand up as if for the "Marseillaise," stand up as if for the Russian national anthem, stand up as if for "God Save the King," stand up as if before the flag. And finally, stand up before Dada, which represents life and which accuses you of liking everything for reasons of snobbery as soon as it costs a lot of money.

You have sat down again? Very well, that way you will pay more attention to me.

What are you doing here, planted on your backsides like a load of serious-minded morons—because that is what you are, serious, isn't it?

Serious, serious, serious to the point of death.[27]

To shroud itself in spectacle, to appropriate all the trappings of the variety show, meant that Dada now had need for the theatrical devices of set, and decor, and costumes. And it seems that for this first foray into the theatrical realm, it was Picabia who provided all of these for the Dadaists. This is where *Danse de Saint-Guy* enters the situation of 1920.

No photographs have survived of Picabia's set, but we do have the testimony of Dada's perhaps sole sympathetic critic of the 1920 season, a critic who described in just enough detail Picabia's sets and costumes for us to reconstruct the scene, and for us to understand the place of *Danse de Saint-Guy* within this context. It is unclear whether the set was there during the entire manifestation, or only during the play by Tzara, *The First Celestial Adventure of Mr. Antipyrine*, which came at the demonstration's end. But it is clear that, in many ways, Picabia's set for the Maison de l'Oeuvre existed as the structural opposite of a set with which we are familiar, the set that Picabia went on to design for his 1924 ballet *Relâche*. For, instead of a "curtain" of lamps paradoxically set up *behind* the performance and aimed out at the audience potentially to blind them, Picabia's earlier Dada set design was set up *in front* of the stage in such a manner that the spectators had to gaze through it. This is how the "sympathetic" critic described the scenery:

———

The costumes were surprising, unpredictable, ridiculous. They clearly evoked drawings as imagined by the insane and perfectly corresponded to the unimaginable text of Mr. Tristan Tzara. . . . The set—placed in front of the actors and not behind them—the transparent set—made up of a bicycle wheel, several ropes hung across the stage and frames containing hermetic inscriptions ("Paralysis is the beginning of wisdom," "Stick out your arms, and your friends will cut them off," etc.)—completed the ensemble perfectly.[28]

With this description in hand, we can begin to see how *Danse de Saint-Guy* was actually a fragment, an offshoot, perhaps even a condensation—something like either a preliminary sketch or a posthumous recapitulation—of the larger Picabia set for the Maison de l'Oeuvre. We can begin to see that there was a context too for the extraordinary form of *La jeune fille,* and the silence that greeted it becomes, given this context, a bit more surprising. The critic, after all, understood Picabia's gambit to create a literally "transparent scenery"—understood, that is, the embrace by Picabia at this moment of transparency as one of the defining tropes of his work. The other Dadaists understood the set as a declaration of transparency as well.[29] The critic did not, however, get the reference to Duchamp.

For, of course, Picabia's set for the Maison de l'Oeuvre can only be described as an homage of sorts to the work of Duchamp. Typical of the dialogue the two were still having at this time, it shows Picabia returning to and developing gestures by Duchamp from the past decade, pushing these gestures further, even turning them back upon themselves. Duchamp would return the favor, and the dialogue must not be narrated as one-way. At times, however, Picabia's turn to Duchamp took the form of simple appropriation: thus the bicycle wheel, hanging, in Georges Hugnet's (second-hand) description, before the stage with the strings radiating out from it. The bicycle wheel was not an innocent choice on Picabia's part: it was one of the first works by Duchamp to incorporate "transparency" into its structure, as one could easily gaze through the spokes radiating out from the object like so many graphic lines (Duchamp's choice was not innocent either). In fact, "motion and transparency" were as much a part of Duchamp's

Bicycle Wheel as they were of Picabia's later *Danse de Saint-Guy,* if one imagines, as Duchamp did, the bicycle wheel in motion, spinning round and round, making the work not only a step toward the readymades but the first step toward the artist's later rotoreliefs as well.[30]

If Picabia's appropriation of the *Bicycle Wheel* and its linear spokes involves the Maison de l'Oeuvre set within the larger Dada investigation of drawing, that involvement was only compounded by the mass of strings stretched across the stage that day. It has hardly been noticed, but there exists a recurrent, persistent use by the Dadaists of string as an objectified form of drawing, a move and a trope that would repeatedly confound the boundaries between painting and collage, producing a twisted knot of connections between the readymade and drawing, between real objects and the laws of graphic production. That Picabia's set involved itself in this investigation of drawing provides the main reason for my extended treatment of the set here, within an excavation of the situation of Picabia's graphic experiment with *La Sainte-Vierge* and *La jeune fille.*[31] Duchamp made a first stab in this direction with his studies for the *Large Glass,* especially in his *Chocolate Grinder No. 2,* of February 1914. There, the precise graphic depiction of the first *Chocolate Grinder* of 1913 was overlaid with threads, threads that rendered the key lines of the depiction in cold, dry strokes and were sewn by Duchamp directly onto the canvas surface. The geometric precision of this procedure was immediately overturned in the *Three Standard Stoppages* that so captivated Picabia, with its three separate meter-long strings dropped from a height of one meter and affixed onto canvas strips, a series of linear drawings deformed according to the laws of chance. And it does not seem to stretch the point to see this allegory of drawing as string continued into the arena of the assisted readymades, specifically in Duchamp's *With Hidden Noise,* with its taut ball of twine imprisoned between two brass plates. It provides as well, I would argue, a reference, even a key, to Man Ray's enigmatic 1916 painting, *The Rope Dancer Accompanies Herself with Her Shadows,* or to the later rayographs that he produced that repeatedly returned to the impression of string on photographic paper. Jean Arp, among others, also turned to this conflation of drawing and string, but only later, by the late 1920s, by which time this device, at least among the avant-garde, had become much more widely known.

———

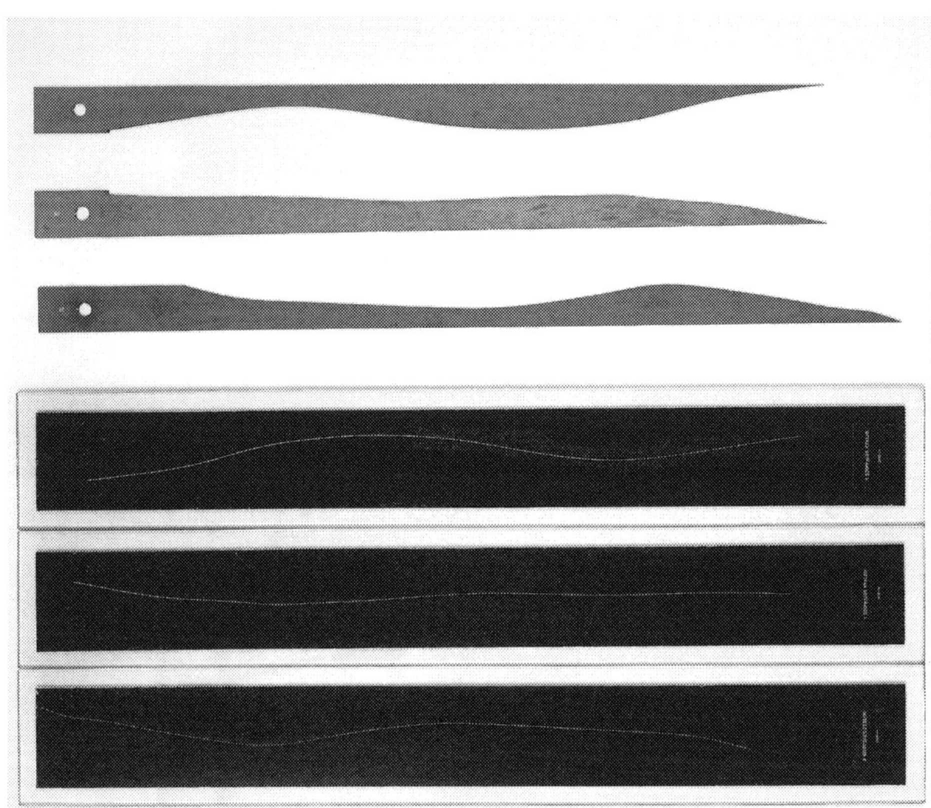

Marcel Duchamp, *Three Standard Stoppages* (*Trois stoppages étalon*), 1913–14. Assemblage: three threads glued to three painted canvas strips, $5^{1}/_{4} \times 47^{1}/_{8}''$, each mounted on a glass panel, $7^{1}/_{4} \times 49^{3}/_{8}'' \times {}^{1}/_{4}''$; three wood slats, $2^{1}/_{2} \times 43 \times {}^{1}/_{8}''$, $2^{1}/_{2} \times 47 \times {}^{1}/_{8}''$, $2^{1}/_{2} \times 43^{1}/_{4} \times {}^{1}/_{8}''$, shaped along one edge to match the curves of the threads; the whole fitted into a wood box, $11^{1}/_{8} \times 50^{7}/_{8} \times 9''$. The Museum of Modern Art, New York. Katherine S. Dreier Bequest. Photograph © The Museum of Modern Art/Licensed by SCALA / Art Resource, NY. © 2005 Artists Rights Society (ARS), New York/ADAGP, Paris/Estate of Marcel Duchamp.

I have purposely left one of Duchamp's string works to the end, for if any-thing it seems the most crucial to Picabia's *Danse de Saint-Guy* and to the set that he produced in 1920. This would be Duchamp's *Sculpture for Traveling* of 1918, a collapsible "sculpture" made of strings and shredded rubber cut from bathing caps that could be stretched in various configurations throughout the space of a room. We have photographs of the sculpture, threading its way through Du-champ's studio in 1918, coiled like a wayward snake around—what else?—the *Bicycle Wheel* in the middle of the space, or casting its shadow like a repulsive cob-web amid the other readymades in the photograph "Shadows of Readymades" that was produced in connection with Duchamp's last painting *Tu m'* of that same year. It seems that Picabia's set for the Maison de l'Oeuvre was his "version" of the *Sculpture for Traveling*. We can assume that he knew the piece, as—true to its title—we know that Duchamp took it with him when he left New York for Ar-gentina in 1918, and that after his year in Argentina, his next stop was the six months he spent living in Picabia's apartment at the end of 1919, leaving only just before the commencement of the Dada season of 1920.[32] If the *Sculpture for Traveling* did not make it to Picabia's apartment—the original supposedly rotted away "after a few years"—surely its memory did, and Picabia's set continues the dialogue. Except now, the *Sculpture for Traveling*'s various impediments and opac-ities would be retooled by Picabia as a web of transparency, a sceno-"graphic" in-scription made literally through which to see—less a sculpture invading space than a drawing throwing off lines.

Duchamp, in his own laconic way, would answer this reconfiguration. It took him until 1942, moving the concept slowly from the studio to the exhibi-tion space, with his *Sixteen Miles of String* installation at the First Papers of Surreal-ism exhibit in New York, another cobweb of string threaded in every direction throughout the exhibition space, more or less blocking the other artworks from view. Still for Duchamp perversely tied to measurement and objectified as string, drawing here became less a form of transgression than of interdiction, a new form of opacity and taboo—not a stage set, nor a frame, but an obliteration, a veiling, an obfuscation, an obstruction, a negation. With this, we have arrived at a more complete picture of the dialogue that was circulating around new forms

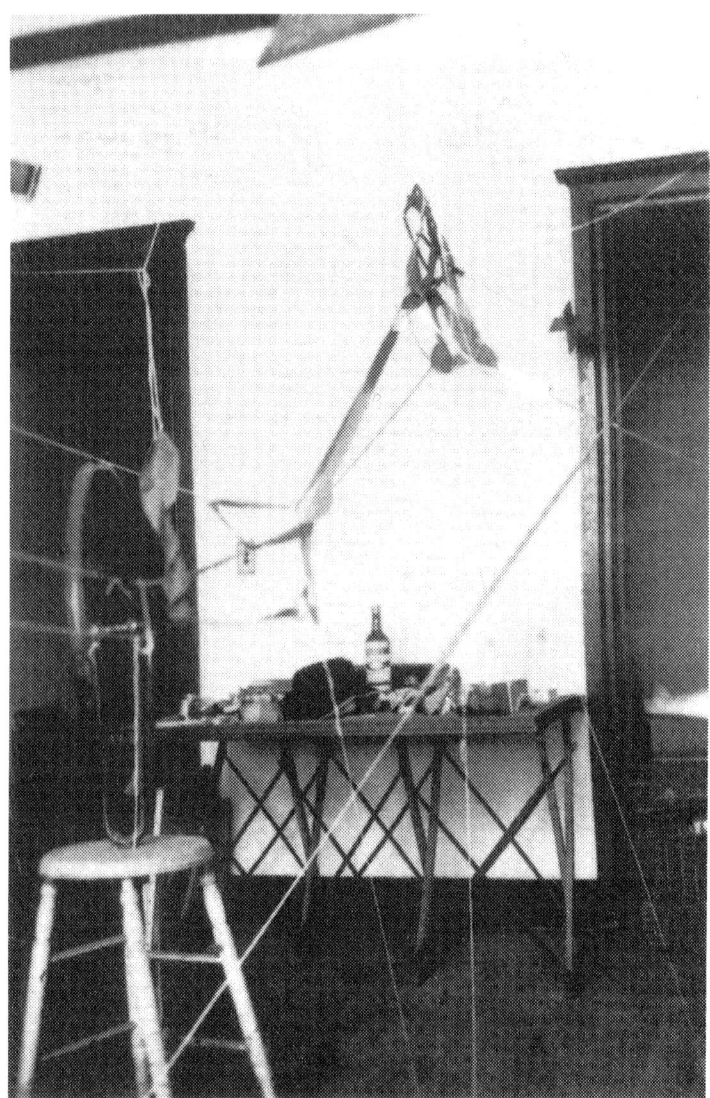

Marcel Duchamp, *Sculpture for Traveling,* 1918. No longer extant. © 2005 Artists Rights Society (ARS), New York/ADAGP, Paris/Estate of Marcel Duchamp.

of drawing within the Dada milieu. We are in a position to understand the high stakes, in 1920, resting on the contested site of drawing. We can begin to see how the Maison de l'Oeuvre contained a great argument, on Picabia's part, about the status of drawing, and of Dada's actions on it. That is my claim. This is the situation in which we must begin to position *La Sainte-Vierge* and *La jeune fille*. And yet the situation becomes only more complex.

Listen again to the art historians, to the few—two in fact—who have bothered to notice *La jeune fille* since Michel Sanouillet's passing mention forty years ago. They see neither transparency, nor an investigation of drawing, nor a dialogue with Duchamp. But they remind us of something this chapter seems to have skirted thus far, and which is unavoidable (central). Perhaps the reader has been incredulous. For the hole, offers one, has "sexual implications," of course. Somewhat less timid, the other offers no quarter. The hole's diameter, he notices, "is that of a penis."[33]

A punch line has been delivered: a drawing that is a hole would be a drawing that one could fuck, a drawing—or so the schoolboy prank goes—that is a cunt. But perhaps this is too vivid, even for Picabia (one may doubt it: this is the same artist who, just a year earlier, had entitled one of his paintings *Vagin brillant,* the *Shining Vagina*).[34] Like the flat-line collapse of individual subject and machine in his mechanomorphs, Picabia now collapses (somewhat more problematically) the female sex with its sex, producing a transformation of artistic practice in its wake. For of course both *La Sainte-Vierge* and *La jeune fille*—in fact Picabia's entire Dada production—tie drawing to what must be called an allegorization of desire, part and parcel of what has only recently come into view as the larger Dada project of the libidinalization of art practice in the wake of modernism's manifold bodily or corporeal repressions.[35]

And yet the collapse of woman and sex, of art and desire more generally, emerges as more complicated than Picabia's literal (obscene) gesture might at first suggest. In this case, Picabia presents us in *La jeune fille* with the form of the circle, a form he will deploy obsessively, repeatedly, throughout the full range of his Dada drawings, from the 1910s into the '20s. There, this form operates not only in relation to the specifically French version of abstraction that, from Robert Delaunay to Frantisek Kupka, had seized upon the circle as the preeminent avatar of abstract form, but also slides into Picabia's obsession with machines throughout his own mechanomorphic period: the circle as a mechanical gear, whirling, churning. What has been missed, however, is how it also provides Picabia with his preferred slip into the realm of what the psychoanalysts call the *part object*. I will return to this collapse more fully in later chapters, but for the moment one can point to a simple demonstration that Picabia made, four years after *La jeune fille,* of the slippage between circle and body. This occurred in a page from the program of his ballet *Relâche,* as the nested circles that Picabia repeatedly employed at this time, rotated 90 degrees from the picture plane, become readable as so many breasts crowned by a perfect nipple: the breast, the preeminent part object and lost object—*le sein des seins*—as the Dada version of the modernist structure of a *mise-en-abyme.* And so the circle wheels off, in Picabia's Dada work, into a series of gears, radiating suns, electrical lamps, but also all the bodily forms of the part object: breast, navel, eye, mouth, anus, and of course genital "hole." In this, modernist abstraction was recoded, by Picabia and the other Dadaists, as a field of fragmentary, throbbing body parts.

The pairing of *La Sainte-Vierge* and *La jeune fille,* however, makes this marriage between abstraction and desire literal, or better, structural. We are at an originary—or at least defining—moment of Picabia's Dada project. The libidinalization of drawing would not merely be a matter of representation, even of figuration, as if modernist abstraction could be countered by simply inserting pictures of outré objects, by substituting images of bodies for questions of form. The libidinalization of drawing would be precisely a question, itself, of form, and of procedures as well as processes. For if *La Sainte-Vierge,* formed through chance, attaches itself to the inimitable, *La jeune fille,* through its definition of drawing as contour and as cut, becomes imaginable as the matrix of its own infinite reproduction—drawing as a stencil, to be reproduced through tracing, a procedure that opens on to almost all of Picabia's future work. It is in this sense that the drawing, originally from Tzara's collection, that the art historians have called *La jeune*

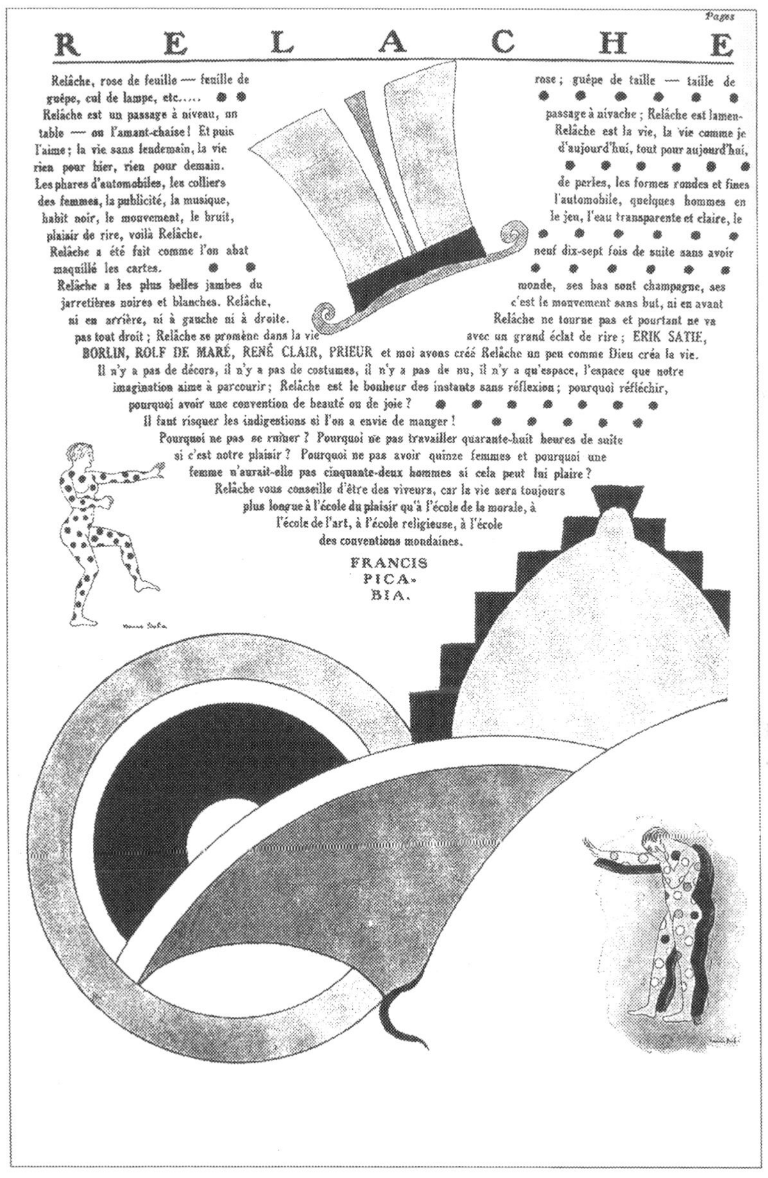

Francis Picabia, page from the program of *Relâche,* special issue of *La Danse,* 1924. Image courtesy Comité Picabia. © 2005 Artists Rights Society (ARS), New York/ ADAGP, Paris/Estate of Francis Picabia.

fille's "maquette" may in fact be *its* product, its spawn. Or, just as plausibly, along with the *Proverbe* version, both works—one on paper and another in a magazine—could be seen as "maquettes." For they were both *invitations to proliferation,* the maquettes, or better, matrices for the production—whether literally or conceptually—of other, later works like Picabia's *Volucelle,* a random accumulation of stenciled circles, one of many such works in the artist's oeuvre. Conceived in this way, drawing becomes a literal process of mechanized reproduction, fecundated not by the penis but by the pen. But reproduction, for Picabia, never remained simply a mechanical process; it was conceived, instead, as both machinic *and* bodily, both technical and corporeal, with reproduction understood in its full sexual sense, marching indeed to the drum beat of desire and the bodily drives. Which is to say: Mechanical drawing in Dada initiated not just a regime of the copy. It let loose drawing as a form of promiscuity.

Promiscuity, virgins, and whores: the structure of desire being explored by Picabia obviously flirts with misogyny. But I would suggest, contradicting much of the recent feminist literature on Dada and Surrealism, that this structure also skirts it, courts misogyny perhaps to move against it. If *La jeune fille* begins with a misogynist collapse of woman and genital, the work's promiscuity of form ensures that this collapse will not produce the ability to *identify* one with the other. For *La jeune fille* was not a project allied with identity. Instead, the work engaged difference; it produced the very labor of formal slippage, the endless transformation of one form into another, which is not the same thing as their equation. It would imagine a model of endless proliferation.

Of course, as with *La Sainte-Vierge,* it must be suggested again that *La jeune fille* is abstract in the deepest sense of the word—not an image "of " anything at all, surely not a woman or her sex. In a certain flat-footed way, its captioning might have less to do with the figure of woman than with what Dada imagined as a "bachelor machine." Typically, outrageously, Picabia makes this conceptual tactic of the Dadaists a literal one, offering up a "drawing" that could also be conceived, if not used, as an absurdly simply machine—ineffectual and painful at

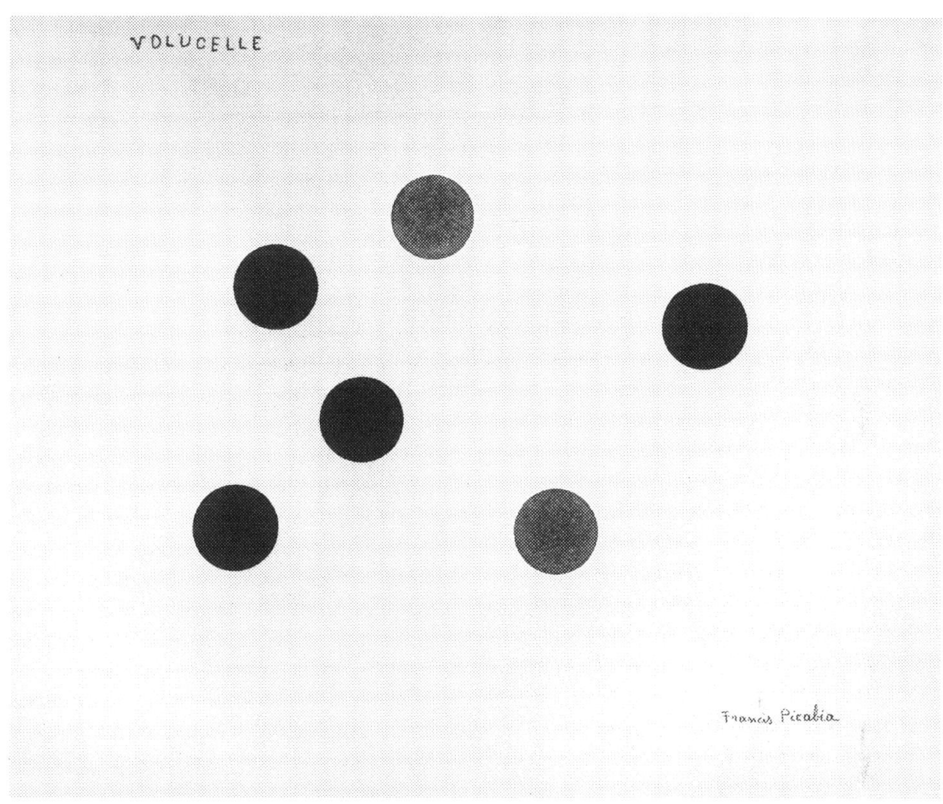

Francis Picabia, *Volucelle I*, 1922. Watercolor on cardboard, 60 × 73 cm (23⅝ × 28¾″). Private Collection Image courtesy Comité Picabia. © 2005 Artists Rights Society (ARS), New York/ADAGP, Paris/Estate of Francis Picabia.

that—for male masturbation. Or, perhaps simply for the nonproductive prolongation of (male) desire. By this I mean to point to the fact that *La jeune fille*'s genital reference might be to the phallus more than anything else, as its second caption points in the direction of a play on the term for a "cock ring." Today, the French use the English term themselves, but Picabia's caption *bracelet de la vie,* placed around the hole in Éluard's magazine, approaches the status of another homophone or pun. For *le vit* is one of many slang terms in French for "penis." And thus behind the "bracelet of life" there may be the evocation of a *bracelet du vit.*[36]

Identity was thus not the tactic of *La jeune fille.* Identification: perhaps. We do face an artistic strategy that seems to open itself to proliferation only by aligning itself with—only by identifying with—the figure of woman or femininity, a gender and a sex. The engagement of *La jeune fille* with multiplicity, its matrix function, perhaps arises here. And along these lines, we can observe that, in some way, such was the purpose of the trope of the *jeune fille* in Picabia's work. Over the course of Dada's existence, this term became Picabia's code for an artistic strategy of the multiple, bodied forth in a chain that stretches through all of his Dada work. This chain thus embodies a kind of proliferation in Picabia's production. But it also serves as a figure of proliferation more broadly.

For *La jeune fille* did not only exist as one of a pair, in dialogue with its twin, *La Sainte-Vierge,* but arrived as the culmination, for Picabia, of an investigation that dates back at least to his cubism and runs through the entire series of the mechanomorphs. Already in 1912, we find Picabia entitling one of his cubist works *Jeune fille,* a dour image of a "girl" in profile, reduced to broad, largely unmodulated planes of pigment running through a limited palette of gray, orange, pink, and white. But this was only the beginning; at every turn in style and with every shift in form that characterized Picabia's progress through the next decade, we encounter another version of *La jeune fille,* an encounter that proclaims both the consistency of Picabia's project and the utter lack of monolithic effect produced by the way in which he went about it.

Each reiteration of the chain was different. Central to his "Orphic" work, in 1913, Picabia painted *Udnie,* a work with a title that has been thought, anagrammatically, to encode (most of) the word *nudité* and included a subtitle when first exhibited that has often been forgotten: *Udnie (jeune fille américaine: danse)*. For a time, the *jeune fille* continued under this American guise. Unveiling the first mechanomorphic drawings in the pages of *291* in 1915, Picabia offered object portraits of Marius de Zayas, Alfred Stieglitz, or Paul Haviland, accompanied by the exacting depiction of a spark plug that was christened *Portrait d'une jeune fille américaine dans l'état de nudité*. Altering the form of the mechanomorphs already in 1917—from a form of readymade mechanical drawing to the actual readymade appropriation of photography—Picabia placed a retouched image of a lightbulb on the cover of his magazine *391*, an image that then earned the linked title *Américaine*.[37] But the series of the *fille* was not finished. It would surface, too, in a drawing style that Picabia developed contemporaneously with the first mechanomorphs, a sort of free-floating, rapid, even incomplete tracing that characterized a work such as *Fille née sans mère*, circa 1915, a drawing that eventually shared its title with a series of subsequent paintings and a book of poems and drawings in 1918. It has been argued that this book's title, *Poèmes et dessins de la fille née sans mère*, could best be translated "Poems and drawings *by* the girl born without a mother"; we thus see Picabia, by 1918, articulating his writerly and artistic production as a project that did not merely take the female as an object, but as the imagined generative subject of his production as well, a position with which Picabia continued to identify.[38]

The chain was not finished. Contrary to some claims, this book was obviously not the last of the *filles* either.[39] The year 1918 also saw the production of another painting, *Esprit de jeune fille*, a mostly abstract affair that, in looking forward to the 1920 work, consisted of variations on the form of a black circle. The painting was inscribed to a Dr. Brunnschweiler, a Swiss neurologist who treated Picabia and was also the subject, along with two other doctors, of the dedication of *Poèmes et dessins de la fille née sans mère*. In 1920, however, this dedication was reversed. Picabia's key 1920 text of Dada "philosophy," *Jésus-Christ Rastaquouère*, was in fact inscribed *Je dédie ce livre à toutes les jeunes filles*—"I dedicate this book to all young girls." Wry, arch, full of braggadocio, intoning the blasphemy suggested by the book's title: these could be some characterizations of Picabia's dedication. But it seems impossible, as with so much else in Picabia's production, not to read this dedication on a double level, as a recapitulation, as a call to memory of all the

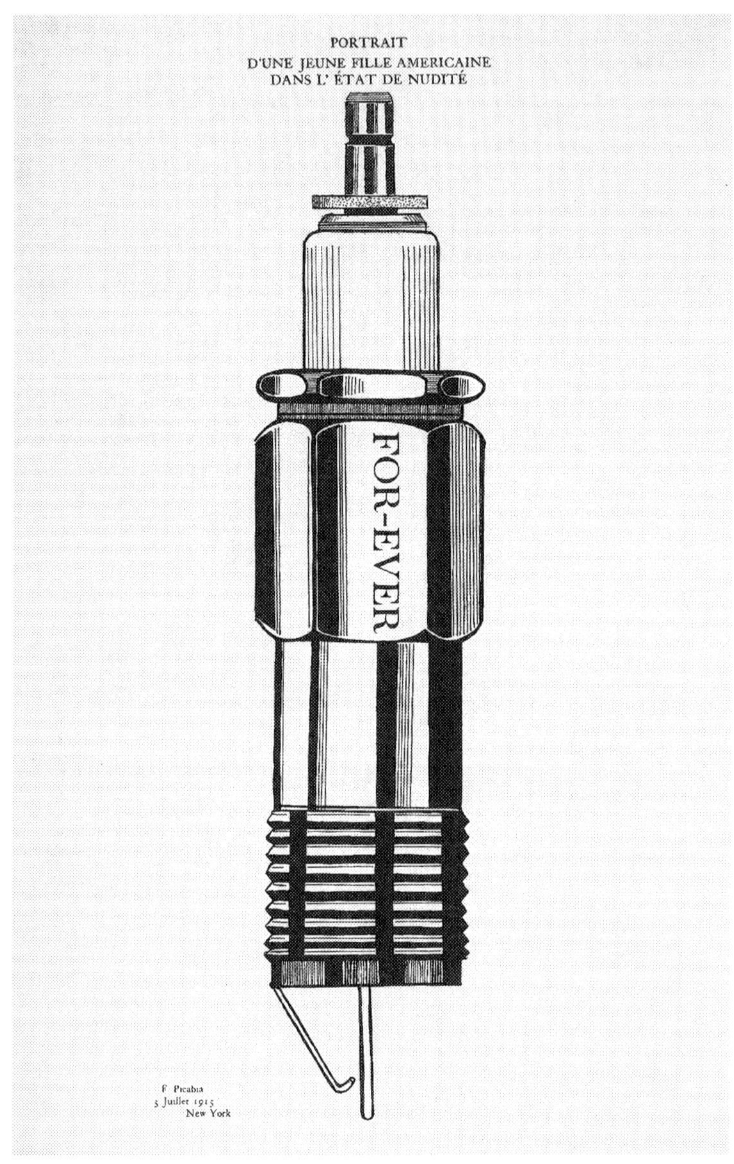

Francis Picabia, *Portrait d'une jeune fille américaine dans l'état de nudité (Portrait of a Young American Girl in the State of Nudity)*, 1915. Published in *291* 5–6 (July–August 1915). Research Library, The Getty Research Institute, Los Angeles. © 2005 Artists Rights Society (ARS), New York/ADAGP, Paris/Estate of Francis Picabia.

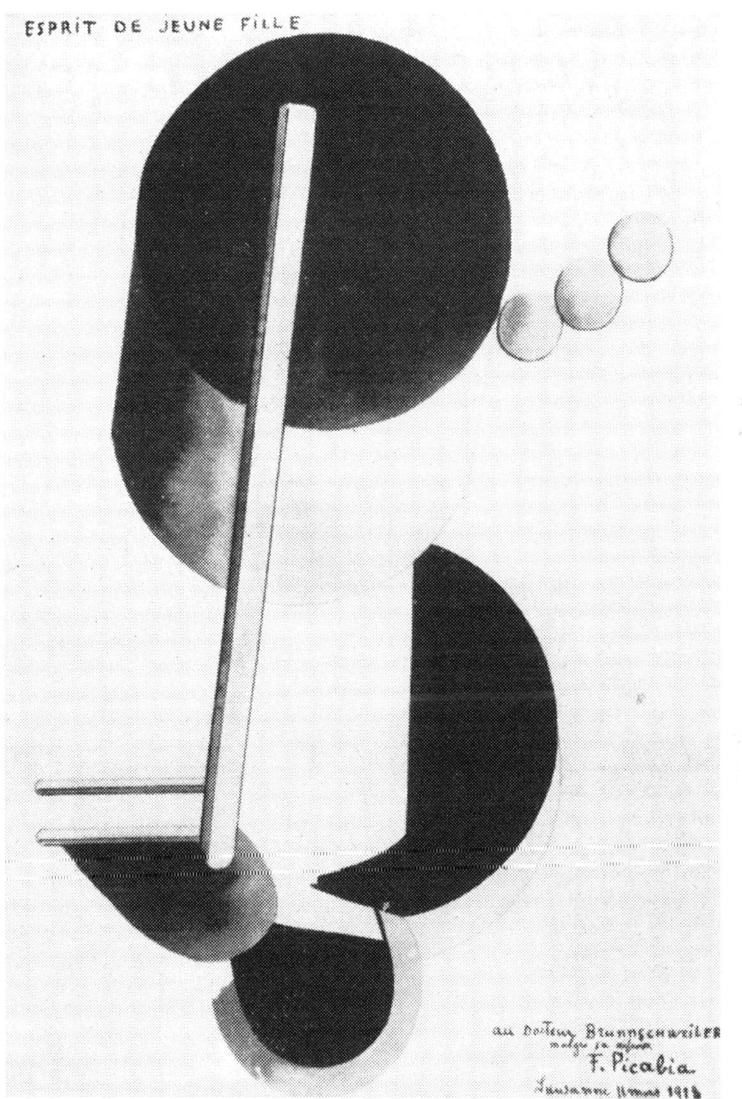

Francis Picabia, *Esprit de jeune fille,* 1918. Private Collection. Image courtesy
Comité Picabia. © 2005 Artists Rights Society (ARS), New York/ADAGP,
Paris/Estate of Francis Picabia.

jeune fille works that had by 1920 been completed by the artist, from the recent hole in Éluard's magazine back to the moment of Picabia's discovery of cubism.

To miss this would be to miss the way in which the entire series had been a response, indeed an attack, on cubism itself. Dada has been perpetually described as a project of "anti-art," but to understand it in the context of 1920 is to acknowledge the specificity of its attack, not simply on art in general, but on cubist modernism in particular. To represent *la jeune fille* was not so much to play with the representation of "woman" in some sort of artistic void, as it was— precisely and specifically—to reflect immanently on the *conventions* of that representation, and to point to and contest the fact that the *jeune fille* had become one of the accepted, even naturalized—and thus traditional—categories of avant-garde artistic production. Picabia made this fact clear on the cover of the number of *391* that has concerned us so much here, with the issue that was distributed at the Maison de l'Oeuvre, in a manifesto printed beneath Duchamp's "Tableau Dada," Picabia's reproduction of *L.H.O.O.Q.* The entire manifesto was an assault on Cubism:

> The cubists . . . think that Dada can prevent them from practicing this odious commerce: to sell art for a high price.
> Art costs more than sausage, more than women, more than anything. . . .
> No more fly shit on the walls.
> There will be some no matter what, obviously, but a little less. . . .
> Cubism represents the dearth of ideas.
> They have cubed the paintings of primitives, cubed African sculptures, cubed violins, cubed guitars, cubed illustrated newspapers, cubed shit and the profiles of young girls [*jeunes filles*], now they will have to cube money!!![40]

This is a very different kind of chain, a proliferation of disparate objects that in fact enacts a repetition of deadening sameness. The *jeune fille* emerges from this manifesto as one of the conventions of the cubist repertoire, a lifeless object among many submitted to the homogenizing effects of what had become, by 1920, a painterly "style" (the manifesto's "ils ont cubé . . . cubé . . . cubé"). The academicization of this style was one target of the Dada attack, and issue 12 of *391* was a declaration of war on its foremost perpetrators: Albert Gleizes, Jean Metzinger, and the other members of the Section d'Or. "Pablo Picasso, Juan Gris," intoned Picabia on page 5, "your cubist colleagues claim that you took everything from them: this is precisely the impression that they give me!" And if issue 12 of *391* began with the assault of this Dada manifesto upon cubism, it concluded with a scathing account on its back page of the recent expulsion of the Dadaists from the Section d'Or itself.[41]

The persistent target of Picabia's "Dada Manifesto," however, was not only the academicization of the cubist style, but its commercialization, and thus the eruption of the commodity as a recuperative force within the very heart of the avant-garde project. And so too we have, throughout the issue, attacks on the centers of this recuperation, this initial commodification of the cubist avant-garde, such as the gallery of Léonce Rosenberg, a perpetual victim of Picabia's Dada barbs.[42] If, as we have seen, one motive behind Picabia's counterattack with *La Sainte-Vierge* and *La jeune fille* had been the rationalization of drawing upon which French modernism had embarked—the reduction of drawing and artistic production to the principle of abstract exchange—this reduction carried with it, as if inevitably, the commodification of artistic practice. Under the banner of rationalization, French modernism had heralded the entrance of the commodity into the logic of the avant-garde on every possible level.

To miss this, finally, would be to miss the fact that Picabia's *La jeune fille* operates on the banalization of cubism immanently, as it were. The full chain of Picabia's *jeunes filles* repeatedly pits multiplicity and transformation against the rigidity of equivalence, but the 1920 work has its own lessons to teach. If the cubist avant-garde can be understood as one of the drawing's targets, it immediately becomes apparent that Picabia mounts this attack in the language of cubism itself. For to create a drawing that is an incised hole—a machine for proliferating line as a function of stenciled contour—is to return to the idiom of cubism's most radical moment. It is to turn one of cubism's most effective weapons against itself. It is, in fact, to look back to collage. And it is to understand one of the lessons of cubist collage all too well: drawing, quite literally, had at the moment of collage been made a function of contour and the cut, and the potential result of this was not academicization and commodification, but a radical reorientation of art practice toward absence and loss.

☞

The cut, indeed, had been the medium of collage, perhaps its most fundamental procedure. For the medium of collage was not paper, or canvas, or pencil, or paint; it was not a material, but rather a process, even what I have been calling an operation. Laying down their brushes, putting away their pencils, Picasso and Braque had taken up their scissors and their razor knives, transforming graphic production into a repeated process of literal incision, reducing the creative act to the endless proliferation of contoured shape and the arrangement of these shapes on a surface. Drawing, in collage, emerges as a *subtractive* process, with our experience of line newly dependent on gaps and divisions, on the inescapable fact that something has been removed, that matter has been cut away, and that we are gazing at a field of parts and pieces, an accumulation of broken fragments.

That this—no matter its glaring obviousness—has been a particularly repressed understanding of drawing in collage is proven by the modernist recuperation of collage as the moment when the flatness of the picture plane was declared most clearly, even without ambiguity. According to the modernists, the two-dimensionality of pictorial production, one of its essential limits, was made self-evident in collage, fully present to perception as never before, as the flatness of each collage element glued onto its flat ground provided a resounding echo and a reflexive acknowledgment. Collage, in this sense, would repeatedly accumulate painting's self-evident flatness, presenting it again and again as an undisputed modernist fact. But, of course, we should beware of the compensatory logic of accumulation, and of the glaring lack that repetition may attempt to mask. For collage, contrary to its positioning at the hands of the modernists, did not found itself as a declaration of presence, but as a mode of representation based on absence. As Rosalind Krauss explains:

As a system, collage inaugurates a play of differences which is both about and sustained by an absent origin: the forced absence of the original plane by the superimposition of another plane, effacing the first in order to represent it. Collage's very fullness of form is grounded in this forced impoverishment of the ground. . . . It is here that we can see the opening of the rift between collage as system and modernism proper. For collage operates in direct opposition to modernism's search for perceptual plenitude and unimpeachable self-presence. Modernism's goal is to objectify the formal constituents of a given medium, making these, beginning with the very ground that is the origin of their existence, the objects of vision. Collage problematizes that goal, by setting up discourse in place of presence, a discourse founded on a buried origin, a discourse fueled by that absence.[43]

If each collage piece, as Krauss asserts, masks and then repeats the image's ground, thus marking this ground as physically absent—and consequently open to the project of being figured through representation—to conceive drawing as a function of the cut only compounds this procedure of loss.[44] For, indeed, the shape of each collage piece can never enter our field of vision as fully present, as each shape cannot escape its formation by what artists, in their elementary education in drawing, learn to call "negative space," as contour becomes a result of what is not there, haunted quite literally by what has been taken, if not ripped, away. (A major collage such as Picasso's *Bottle of Suze* only intensifies this experience, deploying many of its contoured fragments *as* negative space, piling negation upon negation, multiplying the dependence of the entire image upon the play between presence and absence, or producing absence, rather, as a kind of literal presence.) Collage fulfills the destiny of drawing as the creation of contour and shape, literalizing that destiny and accumulating these shapes with endless precision; but drawing, in this form, only accumulates its destiny as a sum of destructions. In this form, moreover—through collage's literalization of drawing as a procedure of the cut—drawing would actually be wedded to waste, with the birth of each collage shape accompanied inevitably by the soft fall of a discarded scrap onto what we

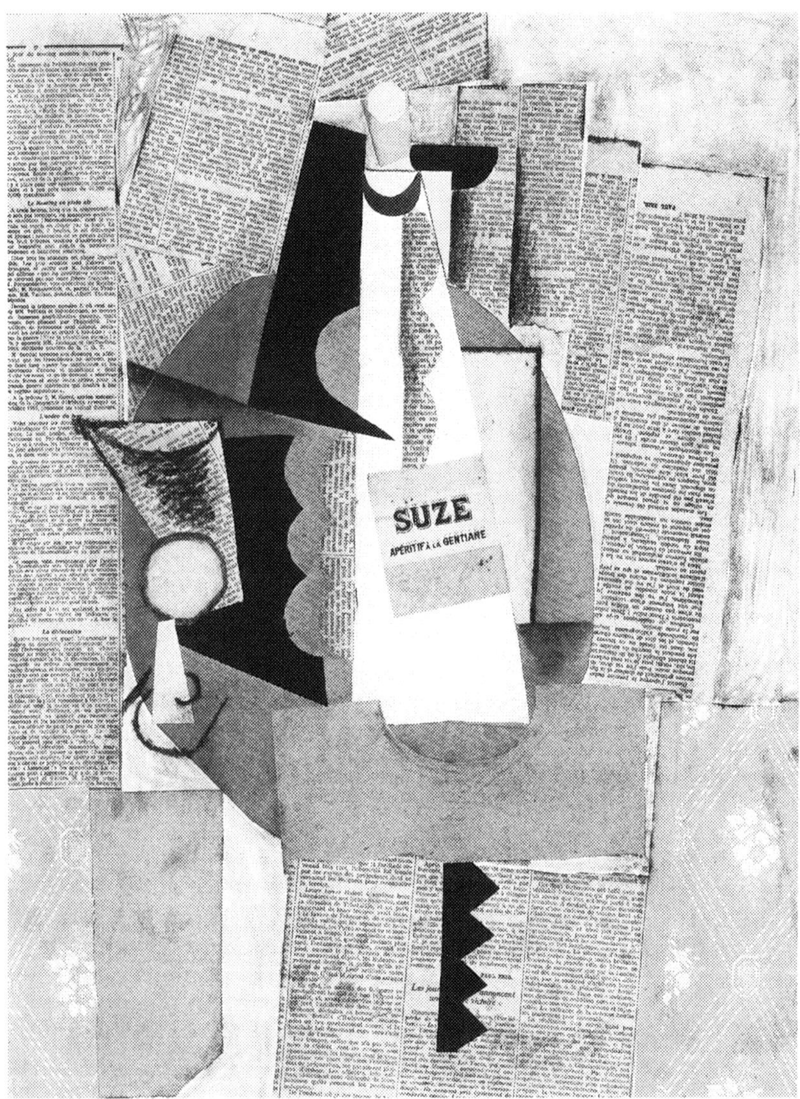

Pablo Picasso, *La bouteille de Suze (Bottle of Suze),* 1912. Pasted papers, gouache, and charcoal, 25³/₄ × 19³/₄″ Mildred Lane Kemper Art Museum, Washington University in St. Louis. University purchase, Kende Sale Fund, 1946. © 2005 Artists Rights Society (ARS), New York/ADAGP, Paris/Estate of Pablo Picasso.

can only imagine as the collage artist's cluttered floor. The cut would depend on—would produce—the cut away, the cast off, the *disjecta membra* of form.

This is precisely the object that Picabia presents to us in *La jeune fille*: we encounter here the detritus of the collage process, the negative of a collage fragment's positive, the discarded ground of the cut—but the matrix too, in this guise, of the contoured form on which collage depends and which Picabia projects as a model of endless proliferation. If this interpretation seems too pat—if the reader stands incredulous before the claim that Picabia even understood the ramifications of cubist form,[45] never mind that his drawing-as-a-hole participated in an immanent critique of cubism, in a recoding of its procedures as in some way excremental and destructive—we have only to look more closely at the internal development of collage itself. To do so is to register that such a recoding was well within the collage artist's own understanding of his reconfiguration of the practice of drawing. To do so is to consider another hole.

"Trou ici," Picasso wrote across the bottom of one of his most important collages, *Still-life "Au Bon Marché"*—"hole here." And indeed we see what appears to be a visual hole, or at least a jagged gap, incised into the readymade ground of the collage surface with the relevant words suspended within it. Here, Picasso seems to signal not only the collage cut's involvement with gaps and voids, but the necessary impediment collage had inserted into the age-old game that painting carried on with vision and illusion, sacrificing its objecthood to the piercing of the picture plane precisely by the effects of painterly illusion, enticing the viewer into a concomitant plunge into represented depth. Collage, of course, was especially sensitive to the painterly logic of surface, to the physical literalness of this surface, as never before. And Picasso's *trou* marked no exception to this attentiveness, as it in fact existed itself as an illusion, and not as a literal hole at all. For what reads, visually, as an incised hole in Picasso's ground was actually a zone of pigment built up *on top* of the ground, a declaration and opacification of the surface, and thus another representation by Picasso of a quality ("depth," "hole," "the cut") in the absence, indeed through the structural reversal, of its physical literality. Picabia's gambits, by contrast, persistently embraced a strategy of literalness, and indeed exacerbated the literalization already implicit in collage's

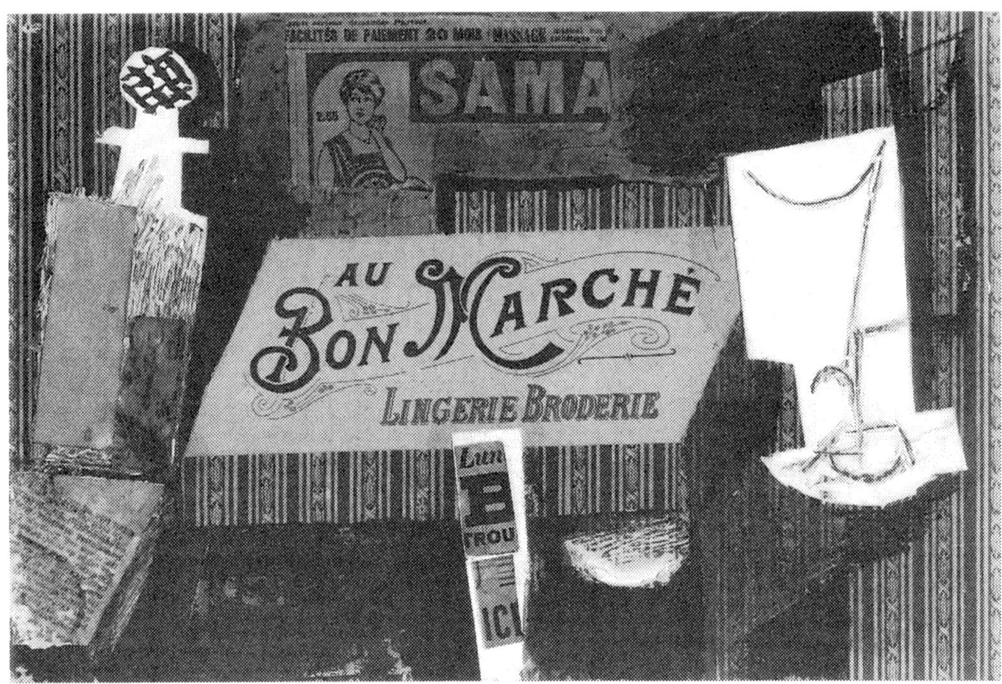

Pablo Picasso, *Still-life "Au Bon Marché,"* 1913. Oil and pasted paper on cardboard, 23.5 × 31 cm (9¼ × 12¼″). Ludwig Collection, Aachen. © 2005 Artists Rights Society (ARS), New York/ADAGP, Paris/Estate of Pablo Picasso.

recoding of drawing as cut. And in another example of *La jeune fille*'s existence as a negative of the formal aspirations of the collage process, as a revelation of the negative ground from which cubist form would emerge, Picabia's hole embraced transparency over opacity, literality over representation, sacrificing the ground of modernist form to a piercing of the surface that cubist collage took so many pains to cover over, to thicken and to defend.[46]

This sacrifice was larger than Picabia's demonstration at the Maison de l'Oeuvre; it was one of the lessons of Dada. At precisely the moment when the cubists began to retreat from their greatest invention, the Dadaists embraced the cut as a central procedure of their work—Picabia was not the only artist to re-code the cut of collage as a procedure of destruction and negation. How else should we explain the sudden appearance of the jagged, knifing forms of Duchamp's *Three Standard Stoppages,* where the scissors of collage were put aside for the saw? Duchamp immediately submitted the procedure of collage to the violence of the cut, producing another type of matrix work, a machine for stenciled contour every bit as effective as Picabia's later *La jeune fille,* if not more insistent on the cut's involvement in waste, in the negative of form, in what I have christened its *disjecta membra.* And the saw became the favorite instrument of another Dadaist, namely Jean Arp, who married his project in the 1910s to the vast proliferation of contoured, cut-out shapes, accumulated persistently into three-dimensional accretions through his wood reliefs. By the 1920s, still developing the lessons of contour and cut that he had learned from cubism, Arp too began to incorporate cut-out holes into and through the very surface of his abstract paintings. But the undoing of modernist form through the strategy of its *disjecta membra* had already been Arp's as well in the 1910s, in his collages "arranged according to the laws of chance," or in works like Man Ray's *Rope Dancer,* both built up from the rejected negatives of the cutting or collage process, dumped like so much trash onto a horizontal surface, whether work or floor.

And so we need to alter our narratives of Dada's relationship to cubism, to collage, and to modernism more generally. If one form of that narrative has seen collage—with its embrace of mass-produced materials—as the first step toward validating Dada's subsequent elaboration of readymade strategies, we need to complicate that simple progression. We may need to alter our understanding of Dada readymade strategies (the plural is the key) altogether, beyond the embrace of the mass-produced, with all the productivist ambitions that this embrace is seen to subtend. For Dada took from collage not just the validation of the mass produced, but the logic of the cut, a logic it exposed as subtractive, as destructive, as excremental, and thus as violent to the productive imperatives of modernist form.

It was not a coincidence that, twenty-five years after the Maison de l'Oeuvre demonstration, advanced painting and drawing arrived at the same structural opposition explored by Picabia, between a drawing that negates its traditional function of defining contour, and drawing as a cut and a hole. One thinks of Jackson Pollock's initiation of the "drip" technique, but also his turn, within the logic of the drip paintings, to the use of cut-out shapes, as in *Out of the Web* (1949). But one could think too of Lucio Fontana's simultaneous commencement, in 1948, of works that he called "Holes," or of the later turn to completely reconfigured procedures of cutting and subtraction among the artists whose work would be called, however erroneously, conceptual art—think of Gordon Matta-Clark's *Conical Intersect* from 1975.[47] Something essential about the very nature of drawing is at stake with this opposition; a logic is being divulged. If this chapter has set out to prove anything, it is that the actions of Dada, so often dismissed as "anti-aesthetic," as so many anti-art jokes and scandalous one-liners—a drawing that is a cunt, or a cock-ring—actually organize themselves simultaneously in relation to the crucial problems of modernist art and form. They subject these problems, however, to another logic, to a different set of procedures, that has made them invisible to the vision of modernist art history to this day.

Michael Fried, for example, in his important modernist interpretation of Pollock's drip paintings, has provided many of the terms of my discussion here. Locating in Pollock's allover drip paintings a "transcendence" of drawing's involvement in defining contour, a line that would contain no shape, Fried traces Pollock's move to incorporate cut-out shapes into his paintings as a technique to allow figuration to return within the dematerialized surface of his "optical" skeins.[48] The logic of this argument is dialectical, it involves a sublation: drawing, by first negating its traditional function, arrives at a fuller combination of both figuration and abstraction, achieving both the opticality of nonobjective line and the contour of the cut without recourse to the tactility and the objecthood still latent in the task of contour-defining line. Fried is quite explicit about the dialectical nature of this argument, isolating what he calls a "dialectic of modernism," an ideal of radical objective critique, understood by Fried through the lens of a philosophical lineage that he claims includes Hegel, the young Marx, the Lukàcs of *History and Class Consciousness,* and the philosophy of Maurice Merleau-Ponty.[49] For Fried, modernism, at its best moments, would be eminently, endlessly dialectical.

A sublated structure, a higher synthesis, a transcendence of drawing itself: Picabia's experiment obeys a different logic. It splits drawing in two. It provides a dichotomous, nonresolvable, ambiguous structure: no sublations here, nothing to be resolved. It orients drawing not toward the productive plenitude of modernist form, but toward loss. And with this reorientation comes no unity, only division.

We should remember that when Walter Benjamin turned his attention to the fate of the work of art under a regime of mechanical reproduction, he turned his attention specifically to Dada, and, what's more important, he arrived at a conclusion that seems at first glance exceedingly close to this experiment by Picabia. The traditional work of art, singular and original, was deemed "auratic" by Benjamin, tied to the sphere of the sacred with its cultic functions of ritual and hierarchical division, whereas the mechanically reproducible work signaled the destruction of aura and a concomitant fall of art into the world of the profane.[50] Picabia's two drawings seem to enforce this diagnosis, deploying as they do a notion of the sacred—*La Sainte-Vierge*—and an embrace of the profane—*La jeune fille*—that turn around this self-same axis, this dichotomy, of inimitability and reproducibility, of the singular and the multiple.

But we should not be too quick to map Benjamin's concerns onto Picabia's. For one, Picabia does not present his drawings as two, dialectically related moments, with one preceding and one following, a narrative of the fall from the sacred to the profane. He embraces Benjamin's two "moments" at one and the same time, as two necessary halves of the same operation, a splitting in two as opposed to a dialectical evolution. And moreover, neither of Picabia's works truly engages Benjamin's notion of a singular "aura"—both, in fact, were introduced by Picabia into networks of reproduction, produced in hundreds of disposable copies through the magic of technical reproduction in the context of the Dada magazines. But, by placing his drawings into this network of art's consumption, into the space of the magazines, Picabia disseminated two examples of artworks that in fact *cannot* be consumed. On the one hand, there is the irreproducible drawing, the inimitable image that becomes inassimilable to the task of the copy; on the other, there is drawing as a cut and a loss, a machine for producing copies that will never manage to replicate the form of their original, that will never duplicate the absent form of the cut itself. Rather than Benjamin's twin notions of aura and technical reproducibility, Picabia offers up drawing as a form of the inassimilable, a caustic thing as jarring as the proverbial bone that sticks in one's throat.

Procedures of loss, impossible objects, drawing as inassimilable, splitting in two: we are far from the concerns of the modernist work of art, far too from all the concerns of dialectics (whether idealist or materialist) on which the modernist work depends. But neither have we arrived at a moment when modernism was simply rejected, negated in an easy move of pure opposition: the solution of "anti-art." Rather, we face a situation where the modernist work—but also the work of modernism, or even modernism *as* work—would be unworked, or, as the French can put it, *dés-oeuvré,* through a confrontation with the very logic of its own system, and through an exposition of that system's limits.

Some years after the conclusion of Dada—but not, significantly, untouched by its activities—the dissident Surrealist Georges Bataille gave a name to such an operation.[51] Or rather, he gave it a plethora of names, the sedimentation of naming being, in fact, one of the certainties that such an operation made problematic. At first, this operation was called *dépense* or expenditure, or heterology, or the "formless" (*informe*); later, broadening his thinking, Bataille began to approach it through the terms "communication," or "erotism," or "sovereignty," or eventually, a "general" or "sacrificial economy." By that point, Bataille's thinking of a "sacrificial" operation was wedded to a thinking of the sacred, by which one means here a thinking of all that resists the rationalizing imperatives of modernity, the instrumental reduction of thought and object to the status of what Bataille called "the thing." And if loss and destruction were central to the activities of Dada, so too were they primary in Bataille's thinking of the sacred and of sacrifice.

"From the very first," wrote Bataille, "it appears that sacred things are constituted by an operation of loss."[52] And like Picabia's demonstration at the Maison de l'Oeuvre, the effects of this operation could be described only through the language of splitting and contradiction, through that which denied the unity and self-adequation of the modern "thing." For what is sacred, according to Bataille, "not being based on a logical accord with itself, is not only contradictory with respect to things but, in an undefined way, is in contradiction with itself. This contradiction is not negative: inside the sacred domain there is, as in dreams, an endless contradiction that multiplies without destroying anything."[53] More than anything else, a sacrificial operation would set itself against modernity's world of enshrined production, its idolatry of reified and isolated objects called commodities, its obsession with activities of conservation and preservation. All of this Bataille denigrated as belonging to a "restricted economy," an order of things dedicated to the postponement of loss in any form. In the realm of philosophy, Hegel's dialectic was Bataille's primary example of such an economy (Bataille called Hegel's system the "philosophy of project," or of "work"), with its insistence that even the negation of a thing, its utter contradiction, could be put to work through the operation of sublation, an appropriating synthesis that eliminates, preserves, and transcends the negative all at the same time.[54] Instead, the countermodel of a sacrificial economy was dedicated to absolute consumption, to the relationality of the gift as opposed to the reification of the commodity, to the intensities of immediate use and utter loss over any concern for preservation. There are, for Bataille, things one can lose, things that can never be regained. There exist contradictions that can never be overcome. For a work of art to engage with such an economy would mean that, properly speaking, it could no longer be a "work" at all. It could take up its existence only in relation to that which causes the "work" to cease to be. Which means that it could found itself only on the loss of its own foundations. This is, at least in part, what Bataille understood as sacrificial.

The imperatives of a sacrificial economy thus describe rather well the logic of Dada's assault on modernism and modernity. For, with Dada, there would be *gifts* (as Man Ray demonstrated in 1921); objects were made to be destroyed. Sculptures were made for "traveling," in the case of Duchamp, only through procedures of destruction and of loss. Diagrams might be embraced for their transformational logic, their dedication to mobility and change, but they too would be allowed to rot out, to fall into disuse and disrepair. Geometry textbooks were left out in the rain, their rational laws ex-posed to that which would destroy them. Such an object was christened an *Unhappy Readymade.* It was itself given as a gift. But Dada readymades could also be "assisted" or "reciprocal," graffiti scrawled across an artwork, a "Rembrandt used as an ironing board." Imagine hammers striking metronomes. Irons made useless for housework, but not for violence. Books crumbling into dust. Bathing caps shredded into pieces. Lampshades taken apart and unfurled. The Dada readymade can hardly be read (cannot only be read) as a capitulation of art to the regime of the commodity. Commodities were lost, not produced, by Dada. Objects would be destroyed.

And artistic mediums were opened to loss as well. This, during the years of Paris Dada, was one of Picabia's central concerns. Each one of the chapters that follows will expand on this. If, by 1920, it had already become clear how central the medium had become to modernism's project—a "restricted" project (in the Bataillean sense) of the reduction and delimitation of a given medium's properties, of the rationalization and infinite progression of this delimited system as a language—it was just this logic that Picabia set out to undo. And, with *La Sainte-Vierge* and *La jeune fille,* we witness Picabia waging his assault on modernism from within, using the techniques and the language of visual modernism itself.

For Picabia's two drawings do reduce the medium of drawing to its most basic, even essential, components. Drawing's function—of providing contour and its delimitation—was put into play. But there was no telos to this experiment, no direction, and no summation. Drawing here did not negate its traditional function only to incorporate its own negation into a higher unity, a transcendent synthesis. This is the modernist move par excellence, a move wherein we see the utter dependence of modernist strategies on the dialectic, on sublations of structuring oppositions, familiar contradictions such as figure and ground, color and line, vision and touch. Modernist abstraction—at what has been described as its best moments—becomes the very image of such sublations.

Picabia's experiment undoes the work of this modernist dialectic, and thus "unworks" the modernist work of art that such a dialectic produced. With Picabia, it was never a question of dialectics, but of another operation, one that Bataille also called "transgression." To say this may sound familiar, indeed banal. After all, we often refer to the Dada and Surrealist movements as part of what is called the "transgressive avant-garde," usually in opposition to what is called a modernist or formalist project. But I think that we hardly know yet what this word "transgressive" means.[55] We hardly know how to discuss it (transgression, in the end, may broach no discussion). And to oppose transgression to the concerns of form would be to miss the point entirely.

The experience of transgression positions the negative as a limit, something one can cross—transgress—but never surpass, an experience of absolute finitude and singularity. It concerns an exposition of a quality to its outside, to that which it is not, to the absence where one could say it ceases to be. Meaning, for example, must be pushed to its limit, to the point where it touches absolute nonmeaning. As Denis Hollier has described this logic in a different context: "To have a sense, for Bataille, is to be constituted by that which negates one. Nothing is meaningful, nothing makes sense, until confronted by its negation . . . . A thing's sense is the rupture of its identity, that which exceeds it, that by means of which it exceeds and is not itself but that which is beyond it, or its absence."[56]

———

Bataille's examples of such a logic are legion, and often apocalyptic: social life defined by the festival, the paroxysm that dissolves its structure; life's meaning as death, the limit at which its noisy exuberance passes into silence. The negative and contradiction here are not put to work, as in the dialectic. Rather, they halt the possibility of any further work, providing the singular dynamic of "unworking," touching a limit where transcendence succumbs to finitude and to loss.[57]

Such would be the sacrificial movement to which Picabia subjects drawing, and by extension, the modernist concern with drawing's delimitation. At the Maison de l'Oeuvre, drawing was not aligned with the reduction, the sublations, and transcendence of modernist form, but with the contradictory splitting that Bataille saw as emanating from the working of a sacrificial economy—a cipher of its violence against the unity of organic wholes, a product of limited particularity over limitless generalization. Drawing was split in two, tied to procedures of loss and of relinquishment, of excess and internal contradiction: an accidental splash, an actual hole. Producing no contour, creating no form, *La Sainte-Vierge* was no longer a drawing; but it would also not be "not-drawing" either. *La Sainte-Vierge* was positioned upon a limit. But Picabia's demonstration was systematic. On, as it were, the other side of that limit, *La jeune fille* produced nothing but contour; but it no longer could be considered simply a drawing. It was no longer truly graphic, but spatial; no longer an image, but a matrix. Literally, procedurally, drawing had been exposed to its outside. And modernism's quest to define the essence of a medium had thus been exceeded—which is to say not transcended, but rather deflated and undone.

Such a claim may necessitate a new understanding of the aims of what has been called the "modernist project." For at its most radical moments—those moments still richest, I think, in energies available to our present cultural crises—modernism was deeply attentive to what Theodor Adorno called "the waste products and blind spots that have escaped the dialectic [of history]," to the claims of "cross-grained, opaque, unassimilated material."[58] The modernist project attained its most radical moments when, in fact, it was no longer a project at all, when it frustrated the very ideals and objectives that would allow it to be a project—when, for instance, pictorial modernism did not seek the "essence" or defining logic of its media, but rather arrived at moments when this essence could be undone, when the larger logic could be pushed to failure. Roland Barthes, for instance, was describing nothing else in his crucial essay "The Third Meaning," when he isolated what he calls the "filmic" in what, "in the film, cannot be described, it is the representation that cannot be represented."[59] Definitions could be secured only by that which exceeds all definition.

We could claim (we have claimed) that, in 1920, Picabia's experiments with drawing explored nothing else. Like Barthes's notion of the "filmic," Picabia presents us with a notion of the "graphic" as that movement wherein art finds not its law ("drawing is the probity of art"—Ingres), but its transgression.[60] Where art finds not the constructive key to its production, but to its loss.

Such was the shock of the Maison de l'Oeuvre. One could paraphrase what Bataille called his "principle of inadequacy" to give language to this shock. "Man is what he lacks," Bataille once wrote.[61] And so too, for Picabia, drawing had become what it lacks. Drawing had been opened to its outside, exposed to its limit. It had become a thing of which one could almost have no conception: a stain upon the field of vision, or a blind spot excised from the same. At this moment, in 1920, a (modernist) paradox was suddenly made clear: pushed to its limit, to draw would be no longer to draw. For a moment, drawing had become sacrificial.

What is left to say of Picabia's experiment in 1920? How should one conclude? I have been—you might have noticed—finding this task difficult. "Isn't the absence of satisfaction more profound than the feeling of triumph at the end of the work?"[62] Bataille's words. But then again, we are not really at an ending, but a beginning, a multiplication of possibilities. For it would continue to be this sacrificial experience of the limit and its transgression, this exploration of another economy for the work of art—an economy of loss—that would play itself out across the gamut of Picabia's Paris Dada works, visible in almost every example of his experimentation with both verbal language and visual form. The sacrifice was not a traditional origin, a wellspring, or a resource, but it would not let itself be forgotten either. Its silence would have its effects.

One could conclude with that. With silence. Bataille had much to say on this subject, for silence was the destination of the entire sacrificial movement of his thought. Meaning would be confronted with nonmeaning; life with death; and discourse with the immense void of silence. Such was the logic of the limit. As a word, as a signifier, "silence" itself could be considered "sacrificial." Bataille called it a "slipping" word: "I will give only one example of a 'slipping' *word*. . . . I limit myself to the word *silence*. It is already, as I have said, the abolition of the sound which the word is; among all words it is the most perverse, or the most poetic: it is the token of its own death . . . a word which is not a word."[63] And it would, perhaps, be fitting to end this excavation with silence. For with it, we come full circle to the (now understandable?) silence that greeted Picabia's actions at the Maison de l'Oeuvre. (And perhaps now, too, we can sense the irony of the name of this notorious place and Dada event, this setting for Dada's exploration of modernist *désoeuvrement*).

Nothing mitigated this silence: not Picabia, nor the critics, nor the other Dadaists, nor the historians. "A delicate silence surrounds the exhibit of Francis Picabia at Sans Pareil." This is Georges Ribemont-Dessaignes in 1920, describing the reaction that faced Picabia's first Paris Dada exhibition, the April show that opened a few weeks after the Maison de l'Oeuvre. Such was Picabia's fate in 1920. "It is a silence full of the charms of vengeance."[64] *La jeune fille* would be forgotten. It would go unseen, Picabia's critique unheard. But this hardly makes this incident minor. The silence may even be proof of its magnitude. "These judgments should lead to silence and yet I am writing." Again, Bataille. "This is in no way paradoxical. Silence is itself a pinnacle and better yet, the saint of all saints."[65] And thus we could end as we began.

Here is an image of Picabia. For that is what he tells us, calling out from the surface of this seemingly spontaneous image, a thick-skinned, inebriated scrawl beneath which Picabia printed the phrase "portrait de l'auteur par lui-même." Included in 1920 as the frontispiece to his book of poetry entitled *Unique eunuque*—another verbal pun like *le saint des saints,* we notice, that while signifying the

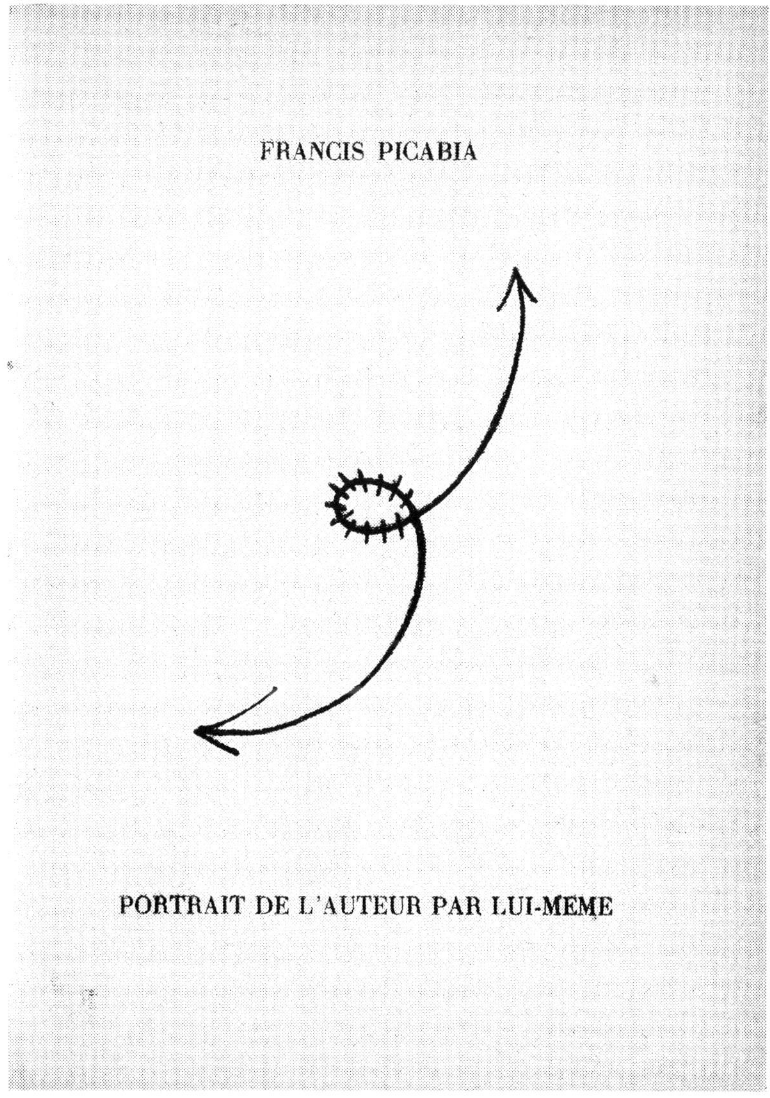

Francis Picabia, *Portrait de l'auteur par lui-même,* 1920. Frontispiece for Picabia, *Unique eunuque,* Au Sans Pareil, February 1920. Image courtesy Comité Picabia. © 2005 Artists Rights Society (ARS), New York/ADAGP, Paris/Estate of Francis Picabia.

absolutely singular (Unique Eunuch) spins through alliteration and, in this case, letter reversal into an experience of the multiple—Picabia offered a self-portrait of himself as a line. The line was vectored and diagrammatic. It pointed, however, at nothing. For this line was no longer the mechanomorphic line Picabia had presented in the 1910s; it shared nothing with that graphic resource of mechanical drawing that has been called "the language of industry," a language, one could say, of work.[66] It instead emblematized a diametrically opposed notion of drawing, a notion that we have been exploring under the nonproductive, transgressive banner of the workless. Tristan Tzara wrote in the preface for Picabia's book what we may take as a motto for lines, and a motto as well for Dada and for Picabia: "Geometry is dry, and old. I've seen a line spurt—bleed—differently. A line that spurts kills theories; and then all we have to do is look for adventure in the life of lines."[67] And so Picabia's drawing of himself as a line doubles over on itself, producing both the strange effect of mirroring, of the duplication of a single linear unit, and the obvious internal contradiction of a line that races in two entirely opposed directions.

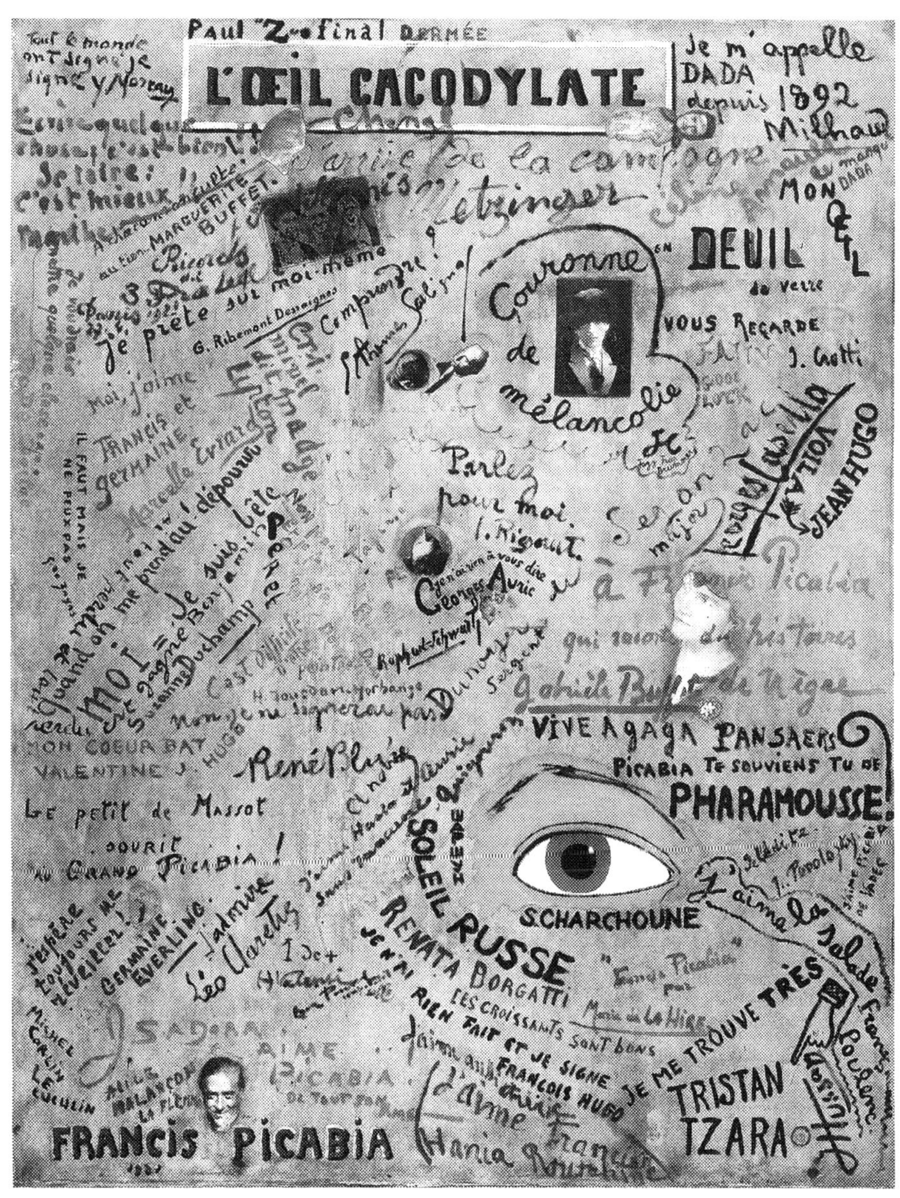

Francis Picabia, *L'œil cacodylate (The Cacodylic Eye),* 1921. Oil with photomontage and collage on canvas. 148.6 × 117.4 cm (58$^1/_2$ × 46$^1/_4$″). Musée National d'Art Moderne, Centre Georges Pompidou. Purchase, 1967. Photo by Georges Meguerdtchian. Photograph © CNAC/MNAM/ Dist. Réunion des Musées Nationaux / Art Resource, NY. © 2005 Artists Rights Society (ARS), New York/ADAGP, Paris/Estate of Francis Picabia.

The Artwork Caught by the Tail: Dada Painting

If it were married to logic, art would be living in incest, engulfing, swallowing its own tail. . . .

—*Tristan Tzara,* Manifeste Dada 1918[1]

The only word that is not ephemeral is the word death. . . . To death, to death, to death. The only thing that doesn't die is money, it just leaves on trips.

—*Francis Picabia,* Manifeste Cannibale Dada, *1920*[2]

Je m'appelle Dada. Here is an image of Picabia. He is staring at us, smiling, his face emerging like an exclamation point from the gap separating his first from his last name. "Francis Picabia," he writes, in letters blunt and childish, projecting gaudily off the canvas with the stiff pride of an advertisement, or the incontinence of a finger painting. (The shriek of the commodity and the babble of the infant: Dada always heard these sounds as one and the same.) And so here again is Picabia. He is staring at us, smiling, a face without a body, or rather, a face that has lost its body, a portrait of the artist under the knife. Decimated. Decapitated. But not quite *acephalic,* to use a term of Georges Bataille: rather the reverse.

For here we do not have the body without a head, but heads without bodies. There is more than one. Picabia may be the only face that meets our gaze, but there is also Jean Metzinger (or Darius Milhaud?), at the top and to the right. And there, just below him, is Jean Cocteau. And there is Gabrielle. And there is Marcel. All so many heads floating free of their bodies, they roll through the space of this painting, turning now this way and now that—backward, forward, sideways, and upside-down—dispersed products of the art of collage practiced in the key of castration. "At the heart of our projects," as Louis Aragon later described Dada's activities in 1921, "there was always the gleam of the guillotine."[3]

These heads, however, had companions. For the heads were joined, not to bodies, but to words. To signatures. So that along with Picabia, there is Germaine. And there is Tristan, and Man Ray, and Georges. And there is Isadora, and Pierre, and Marthe, and Clément, and Suzanne, and Marguerite, and Benjamin. And there is Jean, and Hania, and Darius, and Renata, and Léo, and Michel, and René. And there is Ezra, and Fatty, and Paul, and Alice, and Marie, and Roland, and Serge, and Céline, and Valentine, and François, and André, and Dodo, and Madge, and Marcelle, and Jacques, and Emmanuel, and Magda, and Raphaël, and Hélène, and Yves. And there are many others besides.

Faces and names. Heads and signatures. Photographs and language. These are the signs offered up by Picabia's 1921 painting, *L'oeil cacodylate (The Cacodylic Eye),* perhaps the key "monument" of the brief years of Dada in Paris. Indeed, these are the signs offered up by a painting that seems somehow to be newly *about* the logic of the sign, about the full infiltration of the space of painting by a procession of deracinated signs. For here images, painted images, are in short supply. Picabia provides an eye, a cartoonish, figurative punch line—far from the geometric rigor that characterized the artist's increasingly abstract mechanomorphs—to accompany the painting's written title. But that is about it.

And painted images aren't the only thing suddenly missing. Hair seems to have become a scarce commodity. Picabia has retained his, of course—this was a mane that would accompany him to the grave. But look at Gabrielle. She seems to have given up her locks in return for the plunging blade of her *décolletage,* its point functioning as the flip side of the jagged, ghostly peaks left by the excision of any trace of hair from the photographic image of her face. The scissor did its work on others: look to the completely faded photograph beneath the first word of the painting's title, a blank stain that nevertheless retains the recognizable profile of opera singer Marthe Chenal, conspicuously cropped at the scalp; or find, if you can, the minuscule photograph of composer Georges Auric sprouting the first letter of his last name from the place where once he grew hair.[4] And look at Cocteau. He too seems to exist as a face without a summit, his hair manifestly occluded by the "crown of melancholy" scrawled across his image, two fetishistic woman's gloves substituted for the space above his face. And look at Marcel. In his case, as always, the loss has become real, literal, as Duchamp places two images of himself upon Picabia's painting, two images focused—to a greater or lesser degree—on his gleaming scalp. Amid the panoply of personages and signs within *L'oeil cacodylate,* Duchamp presents himself as bald.

The problem of this chapter will be how to read *L'oeil cacodylate.* Indeed, we face a painting that has more to do with words than with images. The words travel and turn and distend, they shrink and they grow; and yet this is no Dada diagram like so many of Picabia's pieces in the 1910s, surely no poetic calligram. It is a work full of body parts, and yet it hardly seems a bachelor machine. It offers up faces, and yet exceeds the category of the portrait. Instead, *L'oeil cacodylate* was a collective work, a gesture that insisted on the group; but it was made just as Picabia ceded publicly from the Paris Dada group in the summer of 1921, becoming, in effect, the first and most important "dissident Dadaist."[5] None of Dada's central tactics, Picabia's prior tactics, seems to prevail anymore in 1921: chance, readymade, diagram, mechanical drawing. Stylistic inconsistency rubs hands with medium incoherence, suspending the object between text, photograph, and painting. Seemingly, the work's inconsistencies know no bounds.

And yet given the pressure this work puts on loss—the ludicrous loss of hair, the premature loss of Dada—something like an allegorical image begins to form. Its point was tongue-in-cheek, deeply hermetic, perhaps unreadable, even to the majority of the collective that worked to create this painting. Its meaning seems driven home not only by the connotations of disease and emasculation carried by all these hairless faces, but by the one image that manifestly contradicts the hairlessness, or at least (literally) redirects it: the photograph by Man Ray of a woman smoking a cigarette, positioned directly below Duchamp's face. Taken from a radically oblique angle, the one nameless image in *L'oeil cacodylate* reads as reversed, the woman's hair—excessive and thick—splayed out in a tangle as the image's ground, her naked chin substituting itself for the bald pinnacle shared by the other portraits, a summit extended by the appendage of a rigid cigarette.[6] We see something like a body flipped and dehumanized, a face becoming an object— a phallic one, surely, but also one with painterly connotations. In the midst of this scene of medium incoherence, a gesture of self-reflexivity arises. More or less dead center in Picabia's painting, we see something like a face transformed, solidified into a cipher for the "stick with the hairs on its end" that is the painter's brush.

Such a reading is perhaps easier to project onto the image now, with many years remove, as Dada's later progeny have decoded the body in this way with increasing frequency, from Fluxus performances such as Nam June Paik's *Zen for Head,* to Shigeko Kubota's *Vagina Painting,* to Janine Antoni's more recent *Loving Care.* But such an allegory of painting and its renunciation, or corporealization, had its own horizon of expectation at this moment of the historical avant-garde. And it had its own horizon of expectation among the Dadaists, among Picabia's friends. For it had already been a decade since the artist and writer Roland Dorgelès, one of *L'oeil cacodylate*'s signers, had taken the step of attaching a loaded brush to a donkey's tail, allowing it to swish and sway, and submitting the resulting painting to the Salon des Indépendants under the pseudonym Boronali.[7] Dorgelès's action attained immediate currency among the European avant-garde, spawning a Russian exhibit in 1912 entitled "The Donkey's Tail," and inspiring the young Max Ernst at the same moment to dash off a drawing with roughly the same title. And it was a *blague* that the Dadaists began to incorporate into more and more of their own actions.

We find oblique reference to it at the moment of the emergence of Duchamp's readymades, in the flurry of written responses produced to protest the rejection of *Fountain* from the Independents Exhibition of 1917 in New York. "I suppose monkeys hated to lose their tail," the Dadaists intoned, in the opening lines of their defense. "Necessary, useful and an ornament, monkey imagination could not stretch to a tailless existence (and frankly, do you see the biological beauty of our loss of them?), yet now that we are used to it, we get on pretty well without them." Evolution was invoked, from monkey to man, but also implicitly from painting to the readymade, from the stick with bristles to the head with hairs, from the paint brush to the intellect, as the writer concluded, "But evolution is not pleasing to the monkey race; 'there is a death in every change,' and we monkeys do not love death as we should."[8] Later, Man Ray entered the fray, announcing that such a dynamic was definitive for Dada: "Dada is a state of mind. It consists largely of negations. It is the tail of every other movement."[9]

And Picabia, more than any of the others, made this dynamic his own, made his own, that is, both the radicality and the rear-guard nature of Dorgelès's sneering prank. This is a story that has not yet been told. It is a story surrounding the birth and immediate deployment of the practices we now call readymade. It is a story lying behind the ragged surface of *L'oeil cacodylate,* but not, however, as a key to help us unlock or otherwise decode the work, if such a thing were possible. It is an allegory that is actually more of a structure, more of a logic, than a parable. It is a structure that, in 1921, opened once more onto loss. And yet in 1920, as Paris Dada began, the notion of an artwork and its tail had already taken center stage.

Tableau Dada I. Always the literalist, he had been thinking of calling the piece a "tableau vivant."[10] Instead of a painting, thought Picabia, he would present a living creature, a live monkey, as a work of art, escaping thereby the paralysis of representation, the inert lifelessness of the aesthetic for the immediacy and movement of life itself. (Dorgelès and his donkey would be exceeded in turn.) No monkeys, however, presented themselves for the task. In the end, Picabia was forced to go to the toy store instead of the pet store, where he purchased a stuffed monkey, a monkey that soon found itself attached to the center of an otherwise blank canvas.[11] Words were scrawled around this monkey. "Natures mortes," Picabia inscribed it, reversing his original title. "Still lifes," the painting declaimed, and immediately explained itself, with words running like obscenities across the expanse of a schoolboy's desk: "Portrait of Cézanne, Portrait of Rembrandt, Portrait of Renoir." Deadbeats.

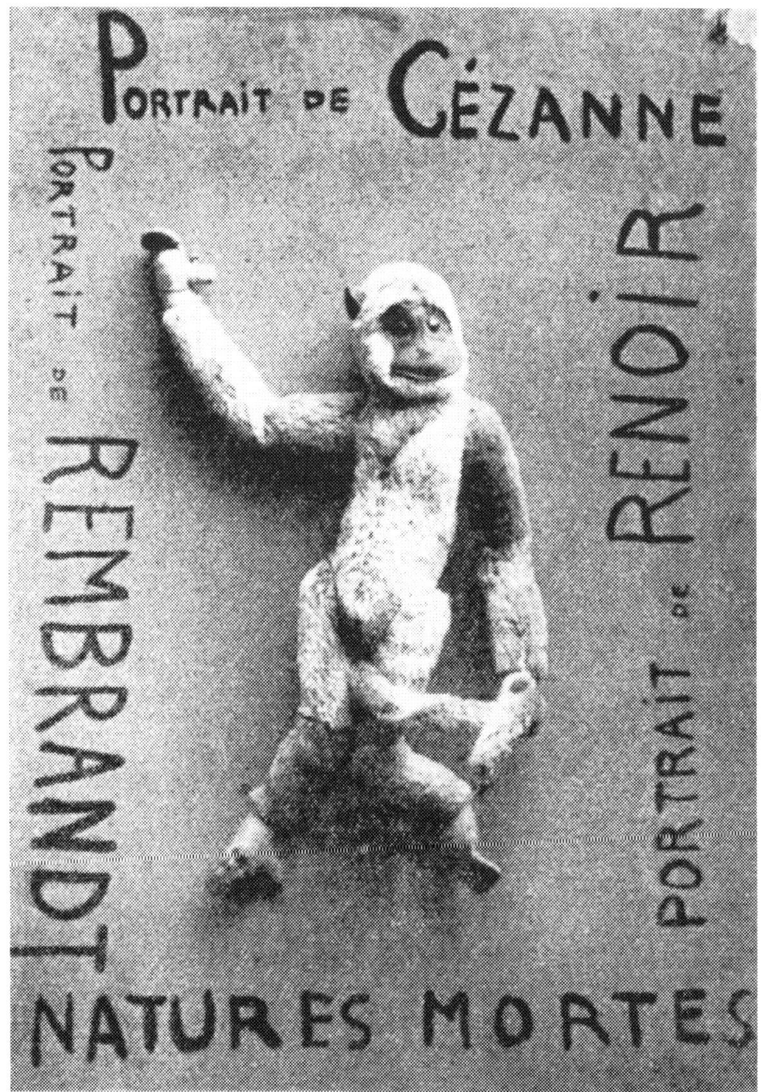

Francis Picabia, *Natures mortes,* 1920. Toy monkey and ink on cardboard. No longer extant. © 2005 Artists Rights Society (ARS), New York/ADAGP, Paris/Estate of Francis Picabia.

We can imagine the jeers and whistles of the crowd, as they became aware of the nature of what they were viewing. For Picabia's *Natures mortes* was presented not in a museum or a gallery, but on the stage. It was the penultimate act of the Dada Manifestation on 27 March at the Maison de l'Oeuvre. As we know, it had already been a long evening, full of spectacular transgressions, before *Natures mortes* was wheeled out at the manifestation's end. But what would this audience have seen? What would they have understood?

We may doubt that they understood the complex circumstances linking this object to the readymade strategies that had been developed recently by Picabia's friend, Marcel Duchamp. In *Natures mortes,* Picabia presents a readymade, but, typically, insists on attaching this object to a canvas surface, forging an indissoluble link between the readymade and painting, a bond that somehow resists easy resolution into the category of *collage,* just as it does not quite enter the free-standing object domain of *sculpture* (a step definitively taken by Duchamp's readymades). Duchamp's insistence that the readymade emerge only as the product of a collision between a chosen commodity object and, just as important, a verbal inscription—their "rendezvous" as he might have put it—this was followed by Picabia. But Picabia's readymade stubbornly clings to the domain of *painting*—a domain whose certainties and conventions, however, now find themselves brutally eviscerated. The title, "Natures mortes," punctuates this connection, calling up painting's traditional genre of the everyday, a genre that the readymade object might be said radically to displace, through a reification that Picabia, again, seems to evoke directly in his title ("still life" in French keeping the connotation of death, of dead nature, that every reification embodies).

But Picabia's *Natures mortes* just as directly evokes the category of the *portrait*—painting's other, and recently outmoded, mainstay—recalling in this the fact that, for Picabia, the readymade had always been, at least in part, an avatar of the portrait. The portrait had been the central terrain of the mechanomorphs that Picabia initiated in 1915, already translating Duchamp's readymade strategy into the domain of the pictorial, with so many close friends and subjects— Alfred Stieglitz, Marius de Zayas, Paul Haviland, Marie Laurencin, Guillaume Apollinaire, Gabrielle Buffet, Picabia himself—replaced by an endless series of diagrammatic machines. Robotic and automated, Picabia's conception of the readymade presumed a conception of the subject. Except in this case, that subject was newly multiple—Cézanne, Rembrandt, Renoir—as Picabia's repetitive inscriptions invoked Modern and Old Master alike, wavering as linguistic signs between the authority of the signature and the regressive violence of the graffito.[12]

We may assume that the audience understood this violence. For the "still lifes" represented here place Cézanne, Rembrandt, and Renoir firmly on the side of the dead, swept aside like so many distant memories—along with the conception of art and of painting that they embody. "I abhor Cézanne's painting, it bores me," Picabia had petulantly announced on the cover of his magazine *391* just one year earlier. And here, three masters of painting's attachment to nature—its replication of the visual motif, its copying of sensuous appearance—are depicted as a leering monkey, Picabia's nod to the allegorical tradition of considering art as the proverbial "ape of nature." It is this allegiance of painting to mimetic activity, its very foundation in the act of copying, that Picabia now declares *bête,* in every sense of the French term. He also proclaims, in this, the death of the mimetic paradigm, its reduction to nothing more than a lifeless stuffed animal, pinioned to its canvas like a specimen in a taxidermist's shop—or a mere painting on the wall of a museum.

The audience would have understood this, I think. But they also would have seen the tail—indeed, this aspect of *Natures mortes* cannot be missed, though I know of hardly a commentator who has since bothered to mention it. Perhaps some things are too obvious to be seen. Picabia's monkey pulls its tail through its legs, grasping its generous length and ridiculously proffering it straight toward the viewer. And since this story of an artwork and its tail is a French story, such an action has a certain valence, attaining the status of a—typically Dadaist—visual pun. For the word in French for tail is *queue.* But *la queue* is also one of many French slang terms for the penis.

By now, the reader will hardly be surprised that Picabia was deeply invested in this pun. It can be seen elsewhere in his Dada work, surfacing, for example, as the "key" to the title of the book-length poem that he had just published in February of 1920, *Unique eunuque (The Unique Eunuch).* Here, the two words of the

FRANCIS PICABIA

UNIQUE EUNUQUE

AVEC UN PORTRAIT DE L'AUTEUR PAR LUI-MÊME
PRÉFACE PAR TRISTAN TZARA

AU SANS PAREIL
37, AVENUE KLEBER, PARIS

Collection DADA

Cover of Francis Picabia, *Unique eunuque* (Paris: Au Sans Pareil, 1920). Image courtesy Comité Picabia. © 2005 Artists Rights Society (ARS), New York/ADAGP, Paris/Estate of Francis Picabia.

title almost trip over each other, performing audibly like twins with just the slightest of differences, and with a repetition redoubled by the "que" at the end of each word—their tails, as it were. But the title also begins to figure a sort of mirror reversal, as the last two letters of *unique* flip around into the first two letters of *eunuque,* a device that finds its elaboration within the body of the poem itself. An accumulation of terse, fragmented, one could almost say "castrated" verses, *Unique eunuque,* indeed, was famous among the Dadaists for its creation of poetic language through the mechanical device of sheer reversal, presenting language as if seen in a mirror, run backward against the onward rush of both time and communicability:

> Allemands les déteste je
> Guerre la pendant que cela pour est'c
> Possible loin plus le resté suis-je
> Maintenant je vais tâcher de les voir de plus près
> Avant comme. . . .[13]

But in the reversal of *Unique eunuque*'s title, one cannot escape the surfacing, again, of the word *queue,* a homophonic extension of the repeated "que" in which each word ends. Picabia's title looks forward, in this, to such Dada puns as Duchamp's texts inscribed on his optical disks, especially the one that reads "L'aspirant habite Javel et moi j'avais l'habite en spirale," a pun that repeatedly offers up the word *la bite* from its alliterative rush, this being another French slang term for the penis. A figure of castration, of the absolute absence of desire, and of singularity, the title *Unique eunuque* operates a machine of connotations that overrides its denotation, opening up the "eunuch" to the condition of multiplicity and the (impossible) resurfacing of *la queue.*

And with this, we can begin to envision the initial sense of this story, of the artwork and its tail. That sense goes something like this: the artwork exposing its tail founds itself upon the remnants of its medium conventions, recycling as dead things mimesis, Old Masters, the functions of signature and of genre. It replaces these things with names and objects, language and the readymade. It turns

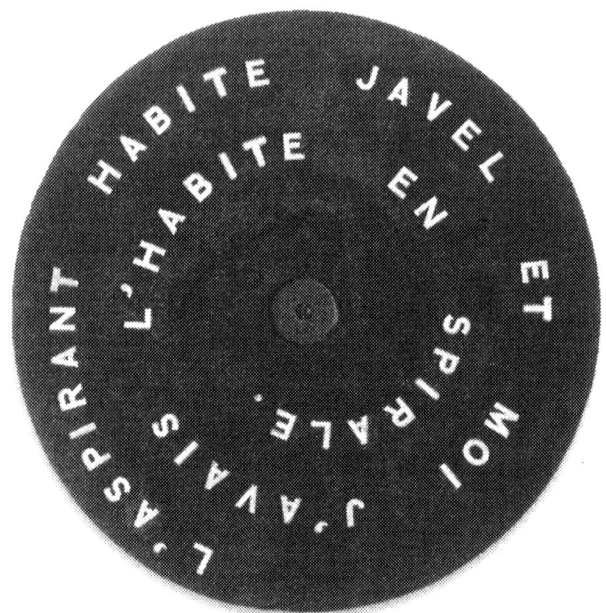

Marcel Duchamp, *Disc inscribed with pun,* 1926. "The aspirant inhabits
Javel and I had a spiral-shaped penis." For use in the film *Anémic cinema,*
produced by Duchamp with Man Ray and Marc Allegret, 1925–26;
white letters pasted on cardboard, painted black, mounted on phono-
graph record, diameter: 30 cm (11^{13}/$_{16}$″). Collection Caroll Janis, New
York. © 2005 Artists Rights Society (ARS), New York/ADAGP,
Paris/Estate of Marcel Duchamp.

what might otherwise seem a self-reflexive gesture not into that which isolates the essence of a medium, but into a self-destructive operation, a loss of essence and foundations, an absurdist circling back upon them like the figure of a snake swallowing its own tail. But in *Natures mortes,* to expose the tail within (of ?) the work of art was also to allow a specific figure to arise. It was to allow the phallus to emerge within the scene of representation. For the phallus would surface from this scene of loss, an impossible resurgence not unlike the pun of *Unique eunuque*—a resurrection in the face of a stated elision. It was Picabia's mission during his Dada years to explore the full significance of what exactly such an emergence would entail. And he was not alone.

One month after the performance at the Maison de l'Oeuvre, just as the critical furor was beginning to fade, Picabia published a reproduction of *Natures mortes* in the first issue of a new magazine that he had founded entitled *Cannibale.* With no explanations given, Picabia's piece was reproduced alone, with Picabia's name printed laconically below it, and a new title above, a title that functioned more as a parodic attempt at classification than at nomination. "Tableau Dada," Picabia lectured, attaching the label to the piece like a professor hammering home a crucial point on the blackboard: Dada Painting.

Tableau Dada II. The category already existed. Picabia had actually inaugurated it at the moment of the manifestation at the Maison de l'Oeuvre, attaching the label, upon that occasion, to a work by Marcel Duchamp. While the Dadaists performed their antics on the stage, the Dada periodicals circulated throughout the hall. And on the cover of the artist's twelfth issue of *391,* Picabia reproduced an image of the *Mona Lisa,* defaced by an improbable, ludicrous handlebar mustache. The piece hardly needs introduction. But this was not Duchamp's *L.H.O.O.Q.,* not exactly. Duchamp, who created that work at the end of 1919 while living for a short time with Picabia in Paris, had left for New York at the beginning of 1920, just as the first Paris Dada season began, taking *L.H.O.O.Q.* with him. Appropriating Duchamp's work, Picabia replicated the piece for his magazine—art can be defaced by anyone, the graffito respects no authorship, the assisted readymade would be collective—although Picabia elided his agency here, announcing unequivocally above the image: "TABLEAU DADA by MARCEL DUCHAMP."

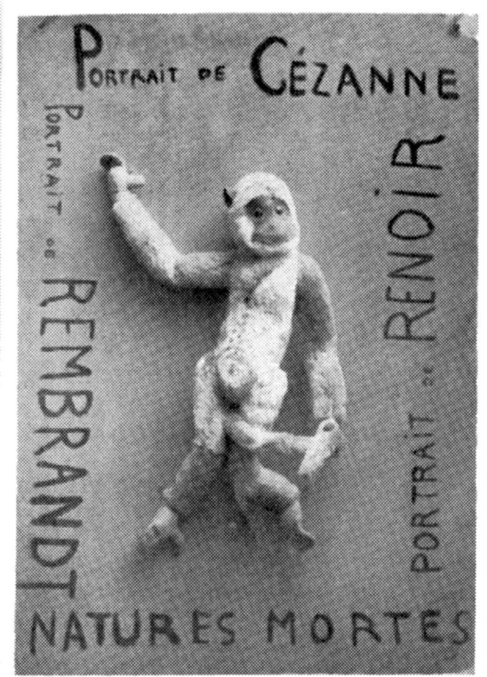

Francis Picabia, *Tableau Dada (Natures Mortes)*. Reproduced in *Cannibale* 1 (25 April 1920). Beinecke Rare Book and Manuscript Library, Yale University. © 2005 Artists Rights Society (ARS), New York/ADAGP, Paris/Estate of Francis Picabia.

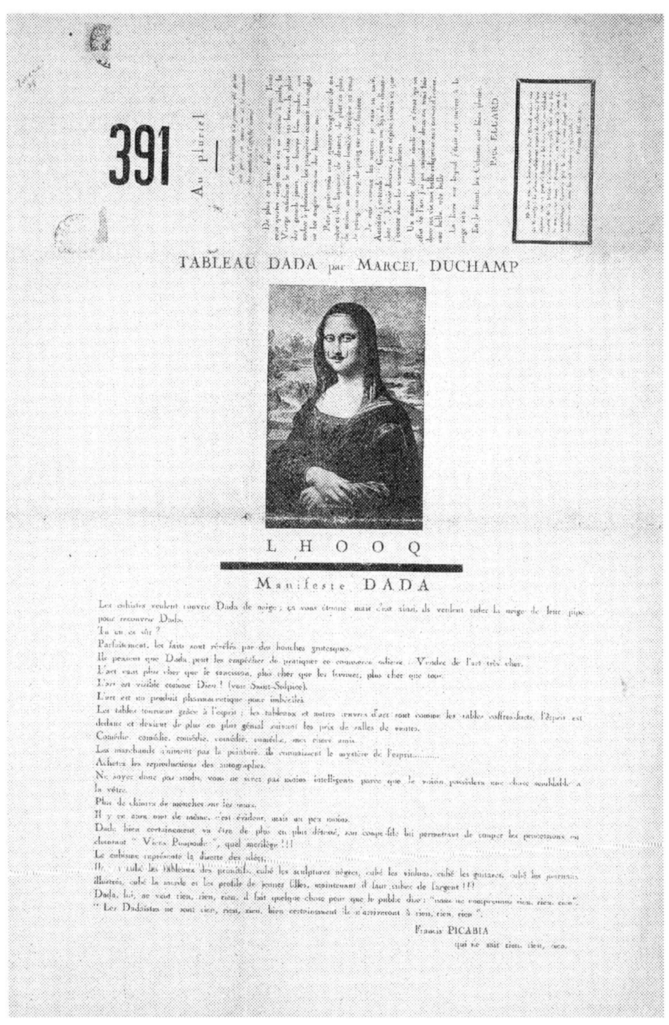

Francis Picabia, *Tableau Dada by Marcel Duchamp (LHOOQ)*. Reproduced on the cover of *391* 12 (March 1920). Research Library, The Getty Research Institute, Los Angeles. © 2005 Artists Rights Society (ARS), New York/ADAGP, Paris/Estate of Francis Picabia.

Paired with *Natures mortes,* the other "Tableau Dada" that was presented on the stage that day, a category was under construction.

That category turned, again, on the relationship between an artwork and its tail. Defacing his reproduction of the *Mona Lisa,* Duchamp added both a mustache and a goatee—a beard, in the words of one critic, "from whose point there hangs something resembling a short black tail."[14] Beneath the image, Duchamp scrawled his well-known pun "L.H.O.O.Q." like an allegorical subscript, an appendage that commands the viewer to "LOOK!" as its English homophone, while spelling out—when pronounced letter by letter in French—"elle a chaud au cul": she has a hot ass. The "Q" at the end of *L.H.O.O.Q.*—the letter with a tail—becomes not a *queue* here, but a *cul:* not a tail, but an ass, not the phallus, but a hole. And yet. The *Mona Lisa's* "cul" is precisely what does not present itself within the scene of Leonardo's representation; it is off-scene, beyond the frame, outside the work. Look again, however, at Duchamp's mustache and beard: they form two inverted *V*s, "mirror images of each other—and . . . also fairly standard iconographic representations of a woman's pubic hair." The hole has migrated upward, into the work itself. And yet the effects of this excluded object's surfacing are immensely confusing. As the critic that I have been citing, Susan Suleiman, has explained: "It would appear that by a humorous 'displacement upward,' Duchamp has produced not, or not only, the Mona Lisa as a sexpot . . . nor the Mona Lisa as a young man, but the Mona Lisa as a phallic mother (pubis plus 'appendages')—indeed a phallic mother doubly marked, redundantly phallic."[15] And when Picabia replicated *L.H.O.O.Q.* for the cover of *391,* he "shaved" the goatee and emphasized the mustache, thickening and lengthening its hairy bulk, turning the handlebars into erections that rhymed with the phallic tail of his own *Natures mortes.*[16]

And so, given all of this, what exactly would a "Tableau Dada" be? What was this lesson of the Maison de l'Oeuvre? Learning from *Natures mortes* and *L.H.O.O.Q.,* a Tableau Dada necessarily engaged the question of language—but language turned against itself, the twisted language of the pun. It reconfigured the status of the mark—of writing, of drawing—as a form of the graffito, striking with violence against the proprieties of representation. It enacted a thematics of

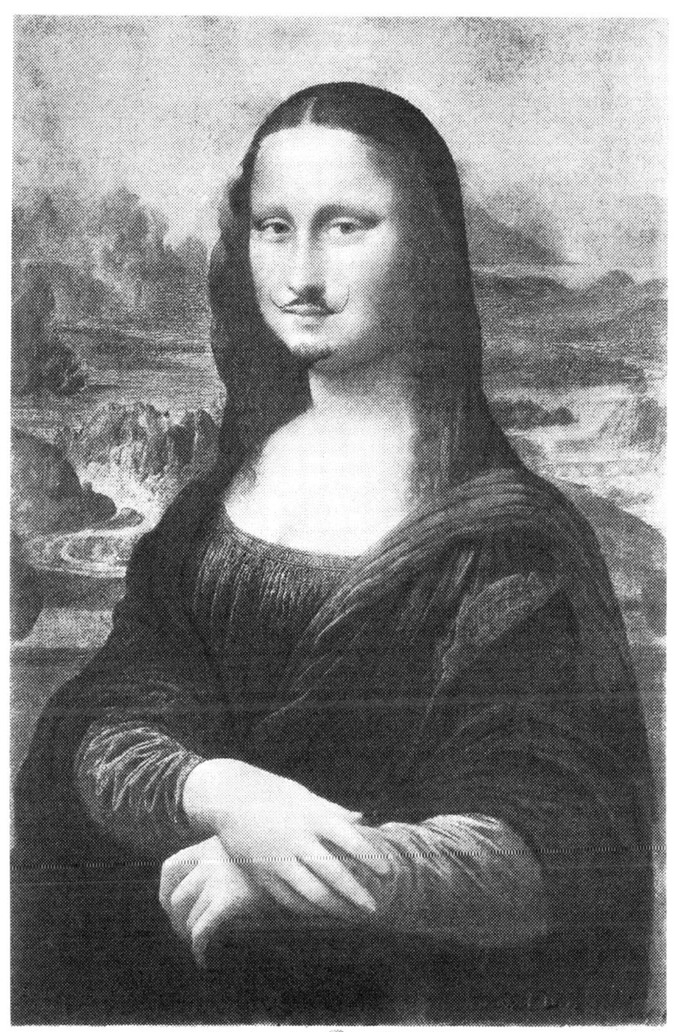

Marcel Duchamp, *L.H.O.O.Q.*, 1919. Collotype hand-colored with watercolor, $7^5/_8 \times 4^{13}/_{16}''$. Private collection. © 2005 Artists Rights Society (ARS), New York/ADAGP, Paris/Estate of Marcel Duchamp.

castration—suggested, in the closely squeezed legs of Picabia's monkey; denied, in the presence of Duchamp's phallic Mother; and redoubled, in Picabia's erasure of *L.H.O.O.Q.*'s facial goatee or tail.[17] Everywhere, the phallus was put into play, entered into the scene of representation, grasped, pointed, appended, displaced. Improper uses of the phallus were imagined: masturbation on the one hand (Picabia's *Natures mortes*), incest on the other (Duchamp's *L.H.O.O.Q.*). And, finally, a Tableau Dada struck against the rule of the artistic Old Master—Rembrandt, Cézanne, Renoir, Leonardo—fusing the Dada attack on painting with a psychic transgression of the Law of the Father.

Money dries up on the rocks . . .

—*André Breton, in* Claire de terre *(1923)*

The general equivalent. Language, the Phallus, and the Father: We are in the presence of three major avatars of what Jean-Joseph Goux has taught us to call *general equivalents.* Simply put, a general equivalent represents a standard measure—that object against which others are compared, making disparate things commensurable, rendering them in some sense equal, opening up the question of an ordered system of substitutions or exchange, and with that, the correlative question of value. Goux borrowed the term from Karl Marx, from his momentous analysis of the genesis of the value form and of money in the early pages of *Capital* (Marx also employs the term "universal equivalent").[18] It is an analysis that Goux has extended from economics across the systems of semiotics, psychoanalysis, and philosophy, tracing a logic that can be contained in the following assertion: the *Father* becomes the general equivalent of subjects, *Language* the general equivalent of signs, and the *Phallus* the general equivalent of objects in a manner structurally homologous to the system that allowed *Gold* to attain the role of the general equivalent of commodities. For Goux, the "process of symbolization" at large follows the specific logic revealed in Marx's analysis of the genesis of money.

In what Goux calls Marx's "genealogy of values," his archaeology of the "genesis of the value form,"[19] Marx posits four developmental stages. The first phase, the "elementary" or "accidental" form of value, entails the placement of two isolated commodities in a relationship of equivalence with one another—but with no other commodities. This relationship of equivalence Goux describes as primarily *visual*. It is also based on the recognition of likeness, a quest for *similarity*. It is a "specular relation, a mirroring," Goux asserts (N, p. 13): one commodity finding its value in the body, in the image of the other. In this, the accidental form of value becomes something like what Jacques Lacan might call its "Mirror Stage"—an operation that depends on "an identification with the image of the *like*" (N, p. 14). However, based on this exclusive identification, the elementary form of value "cannot place a commodity in a relationship of exchange with more than *one other* commodity" (N, p. 14).

In a subsequent development, a second form—the "total" or "extended" form of value—arises to place the commodity into what Marx calls "a social relation." The commodity becomes a "citizen of the world."[20] Ripped free from its original identification, it now can be compared not only with another particular commodity, but with "the world of commodities in general," in a series of "infinite relations" of equivalent forms that psychoanalysis might be tempted to call polymorphous. To use Marx's example: "20 yards of linen = 1 coat or = 10 lbs. tea or = 40 lbs. coffee or = 1 quarter corn or = 2 ounces gold or = $\frac{1}{2}$ ton iron or = etc."[21] This situation involves a series of fragmentary equivalent forms and identifications of value that are mutually exclusive. It produces a situation "of rivalry, of crisis, of conflict" (N, p. 15). For Marx, this expanded value form has "defects." For one, "the relative expression of value is incomplete because the series representing it is interminable." It is thus "liable at any moment to be lengthened by each new kind of commodity that comes into existence," producing a "many-colored mosaic of disparate and independent expressions of value."[22] An economy of one commodity after another, one equivalence after another, represents an economy without a single or unified principle of order, and thus without a Law.

The third, or the generalized, form of value resolves this conflicted state. Now, one single denominator rises to measure the value of all other commodities. Commodities are no longer frozen in a single identification with a similar commodity, nor in a polymorphous series of fragmentary equivalences: they all express their value now in the body of the same commodity, a rationalization that Goux characterizes as "*reason* itself . . . it introduces measure into the community" (N, p. 16). All finding their value in the same mirror, different commodities can now communicate with one another through that common ideal. And so in its fourth, and final, form—what we now recognize as "the money form" of value—the world of commodities converges on this exclusive value form, which, historically, in the Western system, has been gold. The accession to the money form of value entails a homogenization of the world of commodities, and an intense "centralization" around the exclusive form now deemed to confer value. A symbolic economy takes definitive shape, characterized not just by random or disparate exchanges, but by what Goux describes—in words with ramifications much larger than simply monetary economy—as a "scientific system of 'metaphors,' a regulated process of equivalents and substitutions" (N, p. 21). With the rise of the general equivalent, a "principal axis" now exists, a "central and centralizing metaphor that anchors all other metaphors," a "fulcrum of all symbolic legislation" (N, p. 21). In a word whose importance for Dada has been clear since Duchamp created his *Three Standard Stoppages* in 1913, what now exists is "the locus of the *standard* and of unity, totemically implanted in the center of the tribal space" (N, p. 21).[23]

The money form of value thus solves what Goux has called a crisis. Upon this resolution, Goux constructs his first homology: the relationship to the other must be construed analogously to the appearance of money. "At a certain point in ego formation," Goux writes, "the FATHER is chosen to resolve a situation of conflict. . . . the father becomes the sole reflecting image of all subjects seeking their worth" (N, p. 17). And further: "The passage from the extended value form . . . to the generalized value form . . . parallels the resolution of the oedipal crisis" (N, p. 17). But if psychoanalysis teaches us anything, it is that not just any father will serve in this role of measure, distribution, and valuation. To become the general equivalent, the father must be *killed,* mediating between subjects "only provided that he is separated from the group of people, that is, expelled into transcendence" (N, p. 18).

Here we encounter perhaps the central characteristic of general equivalents: to function as the privileged site of measure, to enact the law, to rule over (evaluate) the generalized world of objects or commodities, the general equivalent must undergo a process of radical exclusion. "The law is excluded from the system over which it exercises jurisdiction," as Denis Hollier explains. "The common measure, paradoxically, has an uncommon origin: in a transcendent place whence all its power is drawn. The homogeneous is therefore, by definition, under the domination of the heterogeneous and the law is outside of the law."[24] Social life founds itself upon the *murder* of the Father. Taken out of circulation, put on reserve, gold gets hoarded in banks, never to be seen again.

Nowhere is this radical exclusion of the general equivalent more obvious than in the world of sexual desire or the drives, with the ascension of the Phallus to the general equivalent of objects.[25] For here too, psychoanalysis has isolated four developmental "phases" or stages, a homology between Freud and Marx that Goux will not allow to be left to chance. For Goux, the essential point is this: the "genesis of every major symbol" can be seen as "isomorphic to the discrete genetic phases of the monetary form" (N, pp. 20–21). The origins of money unlock the origins of symbolization in other domains of human culture, revealing a hidden but shared structure or history, and parallel modalities of investment as well as orders of control. The psychoanalytic "oral phase," for example, with its incorporative mode of identification, corresponds in Goux's schema with Marx's first or "elementary" form of value. Subsequently, with the explosive increase in part objects and their slippery relations of metonymy—breast equals nipple equals finger, eye equals mouth equals anus, excrement equals child equals penis—we enter the second, "extended" form of value and the "anal stage" of libidinal development, a mode of conflict and crisis with a complete lack of any generalized form. Once again, however, a single element from among the part objects will be set up against all the other objects, regulating their exchange and applying its standard of value. That object is the phallus; the stage of the "generalized value form" parallels the phallic phase of libidinal development. All the partial objects and partial drives are now organized, centralized around this exclusive form, concluding with the "genital" stage and organization of the drives—corresponding to the fourth, or the money form, of value.

But once again, the phallus must be excluded from the part objects whose commerce it rules; "the phallus cannot enter into a relationship that gives it a price" (N, p. 22); it is priceless, outside the system of exchange. We are those strange beings, as Lacan once mused, who seemingly can accede to our sexuality only on the condition that we are threatened with its loss: pleasure becomes a function of privation, just as wealth becomes real only by being spent:

> The object that functions as equivalent, the sexual organ, is necessarily excluded from the imagined body and from the world of objects of the drive in a logical "operation," a *castration* that dramatizes the phantasmatic element. Castration, the elision of the phallus—however bloody or bloodless the enactment of the scenario—is none other than the syntactic exclusion of the general equivalent from the world of relative values (of part objects). (N, p. 23)

Castration does not destroy the phallus; rather, the elision creates it. Put on reserve, the phallus can no longer be regarded merely as an organ, or as a material thing. It has become, instead, a signifier as well as an ideal, regulating the order and facilitating the movements of exchange.

The general equivalent, then, regulates the circulation of exchange-values by being put on reserve. To enter into exchange, a product must delay its use, postpone its consumption (its destruction), for as long as possible; exchange-value is founded on the renunciation of use-value. As Picabia seemed to express this lesson of modernity at the moment of Dada: money doesn't die, it simply leaves on trips. The general equivalent, regulating this delay, becomes the very principle (the fulcrum) of all exchange. Other exchanges (other economies) may have been possible before it, but none will be remembered in its wake. As a usurper that nevertheless lays claim to being the very foundation of exchange, the general equivalent consequently becomes that which is useless (gold), an item of pure excess, a surplus. Dominant symbolic economies—that of commodities, or of subjectivity, or of the linguistic sign—depend on an identical triple logic of transcendence, abstract or mediated exchange, and exclusion. The general equivalent's primary functions of being a measuring standard (transcendent), a medium of exchange (abstract), and a reserve (excluded), depend on these three dynamics.

At the moment of Dada, however, other questions were asked of symbolic economies—of the very form and logic of the process of symbolization that the general equivalent founds. Picabia's category of the "Tableau Dada" seemed to isolate—to fixate on—the general equivalent in its primary forms. I want to assert that this is far from an accident. The very basis not just of an artistic medium, but of symbolization itself seemed to be at stake. And given the logic of the general equivalent, Dada in 1920 instead seemed to ask: What would happen to a symbolic economy if the general equivalent's transcendence were denied? As opposed to submitting to abstract exchange, what would it mean if the general equivalent were used, without delay? And instead of being placed on reserve, what if the surplus was spent? What if money, contrary to Picabia's dictum, could die?

One answer to such questions came again only after Dada, from another scene of dissidence. For to deny the general equivalent's exclusion would be to enter into the domain of what Georges Bataille later conceived of as *dépense,* a wild, unthinking expenditure without reserve.[26] Losing their ideal mirror, things would become *unequal,* the mediation of exchange usurped. Dada, it seems, had stumbled upon this strategy of expending the general equivalent long before Bataille gave it a name.[27] General equivalents would be taken out of reserve and placed back into use: Father, Phallus, Language. This is one lesson, if I am correct, of the Tableau Dada.

For general equivalents cannot abide immediate use—that denial of the delay of exchange that allows them to regulate the scene of equivalency—or even immediate exchange, the exchange of one use-value for another (barter), bypassing the abstract mediation of monetary law (N, pp. 36–38). Proper exchange can only be indirect. In the sexual sphere, the phallus as general equivalent denies both immediate use (masturbation) and direct exchange (incest, the refusal to submit one's sexual object to the abstract circulation whose laws were long ago discovered by Levi-Strauss). But these are precisely the two scenarios imaged forth by the Tableau Dada: the phallus will be entered into the scene of representation, its exclusion denied, its substance used (*Natures mortes*) or then directly exchanged (*L.H.O.O.Q.*). The phallus becomes a part object once more. The Dead Father too is revived, only to be submitted to the dissemination of reproduction beyond the rule of the One; language ceases to guarantee its singular nominations in the play of the pun. Denominations, in other words, default. "'Values' vanish when either direct exchange (purchase in kind, or incest) or immediate use is practiced" (N, p. 38). What Goux calls the *mono*-form, the form of the One, would be displaced: a challenge in these symbolic registers to phallocentrism, logocentrism, patricentrism.

Art history has mostly missed Dada's specific challenge to such symbolic economies owing to the field's curtailed understanding of the Dada strategy of the readymade. For it can be presumed that Dada stumbled onto its larger challenge to the founding logic of symbolic economies through the readymade: a challenge to art, painting and sculpture especially, fomented by collapsing art's practice with the form of the commodity. The commodity did not only provide Dada with an engagement with mass culture, a disavowal of originality, a questioning of medium-specificity, or a challenge to ontological definitions and contextual frameworks for art. It did not concern only the critique of institutions, surely not only the displacement of the contemplative vocation of art with the real use-value of the everyday object. With the readymade, Dada confronted the commodity in its totality, an object split at its core, riven into the opposed modalities of use-value and exchange-value. *Equivalence* was everywhere at issue for the readymade—which is another way of saying that the readymade confronted Dada with the issue of the general equivalent.

The lesson for art history—the lesson of the readymade—is this: Dada's confrontation was not just of art with the commodity. Dada entailed a challenge closer to Marx's concerns in *Capital,* a confrontation of art with *money*—the principle of the circulation of commodities and their abstract equivalency. And thus, we might speculate that Dada followed this mode of equivalence—followed money—into the heart of the more general logic of symbolic economies. Indeed, almost as soon as the issue of the readymade had been raised, Dada would take the money form as its form, as its very entrance into form.

Dessin Dada I. Just two months after the October 1919 creation of *L.H.O.O.Q.,* on December 3, 1919, Duchamp brought to completion a piece that he entitled *Tzanck Check.* He always insisted on the connections between the two. Instead of an art reproduction, *Tzanck Check* presented a larger-than-life facsimile of a bank check. Signed and dated by Duchamp, the "check" was made out to Daniel Tzanck, a Parisian dentist, in the amount of $115 U.S. dollars drawn upon an institution called "The Teeth's Loan and Trust Company, Consolidated." Although the piece appears to be mechanically printed, it was in fact entirely hand-drawn by Duchamp, with the exception of the background of the lower-half of the check, marked repeatedly by a miniature rubber stamp that Duchamp had created especially for the task. Like the intricate designs on currency that are meant to discourage forgery, the stamp stammered "the teethsloanandtrustcompany-consolitated" [*sic*], over and over; the word "Original" was printed vertically in red capital letters across the piece. Still living in Picabia's apartment at this moment, Duchamp allowed Picabia to reproduce the *Tzanck Check* as he had *L.H.O.O.Q.* during the subsequent ruckus of the first Dada season in Paris. It appeared in the premiere issue of Picabia's *Cannibale,* along with the image of *Natures mortes.* And Picabia continued his nominalist games. The piece was labeled a "Dessin Dada." Dada Drawing. Another category was under construction.

It was a category immediately infected by the condition of forgery. For if the Tableau Dada that is *L.H.O.O.Q.* entered the realm of the graffito through its defacement of a readymade commercial art reproduction, the Dessin Dada that is *Tzanck Check* proclaimed itself a counterfeit—despite its written protestations of "originality"—through its embrace of precise mimetic craft.[28] With hindsight, this condition of the counterfeit can be seen to infect the entire series of "mechanical drawings" that had up until this point been completed by both Picabia and Duchamp, a series of which *Tzanck Check* can be said to be a logical extension, even a fitting culmination. But it must immediately be noticed that Duchamp does not counterfeit the money form directly here—*Tzanck Check* is

DESSIN DADA

Marcel DUCHAMP.

Carnet du Cuculin

Les littérateurs et peintres cubistes veulent être sérieux, pour cela ils pensent à la grande beauté des édifices américains " gratte-ciel ". Il y a en France des fruits qui s'appellent " gratte-culs "

Un de nos amis à qui je demandais des nouvelles de Picasso, m'a déclaré qu'il était dans son bureau, c'est peut-être vrai.

Marcel Duchamp va mieux, il boit de l'huile de foie de morue ; il y a beaucoup de femmes en Amérique et peu de whisky.

La nouvelle Revue Française me fait penser à une maison de santé dont les pensionnaires s'ils n'y meurent pas, ne peuvent sortir qu'idiots —

Jacques-Emile Blanche est un vieux peintre, mais un jeune cerveau.

Picabia m'a dit qu'il trouvait la peinture de Segonzac et de Moreau " Très bien ", ce que fait tout de même l'amitié ! —

Albert Gleizes est un bourreur de crânes !

Marcel Duchamp, *Dessin Dada (Tzanck Check)*. Reproduced in *Cannibale* 1 (April 25, 1920). Beinecke Rare Book and Manuscript Library, Yale University. © 2005 Artists Rights Society (ARS), New York/ADAGP, Paris/Estate of Marcel Duchamp.

not exactly a form of currency, it does not counterfeit the general equivalent. Rather, it entails a copy of a bureaucratic document—a check—that functions as a *demand* for currency, as a promise that the general equivalent will be provided, that value will (eventually) be procured, with, as Duchamp might say, "all sorts of delays."

Thus the currency "function" of Duchamp's *Tzanck Check* is no longer the same as the circulation of the sign supported by mechanical drawing—the *Large Glass* or Picabia's mechanomorphs—in the 1910s. Following the thread leading from the readymade to the money form, Duchamp arrives at a sign for money that is not exactly money at all. Instead, pushed to an extreme level of engagement with the commodity and the money form, the Dada work of art becomes a pure token—an offering made in the place of money, a marker in fact of where money, one might say, *is not*. *Tzanck Check* hardly amounts to the apotheosis of Dada's engagement with the general equivalent. The work, and the Dessin Dada more generally, begin to put on the record that the symbolic economy of the general equivalent had itself entered into a deep historical crisis.

More specific than the money form, a check includes, as Dalia Judovitz has described it, "a blank (the addressee), a bank (institutional endorsement), a date, and a signature (individual endorsement)." Another homology is being constructed:

> These institutional markers that define the legal identity of a check also define the institutional parameters of a work of art. The anonymous spectator of the work of art occupies the blank space of the addressee, while dates are essential to both art and business. The author's signature, however, acts as the guarantor of the authenticity of the work, as well as the general guarantor, the "bank" (the artist's reputation that backs this particular issue of the work).[29]

Duchamp here reinscribes aesthetic experience as an explicitly financial transaction. And yet in so doing, the drama of *Tzanck Check* becomes a drama of what we might call *convertibility*—of whether the demand for value will be answered, the promise of money procured, the quantification of aesthetic pleasure achieved. Newly essential to such an endeavor are all the legal institutions required to shore up this traffic in the general equivalent. And so Duchamp invokes the newly conventionalized *authorizing* function of the (artistic) signature, as well as the *institutional* functions of the corporation or the bank.

The correlative of the bank in the artistic sphere would be the museum; as Jean Baudrillard has expressed this condition: "The museum acts as a *guarantee* for the aristocratic exchange. . . . Just as a gold bank, the public backing of the Bank of France, is necessary in order that the circulation of capital and private speculation be organized, so the fixed reserve of the museum is necessary for the functioning of the sign exchange of paintings. Museums play the role of banks in the political economy of paintings."[30] At the moment of the creation of *Tzanck Check,* however, museums of modern art did not yet exist (despite the pleas of precisely one Daniel Tzanck that just such an institution be created in Paris).[31] No reserve had been established. Or rather, since the reserve (the museum) did exist, it was merely the fate of the modernist work of art at first to exist without one. The general equivalent of (modernist) painting was not yet fixed, which might also be to say that the general equivalent of painting itself had perhaps become—recently, as a result of modernism—unfixed.

This is the crisis of the general equivalent to which the Dessin Dada begins to give form. Duchamp's *Tzanck Check* literalizes the consequences of this unbinding on the very concept of artistic and symbolic value. The work's literal value becomes free-floating, abstract, and speculative, despite the fact of Duchamp's having "drawn" upon precisely $115 dollars of U.S. funds. In 1940, Duchamp informed his patron Walter Arensberg that it was possible to buy back the drawing from Tzanck for precisely $50 dollars. But then later, talking with Pierre Cabanne, Duchamp declared, "And I bought it back twenty years later, for a lot more than it says it's worth!"[32] Value, here, has become unhinged. The artwork itself has become a form of expenditure. Falling outside of both capitalist and artistic economies alike, the work insinuates itself into another economy, the reciprocal economy of the gift.[33] And just as at the moment of the inauguration

of the readymade, the only object anchoring any of these vectored movements—
from the relationality of the gift to the erratic leaping of financial speculation—
will pass beyond the fiction of a "Teeth's Loan and Trust Company" or even the
counterfeit authority of the check. It will instead fall to the immense importance
now weighing on the signature: Marcel Duchamp.

Dessin Dada II. Duchamp's *Tzanck Check* had to wait almost a year to find its cat-
egorical sibling, its Picabian double. But that double would come. In the November 1920 issue of *391,* Picabia published a second "Dessin Dada," an image
printed on the magazine's cover. And although almost every work Picabia completed during the early 1920s could be included in the exploration of the characteristics of a "Dada Drawing," this piece was the only one to be given the
all-important *name,* as Picabia completed his quixotic task of creating categories
of just two starkly juxtaposed objects. Picabia's *Dessin Dada* consisted of the photographic reproduction of a Pari-Mutuel horse race ticket, presented without
further alteration or additions.

The drawing, thus, was a simple readymade. It did not attempt to lift a discarded object into the realm of the aesthetic through the twists and turns of
aleatory recombinations, as did, say, the *Merz* collages of Kurt Schwitters, often
replete with such everyday refuse as discarded tickets and buttons. Like the other
readymades, it insisted only on the addition of a title, of a name, and an authorizing signature, the name of "Francis Picabia" printed lazily below. But actually,
one might wonder if this signature stood entirely alone. Another signature—a
particularly biting, if not monstrous one—stood directly above the *Dessin Dada.*
Like a multiheaded hydra, the signature that Picabia placed above his *Dessin Dada*
emerged from a photographic reproduction of a letter written by one of the
central masters of drawing within the French tradition, namely Jean-Auguste-
Dominique Ingres, the artist upon whom so many artists in postwar France were
calling during these years of antimodernist reaction, the so-called Return to
Order.[34] "Copy of an Ingres autograph," Picabia's *391* announced: except the
autograph had been tampered with. The signature had become an amalgam, a
multiplicity, a sign with double valence. It had become a hybrid, mixed thing.

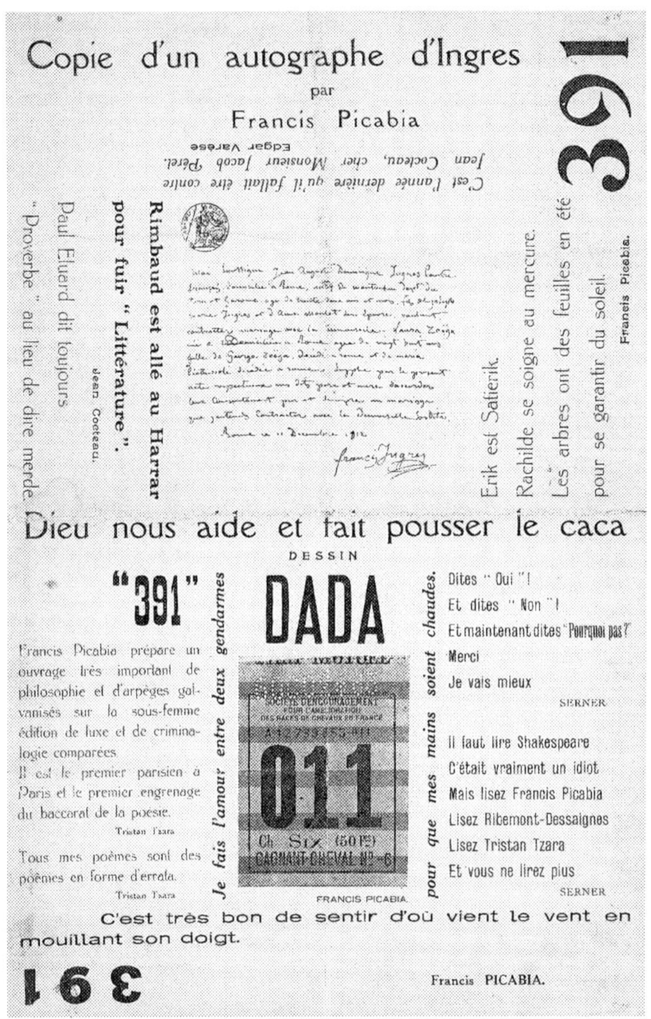

Francis Picabia, *Dessin Dada,* reproduced in *391* 14 (November 1920). Research Library, The Getty Research Institute, Los Angeles. © 2005 Artists Rights Society (ARS), New York/ADAGP, Paris/Estate of Francis Picabia.

For Picabia added his own first name to Ingres' signature. Francis Ingres. The signature, too, was now infected by the condition of the counterfeit, of forgery.

But then the associations begin. Picabia's *Dessin Dada* consists of a series of inscriptions (serial numbers, letters, a numerical price, phrases), a couple of lines, and a starkly repeated alternation of horizontal stripes. It recodes, in this way, those previous combinations of lines and inscriptions that were Picabia's mechanomorphic drawings, a reinscription toward the realm of the geometrical and the abstract. The *Dessin Dada* becomes, with this, what we might call a readymade abstraction; it links, indissolubly, as did so much of Picabia's subsequent work, the readymade to abstraction. The two aesthetic phenomena, so often seen as diametrically opposed reactions to modernity, were now forced—like "Francis" and "Ingres"—however monstrously to coincide.

And value was put into play. Like Duchamp's *Dessin Dada,* Picabia's piece continues to develop the punning multivalency of just what exactly the action of "drawing" could now be seen to mean. To "draw" no longer denoted merely the action of picturing, of creating a form; a Dada drawing also calls on the use of the word that entails financial "drawing" upon a monetary fund; and it just as much evokes "drawing" in the sense of "to pick or choose," with the connotation of gambling and chance, as in the "drawing" of a lottery ticket. "Choosing" was, of course, the action perhaps most associated with the promulgation of the strategy of the readymade; but then again, so were the vagaries of chance procedures. And here these dual actions were immediately translated into the realm of value, a value that Picabia projects as double, as unstable, as undecidable. For we are in the presence of the readymade as a gambling ticket. The question immediately arises: Is the ticket used, discarded, something like the random litter of lottery tickets that one finds on the streets of the city, the detritus of innumerable dreams, wishes that have gone unfulfilled, their tokens now useless—ciphers of pure loss, beyond exchange? Or is the ticket a winner, with exchange-value to be redeemed? The *Dessin Dada* transforms a formula that has, for so long, been seen to describe the actions of the Dada readymade: the alchemical conversion of everyday dross into the gold of the aesthetic. Far too simple, this formula will now be opened on both of its sides, unbinding the relative value or worthlessness of each, testifying to a sudden, epochal *coincidence* of dross and gold, of refuse and of riches. The *Dessin Dada* brought together value and the gift, value and waste. It flirted with currency and the money form, only to move from money directly to an abstract token for its existence, a token in each case potentially too full, excessively replete—or conversely empty, hollow, a void.

> Alas, the best thing that man has managed to do with gold is to make twenty franc coins. . . .
>
> —*Francis Picabia, "Trompettes de Jericho," 1922*[35]

The token sign. We are not finished with Goux's theory of the general equivalent. For if the Dessin Dada did not engage in precisely the same expenditure of the general equivalent that I have proposed as the lesson of the Tableau Dada, it prioritized the general equivalent nonetheless, turning specifically, and for the first time, to the intersection of Dada techniques with the actual sphere of monetary economy. The lesson of the Dessin Dada would be that the actual structure of the general equivalent had undergone, historically, a profound change. Goux has theorized this transformation, locating its culmination around the years of World War I. The simultaneity with the inception of Dada is no coincidence. The transformation of the general equivalent presents us with a theory of the structural conditions of possibility of those very techniques now called "readymade."

Around World War I, the representational, convertible economy of goldbacked money—of what was called the gold standard, of gold as the general equivalent of products—collapses.[36] At this time, gold money disappears in France, and, by 1919, Britain, for one, was circulating bank notes without gold backing. Supposedly a series of temporary, war-time measures, convertibility was in fact never reestablished in any of the Western economies. Money now forever loses its backing in gold. We witness with this transformation not an anarchic expenditure of the general equivalent's reserve; this is not the solution of Dada, nor of Bataille. Gold would not regress to the condition of a part object among part objects, another commodity drifting through the world of shiftless products. The loss of convertibility, rather, testifies to a *further abstraction* of the process that promoted gold to the general equivalent of commodities, of the evolution that instituted currency, or the money-form, as the organizing system of the symbolic economy of values. The money-form's *representational* logic had been undermined, in a vast sweeping away of the last material vestiges tying currency to a referent in the real world—to an actual object, an anchor, namely, gold.

For Goux, this crisis in the convertibility of the money-form parallels a concurrent series of other representational crises: the contestation of realism in the novel, the relinquishment of figuration in painting, and Saussure's momentous severing of linguistic signs from their referents in the real world. As with the inconvertible money-form, the inauguration of what Saussure termed the differential sign led to a situation where signs were seen to refer to other signs, not to actual things, and where linguistic meaning was now seen to be derived from a system of purely internal relations, without any external anchor. In these varied cultural and symbolic realms, we are witnessing a process that Goux calls—in a phrase reminiscent of one of Max Weber's more famous proclamations—"the disentwining of the functions of the general equivalent in modernity" (CL, p. 138).

These functions, historically, amount to three major operations. Goux explains: "Precious metal that becomes money through an evolution in the forms of exchange comes to fulfill three quite distinct functions: (1) that of the *measure of values,* (2) that of the *means of exchange,* and (3) that of the *instrument of payment* and of *hoarding or reserve*" (CL, p. 33). As a measure of values, the general equivalent fulfills its original function as a standard, a primal function, Goux observes, in that the general equivalent has historically emerged as a unit of measurement before all else. But for gold, say, to function as a measure of values, it need not be physically present or available (prices can be fixed without it); gold represents in this a concept of *ideal* value; and Goux calls the general equivalent in its measurement function an *archetype.* For exchange, however, to take place through the delay, the indirect detour, of monetary law, the general equivalent must be present in a substitute form (money circulates in a representative mode); indeed, making the substitution of exchange possible, the general equivalent's own replacement by substitutions, by conventional symbols, may be regarded as an inevitable, logical process, a requirement of the money-form itself; and this means of exchange Goux terms the general equivalent's *token* function. Ultimately, however, beyond the circulation of exchange or the valuation of a standard measure, economic *payments* must be made, the balance of debts redressed, or real treasures amassed; no longer working as a transcendent ideal, nor circulating in substitute form, the general equivalent in its third function becomes that source of the real existence of money that Goux terms the *treasury. Archetype, Token, Treasury*: the general equivalent's functions come to be split into three different "ontological registers," divided by Goux—in a Lacanian turn of phrase—into their respective modalities of the Ideal, the Symbolic, and the Real.

With the loss of convertible, gold-backed currency, the symbolic register of the general equivalent ascends to a position of dominance over both its ideal and real registers; inconvertible, free-floating *token* money now circulates beyond the reach of the fixed standard of the Archetype or the actual reserve of the Treasury. A system of economic legitimation based on *representation* has been dissolved (paper money = gold), replaced with another, less transparent legitimizing system. The transparent value of gold-backed, convertible currency has been replaced by the inconvertible token sign governed by the legal apparatus of the bank; a liberal capitalist economy gives way at just this moment in the West to a system of monopoly capitalism. The previous interplay of the three registers of the general equivalent has been submitted to an intense process of modernization, rendering them in this way autonomous and thus completely split off from one another. This dissociated condition—what Deleuze and Guattari mean by their term "deterritorialization"—privileges the inconvertible sign, but also institutes a new "regime of noncoverage" (CL, p. 121), governed, in Goux's words, by the "universal despotism of the token" (CL, p. 139).

A "regime" and a "despot"—the words are not chosen lightly. For, under capitalist modernization, every dissociation renders necessary a further reassociation; every "deterritorialization" calls up a more encompassing "reterritorialization"; any process of autonomization yields not only a realm of freedom but a more pure enslavement. For values to be assured, the natural right of gold-backed currency will need to be replaced by the immense apparatus of legal convention, centered on the State and the Bank. The ascendancy of the purely Symbolic general equivalent will require a vast investment in the newly enlarged power of the Law. Right will be replaced by "trust," and the State will now even write on its monetary bills, on its token signs, "In God We Trust." Looking to the monetary realm, artists will bank on a "Teeth's Loan and Trust Company." The transcendent site of Measure has been displaced; guarantees no longer exist.[37]

And so the despotism of the token reveals itself to be a paradoxical regime, rife with internal contradictions. Having lost its representational ground, the tokenized monetary sign can no longer be said to represent *anything at all,* being itself of no intrinsic value. Token money no longer remains representational. In money's "conventional" or "fictive" form, "there is no longer any guaranteed backing, either in fact or by right: this is the monetary regime of the *empty repository.* Strictly speaking, this case cannot even be described as one of substitution, since the paper represents *nothing* but a purely conventional notion of value" (CL, p. 127). Guaranteeing the value of monetary tokens that "arise from its own site" and yet remain inconvertible, the Law in fact ensures that money will now be exposed as *valueless:* "The law guarantees value only as *empty value.* The only value signs have is the value conferred upon them by the law, and this value is at bottom an *absence* of value, since the paper note (a mere token) is not convertible" (CL, p. 128). Keyed now to a vast economic system, the token sign refers not to any external object but only to itself, to the very system of value, a condition that paradoxically confirms the token's (real) worthlessness. The token sign speaks thus with a forked tongue, inaugurating what we might call a double language.

This double language helps explain the two major artistic innovations that ran parallel to the economic transformation Goux describes, and to which in some complex sense they are linked: modernist abstraction and the Dada ready-made. For both are fully dependent on a regime of the token sign. Pictorial abstraction's rejection of mimesis, of figurative representation, parallels the general equivalent's transformation from an object to be represented (a standard) to an inconvertible circulation of token signs (a system). Both abstract art and the transformed general equivalent depend on a new relationship to what Goux calls the *unrepresentable*: "[The] operation of virtualization [resulting in the token

<hr>

sign] . . . guarantees the unmotivated sign not by means of material reserves that govern the standardization in gold but by an invisible, potential 'coverage,' a reality that is not only more abstract than the standard but utterly unrepresentable. Instead of referring to a valuable *thing,* this sign refers directly to the general substance of values, to the cause that produces values."[38] With this diagnosis, we have as well a reasonably precise description of the effects of the inauguration of abstract art and of the entire self-reflexive system of modernism in the visual arts that such a rupture was seen to define.

The token sign directs attention back onto the system within which it circulates, the structural conditions of its own production. It might even be said to refer to nothing else but these structural conditions. However, no longer backed by right but by the Law, by a system of convention, the token will also expose the *emptiness* of these conventions, of their nature as mere convention. The Law will summon up—that is, *produce*—the figure of the Criminal, just as the prohibition of taboo institutes the absolute necessity of transgression. And with this we realize the profound manner in which the readymade must be seen as linked to modernist abstraction, as the obverse side of the same regime that instituted the very possibility of abstract art: the rule of the inconvertible token sign. We can also begin to understand the tissue of connections linking readymade practices to other Dada strategies of parody and pastiche. For if, in the economic realm, the token sign can be seen as the quintessence of the money-form itself (its abstract, token existence holding up a mirror to the circulation and the substitutions of exchange that the money form of value inaugurated), the token is also "a parody of money." The token "imitates gold money just as the monkey apes the man. This toy monkey-money makes a mockery of what it mimics" (CL, p. 14).

These words could have been written directly for Picabia, for the critique of painting that his *Natures mortes* conveys, or for the vast, repetitive system of parody and pastiche that his work would later enact. In the wake of Dada, Picabia's lifelong dedication to the copy, his initiation of an aesthetic system of perpetual parodic acts, embraces the mimetic copy only in its absolute bankruptcy—a bankruptcy in the face of the unrepresentable nature of the token sign, but also, one realizes, a bankruptcy on which the token sign will be founded.[39] Parody, in this modernist sense, must be seen as the structural twin of abstract art. Abstraction makes an aesthetic project of the unfixed nature of the token sign, of its newly deterritorialized inauguration as a true *sign*; parody presents an (anti-)aesthetic critique based on the groundlessness of this unfixing, its second-degree imitation of a more profound imitation, its newly debased status as a parodic *token*.

True signs and parodic tokens: the inconvertible token sign legitimates both strategies from within its inherent system of possibility. Both strategies belong, as Goux puts it, to the same historical moment:

> To abandon *covered* or convertible language for language *without backing* is to leave behind all illusions of an objective reality to be reflected or of a subjective reality to be expressed. And here two solutions suggest themselves: one would aim directly at an a priori and abstract construction, producing a crystal that refers only to its own formal regularity and its intrinsic relational coherence; the other, in a seemingly opposite movement (which actually belongs to the same moment), would register the radical absence of any transcendental treasury of meaning, debunking the illusion of an extralinguistic referent and affirming in a tragic key the *play* of a floating signifier now recognized as meaningless. (CL, p. 19)

If the word "Dada" whispers through Goux's characterization of this second solution (despite the invocation of the tragic dimension of the development, a modality not usually associated with Dada's putative symbolic games, but perhaps useful now to begin to consider), we cannot of course reduce Dada and its primary technique—the strategy of the readymade—to the promulgation of parodic tokens alone. For the strategies of Dada—brought into being by the new possibilities opened up by the regime of the token sign—did not only exaggerate, or even exacerbate, the "despotism" of the token, but also, in many ways, contested the new order of signification that the token promised. The Archetype and the Treasury functions of the general equivalent, its Ideal and Real registers, were not left fallow by Dada, superseded in the grand rush of abstraction offered up by the circulation of a token currency. As we have already seen with the *Tableau Dada*, operations on the general equivalent—however newly transformed—would be explored. And new orders of signification would be imagined.

Bankers are artists and artists are bankers. . . .

—*Francis Picabia, "Instantanéisme," 1924*[40]

Junk bonds. Now we are in a position to comprehend the stakes of one of Marcel Duchamp's more elusive projects, a piece that served as a sequel to *Tzanck Check*'s engagement with monetary economy, closing the years of Paris Dada just as *Tzanck Check* had stood at their inauguration. It was a piece that answered the challenge of Picabia's *Dessin Dada* as well. I refer to Duchamp's *Monte Carlo Bond* of 1924. Here, Duchamp formed a "joint stock company" whose aim it was to exploit the roulette tables of the Monte Carlo casinos. A limited edition of thirty bonds were to be printed by Duchamp and offered for sale at 500 francs each, in order ultimately to raise 15,000 francs that could be invested in the casinos by the "company." The bonds were redeemable by "artificial drawings" and were meant to pay their owners the exceedingly high interest of 20 percent. Beyond the bureaucratic operations of the bank figured in *Tzanck Check, Monte Carlo Bond* appeared under the guise of an alignment of art with an imagined corporate structure and the trappings of investment. In reality, however, the *Bond* conflated art, like Picabia's *Dessin Dada,* with gambling.

The consequences of this conflation relate directly to the structure of inconvertibility that now belonged to the general equivalent in its monetary form. If *Tzanck Check* dramatized the crisis of convertibility, this was signaled by the temporal delay in relation to value that the check as a document embodies. Unlike Duchamp's previous readymade objects—the shovel, coat rack, comb, bottle-dryer—*Tzanck Check* has absolutely no physical use. A check, especially a parodic copy of a check, has no use-value; it exists as a pure embodiment of the delay of exchange, a concretization of exchange as indeed a process of delay and of postponement. As a form of pure (even purified) exchange-value, *Tzanck Check* thus carries the question of value away from the material dimension of use

---

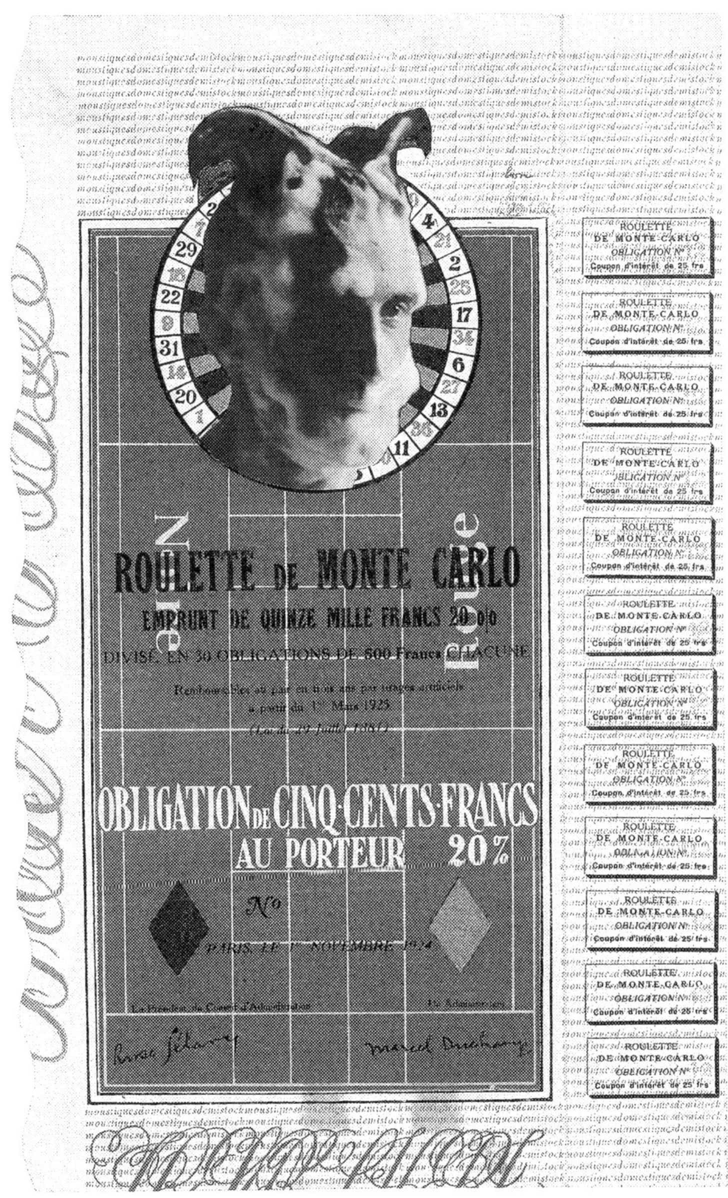

Marcel Duchamp, *Monte-Carlo Bond,* 1924. Photocollage on colored lithograph, 31.2 × 19.3 cm (12¹/₄ × 7¹/₂″). The Museum of Modern Art, New York. Gift of the artist. Photograph © The Museum of Modern Art/Licensed by SCALA/Art Resource, NY. © 2005 Artists Rights Society (ARS), New York/ADAGP, Paris/Estate of Marcel Duchamp.

just as surely as an abstract painting floats free of the task of representing the objects of the world.

By contrast, *Monte Carlo Bond* no longer takes the concomitant crisis of the convertibility of this purified exchange-value as a problem—to be parodically shored up through the fiction of a bank, or authorized by the stamp of a signature—but as a given. Inconvertibility becomes the *Bond*'s structure, and the paradoxical (because groundless) ground of its critique. Imitating the trappings of financial investment, *Monte Carlo Bond* reveals capital and the general equivalent form to have become completely speculative. The economists call this the "filiative" mode of capital—a paradoxical term, since the "father," or the paternal "model" more generally, is precisely that from which such capital departs. Filiative capital refers instead to the potential begetting of money from money itself, a kind of autogenesis without any reference to an outside, "real" world or the traditional realm of commodities.[41] If the tokenized, inconvertible general equivalent required an entirely new apparatus of the Law, the State, and the Bank to fill its newly emptied, husklike form, Duchamp deploys the free-floating nature of the token to enact a deterritorialization beyond the capacities of the Law to fill that form. In the wake of the transformation of the general equivalent in the early twentieth century, Western economies did see a vast investment of capital in the forces of production and of industry. Beyond this "reterritorialization," Duchamp envisions an investment of capital in itself (not, we might say, art for art's sake, but capital for capital's sake): capital's rending transformation into a purely speculative, filiative mode that escapes the bounds of production. More abstract even than the form of a token currency, such a structure's dominance in our own time as the abstract existence of money is what we now call "finance capital."[42] But at the moment of modernism it was a form that was still wild, anarchic, capable of being tendered against the dominant structures of the Law on which the modernist token depended.[43]

Despite Duchamp's reference to the casino games as "mines" in the "company statutes" on the back of the *Bond* (referring his investment plan to the earth as much as to the gold standard, to the "territorial" base that I am otherwise saying the *Bond* escapes), despite too Walter Benjamin's well-known comparison between the experience of gambling and the modern phenomenon of work in the production line, the destination of *Monte Carlo Bond*—its investment in gambling—only furthers this critique.[44] It compounds the fierce transgression that this piece offers to the structures that arose to counterbalance the new inconvertibility of the token sign, structures that attempted to harness the new abstraction of inconvertibility toward purely productive ends. For *Monte Carlo Bond* ties inconvertibility inexorably to loss, to the bankruptcy and waste that Bataille would later name *dépense*. We know that Duchamp made a point of paying his 20 percent dividend to at least one of his investors, the Parisian patron of the arts Jacques Doucet.[45] At least for Doucet, inconvertibility did not result in bankruptcy, in an investment dedicated to complete and utter loss. But this was the exception. Attempting to bring the "logic of chess" to a game of chance, *Monte Carlo Bond* was doomed from the start, wedded inevitably to failure. Chance would tolerate no systematization. And as it had in so many pieces by Duchamp since the crucial *Three Standard Stoppages* of a decade before, a system was opened up to a procedure that exceeded it, its strategies of generalization thwarted, returned to a singularity in the face of which the abstract system would collapse.[46] In *Monte Carlo Bond,* money and value enter into a pact with the devil, dedicating themselves to an investment in their own loss.

And once again, the artist's signature was the only redeemable entity in the totality of this loss, the only anchor onto which value could descend. "If anyone is in the business of buying art curiosities as an investment," hawked the avant-garde journal *The Little Review* in 1925, "here is a chance to invest in a perfect masterpiece. Marcel's signature alone is worth much more than the 500 francs asked for the share."[47] But Duchamp's signature on the *Bond* was deeply paradoxical, no longer singular—as at the moment of *Tzanck Check*—but already itself submitted to a process of doubling, of splitting, of multiplication. Signed "M. Duchamp, an administrator," the *Bond* was also endorsed by Duchamp's alter ego, "Rrose Sélavy," the "Chairman of the Board." The signature was put into play in *Monte Carlo Bond,* made suddenly incommensurable with its former authorizing functions: How else than as newly inscrutable, fragmented signatures should we read the excessive, curling, calligraphic lines cropped into obscurity on the left and bottom edges of the *Bond*? We know that André Breton, busy founding Surrealism in Paris at just this moment, frowned upon what he saw as the complete and utter frivolity of Duchamp's activities around the *Monte Carlo Bond*. But there is a dead seriousness in this play to which Breton was undoubtedly deaf, a seriousness that goes beyond any of the quests for subjective liberation on which the Surrealists would later embark. The signature would become newly multiple, played out across the scene of Duchamp's *Bond*. And we are not surprised to witness with this as well the return of a structure, even a thematics, of what I have been calling the artwork's "tail."

For there, right on the surface of the *Bond,* is Duchamp in his ridiculous mask of shaving cream, a photographic portrait by Man Ray collaged onto each copy of the *Bond*. His features masked by an accumulation of foaming cream, Duchamp has shaped his hair into two large horns, projecting into the air and outside the space of the roulette circle that otherwise frames his face. The image rhymes, in this way, with the defacing mustache and beard that Duchamp had appended to *L.H.O.O.Q.* five years before: the appendage as tail, as horn, as beard, and as phallus. Castration was again suggested (in Duchamp's decapitated head floating on the roulette wheel) and denied (in the excessive bulk of the horns and beard built out of the mass of shaving cream). We have returned to the mechanics of the artwork and its tail. And it would now be the signature itself—with all that it was seen to secure, from subjective identity to the value of the art object in general—that was entered into the scene of representation, toppled from its transcendent position as a potential general equivalent within the system of modernist painting, erupting from and expending a reserve that painting perhaps no longer even knew itself to require.

But inasmuch as Duchamp's activities during the years of Paris Dada are still too poorly known, it has been forgotten that there was already a secret history for such an expenditure. Indeed, this expenditure had already taken place. The signature had already been transformed into a pure token. And it had already been entered anarchically into the scene over which it was meant to rule, in 1921.

For such were the stakes of Picabia's premature farewell in that year to Dada. Such were the stakes of *L'oeil cacodylate.*

> One may conceive of a painting that realizes and abolishes itself in its signature, which is only a signature.
>
> —*Jean Baudrillard*[48]

> A framer [*doreur-encadreur*] who works for the Salon d'Automne often becomes a framer of horrors [*encadreur d'horreurs*].
>
> —*Francis Picabia*[49]

Painting caught by the tail. In a short but suggestive essay, Rosalind Krauss has argued that the readymade's discursive form was that of the "commodity-in-circulation."[50] Existing as real objects, sometimes signed and titled (such as Duchamp's *Fountain*); as the photographs of such objects circulating in the Dada periodicals; or in the form of the mechanomorph, utilizing industrial procedures to multiply drawing within the pages of these same publications, the readymade exploited the specific conditions of possibility of the commodity, forcing these conditions into dissonance with the older requirements of traditional high culture. As an object of economic exchange and circulation, the commodity was now echoed by the readymade's demand for a multiplied artistic subjectivity, ripped free from the bonds of the uniqueness of the individual; it legitimated the readymade's embrace of "deskilling" on the level of its production, falling into parallel modes of mass, mechanical procedures; and the commodity inspired the readymade's embrace of the peculiar trajectory of reification, a process that divorced form from context as well as content, spewing deracinated images across the spaces of the media without any sign of a destination beyond exchange. This last effect was visible in the readymade's dissemination, with the striking emptiness of the page on which Picabia, for example, suspended *Portrait d'une jeune fille américaine dans l'état de nudité* or *Américaine,* his decontextualized spark plug and his lightbulb, or Duchamp his *Chocolate Grinder.* The readymade, as Krauss depicts it, had become a "token," a "depthless sign of equivalence within a system of pure exchange."[51]

But if the readymade's particular bite lies in its critical mimicry of the structure of the commodity, Krauss also envisions another relation to that structure, one that resists its embrace of exchange, and that she sees beginning in the Dada photographs of Man Ray. In these photographs, Man Ray offered up images of mechanical objects in obvious dialogue with the readymades of Duchamp and Picabia, but then within many of these images insisted on the inclusion of a variety of cast shadows—shadows that, according to Krauss, tie their objects to the specific time and site of their production as photographic documents. Throughout his Dada and later Surrealist work, Man Ray would think of the photograph as the residue of a specific event rather than as a circulating multiple.[52] And thus, Man Ray's version of the readymade valorized particularity over generality, the concrete weight of context over the airy movements of the decontextualized status of the token. The readymade, in Man Ray's hands, becomes critical for Krauss inasmuch as it presents an object newly able to "hold out against exchange."[53]

But Man Ray was not alone in this understanding of the readymade. If my argument can be telescoped by saying that the logic of the readymade opened up for the Dadaists a concept of critique not far from Georges Bataille's later notion of expenditure, the logic of exchange was to be contested all along the line. In the work of Duchamp, of Picabia, and of Man Ray, the readymade was understood, in its various instances and at various times, as both a deracinated token *and* as an object with the power to hold out against exchange. In this, the readymade might be said not simply to be modeled on the form of the "commodity-in-circulation," but also to play out the constitutive breach in the structure of the commodity, its fissuring into the opposed entities of use-value and exchange-value, restated globally within capitalist economies as the opposition between labor and capital. This split, and these two understandings of the discursive form of the readymade, could even be present simultaneously in a single Dada work, tugging internally against the artwork's last vestiges of organic coherence. Such works would articulate the readymade's (and the commodity's) impossible,

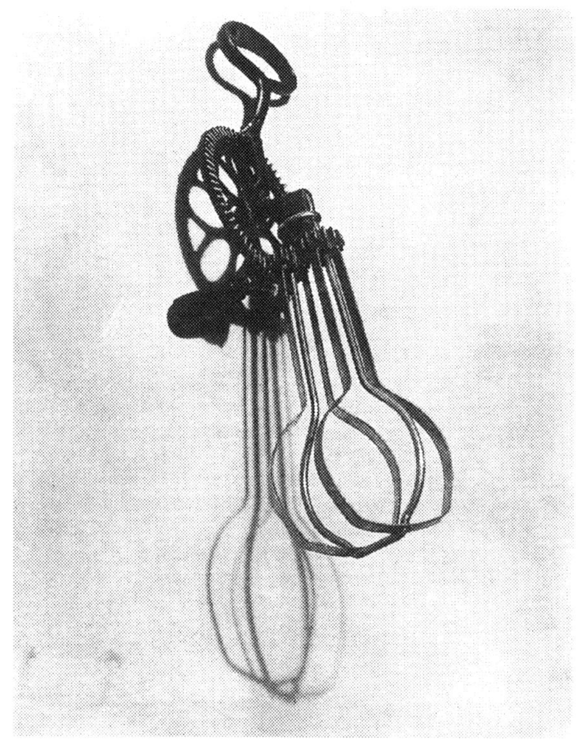

Man Ray, *Man,* 1918. Gelatin silver print. Collection of Frank Kolodny. © 2005 Artists Rights Society (ARS), New York/ ADAGP, Paris/Man Ray Trust.

rending division—the readymade's existence, even, as a form of insurmountable contradiction. This ruptured condition could serve, for example, as a good description of Picabia's drawing *Francis Picabia*.

Sometime during 1920, Picabia signed his own signature as a drawing, which is to say that he signed his own signature as a readymade. It was an extraordinary gesture, deeply complex and immensely ludicrous at the same time—the only tonal key that Picabia's work ever knew. It was as if Picabia were saying that the entire logic of the readymade could be reduced to the authorizing gesture of the signature, a gesture that proclaims the artistic author's choice, and that elevates the chosen object into the domain of art. But here Picabia signs the authorizing gesture itself; he signs, that is to say, a sign(ature), placing the logic of the readymade *en abyme*. Redoubled as if from within, the drawing *Francis Picabia* seems to recast the readymade strategy within the domain of reflexivity, imaging forth the repetitive structures of logically nested forms that had come to characterize abstract painting and the formal imperatives of modernism. We are no longer surprised by this convergence.

And perhaps in a form more radical than any that had yet been imagined by the visual avant-garde, the work of art was reduced to a purely linguistic existence. It traded its older, painterly forms for the form of language. And it now became a true instantiation of "pictorial nominalism," for the specific form of language into which the artwork retreated was the name. In this instance, the withdrawal of the work of art into language occurs only through the isolation of that form of language that had always been accepted, at least since the onset of modernity, within the visual forms of painting. As if bubbling up from its conventional site on the bottom of the painted surface, the signature erupts into the center of the scene of representation, no longer a supplement but the very substance of the work of art.

Reduced in this way to language, the work of art assimilates itself to a form of the genral equivalent just as much as those Dada works that embraced the forms of monetary economy—language being the general equivalent of signs as money is the general equivalent of products. Pried loose, however, from its position on the base of the painted image, the signature in *Francis Picabia* could

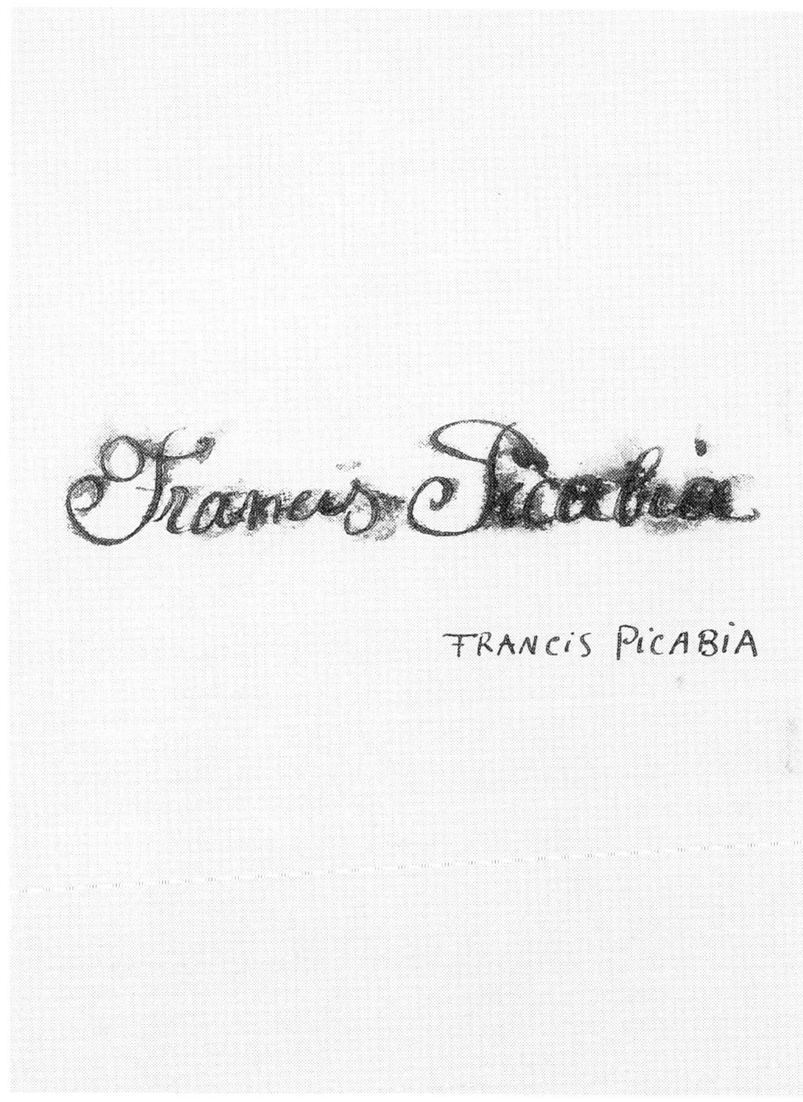

Francis Picabia, *Francis Picabia (Francis Picabia by Francis Picabia),* 1920 [–1922]. Ink on paper, 32.4 × 25.3 cm. Musée d'Art moderne de la Ville de Paris. © 2005 Artists Rights Society (ARS), New York/ADAGP, Paris/Estate of Francis Picabia.

no longer be said to act as an anchor, nor a standard. It was no longer that visible sign that, as Baudrillard puts it, imparts upon the painting a "differential value," bestowed by "the ambiguity of a sign that does not cause the work to be seen, but to be recognized and evaluated in a system of signs, and which, while differentiating it as a model, already, from another perspective, integrates it in a series, that of the works of a painter."[54] The artistic signature, as Baudrillard understands it, indexes the uniqueness of the artistic creator only through a form of language capable of infinite reproduction; it governs the "sign-exchange" of paintings by guaranteeing the painting's singularity only through its paradoxical insertion into a logic of the series.

With perverse precision, and in reverse, Picabia articulates Baudrillard's logic of the signature. Instead of the painting, the signature itself was submitted to the logic of the series. It was doubled, multiplied, but also somehow emptied at the same time, like an old sponge out of which the last drop of liquid has escaped. This condition—multiple yet empty—is a condition that we now recognize as the paradoxical, oppositional existence of the parameters of the token sign. And on the one hand, Picabia's signature fully assumes the dire responsibilities of a token existence, with the smaller of the two signatures newly cut off from any singular, outside anchor (as a signature that signs another version of itself with which, however, it is not identical), while still maintaining the primary form in which Picabia's signature circulated from work to work as the representative sign of his creation.

On the other hand, however, Picabia begins to figure a version of the signature that resists the imperatives of the token, inserting a bit of visual noise into the seamless operation of art's reduction to language as a form of the general equivalent. For the signature that Picabia has signed sets itself apart from Picabia's conventional signature by appearing in the form of a somewhat florid, grand calligraphy; and its ink, while still wet, has been smeared into the page, reducing the signature almost to the point of illegibility. In this regard, the larger signature in *Francis Picabia* emerges as the direct progeny of Picabia's *La Sainte-Vierge*. The inimitability of that gesture, the production of an image that remained absolutely singular through its embrace of chance and accidental procedures was now extended through the medium of ink to the form of Picabia's signature—and beyond it, to the form of language, and thus of the general equivalent. For this signature too becomes unique, inimitable, resolutely tied to the surface on which it is inscribed, contrasted in every way to the second signature that then comes to mark it, to sign it, in a form and a gesture of the multiple. Like the larger discourse of the readymade, the signature—one of the forms in which Picabia understood the readymade to operate—was split into two contradictory halves: a token, circulating in a space of equivalence buoyed by exchange, but also an object exhausting itself in its context, holding out to the last against exchange.

Both artistic identity and the economy of the art object begin to be exceeded in this double movement, opened up, as it were, on two opposing sides. As a token, the signature no longer retains the power to refer the work to a singular author, but rather might be said to point to a free-floating space of equivalence where individual identity cedes its place to a multiple artistic identity, to the fungible, leveling form of the identical as such. As an object holding out against exchange, the signature authorizes nothing, regressing violently toward the singular state where it can no longer even be said to equal itself, and where consequently the logic of identity collapses.

And Picabia continued, inexorably, to draw out the repercussions of this double logic. It led him, propelled him, to the creation of his most important work of 1921—perhaps the most important work of his entire career—the dissident painting *L'oeil cacodylate* that was displayed that year at the Salon d'Automne. The painting's origins lie in the previous spring. After provoking another public scandal with two works presented at the 1921 Salon des Indépendants, Picabia retreated from public activity just as the "Grande Saison Dada" was announced. The reason given for this was illness, an "ophthalmic malady" or eye disease, and a poor reaction to the drugs used to treat it.[55] Beginning in April 1921, then, the public events of the new Dada season proceeded without Picabia. Under the cover of sickness, Picabia invited his friends instead to his home in order to contribute to his latest work, a painting that was created in the face of a stated inability to continue to be able to paint.

Around the middle of May, however, the excuse or fiction of illness no longer remained. Disgusted with the events of the 1921 "season"—especially the contributions of Breton and Aragon, such as the mock trial of writer Maurice Barrès—Picabia announced his defection from the movement. "Profiting from ideas disgusts me," Picabia wrote, in an essay published on 11 May. "The Dada spirit only really existed from 1913 to 1918. . . . I am sorry if, with these lines, I'm wounding friends whom I love dearly, or disturbing certain colleagues who perhaps are counting on a profit from Dadaism." Dada, for Picabia, was bankrupt: "Money itself has value—or it doesn't; paper would perhaps be worth more than gold if it were given to me to discover gold mines as large as the coal pits of Cardiff." Dada had become a empty token, a corpse of its former promise: "An unserious man is one who confuses interest with capital, and doesn't seek to make dollars with his ideas. . . . Dada, you see, was not serious, and that is why it won over the world like wildfire. If some people take it seriously now, that's because it is dead."[56] With this, Picabia's participation in the "official" life of the movement simply ended. And yet again, rather than an endpoint, this sacrifice was only a beginning: Picabia's dissidence in fact galvanized the other Dadaists, propelling the movement's actions onward for several more years at least. And the defection propelled Picabia's critical gestures of that spring and summer of 1921.

At precisely the moment of his defection, in May, the Dada editors of *Littérature* published an advertisement seeking collaborators among the anonymous perpetrators of certain public graffiti, collaborators needed to produce a "mural supplement" for the magazine.[57] It hardly seems a coincidence that it was Picabia himself who took up this ironic challenge, producing in *L'oeil cacodylate* his own "mural" where a collectively accumulated array of tags and phrases by a vast number of his friends was allowed to fill the full extent of a previously blank canvas, wedding in this way the signature to the odd temporality and structure of the graffito.

Such a convergence—of the signature with the violence of the graffito—had been achieved before in Picabia's art. We remember, in fact, that this marriage was already one of the parameters within which language was defined by the moment of Picabia's *Natures mortes,* by the moment, that is, of the Tableau Dada.

The connection between these two works, between *Natures mortes* and *L'oeil cacodylate,* was not something Picabia would let his viewers forget.[58] As if one was the consequence of the other, as if the two works occupied flip sides of a problematic on which the artist had situated his reading of the readymade, Picabia went on to evoke the critique of *Natures mortes* in the initial words of his public defense of *L'oeil cacodylate* at the time of its first exhibition in the fall of 1921:

> The painter makes a choice, and then imitates his choice so that the deformation constitutes the Art. *Why not simply sign this choice instead of making like a monkey before it?* There are certainly enough accumulated paintings, and the sanctioning signature of artists, uniquely sanctioners, would give a new value to works of art destined for modern mercantilism.[59]

This is the closest Picabia ever came to defining his understanding of the readymade, as he traces a logical, conceptual arc leading from the parody of *Natures mortes* to the new conception of the art object embodied in *L'oeil cacodylate*. In the same essay, he then defended the procedures of this painting in words that we should follow closely:

> My paintings are taken as works of little seriousness, because they are done without the hidden motive of speculation and because I produce them while enjoying myself like someone who is playing a sport. Look, boredom is the worst disease and my great despair would be precisely to be taken seriously, to become a great man, a master—a man of the intellect that one seeks out on account of his decorations, his connections and because he does well at dinner parties, where those who eat the most are the people who have the least in their stomachs! You see what I am trying to say, minister artist, deputy artist! But I—as I have written so often—I am nothing, I am Francis Picabia; Francis Picabia who has signed *The Cacodylic Eye,* in the company of many other people who have even been so kind as to inscribe a thought upon the canvas! This canvas was finished

when there was no longer any space on it, and I find this painting very beautiful and harmonious; it is *perhaps* that all my friends are artists just a bit! It has been said that I would compromise myself and compromise my friends, I have also been told that this is not a painting. I believe that there is nothing as compromising as, perhaps, not to compromise oneself. . . . This is why my painting, which is framed, made to be hung upon a wall and looked at, cannot be anything else but a painting.[60]

"I am nothing, I am Francis Picabia": As a "painting," *L'oeil cacodylate* was filled, from one end to the other, with signatures; it was covered, too, with hermetic, graffiti-like inscriptions, a vast, vibrating mass of language heaped on the canvas.[61] Picabia, we may assume, started things off, printing the title in block letters across the top of the piece, painting a large, exorbited eye just below the center, and, most important, signing and dating the piece in an almost conventional manner, on the bottom left-hand side. Around this basis, the signatures began to gather.

God has only ever cured the sick.[62] The title is, of course, strange, by now hermetic, lost to the conventions and the common knowledge of its time. It had its origin in Picabia's supposed illness, the eye problem that necessitated treatment with "cacodylic" acid, a solution of methyl and arsenic that gives off noxious fumes. And so *L'oeil cacodylate* was presented under the sign of failure: the failure of Picabia to continue to be able to paint; the failure, at least momentarily, of the proper workings of vision. And, more locally, the painting was part of the failure of Picabia to participate in the public activities of Dada in 1921, and his subsequent break with the movement. In the wake of this schism, by the summer of 1921, as Picabia and the Dadaists began to hurl insults at each other, we hear such rhetorical feints as these: "My dear Francis. You are cured, is it for a long time? To the extent that I know you, your sicknesses seem to me to be the best of your distractions." That was Gabrielle Buffet. But then there was Jean Cocteau, proclaiming Picabia cured of a sickness that can only take the name, now, of Dada: "After a long convalescence, Picabia is cured. I congratulate him. I actually saw

Dada leave him by the eye."[63] This is part of the artistic horizon to which *L'oeil cacodylate* responded, and into which it must be inserted. On the one hand the painting was a massive monument to failure, a monumentalizing of Picabia's embrace of failure. Perhaps we must even begin to see the work as a fitting testament to a larger failure, to the rapid dissolution of the "official" life of the Dada movement in Paris, scarcely one year after it had been born.

And yet we simultaneously read the accumulation of signatures spread out across the expanse of this painting as the evocation of something like a social space, an engagement with a set of common, non-art practices. We can read the painting as if, for example, it were a greeting card, or rather a get-well card, something not unlike the object produced by the convention of visiting an ailing friend and, perhaps, signing his or her cast. Picabia—or so the stories tell us—actually did set up the canvas on an easel positioned next to his bed, where, for the duration of his illness, friends were invited to sign the work.[64] The painting was a monument to failure, yes, but it was also an inscription, a recording—which is, after all, another function of the monument—a memorial to the modes of sociability that failure can subtend.[65] Such were Picabia's hopes for the Dada group he was simultaneously leaving behind. And such were his "hopes" for art.

God helps us and makes shit grow.[66] Of course other social spaces were evoked by this painting, other practices engaged by its form (or lack thereof). Few would have missed the convenient slipping, the rhyming, of the *cacodylate* of the painting's title with the child's word, in French, for excrement, propelling the eager viewer from the admittedly hermetic title of *L'oeil cacodylate* to the more scatological, but understandable, *L'oeil caca*: Eye shit.[67] Such a reading itself rhymes with Picabia's assimilation of language within his Dada work to the status of the graffito, and to the space—of liminality and obscurity—within which the graffito is most at home. The critics, at least, understood Picabia's work in this manner. Chances to associate Dada with excrement were hardly ever missed. "Pipicacabia," one aspiring wit baptized him. And so another model for the painting's accumulation of signatures lies in what a critic of the 1921 Salon d'Automne isolated in the following way: "Mr. Picabia exhibits the interior of a *pissotière* howling with truth."[68] *L'oeil cacodylate* brought the space of the bathroom into the space of art, the language of the toilet into the idioms of the aesthetic. The memory of Marcel Duchamp's *Fountain* could not have been far from Picabia's thinking at this moment. For such was one of the trajectories of the readymade, running from Duchamp's false signature, "R. Mutt," scrawled like a graffito across the porcelain sheen of *Fountain,* to the riot of names spread out like stains across the desiccated canvas that is *L'oeil cacodylate.*

I am now called you.[69] But some additions were anodyne, almost childlike in their regressive return to the hermetic, complicitous conventions of the grade school autograph book, echoes of so many schoolmates greeting their friend as if on the last day of class.[70] "The croissants are good," Renata Borgatti reminds us.[71] "My heart beats," signed Valentine Hugo. "Little [Pierre] de Massot smiles at the Great Picabia!"—a message from a protégé. And then there were the professions of love: "Isadora [Duncan] loves Picabia with her entire soul"; "I love Francis," from Hania Routchine ("I love Auric too"); "I love Francis and Germaine [Everling, Picabia's companion]," signed Marcelle Evrard. "I love salad," Francis Poulenc confessed, adding a comical twist to this sort of thing.

But not all of the inscriptions, nor all of the signatures, were so friendly. There was Picabia's recent enemy, Metzinger, scrawling "I come from the countryside," across the top of the work;[72] and there was none other than Dorgelès's faded gem, a dismissive poem composed in Picabia's "honor": "Non, je n'en reste pas baba / Et je jure chez Picabia / Que je n'aime pas Dada [No, I am not dumbfounded / And I swear in the house of Picabia / That I do not love Dada]." There were puns—"Man Ray, directeur du mauvais movies," written upside down— and wordplay: "Mon oeil en deuil de verre vous regarde," signed Jean Crotti.

Other signatures, other inscriptions, were less whimsical, more engaged with the implications and the questions raised by Picabia's sudden collectivization of the procedures of the readymade. "'Francis Picabia' by Marie de la Hire," one friend of Picabia's wrote, an advertisement for her 1920 book, the first monograph on Picabia ("I am publishing it," the gallerist Povolozky reminds us just a few inches away). In this context, however, the inscription hardly remains

a simple advertisement, as de la Hire's writing seems to split, not into mono-
graphic title and author, but into two separate signatures—Francis Picabia and
Marie de la Hire—performed, paradoxically, by one and the "same" person, an
object lesson for the larger procedures enacted in the painting.

Other inscriptions were less fortuitous, more programmatic in their concentration on the new status of language within *L'oeil cacodylate*. "*Je me trouve très
Tristan Tzara* [I find myself very Tristan Tzara]": such was Tzara's alliterative, tautological addition, the emptiness of which was only underscored by a painted
hand pointing with its index finger at Tzara's signature itself.[73] As usual for Tzara,
and in an echo of the adjacent announcement of Marie de la Hire, the inspiration for this painted hand comes of course from the world of primitive advertisements, but the gesture seems more intent on underscoring the inherently
indexical nature of any signature, especially in its version as graffito. The index,
prototype of an "empty" sign, can be filled only in the act of its production, and
the indexical signature thus comes to proclaim the presence of the signer only in
his present absence, as a record or trace relegating his actual presence to an un-
specified moment in the past. In the face of such a demonstration, one ines-
capably confronts the potential of every signature—as an index—to be opened
to the radical absence of its signer, to be, in other words, radically empty. This is
the logic of the signature that Tzara's gesture seems to imply, and that Jacques
Derrida has isolated:

> By definition, a written signature implies the actual or empirical
> nonpresence of the signer. But, it will be said, it also marks and re-
> tains his having-been present in a past now, which will remain a fu-
> ture now, and therefore in a now in general, in the transcendental
> form of nowness [*maintenance*]. This general *maintenance* is somehow
> inscribed, stapled to present punctuality, always evident and always
> singular, in the form of the signature. This is the enigmatic original-
> ity of every paraph. . . . [But] the condition of possibility for these
> effects is simultaneously, once again, the condition of their impossi-
> bility, of the impossibility of their rigorous purity. In order to func-

tion, that is, in order to be legible, a signature must have a repeatable, iterable, imitable form; it must be able to detach itself from the present and singular intention of its production. It is its sameness, which, in altering its identity and singularity, divides the seal.[74]

And now we can understand the various other markers that arise within *L'oeil cacodylate* to rhyme with Tzara's indexical, pointing hand, so many attempts at anchoring the unanchorable split in subjectivity initiated by every written signature, strategies to fill the hole that now yawned from beneath its traditional form: the dates, for example, inscribed near several of the signatures, locating their enactment at a specific moment in the past, indexed as such; or the "Voilà" of Jean Hugo, an indexical word circling back on this signature through the similarly indexical device of a diagrammatic arrow like Tzara's pointing finger; or, more important, the few photographs collaged here and there across the surface of the work.

For there, above his signature, is Picabia's smiling face, and there, beneath her own writing, is the cut-out photograph of Gabrielle Buffet. There is a manipulated portrait of Metzinger (or of Milhaud), and another of Jean Cocteau, surrounded by his masochistic "crown of melancholy." There is the miniature Auric, and the faded void of Marthe Chenal. And then, there is Duchamp, his own, now deeply faded signature supported by not one, but two photographs. This is crucial: like Tzara's tautological signature redoubled by its empty, indexical sign, all of these signatures—Picabia, Buffet, Cocteau, Duchamp—were redoubled, echoed by a second form of indexical sign. As index refers to index, from the signature to the photograph, the effect of anchoring would hardly be achieved, the filling would not take hold, as the photograph, like the signature, arrives in a tense keyed resolutely toward the past, securing absence in the present. And again like the signature, the photograph also bears its own relation to the condition of the multiple, spun out through a logic of serialization in which each individual instance of a photograph presents itself as only one of a potentially infinite number of copies.

The signature was thus emptied in *L'oeil cacodylate,* placed before us as yet another avatar of the free-floating token, circulating in a space void of any outside anchor or transcendental standard. And we witness, across the panorama of this work, so many subjects inserting their signatures into the space of Picabia's oeuvre, condemned by the logic of the graffito to emerge within the scene of representation as criminals, trespassers on the property of the Other. "*Criminel dit Madge Lipton*": at least one of the signers made this condition explicit. *L'oeil cacodylate*'s collaborators thus emerge within the field of the painting as radically absent, prisoners of a newly articulated logic—of the signature, of the graffito, of the index—where, to paraphrase Rosalind Krauss, the signer was literally cut away from him- or herself, as if "he had gone up to a mirror to witness his own appearing and had smashed the mirror instead," voiding his or her actual presence, leaving only a transgressive mark.[75]

Not coincidentally, the vast majority of the inscriptions upon *L'oeil cacodylate* become intelligible as reflections, commentaries, on this development, as verbal enactments of the subjective deflation now inflicted on the form of the signature. Tzara's inscription, again, is key in this regard. If his signature emerges only to marry this linguistic form to the empty circularity of tautology ("Je me trouve très Tristan Tzara"), the inscription simultaneously suggests an alternative reading, one legitimated by Dada's persistent play with homophones: "Je me trouve très triste" ("I feel very sad"), a pronouncement that erupts from within the logic of Tzara's written statement to produce the subjective parallel of its otherwise nonsensical linguistic form.

But there were also many protestations of impotence among the signers, flat confessions of the new impossibility of painting itself ("It is difficult to be a painter"—H[élène] Jourdan-Morhange), or of general turpitude ("Laziness"—Alice Malançon), or of the impossibility of producing a meaningful mark ("I would like to insert something . . . ," complained one signer—Dodo Doilac—to which [her husband] Georges de Zayas answered, a few inches away, "One must but I cannot"). If Cocteau and Tzara strike the requisite tone of melancholia within the work, others directly invoke loss, such as Benjamin Peret: "I have lost everything and everything lost is gained." Some signers made obvious admissions ("I haven't done anything and I sign"—François Hugo), but there were also gestures of refusal ("No, I will not sign!"). The condition of silence was imposed ("To write something is good, but to be silent is better," cautioned Marthe Chenal), while others, like Georges Auric, invoked this same silence, this emptiness, while inscribing their words nonetheless: "I have nothing to say to you."

Most poignant, in this regard, was perhaps the large inscription surfacing just above the center of the painting, just above, that is, Auric's confession: "Speak for me," one signer writes—the future suicide Jacques Rigaut—a commandment in the form of an admission. If one understanding of the import of *L'oeil cacodylate* reads the work as a gesture whereby the artist cedes his privileged place to a potential collectivity, to a vast group of artists and nonartists alike, that gesture's utopianism finds itself everywhere undermined. Language, the language and speech of others, indeed rises up into the space of "Picabia's" painting, only to display itself there as a form of emptiness and of castration, of impotence and passivity alike.

And no less a commentator than Gabrielle Buffet ultimately registered, even thematized, this emptiness, the paradoxical version of multiplicity by which *L'oeil cacodylate* displaced the traditional, singular functions of authorship: "À Francis Picabia qui raconte des histoires de Nègre." Buffet here invokes the problematic manner in which French speakers still, to this day, speak of someone who writes in the place or manner of another. For the word *nègre* remains the colloquial term for that abdication of authorship that in English we call, so much more poetically, and in this case appropriately, a *ghostwriter*.[76]

So we have returned to a problematics of the name, of nominations and, inevitably, of their economic correlative, denominations. *L'oeil cacodylate* everywhere summoned up figures of displaced authorship, from the criminal to the ghostwriter to the pseudonym ("Picabia, do you remember PHARAMOUSSE?," the Belgian Dadaist Clément Pansaers wrote, just below Buffet's inscription, his question mark transformed into an excessive spiral or a tail, his reference to one of the oldest pseudonyms under which Picabia had once published his writings in the magazine *391*). *L'oeil cacodylate* was given over almost completely to language, to writing in its dual guise as alternately graffito or signature, ceding the visual codes of painting to the coding of linguistic form. The painting thus stakes its critique on yet another manifestation of the general equivalent, no matter how tokenized and empty it had become.

But as by now we would expect, Picabia does not allow the general equivalent to reign supreme over the desiccated surface of this painting, transcendent and (physically, materially) excluded, a standard and an anchor simultaneously enacting the valuations that any general equivalent serves to promote. The signature was not left on the base of the painting—it was not allowed to remain the basis of painting—governing the artistic object's insertion into a series (that of the author), a series that ultimately allows its easy intellectual or economic consumption. The signature here was *used,* grasped physically in its indexical and messy singularity, spread out in all its evacuated thickness across the expanse of the picture plane.

Another avatar of the tail, of that which is excluded in the form of the Law, the signature here surfaces within the scene of representation. And this movement could be restated by observing that Picabia does not counter the token function of the general equivalent by returning it to its measurement function, displacing the Symbolic for the Ideal; rather, deflated and devalued, the general equivalent erupts in what Goux has allowed us to see as the paradoxical mode of the *Real.* Emptied as a standard, but no longer promiscuously equivalent in its guise as a token, the general equivalent's regression to this mode simultaneously freezes the art object, projecting it as something inimitable, nontransferable, produced violently on the spot. And it splits the artistic subject, multiplying its physical signs beyond the capacities of the name to contain them, transforming this subject beyond all recognition.

Coda. We should let Duchamp have the last word. For we must admit that if this chapter has been in part about a brief moment in the crucial dialogue between Duchamp and Picabia, a moment in which Duchamp's conception of the readymade was recast as a mode of what we can now call expenditure, it was a "dialogue" enacted mostly on Picabia's turf, and largely by his rules. But Duchamp knew Picabia's game. Having initiated the strategy of the readymade, he could appreciate Picabia's assumption of his own ideas in the form of dispersal and dispossession, as a form that indeed obviated the proprietary functions of authorship and the ability to "own" any ideas whatsoever. Duchamp radicalized Picabia's reading of the readymade as a form and a function of the signature.

Pasting two photographs of himself on *L'oeil cacodylate,* Duchamp returns us to the moment of 1919, to the moment when this entire dialogue began. For the two included photographs are different versions of a self-inflicted alteration to his appearance that Duchamp had performed in 1919, and that he later called *Tonsure.* Initially, he shaved his entire head, and the image that has come down to us is of a rather grim Duchamp, bald and hardly recognizable. But later, by the time he was in Paris with Picabia, the shaving had become more strategic; it there took the form of a shooting star traced on Duchamp's scalp, the very image of the fugitive, the momentary, the transient. It took the form, that is, of a star and its tail, extending to Duchamp's own body, in the mode of subtraction, the procedures of addition he was simultaneously enacting upon the *Mona Lisa.*[77] And with these photographs, Duchamp explicitly inscribes upon *L'oeil cacodylate* the dynamic that I have here been calling the relationship between an artwork and its tail.

Furthering Duchamp's photographic play with his physical appearance, Duchamp's signature took the form of an extended pun, a pun that took subjective identity as its very substance: "en 6 qu'habilla rrose Sélavy—Marcel Duchamp." It was a pun that Duchamp had just recently published, in a slightly different form, in Picabia's dissident broadsheet *Le Pilhaou-Thibaou;* indeed, it was the first published example—after the language play that had been included in Duchamp's previous paintings and readymades—of the series of puns that Duchamp continued to work on for his entire life. In Picabia's magazine, Duchamp's first pun took the form of a playful rewriting of Picabia's name: *mâcheur Fran/cfort sau/cisse Pisqu/e quand elles] habilla. Marcel Duchamp (RROSE SELAVY).*[78] Homophonically, and minus the additions in brackets, the pun proclaims with an unmistakable lisp "Monsieur Francis Picabia." Transferring this pun to *L'oeil cacodylate,* however, the lisp turns into a stutter, recasting Picabia's name in the mode of castration, slicing off both of its primary initials, his signature's first syllables: . . . *ancis* . . . *cabia,* or, using Duchamp's homophones, *en 6 qu'habilla.*[79]

Wedding the French verb *habiller* ("to dress") to the first name of his recently invented alter ego Rose Selavy, Duchamp altered that alter ego's initial spelling, adding a second "R" to "Rose" in both *Le Pilhaou-Thibaou* and on *L'oeil cacodylate*. He never dropped this spelling, and what has been forgotten is the manner in which it arose from a hydra-figure not unlike "Francis Ingres," from the collision now of Picabia and Rose Selavy, from the conjunction of the word *habilla* and the name Rose, suggesting another French word to Duchamp, another homophone, the verb *arroser* ("to wet or sprinkle"). To say *en 6 qu'habilla rrose Sélavy* is, first, to invoke the terminology of fashion—one can *habiller Paul Poiret,* or, in Duchamp's version, one can *habiller Rrose Sélavy*—and Duchamp here consequently attaches that parlance to the surfacing of the verb *arroser,* projecting fashion's transformations into a connoted realm of liquidity and of dispersal.

Duchamp knew Picabia's game. He took it one step further. He did not sign *L'oeil cacodylate* as simply Marcel Duchamp, but as "Picabia." If Picabia willfully steals the readymade idea from Duchamp, productively (mis)reading its denial of authorship, Duchamp steals the misreading back in turn, signing "Picabia's" work as "Picabia dressed up as Marcel Duchamp." The signature here was no longer singular—it was turned against itself, knotted up, allowed to trip, to stumble, to fall. It would become double, triple—FRANCIS PICABIA RROSE SÉLAVY MARCEL DUCHAMP—perhaps even more, for instance, the form of six: *en 6 qu'habilla rrose Sélavy Marcel Duchamp.* Once again, the mono-form, the form of the One, was displaced.

Dada's strategy has become clear. From the Phallus to the Father, from the money-form to language, the general equivalent was one of the grounds of Paris Dada's experiment. It is for this reason that value and economics become such crucial questions for Dada, smuggled in through its actions upon the general equivalent in its various symbolic forms. It is also the reason that Picabia's insistence on remaining close to traditional mediums like drawing and painting—as opposed to the whole-scale rejection often attributed to Duchamp and his readymades—begins to look important again and critical to reclaim.[80] For the strategy of symbolic economies does not jump immediately from the abandonment of painting to the critique of art's institutions, a narrative often associated with

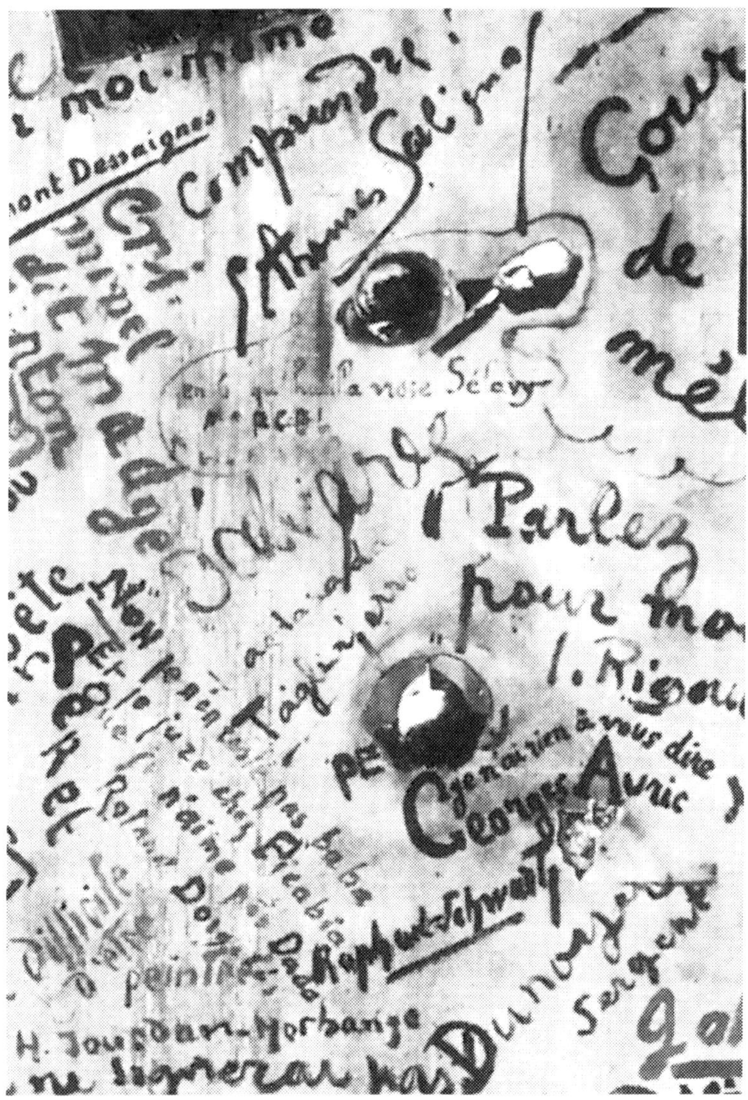

Detail of *L'œil cacodylate,* 1921. Documented before fading of center signatures.
© 2005 Artists Rights Society (ARS), New York/ADAGP, Paris/Estate of Francis
Picabia.

Dada. Rather, it retreats to a given medium category to open onto a larger representational logic, a logic of the sign. Isolated, for example, in relation to the restricted field of painting, this sign logic opened onto much wider realms, being a shared condition of modernity. Paradoxically, then, for Dada, or for Picabia, to *retreat* into a medium was in fact to *attach* Dada's critique to actual historical conditions all the more emphatically. And thus we might also claim that, ultimately, the frame questioned by the Dada readymade was not simply an artistic institution at all—museum or gallery or beyond. Neither was it only a set of artistic conventions. The frame that the Dada readymade opened onto was the defining logic of symbolic economies—a system of which art and its mediums were a part, but that also regulates and supports a vast range of other human activities. However, as we will see in the next chapter, if the questioning of specific artistic mediums via the readymade led Dada to the logic of symbolic economies, questioning these economies led Dada back just as surely to a series of far-reaching transformations of the mediums of art themselves.

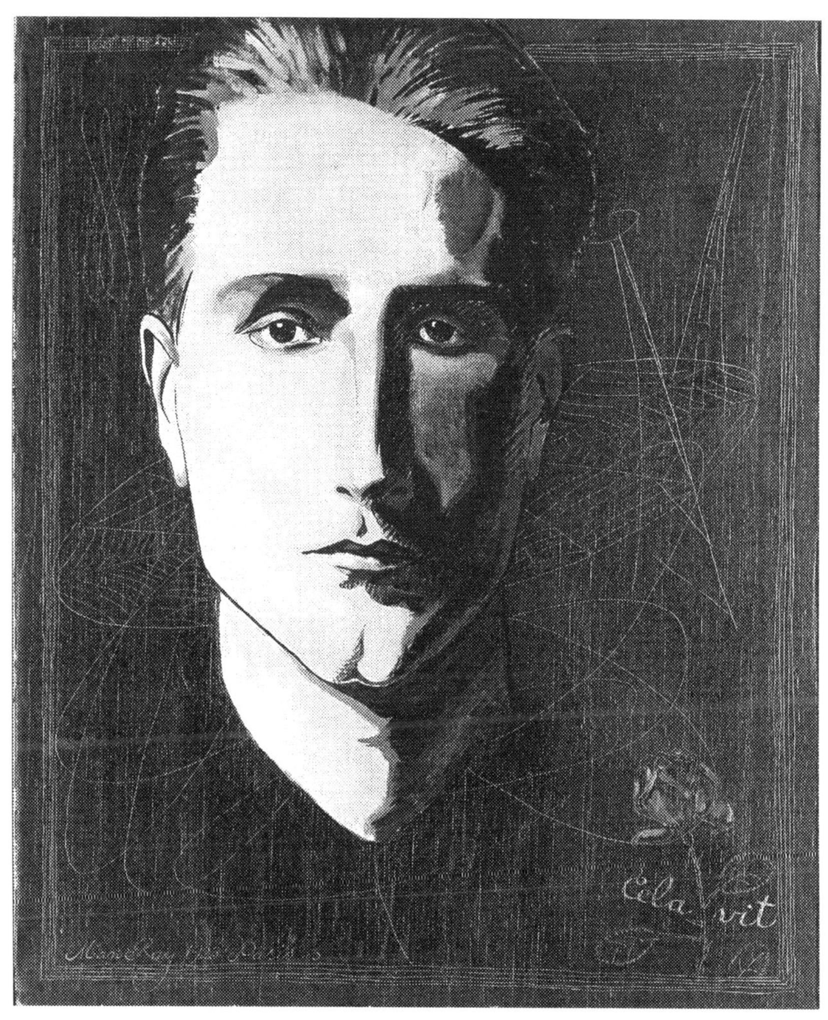

Man Ray, *Portrait of Rrose Selavy,* 1923. © 2005 Artists Rights Society (ARS), New York/ADAGP, Paris/Man Ray Trust.

3

———

Man Ray, n. masc., synon. de joie jouer jouir.

—Marcel Duchamp[1]

Here is an image of Duchamp. Surfacing from the darkness, his head floats—a face without a body—upon a faint tracery of lines, as if emerging from a delicate spiderweb, as if this face were a bud amid a series of looping petals. Painted in Paris in 1923, Man Ray's portrait of his friend does include a flower, but shunted to the lower right-hand side. It is, not coincidentally, a rose. Entangled with the written inscription "Cela vit," the flower and the words create a "synonym," and a crossing of word and image that this chapter will explore. For in the traditional place of the signature, Man Ray rewrites Duchamp's authorial pseudonym, Rrose Sélavy, transforming the false name into a living thing and a sign or an offering of love. And this crossing of the visual and the verbal allows Duchamp's name to escape the condition of the singular yet again.

In what follows, I want to take Man Ray's transformation of Rrose Sélavy quite seriously. Usually rendered as a pun meaning *Eros, c'est la vie* or "Eros, that's life," the homophone offered by Man Ray arrives at a different destination. *Cela vit*: We know, from Picabia's puns surrounding *La jeune fille,* that we could be facing another inscription of the phallus (*C'est le vit*). But this is not, to twist the usage, the Dead Phallus, the general equivalent on reserve: Dead Father, castrated Phallus. Instead Man Ray's phrase is an assertion of life, *cela vit* meaning "that lives." And thus we also face a shift in register and in tone from Duchamp's original pun. Between *c'est la vie* and *cela vit,* between the passive surrender of "that's life" and the joyous affirmation of "that lives," there is, indeed, a world of difference.[2] In the phrase's optimism, in its affirmation—from "that is (just) life" to "that (there) is living (alive)"—we sense the opening up of signifying conditions that exist in opposition to everything that we have been taught to expect from Dada.

I want to explore these signifying conditions by turning to a photograph by Man Ray that has remained marginal in all the accounts of Dada and Surrealist photography within which the artist nevertheless serves as the central figure. I am not thinking of Man Ray's photograph of the egg beater and its shadow, nor of the ashtray overturned, nor of the ghostly rayographs, nor of the gleaming nudes. I am thinking of an image from 1920 usually identified simply with the title *Portemanteau* or *Coat Stand.* The marginality of the photograph in the critical literature should, however, strike us as strange. Indeed, it was this image that Man Ray chose to reproduce in April 1921 in the one existing issue of *New York Dada,* a publication that might be said to define—if anything could—the practice of what paraded beneath the label "Dada Photography."

For Man Ray filled *New York Dada* with photographs. Along with Man Ray's *Portemanteau,* there was a contribution from Alfred Stieglitz, namely his crucial and uncharacteristic *Portrait of Dorothy True.* And from the hands of Man Ray himself, there was the journal's cover image of Marcel Duchamp dressed up as Rrose Sélavy, refashioned by Duchamp into the packaging of a faux-perfume bottle, an "assisted" readymade that Duchamp named *Belle Haleine, eau de voilette.* There were also other "collaborative" images, such as the several nude portraits by Man Ray of the Baroness Elsa von Freytag-Loringhoven at the issue's end. In this plethora of rather disparate photographic reproductions, *New York Dada* seems at first to have only one common denominator, and it surely makes one thing clear: the practice of Dada photography cannot be separated from a reflection on the image of woman. And with this thought, other connections slowly suggest themselves.

Most of the images in *New York Dada* seem to be about "veiling," about an intimation that something is hidden, perhaps enigmatically, within the image: Man Ray's *Portemanteau* depicts this literally, with a woman's body partially hidden behind a coat stand, and Duchamp's *Belle Haleine* writes it verbally, subtitled as it is *eau de voilette* or "veil water." Stieglitz's *Portrait of Dorothy True* could surely be said to foreground an optical veiling as well. Technically, the work is a double-exposed image in which two photographs interact: a tightly cropped picture of a striding woman's calf and foot, wrapped in a black stocking and stuffed into a too-small high-heeled shoe; and, along with this, an image of a woman's face, just visible in the black fog of the monumental stocking. The only images that seem to set themselves against this general formal preoccupation with veiling are the "exposed" images of the Baroness, who appears nude in her portraits. But then, of course, the images of the Baroness perhaps reveal the more general logic of the other photographs' traffic with both images of women and techniques of veiling: the engagement of all of the images in *New York Dada* with a logic of what we can call the fetish.

For a variety of discourses, a fetish object involves at its base a process of displacement. In the anthropological and economic discourses from which the term originated, a fetish emerges from a confusion of the animate and the inanimate, an attribution of life and power to a dead thing that borrows this power from someplace else (the primitive fetish, the commodity fetish). Within psychoanalytic discourse, a fetish is also a displaced substitute, an object that allows for the disavowal of sexual difference through its continued attribution of the phallus to the mother. All of these understandings of fetishism seem to be in place in the images from *New York Dada*.[3] Collapsing female part-object and shoe, Stieglitz's photograph represents a classic sexual fetish; Duchamp's perfume an engagement with the commodity fetish; and Man Ray's *Portemanteau* an opening onto fetishism and fashion, which of course subsumes both commodity and sexual fetishism, just as Duchamp's fashion plate and Stieglitz's modern shoe also emerge from fashion's milieu. And if Man Ray's photograph somehow subsumes the logic of the others that surround it, the artist seemed at pains to foreground this centrality with the captions, even an alternate title, with which he accompanied it.

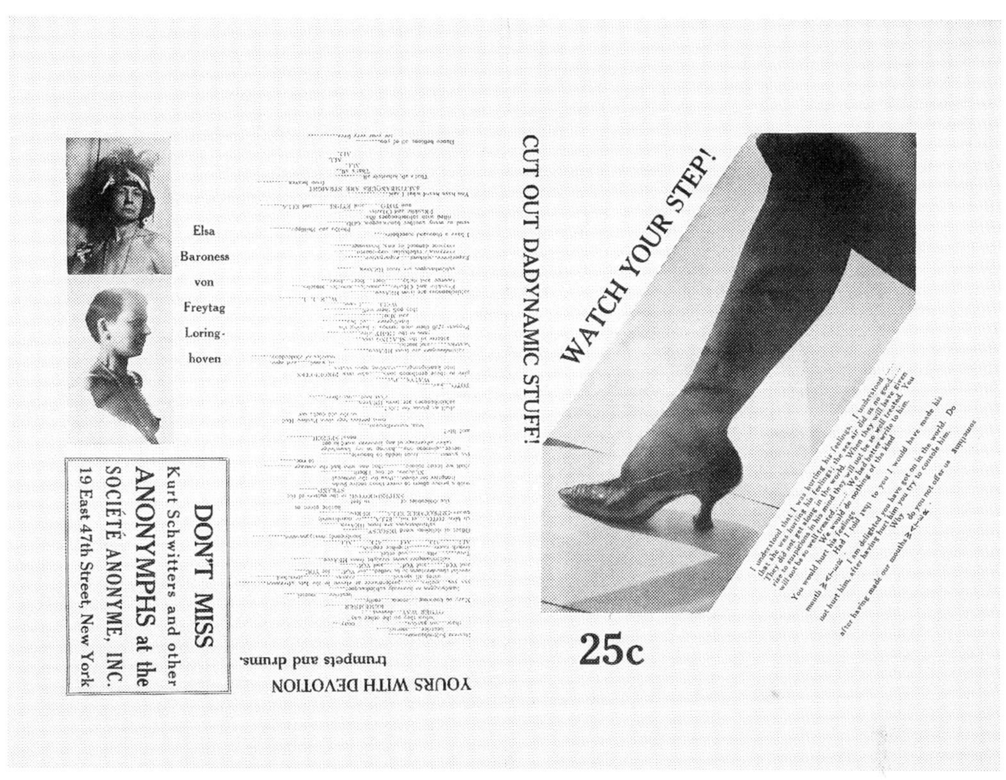

Man Ray and Marcel Duchamp, *New York Dada,* 1921. Beinecke Rare Book and Manuscript Library, Yale University. © 2005 Artists Rights Society (ARS), New York/Man Ray Trust/Estate of Marcel Duchamp.

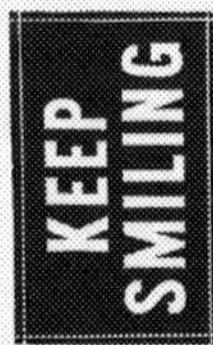

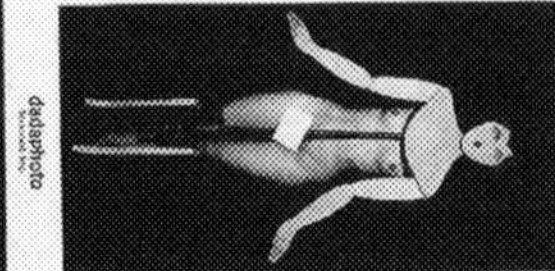

EYE-COVER   ART-COVER   CORSET-COVER
AUTHORIZATION

NEW YORK-DADA:

You ask for authorization to name your periodical Dada. But Dada belongs to everybody. I know excellent people who have the name Dada. Mr. Jean Dada; Mr. Gaston de Dada; Fr. Picabia's dog is called Zizi de Dada; in G. Ribemont-Dessaignes's play, the page is likewise named Zizi de Dada. I could cite dozens of examples. Dada belongs to everybody. Like the idea of God or of the tooth-brush. There are people who are very dada, more dada; there are dadas everywhere all over and in every individual. Like God and the tooth-brush (an excellent invention, by the way).

Dada is a new type; a mixture of man, naphthaline, sponge, animal made of ebonite and beefsteak, prepared with soap for cleansing the brain. Good teeth are the making of the stomach and beautiful teeth are the making of a charming smile. Halfalalah of ancient oil and rejection of rubber.

There is nothing educational about my choice of Dada for the name of my review. In Switzerland I was in the company of friends and was boosting the dictionaries for a word appropriate to the sonorities of all languages. Night came upon us when a green hand placed its richness on the page of Larousse—pleasing very graciously to Dada—my choice was made. I'm a cigarette and drank a demitasse.

For Dada was in no way seeking and to lead to no exploration of this offshoot of relationship which is not a dogma nor a school, but rather a reconciliation of individuals and of free hearts.

Dada existed before us (the Holy Virgin) but one cannot deny to magical power to add to this already existing spirit and impulse of penetration and discovery that characterizes its present form.

There is nothing more accomplished than Dada.

Nothing more indefinable.

With the best will in the world I cannot tell you what I think of it.

The journalists who say that Dada is a pretext are right, but it is a pretext for something I do not know.

Dada has penetrated into every frontier; Dada is the best paying concern of the day.

Therefore, Madam, be on your guard and realize that a ready-made product is a different thing from a glossy label.

Dada abolishes "nuances." Nuances do not exist in words but only in some atrophied brains whose cells are too narrowed. Dada is an anti-"nuance" cream. The simple motions that serve as signs for declamation are quite adequate to express the free or free experience we have discovered within 7 or 8,000 years. Dada offers all kinds of advantages. Dada will soon be able to boast of having shown people that to say "eight" instead of "left" is neither less nor too logical, that 2765 — 34; that yes — no. Strong believers are making themselves felt in politics, in commerce, in language. No whole world and what's to it has glid to the left along with us. Dada has mounted its springs into hot bread, to speak. Regionally into language. Little by little (large by large) it destroys it. Everything collapses with logic. And we shall see certain liberties we constantly take in the sphere of sentiment, social life, morals, once more however normal standards. These liberties no longer will be looked upon as crime, but as ideas.

I will close with a little international song: Order from the publishing house "La Sirène" 7 rue Pasquier, Paris, Dadaconcue, the worst of dadas from all over the world. Tell your bookseller that this book will soon be out of print. You will have many agreeable acceptance.

Read Dadaglobe if you have troubles. Dadaglobe is in press. Here are some of its collaborators:

Paul Citroen (Amsterdam); Baader Daimonides; R. Hausmann; W. Heartfield; H. Hoech; R. Huelsenbeck; G. Grosz; Fried Hardy Worm (Berlin); Clemens Pasuetez (Bruxelles); Mac Robber (Calcutta); Jacques Edwards (Chili); Baargeld, Arnauld v. Dadgeldoben, Max Ernst, F. Huelsrich (Cologne); K. Schwitters (Hannover); J. K. Bonset (Leyden); Guillermo de Torre (Madrid); Gino Cantarelli; E. Bacchi, A. Fiozzi (Mantova); Kroscnick (Moscou); A. Vagts (Munich); W. C. Arensberg, Gabrielle Buffet, Marcel Duchamp; Adon Lacroix; Baroness v. Loringhoven; Man Ray, Joseph Stella; E. Varese; A. Stieglitz; M. Hartley; C. Kahles (New York); Louis Aragon; C. Brancusi; André Breton; M. Buffet, S. Charchoune; J. Crotti; Suzanne Duchamp; Paul Eluard; Benjamin Peret; Francis Picabia; G. Ribemont-Dessaignes; J. Rigaut, Soubeyran; Ph. Soupault, Tristan Tzara (Paris); Mehdilea Viebher (Prague); J. Krols (Rome); Arp; S. Taeuber (Zurich).

The incalculable number of pages of reproductions and of text is a guaranty of the success of the book. Articles of luxury, of prime necessity, articles indispensable to hygiene and to the heart, toilet articles of an intimate nature.

Such, Madame, do we propose for Dadaglobe; for you need look no further than to the row of articles prepared without Dada to account for the fact that the train of your heart is chopped; that the so precious enamel of your intelligence is crushing; also but the presence of these tiny wrinkles still imperceptible but nevertheless disquieting.

All this and much else in Dadaglobe.   TRISTAN TZARA.

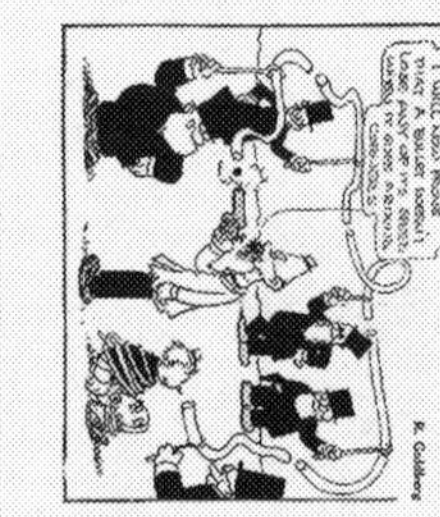

VENTILATION

On the question of proper ventilation opinions radically differ. It seems impossible to please all. It is our aim, however, to cater to the wishes of the majority. The conductor of this vehicle will gladly be governed accordingly. Your cooperation will be appreciated.   DADATAXI, Limited.

PUG DEBS MAKE
SOCIETY BOW

Maiden the day May Make a Couple—
Coming Out Party Next Friday

The first of these captions was writ large, like a sign: "KEEP SMILING." While humorous and friendly enough, the sign appears enigmatically paired with the image that we see. "EYE-COVER ART-COVER CORSET-COVER AUTHORIZATION": this seems to serve as title to the letter by Tristan Tzara authorizing the free use of the name Dada ("Dada belongs to everybody"), a text printed beneath Man Ray's image. Yet the title's repetition of the word "cover" seems to rhyme with what a *manteau* is in French—a cloak or a coat, but also figuratively a mask, a veil, or a pretense—and which this specific *Portemanteau* explores as its basic structure. Man Ray's image "carries" one more caption, the most important for our purposes: he calls the work a "dadaphoto"—itself sub-titled "Trademark Reg."—as if this were the image that defined the very practice of Dada photography.

To copyright if not commodify the form of the Dada photograph, to register if not regulate its appearance through the device of the brand name, seems entirely in character with the "authorization" that the New York Dadaists sought from Tristan Tzara to borrow the European movement's name, or with schemes hatched in New York by 1920 such as the "Société Anonyme" or Marcel Duchamp's one-time desire to market internationally the word Dada itself as a piece of jewelry.[4] Man Ray later spoke in similar terms of the publication of *New York Dada* as a form of "legalization" of the movement:

> In 1919 [*sic*], with the permission and with the approval of the other Dadaists I legalized Dada in New York. Just once. That was enough. The times did not deserve more. That was a Dadadate. The one issue of *New York Dada* did not even bear the names of its authors. How unusual for Dada! Of course, there were a certain number of collaborators. Both willing and unwilling. Both trusting and suspicious. What did it matter? Only one issue. Forgotten—not even seen by most Dadaists or antidadaists. Now, we are trying to revive Dada.[5]

According to this account, the publication of *New York Dada* (however inexactly remembered) represented a "Dadadate," and it contained a "Dadaphoto." To create such a category of image in 1921 reaches beyond the bureaucratic trappings of New York Dada strategies, however, to connect to the recent activities of Dada in Paris, and to its series of similar anticategorical Dada categories. It is for this reason that I take this detour into Man Ray's work.[6] It would seem that Man Ray's *Dadaphoto* poses a quite specific response to Francis Picabia's quest, throughout the year of 1920, to "invent" new categories of artistic objects such as "Dada Painting" and "Dada Drawing," the Tableau Dada and the Dessin Dada.

One difference immediately asserts itself: the *Dadaphoto* shifts its label more aggressively to the realm of the commodity or the brand name than was the case for the seemingly pedagogical demonstration of Picabia's categories. Man Ray presents not a *Dada Photograph,* but a *Dadaphoto,* evincing a collapse of formality in tone if not linguistic differentiation altogether. And if a central strategy of the Tableau Dada and the Dessin Dada was to engage with the general equivalent— denying its reserve, contesting its structural exclusion, submitting the equivalent to use, potentially laying waste to the foundation of a given symbolic economy— Man Ray's category of the *Dadaphoto* evinces no such engagement with the general equivalent at all. For here no trace of Phallus, or Father, or Language, or Money can be discerned; the *Dadaphoto* hardly seizes on the general equivalent, and surely does not subject its forms to direct manipulation. This is perhaps not entirely surprising; to locate such a strategy within what Picabia nominated as "Dada Painting" and "Dada Drawing" is to witness the general equivalent contested upon the site of tradition, upon the mediums delimited and legitimated by history, and that the avant-garde had set out to contest. Photography, by contrast, was a new form for the avant-garde. Not legitimated by tradition, it did nevertheless pose the question of exchange at the very heart of its operation as a form of mechanical reproduction, opening up perhaps—and it will be my thesis that such was the case for the *Dadaphoto*—entirely new forms of exchange, new modalities of visual equivalency, an entirely other symbolic economy.

Indeed, exchange of some sort seems to be at the heart of the image that the *Dadaphoto* offers. Describing what we might see in this photograph has not proven easy for those few commentaries that exist on the image. A female body, nude except for a single black, knee-high stocking (à la Stieglitz), stands behind

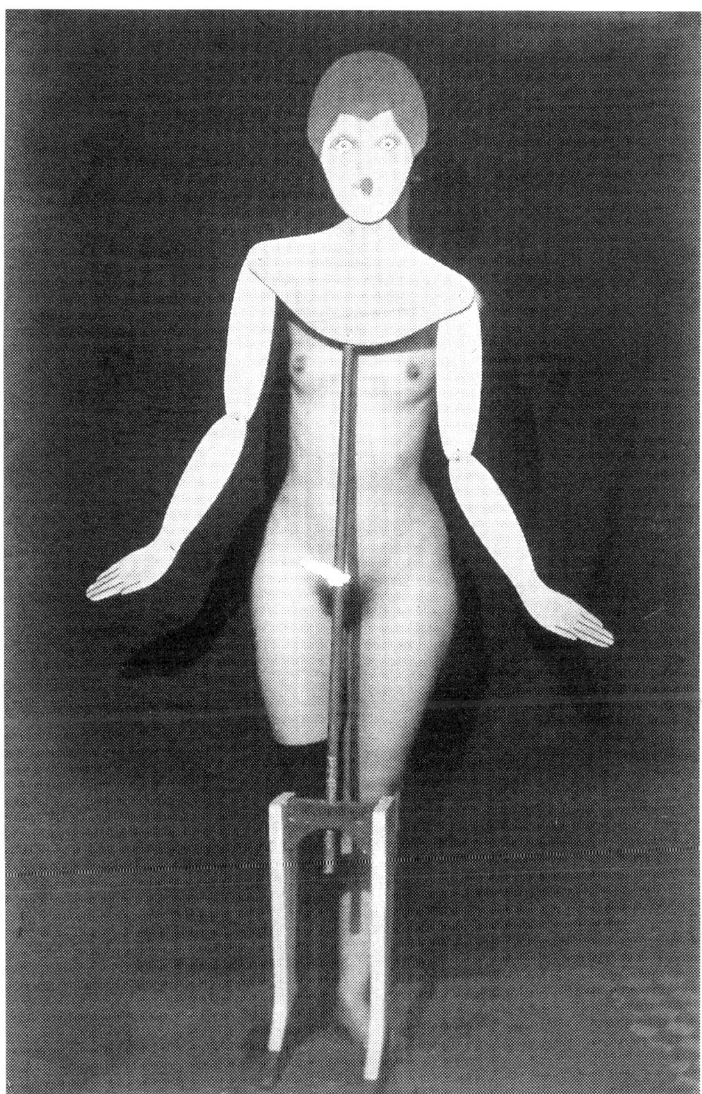

Man Ray, *Portemanteau (Coat Stand),* 1920. Silver salt print on matte paper, 40.4 × 26.9 cm. Musée National d'Art Moderne, Centre Georges Pompidou. Photo by Jaques Fanjour. Photograph © CNAC/MNAM/Dist. Réunion des Musées Nationaux / Art Resource, New York. © 2005 Artists Rights Society (ARS), New York/ADAGP, Paris/Man Ray Trust.

a coat stand of a sort, one itself transformed into something like a caricature of the female form, a cartoon affair of moveable arms and a wide-eyed face, mouth agape, an object suspended illegibly between evoking a sex toy, a fashion manne-quin, and a carnivalesque theatrical prop. At its best, for some, the interest of the *Dadaphoto* lies in how it provides literal form to the repeated "anthropomor-phism" of the Dada readymade or mechanomorph, illustrating directly the bod-ily evocations that ring out from beneath snow shovel, or camera bellows, or egg beater.[7] At its worst, for others, the image confirms the clear misogyny of the Dada project, its need to contain actual female bodies within the iron-clad, man-made forms of industrial modernity.[8] Both of these explanations seem entirely too "quick" to me. For we do not yet understand what the "anthropomorphism" of the readymade might in fact entail. And despite the explicit caricature—despite, too, the fetishism of all the images in *New York Dada*—misogyny might be the inversion of the project that the *Dadaphoto* could be said to sustain.

To restate what the *Dadaphoto* gives us to see, and to do this more slowly: A nude female body stands behind a readymade object, a modified coat stand. This readymade "masks" the full extent of her bodily form; at times, for example around the visual incident of the otherwise ludicrous single black stocking, the female form seems to fuse—in an amateur theatrical sort of way—with the ob-ject that stands before it. Two entities, a body and an object, stand in relation to one another. They seem "drawn" to each another, "rhyming" their visual forms. While the coat stand caricatures or imitates quite openly the female form, the nude body too reciprocates this imitation, rigidifying its vertical stance, con-forming to the object's lines, receiving its shadows. A doubling of sorts takes place; a form of "correspondence" seems on offer.

It will be my contention that the *Dadaphoto* presents not the engagement with the general equivalent of the Tableau Dada or the Dessin Dada, but what might be imagined as a dynamic existing on the other side of the latter's opera-tions. If, previously, I have explored the Dada strategies that set out to rupture a dominant symbolic economy, here I want to detail a linked Dada strategy that in-volves exploring the alternate symbolic economies let loose by this rupture, the repressed or utopian systems, and the new possibilities of meaning and value, that they allow.

As a photograph, the *Dadaphoto* prioritizes a new form of exchange. It concerns itself with equivalency, with objects both doubled and corresponding. But the equivalency of such a photograph will now be that which is let loose by an exchange beyond the Law of the general equivalent. This is an equivalency, an exchange, that will force us to find in the Dada practice of photography a new definition of the photograph itself. It is an exchange whose stakes are inordinately high. In the *Dadaphoto,* we witness an intimation of an exchange not of what Karl Marx called either "relative" or "equivalent" forms of value, but rather of what film theorist and philosopher Kaja Silverman has recently called a form of "absolute" value.[9]

☞

In a recent book and a series of subsequent essays, Silverman has attempted to theorize a redemptive relationship to vision that she calls, using a term from Hannah Arendt, "world spectatorship." Embracing "a kind of looking which takes place *in* the world, and *for* the world," Silverman's world spectator departs radically from the "denigration of the visual"[10] prevalent in most forms of poststructuralism and contemporary film and photographic theory, seeking instead "a kind of looking which not only stubbornly adheres to phenomenal forms, but also augments and enriches them" (WS, pp. 2–3). Her model for this utopia of visual enrichment is decidedly psychoanalytic; this is an account that attempts in the most accurate of ways to theorize how we as subjects can be said to love the world.

Crucial to Silverman's account is the phenomenon that she names "perceptual identity": we "see" something, from a Freudian psychoanalytic perspective, only when an external stimulus or perception can be bound to a chain of visual memories in the subject, only when the outside world can be "touched" by the previous affective ties of the psyche. We care for the outside world—we "see" it—only when we can displace onto its objects the love we once held for a past object of desire. The ability thus freely to displace affect onto the world becomes the focus of Silverman's form of visual ethics; the more that displacement can move from the subject's past into the world, the more we can "see" and ultimately love. "Every act of visual affirmation," Silverman writes, occurs "via the visual *reincar-*

nation of previous incarnations [of the object of desire]," defining the world spectator as "consequently not just someone to whom the past returns, but someone who holds himself open to the new form it will take—who anticipates and affirms the transformative manifestation of what was in what is" (WS, pp. 24–25).

The contiguity of world and psyche at the heart of perceptual identity depends on a mode of symbolization that can transfer affect. In a later essay, Silverman describes such forms of the "conveyance of affect," the symbolization characteristic of a "libidinal conveyance system" that founds a "symbolic order . . . without either unity or closure."[11] Here too we face a mode of symbolization that depends on a psychoanalytic model: rather than "directly evoking a signified, as it does in Saussure's account of the sign," the signifier that Silverman seeks to describe "refers back to a previous one, which itself does the same" (GL, p. 12), a chain of signifiers corresponding to the endless displacements of the movement of desire. In fact, such a signifier would be a "redemptive form," set against the Saussurean model of the sign and ultimately "capable of raising the world from the grave to which the linguistic signifier has consigned it" (GL, p. 10).

Language, in Silverman's account, is "inimical to affect" (GL, p. 20), an impoverished form for its conveyance. The linguistic signifier exists in fact in opposition to all that would support the project of what Silverman also calls libidinal communication: "The linguistic signifier is prototypically closed: closed to affective transfers, closed to other linguistic signifiers, and closed to the world" (WS, 101). Saussurean linguistics, at least, insists on the *delimitation* of the "linguistic entity," its separation "from everything that surrounds it on the phonic chain."[12] As Silverman explains:

> This notion of delimitation also appears at every other point in Saussure's account of the linguistic sign. The abstract *langue* or language system is detached from the real; every element within it means not through reference to what resides outside that order, but only through the ways in which it differs from other elements within it. A signifier is also properly closed in relation to the signified, and vice-versa; although poetic usage can motivate the relation between

the two in all sorts of ways, those signs in which there is no communication between them better exemplify the workings of language
than those in which there is. Finally, although our concrete utterances have the power to work transformatively upon our abstract
language system, *parole* is every bit as respectful of the discrete nature
of individual words as is *langue*. When we speak "well," we *articulate*:
we clearly separate each of our words from those which precede
them, and from those which come later. (WS, p. 104)

This description will hopefully not sound strange to those readers familiar with
the basic outlines of Saussurean linguistics. And yet further, this system of "separation" should also strike the reader as evocative of all that I have had to say about
the system of the general equivalent. Indeed, we are listening in Silverman's summation to the reasons that led Jean-Joseph Goux to nominate Language as the
general equivalent of signs.

When functioning in this mode—according to the logic of the general
equivalent—language will be attached to what Freud calls the "secondary process":

When words are most conventionally "word-like" . . . they bring
displacement to a halt. They do so by insisting upon difference, over
and against similarity and contiguity. Indeed, in a certain sense, the
linguistic sign is nothing *but difference.* "Mother" signifies "not father,"
"not brother," "not sister," etc. When we write or speak, we also ar
ticulate our words, i.e., we "cut" them off from each other graphically or acoustically. Even the "arbitrariness" of the linguistic sign
represents part of this process of differentiation. The lack of affinities between it and the referent, as well as between the two terms out
of which it is itself comprised, puts further obstacles in the way of
libidinal transfer. The linguistic sign is consequently a poor conveyer
of affect. . . . Freud associates the linguistic signifier with the "secondary process," which predominates at the level of the preconscious. (GL, p. 20)

What this description obviously begs is a specification of those characteristics
that pertain to the mode of symbolization that psychoanalysis calls the "primary
process," a mode of symbolization belonging to the unconscious and lying—in
this account at least—outside the linguistic model, lying—for my account as
well—outside the system of the general equivalent.[13] It is to the primary process that Silverman turns for her model of "affective transfer" or "affective symbolization"—a symbolization inherent not in linguistic communication but in
what Silverman calls the "perceptual signifier"—a process that she describes as
the drive "to make repressed visual memories once again perceptually available"
(GL, p. 20). Dependent on visual affinities, similarity, and contiguity, the affective transfer of the primary process corresponds to the activity that psychoanalysis calls "displacement"—an activity that comes with an all-important twin
and corollary, namely, "condensation."

It was perhaps disingenuous of me to observe earlier that nothing in Man Ray's
Dadaphoto relates to the forms of the general equivalent explored in Picabia's categories of the Tableau Dada and the Dessin Dada. We do face, at least in the version of the image published in *New York Dada,* a thematic of castration, and thus
in some way of the Phallus, every bit as strong as that witnessed in Duchamp's
L.H.O.O.Q. Visible in the current form of the print only as an actual tear on the
photograph, when published in *New York Dada* the female body in *Portemanteau*
carried a white stamp placed over her genitals, a literal postage stamp that voided
the space of her sex. In a historical moment that saw the editors of the avant-
garde journal *The Little Review* brought to court on obscenity charges for the
publication of sections of James Joyce's *Ulysses,* it has usually been supposed that
this (eventually removed) stamp served the purpose of protecting *New York Dada*
from similar charges of pornography. And yet this was a visual "obstruction" or
deletion that both looked back to Man Ray's previous journal publications (the
play with deletion and censorship in the 1915 *Ridgefield Gazook*), and also would
remain characteristic of his subsequent artistic procedures. Given the parameters
of the photograph, it is also a deletion that becomes extremely evocative of the
elision of castration itself.

In the moments leading up to the production of *New York Dada,* Man Ray had assisted Duchamp on an infamous film project that itself engaged a thematic of castration, perhaps more directly than any other Dada work. This was Duchamp's attempt to film the shaving of the Baroness Elsa von Freytag-Loringhoven's pubic hair, a project of elision in which Man Ray was to serve as both cameraman and "barber." "While helping Duchamp with his research," Man Ray remembered, "I had shot a sequence of myself as a barber shaving the pubic hair of a nude model, a sequence which was also ruined in the process of developing and never saw the light."[14] At first understandable only, if at all, as an avant-garde strategy of mimicry that seizes on the subcultural *frisson* of pornography, Duchamp's lost project perhaps makes more sense when seen in light of his own attempts to libidinalize art—the work of his *The Bride Stripped Bare by Her Bachelors, Even.* For Duchamp's film produced another understanding of the "stripping bare" of a female body, a denuding that curiously inverts, with almost 180 degree precision, the activity of the traditional painter. Rather then continue to employ the bodily prosthesis of the paintbrush—the "stick with hairs"—to add material to a canvas, Man Ray as Duchamp's "barber" used an everyday item to subtract hairs directly from the female body. And this inversion of painterly activity now linked painting to castration, the abandonment of the brush with the activity of elision, perhaps asserting that the transformation of painting necessarily involves the stark confrontation with sexual difference and also the exploration of a new symbolic economy of both the painterly and the libidinal object.

Potentially linking this lost film project to the *New York Dada* photograph, it has recently been asserted that the female model in Man Ray's *Dadaphoto* is in fact the Baroness herself.[15] Perhaps this is an attribution aided by the stamp that Man Ray placed on the image in *New York Dada,* for the Baroness was known not only for her nude modeling but for her performative masquerades, one aspect of which often included placing postage stamps on her own body. Man Ray did once cryptically describe the *Dadaphoto* as "conceived for a friend [a male friend, *un ami*],"[16] an explanation that may link the photograph to Duchamp and his film. Whatever the case—and whether the *Dadaphoto* depicts the Baroness or not—Man Ray did in fact link the *Dadaphoto* to the Baroness film. When published in April of 1921, the *Dadaphoto* in *New York Dada* was placed on the same page as a letter from Tristan Tzara authorizing the spread of Dada to New York. And just two months later, in June, when Man Ray wrote a response to Tzara's letter, that letter now placed the sole surviving film stills from the aborted Baroness project on the page with his text. In fact, it is in the relation of these film stills to the letter's text that we discover something like a key to a crucial structure paralleled by the visual form of the *Dadaphoto*.

Offering up the lack of the Phallus in a form of extraordinary display, and with seeming gleeful abandon, the Baroness's shaved body in the Duchamp/Man Ray image is made to function in Man Ray's letter in relation to written language. However, in contradistinction to all we have been saying about the symbolic economy of the linguistic signifier, Man Ray's initial language in this letter is not very well "articulated" in the Saussurean meaning of the word. It seems to operate in a quite different way. Stretching from end to end of the white page, the letter begins with a stuttering line, avoiding through repetition the clear pathways of sense:

MERDELAMERDELAMERDELAMERDELAMERDELAMER
de l'a [　]merique!

Usually understood too quickly as an expression of boredom and disgust (*merde*) with America, Man Ray's opening salvo has been read as a prelude to his imminent expatriation from the United States and his July 1921 arrival in Paris, where he would join the Paris Dada group ("Dada cannot live in New York," Man Ray's letter continues). However, the opening line is of course properly unreadable, as it throws up an almost infinite number of possible "articulations," playing on a set of several recognizable French words or homophones, before announcing "From America!":

MER   = Sea
MÈR[E] = Mother
MERDE = Shit
AMER   = Bitter

292 J. Doucet

MER DE LA MER DE LA MER DE LA MER DE LA MER DE LA MER

de l'a merique !

Cher Tzara — dada cannot live in New York. All New York is dada, and will not tolerate a rival, — will not notice dada. It is true that no efforts to make it public have been made, beyond the placing of your and our dadas in the bookshops, but there is no one here to work for it, and no money to be taken in for it, or donated to it. So dada in New York must remain a secret.

No additional sales have been made of the consignment you sent to "Société Anonyme". The "anonyme" itself does not sell anything.

Man Ray, *Letter to Tristan Tzara,* June 1921. Bibliothèque Littéraire Jacques Doucet, Paris. © 2005 Artists Rights Society (ARS), New York/ADAGP, Paris/Man Ray Trust.

Descending to the level of the excremental (*de la merde*), or announcing something coming "from the sea" or "from the mother" (*de la mèr[e]*), language here seems freed from its existence as a mode of the general equivalent. For it is constructed on the one hand by the work of condensation, producing from an entire phrase or sentence what we might call a massive "portmanteau" word, a word made up of other words. In this, Man Ray's line seems given over to that of which language should not be allowed to partake, namely displacement and the primary process. Inhabited by the workings of affective transfer, other readings of the statement thus arise, in a spiral not of nonsense but of expanding meanings, ranging from the scatological to the melancholic, from violence to love: "*MER DE LA MERDE* [Sea of Shit . . . Mother of Shit]," the passage yelps. "*MERDE DE LA MER* [The Sea's Shit . . . The Mother's Shit]," it whines in mirror reversal. The possible readings don't end here: "*MERDE L'AMER DE LA MER* [Shit, the bitter(ness) of the sea . . . Shit, the bitter(ness) of the mother] . . . *MER DE L'AMER* [Sea of Bitter . . . Mother of Bitter] . . . *MER DE LA MER* [The Mother's Sea . . . the Mother of the Sea . . . the Mother of the Mother . . . The Mother's Mother (an Ur-Mother?)]." The spiral of readings could continue.

Attached to this stuttering line of displacements and condensation, it is as if the transgressive image of the nude, shaven Baroness has given its libidinal charge to the words themselves, causing this explosion of articulation and of sense. Indeed, the condensation represented by this collision of words and letters is only redoubled by another, more momentous condensation, a form of deep affinity—that of the body of the Baroness to the experimental phrase presented by Man Ray. We witness a form of fusion, a verbal–visual crossing where the Baroness's body and its placement allows the body to begin to act like a letter, forming in its pose the shape of the first letter from the word "Amerique," namely the letter *A*. But this crossing extends in both directions, allowing the body to become a letter—to become an entity that we recognize as a signifier—but also forcing language now to devolve from the word into pure sound (the purring, alliterative stutter of the phrase), or into pure visual image. For we could reverse our description of the Baroness film still, seeing now how the letter or the linguistic signifier *becomes a body* as it emphasizes its visual—as opposed to merely linguistic—nature.

<hr>

The product of such transformation is that the letter will now carry that body's erotic charge. We are witnessing the operation of affective transfer. As in the *Dadaphoto,* with its ricochet of body and readymade, here the Baroness's body corresponds to another object through similarity and contiguity, but this time it is aligned not with a readymade but with a letter (the letter *A*). Stated in a different way, "language" in this document seems not to operate in the Saussurean manner, where a signifier refers to a signified, but opens up an abyssal chain, with the female body—perhaps even and figuratively the "mother" that whispers through this line's aggressive stutter—now standing *behind* the letter or the word, a support for its libidinal charge.[17]

And we could restate this: In Man Ray's letter to Tzara, language exceeds its existence as a system of the general equivalent through intensifying a form of exchange, just as the original film project of Man Ray and Duchamp might be described as exceeding the parameters of the symbolic regime of castration by refusing to allow it to remain a symbol, intensely inserting the literal "fact" of castration into the visual realm.

The psychoanalytic model of symbolization characteristic of displacement finds its origins in an economy we might begin to call "maternal." Considering Dada's turn to such symbolization, we might also need to begin to recognize that the movement's challenge to patriarchal and phallic economies lies in an exploration—however halting, tentative, even unfulfilled—that also depended on a maternal symbolic economy.

Rather than relating a signifier immediately to a signified, displacement presents a sign of affect that relates the signifier to a chain of other, preceding signifiers, a chain of objects of desire. The story of displacement that Silverman tells focuses intently on Freud's claim—in texts like *The Interpretation of Dreams* or "The Unconscious"—that "every signifying act in a given subject's life refers back, in some ultimate sense, to a primally repressed term, which is most frequently the mother" (GL, p. 12). We are forced—by the kinship structure, by the Oedipus complex—to displace away from the mother throughout our lives onto other substitute objects. The result, for Silverman at least, is not an "abandon-ment" of the original lost object of desire, nor a diminution of a primary affect. Rather, affect can be transferred, and displacement opens up a "qualitative com-plexification" (WS, p. 119), a means of elevating that which served as the "first" term, connecting it to "a host of related memories and thereby expand[ing] its field of meaning" (WS, p. 119). Affect, through this process, can in fact grow and thus evolve.

Rejecting the Saussurean or linguistic model of signification, Silverman's description of affective symbolization might seem unfortunately regressive, an anchoring and thus fixation of the mobility of meaning in the figure (and the meaning) of the mother. Ultimately, however, this is not the case; the opposite would be more true. The mother is a "first signifier" for an even greater loss, one that cannot and will never be symbolized, but that places the drive toward sym-bolization itself in motion.

> Within the Freudian model [of symbolization], this regressive jour-ney finally leads to a term capable of functioning as a signified. This is of course the mother. In my view, however, the mother does not constitute the full stop of meaning. She classically provides the first signifier for a more primordial loss: the loss of what Lacan variously calls "presence," "being," or the "here and now." Unlike the other signifiers of the *hic et nunc,* though, she has nothing to which she can refer back. What she stands in for psychically cannot provide this function, since it is precisely what escapes signification. Although serving as the support for libidinal symbolization, the mother is con-sequently devoid of semantic value. It is not she who gives all of the other signifiers of desire their meaning; it is, rather, *they* who deter-mine what *she* can mean. To go "backward," libidinally speaking, also is not finally to touch "ground"; it is, instead, to apprehend the groundlessness of all signification. (GL, p. 13)

For Silverman, this groundlessness is "liberating" (GL, p. 13).[18] Operating in the absence of an anchor in this way, operating in a close bond with absence itself, libidinal transfer can work freely, with no bounds on its form, with no constraints on which directions it may ultimately take.

It would be all-important to keep open the groundless ground of the signifying chain, the groundless ground that the mother—or what Silverman elsewhere calls the "maternal signifier"—represents. However, in the normative account given by psychoanalysis, all sorts of obstacles arise to threaten this openness. Although again this is not the term that Silverman (or Freud) uses, one of these obstacles will be the installation of the general equivalent at the heart of this symbolic economy. It is an obstacle that thus also signals the repression of the earlier economy itself.

With the onset of the Oedipus complex and the castration crisis, with the ascension of the Father and Phallus to the position of general equivalent of subject and object alike, a massive challenge to the position of the mother in the economy just described takes place. What psychoanalysis strangely calls the "negative" Oedipal mother will be replaced by the "positive" Oedipal mother of castration, the mother of insufficiency and lack from whom we will displace ever more according to the dictates of the paternal Law.[19] Ultimately, this positive Oedipal mother is not the one to which Silverman has devoted her account of libidinal transfer. In fact, the discovery of "anatomical difference," Silverman affirms, leads to a "mortification of language," one even more severe than the blow dealt by the linguistic signifier, and which Silverman sees potentially as "the atrophy of signification itself" (GL, p. 23).

Silverman's description of this atrophy follows closely the installation of the general equivalent at the heart of the subject's symbolic economy. This installation is also a usurpation, a rigidification of the operations of desire. "A language dies," Silverman mourns, "when one of its signifiers succeeds in passing itself off as the signified to which every other signifier ultimately refers." This is the mother's psychic function, but as we have seen the maternal signifier stands in this privileged place only in a "groundless" way, and in such a way that later symbolizations retroactively determine her meaning. The usurping signifier commands a very different relationship to displacement. And so Silverman continues:

This imposture requires two steps. First, a signifier must present itself as autonomous and self-defining by erasing the prior signifier or
series of signifiers upon which it relies for its meanings. Then it must
install itself in the place of origin. As we have seen, although the maternal signifier actually occupies the latter position, it is incapable of
masquerading as a signified, since there is no earlier term to which
it can ever refer. It marks the site where meaning finally and fully
fails. It is classically the paternal signifier which claims to constitute
the bedrock of meaning, and it does so by writing over the maternal
signifier. (GL, p. 24)

This is a close description of the process that Goux calls the "ascension" of the
general equivalent of the Dead Father and his Law, or what Lacan called variously
the Name of the Father or the "paternal metaphor." It is obvious that Silverman
sees the "maternal metaphor" as more crucial for psychic life than the installation
of the paternal metaphor as described by Lacan. For without the mother and her
"failure" of meaning, "there can be neither signifier nor passion of the signifier"
(WS, pp. 122–23). It is she who gives rise to the free form of displacement,
which then reciprocally determines what she can mean. And consequently, Silverman concludes, "in spite of all of the social and ideological encroachments that
work to impose retroactive restrictions upon her, our originary love-object may
be the closest any of us ever comes to pure limitlessness" (WS, p. 123). We must
understand the challenge of the following imperative: "It is through loving the
mother that we are able to love the world" (WS, p. 123).

Loving the mother in the manner that Silverman desires is no simple affair.
It seems almost impossible to think what this might mean. It would involve accessing the mother at a level beyond or before that installed in the Oedipus complex,
accessing the maternal signifier in a mode not sanctioned by castration, by the
Father, by the Law. In my account, it would mean imagining libidinal transfer
from the mother in a series of exchanges not under the sway of the general equivalent. And to describe the form this would take, Silverman reaches back in the psychoanalytic story to what we can define as "forgotten form[s] of symbolization,"

one of which is that which inheres in the working of female subjectivity prior to the castration complex, a mode of relation to the mother that Silverman calls "Girl Love." This is a "love" beyond or before the Law, a love that gives affective transfer its true form. "By uncovering the maternal signifier" usurped by the Law of the paternal metaphor, such love shows "the father to have only borrowed 'clothes.'" The chain of libidinal transfers and the visual possibilities for perceptual identity would be set free, giving us "access to an entirely new kind of symbolization—one without either authentication or limits" (GL, p. 24).

The picture of Man Ray's photography that we have inherited from the recent literature sets itself against many of the terms that this chapter has been exploring. In fact, the most advanced approach to Dada photography reads Man Ray's practice as offering up a series of objects "able to hold out against exchange."[20] This is a reading that sees Man Ray's photographs holding out, in a specifically photographic manner, against the regime of general equivalency—so many readymade objects of economic exchange tied to a specific spot by the actions of cast shadows, by a redoubling of photography's existence as material trace, as an index.

Linked and older accounts of Dada and Surrealist photography saw the doubles created in crucial early photographic images by Man Ray such as *Homme* and *Femme,* the object doubled by its shadow, as not only a homage to Marcel Duchamp's concern with shadows and the indexical sign, but a specifically photographic concern with doubling.[21] This doubling could be given over to a reading that saw it in analogy to the form of double articulation or repetition that within linguistics creates the base condition of meaning, the signifier of signification—in primal words like "mama" and "papa"—thus seeing in the avant-garde deployment of photography a true concern with the photograph as a form of the "graphic," as an invasive mode of "writing" inserted into the domain of modernist visuality.

Inasmuch as I have been investigating how Man Ray's Dada project might at times be given over not to holding out against exchange but to repressed forms of exchange—to an exchange almost without limit—and also to how his practice of photography might challenge the limitations of the linguistic signifier, this reading departs from those earlier accounts. What I am seeking is not the insertion of "writing" into modernist visuality, but a new or redeemed form of visuality counter to modernism's concerns. This Dada search also necessitates a new model of the photographic, one implicitly introduced in Silverman's recent work as well.

"I never worked as Duchamp did," Man Ray once asserted. "I never said that objects were *readymade*. Duchamp found it revolutionary simply to place a phrase or his name on an object found at the hardware store. No: I needed not one thing but two things. Two things which, in themselves, had no relation and which . . . I placed together to create by contrast a sort of plastic poetry."[22] Man Ray called his creation of objects—almost invariably made to be photographed—not a practice of the "readymade," but instead "Objects of My Affection." Accentuating the "ludic" or the "popular," as Rosalind Krauss has observed,[23] Man Ray's moniker also prioritizes *affect,* prioritizes—perhaps—love. It is in this light that I want to see the "plastic poetry" that Man Ray derived from the collision of at least two objects as a figuration of the chain of signification at the heart of affective transfer, of its operations of displacement and condensation.

The *Dadaphoto* gives us the new perspective on Man Ray's objects and photographs that we need to begin to open up this reading. In this image, the *portemanteau* or depicted "coat stand" has a strange relationship to its normative function, as it is not serving immediately as an armature for other objects to be placed on, ultimately to cover it up, but itself serves to mask another object, to stand before and in front of the female body (of the Baroness? of the "mother"?).[24] In fact, the *portemanteau* depicted here performs an inversion of its traditional function, a precise reversal too, we might say, of modernist concerns with structural transparency, as an internal armature—a coat stand—comes to be placed as an external skin on other objects, operating more like a surfacing of the repressed.

This is, then, a *portemanteau* that has its own armature standing behind and beneath it, which "carries" its form and perhaps even depicts in this a model for what we might say was Man Ray's or Dada's particular model of the photograph (Stieglitz's *Portrait of Dorothy True* could be opened up by all that I am in the process of saying, for example). We seemingly face an intimation of a chain of signification, a set of visual displacements propped upon one another, and this chain forms the basis of what the *Dadaphoto* entails.[25] This chain also reconnects us to the female form, which I am reading also as a figuration of the maternal signifier, beneath the appearance to us of the world's objects and its forms, operating not according to a regime of differentiation and separation, but instead of radical contiguity and similarity.

Everywhere we look in Man Ray's photography, we can see intimations of this same chain of signifiers, the tools of "perceptual identity" opening up the possibility of "affective transfer." We also often find the photograph conceived not only as the form of the conveyance of affect, but as a form propped upon—if not defined by—the female form or body. Reconceived in this way, the photograph becomes the sign of a more general Dada project.

Such is the case with Man Ray's *Woman*. Here, as in *Man* (in one print later itself retitled *Woman*), an object is doubled by its shadow, which now in the wake of viewing the *Dadaphoto* we can begin to see in a new way. As in the *Dadaphoto*, we see "two" objects, a chain of signifiers, or we see, conversely, an object displacing its form onto and into the world, producing the contact and the contiguity at the basis of libidinal transfer as much as it is at the basis of the indexical photographic sign itself. We also see the "condensation" of these two objects, the invention from this libidinal transfer of what we must call a "new," expanded form.

What separates *Woman* from *Man,* however, is the intensity of the former's introspection, the mode in which this image also reflects on what a photograph might be thought to be. Of course the objects that make up Man Ray's *Woman* are everyday objects, objects from the domestic sphere formerly of woman and mother alike—clothespins, for example—but they are also tools of the photographer's trade, and bind or fuse the objects that go into the production and development of the photographic image with, once more, the form of woman or the mother.

To see the doubles and shadows in Man Ray's photographs as not only—or merely—indexical signs that betray a self-reflexive photographic logic, to see these signs instead as a self-expansive intimation of a chain of displacements that

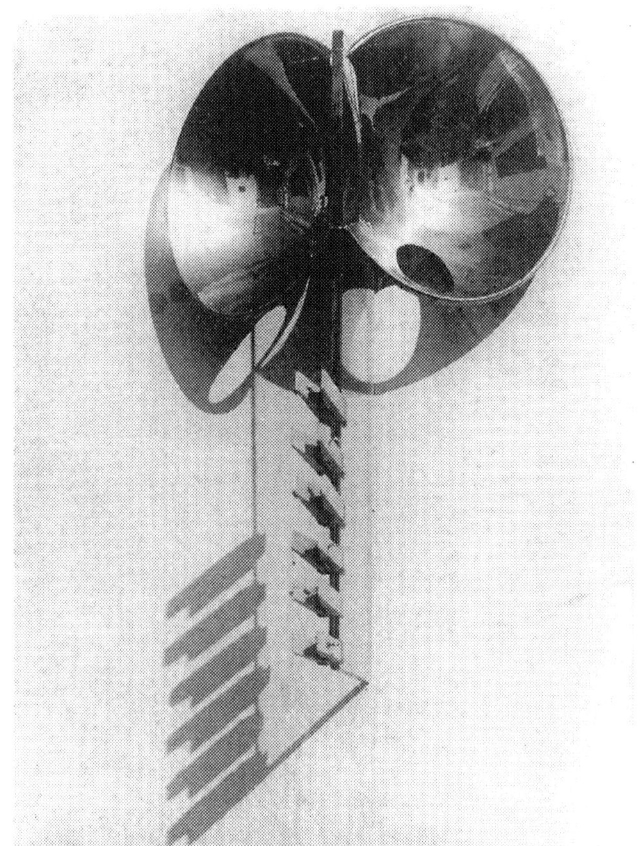

Man Ray, *Woman,* 1918. Gelatin silver print, Gilman Paper Company Collection. © 2005 Artists Rights Society (ARS), New York/ADAGP, Paris/Man Ray Trust.

the photograph can also carry, is to link such images to the manner in which Man Ray often expanded the "life" and affect of a given work. I am thinking in this regard of a photograph that Man Ray entitled *Moving Sculpture,* a still image of laundry on a clothesline fluttering in the wind. Another typical Dada engagement with the everyday—a space and "economy" once associated almost exclusively with the feminine—*Moving Sculpture* also exists as another sign of Man Ray's dialogue with Duchamp, as the image's wafting laundry recalls Duchamp's photographic experiments on what he called the *Draft Pistons,* from the section of his *Large Glass* devoted to the figure of the Bride. And yet, as an everyday image of hanging clothes set out to dry, *Moving Sculpture* must be connected directly to the "sculpture" of a clothes "hanger" that Man Ray's *Portemanteau* also depicts. We are in the presence of another object related to what we might now call Man Ray's principle of the *portemanteau,* and of the *Dadaphoto,* a principle operating along the line of a chain of billowing displacements.

In this regard, Man Ray's title *Moving Sculpture* resonates in two significant directions: toward a sheer engagement with mobility, which would be linked to the exploration of signifying chains, of the photograph no longer thought of as "retentive" and fixed, but as open and connected to a chain moving both backward and forward in space and time. And Man Ray's title also prioritizes the fact that such displacement might be seen as "moving" in the emotional sense. In fact, Man Ray constructed as one of his most important pieces a literal "moving sculpture," the ticking metronome used as the basis for the artist's *Object to Be Destroyed.* This is a piece whose own understanding of that which is "moving" was itself double, as it was this object that opened up the dynamic of what Man Ray referred to as the "destructible" or "indestructible" object around a logic of photographing and remaking the object, the object's disappearance and its subsequent reproduction in a new form.

Object to Be Destroyed was a sculpture that reversed the dialectics of *Moving Sculpture*; instead of a fixed photographic image of moving objects, the piece now put the photograph into literal motion, attaching a photographic image of a woman's eye to the metronome's ticking hand. For Man Ray, setting the photograph into motion in this way was not simply an opening of the piece onto an

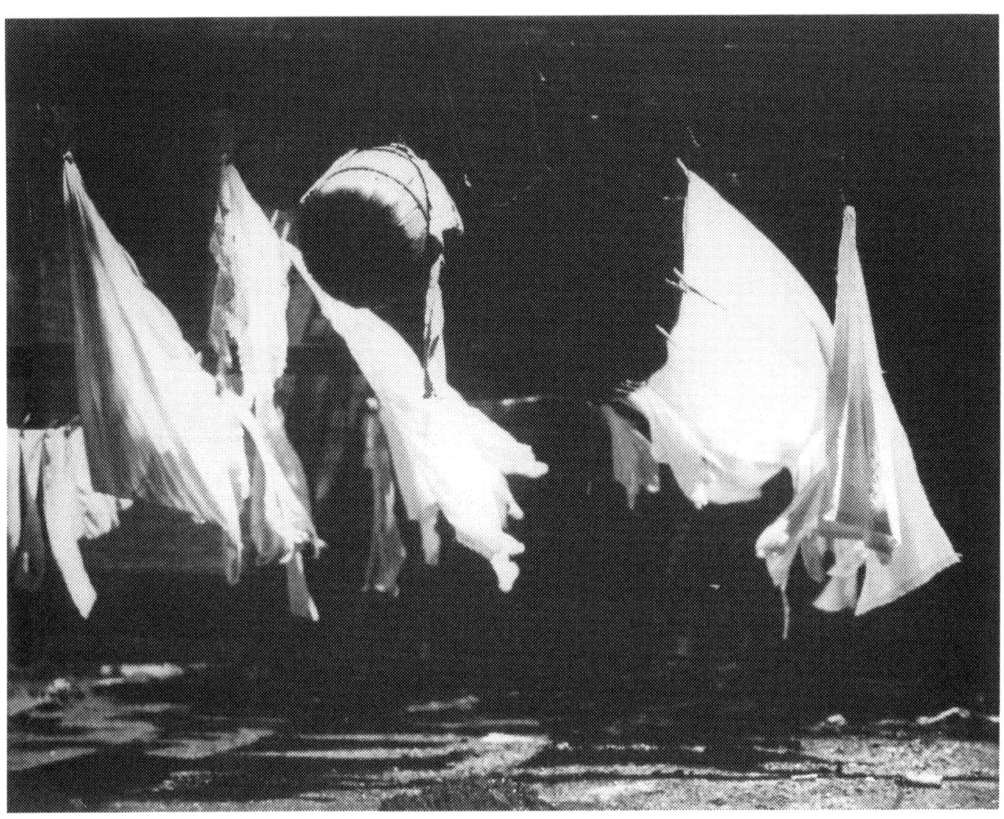

Man Ray, *Moving Sculpture,* 1920. Photograph. Image courtesy National Gallery of Art, Washington. © 2005 Artists Rights Society (ARS), New York/ADAGP, Paris/Man Ray Trust.

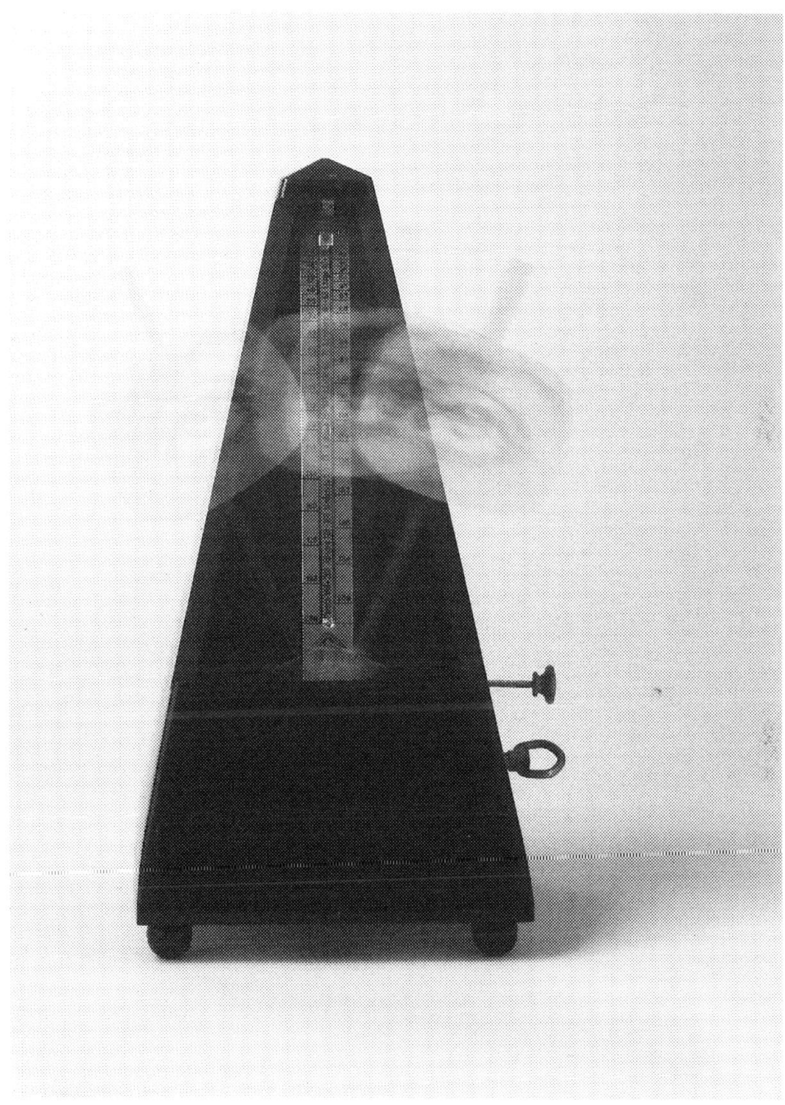

Man Ray, *Object to Be Destroyed,* 1923 (1965 edition). Metronome with moving photograph attached, height: 22 cm. Moderna Museet, Stockholm. © 2005 Artists Rights Society (ARS), New York/ADAGP, Paris/Man Ray Trust.

incipiently cinematic dimension; it linked the photograph once more to the object of desire, and specifically to the implicitly maternal *Lost Object* as Man Ray in fact named a later reconstruction of the piece. From the "lost object" to the "indestructible object," from destruction to rebirth, we follow once more the effects and the characteristics of the signifying chain.[26]

As Man Ray's *Moving Sculpture* attests, it should by now be clear that a strange node of connections existed in Man Ray and Duchamp's Dada practice around what I have been calling *portemanteau* objects. For of course, if the *Dadaphoto* was "conceived for a friend" and that friend was Duchamp, we must register the photograph's response to those two of Duchamp's previous readymades that were themselves *portemanteaux* of a sort: Duchamp's *Trebuchet* and the hanging *Hat Rack,* one readymade infamously nailed to the floor in Duchamp's studio, the other suspended from the ceiling.

Duchamp's name for his practice of choosing store-bought (not always industrial) items—the "readymade"—was in fact a term that came from the garment or fashion industry, and so these objects expand on that sartorial and commercial, supplemental and bodily origin. And yet what has always seemed to me crucial about both of Duchamp's *portemanteau* readymades is not just their domestic or everyday status, nor their existence as somewhat creaky "industrial" objects, nor their own concerted anthropomorphism, their phallic limbs or spidery appendages, their closeness—as the kind of supplemental armature that any coat stand is—to the human body. What seems crucial about both readymades is their internal repetition, their concatenation of the same series of four hangers in *Trebuchet* or the identical "arms" in *Hat Rack.* This registers something like an industrial logic of seriality to be sure. But perhaps one can also press its reading into the domain of what we might call the libidinal chain of signification that this chapter has been exploring. The displacement at the heart of the alternate symbolic economy reclaimed by Dada might also be seen, that is, as internal to the mode of artistic production that the Dada readymade and photograph represented.

These *portemanteaux* in fact found themselves repeated, remade or resignified, in vastly different circumstances, much like the future life of Man Ray's

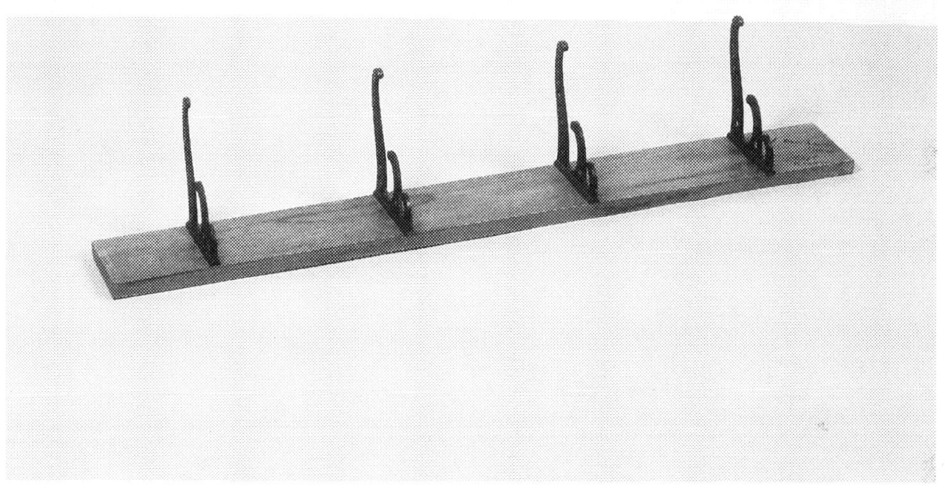

Marcel Duchamp, *Trébuchet (Trap),* 1917 (1964 edition). Assisted readymade, 19 × 100 × 13 cm. Musée National d'Art Moderne, Centre Georges Pompidou, Paris. Photograph © CNAC/MNAM/Dist. Réunion des Musées Nationaux / Art Resource, New York. © 2005 Artists Rights Society (ARS), New York/ADAGP, Paris/Estate of Marcel Duchamp.

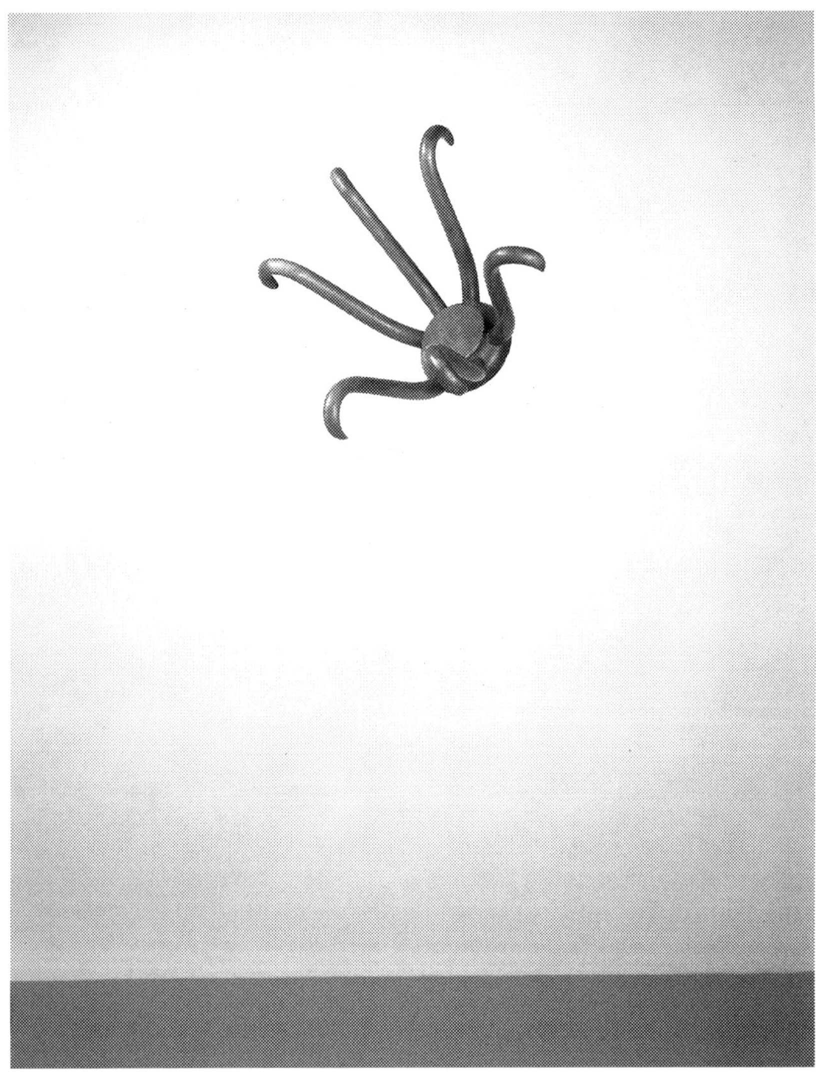

Marcel Duchamp, *Hat Rack,* 1917 (1964 edition). Assisted readymade, height: 27 cm, diameter: 44.5 cm. Musée National d'Art Moderne, Centre Georges Pompidou, Paris. Photograph © CNAC/MNAM/Dist. Réunion des Musées Nationaux/Art Resource, New York. © 2005 Artists Rights Society (ARS), New York/ADAGP, Paris/Estate of Marcel Duchamp.

Object to Be Destroyed. Most famously, this occurred at the 1938 Surrealist Exhibition in Paris, presided over by Man Ray and Duchamp, who took the opportunity here and in later Surrealist exhibition designs to revive a host of Dada strategies if not actual Dada objects. With the mannequins installed in the "Surrealist City" at the 1938 exhibition we have a direct evocation of the mannequin-object of the *Dadaphoto,* an evocation made iron-clad by Man Ray's placement of a *portemanteau* next to his own mannequin at the exhibition. This object was later separated off from the female body to become Man Ray's *Porte-manteau esthetique* of 1938. Like *Trebuchet,* it presents a series of hangers, in Man Ray's installation now actually hung with coats. And in his autobiography *Self Portrait,* Man Ray claimed that Duchamp proposed simply to use his mannequin as "a coat rack."[27] In actuality though, what this meant is that Duchamp dressed his mannequin as a man, attiring it in a reversal of his own masquerade as Rrose Sélavy with suit jacket and men's clothes.

But Man Ray had already resignified the *Dadaphoto,* attached it to another chain, at the very moment of its production. Produced initially in 1919–1920 (which perhaps explains Man Ray's misremembering of the 1921 date of *New York Dada*), the *Dadaphoto* paralleled Man Ray's object *Obstruction* made at this same time. *Obstruction* is an "object" constructed from a series of identical clothes hangers, once more carrying the logic of the *portemanteau* forward. As Man Ray once described the mode of assembly of this item:

> You begin with one hanger attached to the ceiling. In the two holes at the extremity of the hanger introduce the hooks of two more hangers. Into these hooks eight hangers and so on until the sixth row has thirty-two hangers. Of course, if enough hangers are available, this mathematical progression may be carried onto infinity. The increasing confusion is apparent only to the eye and is to be desired.

As perhaps was the case with the *Dadaphoto,* Man Ray evidently thought of this object as his answer to the structurally transparent forms of modernist abstraction (in other descriptions, he played on the homophony between "abstraction"

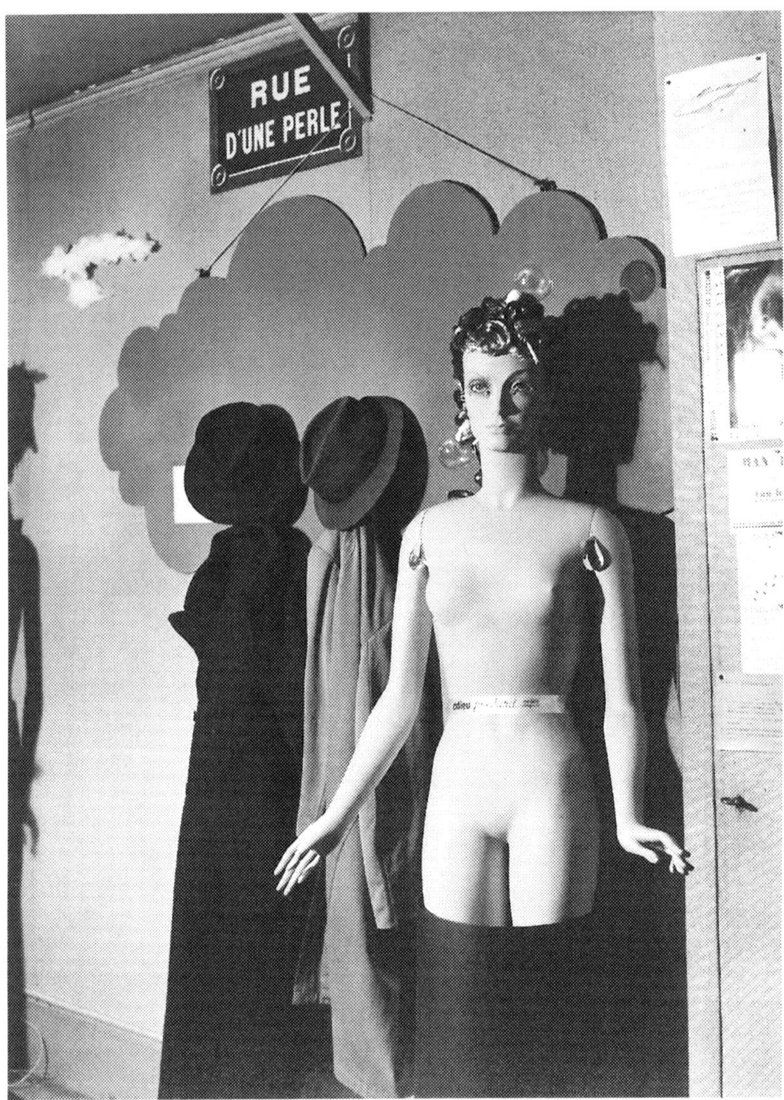

Man Ray, *Mannequin,* for *Exposition Internationale du Surréalisme,* Galerie Beaux-Arts, Paris, 1938. © 2005 Artists Rights Society (ARS), New York/ADAGP, Paris/Man Ray Trust.

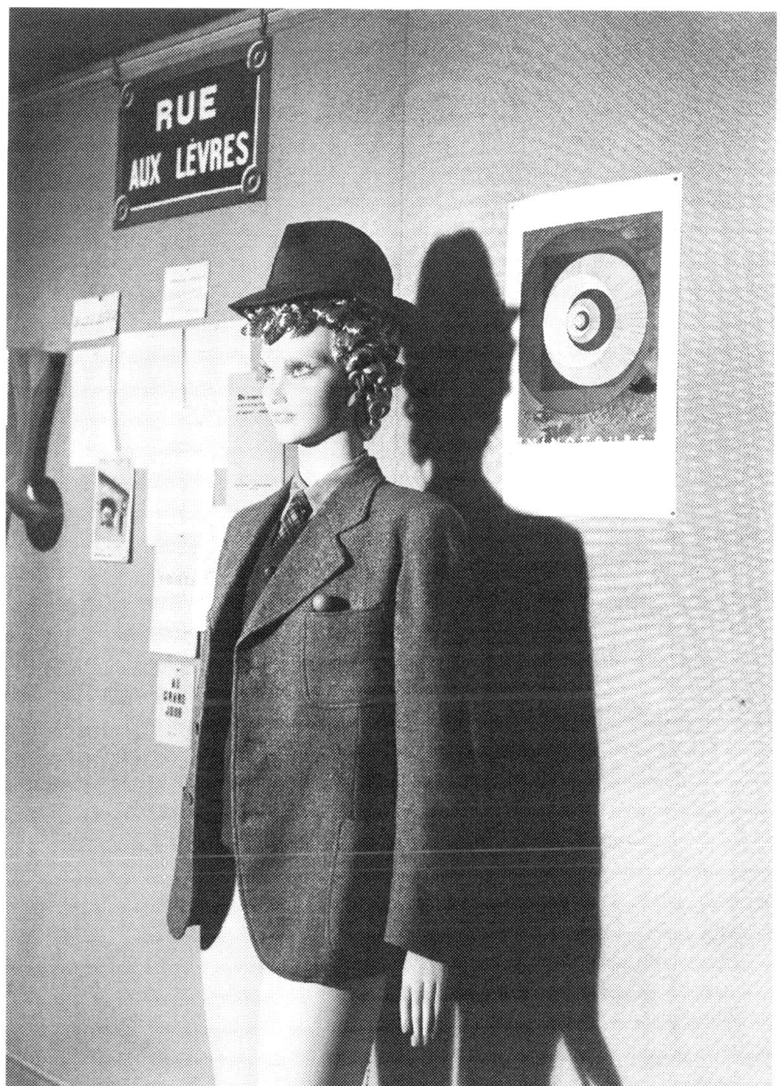

Duchamp, *Mannequin,* for *Exposition Internationale du Surréalisme,* Galerie Beaux-Arts, Paris, 1938. © 2005 Artists Rights Society (ARS), New York/ADAGP, Paris/Man Ray Trust.

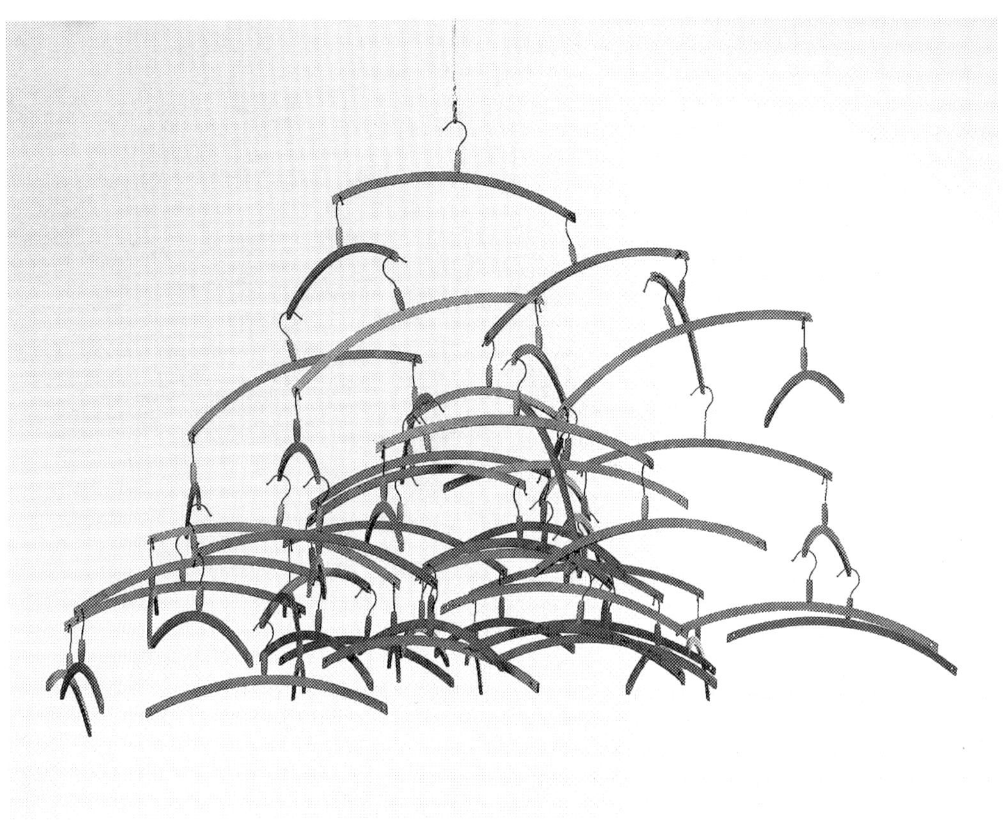

Man Ray, *Obstruction,* 1961 (replica of 1920 original). Sixty-three wooden coat hangers, $110 \times 120 \times 120$ cm ($43^5/_{16} \times 43^1/_4 \times 47^1/_4''$). Moderna Museet, Stockholm. Image courtesy National Gallery of Art, Washington. © 2005 Artists Rights Society (ARS), New York/ADAGP, Paris/Man Ray Trust.

and "obstruction" as words).[28] Indeed, what needs to be explained in approaching the connection of *Dadaphoto* and *Obstruction* lies, first, in the ways in which each is involved in masking, in the creation of sedimented layers, in visual "obstruction." This is a concern that runs throughout Man Ray's project, especially in the Dada moment, from the model standing behind the coat stand in *Dadaphoto,* to the white stamp occluding her genitals, to the visual barrier of *Obstruction,* or the underlying "mystery" of the wrapped objects of *Enigma of Isidore Ducasse.* But what also needs now to be registered is how this visual layering characteristic of the logic of the *portemanteau* was refigured in *Obstruction* as a literal chain of objects, emanating in a proliferation whose extent could be, for Man Ray, "infinite."

It would seem that the *Dadaphoto* has been marginalized in accounts of Man Ray and the Dada movement because it presents, initially, the least "photographic" or self-reflexive of the artist's productions. In other words, the modernist bias of our approach to Dada and other antimodernist avant-gardes still shows. And yet Man Ray obviously considered the *Dadaphoto* to be in some way central to his project. The "doubling" of the *Dadaphoto* is not immediately, or procedurally, related to the photographic apparatus (like the shadows or the ashes in other Man Ray photographs). It presents a doubling, rather, that takes the photograph *outside of itself,* which is another way of understanding what the activity of displacement might in fact entail. And yet in so doing, the *Dadaphoto* does in the end present a reflection on what the photograph might be thought to be. This new conception of photography in turn helps us to understand in new ways the centrality of photography to the Dada movement. It helps us as well to argue for the renewed centrality of Dada uses and conceptions of the photograph to the problems and artistic practice that we face today.

For to model photography on that which Silverman calls the "maternal signifier" is not an unknown proposition within photographic history and theory.[29] Silverman reminds us that our greatest elegy to the medium, Roland Barthes's *Camera Lucida,* presents nothing but this reconception, the search in photography for a lost object, indeed, for the mother. However, Barthes's mournful search also represents the acme of a certain understanding of photography's "indexicality" and "pastness," a theorization emerging like the Owl of Minerva only at the moment of the radical technical transformation of photography that we have since observed. At the present moment, we need to begin to reclaim other models of the photograph than the one that reaches its climax in Barthes's account. "In *Camera Lucida,*" Silverman writes, "Barthes makes painfully evident the temporal limits of the conventional analogue image. The photograph in which he is able to see his mother does not return her to him; it merely says, over and over, 'this was'" (GL, p. 25). The reconception proposed by Silverman then recodes Barthes's account. The model of affective transfer, or what Silverman also names "girl love," is not based "upon representational access to an irretrievably lost mother, but rather upon her recovery in a new form." And so "it can neither be depicted nor enabled by a photograph whose value is primarily indexical. It requires one capable of assuming its place within a *chain of signification*" (GL, p. 25).

This is the chain that the *Dadaphoto* and its "two-layered palimpsest" might be imagined as presenting—self-reflexively, but also self-expansively. This was a statement and thus a model of the photograph where we are shown visually that "everything we see is propped upon something we have previously seen— that perception is a semiotic event." Every photograph is this kind of double, then, a double of that which has already been seen, a visual object fully dependent on a structure of "seeing again." And the transfer of affect thus enabled simultaneously "releases photography from the univocality of the 'this-has-been,' and into the open-ended temporality of 'becoming'" (GL, p. 25).

Like "the signifiers leading back to the mother," the nested objects of Man Ray's images and of the *Dadaphoto* also figure the "path of displacement away from her, and the infinity of directions in which it can move." To enter into such an understanding of Dada photography is to enter a new conception of the signifying conditions of Dada in general. It is to find in the Dada photograph a modality of visual exchange based on contiguity and similitude, one that is groundless in its operation and infinite in its capacity for affirmation. It is to enter a symbolic order deprived, joyously, of the Law of the General Equivalent.[30] For the symbolic order of girl love or affective transfer, the world loved according to the metaphor of the mother, would be an order that "has ceased to be the domain of the law, and become instead the domain of love" (GL, p. 27). It is thus hardly an "order" at all.

It is in this way, finally, that I understand the additional label "KEEP SMILING" attached to the *Dadaphoto* in *New York Dada*. We sense here that the chain of signifiers of Dada symbolization itself is opened onto love and thus to joy. What is joyful in Dada, in fact, is the displacement of signifiers, and their endless expansion. What is joyful is the transfer of affect, and thus of love. And it is this "joy" that returns us, in the wake of our detour through Dada photography, to Picabia and to the beginning of the end of his Paris Dada years.

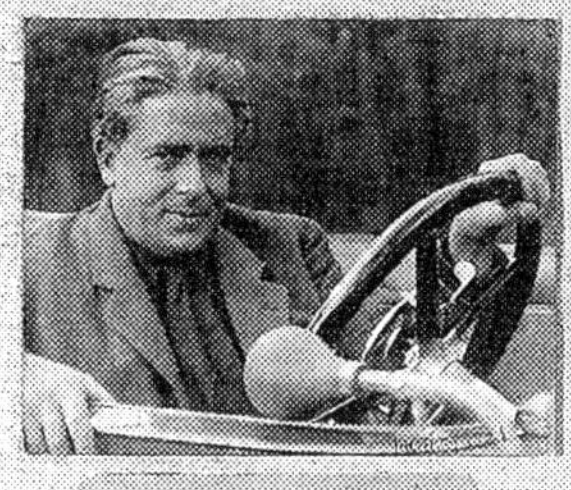

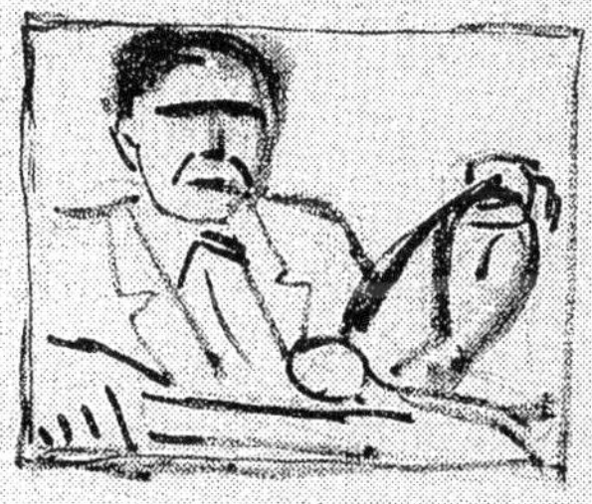

Francis Picabia, *The Merry Widow,* 1921. Oil, paper, and photograph on canvas, 92 × 73 cm. (36$^{1}/_{4}$ × 28$^{3}/_{4}$″). Private Collection, Paris. © 2005 Artists Rights Society (ARS), New York/ADAGP, Paris/Estate of Francis Picabia.

Prolem sine matre creatam: Dada Abstraction

Solitude can be compared to a lamp that fucks.

—*Francis Picabia, "Un effet facile," 1922*[1]

It is clear that the world is purely parodic, in other words, that each thing seen is the parody of another, or is the same thing in a deceptive form.

—*Georges Bataille, "The Solar Anus," 1927*[2]

DE TE FABULA NARRATUR

Here is an image of Picabia.[3] He is smiling, or he is not. For we stare at two images of Picabia: a photograph and a drawing. They seem related to one another, a duplication or a proliferating chain, like two stills flitting by in a film strip. And yet they are not exactly the same. The photograph was a gift from Man Ray, and in it we see a portrait of the artist as a race car driver, with Picabia married to his machine, holding on tight to its various parts. However, despite this conjunction—of artist and machine, and of photography and drawing—Picabia titled the work in which Man Ray's image appears a "widow." And notwithstanding the evidently grim result of the drawing's automatization by the photograph—for Picabia's "self"-portrait seems to have been copied off of the gleaming surface of his image at the hands of another—the artist called this widow "joyous."

A year before Picabia produced *La veuve joyeuse (The Merry Widow)*, Duchamp had inaugurated his authorial alter ego Rose Sélavy with a 1920 construction in which a simulated French window became (through its title) a *Fresh Widow.* The "Bride" of Duchamp's *Large Glass* had been severed from her Bachelors—painting and drawing had been abandoned—becoming mournful and dark in the process, a completely opaque object that reversed the earlier Dada work's transparency through the substitution of black leather panes in the place of glass. Picabia's "widow," by contrast, seemed less a severance—less a disjunction—than a conjunction, a scene of combination and admixture. It was a "joyous widow" rather than a melancholic one; proliferating (a figure of promiscuity?) rather than closed up and shut off. It was, we might imagine, a "widow" let loose or "liberated" beyond the reach of the (patriarchal) law. But within the formal terms of Picabia's collage, what would this "liberation," this "joyousness," mean?

More directly than Duchamp's 1920 construction, Picabia's *The Merry Widow* reiterates the form and the terms of the *Large Glass (The Bride Stripped Bare by Her Bachelors, Even)*. Like the allegorical self-portrait contained in the *Glass,* Picabia presents a doubled self-portrait, a single self-image erupting into two. More, this multiple self is now presented in the vertical format of the *Glass,* as if with two "zones" one atop the other.[4] Photography was above and Drawing below, an allegory of artistic media—like the Tableau Dada or the Dessin Dada or the *Dadaphoto*—distilled from Duchamp's original plan to have the zone of the Bride, above, explicitly determined by the methods of photography, and the Bachelors, below, the products of mechanical drawing. *The Merry Widow* thus reiterated the central position that photography occupied at the heart of the Dada project.

We have seen, with Man Ray, how radically the Dada models of photography depart from traditional definitions of its properties, indeed, how photography for Dada opened up a scene of alternate or entirely repressed symbolic economies. Ironically, for Duchamp, photography was to have determined the "abstract" portion of his *Glass,* the zone of the Bride contrasted in every way with

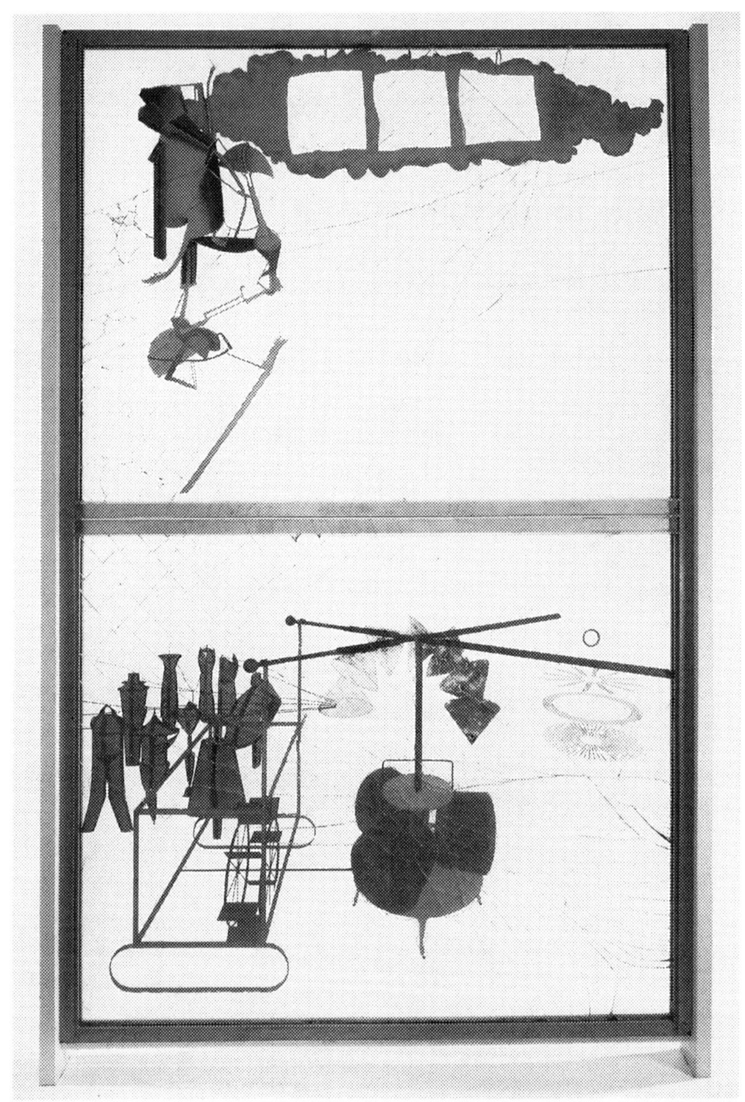

Marcel Duchamp, *The Bride Stripped Bare by Her Bachelors, Even (The Large Glass),* 1915–1923. Oil, varnish, lead foil, lead wire, and dust on two glass panels, 277.5 × 175.9 cm (109¼ × 69¼″). Philadelphia Museum of Art, Bequest of Katherine S. Dreier. Photograph © Philadelphia Museum of Art / Art Resource, New York. © 2005 Artists Rights Society (ARS), New York/ADAGP, Paris/Estate of Marcel Duchamp.

the perspectival and representational space preserved in the zone of the Bachelors below. The photograph in Dada thus was also somehow linked to gender and femininity again, or from the start. And in this vein, we must observe that photography had been crucial to the entire series of mechanomorphs that Picabia had been producing since 1915, initiating them at the same moment as Duchamp's first efforts toward the *Glass.*

There was, for example, the crucial—initiatory—1915 depiction of Alfred Stieglitz as a camera. Or there was the slightly later *Portrait of Max Goth,* an image like *The Merry Widow* holding photography and drawing in suspension, with one literally supplanting the other, automating it from within—a photograph of the sitter's face, like the signs that would eventually float through Picabia's *L'oeil cacodylate,* attached to a line drawing of his body. With such images, we can begin to see that for Picabia the readymade, as a Dada strategy, was always inherently connected to the photograph. If Picabia's mechanomorphs pictorialized Duchamp's readymades, returning them to the scene of representation, turning their found object status into an industrially drawn image—created by tracing, by stencils, by ruler and compass—the new conditions of such an image were attached by Picabia to the machinic form of image production that is the photograph: infinitely reproducible; physically tied to its referent; disconnected from the expressive control of its author; and freed from the traditional skills of previous modes of image making.

The mechanomorphs, like Duchamp's *Large Glass* alongside them, were an example of "photography by other means."[5] And yet, the initial trajectory of the mechanomorph was, as in the *Portrait of Max Goth,* one of supplantation, the photograph's eventual displacement of the traditional media of art altogether. Already by 1917, just two years after the initiation of the series to which the *Portrait of Stieglitz* belongs, Picabia dropped the pretense of drawing altogether, selecting actual photographs that were altered in minor ways and published, readymade, as mechanomorphs on the cover of his magazine *391* (for example, *Américaine,* or *Peigne,* a title shared by one of Duchamp's most important readymades).[6]

The Merry Widow returns to the earlier promise of the mechanomorphs as a kind of "photography by other means." Now drawing and painting were not

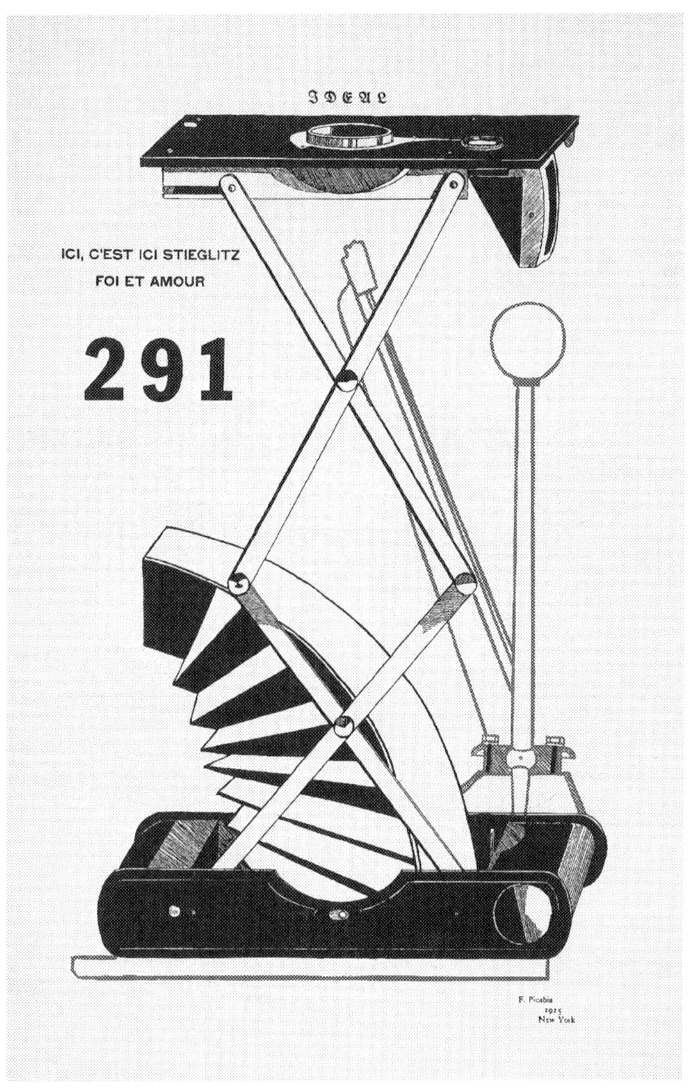

Francis Picabia, *Ici, c'est ici Stieglitz,* 1915. Published in *291* 5–6 (July–August 1915). Research Library, The Getty Research Institute, Los Angeles. © 2005 Artists Rights Society (ARS), New York/ADAGP, Paris/Estate of Francis Picabia.

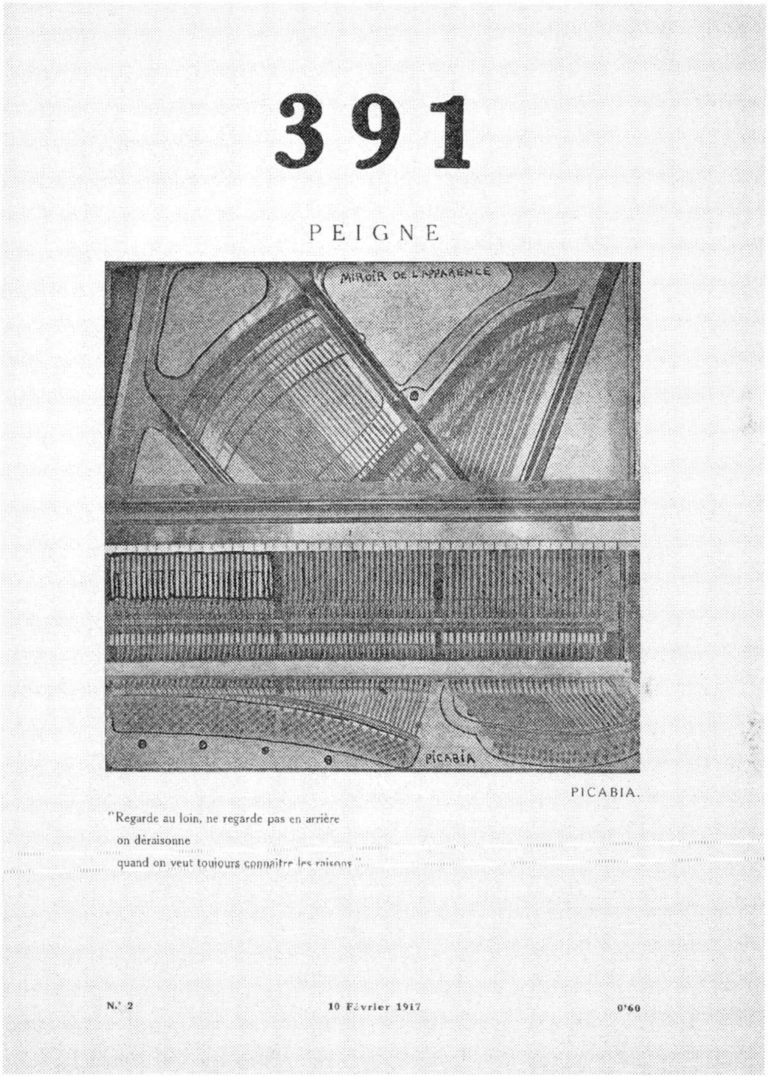

391

PEIGNE

Francis Picabia, *Peigne (Comb)*, 1917. Cover image of *391* 2 (February 10, 1917). Research Library, The Getty Research Institute, Los Angeles. © 2005 Artists Rights Society (ARS), New York/ADAGP, Paris/Estate of Francis Picabia.

replaced by the photograph, but were *infected* by it, as drawing became a product of the photographic, copied or directly traced off of the photograph's mechanically produced surface. Picabia's clarification of *this* model of the mechanomorph (my point is that there was not just one) seems to have been provoked by quite specific events. For Picabia's *The Merry Widow* was created in response to the exhibition of *L'oeil cacodylate* in the late fall of 1921.

As was so often the case for Picabia, *L'oeil cacodylate* had been submitted in 1921 to the Salon d'Automne as part of a deliberate pair. Like *La Sainte-Vierge* accompanied by *La jeune fille,* or like Picabia's submission to the 1921 Salon des Indépendants of two paintings with linked but opposed titles, *La lierre unique eunuque (Unique Eunuch Ivy)* and *Le double monde (The Double World),* these pairs circled repetitively around the condition of the inimitable and the copy, the unique and the double. Thus the companion of the singular *L'oeil cacodylate* was titled, appropriately, in the mode of the multiple: *Les yeux chauds (Hot Eyes).* And this painting (now destroyed) was a mechanomorph.[7] It contained both figurative and machinic elements, kitsch colors, diagrammatic lines, and written inscriptions, appearing as a kind of object-portrait or dubious "homage" (as it was emblazoned) to the Salon president Frantz Jourdain. For the first time, however, in the face of this painting, Picabia's mechanomorphic method was discovered. The French newspaper *Le Matin* published an exposé, having located in a popular science journal the diagram (for part of an airplane turbine) that Picabia precisely copied to produce the piece. The two images were reproduced together, showing even some of the painter's "poetic" inscriptions to have been copied entirely from the diagram. Picabia's response: "I congratulate the newspaper *Le Matin* not only for having discovered the secrets, but for understanding them."[8]

The Merry Widow was another response. The work of appropriation or the copy that lay at the heart of Picabia's mechanomorphs was both confirmed here as a photographic principle and (however subtly) shifted. Now, rather than being replaced by the photograph, the work of art starts from it. Or rather, it departs from it. The photograph lies as an initial model for the work of art—a model that does not replace but lies in communication with both painting and drawing, which proliferate from the photograph as starting point. However, to place the photograph at the origin of the work of art is to place what has been called a "copy without an original" at this place of origin, an origin that then must be described as without origin. We seem once again to have veered close to the groundless ground that belongs to the maternal signifier, or at least to a symbolic economy outside the law of the general equivalent form. It was such an economy that now allowed Picabia to begin to shift the terrain of the form of the mechanomorph.

That this terrain *was* being altered Picabia made clear at the beginning of 1922, when *The Merry Widow* was submitted with its own companion piece to that year's Salon des Indépendants. The "widow's" partner was given the unusual title *Chapeau de paille? (Straw Hat?),* its strange concluding question mark enlivened into another spiraling tail. Again Picabia's pairing was made explicit on the level of titles, in this case a product of both stemming from the milieu of music and the theater, being appropriations of two specific comic operas, Franz Lehár's *La veuve joyeuse* (1905) and Eugène Labiche's *Un chapeau de paille d'Italie* (1850).[9] The latter opera, perhaps significantly, is the story of the search for a feminine lost object, an erotic object, a precious Italian straw hat stolen during a *liaison dangeureuse.*

Liaison or linkage in some way represented the stakes of Picabia's work. For *Straw Hat?* returns to the mechanomorph as Dada diagram, examining both the mechanomorph's lines and its verbal inscriptions as so many relational vectors and connection points.[10] Here, a dissolute string links two readymade objects and two names: Picabia's printed on his calling card, cut out in the shape of a heart (or palette); and singer Marthe Chenal's on the invitation to her 1921 New Year's Eve party, planned by Picabia, the "Reveillon Cacodylate." Along with this, a line of text borrows the teasing device of Duchamp's relational title *Tu m'* of 1918, opened as it is to a connection with the activity of the reader or spectator, invited to fill in the blank: "M. . . . . . . pour celui qui le regarde!"

However, in *Straw Hat?,* both these directional vectors cross over one another, forming an unmistakable X, as if the very space and immaterial linkage of the Dada diagram were being self-consciously canceled or indeed crossed out. Instead, in *Straw Hat?* the diagrammatic line becomes singular and opaque, less an immaterial connection or vector than the scene of a kind of graphic thickening,

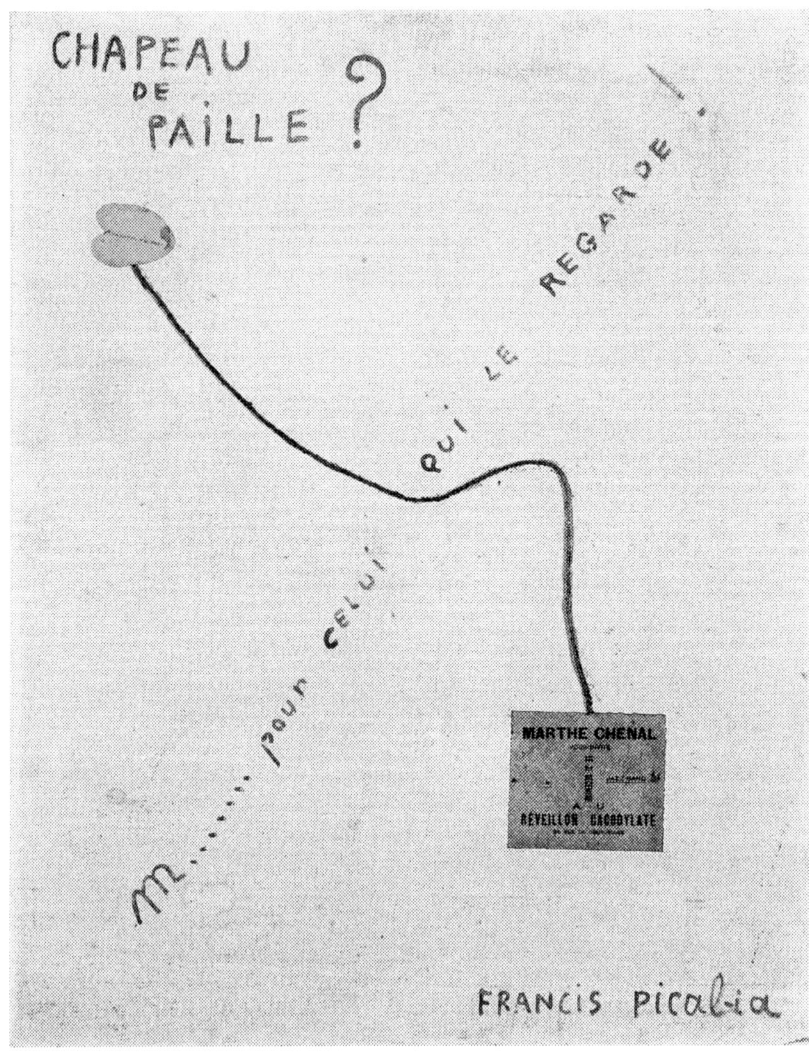

Francis Picabia, *Straw Hat?*, c. 1921. Oil, string, and invitation card glued on canvas, 92.3 × 73.5 cm. Musée National d'Art Moderne, Centre Georges Pompidou. Photograph © CNAC/MNAM/Dist. Réunion des Musées Nationaux/Art Resource, New York. © 2005 Artists Rights Society (ARS), New York/ADAGP, Paris/Estate of Francis Picabia.

a viscousness, as Picabia's "line"-as-string lands with a thud on the empty canvas, the chance operations of the *Three Standard Stoppages* played now against not only the general equivalent as standard or as measure, but the flow of diagrammatic form.[11] And similarly, Picabia's formerly "poetic" verbal inscriptions become less a series of lines of flight than an assault and a graffito once more, the open-ended "M. . . . . . ." calling up inevitably the Dadaists' favorite exclamation: *Merde*. Shit for whomever looks at this! Or better: Fuck anyone who looks at this.

It was just this message that the Salon des Indépendants received when Picabia's two works—in a forgotten replay of Duchamp's testing of the Society of Independent Artists in New York with his readymade *Fountain* in 1917—were categorically refused.[12] One contained an "obscenity."[13] The other, a photograph. Somehow, these two things were linked, and as the Salon was dedicated to painting, neither would be allowed. However, the Salon committee raised no objection to yet a third submission on Picabia's part. It involved another "image" of Picabia. We have seen this one before. We have seen Picabia standing calmly behind his *Danse de Saint-Guy,* transforming the gutted frame with its abstract (diagrammatic) tracery of strings and inscriptions into another version of a self-portrait. An empty frame, at least, was recognizable, acceptable, the last stand of the painterly medium, reduced to its most pitiful zero degree.

The Salon committee in 1922 seems, however, to have missed the X that the strings of *Danse de Saint-Guy* also trace, echoing the ruined diagram of *Straw Hat?*. It surely missed the manner in which the piece arrived as an even more radical fusion of the rejected works, neatly condensing their opposed lessons. It is for this reason, we may assume, that Picabia resurrected his demonstration of 1920 for its first public showing in 1922. Image and line were at stake, transparency and opacity both in play—however strangely, or rather, incoherently.

Danse de Saint-Guy layered together the two central concerns of the Dada mechanomorph, the photographic or readymade principle of the copy and the relational vocation of the diagram. Both of these Dada terrains—perhaps in their very confrontation—were in flux for Picabia in 1922. Neither would continue to function as they had in the past. *Danse de Saint-Guy* embraced, impossibly, the opposed lessons of *The Merry Widow* and *Straw Hat?,* pitting against each other the transparency of line-as-trace and the opacity of line-as-deposit, roping together the incompatible Dada gambits of the copy and that of chance, the image conceived of as a token or as excremental. And finally, *Danse de Saint-Guy* returned to the mechanomorph as a compulsive imaging of the self, but only a self under the sign of erasure, becoming a self-portrait given over to destruction and to the X-marks-the-spot of utter annihilation.

Picabia's return in 1922 to the mechanomorph carried all the force of a manifesto. And however contradictory this manifesto, *The Merry Widow* thus stood with *Straw Hat?* at the beginning of an aesthetic program, one evidently predicted by the earlier opening salvos of Dada in Paris and the visionary leap of *Danse de Saint-Guy*. Art history has missed entirely this alteration visited upon the mechanomorph in Picabia's submissions to the 1922 Salon des Indépendants, showing the metamorphosis to have been more like a disguise, a thoroughgoing shift indeed. And yet, in 1922, Picabia did vehemently return to the mechanomorphs that he had initiated in the 1910s.

This return could not be missed. In the wake of the scandal of the 1922 Salon des Indépendants, during the spring and summer of that year, Picabia produced some fifty works on paper, all of them mechanomorphs, all of them, however, now strangely verging on the condition of the abstract. In the fall of 1922, he exhibited these new and inscrutable works in the Dalmau gallery in Barcelona, making a largely forgotten trip to Spain with André Breton. These would be—more or less—Picabia's last Dada works. In number, they rivaled the extent of almost all the mechanomorphs that had preceded them. And yet these works, the last mechanomorphs, have never received their due. They have hardly received even the beginnings of an interpretation.

If *The Merry Widow* and *Straw Hat?* provide the basis for sketching the lineaments of such an interpretation, it is due to the manner in which they condense a set of recurring Dada contradictions or oppositions. Impossibly, Picabia now pushed the photograph toward the relational task of the diagram, involving photography in a chain of signifiers, linkages, and transfers. And conversely, the artist pushed the diagram toward the indexical domain of the photograph, entering into a space where the diagram's immateriality collapses, where its virtuality erupts into pure matter or the actual space of the real. Such were the discoveries

of early 1922. These were the oppositions rooted in the torn practice of the earlier Dada mechanomorph, but that only now emerged to produce an aesthetic
that found its full, contradictory, utterly riven flowering in the unexplored
bloom of the last mechanomorphs.

VENI, VIDI, VICI

Here is an image of Picabia. He is not smiling. He stands before the grill of an
automobile, its steering wheel and a single headlight surfacing from the spotted
fog of the old photograph's current decay. Breton's wife Simone must have taken
it, for she is the only one not present, as we witness Picabia posed next to his partner Germaine Everling and pressed up tight against a stooped and swaddled
André Breton, in what seems a stern display of masculine camaraderie.

The couples were on their way to Spain. Picabia had been anticipating the
journey for some time, and in the fall of 1922 curt snippets of his excitement began to surface in the Parisian magazines as publicity for his Barcelona exhibition.
For instance: "My heart beats in leaps and bounds, my blood is a railroad without
stations that leads to Barcelona. My body is a vial of excellent opium that serves to
enchant my free time."[14] Or then again: "In a month, Picabia says, we will go
searching for the sun in Spain; this big yellow car, asleep now in its garage, will carry
us toward Seville, Algésiras, toward oranges, the quivering sea, and red sierras."[15]

Romantic images, poetic images, yet utterly false: the photograph gives up
the lie. If they were searching for the sun, we instead see Picabia and Breton
wrapped desperately against the autumn cold, with Breton protected against the rav-
ages of Picabia's open-air Mercer by both an aviator's helmet and dense goggles,
awkwardly enveloped in a fur coat that he had to borrow from his employer,
the couturier Jacques Doucet. The couples had set off for Spain on October 30,
reaching Marseille soon enough, where the photograph was taken and where
they stopped to visit the Colonial Exhibition. The exoticism of Picabia's predic-
tions instead turned up only a revolting series of reconstituted African villages,
lifeless simulacra of Moroccan markets and American jazz bands, the spectacle of
a degrading primitivism that convinced Picabia and Breton that they had entered

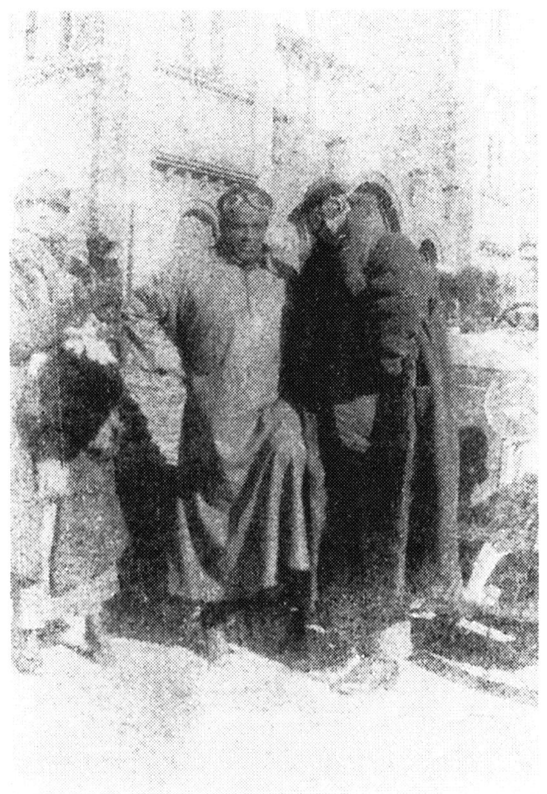

Simone Collinet, photograph of Francis Picabia, André Breton,
and Germaine Everling in Marseille, leaving for Barcelona, 1922.
Archives Sator, Paris.

"a loathsome cemetery in which we are the corpses."[16] After this, Picabia could only improve the mood by forcing Breton to accompany him to Marseille's red-light district, where Breton glared in silence at the prostitutes, reacting with paralysis when one of them jumped out at him and stole his hat. Picabia received a discreet admonition from Simone later that night, entreating him never to take Breton to such places again, as they "depressed him terribly."

And reaching Barcelona on November 7 did not improve the situation. Breton thought the city ugly and disappointing, banal and expensive, finding only Antonio Gaudí's Sagrada Familia of any interest, immediately firing off a postcard of the church to Picasso: "Do you know this marvel?" And then Simone became ill, contracting a debilitating case of salmonella poisoning. Breton wanted to leave at once, but Picabia insisted that they stay for the opening of his exhibition on November 18, and that Breton keep his promise to give a lecture the night before on modern art. Simone was thus confined to her hotel room for the duration of the visit, and Breton kept her company, composing automatic poems that used the discoveries of the recent "sleeping fits"—the experiments with hypnosis that he and the other soon-to-be Surrealists had begun at this point in Paris—as a point of departure.

The photograph of Picabia and Breton on their way to Barcelona was meant to be a *souvenir de voyage*. But this was a trip destined to be forgotten. It was to be relegated to the trash heap of modernist art history, exiled from any of its central accounts, a lonely footnote to the dissolution of the Dada movement by 1922 in Paris. And perhaps this is as it should be. For if Picabia's 1922 exhibition in Barcelona has recently been rediscovered by art historians, they are now calling out for the symbolic status of this trip. It has acquired a meaning. "The trip, in fact, was a symbolic act," writes Jean-Jacques Lebel. "It signaled the end of Dada. The journey, the exhibition and [Breton's] lecture at the Ateneu indicated new directions for both of them [Picabia and Breton]."[17] The trip has become an example. It has been reclaimed for history. And now, we are told, it is intelligible.

But I am not so sure. Breton, always eager to have done with his entire association with the Dada movement, seems at times to agree with Lebel's claim.

His great dirge of the spring of 1922, "Leave Everything," sets the stage for reading the Dalmau exhibition in this way:

> Leave everything.
> Leave Dada.
> Leave your wife, leave your mistress.
> Leave your hopes and fears.
> Drop your kids in the middle of nowhere.
> Leave the substance for the shadow.
> Leave behind, if need be, your comfortable life
>   and promising future.
> Take to the highways.[18]

And Breton retrospectively peppered his varied proclamations of Dada's demise neatly around the fall of 1922. It was August 1922, says Breton at one point, that was "the date of Dada's ultimate extinction." And then later: "By the spring of 1923, Dada, which for over two years had been gravely ill, was now in its death throes. Its last gasp was the 'Gas Heart' evening in July."[19] But which demise was correct? And what exactly was ending here? What does it mean for Dada to end? For it to die? Or rather, what does it mean for Dada to be *declared* dead, for someone to produce a certificate of its demise?

According to Picabia scholar Maria Lluïsa Borràs, the end for Picabia comes down to a simple change in style, with Picabia in her eyes moving away from Dada in 1922 and toward modernist abstraction, toward, in fact, the formal explorations of those artists (some former Dadaists, like Théo van Doesburg) associated with Neo-Plasticism.[20] But Picabia had noisily quit the Dada movement already in 1921, and so other scholars, such as William Camfield, see the source of Picabia's turn to abstraction in 1922 as a product of his association with such alternative Parisian events as Jean Crotti's and Suzanne Duchamp's short-lived "Tabu" movement.[21] Is this the end? Should we take the first artist's cry of "I quit!" as the token of a conclusion?

Again, I'm not so sure. Dada made a habit of enshrining its deserters as the true embodiment of its aspirations—as if to reject Dada, to negate its negations, to kill it, to become its dissident, to cry "PODE BAL" to its official manifestations was the only possible way to save it. Picabia, in this light, might never have been so fully a Dadaist as he was on the day he quit the Dada movement.[22] And so I'm not sure if Picabia's trip to Barcelona in 1922 can be so clearly read (which is to say that I'm not sure that this trip didn't slip out of the history books *precisely* *because* it cannot be read). What did it mean in 1922 to flee Paris and the internecine Dada warfare for Spain? What did it mean for Picabia to return to the same Barcelona gallery where, during the waning days of World War I, he had initiated the magazine *391* as his own personal organ of Dada provocation? What did it mean, in terms of form, to "take to the highways," to send the mechanomorph once more on a voyage, a journey, a long and achingly physical displacement? And, finally, what did it mean to mount one's most artistically ambitious show in years—perhaps the most important exhibition of a lifetime—in a place where hardly a soul would even see it?[23]

I think it means—let me venture this at least—that the whole endeavor was particularly, intimately attached to Dada, to its own brand of inscrutability. It means that the Barcelona show was deeply representative of what Dada means (for me), part and parcel of a movement that was never more powerful than when it was in full flight, or when it was devolving into absolute disintegration. Dada was a complete success in just those moments when it could only be judged a total failure. When it missed its target. When it self-imploded. To proclaim its death was, then, to do its work. It was to reveal Dada's work as a form of death, of non-work, of what I have called "unworking" and dissolution.

For what could be more Dada than this miserable trip that served only as a prelude to Picabia and Breton's absolute break with each other, the end arriving within the space of a year? What could be more Dada than the Sisyphean effort that witnessed Picabia shipping over fifty of his latest works to Barcelona for an exhibition where not a single work was sold, where but a single critic was won over?[24] What could be more Dada than the sight of Breton traveling all the way to Spain, and then waiting two weeks in detestable conditions in order to deliver a lecture to what was, by all accounts, a half-empty hall? Where the crowd that did arrive was invariably hostile, seeking news of Dada's life only to be met with a former leader proclaiming its recent death? What could be more Dada than the following words, Breton's way of negotiating his speech in Barcelona:

> Nonchalance, when it travels abroad, relinquishes most of its prerogatives; otherwise—although I have given little thought to the proper form for a lecture—I would probably behave quite differently with you. As a rule I believe that a critical study is not appropriate in these circumstances and that the smallest theatrical effect would convey my message much more clearly. . . . All in all a sense of provocation is still the most noticeable thing in this domain; a truth will always benefit from adopting an outrageous means of expression. In my case, I am not possessed by the desire to impose my point of view, whatever it may be; indeed I hold it only as long as I have not yet managed to make others share it. . . . But I repeat, we are in Barcelona, and my perfect ignorance of Spanish culture, Spanish desire, a cathedral under construction that I rather like if I forget that it is a cathedral, your climate, and the women I pass on the street who are so delightfully foreign to me have somewhat undermined my natural audacity. I cannot put a name to a single one of your faces, gentlemen, and so I momentarily believe that we have a good chance of understanding each other.[25]

But this was not to be. No one would "understand" each other, and Picabia's Barcelona exhibition gave off the typical Dada scent of dystopia and willful ignorance, a non-engagement with the desires and expectations of its contemporary audience that perhaps remains Dada's most endearing lesson.

For what could be more Dada than the works themselves? The question is coy, for at first glance, one might say, perhaps anything could. A riveting series of "non-objective" works on paper inscribed only with their titles—mixed, for good measure, with another series of slavishly figurative (and ludicrous) images

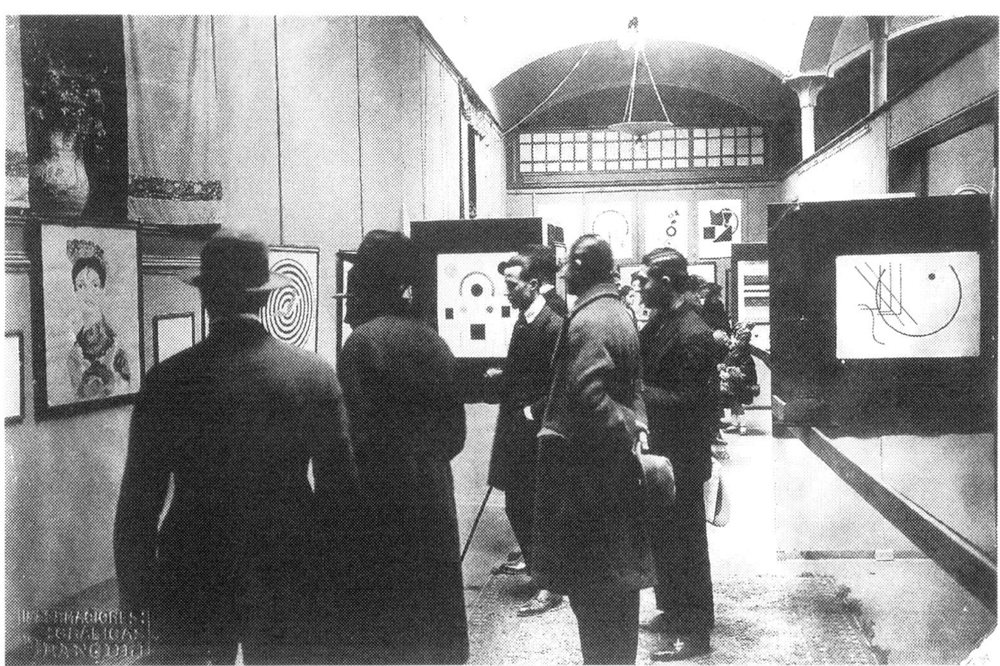

Opening of the exhibition "Francis Picabia," Galerie Dalmau, Barcelona, November 18, 1922. Image courtesy Comité Picabia.

depicting "Spanish women"—most of Picabia's 1922 paintings seemed deeply concerned with the issue of abstraction.[26] For Picabia, one of the first abstract painters in France, this was an old interest from his post-Cubist years, and a mode that the painter seemed to have abandoned by 1915 at the latest, precisely with his initiation of the mechanomorph and his adherence to what would later be called Dada. But on first glance, it appeared in 1922 as though the artist was now moving into a dialogue with the mainstream of European formalist modernism, confirming his friend Breton's desire at that moment for a synthesis of the various aspects of modernist thinking, or as it was still called then, in memory of Apollinaire, *l'esprit nouveau*.[27]

This desire had resulted in the massive failure, in 1922, of Breton's idea for a "Congress of Paris," a plan for a meeting of the leaders of various artistic movements wherein modernism could be isolated and defined in the commonality of its aims. For a while, Picabia had given the idea—however mischievously—his support. And then later that year came the trip to Barcelona, a respite for Breton after the failure of the Congress and the larger failures of Dada, where one might think that Picabia seemed to want to please his friend, exhibiting works that perhaps matched Breton's desires to the letter.

Breton surely claimed a new status for the 1922 paintings. He saw them as utterly breaking with Picabia's previous Dada mechanomorphs: "Given the spirit in which these paintings were conceived, and after having stressed Picabia's first-rate faculty for breaking with the images that others would have been pleased to leave of themselves, is it really necessary to point out that we would be wrong to try to include these latest works in his 'mechanical period'? It would be a veritable confusion, and I see no need to contest so superficial a judgment."[28] But Breton was wrong. The confusion was his. The 1922 paintings *were* mechanomorphs. What could be more Dada than that?

In 1922, Picabia resurrected the mechanomorph. He returned with a vengeance to its fraudulent principles, to its pictorialization of the readymade, to its engagement with a process of the copy and pastiche. But, with the mechanomorph now altered, its form completely changed, this return could not be recognized. Breton, at least, could not even see it—could not know, that is, that these works had nothing to do with formalist "modernism," and that he was most likely being mocked. The last mechanomorphs, then, sabotaging and themselves sabotaged from within, had an audience at their birth that consisted of one, or perhaps even of none. And what could be more Dada than that?

LAUDATOR TEMPORIS ACTI

One leads the people to abstraction. Which is different than the slaughterhouse. But it is also for abstractions that the latter has been readied.

—*Georges Ribemont-Dessaignes, 1920*[29]

The 1922 mechanomorphs do seem abstract. They are an affair of circles and squares, lines, triangles, the precision of geometric form: consider *Fixe,* for example, an apparent cataloging of each of the primary shapes available to the project of form; or *Phosphate* and *Presse hydralique,* with their seemingly random distribution of rectangles and circles; or *Radio-concerts,* with its marriage of such geometries to the inherently abstract ordering principle of frontal symmetry.

Unlike Picabia's first mechanomorphs, these images are not "object-portraits." In the 1915 object-portraits, machine parts—precisely copied and completely recognizable—were given human names: Stieglitz, Haviland, de Zayas. In the 1922 works, by contrast and in reverse, most of the titles refer directly to the world of machines and machine parts, while the visual elements themselves at times suggest the human body, or have become completely unrecognizable.[30]

But the 1922 works, as mechanomorphs, are not abstract. At this moment, Picabia evidently did have the modernist development of a non-objective pictorial language in his sights: Mondrian, Malevich, Lissitzky, Moholy-Nagy. The art historians have shown us to what extent Picabia was actually in contact with such abstractionists as Théo van Doesburg and the Neo-Plasticists; they have shown us how he was aware of the work of Mondrian then being exhibited in Paris; and how, most likely, he had an eye turned toward the outpouring of constructivist work from Germany and from the Soviet Union.[31] (The last mechanomorphs

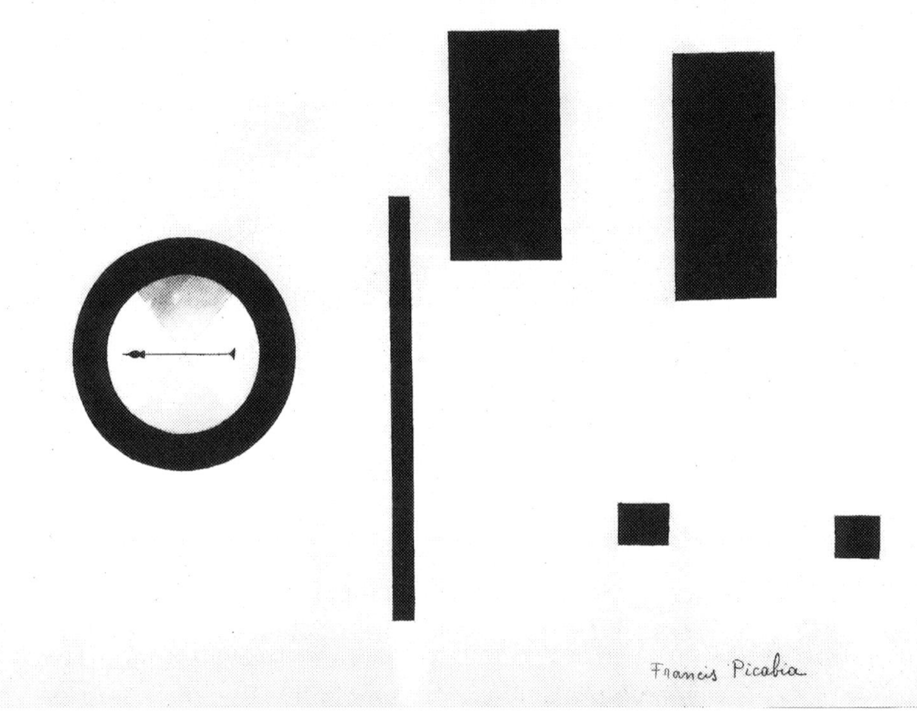

Francis Picabia, *Hydraulic Press,* 1922. Ink and watercolor on paper, 60 × 72 cm. Private collection. Image courtesy Comité Picabia. © 2005 Artists Rights Society (ARS), New York/ADAGP, Paris/Estate of Francis Picabia.

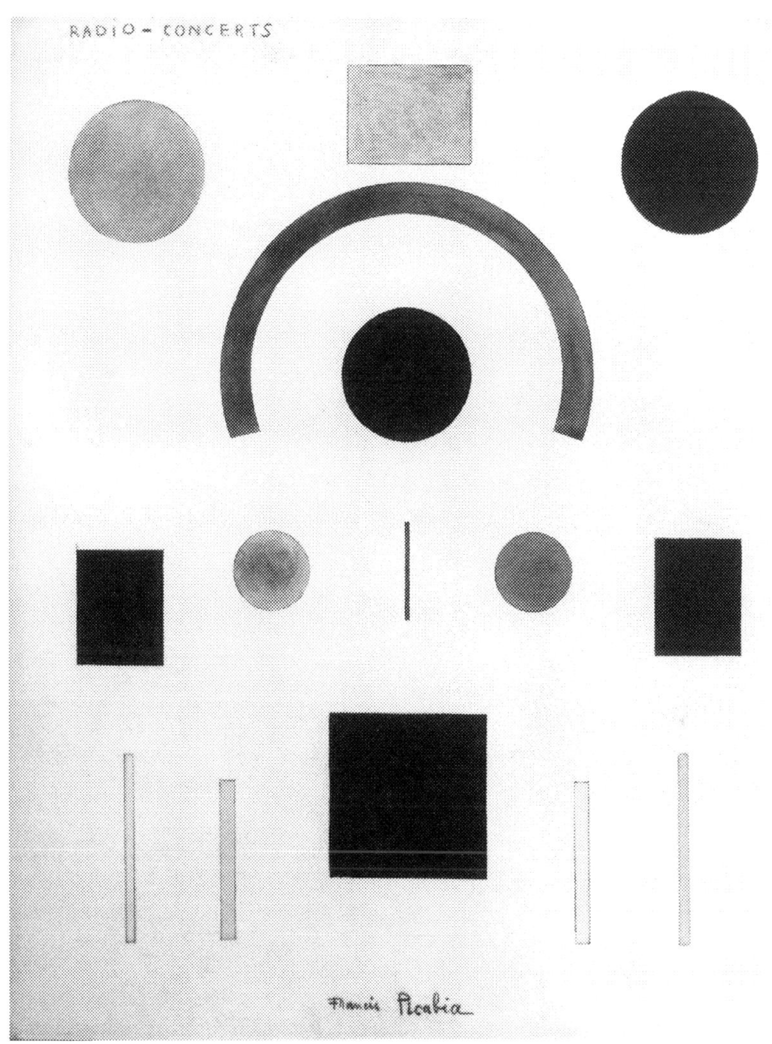

Francis Picabia, *Radio-concerts,* 1922. Ink and watercolor on paper, 72 × 59 cm. Private collection. Image courtesy Comité Picabia. © 2005 Artists Rights Society (ARS), New York/ADAGP, Paris/Estate of Francis Picabia.

seem particularly interested in the Suprematism of Malevich.) Against the development of this united front of modernist abstraction, against this emerging constructivist International—deeply attractive to many of the former Dadaists—the weapons of the mechanomorph were turned: its mechanization of the artistic gesture, its dependence on the photograph, its production through the copy and the trace.

It is to the art historian Arnauld Pierre that we owe the recent discovery that almost all of the 1922 mechanomorphs do have recognizable "sources," culled from a popular scientific journal of the time, a general-readership publication entitled *La Science et la Vie.*[32] Aligning themselves with the methods of the earlier mechanomorphs, both title and image in the 1922 works emerged from these sources: a work called *Cement,* for example, was based on an image detailing "The devices used for testing cement before its use"; the highly schematized *Cellar with Wine Press* emerged from selected elements of a diagram of just that, a cellar outfitted with a mechanical wine press; *Pump* from a photomechanical engraving of a pneumatic pump; *Winding* from a photograph of the "assembly of the winding connections of a turbine." Loosely copied, partially copied, traced or extrapolated, the "abstract" mechanomorphs of 1922 had their sources in photographs, or mechanical diagrams themselves based on photography, their sole purpose to reproduce the machines they mapped as well as to map themselves within the world of mechanical image reproduction.

With this, Picabia drew the worlds of abstraction and photography exceedingly close together, producing a near collision, a painterly game of chicken. Abstraction here was not understood as the opposite of photography, its nonobjective burst into freedom the flip side of the photograph's slavish anchoring in the real world of objects, facts, and appearances. Both shared the same conditions of production; the abstract painting as much as the photograph was produced in series, it utilized mechanical procedures, it rejected the traditional skills of craft and of the hand.[33] Both—the abstract painting and the photograph—were submitted to the regime of the multiple, relegating to the past the experience of the original and the nonreplicable. Some of the last abstract mechanomorphs loudly proclaimed this dependence on the photograph, such as a lost work that we know

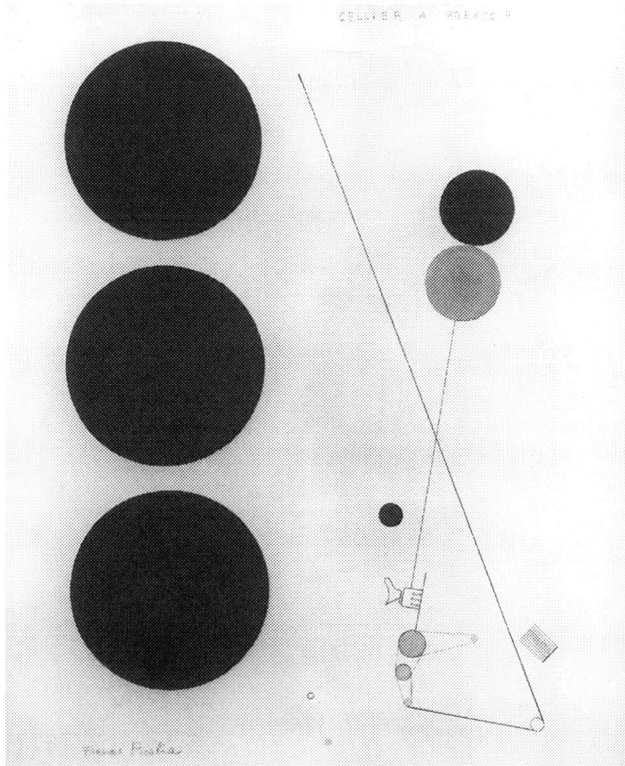

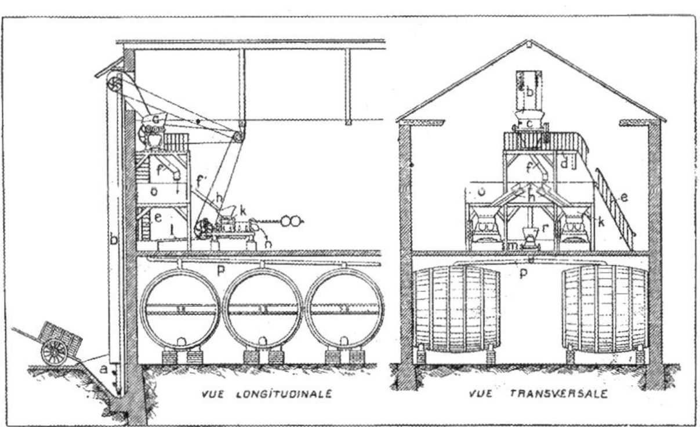

SCHÉMA DE L'INSTALLATION D'UN CELLIER A PRESSOIR CONTINU

a, Conquet de l'élévateur ; b, élévateur ; c, fouloir à grand travail ; e, escalier ; f, coulotte tournante pour vinification en blanc ; f' rallonge de la coulotte pour vinification en rouge ; h, couloir de distribution aux presses ; k, presse continue ; l, écoulement du moût aux presses ; m, réservoir du moût ; o, chambre d'égouttage ; p, tuyauterie des foudres ; r, wagonnet.

Francis Picabia, *Cellar with Wine-Press*, 1922. Ink and watercolor on paper, 72 × 60 cm. Private Collection. © 2005 Artists Rights Society (ARS), New York/ADAGP, Paris/Estate of Francis Picabia.

Source for *Cellar with Wine-Press*. ("Schéma de l'installation d'un cellier à pressoir continu," *La Science et la Vie* 45, June–July 1919, p. 106. Image courtesy Arnauld Pierre.)

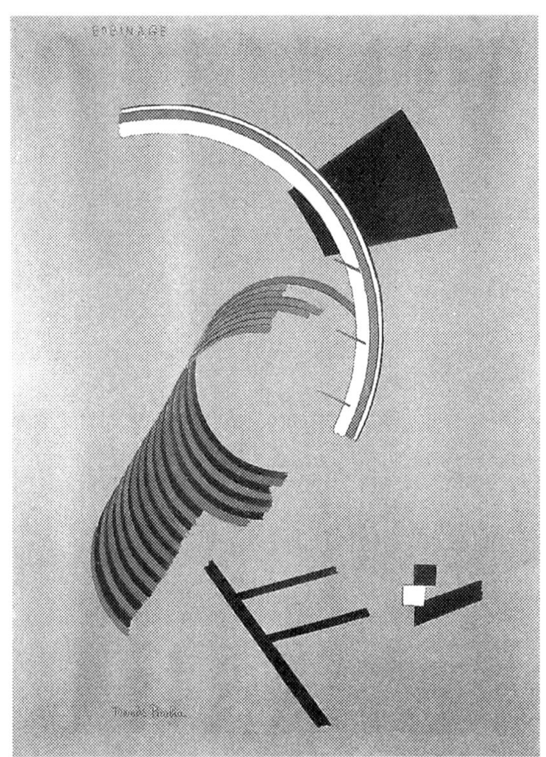

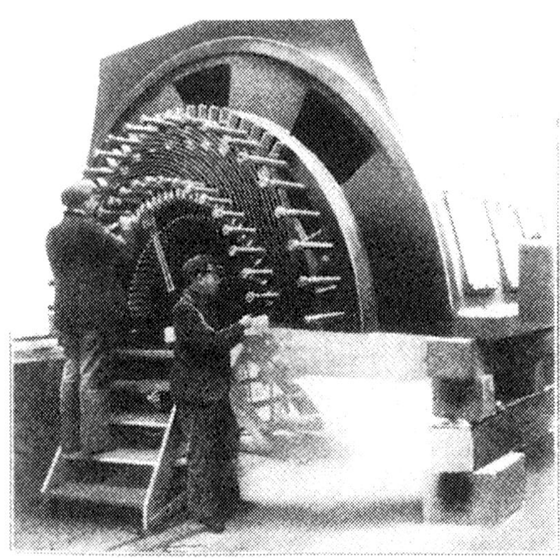

Francis Picabia, *Bobinage (Winding),* 1922. Pencil and gouache on paper, 76.5 × 56.9 cm. Aichi Prefectural Museum of Art, Nagoya. © 2005 Artists Rights Society (ARS), New York/ ADAGP, Paris/Estate of Francis Picabia.

Source for *Bobinage.* ("Montage des connexions de bobinage du stator de l'alternateur," *La Science et la Vie* 63, June-July 1922. Image courtesy Arnauld Pierre.)

was entitled *Shutter,* a work whose source came from a diagram of the lens and internal workings of a camera.[34]

The last mechanomorphs, then, seem to rupture the idealist space of autonomy and creative freedom that some versions of abstraction were claiming for themselves by the early 1920s. Instead of ascending into a weightless realm without objects, into an autonomous space utterly split from the exigencies of the real world and its merely physical properties, Picabia's "abstractions" clung ever more desperately to these physical things. They were copied from the real world. They were, then, not autonomous at all, but repetitive attempts at escape into that precarious "gap between art and life" that has been one of the great legacies of Dada for the art of this century.

But such an interpretation of Picabia's last mechanomorphs would be wrong. Or, at least, it would not be entirely right. For the last mechanomorphs had little connection to the "real world." They were copies of photographs or diagrams—copies, that is, of copies, of what we would be entirely justified in calling a series of visual tokens. More than abstraction and photography simply sharing their conditions of production, there was something in the very experience of photography that Picabia now turned toward an engagement with the abstract. There was something about the scene of anarchic equivalency that photography produced, about the chain of signifiers that it could spawn—about, in other words, its specific symbolic economy and its relation to general equivalency—that pushed the last mechanomorphs into the domain of pictorial abstraction.

And so it might be more accurate to describe the last mechanomorphs as wedding the project of abstraction not to the exigencies of the real, but rather to the wild fluidity of the token. This would be to confront two possibilities for the symbolic economy in which Picabia's abstractions took part. On the one hand, they could turn to the photograph as the machine of anarchic equivalency, as the engine of a proliferating chain of signifiers, ever more distant from a (paternal) standard or from the rule of the general equivalent altogether. This would be to see the last mechanomorphs as a form of abstraction dedicated to an alternate symbolic economy, one that severs painting from its rule, its (mimetic) standard, its Law.

Or, on the other hand, and in a more fraught move, such abstractions could perhaps be seen as marrying themselves in the most radical way to the condition of general equivalency of which the token is a sign. They would make their own the crisis of the general equivalent that within modernity had already toppled the figurative standard, and that represented a further abstraction of its symbolic form. They would embrace the great emptying out of the standard, the new abstraction and depthless mobility of the token, in what could itself be an excessive and anarchic way. Picabia's last mechanomorphs reveal the repressed fact that abstraction and the readymade were simply two sides of the same coin, bound like a pair of Siamese twins around the new conditions thrown up by what I have discussed as the paradoxical regime of the token sign.

The experience of the work of art as a token—either a secondary elaboration or a deracinated copy—that paradoxically twists into a visual apprehension of the work of art as nevertheless unrecognizable, and thus abstract, remains one of the least remarked on but most characteristic aspects of Picabia's work during the Paris Dada period. Far from being an entirely new departure, the last mechanomorphs were the apotheosis of this dynamic in Picabia's work. One of its great and early statements during the moment of Paris Dada was the appropriately titled painting *Le double monde (LHOOQ)* of 1919—one of Picabia's submissions to the 1921 Salon des Indépendants. However, the work made its first public appearance within the context of Dada at a slightly earlier, and rather significant, moment.

Created late in 1919 during the height of Picabia and Duchamp's dialogue—and thus created in tandem with Duchamp's *L.H.O.O.Q.*—*Le double monde* was initially displayed early in 1920, as part of the very first manifestation of the Dada movement in Paris, the "Premier Vendredi de Littérature." Little about this painting has ever been adequately explained, but its title's reference to the condition of the double should have given interpreters an initial clue. And now, thanks to the work of Carole Boulbès, we know that like Duchamp's *L.H.O.O.Q.*, Picabia's painting took Leonardo's *Mona Lisa* as its point of departure. To impose the abstract tracery of *Le double monde* over an image of Leonardo's portrait is to witness how Picabia's looping and seemingly aimless diagrammatic lines trace the major compositional elements of the image, with each crossing

------

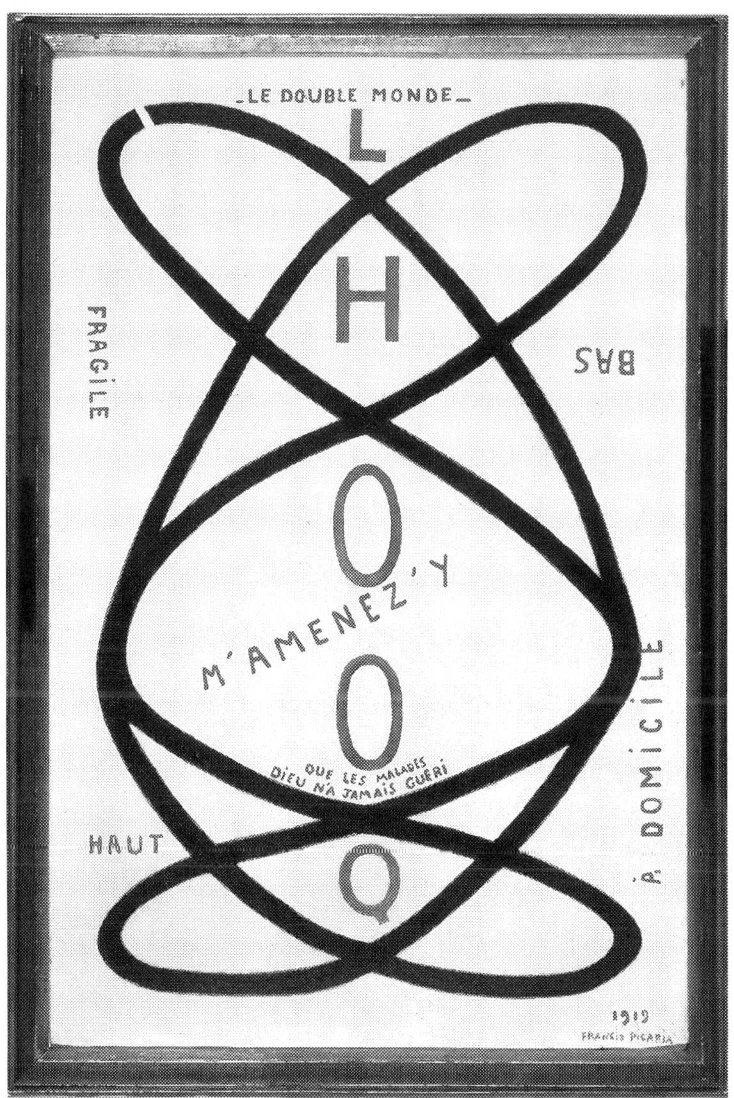

Francis Picabia, *The Double World (LHOOQ),* 1919. Ripolin, oil on cardboard, 132 × 85 cm (52 × 33 ¹/₂″). Musée National d'Art Moderne, Centre Georges Pompidou. Photo by Philippe Migeat. Photograph © CNAC/MNAM/Dist. Réunion des Musées Nationaux/Art Resource, New York. © 2005 Artists Rights Society (ARS), New York/ADAGP, Paris/Estate of Francis Picabia.

point of the design marking an important element of Leonardo's figure: her fore-head, her chin, or the placement of her hands, for example.[35]

Picabia's design emerges as a compositional tracing, something like the "regulating lines" that artists like Amédée Ozenfant and Le Corbusier were soon superimposing over the masterpieces of Western art and publishing in their magazine *L'esprit nouveau,* a series of object lessons proving the overriding rationality of great pictorial art. And even more to the point, Picabia's design, in tracing Leonardo's composition, marks out a series of pictorial zones that—comparing the equally proportioned top and bottom loops against the larger middle section—divide the canvas into three areas corresponding to the precepts of the Golden Section. We can thus read the work as an immediate, arch response to the revival of the activities of the so-called Section d'Or cubists, proclaimed in Paris precisely in the fall of 1919.[36] In postwar France, the rallying cries of aesthetic rationalization had been sounded. "Geometry," as Le Corbusier put it, "is the language of man."[37]

Picabia's image engages with this rationalization, only to turn its procedures to wholly opposed ends. *Le double monde* recasts pictorial rationalization as a process of the copy. It relegates the work of art to the status of a secondary elaboration, a visual token. But the figurative standard—the original of which the copy is now a sign—becomes here not only a figure for the Mother; it becomes opaque, distanced, unavailable, resolved into an indecipherability, a kind of physical remoteness, that pushes the painting into the domain of the abstract. And this abstraction registers its secondariness and its distance from its source—it registers, in other words, its deracination—inscribed as it is with words, labels like those found on a packing crate: "Fragile," "Top" (written on the bottom), and "Bottom" (written on the top, and upside-down). The painting as a packing crate: we confront an image given over to its deracination, ripped free even from the traditional orientation of painting itself, summoning the viewer as it does—through the precise dispersal of its inscriptions—to rotate the work literally in all directions. *Le double monde* is an image rethought as a portable shell wrapped around and over a past reality, an image whose inner source can be sensed in its displacement, but absolutely cannot be seen.

Based, like *L.H.O.O.Q.*, on the *Mona Lisa, Le double monde* may be considered very much another Tableau Dada, concerned as the category was with the general equivalent. The remoteness, the pastness, the erasure of the *Mona Lisa's* form—even as it is doubled and distilled—makes one think inevitably of the affective distance traveled from the maternal signifier, the chain of displacements Dada increasingly made its own, or conversely of the imposture by which the general equivalent came to supplant the maternal signifier's role. *Le double monde* too was a ruined diagram, perhaps a first attempt to bring together the mechanomorph's principles of the photographic copy and the diagram, as its enigmatic tracery reads as a series of diagrammatic lines that now point nowhere—except behind the scene, to the image beneath the work that we see, to the chain of prior signifiers from which it emerges into view, but does not at all resemble. "M'amenez'y," Picabia further inscribed the work, a grammatically incorrect way of saying "Take me there." But this was an invitation to a voyage in the face of the enactment of a deep amnesia, the utter loss of memory and of sense. For *M'amenez'y* when pronounced in French produces homophonically something like *amnésie,* or, precisely, amnesia.[38]

It was a plaintive cry, a hopeless command, a look backward in mourning or in denial, simultaneously an acknowledgment and a disavowal. It was, perhaps, a return of the repressed, an eruption of time past into the supposedly forward-looking scene of abstract art. Here is Picabia's version of abstraction. Here is an image of abstraction given over to its basis in the token, to a potential engagement with the general equivalent and its supposedly rational procedures. But here too is a token made instead to the mother's rule, and thus potentially ruining the rule altogether. Here is an example of abstraction on the run—abstraction as a process of the copy, as a function of deracination, as a true enactment of the modernist tabula rasa, which is to say, an acknowledgment of what this erasure might mean.

And so here, finally, is abstraction as an art of the void, and of the voided—a dalliance with the hopes for a groundless ground, equivalence without a rule. It is no coincidence that when *Le double monde* was exhibited at the first Paris Dada manifestation in 1920, it was paired with a work that we know Picabia entitled *Riz au nez (Laugh in Your Face),* a white chalk drawing on a small blackboard that André Breton presented to the assembled crowd of spectators, only to erase it a moment later before their startled eyes.

UT PICTURA POESIS

More drunks!
More gonorrhea!
More vigor!
More urinary tracts!
More enigmas!

—*Dada slogans,* Dada, *no. 6 (1920)*

The photograph, we have often been told, can only be anchored by its caption. Its particular brand of visual excess depends on language not only to give the photograph direction—to point like a signpost to that portion of its infinite detail that is to be considered significant—but also to give it meaning at all, which the French can more simply designate with the word *sens,* the term for both meaning and direction. Diagrams too rely on this relay between word and image, a hybrid representational condition that perhaps provides the common terrain in the mechanomorphs between photography and the diagram more generally. However, this common ground resists the lessons that we have learned. It refuses, in fact, to be a ground. For language, in the mechanomorph, enters into the space of the caption in order utterly to dissolve its functions.

Consider the earliest mechanomorphs, the object-portraits of Stieglitz, of Haviland, or of de Zayas, for example. In the full, contradictory range of the engagement of the mechanomorph with language, here the written word does seem to function most closely to that of the traditional form of the caption. But we now know that these so-called captions arose readymade from the space of Latin literary references, the dead language of emblematics and formalized expressions, inserting a caesura between caption and image that emerges as a temporal disjunction, a nonalignment of image and word best described by the fragmentations of allegory rather than the clarities of the traditional symbol.[39]

Or consider the mechanomorphic drawing *Paroles (Words)*. Completed around 1918, and thus significantly later than the first mechanomorphs, here language seems to hold absolutely no relation to the image whose lines it follows. This was the most intense moment of Picabia's poetic production, a moment that saw the publication in rapid-fire succession of Picabia's poetry collections *Fifty-Two Mirrors, The Funeral Parlor Athlete, Purr-Verse,* and *Thoughts without Language,* among others, and that almost came to eclipse Picabia's activities as a painter altogether, from which he abstained toward the end of the First World War. Indeed, the words in *Paroles* emerge like lines in a poem, dispersed here and there across the space of the drawing itself. The clearly traced—even recognizable—machinic forms of the image find their reluctant companion in these poetic tags that Picabia totally subordinates to the shapes cut by his mechanomorphic lines. But following these mimetic lines, the words simply throw up any number of verbal enigmas: "Truth resembles death," "Binges of immobile nervous tics," "Treachery," "Sultry worries in the desert," "The height of my grief," "My eyes are no longer misled." Language here belies the token mimeticism of the mechanomorphic drawing. It pushes the supposed clarity of a diagrammatic space—and the readymade copy that is the token—into the "anxiety" of a verbal enigma, a rebus where word and image do not add up, where visual sense is made to succumb to verbal entreaties of wild confusion. Language here takes flight, leading vision away from the image that we see.

Once again, the last mechanomorphs exist as a precise reversal of this former device within Picabia's work. In the last mechanomorphs, we might say, language at long last functions quite literally and specifically as a caption. All of the last mechanomorphic titles, in fact, *were seized on readymade from captions,* taken directly from the explanatory labels affixed to photographs and diagrams in the magazine *La Science et la Vie.* They were readymade captions. But now, the images that they so clearly identified could not be seen as such. They were captions pinned hopelessly to abstractions, disassociated phrases attached to still potent enigmas whose source had now been flipped away from the verbal and into the operations of visual form itself.

One of the last mechanomorphs was entitled *Sphinx.* Picabia knew exactly what he was doing. Title here matches and doubles experience: we face the blank

Francis Picabia, *Paroles (Words),* 1918. Ink on paper, 26 × 34.5 cm. Collection Sylvio Perlstein, Anvers. Image courtesy Comité Picabia. © 2005 Artists Rights Society (ARS), New York/ADAGP, Paris/Estate of Francis Picabia.

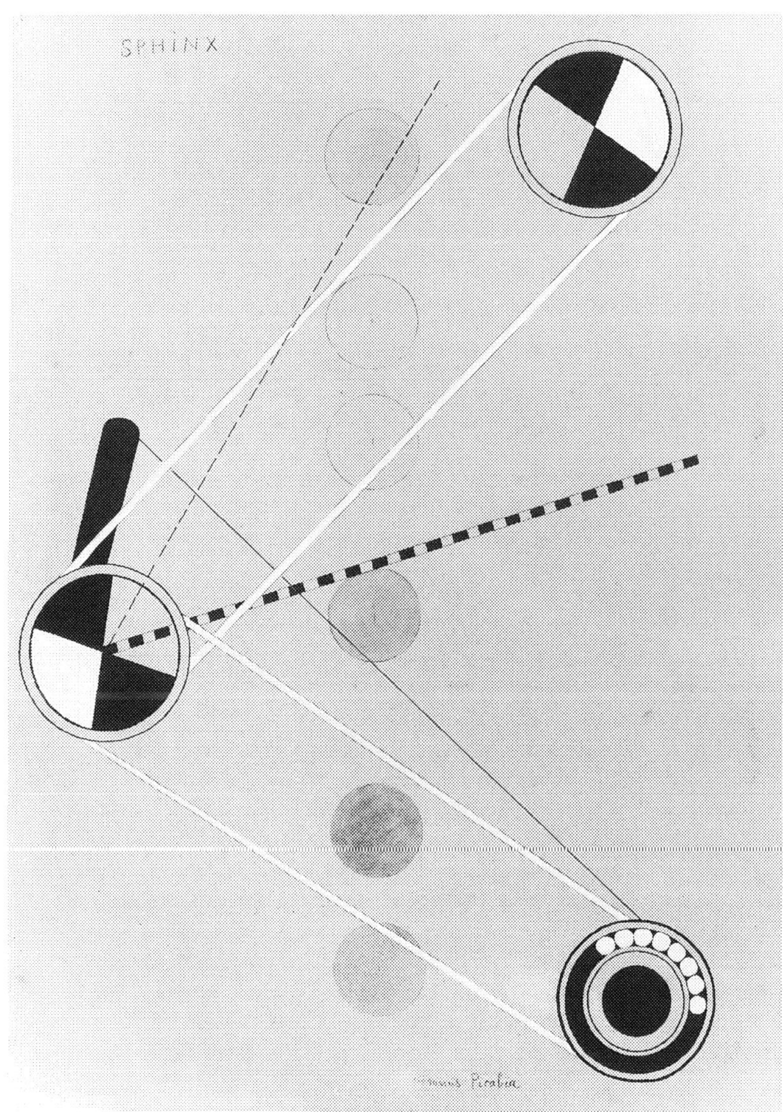

Francis Picabia, *Sphinx,* c. 1922. Gouache, ink, watercolor, and pencil on newsprint, 76.2 × 65.2 cm (30 × 22 ¹/₈″). Photo by F. W. Seiders, Houston. The Menil Collection, Houston. © 2005 Artists Rights Society (ARS), New York/ADAGP, Paris/Estate of Francis Picabia.

stare of the last mechanomorphs as if we had been posed an unanswerable question. It is almost a shame for it now to be revealed that this mechanomorph emerged from the photograph of a machine in *La Science et la Vie* whose caption simply read: "Vue d'ensemble de l'appareil 'Sphinx.'"[40] A view of the assembly of the Sphinx-brand device. Beware an art of false riddles, an aesthetic of deflated mysteries.

IN VITRO

Almost all of Picabia's mechanomorphs made reference to the thematics and the forms of Duchamp's *Large Glass.* This must be admitted up front. The mechanomorphs were begun in 1915, and came to a climax in 1922 and 1923, precisely the life span of Duchamp's work on his *Glass.* Picabia was not interested in hiding this fact. His *Portrait of Gabrielle Buffet* practically screamed it.[41] But the mechanomorphs were not slavish imitations of the *Large Glass*; rather, they elaborated aspects of its thematics and procedures often left unexplored by Duchamp himself.

One of the last mechanomorphs was entitled *Glass.* This work did not illustrate any specific aspect of Duchamp's *Large Glass,* but rather engaged its structure, the literal transparency produced by Duchamp's use of a glass support. Picabia's *Glass* evokes this transparency, as one cannot help but read the painting as the superimposition of two planes, one a double spectrum of horizontal bands standing resolutely in front of a haphazard series of curving lines, lines that seem to be buried *beneath* the picture plane, indeed welling up from below it. In fact, these lines were probably drawn *on top* of the horizontal bands of colored wash, and their random meandering immediately suggests that the lines should be read as yet another of Picabia's references to Duchamp's *Three Standard Stoppages,* and to his figuration of drawing as deposit.[42] We are once more in the domain of *The Merry Widow* and *Straw Hat?,* with their split and their opposition condensed into the procedures of a single work. However, this fact of production does nothing to effect one's visual reading of the lines as buried beneath the horizontal bands that push these lines resolutely and insistently back in space. And this optical experience, of the trace burgeoning up from below the image, of the work as a metaphorically transparent but wholly secondary elaboration through which one

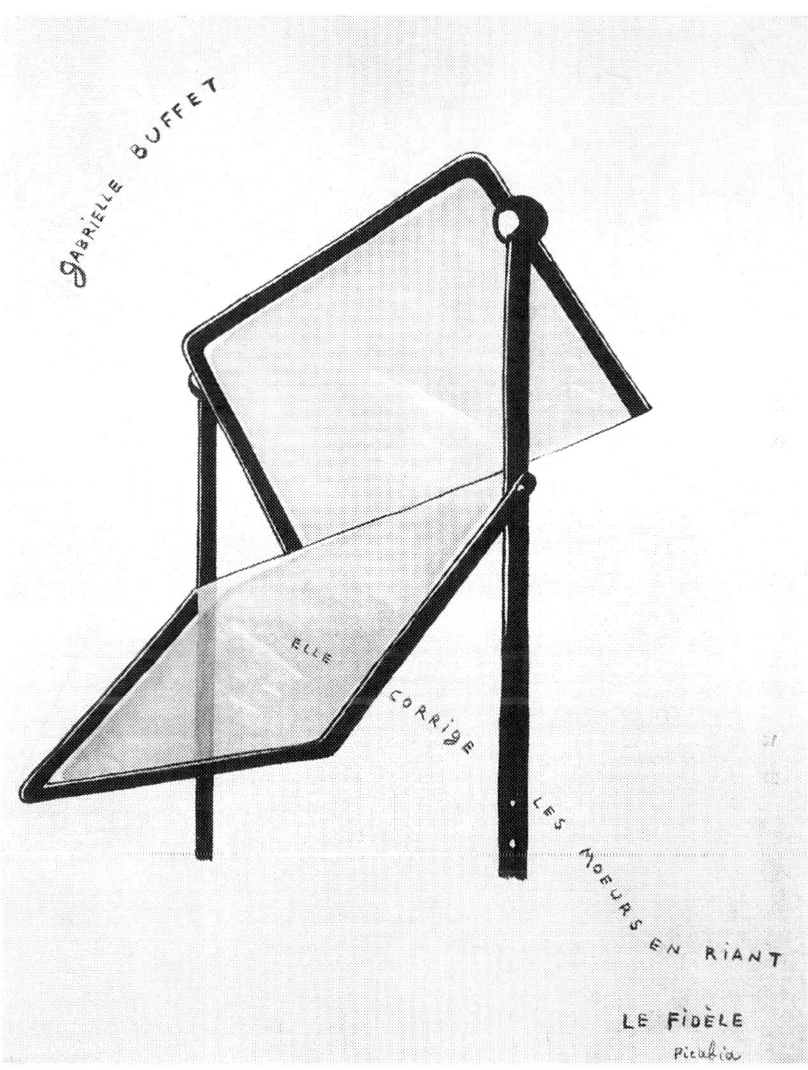

Francis Picabia, *Portrait of Gabrielle Buffet,* 1915. Ink, watercolor, and graphite on paper, 58.5 × 46.8 cm. Collection Staatsgalerie Stuttgart, Graphische Sammlung. © 2005 Artists Rights Society (ARS), New York/ADAGP, Paris/Estate of Francis Picabia.

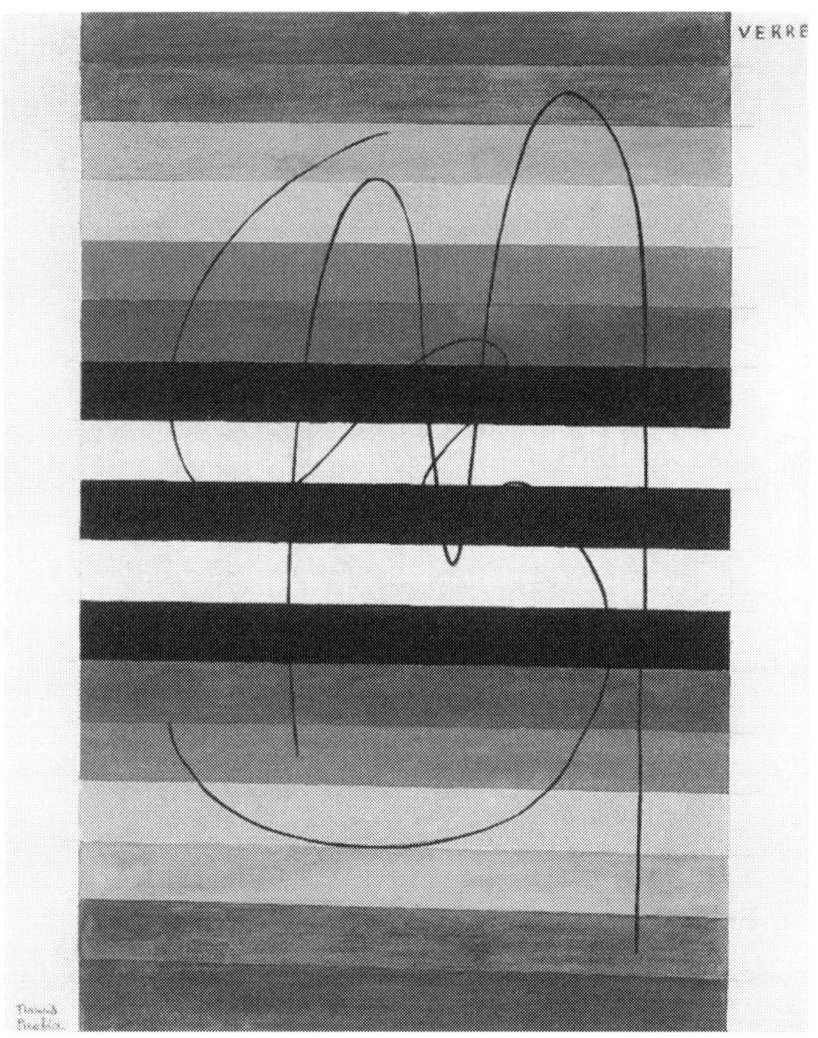

Francis Picabia, *Glass,* 1922. Ink and watercolor on paper, 72 × 60 cm. Private collection.
© 2005 Artists Rights Society (ARS), New York/ADAGP, Paris/Estate of Francis Picabia.

attempts to see—the progeny of a set of displacements or of a signifying chain—
was of course a formal consequence of the elaboration of Picabia's mechanomorphic method, with each image based on an exterior, readymade model, whether
photograph or diagram.

This experience was visible everywhere in the 1922 mechanomorphs:
Embroidery, with its superimposition of traced forms, made this dynamic self-
reflexive, announcing already in 1922 the project of the "Transparencies," as Picabia called those paintings of the late 1920s made up of wildly superimposed
forms copied from (photographs of) historical paintings. But this experience of
transparency and of formal displacement also points us backward (not just along
the signifying chain but within the development of Picabia's Dada work): to the
literally transparent works, *La jeune fille* and the *Danse de Saint-Guy*, that Picabia
produced in 1920; and even further still, to his 1918 book, *Poems and Drawings by
the Girl Born without a Mother*, the closest precedent among the earlier mechanomorphs for the procedures of the last mechanomorphic series.

It is in the drawings for this 1918 publication that one most directly experiences the field of the mechanomorph as one of transparency, that one senses the
displaced presence of an external model for each drawing and perceives the
mechanomorph as an affair of precise and exact but selective and schematic tracing. One hardly needed to know the sources of these mechanomorphs to feel that
this was true. But now that these sources are largely confirmed, the evidence is
incontrovertible. Witness *Cantharides (Spanish Fly)*, or *Voyez (See)*. Both are products of the selective tracing of graphic elements taken from photographs of tele-
phones, two images which were published in the same issue of *La Science et la
Vie*.[43] And no matter how schematic, recognizably iconic elements of these photographs break through into the mechanomorphs that seem now literally peeled
off the photograph's gleaming surface. The tracing at times became more precise
and more complete—in drawings such as *Egoïste (Selfish)* or *Polygamie (Polygamy)*,
for example—and yet, in a typical Picabian dialectic, such drawings only seemed
less iconic, more unrecognizable, in the precision of their conformity to the isolated, rootless forms from which they came.

It is true that Picabia, anticipating the work of Max Ernst, produced the
occasional "over-painting," applying pigment directly to his readymade sources

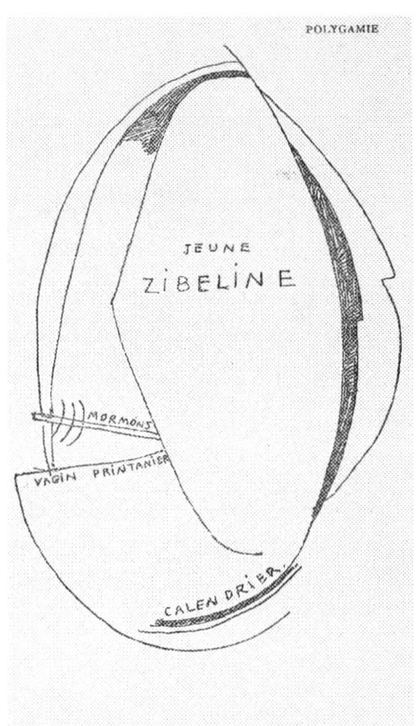

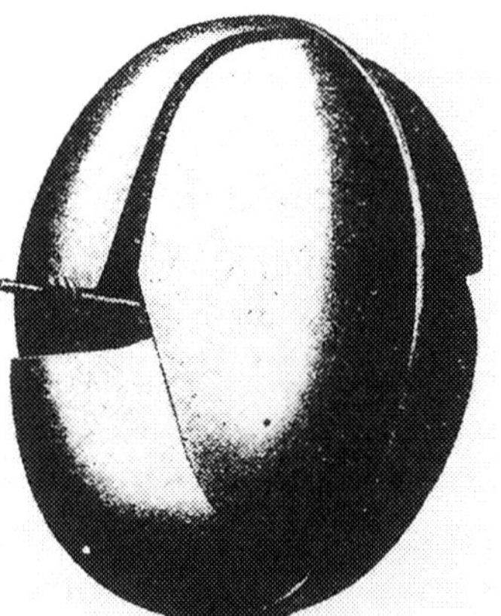

Francis Picabia, *Polygamy,* 1918. From Picabia, *Poèmes et dessins de la fille née sans mère* (Lausanne: Imprimeries réunies, 1918). Research Library, The Getty Research Institute, Los Angeles. © 2005 Artists Rights Society (ARS), New York / ADAGP, Paris / Estate of Francis Picabia.

Source for *Polygamy.* ("Le volant du compteur 'Duplex,'" *La Science et la Vie* 36, December 1917–January 1918, p. 74.)

in a game of opacification and effacement. One of these works shared the same title as Picabia's 1918 book, *The Girl Born without a Mother*; another was called *Mechanism,* with its original source still peeking through, a source that we now know emerged from the same publication, *La Science et la Vie,* utilized for the mechanomorphs from which it otherwise departs.[44] But these were the exceptions. The mechanomorphs that belonged to the series of the *Girl Born without a Mother* privileged transparency; they were formed by the trace; and yet they became unrecognizable, almost uncanny, verging as they do on the condition of the abstract.

And while preserving the mechanicity, the sheer indexicality of the trace, Picabia was not above performing operations on his sources, making them even more disorienting, capitalizing on their inherent decontextualization, rotating them, for example, ninety degrees. Such was the fate of the source that served for *Machines sans but*—"machines without a purpose" or end—a diagrammatic propeller (the tail "end" of a machine) uprighted and thus transformed into something like a blooming flower. Or then there was the source for *Machine des idées actuelles dans l'amour*—a machine of "current notions about love"—a pair of wheels turned and levitated into indecipherability, a throbbing erection of nonsense.[45] It was as if the mechanomorph's abstraction was achieved not only in the partiality of the actions of the trace, but in the rotation of the source itself, uprooted from the frontal, grounded orientation that secured the recognizability—the sense—of its Gestalt.

With this, we witness too that Picabia's copies surely were not tied to the real world, to a fronto-parallel view, to the vertical field of nature and the traditional mimetic copy; they were not anchored in the upright coordinates of human perception. Rather, the mechanomorph occupied the horizontal domain of the printed page, both seeking its sources there and making this page its ultimate destination, landing these images in a dense, reified, and evidently directionless field, that of culture as opposed to nature.[46] The horizontal space of the page served as the fluid ground of the mechanomorph's abstraction, of its visual deracination.

And so Picabia's transparency was not the principle of structural transparency embraced by modernism. It was rather that peculiarly thick transparency

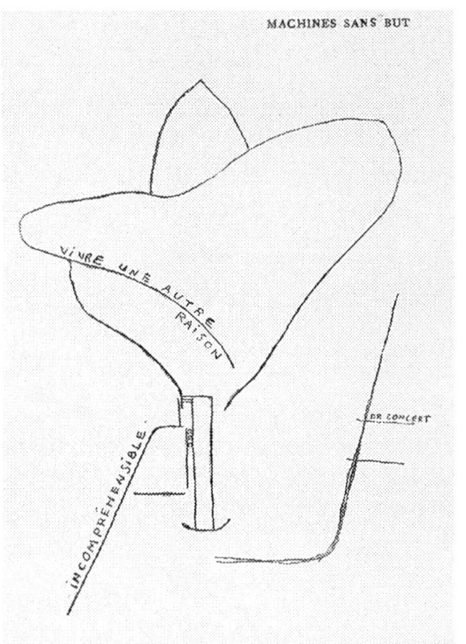

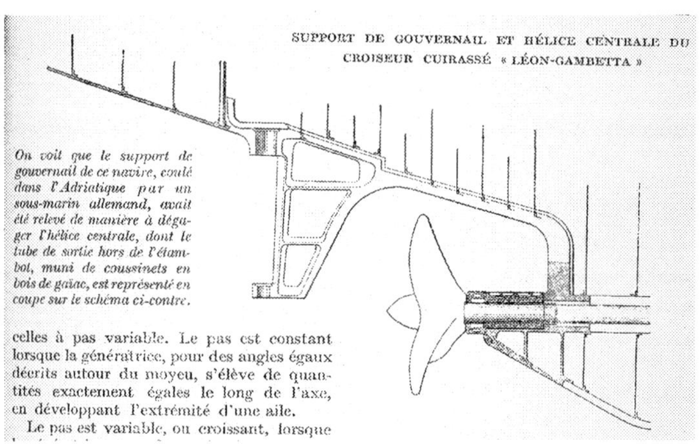

Francis Picabia, *Machines sans but (Machines without End),* 1918. From Picabia, *Poèmes et dessins de la fille née sans mère* (Lausanne: Imprimeries réunies, 1918). Research Library, The Getty Research Institute, Los Angeles. © 2005 Artists Rights Society (ARS), New York/ADAGP, Paris/Estate of Francis Picabia.

Source for *Machines without End.* ("Support de gouvernail et hélice centrale du croiseur cuirassé 'Léon-Gambetta,'" *La Science et la Vie* 37, February–March 1918, p. 225. Image courtesy Arnauld Pierre.)

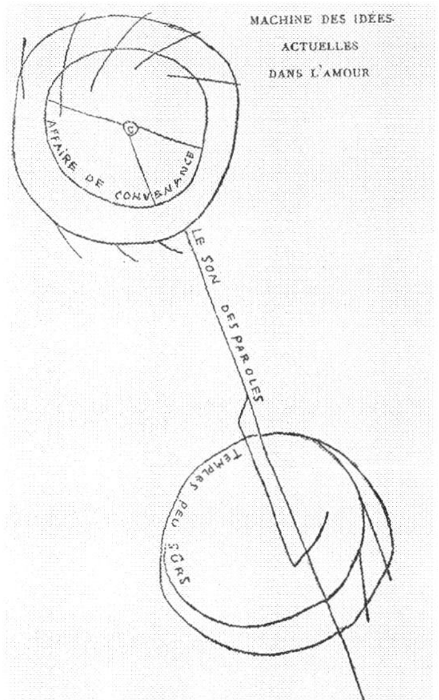

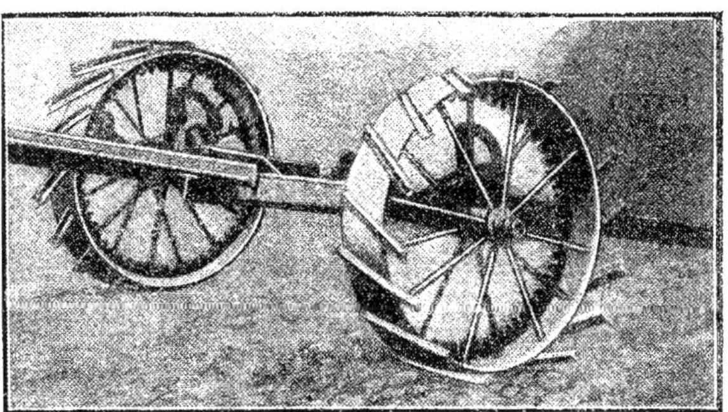

ARRIÈRE-TRAIN SE FIXANT A L'ARRIÈRE DU VÉHICULE
Ce dispositif est celui adopté pour les travaux de l'agriculture.
Les roues métalliques sont munies de cornières pour s'agripper
dans les terres molles.

Francis Picabia, *Machine des idées actuelles dans l'amour (Machine of Current Notions in the Realm of Love)*, 1918. From Picabia, *Poèmes et dessins de la fille née sans mère* (Lausanne: Imprimeries réunies, 1918). Research Library, The Getty Research Institute, Los Angeles. © 2005 Artists Rights Society (ARS), New York/ADAGP, Paris/Estate of Francis Picabia.

Source for *Machine des idées actuelles dans l'amour.* ("Arrière-train se fixant à l'arrière du véhicule," *La Science et la Vie* 37, February–March 1918, p. 267. Image courtesy Arnauld Pierre.)

that belongs to the photograph, where the experience of "seeing through" becomes partial, selective, transparency transmuted into an experience of the opaque. As if to prove this point, in 1920, Picabia exacerbated the relation that his mechanomorphs had to their photographic models, publishing the drawings from *The Girl Born without a Mother* again in the catalog for his first Dada exhibition in Paris. The chain of displacements could continue, and perhaps indefinitely. But this was no ordinary exhibition catalog. Picabia published his mechanomorphic drawings *over* Tristan Tzara's catalog text for the exhibit, in fact on top of all the printed text in the book, so that we see *Libellule (Dragonfly)* running across Picabia's cover, *Vis-à-vis* and *Ventilateur surprise* eclipsing Tzara's text, *Cantharides* canceling the legibility of the catalog's obligatory checklist.[47] Once again, with these images, one faces the mechanomorph as a field through which one attempts to see, but it is a field that threatens to block this seeing nonetheless, verging now on the potentially erased condition of the palimpsest.

PROLEM SINE MATRE CREATAM

Perhaps the first mechanomorph that Picabia ever produced—the origin point is disputed—was also entitled *Girl Born without a Mother*. What is not disputed is the fact that this title, or a version of it, was the most commonly used title during the entire run of the mechanomorph in Picabia's work. It was his code-word for the machine, as well as for the visual emissary of the machine, namely, the camera.[48] But it was also a readymade. Like most of Picabia's early titles, this one came from the list in the *Larousse* dictionary of commonly used Latin phrases. And it strikes me as entirely appropriate that the title standing guard over the entire series of Picabia's Dada mechanomorphs had its origin—or so the dictionary tells us—in that narrative of endless transformation that is Ovid's *Metamorphoses*.

Prolem sine matre creatam: the child born without a mother. In the dictionary from which Picabia lifted this phrase, its origin is given as Ovid, but its usage is given as referring to something that not only has no *mother,* but has no *model—* that is unique, sui generis.[49] Which is paradoxical. For I have been intimating that the maternal, in some way, was definitive for Dada. Picabia's phrase *fille née sans mère* retains a fixation on the female sex and gender: the neutral "child" here

FRANCIS PICABIA

Le grelot d'un chien s'amuse sur une manchette coupe le nez de ceux qui sentent la viande en masturbation.

Francis Picabia mange les hommes s'ils ont dans leur tête des bonbons nus — les microbes et les bonbons grattent la peau de leur cerveau — ils appellent idée le sperme artificiel obtenu par des moyens faciles et rythmiques.

Lorsqu'ils frottent la tête de leur sexe une sonnerie mélancolique à la colique dans le crâne de Monsieur Saturne.

Le cannibale vient sur une ligne fraîche avec une grande mâchoire de fer dans les mains, avec des dents à roues, avec un balai, avec deux pierres de moulin, avec des acides sombres et forts, pour détruire tout ce *qui digère*. Tout ce qui continue le mot, la couleur, la joie est une digestion mortuaire et scientifique ; la discussion, la masturbation, l'explication, l'exaspération.

Francis Picabia envoie des scaphandriers gonflés dans le ventre musical de Monsieur Cormon (on y trouve la propagande pour la couleur bleue des yeux, la pâleur des abatjouraux bords de la mer cubiste et la matière grisâtre des yeux pourris des poissons noircis des pierres en folie)

raccourcis
adversaire
disponible
régime

usage
député
pronostics
profondément
halles

Le bain à l'acide gastrique mange le papier — ne cherchez rien dans ces tableaux, le sujet et le moyen sont : Francis Picabia. Le tableau dada est une douche universelle à l'eau rouge. La nature est ce qui sort des yeux et des doigts — librement — elle a un numéro de téléphone un appartement au Champ de Mars, une voiture de 85 HP, comme l'amitié et la conversation filtrée par le filet du tissu cérébral.

L'art est un poète aux côtes cassées — Picabia casse tous les os et les roses de verre — l'art est un bandage et un livre d'Oscar Wilde — l'art est l'art des artistes — l'art d'être poli avec les événements du jour, susceptible en société, un cochon dans sa cuisine.

Dans toutes les boîtes crâniennes, il y a des lignes pures et une expression de géographie au soleil, il n'y a pas de secret pour les noter — la simplicité s'appelle DADA — ses mouvements détruisent et tuent maintenant — elle ouvre la lumière pour quelques hommes qui regarderont et sauront qu'ils ne trouveront rien. Dans une ampoule, un morceau de cerveau désinfecté — on ne vous offre que la méchanceté et la bonté comme une déclaration en douane sur un sublime boutonnière sagesse sempiternelle.

TRISTAN TZARA

Francis Picabia, catalog for *Francis Picabia: Exposition Dada* (Paris: Au Sans Pareil, 1920). Beinecke Rare Book and Manuscript Library, Yale University. © 2005 Artists Rights Society (ARS), New York/ADAGP, Paris/Estate of Francis Picabia.

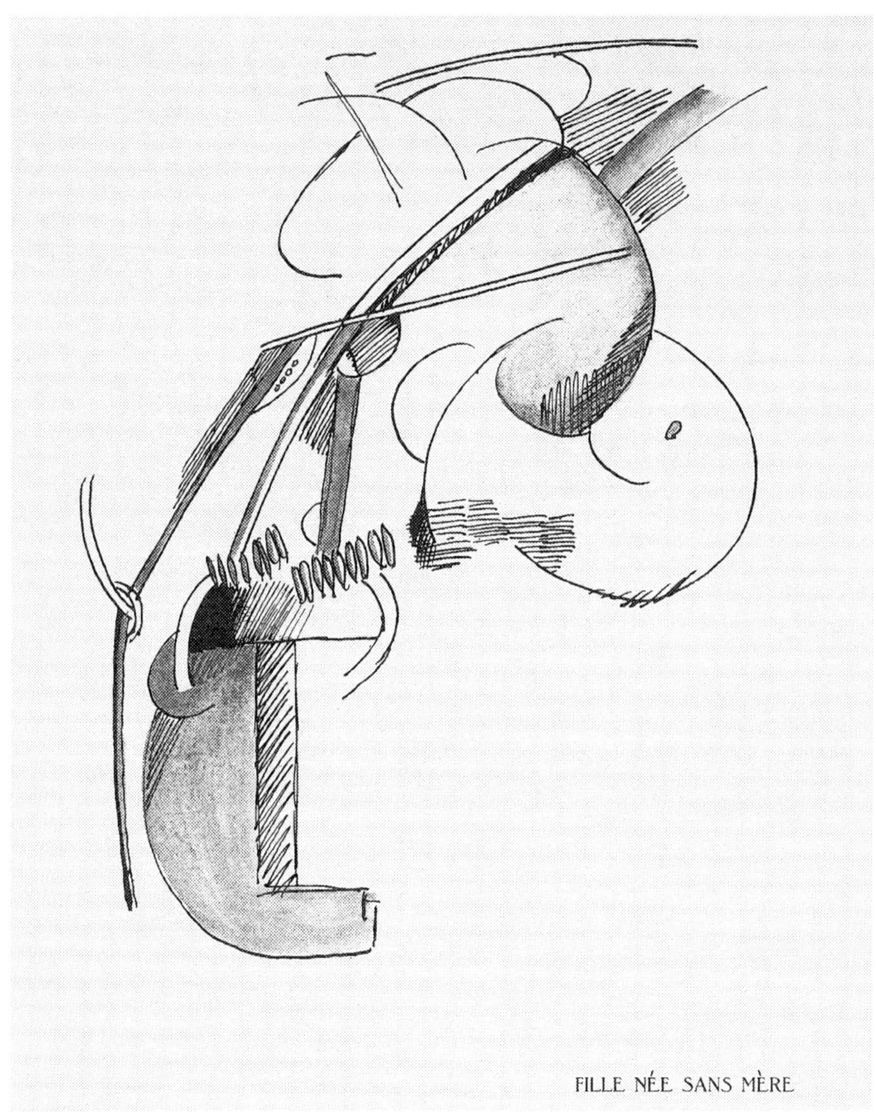

Francis Picabia, *Girl Born without a Mother,* c. 1915. Ink on paper, 26.7 × 21.6 cm (10$^{1}/_{2}$ × 8$^{1}/_{2}$″).
Published in *291* 4 (June 1915). Research Library, The Getty Research Institute, Los Angeles.
© 2005 Artists Rights Society (ARS), New York/ADAGP, Paris/Estate of Francis Picabia.

transformed into a girl-child, a daughter of a sort. But the "absence" of a mother seems immediately to imply, on the most literal level of the phrase, that one has not at all entered into a zone operating outside of the patriarchal order of the general equivalent. Perhaps, however, the motto should be taken as an acknowledgment once more, a kind of mourning: a recognition that the equivalent, as token, operates in a way ever-more forgetful of the maternal signifier, dependent on a rule that represses the groundless ground. This call to memory would then be a way of engaging the token while combating the erasure through which it borrows its power and from which it stems.

But this epigraph or motto—*prolem sine matre creatam,* the child born without mother or model—is paradoxical in an even more direct sense. For of course, as I have been demonstrating, all of the mechanomorphs resolutely had models. This fact has made the industry of "source-finding" that has arisen recently within Picabia scholarship so productive, a potential unveiling of Picabia's artistic method. And yet given the tight marriage within art history between locating "sources" for works of art and the hermeneutical claims of iconography, it is precisely the production of Picabia's mechanomorphs, the method of their formation, that we have yet to understand. We need to define Picabia's relationship to his sources, to his models, and his actions upon these models.

A key, again, can be found in *Poems and Drawings by the Girl Born without a Mother.* In a crucial image from the book—the first drawing that one encounters within its pages—we see a form that evokes perhaps a mechanical fan or ventilator. However, Picabia actually based his tracing not on a form of technological cooling, but on a "hot" image of a sort, a transmitter of both heat and light, an electrical radiator. To this tracing, Picabia offered a name in line with the mechanomorph's origin in the linkage and connection of the diagram form, a title that bespeaks a form of relation, namely, *Vis-à-vis.* And with this title, Picabia included an inscription that seems to define his method throughout the remainder of the mechanomorphs. "That which disfigures the rule," it says. The general equivalent as standard and as measure, the very foundation of the rule: this was precisely what was at stake in Picabia's mechanomorphs. And indeed, one experiences the distance that Picabia sets up between his mechanomorphs and their

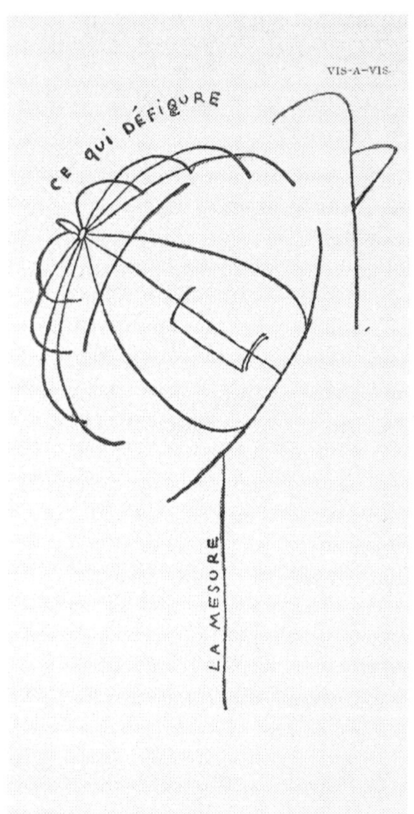

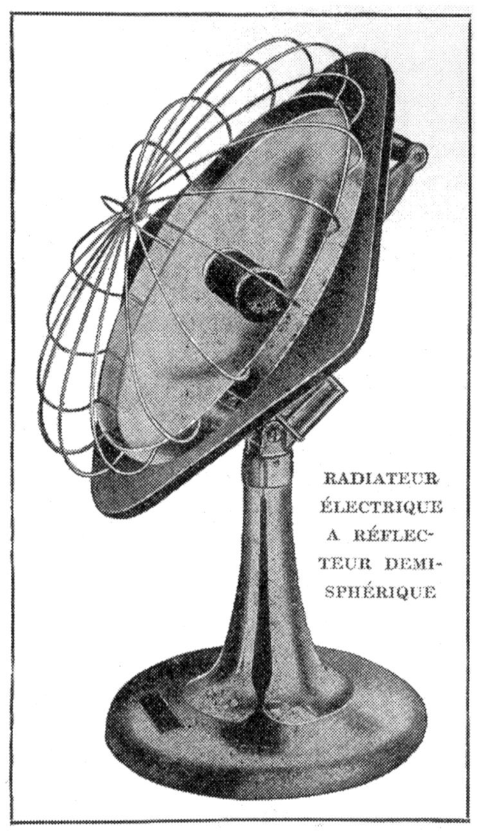

Francis Picabia, *Vis-à-vis,* 1918. From Picabia, *Poèmes et dessins de la fille née sans mère* (Lausanne: Imprimeries réunies, 1918). Research Library, The Getty Research Institute, Los Angeles. © 2005 Artists Rights Society (ARS), New York/ADAGP, Paris/Estate of Francis Picabia.

Source for *Vis-à-vis.* ("Radiateur électrique à réflecteur demi-sphérique," *La Science et la Vie* 37, February–March 1918, p. 315. Image courtesy Arnauld Pierre.)

models, between the trace (in its partiality) and the source (in its full Gestalt), as a mode of disfiguration, an *alteration* enacted upon the model itself.

It should not be surprising by now that I want to use this term "alteration" in the sense that Georges Bataille later gave it, seizing upon the word to embody the destructive impulse that Bataille saw at the basis of all modern art. Art proceeds, Bataille once wrote, "by successive destructions . . . [and] insofar as it liberates instincts, these instincts are sadistic."[50] Bataille's use of the word "alteration" for this destructive process stemmed from the word's root in the ambivalent Latin term *alter,* a word that connoted equally the actions of devolution and evolution, a change in both state and in time. As Briony Fer has described Bataille's proposal:

> Rather than a digression from the concerns of modernist painting, annihilation and obliteration were the concern of modern painting. Doing violence to representation forms the basis, for Bataille, of any representational act. . . . alteration (*altération*) as the basis of drawing . . . involved not only the change from one state to another, but also a succession of changes, each destroying the preceding state. In the act of drawing, a clean piece of paper or a bare wall is in effect "spoilt" and so transformed into something else—a horse or a head, for example; the drawing process, as it continues, subjects the basic figure to further deformations.[51]

Here, I think, we find the description of a process very close to the model of perpetual transformation enacted in the mechanomorphs. Alteration, in its opening onto the dual actions of devolution and evolution, could be compared, in Bataille's words, to both "a partial decomposition analogous with that of corpses and at the same time the transition to a perfectly heterogeneous state corresponding to . . . the *tout autre,* that is, the sacred, realized for example by a ghost."[52] Alteration thus involved the inherently double (and contradictory)—both devolution and evolution, both the material (a corpse) and the immaterial (a ghost)—but it opened onto a process of doubling that produced what we can only call the irremediably singular, the inassimilable (Bataille's "perfectly heterogeneous state").

Art, in the modality of alteration, would strike against the model; it would dirty its support, mutilating it, deforming it. Alteration was not a stable, Platonic affair of mimesis as the experience of the idealized copy, faithful to its model. It instead produced monsters, deviations, deformities—singularities emerging paradoxically in the midst of a process dedicated to replication.[53] And seen in this way, Picabia's 1922 mechanomorphs can be described as internalizing alteration as their (anti-)aesthetic principle. "The painter makes a choice," Picabia had written in his crucial defense of *L'oeil cacodylate* in 1921, "and then imitates his choice so that the *deformation* constitutes the *Art*."[54]

In the variety of Picabia's borrowings, a single model could produce multiple, and completely dissimilar, mechanomorphic copies: witness *Calculator* on the one hand, or *Tickets* on the other. Each abstract mechanomorph emerged as the alteration of its mechanical model, as the loss of the model's uniqueness, an alteration that in effect obscured that model, disfigured it, producing the experience of the abstract out of Bataille's "succession of destructions." The fact that these so-called models were themselves copies—whether the infinitely reproducible photograph or the mechanically produced diagram—only compounds this experience. Internalizing the photographic principle of the copy and the trace, the 1922 mechanomorphs read as abstract *precisely because* they are copies (this is their paradox); they reconfigure abstraction as a *process of the copy*—but copies for which no true model exists, copies that, in effect, destroy the model in a movement that spawns the abstract. We face a form of representation true to the violence that Bataille posited at the basis of representation: a process of reproduction that produces something other than the stable copy and the true double. The last mechanomorphs were copies without originals, "false claimants," to use a phrase from Gilles Deleuze's definition of the simulacrum. "[Iconic] Copies are secondhand possessors," Deleuze writes, "well-grounded claimants, authorized by resemblance. *Simulacra* are like false claimants, built on a dissimilitude, implying a perversion, an essential turning away."[55]

And so the 1922 mechanomorphs were in fact "born without a mother," or a model. They fulfill Breton's early characterization of them as an "art without models," although probably not for the reasons that he thought.[56] "Likeness,"

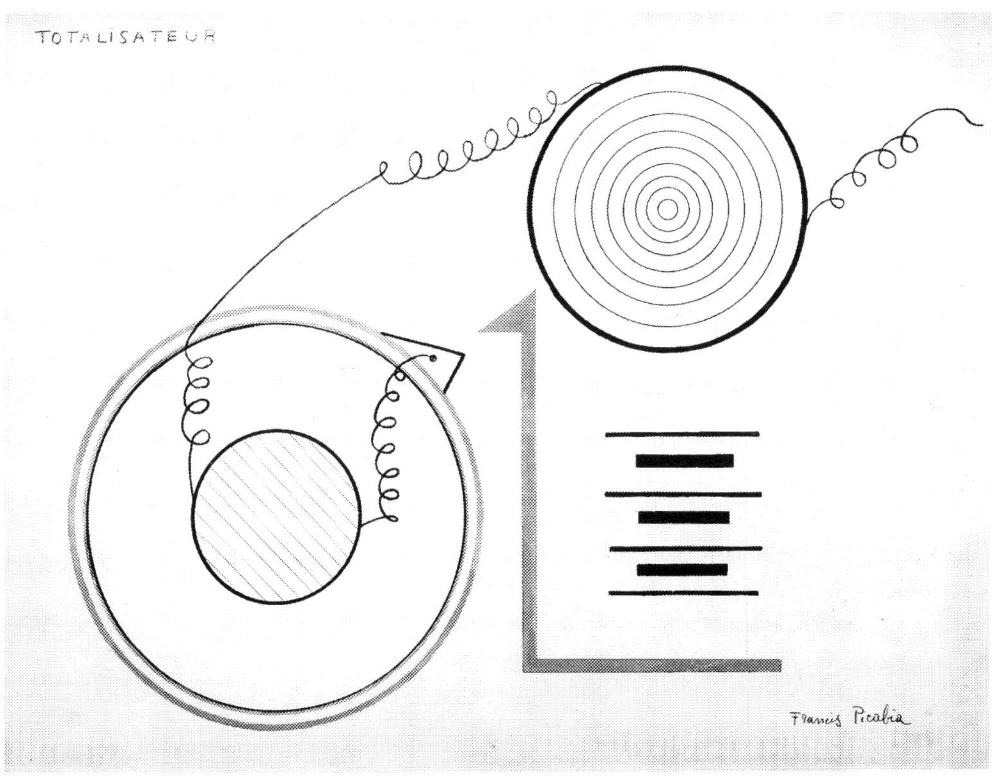

Francis Picabia, *Totalisateur (Calculator),* 1922. Ink and watercolor on paper, 55 × 75 cm. Private collection, Turin. Image courtesy Comité Picabia. © 2005 Artists Rights Society (ARS), New York/ADAGP, Paris/Estate of Francis Picabia.

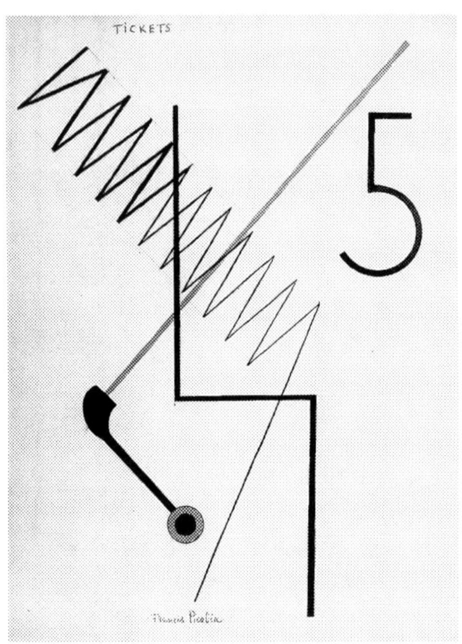

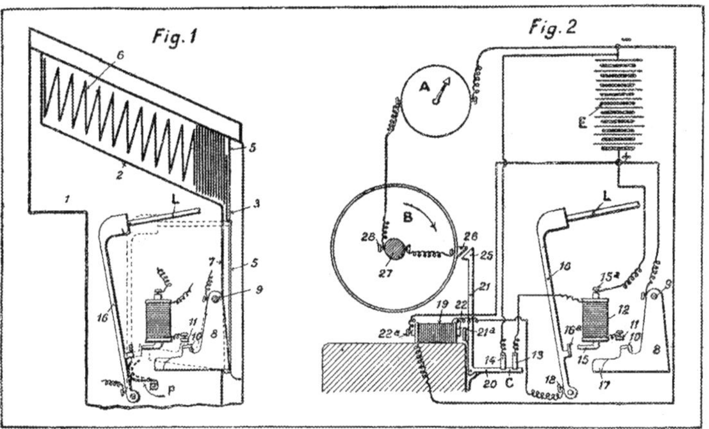

VUES SCHÉMATIQUES DU TOTALISATEUR DE M. KIPARSKI

Fig. 1 : *disposition d'un compartiment ou section d'une caisse à tickets ; fig. 2 : schéma de montage d'un compteur additionnant les tickets délivrés d'une même classe.* — 1, *boîte* ; 2, *plancher incliné* ; 3, *tickets* ; 5, *châssis antérieur* ; 6, *ressort* ; 7, *paroi postérieure* ; 8, *commutateur* ; 9, *axe* ; 10 *et* 11, *contacts produits par le pivotement du commutateur* ; 12, *enroulement d'électro* ; E, *pile* ; 13 *et* 14, *contacts* ; C, *plaque fixée au levier coudé* 20, 21 ; 15, *noyau d'électro* ; 17, *armature* ; 16, *levier* ; P, *ressort* ; L, *doigt* ; 16ª, *plaque de contact du levier* 16 ; 22, *noyau d'un second électro et son armature* 21 ; 23, *ressort* ; 24, *bras* ; 25, *dent du levier* 21 ; 26, *dent du cylindre* B ; 27, *axe* ; 28, *balai relié électriquement au compteur* A.

Francis Picabia, *Tickets,* 1922. Ink and watercolor on paper, 75 × 56 cm. Collection Arturo Schwarz, Milan. Image courtesy Comité Picabia. © 2005 Artists Rights Society (ARS), New York/ADAGP, Paris/Estate of Francis Picabia.

Source for *Tickets* and *Totalisateur.* ("Vues schématiques du totalisateur de M. Kiparski," *La Science et la Vie* 45, June–July 1919, p. 156. Image courtesy Arnauld Pierre.)

as Breton wrote in his catalog essay for the Barcelona show, "Likeness, even a distant one, no longer exists."[57] For the last mechanomorphs were "disfigurations of the rule," a frontal assault on the general equivalent's insistence on the stable origin and filiative model, equivalence twisted into transformation. They had little to do with abstract art's wholescale negation of mimesis, but were instead a shattering of that model (of the model) from within, mimesis and the copy dedicated to failure. They were, indeed, a form of Dada abstraction: failed reproductions, violent abortions of resemblance, a stubborn procession of deviations.[58]

And as if in confirmation of this principle, Picabia produced another version of *Tickets,* another copy, one that even more fully internalized the photographic procedure of the copy and the double. This second version of *Tickets,* in essence, copied itself: it was doubled, fissured from within, folded over around its own central axis, and thus even further disassociated from the external model from which it had been spawned. Here is the copy as a process of destruction, the loss of the original experienced as a disfiguration, an alteration. Picabia entitled this image *Canceled Tickets.*

ECCE HOMO

One must prefer physical pleasure above all but indulge only with oneself; shared passions are like two cars positioned face to face, each trying to make the other back up. I've just sneezed, a little trip through the infinite, now I'm listening to a distant song, the song of the spermatozoa that the allure of my spirit attracts.

—*Francis Picabia, December 1922*[59]

No one has thought to interpret Picabia's last mechanomorphs in their connection to Duchamp's *Large Glass.* But the coincidence that the Picabian mechanomorph appears at the same moment as Duchamp's initiation of the *Large Glass* in 1915, and then climaxes as Duchamp abandons his project, proclaiming it "definitively unfinished" in 1923, should of course not be left a coincidence. The

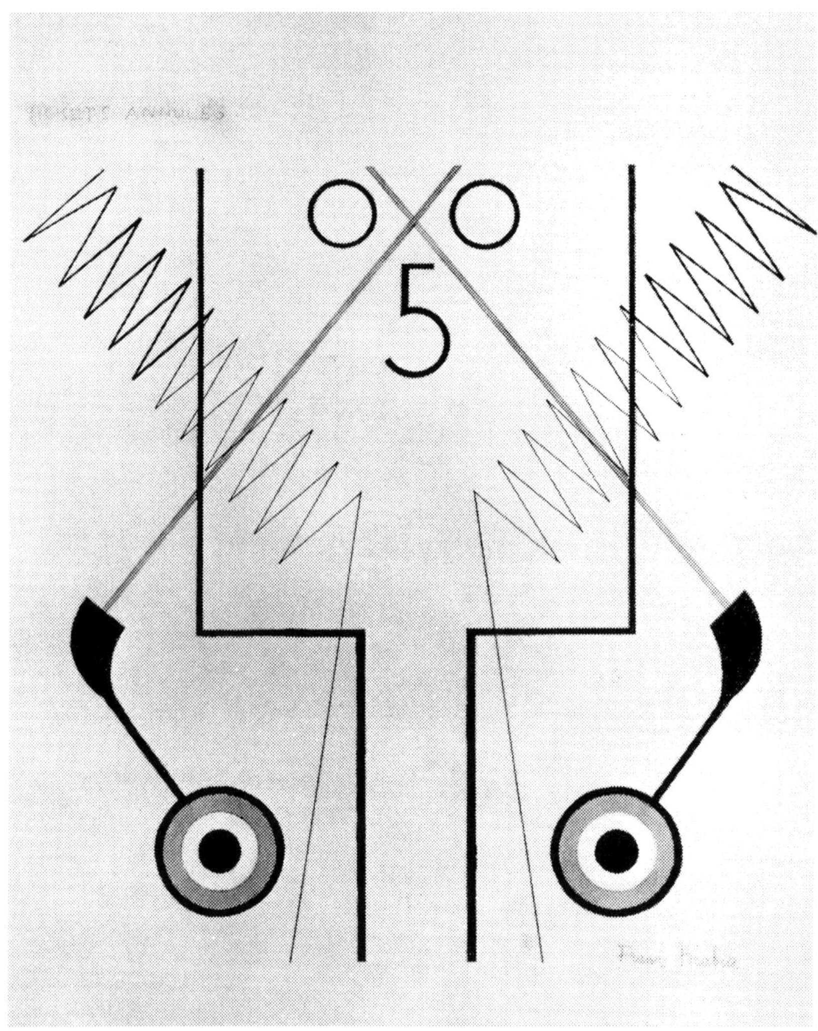

Francis Picabia, *Tickets annulés (Canceled Tickets),* 1922. Ink and watercolor on paper,
71 × 58 cm. Private collection. © 2005 Artists Rights Society (ARS), New York/ADAGP,
Paris/Estate of Francis Picabia.

connection should have been obvious. The mechanomorphs shown in Barcelona were entirely an affair of the bachelor machine, so many progeny of the *Large Glass.*

There was the *Drying Rack,* with its obvious reference to Duchamp's ready-made *Bottle Dryer;* there was the *Grinder,* claiming its own (failed?) filiation to the more famous *Chocolate Grinder* by Duchamp, and that work's subsequent chain of variations leading to its presence in the *Large Glass.* One need list only some of the titles of the works that we know were shown in Barcelona to witness this multiplication of bachelor devices: *Chaff-Cutter, Winding, Hydraulic Press, Fleecer, Calculator, Swiss Machinery, Three-Bladed Cutter, Shutter, Strong Room, Wheelbarrow, Pump, Fuel Pump, Petrol Gas.* All so many echoes of Duchamp's bachelor machine, these works evoke mechanical actions—cutting, winding, pressing, fleecing, adding, clicking, locking, grinding, drying—that I like to imagine in tandem with Picabia's precision actions upon pictorial form. These actions would be Picabia's "Litanies of the Chariot," the song of the bachelor machines from the *Large Glass* that Duchamp imagined as endlessly chanted: "Slow life. Vicious circle. Onanism. Horizontal. Round trip for the buffer. Junk of life. Cheap construction. Tin, cords, iron wire. Eccentric wooden pulleys. Monotonous fly wheel. Beer professor."[60] And indeed, to the satisfaction of the Duchampian sleuths among us, Picabia produced an image that he actually entitled *Chariot,* an image created in the immediate wake of the Barcelona exhibition, with the mechanomorphic bachelor machine transmuted into the stark silhouette of a male form, floating isolated on a riveting field of black and white, like so many prison bars.

Picabia had his own "Litanies of the Chariot." He imagined this litany as what he called the "song of the spermatozoa." This invocation of reproduction reminds us that reproduction indeed was one of the main concerns of the last mechanomorphs. On the one hand, these works embraced the status of the photograph and of the multiple. On the other hand, however, they engaged abstraction only as a procedure—as a product—of *failed reproduction,* as a breakdown of the principles of filiation and similarity, as a process of the copy devolving into the propagation of absolute singularities.

Picabia seized upon the bachelor apparatus as the agent of this failure. The bachelor machine—at least as Duchamp imagined this in his *Large Glass*—produces nothing but failure, or rather erotic incompletion; it is characterized by its

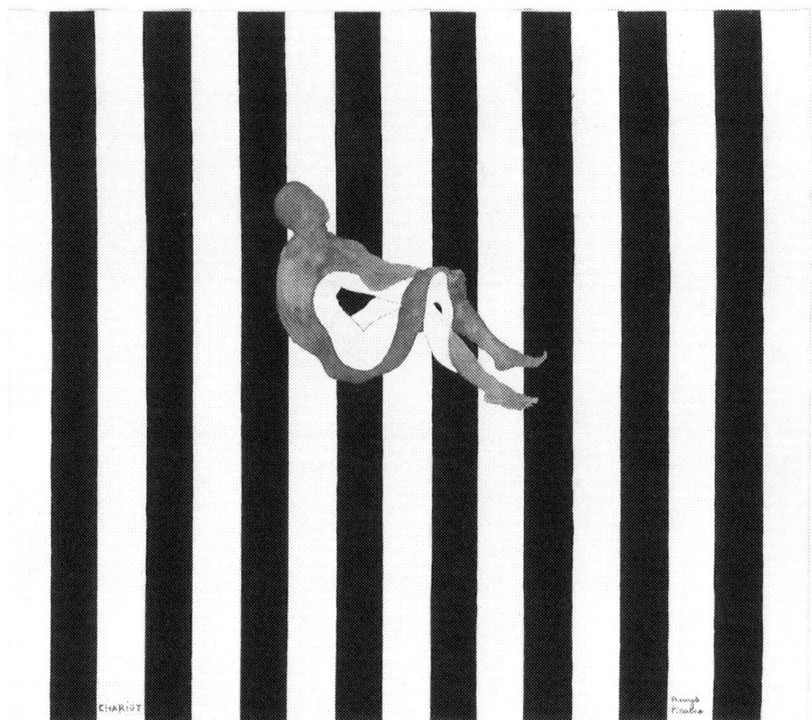

Francis Picabia, *Chariot,* c. 1922–23. Watercolor, ink, and pencil on paper, 60 × 71 cm.
Collection of Clodagh and Leslie Waddington, London. Image courtesy Comité Picabia.
© 2005 Artists Rights Society (ARS), New York/ADAGP, Paris/Estate of Francis Picabia.

isolation, its utter self-enclosure; and it initiates an endless series of connections between its own parts that is simultaneously a disconnection from any incursion of an outside. This isolation remains the visual experience most characteristic of the last mechanomorphs. They are filled with lines and forms teetering into the realm of the unmotivated only by a process of isolation and decontextualization, as if the tissue of connections that would make sense of these forms had been ripped away or suppressed, their drawing a function of subtraction, the elision of what is *not* there. And these forms are then recombined, manipulated, scattered across a representational field on which they will be captured and suspended like a series of helpless prisoners. One notices that almost never does a line in any of the last mechanomorphs touch the framing edge of the picture plane on which it seems to float, recoiling from this edge as if in fear. And although forming no coherent Gestalts, the compositions of the last mechanomorphs are repeatedly formed by being roughly centered; in fact, centering seems Picabia's overriding, if not his only, compositional decision. The effect of both procedures only heightens the isolation of each of the last mechanomorphs, increasing the sense one has of gazing at an immobilized field of specimens, disconnected from any outside domain of which they were once a part.

The last mechanomorphs, then, do not so much *illustrate* the components of the bachelor apparatus as they exist as a series of *enactments* of its procedures, lonely precipitates of the bachelor machine's dedication to onanistic production and to failure. "Comedies of laying bare, machinery of torture, 'automaton accounts' stripped of meaning, faces broken down into cogwheels":[61] such is how Michel de Certeau describes the bachelor machine, thinking of its dual commitment to the actions of *laying bare* ("not an 'uncovering' of truth in the Greek sense, but a stripping down and demystification of the semantic order" [CM, p. 160]) and of the *torture* necessary for this labor. A late mechanomorph such as the black hole that is Picabia's *Décaveuse (Fleecer)* succinctly encapsulates both procedures: its frame studded with nails pointing out at the viewer like a medieval torture device, its title from the French verb *décaver,* meaning to clean out, to bankrupt, to ruin, or to beggar.

De Certeau's account of the bachelor machine depends on a comparison between its various twentieth-century avatars, long ago isolated by Michel

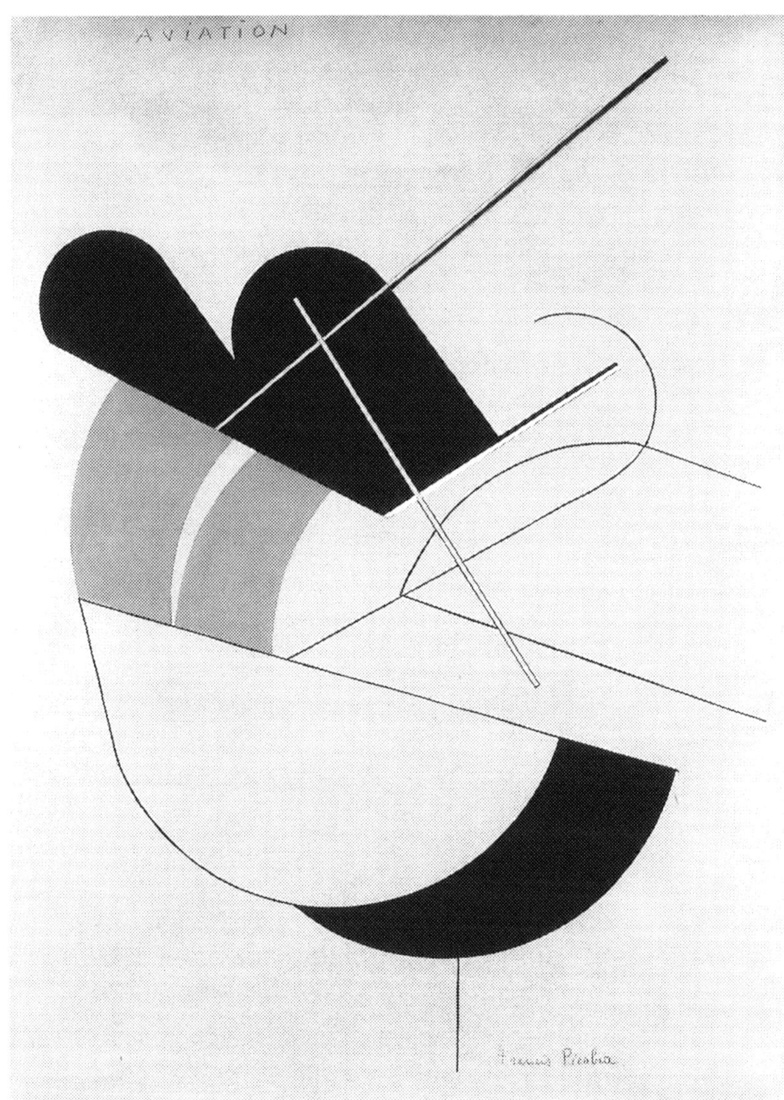

Francis Picabia, *Aviation,* 1922. Pen, ink, and gouache on paperboard, 75 × 54 cm. (29$\frac{1}{2}$ × 21$\frac{1}{4}$″). Museum of Art, RISD, Gift of the Harriet and Bayard Ewing Collection. © 2005 Artists Rights Society (ARS), New York/ADAGP, Paris/Estate of Francis Picabia.

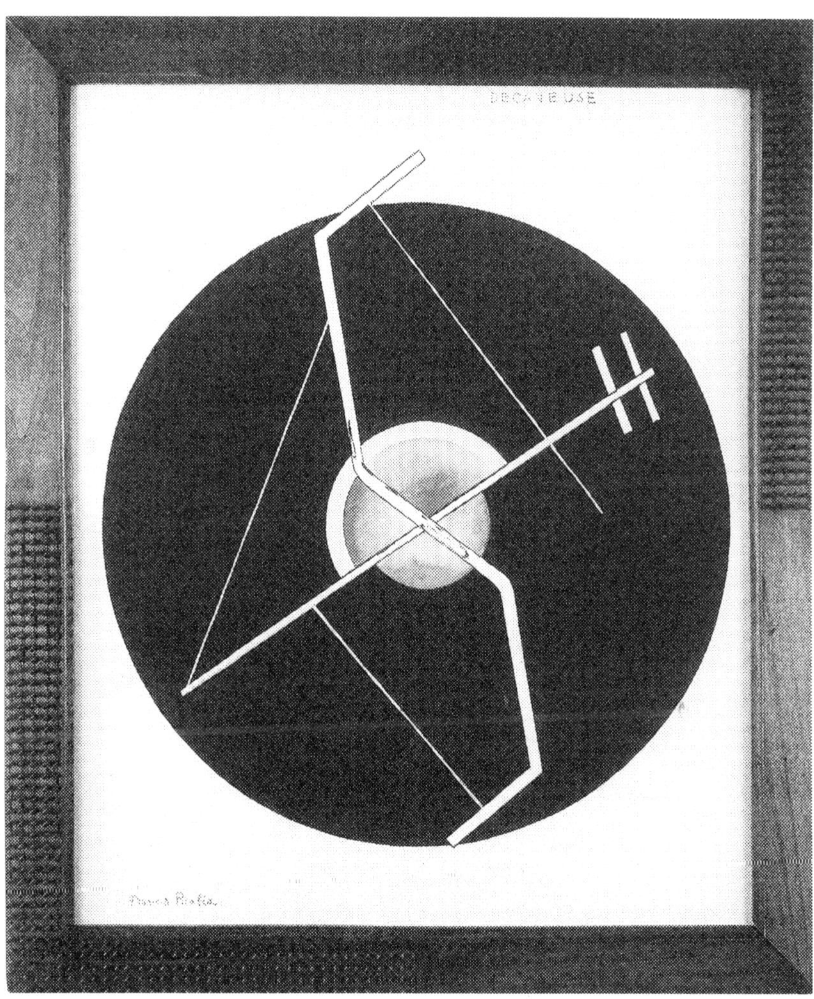

Francis Picabia, *Décaveuse (Fleecer)*, 1922. Ink, watercolor, and gouache on paperboard, 72.5 × 59.5 cm. Collection Mr. and Mrs. George L. Lindemann. © 2005 Artists Rights Society (ARS), New York/ADAGP, Paris/Estate of Francis Picabia.

Carrouges—Franz Kafka's torture mechanism in *The Penal Colony*, Raymond Roussel's machines for artistic production in *Impressions of Africa*, Duchamp's *The Bride Stripped Bare by Her Bachelors, Even*—and the traditional workings of mystical, religious discourse, from which he claims the bachelor machine borrows its dual procedures. "By the twentieth century," de Certeau writes, "all of [the] postulates of the religious *episteme* of the seventeenth century had disappeared." And yet:

> Although they abandon the hypothesis that there is one, traditional, semantic system (meaning is everywhere) . . . [and] though they have finally freed themselves from the need for an institution concealing a truth somewhere in its dark recesses (mysticism arose in relation to a religion) . . . celibatory machines nevertheless practice both the art of laying bare and torture. Theirs, however, is a *linguistic* rather than a semantic labor. It can no longer take recourse in "truth." (CM, p. 160)

The result is an endless writing, a "system of phonetic drift."[62]

The bachelor machine produces what we might call a token language stripped of meaning, a system violently "laid bare," a language divorced from any sense of a source, endlessly recurring and yet sui generis: "The text stands alone. It is the only referential 'body.' It is a substitute (*Ersatz*), kept at a distance (*Locus solus*), of both the speaking subject and the maternal body: one is the absent author (it authorizes nothing); the other is 'tread upon' by a writing which is separated from it" (CM, p. 161). Here we sense the slight but crucial difference between the work of the bachelor machine and the general equivalent as empty—or emptied—token sign. As opposed to the imposture of the general equivalent, the bachelor machine quite precisely refuses to "write over" the maternal signifier, sealing off the groundless ground of the signifying chain. The bachelor machine may stand distant or divorced from the maternal sign—it perhaps registers the loss of this sign and an alternate symbolic economy more broadly—but it will not step in to participate in the series of exchanges that usurp her place. It instead opens up in the place of this usurpation an endless auto-displacement.

De Certeau's invocation of the distance that the bachelor machine takes in respect to the "maternal body" immediately recalls Picabia's invocation of the "girl born without a mother" as the guiding principle of his mechanomorphs. Viewed as a principle of the bachelor machine, such a dynamic emerges as the polar opposite of the misogyny that many feminist critics have lately attributed to Dada's engagement with the machine, as if this engagement were simply a late outgrowth of Marinetti's Futurist rants against the female. Picabia's gendering of this principle as the "*girl* born without a mother" can, I think, be attributed to his interest in Duchamp's conception of the "bride," a necessary component of the bachelor apparatus, a part of its system of "inscription," and, for both Picabia and Duchamp, a figure serving as a synecdoche for abstraction—which, in this case, we might read as a word signifying the unknowable, the empty, the void.[63] "Since laying bare occurs in relation to an impossible incest," de Certeau explains, "the fading away of the 'land' that guarantees language appears both in the form of blasphemies directed against the woman/mother [*mère*] and dreams of the sea [*mer*]."[64] The mother, de Certeau adds, was dominant in mystical discourse—one thinks of the cult of the Virgin Mary, of the innumerable mystics who were themselves female—and yet its exegete "was the clergyman, the male adherent of mystic discourse who expected to receive through its feminine alteration, not his power . . . but the ability to produce and 'speak'" (CM, p. 161).

The bachelor machine, on the other hand, "is the narrative of the *celibate,* in relation to the impossible *mère (mer),* to the female hanged man, to the bride stripped bare" (CM, p. 161). It entails an alteration of—directed against—the self. It reverses the power relations inherent in the older order of things. Its self-enclosure announces a renunciation of the power of introducing the Other into discourse, of claiming and speaking that "truth":

> The celibatory machine . . . has no need to disclose something hidden. A refusal of the title, "son of," is the very principle of this construct featuring the Separate . . . . There is nothing hidden because *exteriority* takes its place. (CM, p. 166)

Filiation fails. The model behind the work misfires. Instead, an outside and a limit are revealed:

> The recognition of an absolute *outside* dispenses with the need to introduce *into* the text a concealed/disclosed allusion to an authority that would make it believable. Mysticism presupposed the internal perception by an ego of its exteriority, in other words, it had to quote the other in the text. The celibatory machine keeps the other outside of itself . . . . The very exactness of its details (each part is a "well arranged item") emphasizes their separation from one another, within systems themselves carefully distinguished. No confusion intervenes to make us forget about difference. The apparatus shines like a blade. It has the cleanliness of a suicide which *makes way* for the world's alterity, with no compensation. (CM, p. 166)

I can think of no better words than the last sentences of this passage to describe Picabia's reconfiguration of abstraction in the last mechanomorphs. "No confusion intervenes to make us forget about difference. The apparatus shines like a blade. It has the cleanliness of a suicide which *makes way* for the world's alterity, with no compensation." Here we encounter the logic behind a practice of abstraction that depends on the copy, a procedure of the copy that produces the dissimilar, an engagement with dissimilarity that generates non-engagement—a circumscribed (self-enclosed, celibate) abstraction of visual unknowing.

Abstraction's boundlessness has no place here, none at all. This is an art of limits, an art proclaimed in the key of dispossession (both of the creator and the viewer). This is an art (de)formed by alteration—and thus an art of alterity, of an outside to be neither transcended nor deflated. De Certeau connected such a logic directly to Georges Bataille, who has been useful to us, at least in part, because he is one of the great inheritors of the tortured labor of the bachelor machine, capitalizing on its central notions of what de Certeau calls the "male divide," the limit, and the preservation of an outside. Bataille's thought contained many examples of his own exploration of language "laid bare." "I think like a girl takes off her dress," Bataille once wrote. "At its most extreme point, thought is immodesty, obscenity itself."[65]

NON LIQUET

One should pay no attention to which sex one belongs. I no longer worry about knowing whether I'm a male or a female, for I don't think that men are any better than women.

—*Francis Picabia, January 1923*[66]

. . . the milky way, that strange hole of astral sperm and celestial urine in the cranial vault formed by the ring of constellations: that open crack at the summit of the sky . . .

—*Georges Bataille, 1928*[67]

And so with the Bachelors comes the Bride. In the Barcelona exhibition proper, "her" presence was registered in the series of ludicrous pastiches that mocked the return to figuration and to Ingres in recent French art, images inserted willy-nilly among the abstract mechanomorphs and that Picabia called "Spanish women." We see one of the *Espagnoles* in the photograph of Picabia's vernissage, surrounded by a group of (real) Spanish men with their backs turned resolutely to the teeming surround of the mechanomorphs, gazing in silent collective perplexity at the figure's bulbous, vacant, slightly *louche* eyes, the single mole punctuating willfully a too-broad left cheek, the preposterous stub of a lit cigarette clenched between teeth and lip.

But in the wake of the Barcelona show, as 1922 slipped into 1923, the bachelor machine for Picabia suddenly became figurative (*Chariot*), and the Bride became abstract, their turn around this formal divide seemingly in alternation, for the moment a product of opposition and of separation. After returning from Barcelona, Picabia submitted a major painting entitled *Volucelle II* to the Salon des Indépendants in February of 1923. A series of perfect circles on another

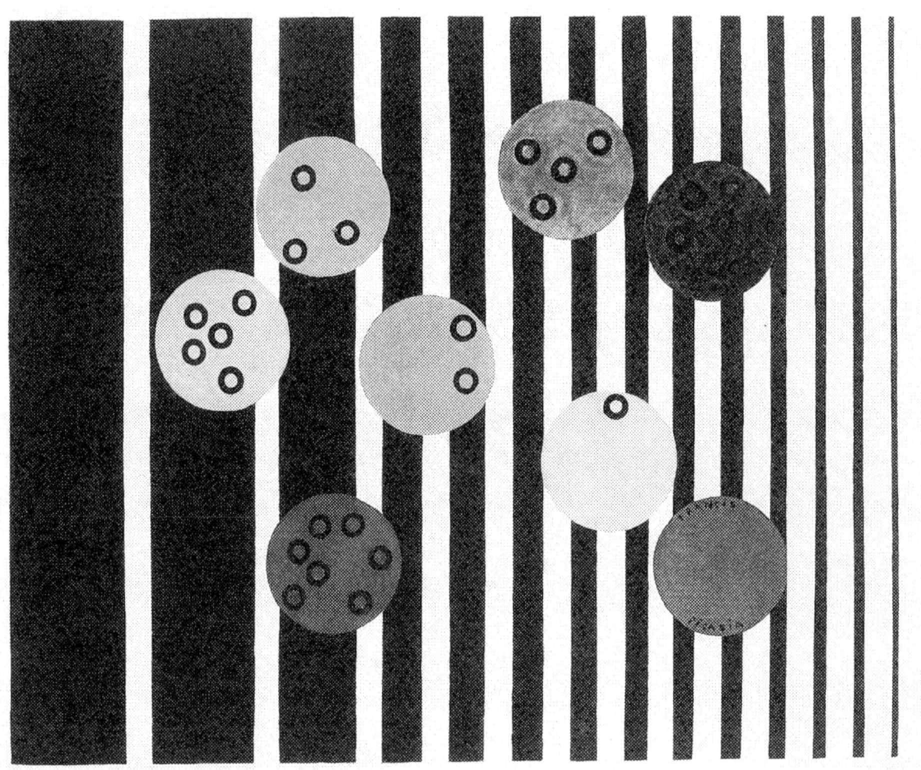

Francis Picabia, *Volucelle II,* 1922–23. Ripolin on canvas, 198.5 × 249 cm. Private collection. © 2005 Artists Rights Society (ARS), New York/ADAGP, Paris/Estate of Francis Picabia.

shimmering ground of black and white, *Volucelle II* has been interpreted as a possible reference to star charts and to constellations—a recurrent fascination for the Dadaists and Surrealists—but no satisfactory "source" for the image has ever been found.[68] What has been missed in this iconographical approach, however, is the admittedly hermetic affiliation of Picabia's title to the *Large Glass*: in French a *volucelle* is a scientific term for a winged insect. And as Michel Carrouges has pointed out, the term for "bride" in French, *la mariée,* is also a slang term for a type of nocturnal insect, a moth.[69] And of course, Duchamp, in his apparatus of notes for the *Large Glass,* referred consistently to one part of the Bride's domain as the "Wasp."

Picabia's title must be understood in this connection: we are facing a mechanomorphic incarnation of the Bride. This is not to say that the iconographer's constellation interpretation is misguided; references to stars and astronomy were indeed common in the 1922 mechanomorphs closest to the form of *Volucelle II*: *Mercury,* for example, or *Astrolabe,* both shown in Barcelona. But of course this too was a theme of the Bride's half of the *Large Glass,* with the Bride's "blossoming" baptized by Duchamp as "the Milky Way."[70]

The lesson of Duchamp's Milky Way—which contained the three "Draft Pistons" formed by photographing the chance actions of wind on a piece of cloth—was the stark formal dialectic between mechanicity and chance procedures, in a knot that tied together tracing, photography, and the aleatory. Beyond the iconographic level at which *Volucelle*'s interpretation has stalled, such was the formal lesson of Picabia's painting as well, the random distribution of his circles played off against their utterly precise and serialized rendition as graphic signs. And so to see the notion of the "Bride" operating beneath the surface of Picabia's *Volucelle II* is not to add another layer of iconographical interpretation to a painting evidently intended to be hermetic—intended, indeed, to call up the entire problematic of what Picabia considered the "abstract." It is, rather, to view the painting, like the last mechanomorphs, as the enactment of a procedure, the laying down of a principle.

I think, then, that the closest thing to a "source" for *Volucelle II* we will ever find is the following project of Picabia's recorded by Breton, a project that scholars formerly thought had gone unrealized. The passage in question comes from Breton's 1921 verbal portrait of the painter André Derain:

> Derain is not a subjectivist. He denies that a collection of indifferent strokes can appear beautiful. The three curves I see here affect me only because they form the astrological sign for Leo. Nothing more premeditated than that. We could say as much about the letters of the alphabet. The appearance of a page of characters in a book is extremely unnerving: to think that *that* can make people act. Derain admits that language (pictorial or otherwise) is a convention, but he believes he can go beyond this. Asked to comment on Picabia's project (assemble some twenty balls in the corner of a pool table, then sweep them forward in a single motion along the felt, photograph the result, and sign it) he demurs. That would be a feat of magic rather than a work of art. In any case, to reach some sort of conclusion one would have to take *several* photos of the pool table once the balls were in place, in order to compare them.[71]

Everything crucial about *Volucelle II* is contained in this passage: the seeming invocation of astrology, the propagation of a system of conventional but projected signs, the outline for a formal procedure melding both chance and photography. And Picabia did make more than one version of *Volucelle II*. We do know that there exists a much smaller, drawn version entitled *Volucelle I*. This image was not so much a maquette for the later painting as it was another, *different* enactment of the same procedures, another random distribution of a series of identical circles. As with *La Sainte-Vierge,* this was then an action that Picabia meant to be repeated, with a different result each time. Traced and formally perfect, however, the circles of *Volucelle* call up nothing in Picabia's art so much as the promise of *La jeune fille*—another invocation, of course, of the Bride—as if the opening up of drawing to its outside, the reconfiguration of drawing as a literal matrix, here found its logical progeny. Drawing as a hole gives rise to the propagation of a series of black holes, the condition of the multiple arising from a foundational loss, from the transparent space of the void.

And if the circles of *Volucelle* were meant to evoke the constellations, we witness here not the gleam of white stars against the black ground of night, but rather a chain of black suns upon the white space of drawing, as if such an evocation of the stars had been given over to a procedure of tonal reversal, assimilated to the negative image that is the characteristic domain of the photograph-as-double. What I would like to call the *Volucelle* "principle," then, is a procedure founded on both the trace and the photograph. It reconfigures the inscription of the Duchampian "Bride" as the production of an abstract form, constructed from a repetitive series of identical signs arranged in configurations that nevertheless result in the propagation of the singular. And as such, abstraction here was not an affair of immanence; it emerged rather from the outside—a giving over of form to a dalliance in the hole of *La jeune fille,* or to the externality that is the photograph.

Abstraction, in Picabia's hands, becomes the sign of that externality, a cipher for the unknowable, a figuration of the limit, and an inscription of failure—of the forms that failure provides. It was understood as a series of signs "stripped bare," predetermined and yet ever-changing, repetitive and yet contingent, systematized and yet utterly meaningless. Abstraction would take refuge in the circle: the shape of form perfected, the symbol of form as endless and inexhaustible, and yet the enactment of form as endlessly undone. Abstraction, for Dada, became in this way an explicitly feminine trope, ever more distant from the paternal equivalent and standard, and from the latter's claims to embody all that abstraction could be within modernity, and all that it would permit.

IN NATURALIBUS

Eyes, hands, legs, and mouths become one when they make love.

—*Francis Picabia, 1924*[72]

It was the circle—now visible in its attachment to the (auto)erotic dynamics of the Bachelors and the Bride—that introduced the logic of the "part object" into the last mechanomorphs. What the psychoanalysts call the part object restructures the field of the object as a field of transformations, never fixed, never unitary, always slipping from one form to the next through a logic of substitution that seems particularly appropriate to our experience of Picabia's mechanomorphs.[73] Indeed, some notion of the part object had always been crucial to the mechanomorph.

We see it already in 1915, with the *Portrait of Haviland,* the represented lamp's improbable cord simultaneously bodying forth a shape recognizable as nothing so much as the human ear. We see it with the *Portrait of Stieglitz,* in the too insistent phallic detumescence of the represented camera bellows. And then again in 1917, with the photograph that served as *Américaine,* the decontextualized lightbulb summoning forth concurrently the round swell of the breast and the upright projection of the phallus.[74] Then too there was *Âne,* or *Ass* in English, a ship's propeller and another tail-end form that—not unlike Duchamp's contemporaneous readymade *Fountain*—promiscuously opens up an entire scene of bodily projections, its blades pendulously suggesting not just the flap of a donkey's ears but also the female breast, the suspension of the male scrotum, and the swing of fleshy buttocks, its central hole following the obscene direction of *Ass*'s punning title into the realm of bodily orifices. In the early mechanomorphs, it is as if the appearance of a series of reified, appropriated machine parts begins to herald a breakdown in the unified economy of the visual field.

Language surely plays its role here, refusing as it does in Picabia's work the adequation between word and thing, between sign and phenomena, crucial to visual identification and to the sense to be gleaned from a purportedly mimetic terrain. It is as if the fixed *unity* of objects, their *singleness,* could no longer be maintained, as the mechanomorph, fusing body and machine, summons up a field of transformations and apparently anarchic visual equivalencies. And the last mechanomorphs turned this field of transformation into a *process,* embraced as the founding logic of their parturition.

This enactment of equivalency hardly brings us back, however, to a space of mythic similarity, no matter Picabia's placement of the early mechanomorphs under the aegis of Ovid's *Metamorphoses.* But neither can the last mechanomorphs' equivalency principle be completely assimilated (or assimilated any longer) to the modern transformations of capital, or to the fluid economy of the general

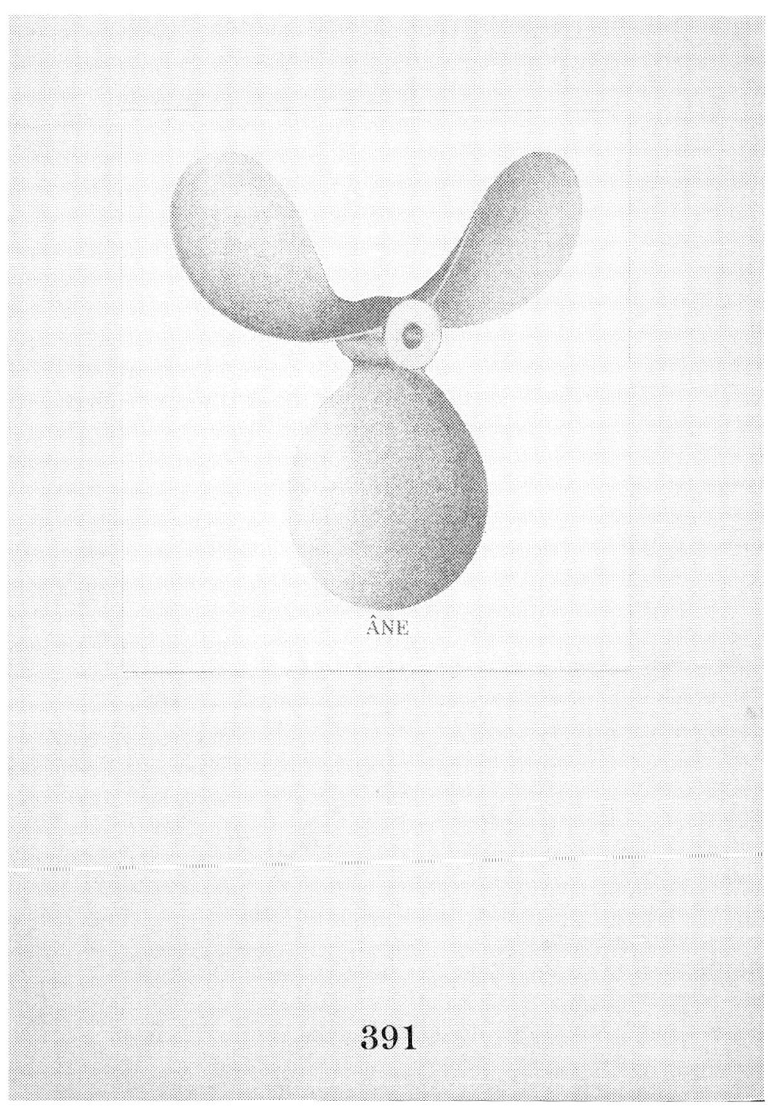

Francis Picabia, *Âne (Ass),* 1917. Cover of *391* 5 (June 1917). Research Library, The Getty Research Institute, Los Angeles. © 2005 Artists Rights Society (ARS), New York/ADAGP, Paris/Estate of Francis Picabia.

equivalent. We are summoned to bear witness to the visual field of an entirely altered economy, a breakdown in vision's inherent search for fixity and stable form, an economy spewing out remainders but gleefully deprived of a common denominator. In the end, the mechanomorph's equivalency principle must rather be compared to the flow of endless difference that belongs to the part object.

The last mechanomorphs witness the part object erupting from within a domain supposedly dedicated to being entirely without objects, the field of modernist abstraction, undoing in this the opposition between figuration and abstraction itself. If, despite the invocation of a mimetic field, the earlier mechanomorphs evinced a repeated fusion of objects perhaps characteristic of the operation Melanie Klein has theorized as "introjection," the last mechanomorphs might be seen as consistently splitting their forms between body and machine, between the figurative and the abstract, more characteristic of the opposed operation that Klein terms "projection." This splitting revolves around the consistent tracing, within the last mechanomorphs, of the circle and its various instantiations.

The circle is the form par excellence of the part object. It makes its appearance in the last mechanomorphs not just as a sign of pure geometry—the circle being precisely that abstract form that absolutely cannot be made by hand, that necessitates mechanical procedures—nor simply as the symbol of so many gears and circular machine parts, but as the avatar of so many part objects, all promiscuously connected through the form of the circle: breast and nipple, eye and mouth, anus and genital orifice. By 1924, Picabia succinctly demonstrated this splitting in the page from the program of his ballet *Relâche* that I discussed in chapter 1, where a geometric series of nested circles abuts the traced contours of a parallel series of female breasts, the fusion of Picabia's previous abstract forms now split into the confused and fragmented impurity of the geometric and the bodily. But perhaps my division is too simple, as the splitting of projection probably can never be so easily divorced from the fusions of introjection, as we witness, across the full panorama of this page, words tracing both a pendulous breast and a perfect circle, periods stuttering into polka dots, bodies de-differentiated by a covering of abstract forms, and abstract forms erupting into the sudden recognizability of bodily pieces.

The economy of the part object does not uphold clear oppositions, the structuring comparisons on which valuation and exchange depend. A certain economy of sense and of form collapses: witness *Optophone*, its title keyed to the domain of sound, but its forms pressuring the limits of vision. *Optophone* layers the figurative on the abstract, merges the pastiched contour of a classicizing silhouette with the mechanical contour of geometric form, and places the genital on the summit—or deep within the vortex—of a modernist nesting of structures creating a reflexive *mise-en-abyme*. We face a mad collapse of the hierarchies of form and of style achieved (but is it an "achievement"?) through the operations of the part object.

In their recourse to the bachelor machine, the last mechanomorphs marry abstraction to the part object. And with this, we feel a thematic echo of the mechanomorphs' formal beginnings in the process of alteration, in the continual transformation of their photographic models and sources. Unfixed and unfixing, the part object signals a loss of identity, a loss of self-similarity, and so too do the mechanomorphs. And as the part object's model of perpetual transformation operates as an anarchic result of desire's basis on the lost object, so too the mechanomorphs emerge into our field of vision as an affair of secondary elaboration, the production of the image as a field of blurred substitutes—displacements along a chain, without ground, without end.

The part object is reductive: it collapses the whole body into a fragment that represents it. But its reduction is not to the singular, or to the One—this is not the reductive impulse that inspired modernist abstraction—for the part object rather seizes upon reduction as a process of multiplication. Consider the almost imbecilic intensity projected by the forms of Picabia's *Lampe,* another work created around or in the immediate aftermath of the Barcelona show: we have traveled far from the simple photographic appropriation of the lightbulb of *Américaine.* Evidently involved in staging both fusion and splitting, introjection and projection, *Lampe* floats an innocuous series of multicolored circles across a progression of rings sprouting gears, an icy face supplanting the luminosity of a machinic bulb, and not-quite-two frozen, cartoon-quality eyes married to the piercing luminosity of the sun. The black orb of an ungainly mole sits again to

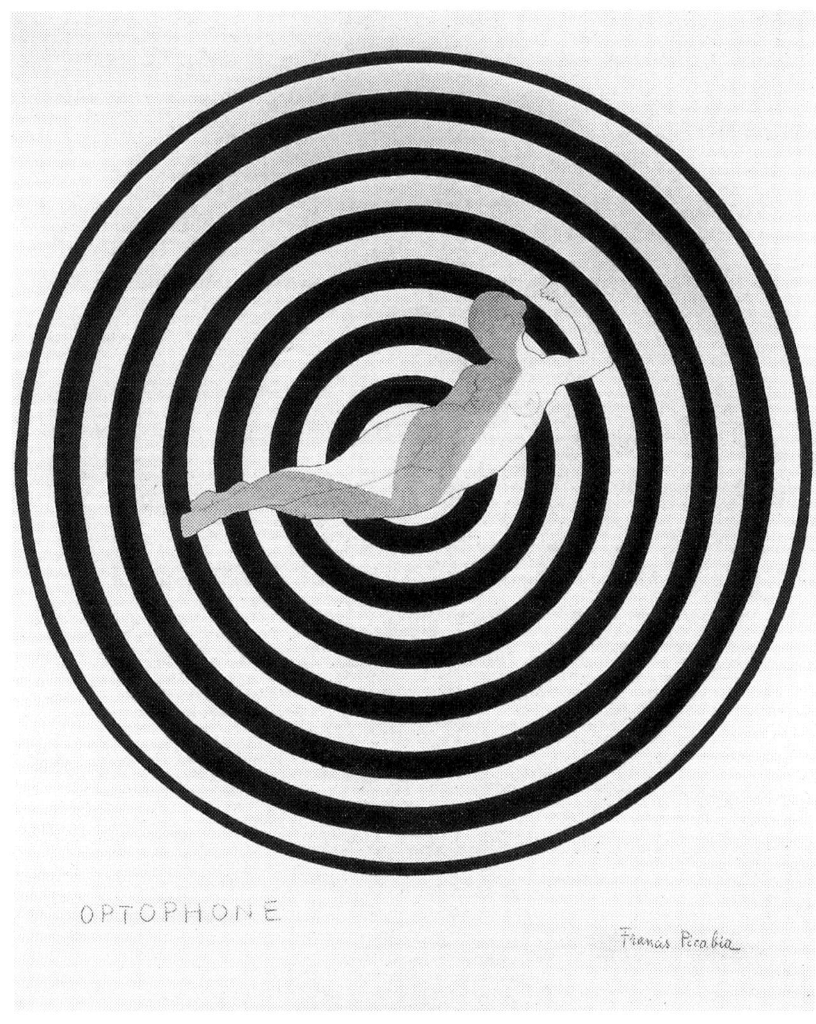

Francis Picabia, *Optophone,* 1922. Ink and watercolor on paperboard, 72 × 60 cm. Private collection. © 2005 Artists Rights Society (ARS), New York/ADAGP, Paris/Estate of Francis Picabia.

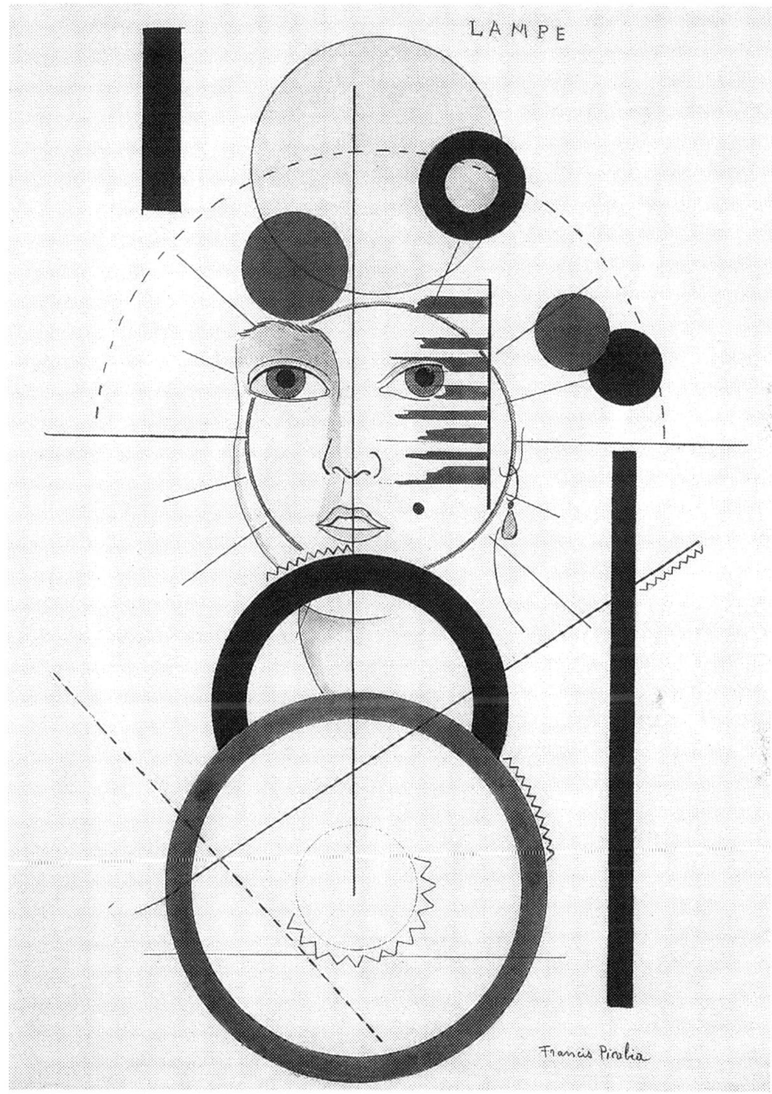

Francis Picabia, *Lampe,* c. 1923. Pencil, ink, and gouache on paper, 62.5 × 47 cm. Collection of Clodagh and Leslie Waddington, London. Image courtesy Comité Picabia. © 2005 Artists Rights Society (ARS), New York/ADAGP, Paris/Estate of Francis Picabia.

the left side of this face, the abscissa and ordinate of geometric form skewed by the eruptions of the body, the arbitrary and the unmotivated overtaking mechanicity (or mechanicity *revealed as* both arbitrary and unmotivated). *Lampe* predicts one of the futures of Picabia's art: an embrace of the figurative-as-pastiche that soon left any concern with abstraction far behind, seemingly authorized by the eruption of the part object within the mechanomorphs.

At their most bald, such pastiches violated the neo-classical body of postwar French art with the hallucinogenic, pornographic intensity of a 1924 drawing such as *Érotique,* a vision worthy of Bosch, with the stark bodily contours of a renewed figurative line doing nothing to stem the tide of transformations initiated by the part object to which this line nevertheless attempts to give form, and from which it takes the modality of its form. Breasts become testicles, or conversely sprout erections. Heads are thrown back, or erupt into throbbing dicks, while tongues slither out from the place of the phallus, connecting bodies both licking and sucking at once, deep within the grip of projection and introjection, splitting and fusion. Asses hang from cheeks like jowls. Or from the chest like breasts. Or from the arm like fists. Nipples merge. A swollen glans becomes a puckered lip, a blushing anus opens wide as a mouth, and a nose sprouts a phallus and violates an anus in its turn. Mouths regurgitate fingers, or become the clenched fist of a penis in full salute. Arms become legs, backs become fronts, and—somehow more obscene than all the rest—a single breast protrudes like a vile lump from the space between a pair of spread-eagled legs. All parts of the body "become one" as they "make love," but none becomes singular, none becomes One, all instead devoted to a new mode of linkage and fusion transformed into a *mise-en-scène* whose only unity is multiplicity.

Line here, we might say, has itself been "stripped bare." It will produce contour, it will cut out the exactitude of mimetic form, but it will be emptied of its former valencies, a promiscuous token as much as a token of promiscuity. To arrive here, however, Picabia's line had to travel from the diagrammatic vector through the abstraction of the last mechanomorphs, through a different but initiatory promiscuity, like that opened up by the slit circles of *Culotte tournante,* for example. And however melancholic the future of Picabia's pastiche would be,

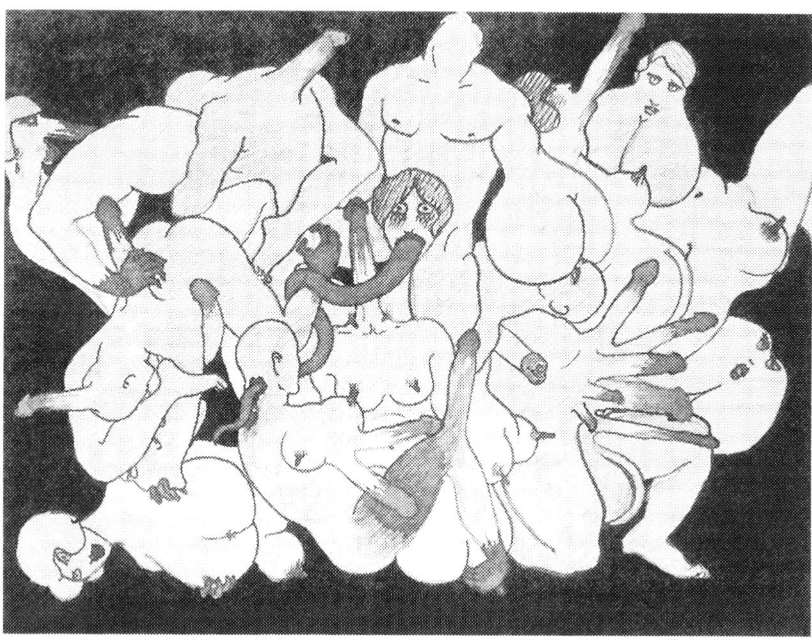

Francis Picabia, *Erotic,* 1924. Watercolor, India ink, and pencil on paper, 45.3 × 30.5 cm. Private collection, Paris. © 2005 Artists Rights Society (ARS), New York/ADAGP, Paris/ Estate of Francis Picabia.

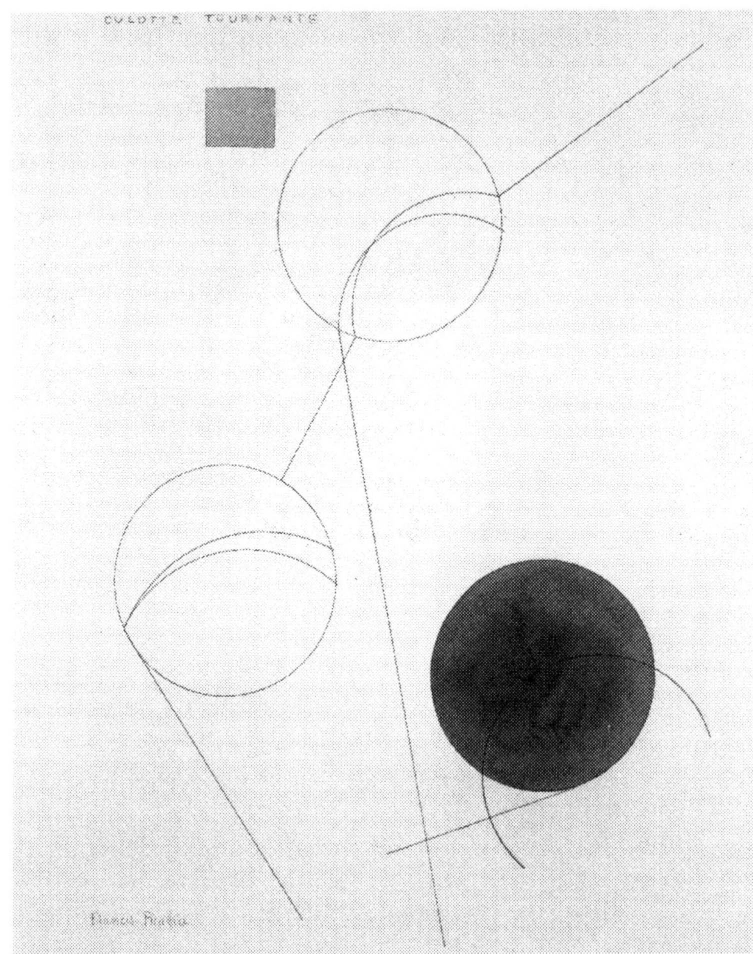

Francis-Picabia, *Culotte tournante,* 1922. Watercolor and ink on paper, 72 × 59.5 cm. Private collection, Paris. Courtesy Galerie 1900–2000. © 2005 Artists Rights Society (ARS), New York/ADAGP, Paris/Estate of Francis Picabia.

there should be no forgetting of the unbalanced, wild intensity of the last mechanomorphs, their short, momentary proposal of a visual abstraction stripped bare. The logic of the sign stripped bare fed Picabia's abstraction, and formed the compulsive logic for the supposed frenzy of his later career.[75]

And so the abstract mechanomorphs, in the end, are not experienced as a refusal of the object, as non-objective paintings. Rather, they reconfigure abstraction as a multiplication of allusions, an affair of too many objects, an overflowing of representation, with the logic of the part object now embraced as the proper domain—or perhaps I should say the improper domain—of an art of the copy, an art truly of the multiple.

NEC PLURIBUS IMPAR

Is the sun modern? No. So what?

—*Francis Picabia, 1924*[76]

It seems no coincidence that so many of Picabia's last mechanomorphs float, dizzyingly, on a field of black and white. We have seen *Optophone,* and *Volucelle,* and *Chariot;* we could add *Conversation I,* a dispersal of headless women, evidently inspired by the work of Max Ernst, cavorting in a manner parallel to the circles of *Volucelle II* on another series of black and white stripes. Creating an effect of movement and optical illusion that is another token of Picabia's intense dialogue with contemporaneous works by Duchamp,[77] these fields of black and white also reduce the ground of the last mechanomorphs to the minimal conditions of graphic inscription, to a system of stark opposition that Picabia immediately deployed—in a crucial painting from the fall of 1922 entitled *The Spanish Night*—in the service of the opposition of the Bachelors and the Bride. But this field of opposition, of reversal, and of illusion—this ground of black and white—is also, we realize, the system of inscription of the photograph. We stare at *The Spanish Night* as if at the scene of painting transformed into a large-scale photographic

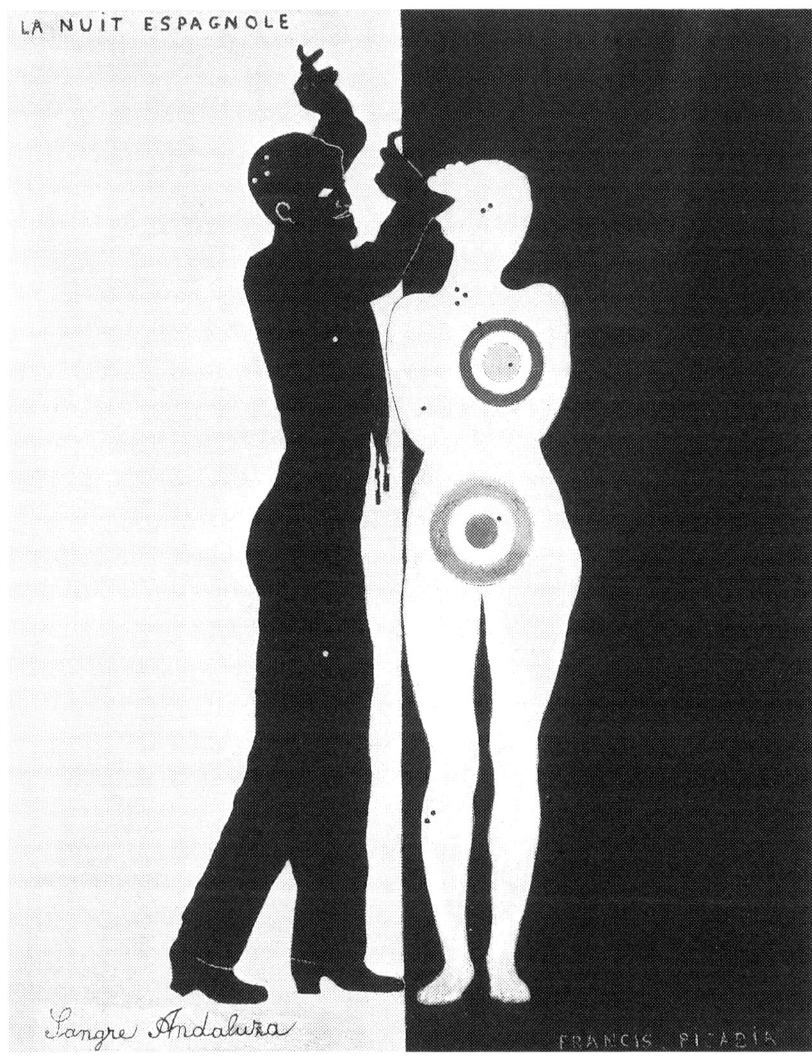

Francis Picabia, *The Spanish Night,* 1922. Ripolin on canvas, 160 × 130 cm (63 × 51″).
Museum Ludwig, Cologne. © 2005 Artists Rights Society (ARS), New York/ADAGP,
Paris/Estate of Francis Picabia.

negative, its field of opposition a product of the tonal reversals crucial to photography's stark dependence on a filmic technology of the negative image.[78]

Beyond the photograph, many of the last mechanomorphs made reference to optical devices. There was *Toton,* its title settling on the French word for a spinning top, its source now located in the science of physiological optics, combining a graph and a diagram of a device called a chromatic gyroscope. And then there was *Jumelle,* its title registering the condition both of the double and the mechanical—translatable as either *Twin* or *Binocular*—its source squarely established in a diagram showing the passage of rays of light through the body and lens of a pair of binoculars.[79] It seems that Picabia presented this painting as a gift to André Breton. It stayed in his collection for many years. And we now can understand why at the end of the '40s—when, shortly before Picabia's death, Breton turned to write his penultimate essay on Picabia—Breton entitled that essay "Binoculars for Blind-folded Eyes."

In his 1922 catalog essay for the Barcelona exhibition, Breton had described Picabia's last mechanomorphs as an art vehemently "without models"; in his later essay he implicated Picabia's work in a logic of blindness. Indeed, one of the 1922 mechanomorphs shown in Barcelona had been entitled *Thermometer for the Blind.* But beyond this titular reference, blindness was the visual model toward which all of the last mechanomorphs were dedicated. The last mechanomorphs read as abstract precisely because they block the recognition of their models; they transform a logic of the trace and the photographic copy into a visual experience of opacity; they present the field of vision as entirely mediated, opened up to the play of substitution and of transformation without origin. Sundered from their models, presenting representation as the scene of alteration, the last mechanomorphs offer up the supposed free play of visual abstraction to the mute numbness of a blind field.

And it had been Georges Bataille's conclusion, upon developing his theory of representation as alteration, that blindness was the visual model that such representational practices enact. In his essay "Sacrificial Mutilation and the Severed Ear of Vincent Van Gogh," Bataille compared his notion of alteration to Van Gogh's infamous act of cutting off one of his ears. This act of "auto-mutilation,"

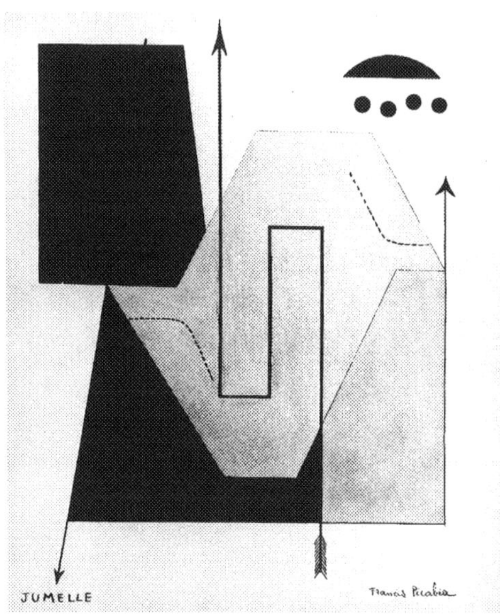

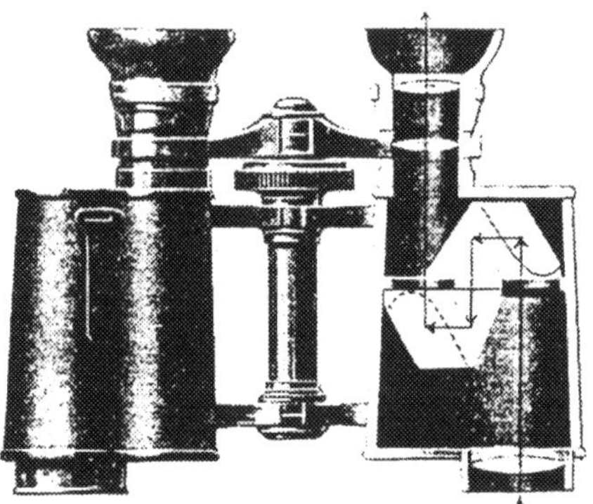

JUMELLE DEMI-COUPÉE MONTRANT LA MARCHE
DES RAYONS LUMINEUX

*La lumière pénètre par l'objectif, se réfléchit quatre
fois sur les prismes à réflexion totale et vient frapper
l'œil après avoir traversé l'oculaire.*

Francis Picabia, *Jumelle,* 1922. Watercolor on paper, 74 × 60 cm. Private collection. Image courtesy Comité Picabia. © 2005 Artists Rights Society (ARS), New York/ADAGP, Paris/Estate of Francis Picabia.

Source for *Jumelle.* ("Jumelle demi-coupée montrant la marche des rayons lumineux," *La Science et la Vie* 64, August–September 1922, p. 233.)

as Bataille called it, produced an alteration on the human body analogous to the practices of destruction Bataille had previously detailed in representational art. As a sacrificial act, it was, in Bataille's words, a "rupture of personal homogeneity and the projection *outside the self* of a part of oneself," producing "a radical *alteration* of the person . . . characterized by the fact that it would have the power to liberate heterogeneous elements and to break the habitual homogeneity of the individual, in the same way that vomiting would be opposed to its opposite, the communal eating of food. Sacrifice considered in its essential phase would only be the rejection of what had been appropriated by a person or a group."[80]

It was an act of alteration that Bataille connected directly to the recurrent experience that one has before Van Gogh's paintings of staring directly into the sun. The sun, Bataille wrote, is "the most abstract object, since it is impossible to look at it fixedly."[81] However, at the same time, if "one obstinately focuses on it, a certain madness is implied, and . . . it is no longer production that appears in light, but refuse or combustion, adequately expressed by the horror emanating from a brilliant arc lamp. In practice the scrutinized sun can be identified with a mental ejaculation, foam on the lips, and an epileptic crisis."[82] Bataille's sun was irremediably double, heterological, split in two: "In the same way that the preceding sun (the one not looked at) is perfectly beautiful, the one that is scrutinized can be considered horribly ugly."[83] And in Van Gogh's assimilation of the eye and the scene of vision to its source in the sun, Bataille hypothesized an excessive identification with the sun in its modality of excess, with Van Gogh's severed ear reconceived as a sacrifice congruent with the sun's gratuitous expenditure, a sacrifice that Bataille saw as only a displaced token of what he called "the most horrifying form of sacrifice," namely the "Oedipal enucleation."[84] Here was the eye given over to the mutilation of alteration, the eye given over to an identification with the sun that results in utter blindness.

It has gone entirely unremarked that Picabia's mechanomorphs present an analogous visual encounter. Beyond the experience of visual opacity enacted by the abstract mechanomorphs, we should now realize that we are summoned, in mechanomorph after mechanomorph, to stare like Van Gogh into a series of blinding sources of light. Once again, we could begin with *Voilà Haviland* and

Américaine, their radiating series of bodily projections fully dependent on our pro-longed stare into two sources of irradiation, our vision filled by the mechano-morph as lightbulb or as lamp. And along with the "celestial bodies" that we now know can be read into some of the abstract mechanomorphs,[85] these works only exacerbated such origins, as staring at stars soon becomes an affair of the mech-anomorph being filled by an endless succession of radiation, from the flame to the spark, from the sun to the eye to the lamp once more. Consider the combustive flash at the center of *Magnéto,* the flame and effulgent sun dominating *Magnéto anglaise*—mitigated, or perhaps tantalizingly emphasized, by a series of floating opaque screens—and the shimmering orbs of *Lampe,* all enactments of the mech-anomorph as the literal engine of expenditure.

In this light, the last mechanomorphs, we could say, had only one sequel: Picabia's 1924 ballet *Relâche* or *Canceled Performance,* where the mechanomorph's representational blindness, its courting of alteration, was violently literalized—made physical in a mode of self-canceling horror. The mechanomorph's en-gagement with blindness was literalized, that is, in Picabia's so-called curtain, a stage-set of some 370 projector lamps backed by reflecting circles, and aimed directly at the audience.

As a ballet, perhaps the only recognizable narrative of *Relâche* seemed to entail the stripping, alternately, of the female and then the male dancers.[86] And thus *Relâche* divulges a narrative, of course, that emerges as yet another rework-ing of the thematics of Duchamp's *Large Glass,* another manifestation of the bachelor machine, another enactment of the artistic procedures of both "strip-ping bare" and of "torture." In one of his many contemporary descriptions of the ballet for the artistic press, Picabia made this engagement with the *Large Glass* explicit, evoking the bachelor machine and particularly Duchamp's description of its "cemetery of uniforms and liveries," that part of the bachelor's domain replete with the "malic molds" that Duchamp imagined as a series of nine represented professions: Priest, Department Store Delivery Boy, Gendarme, Cuirassier, Po-liceman, Undertaker, Flunky, Busboy, and Stationmaster. Here is Picabia's de-scription. We have heard part of it before:

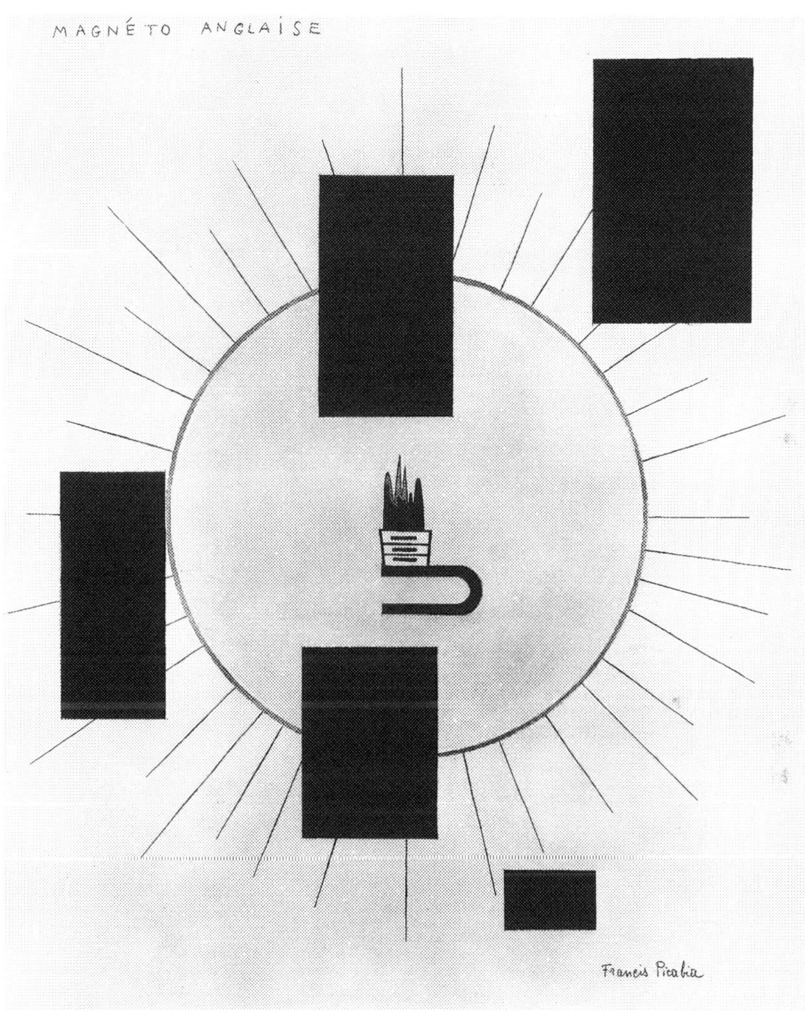

Francis Picabia, *Magnéto anglaise,* 1922. Pencil, watercolor, and collage on paper, 72 × 59.4 cm. Private collection. © 2005 Artists Rights Society (ARS), New York/ADAGP, Paris/Estate of Francis Picabia.

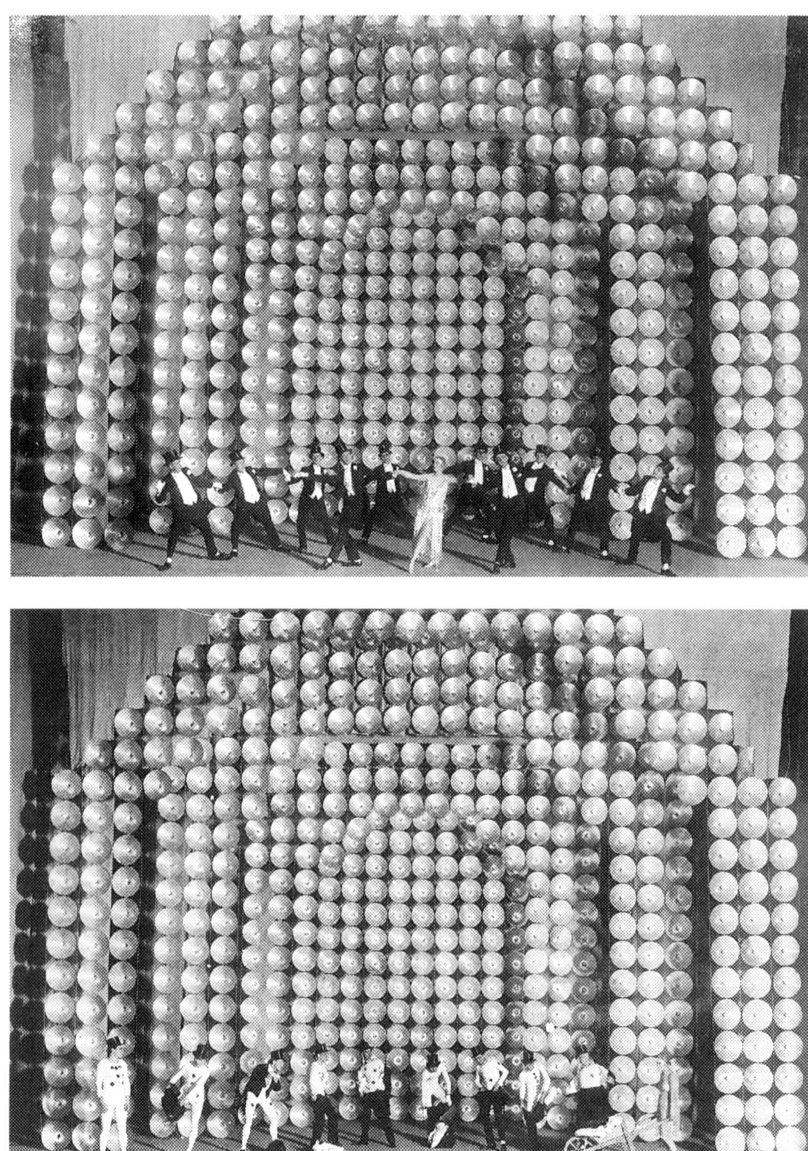

Two stills of the performance and set of Francis Picabia, Erik Satie, and the Swedish Ballet, *Relâche,* 1924. Courtesy of and © Dansmuseet, Stockholm.

Playboys, clergymen, conmen, magistrates, pimps, generals, burglars, dealers, prostitutes, and legislators all become one: they dance before the mirror of the infinite and definite changes of the lights. Eyes, hands, legs, and mouths become one when they make love. The love of life in order to forget life. To forget amidst the filigree of delight, the fragrance of female dancers who are nude and male dancers in black tie.[87]

And as Picabia's bachelors and his bride stripped around their gendered divide, the bride in one act and then the bachelors in the other, they shed modern evening wear to reveal themselves clad only in body stockings covered over in the multicolored circles of Picabia's last mechanomorphs. The body stripped bare dissipated into the abstract, which means, for Picabia, the form of both multiplicity and of desire.

This body could appear, perhaps, in a momentary flash, like the scenario that Picabia imagined simultaneously with *Relâche* as a one-time performance that he entitled *Cinésketch,* remembered today only for a live tableau that it included, constructed once more on the precarious divide of the *Large Glass,* with Duchamp now himself stripped bare, standing nude next to a similarly naked woman that Picabia took pains to identify in his public pronouncements on the piece as "Francine Picabia."[88] Picabia's literalizations would know no end. Like a living version of Picabia's previous painting *The Spanish Night,* and like so much of what Picabia's art became after 1924, *Cinésketch* presented a pastiche, a *tableau vivant,* a painting brought back to life—half-recreated Cranach painting of Adam and Eve, half-lugubrious and outmoded porn scenario—but it founded itself like *Relâche* on a withdrawal from vision, existing only as a momentary tableau sandwiched between long stretches of utter darkness, a scene that Picabia arranged to have illuminated from time to time by something like strobe lights.

The body stripped bare, however, could also disappear in a momentary flash, as *Relâche* employed a diametrically opposed tactic: Picabia's stage set—keyed to the murmuring of Erik Satie's musical score—exploded convulsively into illumination in time with the beat and volume of the music itself. Pulsing rhythmically and repeatedly, these lights flashed into an illumination that could only be experienced by the audience as the literal enactment of blindness, the loss of what was given to be seen. And so *Relâche,* as a spectacle, was indeed canceled, the appropriative logic of vision refused in the searing excess of just that which should facilitate it.

Relâche was another child of the bachelor machine, producing non-engagement with and as the spectacle, parsing out its tortures now to the viewer in the excessive gleam of pain. Blindness, for Bataille, was the experience of vision refusing to appropriate, committing itself instead to a mutilating alteration in which it would be lost, given up and given over to the burning darkness in which it ends. And the mechanomorph too would end here, in 1924, its literalization also the scene of its ultimate closure, with the scene of representation for Picabia—as for Bataille—broached only by what breaches it, the field of vision at its limit experienced only as a modality of blindness. This was a transgressive model of vision, a sacrificial economy. The Dada mechanomorph has been understood as an art of "appropriation" for too long. Its hopes lay elsewhere.

PARTURIUNT MONTES, NASCETUR RIDICULUS MUS

As for me, I wear a blindfold
in order not to see sunsets;
sunsets are not so beautiful
and they would make me cry

—*Francis Picabia, 1922*[89]

To conclude, we need to return to the beginning. We need to return to Picabia's literally transparent work, *Danse de Saint-Guy.* Created first in 1920, it was this piece that Picabia resurrected in 1922, submitting it along with *The Merry Widow* and *Straw Hat?* to the Salon des Indépendants at the start of that fateful year. And some twenty years later, Picabia returned to it again, rearranging and tightening its various strings, clarifying its self-canceling X and retitling the work as well. The painting would now be known as *Tabac-rat*: Rat tobacco. It is a striking,

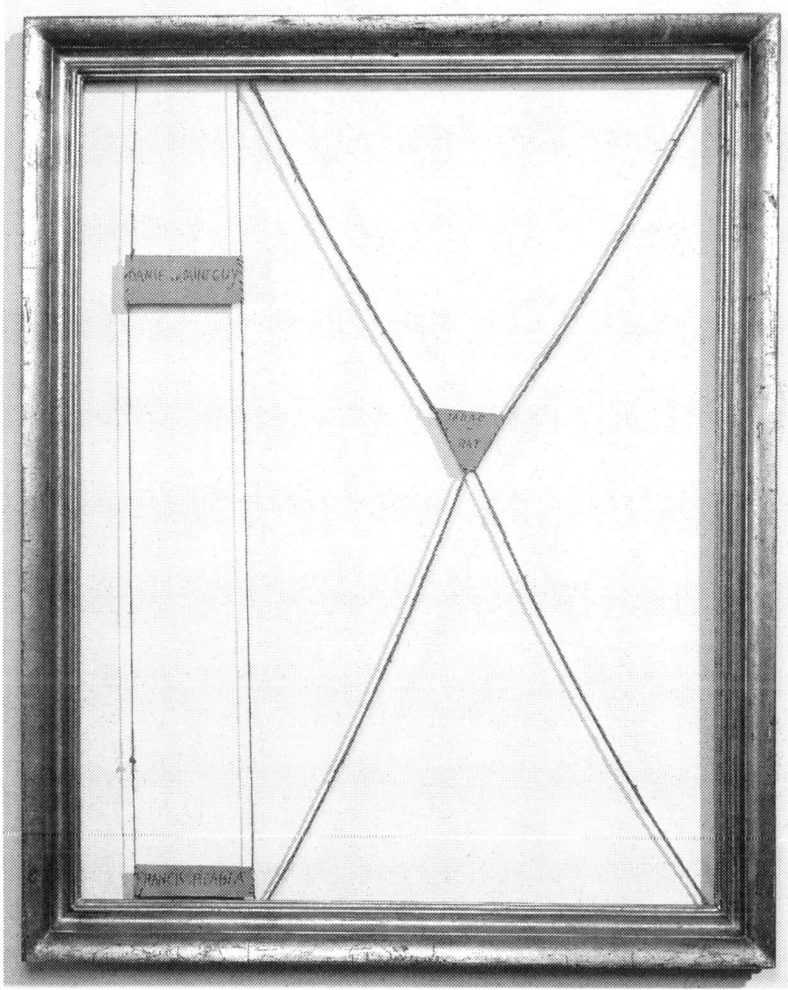

Francis Picabia, *Tabac-rat,* 1920/1948. Twine, board, and ink in open gilt wood frame, 104.4 × 84.7 cm (41$^1/_8$ × 33$^3/_8''$). Musée National d'Art Moderne, Centre Georges Pompidou. Photograph © CNAC/MNAM/Dist. Réunion des Musées Nationaux/Art Resource, New York. © 2005 Artists Rights Society (ARS), New York/ADAGP, Paris/Estate of Francis Picabia.

repulsive confluence of words. Rats occur frequently in Picabia's poems and writings; among other resonances, Carole Boulbès has pointed out that the word, of course—in both French and in English—is an anagram for "Art" itself.[90]

Along with its transparency, in the original version of *Danse de Saint-Guy,* Picabia had sprinkled the work with a series of other words, written inscriptions on paper labels attached to the abstract tracery of its strings. In the wake of the claims I have been making for Picabia's mechanomorphs, these inscriptions now make for some riveting reading. For they evoked castration as well as mutilation: "Hold out your arms," one advised, "and your friends will cut them off." The labels proclaimed an artistic subject on the verge of disappearance: "I am going to sleep," another announced. And they invoked once again the sun: "What a beautiful sun!" a last label exclaimed. Picabia made sure in his written statements about this work to mention its use as a frame through which he liked to stare directly at the sun.[91] And so once again we experience the field of the mechanomorph as a painting literally burnt out, eviscerated, voided of its traditional competencies, a field of destructions evoking absolute transparency and blindness at one and the same time.

Think back to the start of Paris Dada, to *La Sainte-Vierge* and *La jeune fille.* Think back to their structure, to their structural blindness, a stain on the field of vision, or a blind spot cut from the same. The effects of a sacrificial economy continue to be felt in Picabia's art. The mechanomorph internalized them. And in doing so, the mechanomorph also internalized the photograph in its multiple dimensions and effects—as both a mechanical technique and as a mode of vision—including, as in *Relâche,* the photograph's creation of a kind of blind field, as well as its inauguration of a subject, an audience, thrown into illumination only through the paroxysm of its own blinding.

We have reached another understanding, then, of the mechanomorph as a kind of "photography by other means." We can now see that the mechanomorphs, at their limit, attempted to *draw light,* and thus attempted to become literal *photo-graphs.* Like Picabia's *The Merry Widow,* the mechanomorphs brought two mediums together, coarticulating the concerns of drawing and photography. But in attempting to draw light, the activity of drawing in the mechanomorphs is also canceled, suspended, literally blinded. The mechanomorphs were already *relâche*. This, again, is Picabia's version of abstraction, Dada abstraction. For to draw light is precisely what drawing cannot do (this, rather, was always the traditional artistic function of color, as opposed to that of line). It is where drawing loses itself yet again. And it is where drawing loses itself precisely by touching a limit to its form, only to find, in photography, a medium that could present it with its lack, offer it what it is not. It is at this precise limit—the threshold of their insufficiency—where forms open onto other forms.

We can thus see that photography, for Dada, was not merely a force of destruction, a mechanical incursion meant only to dissipate the traditional practice of art, to disperse its conventional mediums. The photograph was a kind of "gift" to drawing. And indeed, on the other side of this limit, the meeting place between drawing and photography, the photograph reaches a limit as well. Drawing was a "gift" to the photograph in turn. The mechanomorph was the staging of this transgressive crossing, with each medium, both drawing and photography, presenting to the other its limit, its lack, its "principle of inadequacy," a mutual recognition around and attraction to that which is missing, the groundless ground beneath each medium's Law. For photography, in the mechanomorphs, while introducing the principle of the graphic deposit and the physical trace, can no longer be considered as a retentive index, an object captured, or frozen, the immobile fossil of visual form. Rather, given over to drawing's scene of graphic alteration, photography succumbs to self-difference, to the voyage of the signifying chain, to an essential loss of fixity. At its limit, photography was opened in the mechanomorph to transformation, to mobility, to becoming. We have already seen, in other arenas, that this was one of Dada's great hopes for photography. One almost imagines that cinema could begin.

QUOD ERAT DEMONSTRANDUM

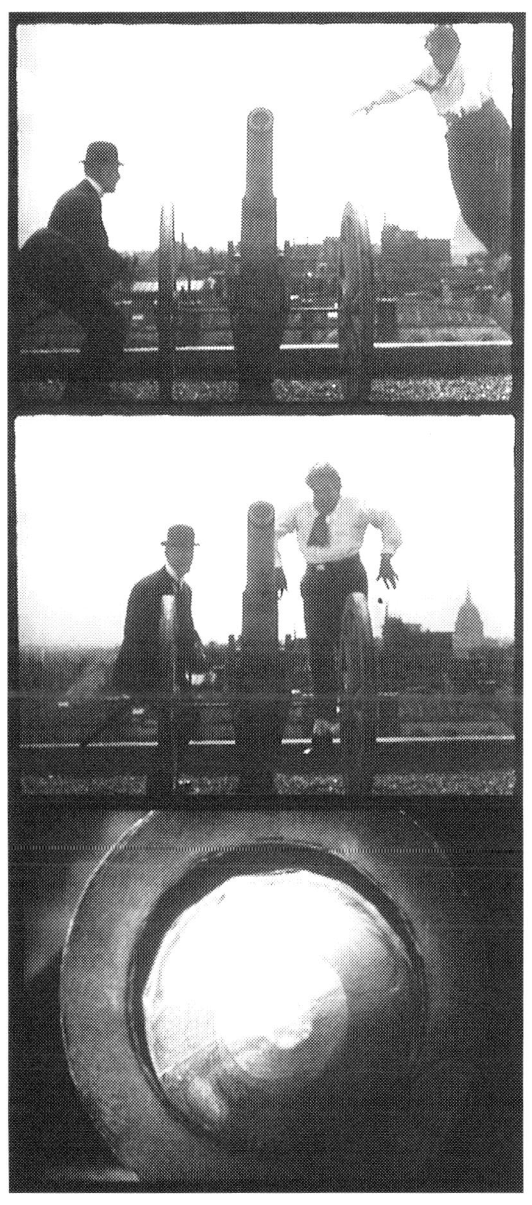

Stills from Francis Picabia, René Clair, and Erik Satie, *Overture to "Relâche,"* 1924.
© Pathé International, Paris.

Intermission: Dada Cinema

One day humanity will play with law just as children play with disused objects, not in order to restore them to their canonical use but to free them from it for good. What is found after the law is not a more proper and original use value that precedes the law, but a new use that is born only after it.

—*Giorgio Agamben,* State of Exception[1]

The high railings of Prospect rippled past their gaze. Dark poplars, rare white forms. Forms more frequent, white shapes thronged amid the trees, white forms and fragments streaming by mutely, sustaining vain gestures on the air.

—*James Joyce,* Ulysses[2]

Here is an image of Picabia. The image is one of many. It comes from a film. When we first see the artist, he is flying in slow motion through the air, like a circus clown or an acrobat, or like, according to some descriptions, a wayward Valkyrie or a corpulent god (Dionysus no doubt) "descending" from the heavens. When we first see him, he is jumping up and down, with a vigor and delight that belie his not-insignificant weight and his age, and that leaves behind the feeble hopping of his pencil-thin companion, the avant-garde composer Erik Satie. The two are on the roof of the Theatre des Champs-Elysées in Paris, home in the early 1920s to the productions of the Swedish Ballet and home to its last and final production, Picabia and Satie's 1924 ballet *Relâche*. The two are jumping, leaping, in slow motion, and the grace of their movements seems to recall the actions not of painters or of musicians, surely not of poets or composers, not even of gods or acrobats, but of dancers.

Dancing is the key reference here, for the image we are watching belongs to a film made by Picabia and the director René Clair that was meant to be projected as a cinematic "overture" to signal the beginning of Picabia's ballet. There would also be an intermission, filled as well with film, a much longer projection that was simply given the site-specific title of what the French call an intermission, namely an *Entr'acte*. This site-specificity was crucial to the film, now a classic within cinema studies, but usually studied without the surround of its larger context. Indeed, the images of the leaping Satie and Picabia are often projected as part of this film, no matter that they were sundered in time by the first act of Picabia's ballet, a performance that they then split in turn.

However, the opening images of the filmed overture were also site-specific, placing the viewer precisely and immediately on the roof of the ballet's theater, looking out over the surrounding buildings of Paris, until a peripatetic cannon makes its way into the shot. This cannon, alone and without aid, gracefully weaves its way across the roof, first in one direction and then the other, spinning around and moving in all directions. This cannon too is a dancer. Or, rather, it begins to make us think in analogical ways about dance and about what dance is. Picabia and Satie bounce slowly toward it, they "dance" around it. They seem to engage in a heated discussion. Satie points through what Brecht would call the "fourth wall," and thus implicitly to the audience. Picabia demurs. Satie gestures, imperiously, again. Picabia concurs. Like aging dandies, they sniff an artillery round in disgust, and load it into the back of the cannon. In sped-up and reversed motion now, they begin their leaps and bounds once more, disappearing quickly from the scene. Looking like a mechanical eye or some other kind of orifice, the cannon fires its volley directly into the camera and by extension the audience. And thus *Relâche* begins.

☞

It was Walter Benjamin who once claimed that in Dada, the work of art had become "an instrument of ballistics."[3] This strange assertion appears in Benjamin's discussion of the anticipation by the Dadaists—in both their performances and collages, in their poems and montages—of effects that could only be realized by a technological transformation, and by a future art: film. "From an alluring appearance or persuasive structure of sound the work of art of the Dadaists became an instrument of ballistics," Benjamin wrote in his essay "The Work of Art in the Age of Mechanical Reproduction." "It hit the spectator like a bullet, it happened to him, thus acquiring a tactile quality. It promoted a demand for the film, the distracting element of which is also primarily tactile, being based on changes of place and focus which periodically assail the spectator."[4] One wonders if Benjamin knew that the Dadaists had themselves produced films; one wonders if he knew *Entr'acte*; one surely wonders why the critic sees Dada as a precursor to the cinema when the latter medium pre-dated Dada by almost two decades. But the critic continued: "Before the rise of the movie, the Dadaists' performances tried to create an audience reaction that [Charlie] Chaplin later evoked in a more natural way."[5]

The basis of Benjamin's comparison of Dada and cinema lay in the mode of apperception that Dada art forced on its spectators, and the aesthetic distance that it, and then film, no longer allowed. "Let us compare the screen on which a film unfolds with the canvas of a painting," Benjamin wrote. "The painting invites the spectator to contemplation; before it the spectator can abandon himself to his associations. Before the movie frame he cannot do so. No sooner has his eye grasped a scene than it is already changed. It cannot be arrested. . . . The spectator's process of association in view of these images is indeed interrupted by the constant, sudden change."[6] Much has been said about Benjamin's idea that film overturns previous aesthetic modes of what he called "contemplation," furthering instead a mode of apperception that the critic named "distraction."[7] But the key idea for me in this passage is the opening onto perhaps a new mode of "association," one "interrupted" but by "constant, sudden change," and that both Dada and film take us there.

Dada's origins lie in an engagement with performance and theater, from the moment that the first Dadaists coalesced in 1916 at the Cabaret Voltaire in Switzerland. Paris Dada, in its own ways, intensified this theatrical origin. We know that Picabia, at the very height of Dada in Paris—after his work as set and costume "designer" for the first season of Paris Dada activity—was contemplating more grand collaborations with musicians and composers, for example in 1921 on an opera with Stravinsky. And by 1923 he was in negotiations with French film director Marcel L'Herbier to produce the script for a movie to star silent film actress Georgette Leblanc, with Marcel Duchamp serving as his mediator to the star.[8]

Neither project came to pass. But cinema did ultimately (and as if inevitably) further intensify Dada's theatrical origins. It provided Dada, in Thomas Elsaesser's words, not only with "a model or metaphor for representing the relation of body to social environment," but also "for conceptualizing the art-work as event, rather than as object, no longer as products but as circuits of exchange for different energies and intensities, for the different aggregate states matter can be subjected to between substance and sign through an act of transposition, assemblage, division, and intermittence."[9] One imagines, too, that cinema served Dada not only in imagining the transition from art object to event, but also as a mode that introduced symbolic possibilities far removed from the stable economies of painting or sculpture, with the cinema as an "assembly" of media that rejected the singular at its foundation, and that supported wholly new modes of the circulation of the sign. Cinema, in other words, might inherently force the issue of an alternate symbolic economy. It is with such goals in mind that one should approach what seems to be Picabia's drive to bring his Dada work to a climax through a project that included the form of film.

By 1924, if Picabia had distanced himself from the remainders of the Paris Dada movement, in fact most of his fellow Dadaists had abandoned the cause as well. This was the year that saw the launch of Surrealism under the control of André Breton. But this was also the year that saw Picabia finally able to realize a major collaborative project for the stage, creating the concept and scenario and designing the sets and costumes for the ballet *Relâche,* with Erik Satie as composer, Jean Börlin as choreographer and principal dancer, and the twenty-six-year-old René Clair as the director of the ballet's cinematic interlude, also scripted (very loosely) by Picabia.

Actually, true to Picabia's long-standing practice of appropriation and pastiche—true to his notion of "dialogue" that this collaborative project radicalized—the concept for *Relâche* seems to have been borrowed, as the Swedish Ballet had originally commissioned Picabia's one-time friend and neighbor, the poet Blaise Cendrars, to create the event. Cendrars had worked with the Swedish Ballet before, most recently in 1923 on *The Creation of the World* in collaboration with Fernand Léger and Darius Milhaud. In the wake of this success, Cendrars began work on a new ballet for the company's next season. The poet decided suddenly to depart from Paris, however, spending most of 1924 living in Brazil. He thus effectively abandoned the Swedish Ballet project, and already, by January of 1924, in the wake of Cendrars's departure, we can document the company's attempts to secure Picabia's full collaboration. This was seemingly done at Satie's prodding, with Picabia's protégé Pierre de Massot acting as intermediary and pleading with the artist to join the endeavor, inviting him to use the opportunity to invent "a new form of Dada perhaps."[10] Before departing, however, Cendrars had already tentatively entitled his unfinished project either *After Dinner* or *Cocktail Party* or, in fact, *Relâche.* It seems that the title for the final ballet was his.[11]

It is a title that, for the English speaker, takes a bit of explanation. *Relâche,* in French, basically means "relax." Spas today in France are sometimes given the name. When used in theatrical parlance, however, on street signs or posters or on schedules, *relâche* indicates the nights when the show, one might say, "does not go on," when there is a break in the production—when there is "no performance" or it is announced "Performance Canceled."

But a quick perusal of any French dictionary multiplies this title's connotations. A *relâche* is an intermission, a discontinuance, a rest, a respite, a form of "relaxation." This, in French, is *relâche* as a masculine noun, but it can also be a feminine one, and as such it also means, significantly, a "port of call" or a putting into or call at a port. It can be a verb, *relâcher,* meaning to loosen, slacken, relax and release, but also to set at liberty, to unbend (the mind), to yield, give up, or abate. That is its transitive form. As an intransitive verb, it means to relax in the sense of "to flag." It can also be a reflexive verb, *se relâcher,* meaning primarily to grow slack or loose, to fall off or to abate, to give way, to sit back, or to get milder (said of the weather). The noun *relâchement* denotes slackening, loosening, slackness, as well as an abatement, remissness, and the laxity of morals—but also the looseness of the bowels. Indeed, as an adjective, in French one can talk of something being *relâché,* that is, lax, relaxed, loose, or remiss, as in *morale relâchée,* loose morals. And *relâchant,* an adjective meaning relaxing or loosening, is also a noun that comprises the word in French for an "opening medicine," or, in other words, a laxative.

The title may have come from Cendrars, but Picabia immediately set about making the word's many connotations his own. We may speculate on Picabia's perverse pleasure at bringing Dada to a close with a performance whose title signified that which is flagging or an abatement, as well as something loose, mild, and relaxing. Given Dada's persistent scatology, we can surely imagine Picabia's embrace of the performance as a metaphorical cultural laxative.[12] The ballet's opening projection with its expelled and smelly cannonball already travels such paths.

But it is *Relâche* in the sense of a cancellation that evidently most enthralled the artist. In fact, one of the legends of the production was that the very first performance of *Relâche,* set for the last week of November 1924, had to be canceled. The work premiered one week later, but on its original opening night, *Relâche* was *relâche.* Supposedly, the principal dancer Jean Börlin fell ill and could not perform, but given Picabia's reputation, the public sensed a hoax, a typical Dada gesture.[13] However, it was only when the production actually opened for its short run in December that the public was exposed to Picabia's full meditation on the dynamics of "cancellation" that *Relâche* now made its own.

For when *Relâche* did open, the audience was confronted with a massive stage set designed by Picabia consisting of some 370 metal reflecting disks, each equipped with a light. These lights perhaps explained the publicity that Picabia had been placing for the ballet, ads that read, in part, "Bring your sunglasses and something to plug up your ears!" The lights were dimmed and lit throughout the performance in coordination with the music, at times fully blinding the audience.

Typical for Picabia, who in his earlier design for the 1920 Dada manifestation at the Maison de l'Oeuvre had offered a stage set arranged in front of the performers as opposed to behind them, the set for *Relâche* utterly *reversed* the function of what a set might be thought to involve. As the director of the Swedish Ballet, Rolf de Maré, put it at the time: "The sets?—They are perhaps not sets, just as the music will and yet will not be music, just as it will be a ballet while not being a ballet . . . That's life as Picabia sees it."[14] Instead of illuminating the stage, Picabia lit the audience. Instead of rendering the performance space legible, he rendered it periodically blinding and blank, a space of "division and intermittence." Instead of providing his performance with a ground, his set ungrounded the ballet. And as opposed to the film that during the intermission was projected onto a temporary screen set up across the ballet's stage, during the dancing, light was projected back into the theater, traveling fully in the other direction. The audience was lit during the performance; the stage illuminated during the intermission. It was in these precise reversals of function and convention that Picabia introduced his public to the larger project of *Relâche,* indeed to an understanding of *Relâche* as a form of cancellation, break, negation. And the reversals hardly stopped here.

Relâche was short: the ballet lasted only some forty minutes, and was presented in 1924 on a bill that included two other Swedish Ballet performances. After opening with Satie's musical overture embellished by Picabia and Clair's filmed "projectionette" as it is sometimes called—the short film of the leaping authors and dancing cannon—the music continued into the body of the ballet proper. The music was raucous, playful, at times infantile and backward-sounding. It was obviously an affair of appropriation, and it shocked some of Satie's own disciples, for instance Georges Auric who then cemented a recent split with Satie by calling the music in print "a miserable pastiche."[15]

By contrast, and by way of explanation, Satie baptized *Relâche* a *ballet obscène,* and announced that he had composed "pornographic" music for its score. This

Pourquoi payer le luxe de votre fournisseur ou son ignorance ?

Pour être un penseur il faut penser.

Pourquoi payer votre fournisseur ou son ignorance ?

Das leben ist ein schöne abord.

Pourquoi payer le luxe ou son ignorance ?

Tout appel non justifié expose aux poursuites judiciaires et du Salon des Tuileries.

Pourquoi payer son ignorance.

C'est ainsi que les saintes images ont une vague odeur de fromage.

Pourquoi ?

Saviez-vous qu'il y a une Adaptation Française ?

E. L. T. MESENS

Le conscient est l'Évolution Dernière et Tardive du système organique, et par conséquent aussi, ce qu'il a dans ce système de moins achevé et de moins fort

Un Instantané te

—— En rêve.

—— Les bordels font une impression très forte,

—— On croirait entrer dans un Conservatoire,

—— Les invalides justifient le cubisme.

Le pôle positif aime le pôle négatif, puisqu'on vit on aime.

J'aime la bière et les roses trémières.

Un homme en costume d'Adam.

Les chats sont heureux de vivre en dessous des chaises.

La vache a du sentiment.

RENÉ MAGRITTE

LES BALLETS SUÉDOIS DONNERONT
LE 27 NOVEMBRE
AU THÉATRE DES CHAMPS ÉLYSÉES

" RELÂCHE "
BALLET
INSTANTANÉISTE

EN DEUX ACTES, UN ENTR'ACTE CINÉMATOGRAPHIQUE
ET LA QUEUE DU CHIEN
PAR

FRANCIS PICABIA
MUSIQUE
D'

ERIK SATIE
CHORÉGRAPHIE DE **JEAN BORLIN**

Apportez des lunettes noires et
de quoi vous boucher les oreilles.

RETENEZ VOS PLACES

Messieurs les ex-Dadas sont priés de venir manifester et surtout de crier : « A BAS SATIE ! A BAS PICABIA ! VIVE LA NOUVELLE REVUE FRANCAISE ! »

" 391 "
N° 19 — PRIX : 2 FRS

Dépositaire " AU SANS PAREIL "
37, Avenue Kléber, PARIS

Le Gérant, PIERRE DE MASSOT

Back cover of the last issue of *391* 19 (October 1924). Research Library, The Getty Research Institute, Los Angeles. © 2005 Artists Rights Society (ARS), New York/ ADAGP, Paris/Estate of Francis Picabia.

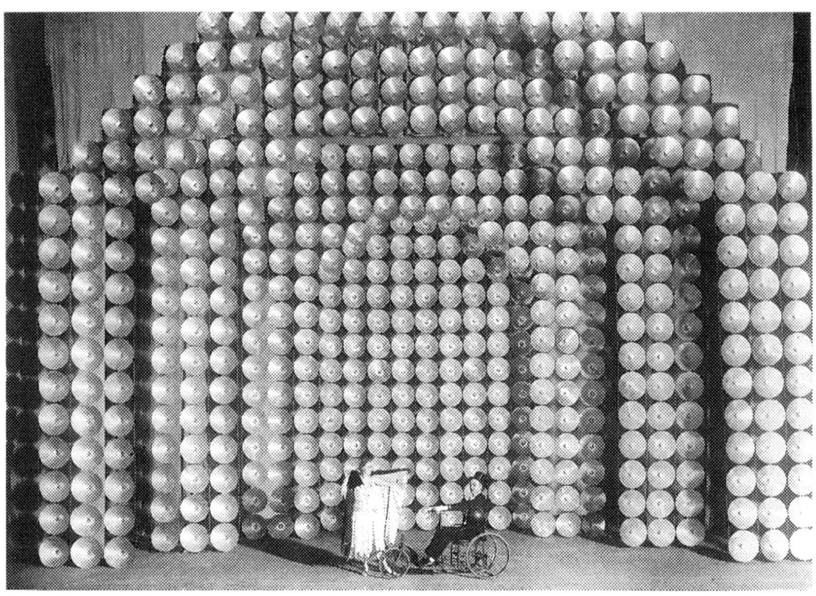

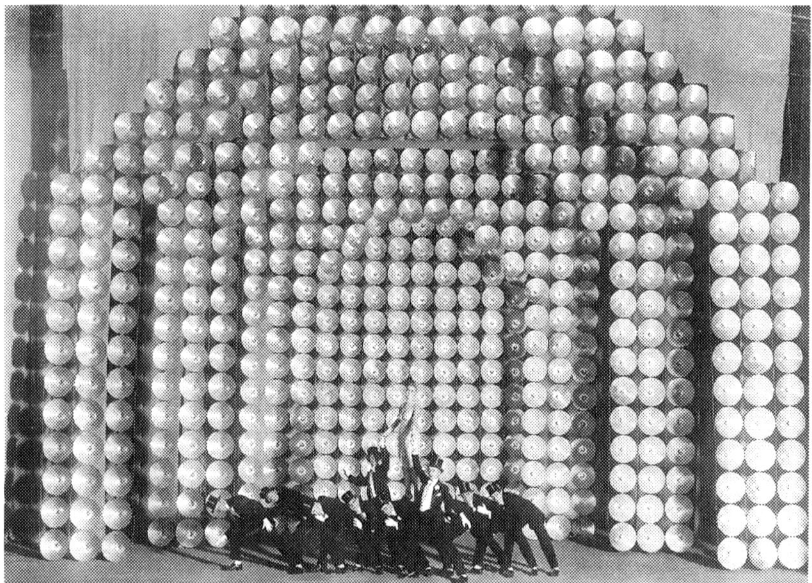

Two images of the performance and set of Francis Picabia, Erik Satie, and the Swedish Ballet, *Relâche,* 1924. Courtesy of and © Dansmuseet, Stockholm.

seems to refer to the fact that Satie's composition quoted over and over a series of then-recognizable popular songs, often bawdy songs, or army songs, with titles like "The Turnip Vendor" or "Have You Seen the Canteen Girl?"[16] We are obviously far from the folk references in the contemporary pastiches of a Stravinsky, as far, perhaps, as the peasant's field is from the urban fairground. Satie explained:

> The music for *Relâche*? I was portraying people "*out on a spree.*" Using popular themes for the purpose. These themes were powerfully "*evocative.*". . . Yes, very "*evocative.*" "*Special,*" even. "*Faint-hearts*"— and other "*moralists*"—will reproach me for making use of these themes. Why should I bother with such people's opinions? . . . The reactionary "*sourpusses [têtes de veau]*" will rant and rail. Pooh! . . . There is only one judge I defer to: the public. It will recognize these themes and will not be in the least shocked to hear them. . . . Aren't they "*human,*" after all? . . . I have no wish to make a lobster blush, or an egg, for that matter. Let anyone who dreads such "*evocations*" retire. . . . I would be ashamed to disturb the smooth and tranquil waters of their serene innocence. . . . I am too nice to want to displease them.[17]

If Satie's music was "pornographic," Börlin's choreography for the production— from the six or so documentary images that survive—seems to have been concerned less with classical ballet than with forms of appropriation linked to Satie's own. The dancing was entirely an exploration of athletic or quotidian movements, so many handstands and piggy-back rides and human pyramids, referencing other locations for dance and human motion such as the cabaret, the circus, the sporting event, and especially, one notices, the tawdry site and the actions of strip-tease.

Perhaps most important, however, while music and dance both looked outside themselves to the appropriation of other liminal or "popular" forms, the two artistic mediums combined, in *Relâche,* only to break into and halt each other's forward momentum. Here was another modality of cancellation. If *Relâche* lasted some forty minutes, we can see today that Satie's score contributes only about twenty minutes of music, and the cinematic intermission adds only just over another ten. The time difference speaks to the crucial fact that musical performance, in this ballet, was designed to alternate for the most part with periods of dancing done completely without music. When the dancers moved, the music stopped; and conversely, when the musicians played, the bodily motion came to a halt.[18]

The most satisfying reconstruction of the performance is that of William Camfield, which looks at the (sometimes contradictory) evidence of Picabia's original scenario and a variety of contemporary press accounts.[19] I will paraphrase this reconstruction here. As the ballet opened, a woman—the principal female dancer, Edith Bonsdorff—simply walked up onto the stage from a seat in the audience. She was dressed in evening wear, a rather spectacular and shimmering cocktail dress that matched the reflective disks of Picabia's set, adorned with jewelry and bangles, and, instead of flats, conspicuous high-heeled shoes. Crucially, she sat and smoked a cigarette while the orchestra played, and subsequently began to dance only when the music ceased. The principal male dancer, Jean Börlin, then joined her, also in formal dress (a tuxedo and top hat); the dancer's first appearance on stage, however, was made in a fanciful wheelchair. "Quickly healed by the allure of Mlle. Bonsdorff," as Camfield puts it, the two engaged in a kind of waltz entitled the "Dance of the Revolving Doors." (Picabia's scenario explicitly called for a revolving door to be placed upon the stage, and for the dancers to use it, circling repetitively, again and again, through its portals in the place of any more elaborate dancing.) Significantly, nine more men in formal dress then joined the dancers on the stage. They also emerged from seats in the audience. The group gathered around Bonsdorff, who reacted by stripping down to rose-colored silk tights, causing the men "to back off momentarily." By some accounts, she also walked over their bent backs "as if they were a bridge," only at last after the final dance of act 1 to be carried off-stage by one of the men.[20] All the while, a fireman—*pompier* in French being also the term for that which is academic—stood to the side of the stage, chain-smoking (another reversal of function?), decorated with the Legion of Honor, and pouring water studiously from one bucket into another.

After the cinematic intermission, a new curtain or backdrop greeted spectators, a kind of mad diagram from Picabia's hands, inscribed with pointless arrows, spirals, and slogans or provocations such as "Erik Satie is the greatest musician in the world," "Long Live Relâche," or "If you are not satisfied, whistles are on sale in the box office for a few cents." Rather than present any kind of recognizable narrative progression—although some critics tried to reconstruct one—*Relâche* then concluded in act 2, as Camfield points out, by simply and diametrically *reversing* the sequence of events of act 1.

The entire ballet proceeded by a structure of reversal. Now the male dancers entered first, followed by Bonsdorff, still in pink tights but carried in on a stretcher, like the "crippled" Börlin at the opening of act 1. (Picabia originally wanted her to descend from the rafters, to which he had also envisioned her raised at the end of act 1; such levitation was instead only to be achieved in Picabia's film.) While she got dressed, the men in turn now began to strip off their clothes, revealing white tights punctuated with the round polka-dots of Picabia's recent abstract mechanomorphs. They danced joyfully around Bonsdorff, and then with disdain around a classical statuette that, by some accounts, came to replace her. All the while, the fireman continued his repetitive movements, smoking and pouring water. Then the male dancers returned to their seats in the audience, while Bonsdorff merely collected their discarded clothing in a wheelbarrow, dumping the evening wear in a disordered pile in the corner. On opening night, she completed her "performance" by throwing a crown of orange blossoms—Picabia's scenario calls this a "bridal crown"—into the audience, where it was placed on the head of none other than celebrity singer Marthe Chenal. Finally, Bonsdorff regained her own seat in the audience, and a curtain descended, in front of which another ballerina—Picabia's scenario specifically calls for a "small woman"—then concluded the event by dancing and miming the words to a completely raucous and double-tempo song that the authors called, enigmatically, "La queue du chien" or "The Dog's Tail."

Strip-tease, music hall, and the circus; reversal, repetition, and violence; mediums that frustrate one another at their meeting point, rather than fuse in some seamless ensemble; nine bachelors and one Bride: Picabia's *Relâche* was far from a simple borrowing of the ideas of Blaise Cendrars. What the critics could

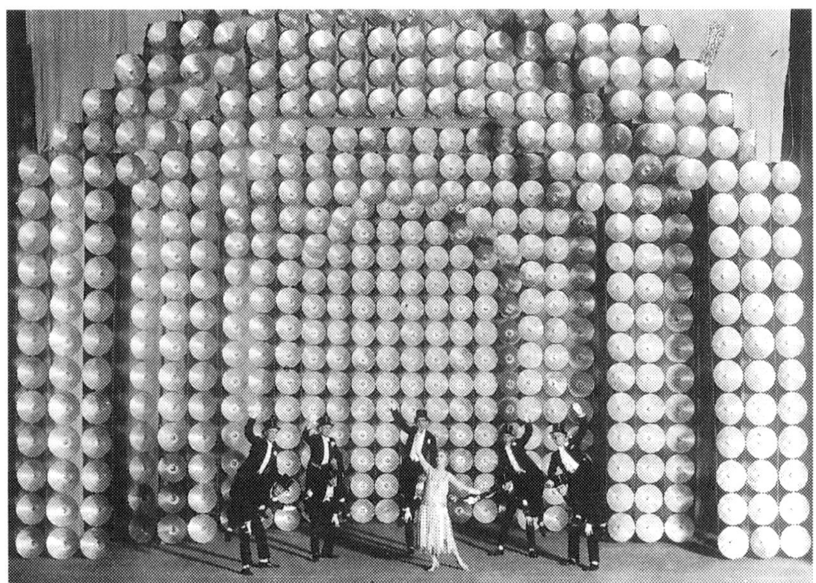

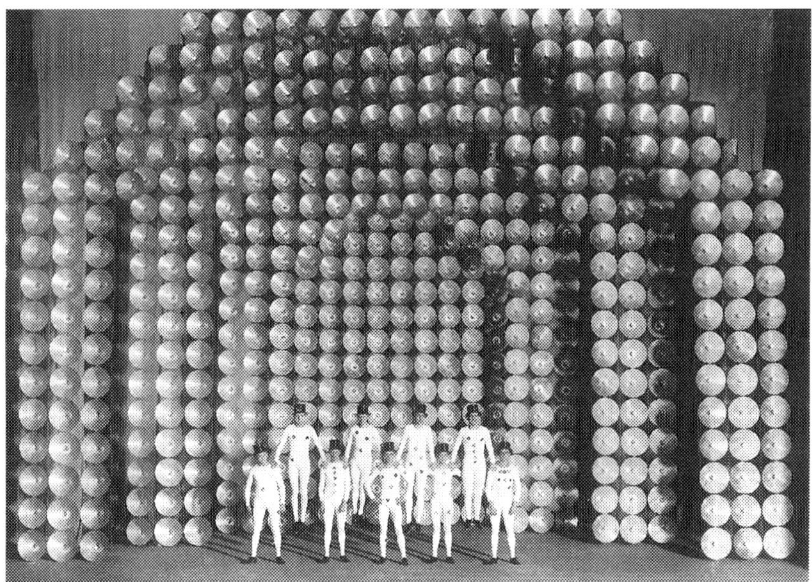

Two images of the performance and set of Francis Picabia, Erik Satie, and the Swedish Ballet, *Relâche,* 1924. Courtesy of and © Dansmuseet, Stockholm.

not then see, however—as no one really yet knew the work in question—was that far from being "fully expressive of Picabia" (as Camfield claims), the entirety of Picabia's scenario *was* "stolen," in a quite direct sense.[21] Just like the score and choreography, this was a work steeped throughout in appropriation. For *Relâche* was a staging, at least in part, of the thematics of Marcel Duchamp's *Large Glass*; it was *The Bride Stripped Bare by Her Bachelors, Even* brought to the stage, to some new meeting place between theater, music, and dance. If that meeting place must be even further expanded to include photography (with the flashing of the set's lights) and of course cinema, the filmed *Entr'acte* too forged its own connections with the *Large Glass*. This was achieved perhaps most directly by casting Duchamp and Man Ray in one of its early scenes, and, most notoriously (and significantly for the context of *Relâche*), in the film's repeated image of a ballerina recorded as if positioned above the spectator, dancing on a pane of glass that we view, in the film, from below—the very *mise-en-scène* of the *Large Glass*, with the Bride above, and her bachelors below. And if Picabia here was once more working in stride with Duchamp, we should remember that within the Dada milieu it had been Duchamp too who had first begun to work with film.

In addition to casting Duchamp in his film, Picabia dropped one major hint that his friend was on his mind during the launch of *Relâche* and its film *Entr'acte*. On the cover of the last issue of his Dada journal *391,* published in October 1924 on the eve of the Swedish Ballet production, Picabia renamed his magazine the *Journal de l'Instantanéisme,* announcing with this a new movement, "Instantanism," that would last "for a little while," coupled with "Dadaism" at the top of the journal's front page. The primary avatar of this new movement was also pictured on the cover in a line drawing that seemed to be a portrait of Marcel Duchamp. To confuse matters a little more, however, the drawing was actually an image of a famous boxer of the day, Georges Charpentier, sketched by Picabia the previous year. Autographed by the boxer, the drawing was then altered again by Picabia, who corrected the image slightly, reinforcing the profile here and there, and then crossed out Charpentier's signature and retitled it an image of "Rrose Sélavy by Picabia."[22]

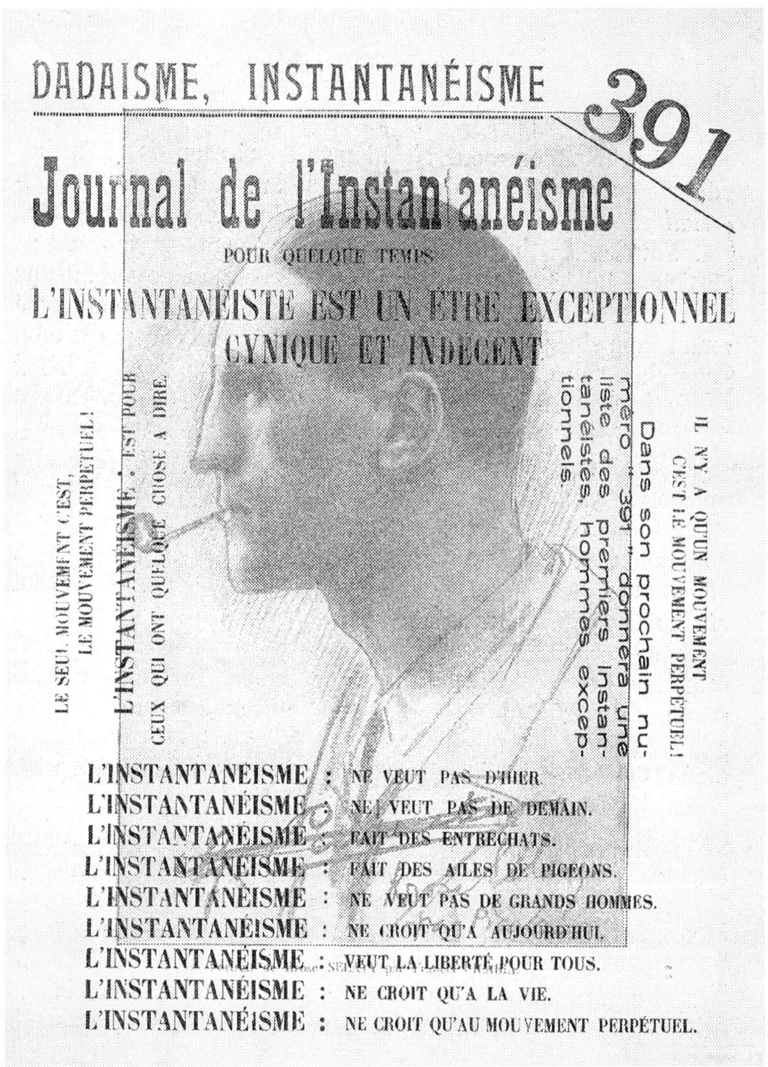

Front cover of the last issue of *391* 19 (October 1924). Research Library, The Getty Research Institute, Los Angeles. © 2005 Artists Rights Society (ARS), New York/ADAGP, Paris/Estate of Francis Picabia.

Picabia's gesture pointed to Duchamp. But this acknowledgment at the moment of *Relâche* only pointed to Duchamp to perform his image in the modality of appropriation, a borrowing of the very contours of another being, another self (and a celebrity at that), splitting the subject and emptying out the figure (and name) of the author at their core—but perhaps also expanding these figures as well. "This substitution of men," Michel Sanouillet once wrote of Picabia's gesture, "is in fact a program."[23] The program is not just cynical, the collapse of artist and celebrity that Picabia's current turn to a major ballet company and to film might otherwise involve. As Picabia seems to have been struck by the resemblance between Charpentier and Duchamp, the portrait of Rrose Sélavy that announces the new movement of Instantanism foregrounds a more profound slippage between beings, a radical connection via resemblance, a new mode of *analogy* between disparate forms. The Dada diagram and its relational web seem to haunt such a tactic. But the kind of visual analogy that Picabia now proffers takes this Dada strategy to entirely new lengths.[24] We perhaps face a key to the central strategy of *Relâche* and *Entr'acte,* and thus to the very culmination of Picabia's Dada project.

Nevertheless, the proclamation of the new movement of Instantanism was evidently parodic, with slogans like "There is only one movement, that is, perpetual motion," and it was another slap in the face of André Breton, one of many barbs aimed by the still-dissident Picabia at the former Dadaists who were gravitating in 1924 toward the new movement of Surrealism. But there was seriousness here as well. With the name of this new "movement," time itself was obviously on Picabia's mind, as he began to work with time-based mediums like dance, music, and film. And yet, to return us to a kind of strategy of doubling and of connection, the word *instantané* in French means both "instantaneous" but also "snapshot," referring directly to the medium that had previously meant so much to Picabia's reformulation of painting and drawing—photography. Thus Picabia's so-called new movement, explicitly linked to Dada in this final issue of *391,* could be translated as both "Instantanism" or "Snapshot-ism." In his advertisements for his ballet, Picabia called *Relâche* not a *ballet obscène,* as Satie had done, but rather a *ballet instantanéiste.* An Instantanist Ballet. A Snapshot-ist Ballet.

With its glimmering set flashing lights at the audience like a group of paparazzi gone mad, *Relâche* does present us immediately with a collision of ballet and something like photography, or at least a "photographic effect." And, crucially, rather than an easy fusion of two separate media, dance and photography, their intertwining here produces the very condition of negation to which the title *Relâche* speaks, with the "photographic" lights of the set literally canceling the visibility of the performance, their stasis freezing momentarily the flow of the ballet's motion. Of course, these "flashes" were articulated in time to another medium, to music, with its percussive beats and shifts in volume, adding another layer of complexity to this collision. And further, we cannot forget the fact that the music in this ballet often itself worked to freeze the flow of the dance, or that conversely, the dance articulated a series of breaks in the progression of the music. But that art forms had entered into intermediary states between one another, and what these forms of admixture might produce—like the sudden translation of Charpentier into Duchamp—seems to be the very stake of *Relâche,* as well, of course, of its intermission *Entr'acte,* which adds cinema to this growing mix, placing it directly between the two sundered halves of the ballet, breaking apart the dance in its turn.

In fact, both titles, both the film and the ballet, speak to intermediary or in-between states, but they do this with a series of significant differences. Both *Relâche* and *Entr'acte* can be translated as "intermissions," although the first means something more like a "break" or indeed a "cancellation," while the latter signals a different form of relaxation, in the sense of an "interlude," or even a "diversion." The first break, *relâche,* signals a negation, while the latter, *entr'acte,* perhaps, a more playful affirmation: a cancellation versus an amusement; a break with a diversion.[25] And yet *Entr'acte* in French literally means "between the acts," inscribing the condition of the "between" into the very heart of Picabia's labor on this project. I want to see this articulation of "between-ness" in the light of the collaborative work Picabia's project initiated between a number of formerly separate artistic mediums.

☞

It should be admitted right away, however, that the admixtures of which *Relâche* and *Entr'acte* partook were not only formal. They were also class-based, and perhaps were this first and foremost. We sense this already in Picabia's travesty of Duchamp as a boxer (or celebrity). And, considering Satie's "pornographic" score for *Relâche,* its dancers outfitted in evening dress and engaging in striptease, the major contribution of *Relâche* to balletic form was its displacement of ballet for the frolic of slapstick and the music hall, the insertion of quotidian and acrobatic movements into the space of dance, or even the subcultural *frisson* of the pornographic into high art. As for showing a film during a ballet, René Clair later explained that Picabia's explicit motivation was to reach back to an early twentieth-century custom, where in *café-concert* intermissions an early film or series of films was often shown.[26] Cinema studies has long established that Picabia and Clair's film, *Entr'acte,* itself reached back to these early or "primitive" films, resurrecting the forms of what has been called the "trick" films of someone like Georges Méliès, the motion studies of Marey, Muybridge, and eventually the Lumière Brothers, or the comic forms of the American films of Mack Sennett, master of the "chase" film and originator of the Keystone Cops series.[27] *Entr'acte,* then, this announcement of the "in-between," looked back to and, more importantly, occupied the precise liminal position of cinema when it had been primarily a proletarian art. And it did this at precisely the historical moment when cinema was attempting to rid itself of this class-belonging, at the moment the medium was forever purged too of its hybrid theatrical roots, the class-bound origins of what has been called the filthy "excrement of vaudeville."[28]

☞

It is time to begin to look at *Entr'acte.* Similar to the unfurling of *Relâche,* the film is not in any straightforward way a narrative film, and so it remains resistant to linear description, or to any summation of its "plot" or events. The great German critic Siegfried Kracauer, however, thought of the film as opposed to abstract film, indeed as representing the concrete "content of a dream," one supposedly dreamt by someone who had "visited a fair" the evening before, thus providing the film or dream-images' manifest content, as the film lurches from shooting galleries to circus arenas to roller-coaster rides and other forms of popular amusement, turned away from their work-a-day reality.[29] It bears stressing, however, that this "dream," if such it is, once again in Picabia's typical manner seems to be "borrowed," the last thing we expect of our dreams (although, of course, Freud would disagree with us): the film's setting runs through the amusement park diversions—especially the shooting gallery stand—that Duchamp long claimed as one of the actual origins for his very idea of the *Bride Stripped Bare by Her Bachelors, Even.* "If the work of another translates my dream," Picabia once asserted, "then his work is mine."[30]

Kracauer's association of *Entr'acte* and dream speaks to the film's creation at the moment of the birth of Surrealism, no matter Picabia's clear hostility to Breton and this movement. But perhaps, for this precise reason, the film's evocation of the dream work was intentional, a deliberate challenge, a fact Picabia seemed to make clear at least once, in his ballet's program, where he wrote: "The intermission for *Relâche* is a film that translates our dreams and the unrealized events that pass through our brains."[31] Surrealism would be outdone before it even had a chance to get off the ground.[32]

Kracauer's reading speaks to the modality of the progression of images and scenes in the film, which in its first half especially seem to flow in "the manner of free associations," as the critic put it, perhaps contradicting Benjamin's interdiction of cinema and the work of association. "The dream images," Kracauer wrote, "are loosely connected in the manner of free associations, drawing on analogies, contrasts, or no recognizable principle at all."[33] From scene to scene, images and shots are matched because of their shape (for example, round objects), their motion (up and down), or their metonymical connections (water in one scene returning in a different manner in the next). And yet even in what amounts to the film's first, associative half, snippets of narrative progression begin to intervene (they will come to dominate the film's latter half).

The film, crucially, starred as its major character the principal dancer from the Swedish Ballet and the choreographer of *Relâche,* namely Jean Börlin, interweaving the two works indissociably. However, Börlin makes his entrance late in the day, and his "screen time" is curiously limited. Instead, the film begins with a series of rhythmic and yet seemingly arbitrary images. We see, in something like this order, an opening shot of upside down rooftops—as if the film begins with the world *in reverse,* or as is more commonly said, the world-upside-down—dolls with inflatable balloon heads from a shooting gallery, and then a ballerina viewed lasciviously from below. She jumps up and down in slow motion on a piece of glass, her tutu expanding and contracting, bloomers parting, garters stretched. We see city lights, car headlights, and disembodied white boxing gloves, sparring like birds over a superimposed image of the Place de l'Opera. There, traffic circulates in perpetual motion. Objects in *Entr'acte* evidently move on their own like the peripatetic cannon, as wooden matches then "dance" magically across the hair of a man seen from above. The man scratches his hair. The matches ignite. The man looks up. Marcel Duchamp and Man Ray play chess on the theater's roof, reacting in shock when the moving traffic of the Place de la Concorde now appears on their game board, the city still in endless agitation, endless circulation. Duchamp sticks out his tongue. Picabia hoses down the board. The water seems, in the next shot, to unloose a drunken paper ship, which rides the "waves" of the roofs of Paris, upon which it is superimposed. The camera "catches" the ship's inebriated reeling, lurching violently from side to side across the cityscape.

The ballerina reappears. For the first time, the camera fixates on her hands, which undulate like waves. A subsequent shot inserts an image of flowing water, a heaving field of ripples and eddies. We pan up and down the ballerina's body. When we pan down from her hands, we see her face for the first time: she is revealed to be a "man," a bearded dancer in spectacles who recalls the visage of Erik Satie (another "Instantanist" portrait?). When we pan up from her ankles, the ballerina reclaims her beauty and regains the female sex, all traces of the beard long gone. From changes in sex, we return to the flowing water, in which now the genders do not so much commingle, as fragments of faces recombine: two eyes, an upside-down chin, the side of another face creating a composite and radically new image of the human visage.

In the wake of this apparition, we then finally come to recognize Börlin, entering the film to play one of its "stagiest" roles as a farcically dressed hunter.

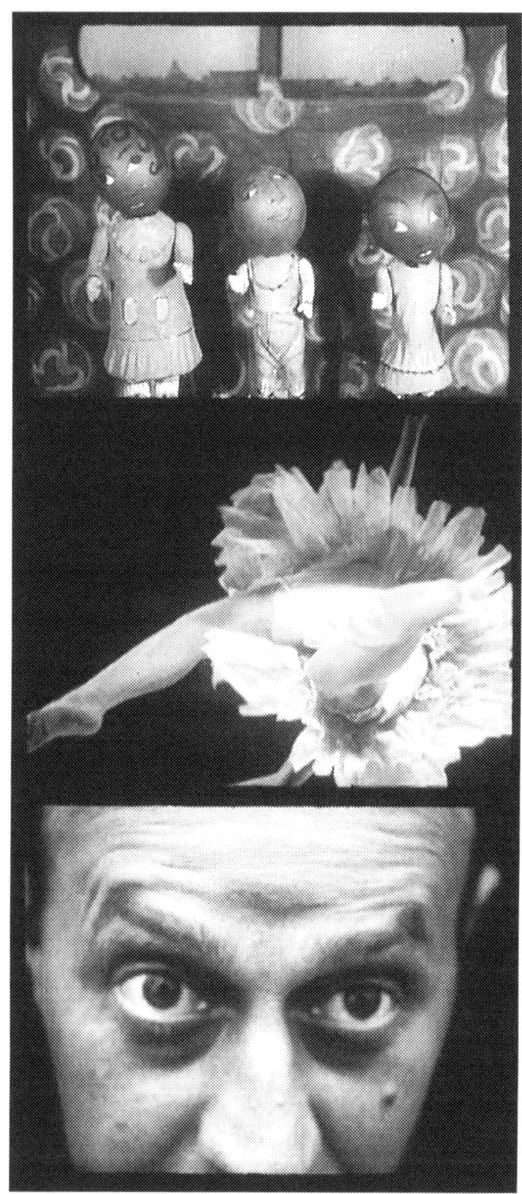

Stills from Francis Picabia, René Clair, and Erik Satie,
Entr'acte, 1924. © Pathé International, Paris.

With some difficulty, the hunter attempts to shoot an ostrich egg supposedly floating on a jet of water—an egg that, in an immediate reversal, in actuality looks with its watery tail like an outsized spermatozoa, and frustrates the hunter's aim by multiplying itself a myriad of times, through the miracles of mechanical reproduction. Upon shooting his target and releasing a bird that circles around to fly to a feather attached to his hunter's cap—reversing the trajectory of his bullet—Börlin is accidentally shot by another marksman, played by Picabia, who supposedly is himself now aiming for the bird. Börlin's body then plummets from the theater roof, the first of at least three indignities that Picabia and Clair's film will thrust upon the dancer (later, he is thrown from a hearse, and then, ultimately, kicked in the head). This death, more or less, ends the first half of *Entr'acte,* which, itself split in two, then begins from this event to follow a more narrative path. We pass to a funeral progression on the way to Börlin's burial, occupying the entire second half of the film.

Now the film runs in a more directional manner, as, according to one film critic, "the funeral cortege is the very model of teleology; it is an end-determined structure."[34] Death, the end and limit of all things, paradoxically driving the narrative forward: one is reminded, however, of Leo Bloom, lost in his thoughts in the funeral carriage on the way to Paddy Dignam's burial, in the Hades section of James Joyce's *Ulysses*: "The carriage wheeling by Farrell's statue united noiselessly their unresisting knees." There, this structure, this device, unites; for a time, death brings a group together. But songs, "a rollicking rattling song of the halls," enter the tram; the city flits by in procession before the characters' eyes; thoughts begin to wander. The relentless engine of death seems to drive the stream-of-consciousness alogic of the narration. And yet at one point, when the carriage comes to a forced halt, Bloom instead fantasizes about a funeral procession gone awry: "Bom! Upset. A coffin bumped out on to the road. Burst open. Paddy Dignam shot out and rolling over stiff in the dust in a brown habit too large for him. Red face: grey now. Mouth fallen open. Asking what's up now. Quite right to close it. Looks horrid open. Then the insides decompose quickly. Much better to close up all the orifices. Yes, also. With wax. The sphincter loose. Seal up all."[35]

By contrast with *Ulysses,* in *Entr'acte* free association had already dominated the film's beginning. By the time of the funeral procession, no "seal" would be possible, and the engine of death indeed runs amok. After Börlin's fall, we begin with the funeral celebration, with such *pompes funèbres* as the French strangely call their mortuaries transformed truly into pomp and a celebration, a fun-house parade, as the mourners file from the "church" to the accompaniment of streamers, while a wind-machine is blowing up the skirts of all the women.[36] Bored mourners outfitted inappropriately in the top hats worn by the dancers in *Relâche* line up behind the hearse, which is bedecked like a carnival float with country hams and loaves of bread. A mourner begins to eat them. The hearse will be drawn by a camel, as if it were a nomad's caravan. Appropriately, the procession begins in slow motion, and instead of walking, the trailing mourners set off after it in graceful leaps and bounds. The ballerina, seen from below, makes her appearance once again, intercut with the scenes of the slow-moving procession. This procession too is a form of dance.

The rest of the film has become famous; summation seems superfluous. As the hearse rounds a faux-Eiffel Tower outside a popular cinema in an amusement park, the carriage breaks away from its camel. Now the film's speed increases, as the mourners attempt to follow a hearse without a head, careening wildly of its own momentum down the city streets. When the oblivious mourners realize that they are following a corpse on the loose, the film increases speed yet again, and more and more citizens join the chase. Eventually, it seems as if the entire city has joined in what has become a race, as bikers pass before our eyes, motor cars careen through traffic, war cripples leap from wheelchairs (as had already happened in *Relâche*), representatives of every class trail the cadaver, and even the *bateaux mouches* and airplanes join the frenzy. The camera work takes over, recording sheer directional movement, most infamously as the film follows the rise and fall of a rollercoaster ride, and then climaxes with the inherent abstraction of high-speed, images of the leaves of trees "streaming by mutely" overhead, as Joyce put it, with "white shapes thronged amid the trees," sustaining "vain gestures on the air." The rollercoaster images are then run not only in reverse but flipped upside down, and the film's opening shots of upside-down rooftops return, finding their companion and culmination at the film's end. And thus the hearse seems finally to flip as well, producing an ejected "coffin bumped out on to the road," rolling like a log into the middle of a country field.

———

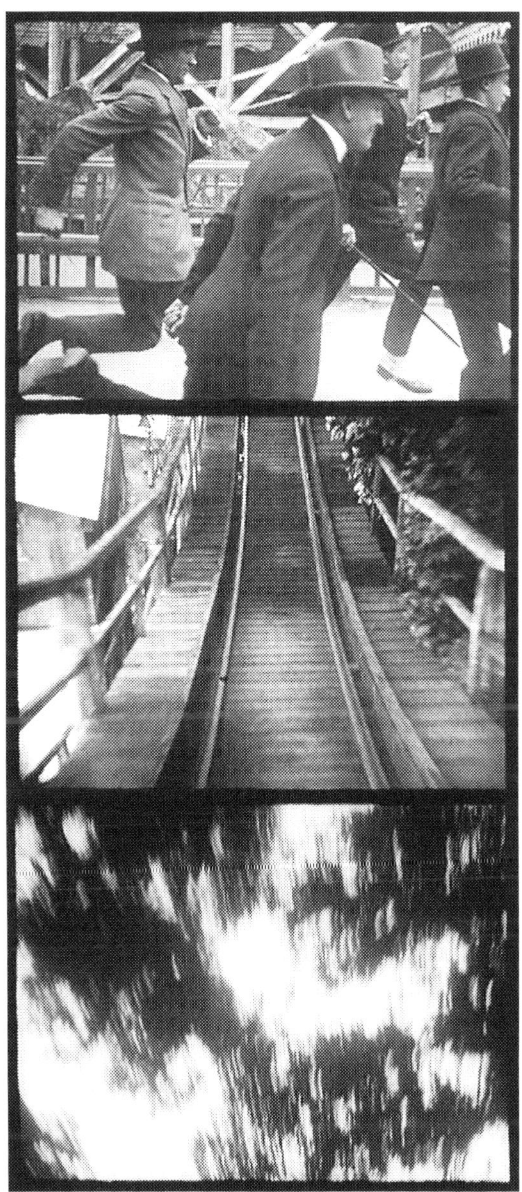

Stills from Francis Picabia, René Clair, and Erik Satie,
Entr'acte, 1924. © Pathé International, Paris.

A small group of panting mourners, representatives of various classes, arrive. Death too, to echo a poet, now dies, its elision will not hold, as even this limit now finds its reversal. The coffin bursts open. From it, Börlin emerges in all his finery, very much alive and brandishing a wand with which, like a magician, he causes each mourner, one by one, to disappear. In the film's final seconds, he turns this wand on himself, fading away before our eyes. The end credits roll, and yet notoriously, from behind the surface of the "screen," the dancer now rips open and leaps through the word "FIN" or "The End," as if to break into the theatrical space like the prelude's cannonshot. The dancer, however, falls flat on his face, and then is kicked in the head, seemingly by the producer Rolf de Maré. While perhaps the dancer has now finally died, this kick sends him traveling back through the screen, via the mechanical magic of reverse motion, reconstituting for a second time the word FIN.

But of course even this is not the end. For if here *Entr'acte* did in fact close, with this virtuoso assertion of a direct cinematic structure of reversal—of protension and retention, forward and back—only seconds later the audience would witness Börlin immediately take the stage once more, to begin his "dancing" in *Relâche,* now itself run like the film in reverse.

Cinema studies, beginning more or less in the 1970s, has approached *Entr'acte* mainly as a formal experiment that undoes or plays with the conventions of narrative cinema. For a film scholar such as Noël Carroll, the disruption of narrative plausibility in *Entr'acte* amounts to an assault on rationality itself, an assault in keeping with what he generally views as the film's "moral immoralism," its stand against the bourgeois vision of social life.[37] This seems an interpretation that cannot see in the film anything but an assault on artistic and social conventions, and surely finds in it no attempt to build other forms from the voided and ossified ones that it attacks.

Other film scholars have more closely followed the precise ways in which narrative causality is foiled in *Entr'acte,* the system behind its voiding of meaning, and thus the alternate symbolic economies that the film might then put in place, the other values it might create. For example, one scholar (Mimi White) points

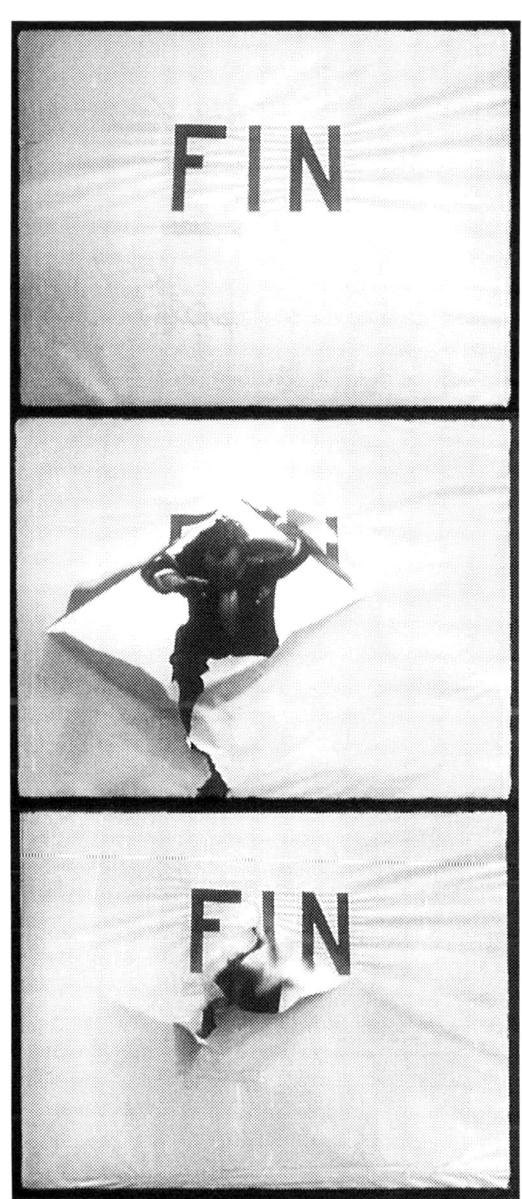

Stills from Francis Picabia, René Clair, and Erik Satie,
Entr'acte, 1924. © Pathé International, Paris.

out that "The film plays with narrative by placing units (identifiable series of shots) in sequence; and against narrative by rejecting the logic of traditional sequentiality, replacing it with a free play of metaphoric and metonymic association while preserving the basic idea of discursive units."[38] These units, in the first half of the film especially, are not randomly strung together; under close inspection, they can be seen as tied together and motivated in an almost infinite number of ways.

In one of the most striking of the film's examples, the scene of the hunter attempting to shoot the egg, we travel through shots that are simply ordered *backward* in relation to a standard pattern of narrative editing. A structure of reversal again rears its head.[39] Things in *Entr'acte* are constantly being "ordered" head-to-tail, and then tail-to-head in turn, in reverse. In this case, we first see a shot of an egg balanced on water, then a close-up shot of a gun muzzle, then a medium shot of the hunter with his gun, and then a long-shot, an establishing shot of the hunter's placement on the theater's rooftop. If these shots were simply reversed, we would be faced with a standard breakdown for a narrative sequence, as White explains: "an establishing shot, a closer shot of the person holding the gun, an extreme close-up of the gun (for impact), and finally a shot of the object at which the gun is being aimed. In the film, however, the object precedes and determines the look rather than vice versa."[40]

The crucial lesson to be learned here, however, is this: By simply reversing standard shot order, meaning is not merely sapped or voided. A whole new series of *connections* comes into play, connections usually repressed by narrative causality. By way of a structure of reversal, and by way of moving directly to the tail—to the end—at the start, we travel from the egg to the muzzle of the gun because both are round objects (a metaphorical connection, one thing is like another), and then from the muzzle to the hunter because of their contiguity (a metonymical relation, one thing being part of the other). The film scholar calls such a technique a "double strategy," for it is one that remains grounded in the order of representation of cinematic narrative while insistently opposing the "logic of conventional narrative structure," retaining the "shot/reaction shot structure," for example, while discarding the temporal and causal logic that underlies it.

Other writers have seen this "double strategy" as indeed more far-reaching in the film, calling its strategies those of a kind of overarching double "parody."[41]

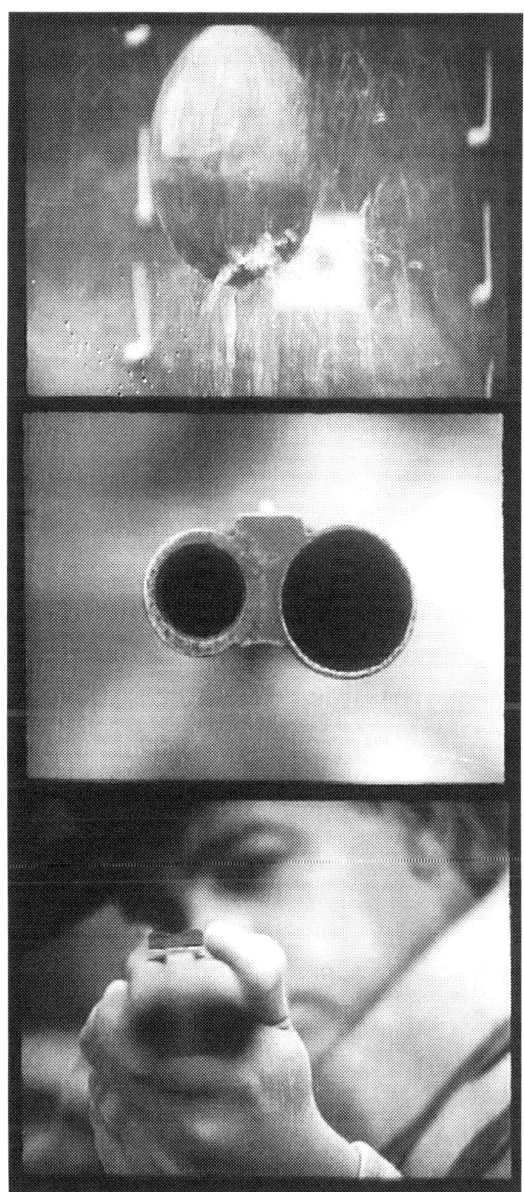

Stills from Francis Picabia, René Clair, and Erik Satie, *Entr'acte,* 1924. © Pathé International, Paris.

Although not stated as such, the logic of sheer reversal is crucial to this claim. According to such an account, the first half of *Entr'acte* parodies the poetic and abstract visual explorations characteristic of avant-garde cinema of the day by inserting stubborn remnants of narrative structures that are ultimately frustrated. An early example of this lies with the shooting-gallery dolls shown at the start of the film. On an abstract or metaphorical level, the dolls seem connected to the ballerina scenes that follow them by the rhythmic movements of their inflating and deflating heads, a motion rhymed with the gravity-bound leaping up and down of the ballerina, a metaphorical connection on the level of shape and motion. However, the dolls' eyes in the first scene seem to look up, as if, in a "point-of-view" shot from a standard narrative sequence, we are being given the "reason" and motivation for why we are looking up at the ballerina in the next shot from beneath. In a slightly later scene, the man whose hair is lit "aflame"—or who conversely is seen simply to be scratching his head (as if confusion?)—looks up in a linked manner, except in this case a sequence of the dancing ballerina had been inserted *before* the image of his upward glance, immediately reversing even this "point-of-view" disruption to the flow of free association.

In a corresponding and opposite manner, however, the second half of *Entr'acte,* with its funeral progression and madcap race, parodies more straightforward narrative films. Now, remnants of poetic and lyrical scene changes more appropriate to avant-garde films erupt to counter the narrative flow (as when the ballerina again appears in the midst of the scene of the leaping mourners, with her leaping compared to theirs). For this argument, the in-between position of *Entr'acte,* the in-betweenness embraced in its title, refers in fact precisely to its place between avant-garde and narrative cinema. It refuses to belong to either practice:

> *Entr'acte* is a double-edged parody, parodying on the one hand the construction principles of cinematic realism in the classical narrative cinema, and on the other, the esthetic practices of the "pure cinema." The film derives its energy from its position between the two discursive traditions, which allows it to play one against the other in a dynamic of double destabilization. For this reason, the esthetic stance

of *Entr'acte* is patently irresponsible, for at any moment it can retreat to the security of one discursive mode while it parodies the other.[42]

Irresponsible, parodic, immoral, irrational: these are the ways in which cinema studies has characterized Dada film.

What cinema studies seems to have missed about *Entr'acte* is the symbolic value system it puts in place in its parody of narrative conventions. Yes, an order of representation here is targeted; and yes, its annihilation proceeds as if from within, via the upending and sheer reversal of that order's conventional symbolic structures. However, in this upending, the cuts between scenes in *Entr'acte* may at first not appear "logical" or motivated by the conventions of storytelling, but they weave a vast tapestry of interconnections nonetheless, a series of exchanges and comparisons whose overall effect is one of a general symbolic contagion.

The entire example of Picabia's Dada years has taught us to be attentive to such strategies of connection or relation, whether diagrammatic, indexical, or otherwise. And thus we might say: As opposed to the sheer nihilism of parody, or the condition of being meaningless, things, in *Entr'acte,* perhaps *mean too much*—in other words, they signify *in excess*—for standard narrative or cinematic conventions to encompass their new modes of existence. There is something *profoundly meaningful* about Dada's sapping or expenditure of the symbolic economies of meaning. Consequently, Dada cinema can hardly be described as consisting only of a strategy of negation; it entailed too a process of intense affirmation.

Above all, and in the first half of the film especially, *Entr'acte* appears dedicated to finding *analogies* between the objects of the world, to finding the qualities and visual characteristics that a host of disparate, seemingly separate objects *share*. Logic and rationality may be supported by the requirements of analysis, the assertion of utter differentiation between all things, a process of cutting and of dissection, of categorization and distinct boundaries. But *Entr'acte* belongs to a different vision of the world; it claims cinema for this different vision of the world. The difference between and the disparateness of objects, in this view, may only be superficial, the thin-skinned appearance masking a far more radical core. Rather, *Entr'acte* dedicates itself to locating the interconnections between formerly separate forms.

The film elaborates two major strategies for establishing such a tapestry of connection. These, in fact, are the cinema's two greatest tools of association, and Picabia's emplacement of them in *Entr'acte* rubs against the dominant modernist models of theorizing the negativity of cinema's strategies via the cut of montage. We are faced instead with a Dada model for the cinema. And these two distinct strategies also explain the split structure of Picabia's film, its two halves sitting together like two foreign languages, yet attempting, nevertheless, to communicate with one another, intercut as they are.

The first of these strategies lies with what could be called *cinematic analogy,* an endless motivating of the arbitrariness of the montage between images through the shared revelation of cinematic motion, the gift that film imparts to all things. Objects are connected in *Entr'acte* because they are "like" one another, in motion, or in speed, or in direction; the film also utilizes motion to align the disparateness of shape and texture. We move, in an endless flow, from the circular, glowing set of *Relâche,* to the round lights at the start of *Entr'acte,* to the round heads of the dolls and the corolla of the ballerina's skirt, to round gloves flitting through the air, to the moving traffic that then follows, to the round-tipped matches that ignite like lights and dance like ballerinas, to the scratching of the round dome of the head which signals an enigma but is also the action that lights matches. And with this, the web of connections in *Entr'acte* has only just begun. In the film's delirious contagion of objects and properties, *analogy* comes to work as a vast connective tissue linking the world together in new, formerly repressed ways, rather than simply analyzing it, dissecting it, tearing it apart and voiding it of meaning.

The second strategy of *Entr'acte* takes motion in the cinema to another plane entirely. The second half of the film, in fact, seems primarily an exploration of motion now disengaged from the anchor of the object, motion becoming a free-flowing enactment of what might best be called a *vector.*[43] Like Dada diagrams, *Entr'acte* devotes itself to a vectorization without object, the full-forward thrust of movement, displacement, sheer relationality without goal. But this is relationality produced by Dada in the wake of the auto-destruction of its own diagrams; or perhaps we might here sense the semiotic project of the diagram redeemed, if not transvalued, its web of exchange set free (beyond measure, beyond rule, after the real or imagined "fall" of the general equivalent). At its most pure moments, rather than "represent" a process of vectorization (as the Dada diagram once did), the film enacts this relational movement physically, imparting its endless lurching directly to its spectators. And the forward or relational thrust of the vector enacted in *Entr'acte* can thus be described in terms similar to the analogy at work in its first half: as that analogy worked everywhere to transvalue the negativity of cinematic montage and the cut, now the vector sutures the film's audience and its spectator, affirming this form of cinematic incorporation for a purpose linked not to its degraded future in mass delusion and the spectacle, but to a more pure form of connectedness and relationality. The progression of *Relâche* too, we realize, was everywhere devoted to a linkage or suturing between audience and spectacle, even if the "marriage" of performance and audience effected by the ballet often proceeded by rendering the spectacle as blank, blinding, a palpable excess pushed beyond boundaries and limits. With this, the "inbetweenness" of *Entr'acte,* rather than amounting to an irresponsible position that refuses to grant any one symbolic language priority over any other, begins rather to seem an almost ethical stance. "Moral immoralism," indeed.

The fact has been consigned to oblivion until now: at the moment Paris Dada began in 1919, Picabia was in a brief but direct contact with Walter Benjamin. Facilitated by Benjamin's relations with the Zurich Dadaists—Benjamin mentions specifically Hans Richter—the critic had been reading Picabia's poetry, and wrote to thank the artist for sending him a book. He also wrote of the "joy" that studying Picabia's work brought him. You are an "artist of correspondences," Benjamin averred, which, "for a long time already, have been the object of my own meditations."[44]

Benjamin's implication was clear. The Symbolist heritage of the "correspondences" survives in Picabia's work, no matter art history's long insistence that Symbolist aesthetics were precisely targeted by Dada as an avant-garde, like the perfume of so many vibrant flowers falling before the aggressive petrol stench of the machine. But instead of seeing this heritage liquidated in the moment of Dada as an avant-garde, one might suggest that ideas such as "correspondence" were only radicalized by artists like Picabia—transformed beyond recognition, but not relinquished.

In fact the idea of the interconnection between objects in the world had always been crucial to Picabia's Dada work, although few aside from Benjamin bothered to notice this. Picabia's aesthetic, from the earliest years of its formation, from Orphism through the Dada diagram or mechanomorph, had been based on the Baudelairean notion of "correspondence," and this (antimodernist) insistence on always stating "this is like that" has perhaps been at the ground of the insistence of art historian after art historian that Picabia's readymade pictures and diagrams yield up simple symbolic and iconographic meanings. But the more radical symbolic meaning of his work, culminating in the project of *Entr'acte,* lies in the contagion of exchanges between disparate realms that correspondence effects, its anarchic analogies and admixtures: between word and image, painting and photography, art and advertising, man and machine, or—to be more specific about Picabia's analogies—a ship's propeller and a donkey, a close friend and a cheap lamp, Marcel Duchamp and a boxer. It is no coincidence that dance was always one of the phenomena that pushed Picabia's work in this regard, along with its corollary of music. We can trace this concern from early paintings based on dance and music such as *Star Dancer on a Transatlantic* to early mechanomorphs such as *Music Is Like Painting* to the "animated" appropriations of photomechanical *391* covers like *Flamenca* or *Ballet mécanique.*[45] The temporal and mobile destiny of mediums like dance and music pushed Picabia to extend even further the Symbolist afterlife of his Orphism into the diagrams of his mechanomorphs, their mobile vectors and their marriage between word and image also so many radical assertions of linkage, connection, analogy. Now we can begin to understand why and how Dada for Picabia came to fruition only in the collaborative project of a ballet and a film. *Relâche* and *Entr'acte* bring this mode of interconnecting objects to a climax in Picabia's work. They were hardly the last gasp of

---

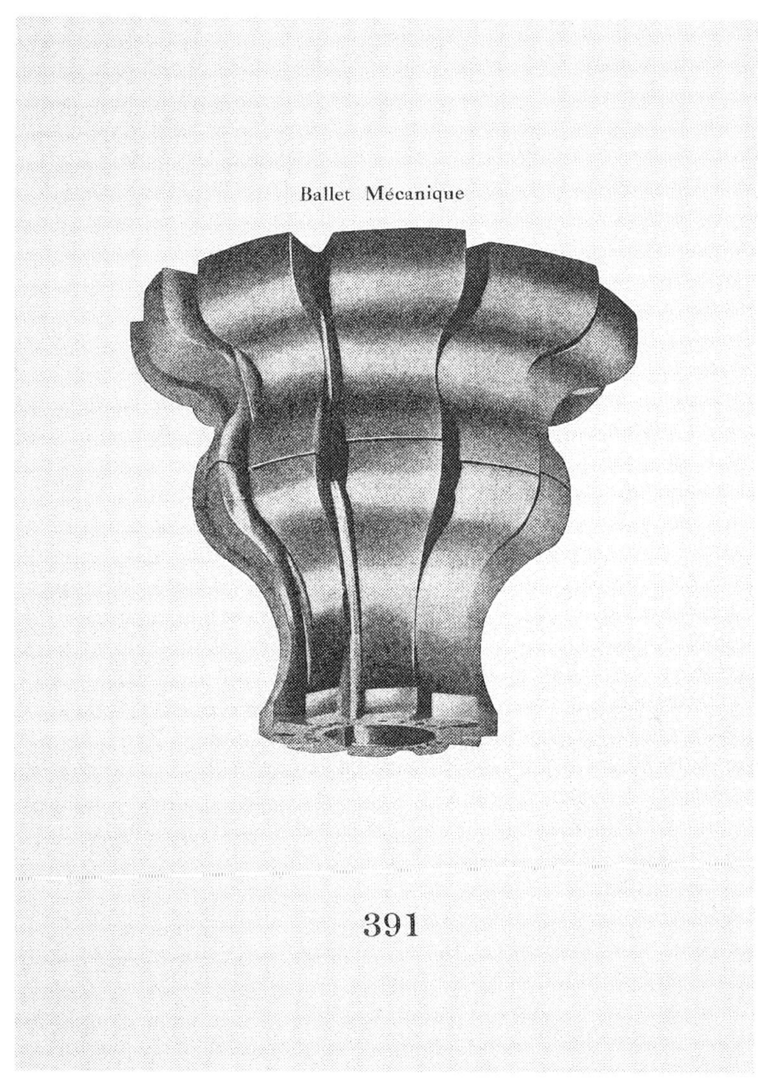

Francis Picabia, *Ballet mécanique (Mechanical Ballet),* 1917. Cover image of *391* 7 (August 1917). Research Library, The Getty Research Institute, Los Angeles. © 2005 Artists Rights Society (ARS), New York/ADAGP, Paris/Estate of Francis Picabia.

the correspondences, but they were inheritors, and for Dada, they were a culmination and a conclusion.

☞

This climax—and here we return to Benjamin's claim that Dada looked forward to the cinema—has everything to do with the existence of *Entr'acte* within the medium of film, its cinematic dedication to an endless transition and becoming. For the French philosopher Gilles Deleuze, cinema's greatest resource and its overwhelming power lie in its endless mutability, its almost abstract dedication to change and to bringing new things to life ceaselessly before our eyes. He would, himself, comment on *Entr'acte* as an important model of this understanding of cinema, seeing in the film's ever-widening stream of images its most crucial contribution—this is Deleuze citing and correcting Jean Mitry, cinema historian and one-time assistant to René Clair—"the dancer's tutu seen from beneath 'spreads out like a flower,' and the flower 'opens and closes its corolla, enlarges its petals, and lengthens its stamens,' to turn back into the opening legs of a dancer; the city lights become a 'pile of lighted [matches]' in the hair of a man playing chess, [matches] which in turn become the 'columns of a Greek temple, then of a silo, whilst the chessboard becomes transparent to give a view of the Place de la Concorde.'"[46] Faced with such a chain of images, linked in their various ways, Deleuze concludes: "These are not metaphors." Rather, for the philosopher, they are implicitly diagrammatic, like a circuit. Such was the nature of the oneiric vocation that Deleuze continues, after Kracauer, to see as central to the image chain in *Entr'acte,* its association of cinema and dream: "the virtual image which becomes actual does not do so directly, but becomes actual in a different image, which itself plays the role of virtual image being actualized in a third, and so on to infinity: the dream is not a metaphor but a series of anamorphoses which sketch out a very large circuit."[47] In this light, the image chain in *Entr'acte* becomes another Dada chain of signifiers, one that Deleuze describes as the sign of "a becoming which can by right continue to infinity."[48] We so rarely, in life, experience in an intelligible way one thing becoming something else. We so rarely experience the breakdown of limits between beings, between things. We so rarely experience *becoming.* Cinema allows us to do so.

———

If cinema studies has ignored, with the exception of Deleuze, the potential power and valence of the connections forged between images in *Entr'acte,* it has similarly ignored the film's site-specificity, its placement in the midst of a number of other art forms, and the potential connections that this "interlude" proposes between these various forms. It has ignored the key to opening up the film that its literal position as an *entr'acte* within a ballet provides.

For example, we have so far completely ignored the music for *Entr'acte,* which is also typical of most analyses of the film. But one cannot discuss the import of this film in the absence of a discussion of its use of sound. In an era of still silent cinema, *Entr'acte* was the first film for which a score was written by an avant-garde composer, and the first as well for which a composition was written methodically "shot by shot," as Clair later affirmed. It is also true that neither film nor score exist as satisfying entities on their own, and this lack of autonomy needs to be explained.[49]

Long understood as an example of what the composer called "furniture music," Satie's score for *Entr'acte* was vastly different from that of *Relâche.* "Furniture" music, for Satie, was music that had become useful—not existing for its own sake, it was something like background music, what we today call Muzak or wallpaper music, a music, in Satie's words, with the "same role as light and heat—as comfort in all its forms."[50] The idea was something like Henri Matisse's infamous desire to produce a form of painting that functioned like a comfortable armchair.

And indeed, in Satie's music for *Entr'acte,* we witness the vast reformulation of musical form that cinema and its exigencies could enact on another medium. Musical "expression" fades away; Satie's pastiches and citations of previous songs are kept to a minimum (the major exception being a parody of Chopin's Funeral March that erupts briefly at the beginning of the film's funeral procession); the music devolves instead into an endless chain of disconnected units, four- or eight-measure-long motifs that could be repeated over and over again to match the progression and changes of scenes in the film. The motifs hold little relation to one another, and are strung together without any attempt at transition, "crazy-quilt style," in the words of one critic, or like the sudden shifting of the gears of a machine.[51]

The use of mechanical repetition was not new for Satie: as early as 1892 he had composed a piece entitled *Vexations* composed of a small musical fragment to be played over and over again some 840 times.[52] It was a performative structure that Satie deployed in the score for *Entr'acte* in order to allow the orchestra's conductor, Roger Désormière, to adjust and repeat segments of music as needed in order to synchronize the film and the sound.[53] Disconnected internally, the music in *Entr'acte* relies entirely on an external, outside force for the rationale of its changes in theme and tone. Cinema provides this external motivation (as well as the very "being," one might say, of the mechanical, repetitive, but lively music: Satie's score was simply entitled "Cinema").

And yet the designation of "furniture music" misleads, for the music acts similarly, that is, externally, on the cinematic images. At times, of course, the music and the film are marked by a set of qualities that they seem to share. As critic Martin Marks points out, the "prevalent characteristics" of the *Entr'acte* score could be said to rhyme with the film, including "*buoyancy,* suggested by the bouncing and dissonant figures which blithely refuse to resolve, *momentum,* sustained by the constant tempo, the lack of cadences, and the grouping of units into four and eight measures, and *discontinuity,* caused by the abrupt shifts which isolate each unit in terms of 'theme,' key area (which is often ambiguous), and texture."[54] In addition, like the return in *Entr'acte* again and again to the image of the leaping ballerina, Satie's score for the film has been described as a form of rondo, returning again and again to a "home" theme. However, Marks avers that this dominant theme is a "home" that is "up in the air"; it is a theme that, like the images it accompanies—bouncing lights, boxing gloves, the mobile matches—"defies musical 'gravity' by refusing to come to rest on the solid ground of an A major chord. Its melody keeps bobbing back up to the pitch just above the tonic."[55]

Such connections between film and music need to be registered; but the more radical linkages seem not to lie in the realm of confluence, or simple rhyme, but on the level of structure, and of the literal externality of image to sound. For Satie's music often cadences and thus underlines the cuts and montage in Picabia and Clair's film, bringing things to a rhythmic stop when the film images seem rather to push connectedness between scenes. One of the first times this happens is with the early images of the drunken paper boat, which never stops moving and imparts its motion to the following scenes, but seems to be "stopped" by a grand four chord "outburst" on the level of the score, which comes to a halt immediately before the change in scene. Such a cadence enforces the jump of the montage like a warning signal, making palpable through sound—but actually through musical "silence," through a sudden abandonment of musical progression—a literal, visual absence within the film. The score "articulates a division between images which the film interconnects."[56] If montage is the invisible force within cinema that creates a film's rhythm—one of the qualities that the temporal art of film could conceivably "share" with music—then it is precisely the invisible "rhythm" of montage and cutting to which the music is attracted, and that it must reveal.[57] Cinema cannot "show" this invisible structure. But the music can.

A form "is" what it "lacks"; Bataille's principle of inadequacy has returned. *Entr'acte* imagined a transgressive movement around a limit, or series of limits, between the forms of dance and music and film, with each medium exposing its limit, its lack, receiving the gift of what it cannot express—the exclusion that structures but also undoes the medium—from the bounty of another form. And *Entr'acte* itself occupied a limit, entering into its liminal site *precisely.* We now begin to see how forms might be said to interact in *Entr'acte,* the true force of its operation of the between: Cinema enters into and alters the structure of musical form, breaking into its totality and sense of sustained development and variation, a music that once broken down in this way could play against the images in turn, to reveal the invisible economy, even the Law, underlying their form, the void that film attempts to cover over, the absent structure girding the very medium of the cinema.

In the wake of registering the precise interaction between the film and the music, several images from the film now begin to look very different. Suddenly, the scene immediately following the revelation of the ballerina as a "bearded" man-in-travesty—the intensely dreamlike sequence of incongruent facial parts recombining in the midst of the endless flow of a body of water—makes claims for perhaps being the most important suite of images in the film. We face a potential emblem for the film's larger operation. Eyes float in space, immersed and fully "liquid," only to be joined by a nose and mouth turned in a different direction (upside-down), and potentially from another face; two profiles arranged in reverse orientation—head to tail, once more—line up to create a strange composite "person." This is one of the key images from *Entr'acte* for it literalizes, on the subjective dimension—on the plane of "being"—the potential chains of connection formed by the other images of the film, its linkages between disparate objects, as well as the entire project in *Relâche* and *Entr'acte* of the linkage or sharing of form. Occurring more or less precisely at the sundered midpoint of the film, it emblematizes too that conjunction of its "associative" and "narrative" halves, the film's internal linkage and fragmentation (if not its larger purpose to link and fragment the entire performance of *Relâche*). And the sutured, multiplied faces become another "expanded" or Instantanist "portrait" predicting the breakdown of boundaries effected by the incorporation of the viewer into the chase scene at the film's end. It is an image sequence that sings quietly of the entire interaction of mediums posed by this film's occupation of the position of a form in-between.

Many images in the film emblematize quite precisely this interaction of mediums. They perform a kind of "sharing" of form, becoming something like the internal signs of a series of art forms themselves beginning to "communicate" with each other. Critics have long been attentive to the play with dance that the film images consolidate. Through the trope of insistent comparison with the ballerina sequences, the film's objects can be described as "dancing," its mourners "dancers" too. But these observed continuities between the film images and dance do not go far enough. For the "continuities" in question operate in fact as another form of chiasmus, of reversal, and this can only be seen when *Entr'acte* functions in its larger context: as dance in *Relâche* was *undone* by appropriations throughout of pedestrian movements, becoming sheer gymnastics, strip-tease, or task-performance, now quotidian activities or everyday things in the film find themselves *elevated* to the condition of dance.[58]

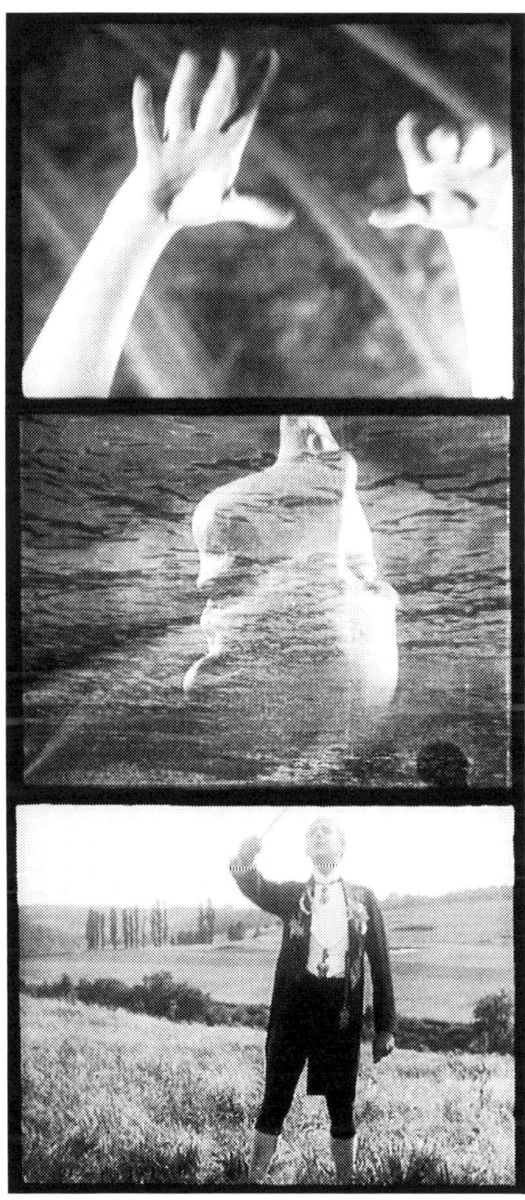

Stills from Francis Picabia, René Clair, and Erik Satie,
Entr'acte, 1924. © Pathé International, Paris.

The chiasmus is a relational form (a reversal of forms) more complex than that of a simple opposition. And indeed, here it effects not a binarism, but a multiplicity. As Börlin, for instance, explodes from his coffin at the end of the film, wildly prancing through an open field, his magician's outfit is belied, to become instead a direct evocation of the leaps and bounds of the ballet dancer and the dance that he will consistently fail to uphold within *Relâche* on the stage. And as he then waves his magic wand in the air, miraculously vanishing the gathered group of astonished mourners like so many signs for the audience's own disappearance during this *Entr'acte,* he again belies his "magical" character, appearing on the screen before us as if he were suddenly a "conductor," directing with his baton the music that we hear. Börlin as conductor: the cinematic image that we see "directs" the sound that we hear. Only when the position between mediums of *Entr'acte* is taken into account can this expansion of form be perceived. And only then can the external revelation of one form to another proceed, as we now quite literally see the cinema directing the musical progression, the external determination of form that the music otherwise undergoes throughout.

But this is a revelation that the film has offered us before, for instance when the ballerina is transformed into a bearded man and suddenly expands into an uncanny analogue for Satie, the score's composer. In this scene, "she" also waves her hands, producing an undulation that is an analogue for the film's liquid "flow," but that also simultaneously and literally conducts the sounds that we hear, like the magician's later baton. Analogy overflows. Chiasmus opens all the images of the film: In *Relâche* and *Entr'acte,* dancers become objects, and objects become dancers. Conductors (composers) become dancers, and dancers become conductors (composers). Montage undoes music, and music undoes—and thus reveals—the montage.

Picabia's project for the Swedish Ballet has been called a venture that "veered more closely towards the Wagnerian concept of the *Gesamtkunstwerk* than had any previous performance."[59] Art history seems to concur with this view, and when it treats *Relâche* and *Entr'acte* at all, it has usually been as late inheritors of the notion of a "total" work of art. The project was long banished from modernism's critical story for precisely this reason, the ballet's utter (indeed comical) rejection of the modernist imperative of medium-specificity. Without the specter of the *Gesamtkunstwerk,* no one seems to know what to do with *Relâche.* And yet *Relâche* is hardly the belated progeny of one of the most fraught dreams of the nineteenth century. For *Relâche* and *Entr'acte* are anything but a *Gesamtkunstwerk.*[60]

Forms, mediums—even objects and beings—come together in *Relâche* and *Entr'acte.* Connection and relation are surely at stake. But the mediums come together precisely *not* to unite, to become One, to become newly Total. Rather they split each other apart. They interrupt each other's limits, in order to be rendered, quite precisely, multiple. Forms come together in Picabia's project to break each other open. They consolidate nothing. Instead, they undo each other's medium conventions, disrupting what we might call the Law that each form excludes in order to define its operation. And as Picabia's project gathered to itself each of the major art forms, like a growing chorus of the Muses, each form turns to the other in order to locate its exclusion, its lack, its outside, undoing the elision at its own foundations.

The mediums come together in *Relâche,* but only through the figure of chiasmus, through reversal, positioned head-to-tail. No parallel orientation of the mediums will be possible; non-alignment is their only form of confluence. Dance will be stopped, not supported, by the music; frozen, not grounded, by the set. It will be undone by pedestrian movements, by bodily activity both aristocratic and proletarian in its origins—incoherent as to its source other than from realms external to those of dance, signaled by the pastiches in the ballet's score. And the dance's "breakdown" will be reversed by its quotidian "redemption" in the form of film. Musical "development" and lyricism collapse, to become instead sheer tempo and pastiche, a structure of repetition or of something like the sonorous equivalent of a collection of cinematic "jump" cuts. The music takes into itself the "hole" at the heart of film. It makes this "hole" appear—to become visible, palpable—during the viewing of the film. Cinema will split in half the ballet, and yet it will be split itself in turn, its narrative vocation foiled by movement of another kind, of entirely other kinds, whether we think of the rhythm of music or the sheer kinetic gyrations of dance. Each medium "combination" produces an undoing.

But to split forms in this way (like the split but communicating zones of Duchamp's *Large Glass*), to undo each form at the limit where it touches another, is also to expand them. We might in fact assert that this confrontation with loss is the only way in which forms can be expanded—as opposed to what occurs in the *Gesamtkunstwerk* model, a totalitarian procedure.[61] This, instead, is a transgressive model of medium-belonging, a "belonging" that amounts in fact to a dispossession. Each medium works "in concert" not to fuse but to frustrate the other. Each is exposed to its inadequacy, its limit, producing a scene of proliferating fragments, with no claim to totality at all.

And this model for the expansion of form—the destiny, it must be said, of the full panoply of Dada's "reinvented" artistic mediums, finally revealed—finds its corollary in the ballet's imagination of a kind of "bachelor machine" logic for combination of all kinds: not just of forms, but of genders, subjectivities, classes. The sexes will come together in *Relâche,* only to split asunder, to work in a marked rhythm of alternation. Such alternations are echoed in *Entr'acte.*[62] Beings in the film are "fused," only to organize their conjunction head-to-tail, a logic of diametric reversal, with no shared orientation in sight. And references to or figures of both the "popular" and bourgeois classes commingle throughout, but not to produce the overarching terror of the People, once envisioned as the highest mission of the idea of the *Gesamtkunstwerk.* The "popular" will be referenced throughout, but without giving rise to an expression of the "People"—admixture without commonality, without universality, bereft of a standard or law.

Relâche instead imagined its relation to the social field as something like what today we might call an "inoperative" community.[63] The only commonality would be the shared experience of blindness and of limits. The only thing that is shared is that which the People lack. The only thing that unites the social field is the force of dissolution. *Entr'acte* chose to portray this by transforming all of Paris into a mad chase after a corpse, a "People" united by one thing only, by death, by their limit, by that which dissolves them at their limit. And so it was in this ballet with form.

But corpses come back to life in *Entr'acte*. Mourning becomes a celebration. And so it was in this ballet with form. Limits were worked on all their sides. Limits could be reversed. Such are the lessons of transgression. Exposed to their outside, to their limit, to the extermination of their being—to the place where they are not—forms expand in more than one direction. Forms can come back to "life."

Picabia offered *Relâche* and *Entr'acte* an unusual sequel, a single offspring without issue, a one-night-only performance on the last day of December 1924—a New Year's Eve performance—that he entitled *Cinésketch*. Here was truly the last gasp of Dada in Paris. But perhaps this performance was less the sequel to *Relâche,* than something like its necessary reversal, its tail. The very name of the performance now imagined the coming-together of mediums—*ciné* and *sketch*—terms for cinema and an informal performance in the theater, or more basically the terms for movement and an informal (but foundational) mode of drawing. Picabia prepared for the tactics of *Cinésketch* with the opening lines of his essay "Instantanism," staging yet another list of reversals, a long imagining of the operations of chiasmus:

> Bankers are artists and artists are bankers; grocers are writers and writers are grocers; cinema is based on theater, and theater is based on cinema; doctors are patients, and patients are doctors. Doctors infect us with their contagious diseases just like the theater has unfortunately injected all of its long-standing maladies into the cinema.[64]

In his Swedish Ballet production, Picabia had brought dance and music into the space of the cinema. But now, in *Cinésketch,* cinema would in turn work out of bounds. Picabia brought the operations of cinema directly to the stage: "Up until now," Picabia explained, in an interview given on the day of the production, "the cinema has been based on theater. I tried to do the opposite, bringing to the stage the techniques and the lively rhythms of cinema."[65]

Instead of charging René Clair with the making of another film, Picabia now invited Clair to stage *Cinésketch,* to organize the lighting and the *mise-en-*

scène. In the face of Picabia's lugubrious scenario calling for various Swedish Ballet members like Börlin, or starlets like the dancers "Caryathis" and "Jasmine," or aristocrats like the Baronness Jeanne "Double" (Lecomte de Noüy), to play the parts of cops and robbers, lovers and chefs—a veritable "Cook, the Thief, His Wife, and Her Lover" to cite a more recent cinematic scenario—Clair divided the stage into three "zones," representing domestic spaces like kitchen and bedroom. In these divided areas of the stage, the actors performed simultaneously, accompanied by a New York jazz band. Clair worked the lights, flashing them on and off from zone to zone in rapid-fire succession, producing a stroboscopic effect, or an alternating illumination of "the three different sections to produce a rough equivalent of montage in films."[66]

Imparted now to the stage, to theater, would be something like the very foundation of the cinematic image, the condition of illusion authorized by the persistence of vision. Such illusion on the stage, however, was ruptured, as the stroboscopic flashing froze the performance, suspended it, instead of unleashing the kinesis of film. And yet to bring montage to the stage would also be to set loose entirely new performative movements, new conceptions of "development" and progression in the theater itself, fragmenting the so-called live action of performance, opening it to the leaps and bounds of film, connection via intermittence. But this was achieved only by bringing the foundational "absence" at the very heart of film to the stage, sharing that absence in turn. The "hole" of film—montage—had first entered music (in *Entr'acte*); now it was unleashed on the central Dada terrain of theater, of performance. Cinema could become (in Dada it became) a kind of model for this "sharing," a model for connection across a gap, a division, the intermittence or absence between frames, or the leap over the abyss that is montage. The result was a kind of incommensurate sharing around a gap, a hole—dialogue in the void.

In *Cinésketch,* however, this space of suspension was also somehow a space of resurrection. Resurrection is of course the precise interval between life and death, the impossible non-space that amounts to neither the one nor the other, the limit itself, although now played in reverse, moved through in a contrary direction. Such would be the logic of allowing one medium to display the elision at the heart of another, bringing to light the excluded Law at the basis of a form,

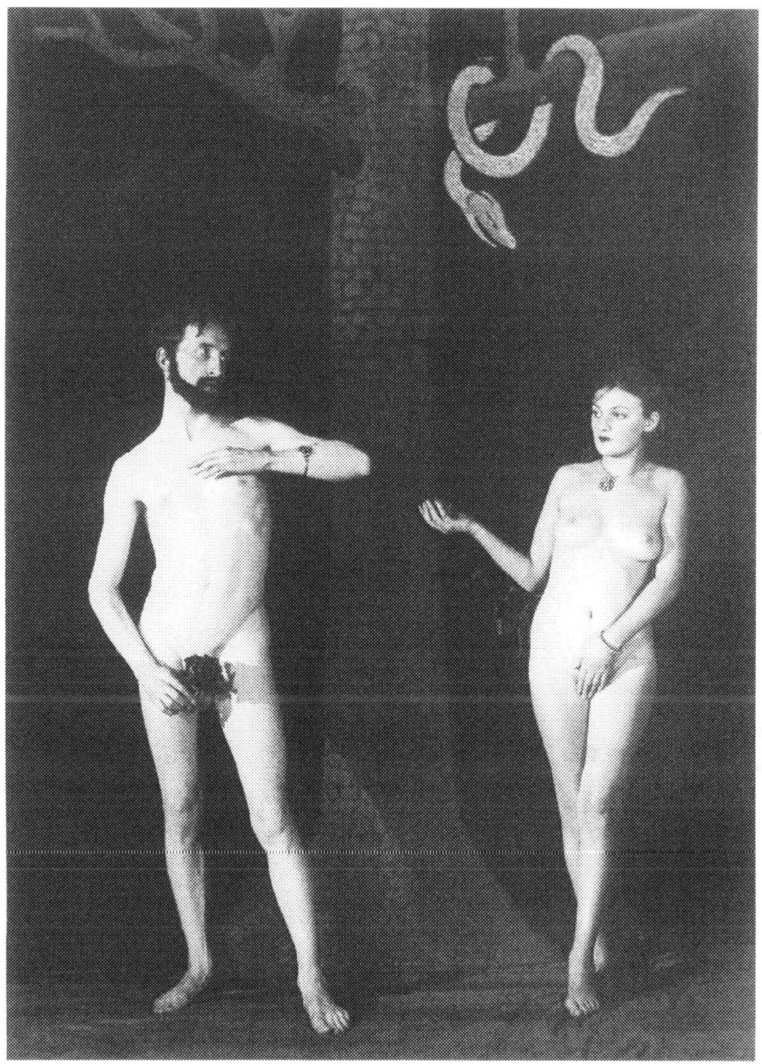

Francis Picabia, *Cinésketch,* 1924. Image of Marcel Duchamp and Brogna Perlmutter. Image courtesy Comité Picabia. © 2005 Artists Rights Society (ARS), New York/ADAGP, Paris/Estate of Francis Picabia.

but only through self-exposure, through exposure to an other. The performance's most famous image—in fact, the only image of it that seems to have been recorded (it is thus something like its "emblem")—is of Duchamp, again cast as he was in Picabia and Clair's film, but now playing the role of Adam, fully nude—exposed, or, of course one should say, *stripped bare*—in a recreation of a painted scene by Lucas Cranach of Adam and Eve. Lit momentarily by the stroboscopic flashing, and inserted repeatedly—one imagines—between the other scenes, this restaging of an Old Master painting was described by Picabia as a form that had been "brought back to life."[67] And here another meaning of the title *Cinésketch* arises, as painting and drawing lurch into suspended animation, producing at the precise interstice of painting, theater, and cinema the ambivalent vision of a *tableau vivant*.

At the end of Dada, we thus come to a reversal of its beginning. Dada in Paris had begun, for Picabia, with death, with art imagined as the very scene of a kind of dying, life frozen into a mortuary relic, a stuffed monkey entitled *Natures mortes*. To reverse that scene would be to explore the terrain of a *tableau vivant*. Theater plays its role in both cases, as it would for the remainder of visual art's development in the long, terrible twentieth century. But if *Cinésketch* must be narrated as a reversal, we realize at this point that it was also a reversal of the artwork caught by the tail, or perhaps it was, simply, that tail, a reversal of a scene of expenditure, the flip side of Dada's war on the general equivalent.

Indeed, one understanding of *Cinésketch* might be to see it as a *reinstatement* of the general equivalent, a paean to the Old Masters as much as a parody, a return to the site of the Law. One reading of the remainder of Picabia's career as an artist would be confirmed here, as in the wake of Dada the painter returned to the history of his medium, exacerbated the work of parody and pastiche, producing painting as a kind of endless catalog of historical citations, a voracious encyclopedia of every discredited painterly "style."

But for Picabia, in 1924, to reverse Paris Dada's originary (primal) scene, to invert *Natures mortes,* could also be read as an attempt to work on the other side of the expenditure of the general equivalent, the far side of a precipitous limit, a labor that we could hardly expect any artist to sustain. Indeed, *Cinésketch* was an "instantanist" apparition, a suspension "for a moment," not the progenitor of an entire career. On the other side of the general equivalent's destruction, there could instead be imagined—however briefly—resurrection, affirmation, death run in reverse, equivalence without a standard, beyond measure, without a Law. In such a space, mediums could combine, and forms exchange places, anarchically, outside of the Law—to the beat, that is, of equivalence without measure. Elision could be reversed. Art might be reborn. Or, given that the *tableau vivant* at which we gaze was a restaging of the suspended moment just before the endless plummet of Original Sin: forever accursed.[68]

Before *Cinésketch,* however, Picabia's *Relâche* already had a tail. In all of his announcements for the ballet, the artist enumerated a third companion to *Relâche* and its cinematographic *Entr'acte,* a finale entitled "la queue du chien": The Dog's Tail. He didn't say, as one can in French, that his ballet would end in a *queue de poisson*—a fish's tail, but also, figuratively, to end by fizzling out, in vain. Such an ending would have matched the connotations of Picabia's title *Relâche.* Instead, the public was presented with a "Dog's Tail."

As ridiculous as it sounds, dog tails had been showing up by this moment in Picabia's art, most notoriously in 1923 in the Salon machine *Dresseur d'animaux.* But even René Clair later claimed that he had no idea what Picabia meant by the idea, and assumed it had been skipped. "For the sake of future historians of the theatre," Clair asserted, "I must add that no one has ever known exactly why this ballet was 'instantanist.' As for the dog's tail, no one saw the shadow of it. But Picabia, one of the great 'inventors' of the day, felt that one invention more or less would make no difference."[69]

Clair was wrong. The shadow was there. The "Dog's Tail" was present for all to "see." It functioned, in fact, as the finale of the ballet. Satie's score explicitly names it. As the ballet's music petered out, the music's tempo slowing almost to a stop in its last moments as all the dancers emptied from the scene, a white curtain fell as if in closure. But this was the same curtain onto which, during the intermission, *Entr'acte* had been projected. And now, in front of it, a tiny ballerina appeared—I imagine her spot-lit—dancing and frantically miming, as if belting out the double-time song struck up by the orchestra. This was the *queue du chien*. It was a music-hall trick, a vaudeville routine. It was the raucous "That's All, Folks" at the end of the show.

It was like the ending of *Entr'acte*. The end would come, and then it would be reversed, the screen ripped open, plunged through, renewed vivacity at the end of all things. As a vaudeville trope, it made explicit the pastiche of popular forms in all of the ballet's other domains. As a mimed song, it positioned mime itself—and potentially mimesis, even the token fraudulence of the mimetic sign—as a kind of connective tissue within the project, linking on another level the music, the cinema, the ballet.[70]

I really have no idea why Picabia called it the "Dog's Tail." The image is vivid. And sure, the artist loved dogs, especially his beloved pet of the Dada years, notoriously appearing in many of their tracts, the famed "Zizi de Dada." The only (admittedly obscure) connection that seems plausible lies in a realm with which we know Picabia was familiar, a realm traversed by his last mechano-morphs, namely astronomy. "Dog's tail" is a literal translation of the word "cyno-sure," a word that we still use today, but that stems in etymology from the Greek name for the constellation Ursa Minor, an alternate name for the guiding star Polaris, the North Star. And consequently, a cynosure is an object that serves as a focal point, a guide, a center of admiration or attention.

At the end—in the end—it was the limit that was being asserted. This was the "tail" to which all was drawn. "That's All, Folks." It was an assertion of the end, the limit—of the People, to the People. And it was the tail-end of Dada as well. In 1915, Dada had begun with a magic trick, the prestidigitator's "*Voilà*." *Voilà Haviland, Voilà Elle, Voilà la Femme*. Picabia would remind us of this in *Entr'acte*. But a decade later, Dada ended with a "That's All, Folks." It ended in a *queue du chien,* with the raucous anticonclusion of the music hall, of vaudeville. It was an end that was also not an end. It was a limit that was also alive.

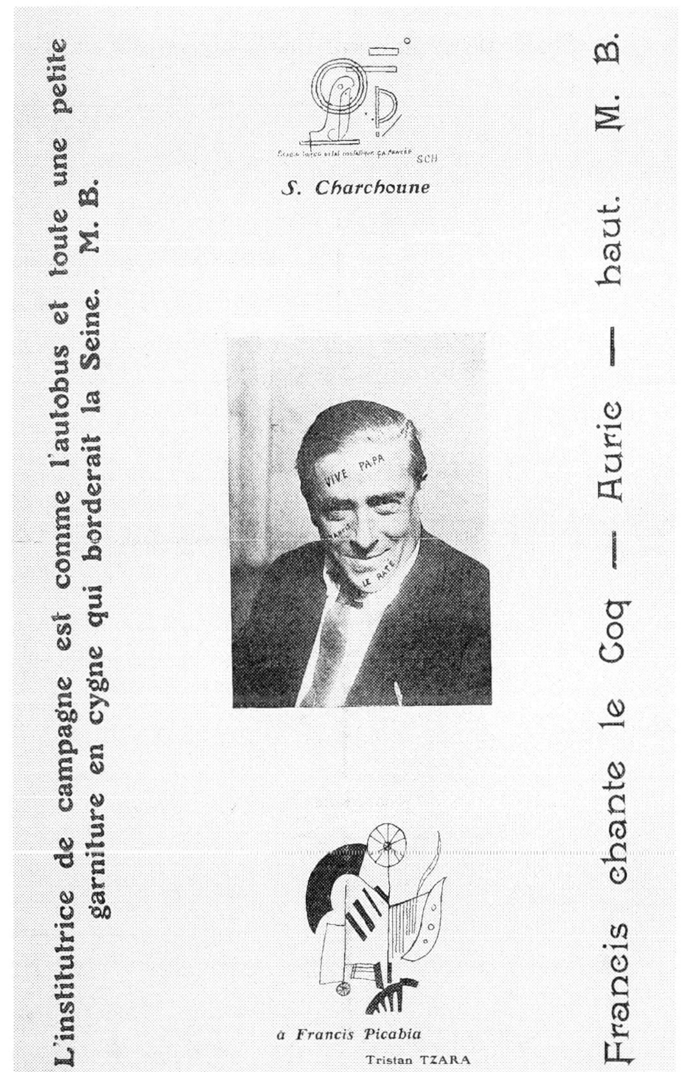

Francis Picabia, *Vive Papa (Long Live Daddy),* 1920. Published in *391* 14 (November 1920), p. 6. Research Library, The Getty Research Institute, Los Angeles. © 2005 Artists Rights Society (ARS), New York/ADAGP, Paris/ Estate of Francis Picabia.

LONG LIVE DADDY: A DADA MONTAGE

I break down in the grasp of infinite tenderness, accepted and finally revolting. Here begins the eclipse of the ego. Night at high noon.

—*Louis Aragon,* The Adventures of Telemachus[1]

— Here is an image of Picabia. He is staring at us, smiling.

— Again?

— He is staring at us, smiling, again.

— It's the same photograph.

— The gleam of his hair matching the sheen of his cravat, he is staring at us, smiling, eyes narrowed, skin bunched, wrinkles spread out like gullies across the leather field of his face. I have been captivated by this smile, by Picabia's smile, for quite a long time now, for years it seems. I have stared at this smile, at Picabia's smile, lips held tight and yet fat, drawn into a grin neither smug nor really defiant. I want to enter into the enigma of this smile.

— What of smiles? What, smiles? Whose are the smiles? Who are they for? And even, who are they? Here they are, the questions, that's all.

— Dada liked smiles. It placed great hopes on laughter. Is it possible to write about this laughter? Such an account surely wouldn't be funny. Nothing kills a joke faster than an explanation.

— It's the *Mona Lisa*

— You mean to say that the smile is an enigma. We are dealing, again, with something like one of Dada's many answers to modernist abstraction. Meaning and meaninglessness are precisely what is at stake. For does one ever search for a solution in the face of an enigma? What would an enigma be that had a solution? Isn't the condition of a true enigma precisely the lack of finding an answer, the suspension of the possibility of its ever being solved? "Why do you write?" the editors of *Littérature* asked the Parisian literary community in 1920. To which Picabia responded

— I really do not know, and I hope never to know.[2]

— It's like *L.H.O.O.Q.* There is a smile and an answer. A joke and a punch line. Writing and laughter.

— It's the image from *L'oeil cacodylate*. It's the same photograph.

— And the same structure, put in place exactly one year earlier. The project of *L'oeil cacodylate* is already announced here. All of Picabia's hopes for Dada can be discerned. The graffito strikes against the image. Words and mechanical reproduction come into play. The readymade cedes its object form and proliferates as a set of now-recognizable signs. Faces and names. Heads and signatures. Photographs and language.

— But there is just one signature. It's Picabia's signature.

— Nothing could be less certain. Do we see "Picabia" written anywhere? Do we see "Picabia" here? And is there only one signature? Can we ever have just one? Does the structure of the signature allow this?

— Artists sign their paintings. Dadaists sign their readymades.

— And Picabia signed his signature. He signed himself a lot. Consider another self-image, a line drawing

— Is it a self-image? A figurative image?

— that Picabia made of himself in 1920, one of the first major irruptions of a return to figuration in Picabia's art during the core years of the Dada movement.

— In 1917 he drew an "American Worker." He also drew a toreador. He drew Marcel Duchamp. And then there is the *Portrait of Max Goth,* the one with a photograph placed over the subject's face. He published them all that year in *391.* The *retour à l'ordre* had already begun. Can we talk of a return to figuration when it comes to Picabia? Weren't the mechanomorphs already "figurative"? Is a photograph figurative? And why does figuration always "return"? To whom is it coming back? It looks like Picasso

— Like a facile echo of Picasso's echoes of Ingres, it was part of a series of line drawings made by Picabia in 1920 and 1921, perhaps as gifts, offering up a panoply of his fellow travelers within the Dada movement: Cocteau caricatured, a sickly Tzara, Éluard with his nose in the air, a proud Breton with jutting chin, a swarthy, fire-haired Soupault, an inconceivably awkward, almost feeble Péret. But Picabia signed his self-portrait in a manner different from all the rest.

— Francis by Picabia 1920

— Things were not always so funny.

— It was as if the subject would be split—would split himself—around the content of the name, the self-portrait delivering up not the self-identical, but the self irremediably split in two. To depict oneself would be to depict an other; it would be to depict the other in the self. And two years later, in the midst of another, more definitive irruption of the figurative within Picabia's work, in the midst of the series of covers that Picabia designed for the Dada journal *Littérature* and matching their regressive graphic style, Picabia produced another self-portrait. This portrait replicated the earlier formula that Picabia had chosen for his signature, ending up just as split

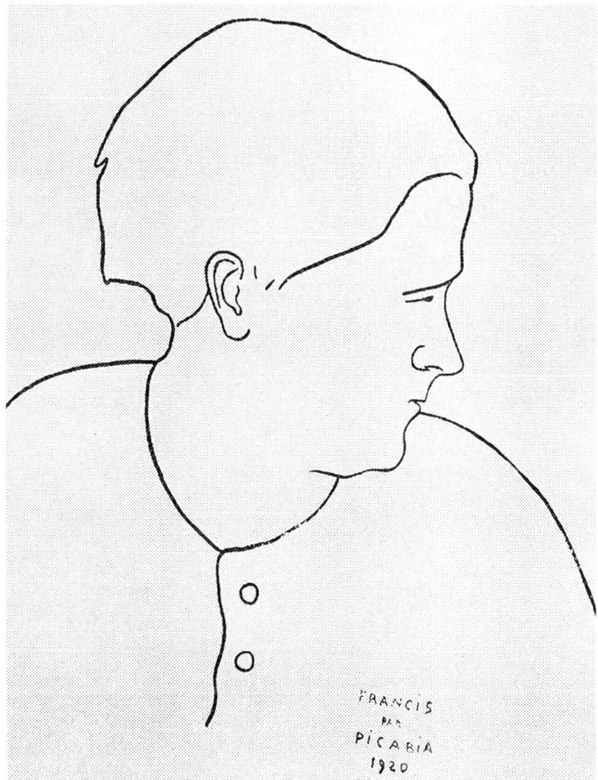

Francis Picabia, *Francis by Picabia 1920,* 1920. © 2005 Artists Rights Society (ARS), New York/ADAGP, Paris/Estate of Francis Picabia.

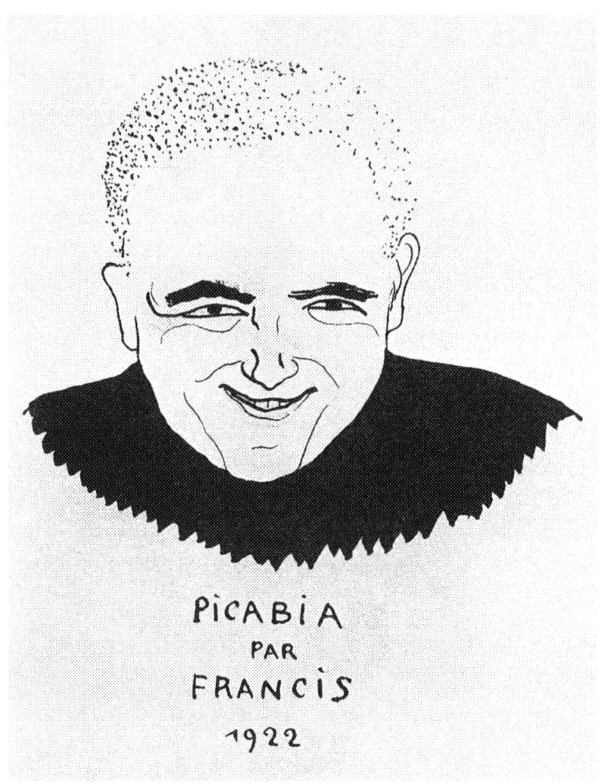

Francis Picabia, *Picabia by Francis 1922*, 1922. © 2005 Artists Rights Society (ARS), New York/ADAGP, Paris/Estate of Francis Picabia.

— Picabia by Francis 1922

— and yet precisely reversed. The subject was split, its image altered, and consequently the self-portrait emerges as an impossible genre, as a genre of paradox, hardly fixed and evidently multiple. For we recognize Picabia in both of the self-portraits here, but in diametrically opposed guises: in the first, looking away from us, a self-image become an object; in the second, staring at us, an image for which we are an object; on the one hand, long-haired and anxious, a graceful silhouette edging into melancholia; on the other hand, shaved and gleeful, a ragged cartoon fixated on the Dionysiac. Riven upon the site of the name, it is as if we witness a fissuring of the personal from the patronymic. It is as if we see first the son, Francis, depicted by the father, Picabia, by the agency of the patronymic; and then we have the father, Picabia, depicted by the son, by a name deprived of the Name-of-the-Father.

— It's a father and a son.

— No. I am not saying anything so simple as that in these two portraits of Picabia we see first the image of a son, and then a figuration of the Father. The situation is much more complex. We see something like a drama of castration, with the anxious son *as seen by* the Father, and the joyous Father *as seen by* the son—visions produced, however, by one and the same subject, and embraced as the aesthetic logic allowing the sudden irruption of a multiplicity of graphic styles. Pastiche as automutilation: line can be "freed," style can become multiple, only in this way. Production as projection: we see figurations of crossed positions, hybrid liminalities, fantasies of a division within the self.

— And so it was with the image of Picabia with which we began. For if in that photograph we see once more the gleeful Picabia, like a joyous, prodigal Father, it is an image offered up again from the vantage point of "Francis," a product of the Son, of the name without a patronymic, signed as it is across Picabia's face.

— Maybe.

— Place the photographic plate of the face in an acid bath.[3]

— Published in *391* in 1920—and linked to the recent publication of Picabia's book of Dada philosophy named after another famous son, *Jésus-Christ Rastaquouère*—the photograph was covered over with words, a tortuous or bachelor-machine vision of language as if branded onto the skin of the body, carved there for eternity like a love note on the bark of a tree.[4] That this was a common Dada fantasy—the subject marked by a deforming facial tattoo, the symbolic regime of language materialized, inscribed on the very surface of the body—can be seen in photographs that we retain of various Dada celebrations, with the most common Dada masquerade consisting simply of the word "DADA" scrawled, for example, across Tristan Tzara's forehead, or ruptured into a resolute "DA" and another "DA" punctuating each of Georges Ribemont-Dessaignes's razor-sharp cheeks, or the points of Picabia's starched collar. It was as if the Paris Dadaists were offering up a performative version of the collage principles applied to the portrait by the German Dadaists, thinking perhaps specifically of the work of Raoul Hausmann. And Picabia reinserted this performance into representation.

— "Long Live Daddy," his inscription salutes, and then signs off, "Francis, the Failure."

— *Rat*: a rat (anagram for art). *Rate*: spleen (also a female rat). *Raté*: Rat-eaten. More commonly, an unsuccessful man (of letters), a failure (in art). A wash-out. A misfire. *Rat*: the word that follows *rastaquouère* in most French dictionaries. Look it up.

— *Jésus-Christ Rastaquouère* was a book about failures, a treatise on failure. André Breton disliked it intensely, he thought it was a failure. Can a book on failure fail? Full of reflections like

— All of the painters exhibited in our museums are painting's failures; one only ever speaks about failures; the world divides up into two categories of men: failures and the unknown.[5]

— Don't forget *rature*: erasure, a word (etc.) crossed out. This will become important.

— Long Live Daddy . . . [Love,] Francis the Failure

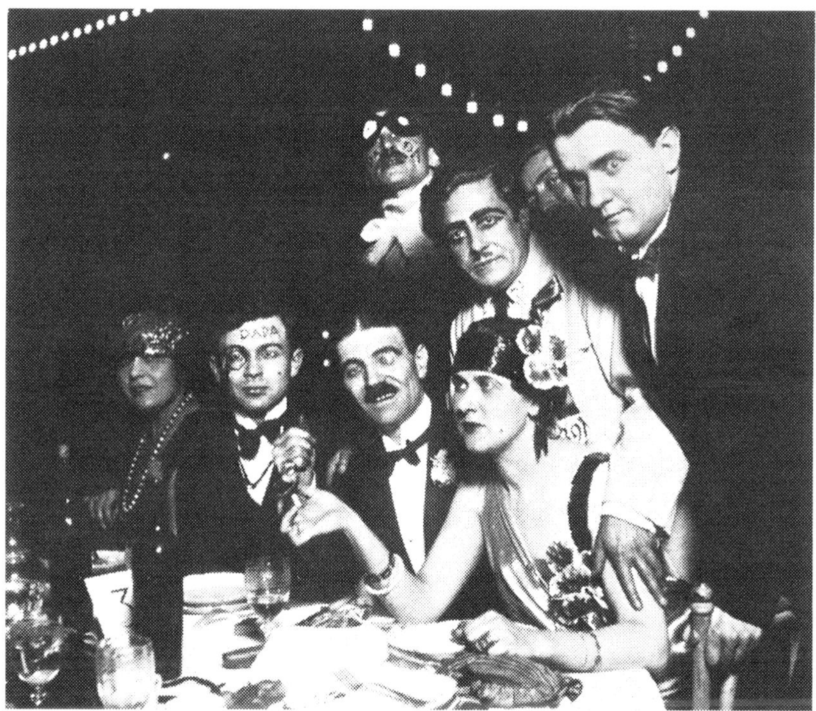

Anonymous, *Dada dinner,* c. 1920–21. Photograph. Bibliothèque Littéraire Jacques Doucet, Paris. © 2005 Artists Rights Society (ARS), New York/ADAGP, Paris/Estate of Francis Picabia.

— Little Francis?

— But then of course one could read the inscription differently, as something like, instead, "Long Live Papa Francis"

— Long Live Papa Francis, the Failure

— It is an image of the son's production of the Father, with the line of filiation wedded to failure; or it is an image of the Father himself under the sign of (an evidently joyous) failure.

— So it's both. It's a father and a son.

— What links them in nature? An instant of blind rut.

— Sabellius, the African, subtlest heresiarch of all the beasts of the field, held that the Father was Himself His Own Son. The bulldog of Aquin, with whom no word shall be impossible, refutes him. Well: if the father who has not a son be not a father can the son who has not a father be a son?[6]

— There was a sketch on the journal's facing page. A sketch of Dada. A sketch in words

— Dada is a fellow without form [*figure*], a face without features and without eyes. A happy engine of pleasure for the imagination, a healthy diversion for the mind. I know him in any case as the best friend one could have, because he is always smiling. . . .[7]

— The undecidability of the image is certain. But we are missing what is obvious. Iconography won't work here; no use looking for the daddy *of* the image, for the daddy *in* the image

— Iconography is a daddy-system of the image. Its *Ur*-formulation begins with a hat being tipped in greeting in the street. This is Panofsky's story. A rather telling story. To understand it, we need to cultivate the "mastery" of "tradition": armed men used to remove their helmets as a sign of peace. A story of chivalry, a rather military story. A story of communication between men, of communication that one is a man. But an Australian bushman wouldn't understand it.[8]

———

— is just that: an inscription within the image. What is certain here is the inscription onto Picabia's work of the *general equivalent,* of the Father-as-general-equivalent.

— Michel Foucault once described this

— The father, as the third party in the Oedipal situation, is not only the hated and feared rival, but the agent whose presence limits the unlimited relationship between the mother and child and whose first, anguished image emerges in the child's fantasy of being devoured. Consequently, the father separates, that is, he is the one who protects when, in his proclamation of the Law, he links space, rules, and language within a single and major experience. At a stroke, he creates the distance along which will develop the scansion of presences and absences, the speech whose initial form is based on constraints, and finally, the relationship of the signifier to the signified which not only gives rise to the structure of language but also to the exclusion and symbolic transformation of repressed material.[9]

— Language, the Phallus, the Father, and Money: here for Goux are the master signifiers—the standard measures—that rule over the respective economies of the sign, the object, the subject, and the commodity. And here too are four of the quintessential arenas of Dada's actions upon artistic and symbolic economies, from the stratagems of Marcel Duchamp's *L.H.O.O.Q.* and *Tzanck Check* to Picabia's *Natures mortes* and *L'oeil cacodylate.* If, as Goux insists, the general equivalent depends on a process of radical exclusion and elision to enact its operations—the fantasy of castration that distinguishes the signifier that is the Phallus from the actual object that is the penis, the primal murder of the Father that produces the introjected function of the Dead-Father-as-Law over any individual figure—Dada opened up another type of operation. General equivalents, in Dada's hands, were taken out of reserve and placed back into use. The reserve, the exclusion, and the excision of the general equivalent were denied. For example, in works from the *Large Glass* to *Natures mortes*—in all the manifestations, that is, of the Dada bachelor machine—the Phallus becomes a part object once more: not a master signifier, but an actual object, not a principle of measured order but an instigator of immeasurable disorder. In *Long Live Daddy,* we witness a similar denial of the Dead Father, of precisely that excision of the general equivalent that places it on reserve.

— A lesson in the war on patriarchy? You can never win by attempting to "kill" the Father. He's already dead, and that's the problem. You have to love him (in a certain way). You have to resurrect him. To keep him from death, from the rule of exclusion. It's a lot of work

— It's easier to scratch the ass than the heart.[10]

— the "rule of exclusion" and expenditure: they sound like the same thing. But they are not. They are utterly opposed.

— No, ambiguously opposed

— *Long Live Daddy*: To declare the Father to be alive would be to allow his *use*; it would be to insert the general equivalent into the scene from which it was to be excluded, and over which it was supposed to rule. It is to allow the Father to be used against the very symbolic regime that he founds, just as the penis-as-part-object can be used against the regimes of both castration and the Phallus. And as the Father is the general equivalent of the economy of the subject, it is not surprising that this engagement with the general equivalent occurs within and upon Picabia's self-image, played out on the terrain of the self.

— the self? But subjective transformation will always be insufficient. Without a parallel transformation of the object, of the institution, of the real . . .

— Indeed, we are in a better position now to understand Dada's persistent interest and play with the genre of the portrait, especially the self-portrait, from Picabia to Duchamp to Man Ray to the Berlin Dadaists. We stand, in fact, in a much better position to begin to understand the full ramifications of the much vaunted "death of the author" that so many commentators have seen beginning in Dada, in Dada's promulgation of artistic strategies of the readymade. This death of the author in Dada cannot be separated from a fundamental investment in the loss of the self, a primary self-dissolution, an economy of the subject that psychoanalysis—beginning at roughly the same moment as the Dada movement—has for a long time theorized under the name

— It's a form of automutilation.

— of masochism. We art historians have hardly begun to realize the deep tissue of connections linking masochism and modernism, lodging an insistent pleasure in the violent destruction of the self at the heart of the cultural aspirations of the avant-garde.

— Of course, aspiration is the wrong word entirely.

— Francis Picabia always attacks himself.[11]

— Exhibitionism and self-display have always been sure signs of the masochist. As Kaja Silverman has explained

— What is it precisely that the male masochist displays, and what are the consequences of this self-exposure? To begin with, he acts out in an insistent and exaggerated way the basic conditions of cultural subjectivity, conditions that are normally disavowed; he loudly proclaims that his meaning comes to him from the Other, prostrates himself before the gaze even as he solicits it, exhibits his castration for all to see, and revels in the sacrificial basis of the social contract. The male masochist magnifies the losses and divisions upon which cultural identity is based, refusing to be sutured or recompensed. In short, he radiates a negativity inimical to the social order.[12]

— It's just gone.

— It's coming round again.

— It's just gone again.

— He is staring at us, smiling, again.

— Picabia did not leave the photograph of himself as a "prodigal" father—defaced by the cutting words of the son—alone.[13] The image would return, and not only in *L'oeil cacodylate*. Just one month after the publication of *Long Live Daddy* in *391,* Picabia busily set himself to cutting out an example of his image, reconfiguring it, and offering it up—offering himself up—as a Christmas gift

— like a severed ear, like that organ (it isn't just any organ) that he is supposed to have sent, dispatched, detached, on a mission, as his representative[14]

— to Hans Arp and Max Ernst in December of 1920. Entitling the collage *Tableau rastadada (Rastadada Painting),* Picabia simultaneously assimilated the cut of collage to the mutilation of his own self-image. Now, a jaunty, ludicrous bowler hat sits perched atop Picabia's head, punctuating the mysterious smile and the giant head that it will stubbornly refuse to fit. A single eye gets ripped from its socket, and pasted down again on an angle, an enucleation surfacing from the realm of horror into the piercing humor of a complicitous wink. The bridge of Picabia's nose and a portion of one cheek are scissored off and out, never to be seen again. A pipe dangles from one nostril, a portion of the hair and forehead go missing, and three gleaming, high-heeled women's shoes now dance around Picabia's face, stepping on each shoulder and sliding down his chest. One shoe sprouts another, descending from the top of the image as if Picabia's head now lay rolling, lopped off and at ground level; a last shoe carries a woman's face within its cavity, a woman staring dreamily off into the distance. And, perhaps most important

— What of shoes? What, shoes? Whose are the shoes? What are they made of? And even, who are they? Here they are, the questions, that's all.[15]

— echoing the obliterations enacted by both the operations of cut and paste, by both the subtraction and the addition of all these bits and pieces, Picabia obliterated part of the former inscription of *Vive Papa*. You have undoubtedly already noticed which part. Picabia placed the word "Papa" under erasure, deleting it with three insistent, steady strokes. Which we could translate, admittedly somewhat literally: The Father would enter the scene of representation only to

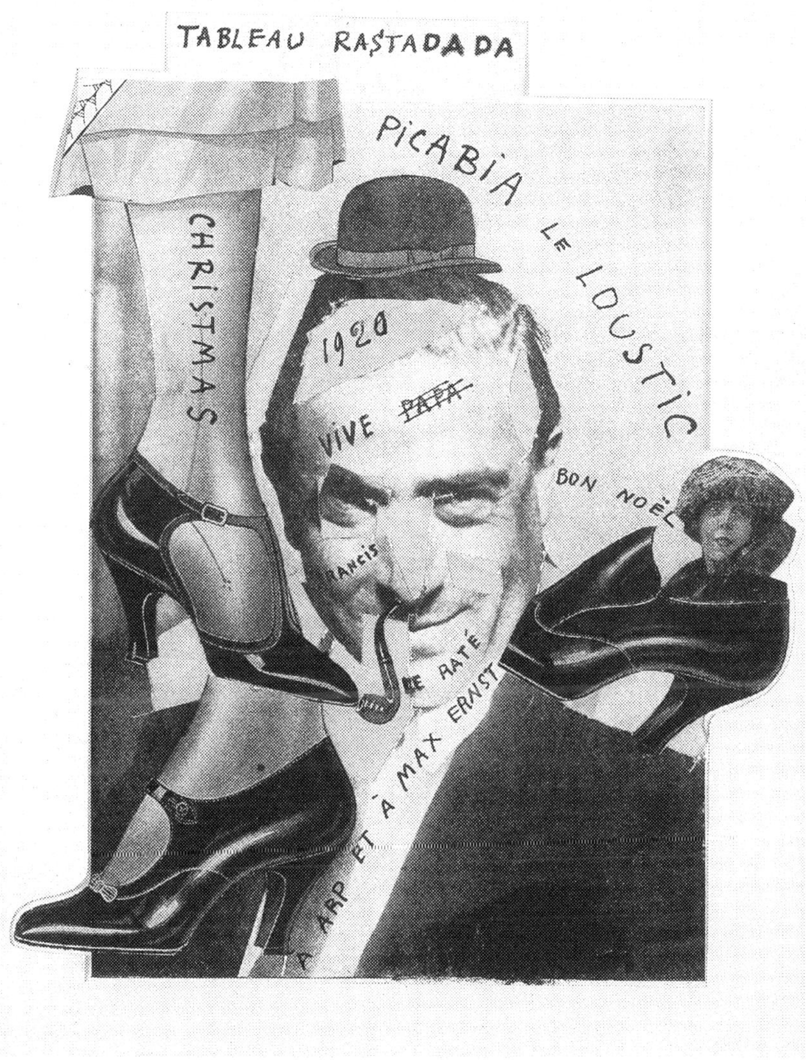

Francis Picabia, *Tableau rastadada (Rastadada Painting),* 1920. Photomontage and collage with ink on paper, 19 × 17 cm. Collection Paul Destribats, Paris. © 2005 Artists Rights Society (ARS), New York/ADAGP, Paris/Estate of Francis Picabia.

be expended, leaving behind this mad image in its wake. To submit the general equivalent to expenditure, to deny the principle of reserve for the operation of use: such is the quintessential Dada gesture. And under the pressures of auto-mutilation, Picabia's image has changed its tune. It sings a new hymn.

— *Long Live Francis,* it now proclaims, *the Failure!*

— Something like an underbelly of modernist techniques of blankness surfaces here, a repressed equivalent for its deletions and negations. The *raté* and the *raturé.* Explain this convergence.

— It is in the account of masochism given by Gilles Deleuze, I think, that the connections between this wild vision and expenditure, between Dada's actions upon symbolic economies and the desperate stakes of masochism, are made most clear.[16] For although he does not put this in the language of the general equivalent that I have been using here, Deleuze depicts masochism as a specific, indeed utopian force to achieve the destruction of the Father, to repudiate the Dead Father as the general equivalent ruling over the economy of the subject. Masochism is the libidinal economy in which the Dead Father's reserve would be denied, with a series of consequences emanating from this denial, operating in its wake like clockwork. Looking closely at the opposed examples of the novels of the Marquis de Sade and Leopold von Sacher-Masoch, Deleuze's thesis contests the continuity between sadism and masochism implicitly ratified in the work of psychoanalysis, as he proclaims sadism and masochism to be fundamentally *discontinuous* entities separated by their opposed operations upon a traditional Oedipal dynamic. For Deleuze, it is sadism that is dominated by a "paternal and patriarchal theme [M, 59]," created of an incestuous union of the figures of father and daughter, an orgiastic union that serves to negate the mother and place the father "beyond all laws [M, 60]." Masochism, on the other hand, is dominated by a figure Deleuze imagines as the "oral mother." Absolutely rejecting the primary assumptions of Sigmund Freud's account of masochism, especially in the well-known essay "A Child Is Being Beaten," Deleuze reverses Freud's scenario, a fantasy in which Freud claims the masochist sets up the father in the role of his beater, only to understand this punishment retrogressively as an expression of

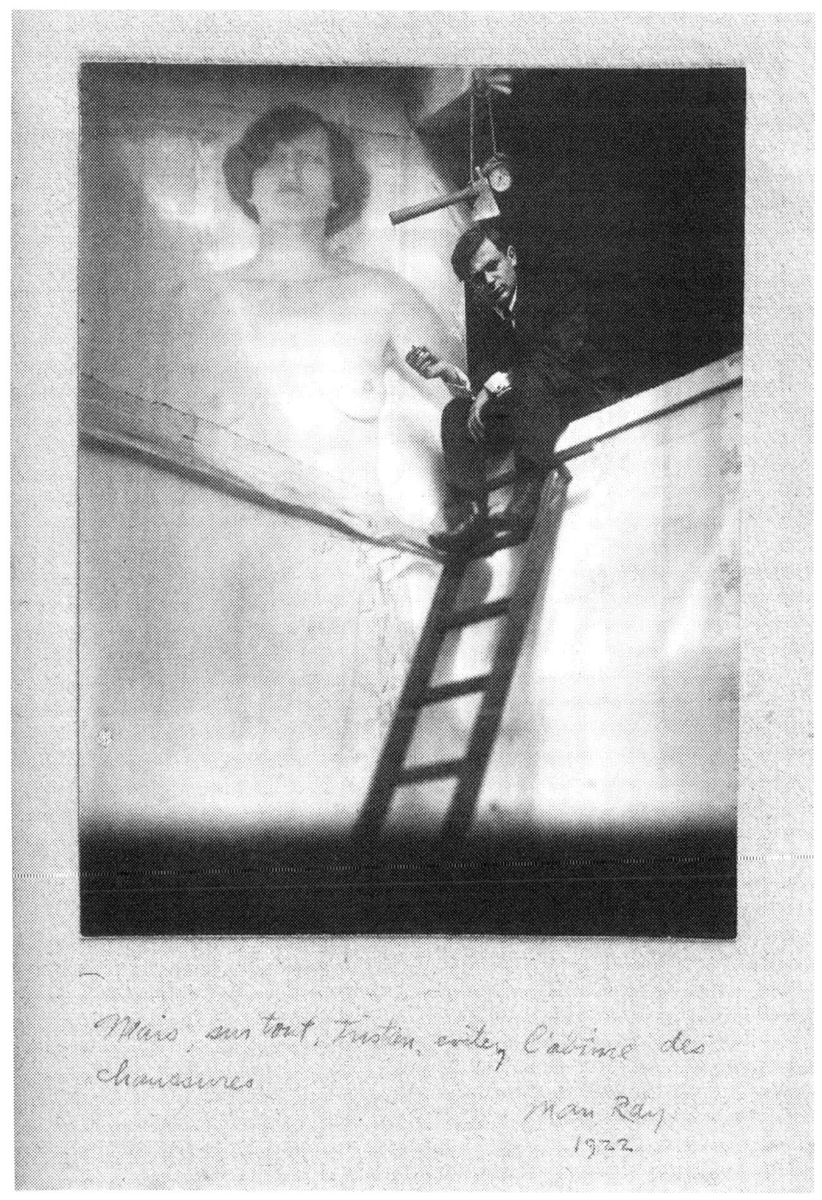

Man Ray, *Tristan Tzara,* 1921. Gelatin silver print, 10.3 × 7.2 cm (4^{1}/$_{16}$ × 2^{13}/$_{16}$″). The Bluff
Collection. © 2005 Artists Rights Society (ARS), New York/ADAGP, Paris/Man Ray Trust.

love from (and for) the Father. In masochism, Deleuze asks, who in reality is being beaten? His reversal is total:

— Where is the father hidden? Could it not be in the person who is being beaten? The masochist feels guilty, he asks to be beaten, he expiates, but why and for what crime? Is it not precisely the father-image in him that is thus miniaturized, beaten, ridiculed and humiliated? What the subject atones for is his resemblance to the father and the father's likeness in him: the formula of masochism is the humiliated father . . . the father is not so much the beater as the beaten [M, pp. 60–61].

— I thought you said that we have to love the Father.

— Yes, indeed. Maybe this is what that would mean. As Freud in fact saw it: a retrogressive expression of love for the Father. Beating as caressing. It is the only way to caress the Father.

— A father, Stephen said, battling against hopelessness, is a necessary evil.[17]

— So the Father isn't gone in masochism? As the general equivalent loses its reserve, as it enters into the scene from which it was to be excluded, it can now be exchanged directly, used, but also used up, lost. Subjects can enter into relations with each other and with the general equivalent directly, relations formerly mediated only by it. The child can take the place of the Father. That is what you seem to be saying. The child can beat the Father.

— The child can beat himself. That is what Deleuze just said. He is caressing himself. It's masturbation

— But someone is missing, however, here. Where is the mother? What relations can she now support? Where is she hidden?

— she's in the shoes

— No, those are Picabia's shoes. He was very proud of his shoes. He wore high-heeled boots. He talked about them all the time

— P.S. EVERY MORNING I PUT ON MY BOOTS[18]

— Sixty-four pairs of boots![19]

— Masochism, according to Deleuze, relies not upon a pact between father and son; it is, rather, a mode of alliance between the son and the fantasized figure of the oral mother, called "oral" by Deleuze because she is invested with the powers of both sexual pleasure and punishment. For, in masochism, the site of the Law does not lie empty. It is not discarded, but as in the strategies of parody, the Law will be used, and used (treated) badly. Perhaps reversed. If the son commits himself to destroying the Father in himself, repudiating the very principles of male virility, he simultaneously attributes the phallus to the mother, producing a femininity "posited as lacking in nothing and placed alongside a virility suspended in disavowal [M, p. 68]." For Deleuze, masochism surely then also disavows the mother, but in an ideal, "positive" manner (she is "identified with the law"), as it simultaneously disavows the father in the mode of invalidation (he is "expelled from the symbolic order [M, p. 68]"). Deleuze's fantasy is absolute: "*It is not a child but a father that is being beaten.* The masochist thus liberates himself for a rebirth in which the father will have no part [M, p. 66]." More precisely, it is the Father's "likeness" in the son that is beaten, the latter's "resemblance" to the Father that is dissolved, as if it is the very principle of identity, of sameness, of filiation that must be broken, with the (patriarchal) standard now shattered beyond all repair.

— Daddy you scare me. Daddy, please scare me.[20]

— Fatherhood, in the sense of conscious begetting, is unknown to man. It is a mystical estate, an apostolic succession, from only begetter to only begotten. On that mystery and not on the Madonna which the cunning Italian intellect flung to the mob of Europe the church is founded and founded irremovably because founded, like the world, macro and microcosm, upon the void. Upon incertitude, upon unlikelihood. *Amor matris,* subjective and objective genitive, may be the only true thing in life. Paternity may be a legal fiction. Who is the father of any son that any son should love him or he any son?

— What the hell are you driving at?

— I know. Shut up. Blast you. I have reasons.

— Are you condemned to do this?[21]

— I thought that you said that we have to resurrect the Father.

— YOU DON'T UNDERSTAND RIGHT WHAT WE ARE DO-ING. WELL DEAR FRIENDS WE UNDERSTAND IT EVEN LESS. WHAT JOY HUH YOU ARE RIGHT. I WOULD LOVE TO SLEEP WITH THE POPE AGAIN. YOU DON'T UNDERSTAND? ME NEITHER HOW SAD.[22]

— Shattering the patriarchal standard will be a form of resurrection, almost a redemption. It's like. the shattering of the representational paradigm in the early twentieth-century, the sudden dissipation of the gold standard of mimesis.

— If those two things are linked, you have to listen to this. We could imagine here an entirely new perspective on modernism, on the avant-garde, on the readymade or pictorial abstraction. We would have to rewrite the whole story. It's Michel Foucault again

— It is not in . . . functional terms of deficiency that we understand the gap which now stands in the Father's place. To be able to say that he is missing, that he is hated, excluded, or introjected, that his image has undergone symbolic transmutations, presumes that he is not "foreclosed" (as Lacan would say) from the start and that his place is not marked by a gaping and absolute emptiness. The Father's absence, manifested in the headlong rush of psychosis, is not registered by perceptions or images, but relates to the order of the signifier. The "no" through which this gap is created does not imply the absence of a real individual who bears the father's name; rather, it implies that the father has never assumed the role of nomination and that the position of the signifier, through which the father names himself and, according to the Law, through which he is able to name, has remained vacant. It is toward this "no" that the unwavering line of psychosis is infallibly directed; as it is precipitated inside the abyss of its meaning, it evokes the devastating absence of the father through the forms of delirium and phantasms and through the catastrophe of the signifier.[23]

— A catastrophe?

— The Oedipal tenor of Picabia's Dada production has been entirely missed, and thus, of course, specific perversions of that dynamic have of course not received their articulation.[24] No one has seen the Father's (lack of) place in the mechanomorphs, for example, not even when faced with the ridiculous specificity of a drawing such as *Le Papa,* a gear transformed into a circular saw

— all teeth and blade

— inscribed "Make Love," a representation of the Father as a castrating force that is nevertheless aimed to self-destruct, with the glistening blade threatening the title of the work itself, a second away from severing off its own name. And few have pointed out the images of male sexual oblation within the mechanomorphs, such as we witness in the drawing *Hermaphrodism,* published in Picabia's 1918 book

— That's one of Deleuze's claims. Androgyny is characteristic of sadism; hermaphrodism the sign of masochism.

— *Poems and Drawings by the Girl Born without a Mother,* inscribed across its machinic tracings "sperm," "sexual apparatus," "oviduct," and finally, and tellingly, "chopped male [*mâle haché*]."[25]

— No one forgets Picabia's life though. That he was raised in a household almost entirely peopled with men: father, uncle, grandfather. That his mother died when he was a child.

— But the mother is there, in the work. And no one talks about this. She is there, as a figure, in many of Picabia's poems. For example, "*Télégraphie sans fils*"—"Wireless Telegraphy," but also "Telegraphy without a son," without descendents, also included in *Poems and Drawings by the Girl Born without a Mother*:

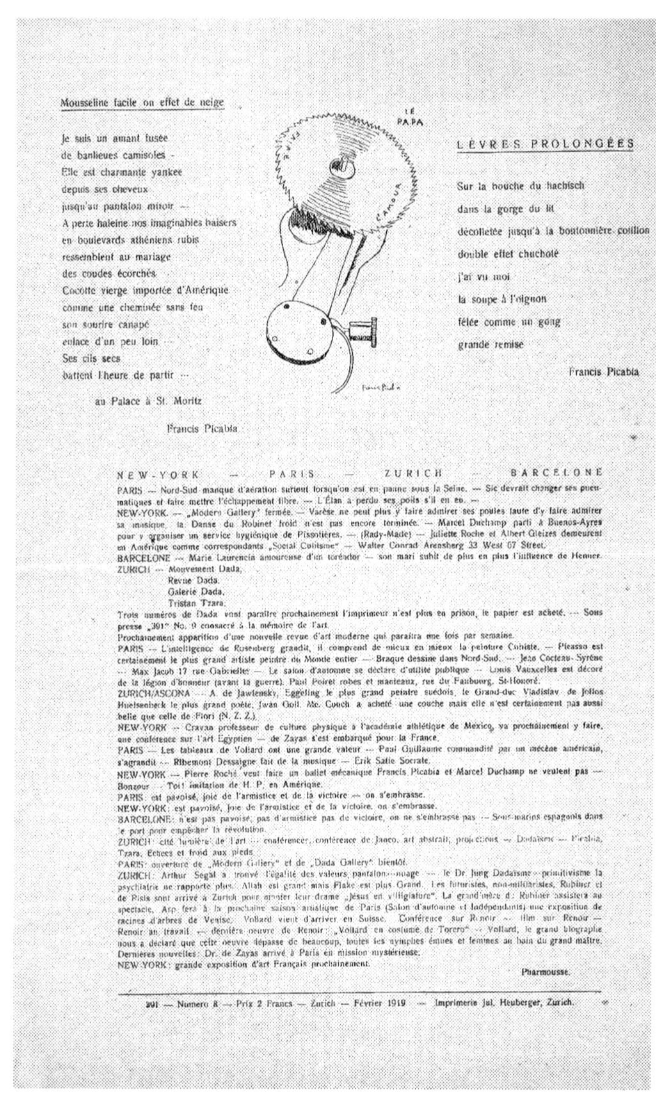

Francis Picabia, *The Daddy,* 1919. Reproduced in *391* 8 (February 1919), p. 8. Research Library, The Getty Research Institute, Los Angeles. © 2005 Artists Rights Society (ARS), New York/ADAGP, Paris/Estate of Francis Picabia.

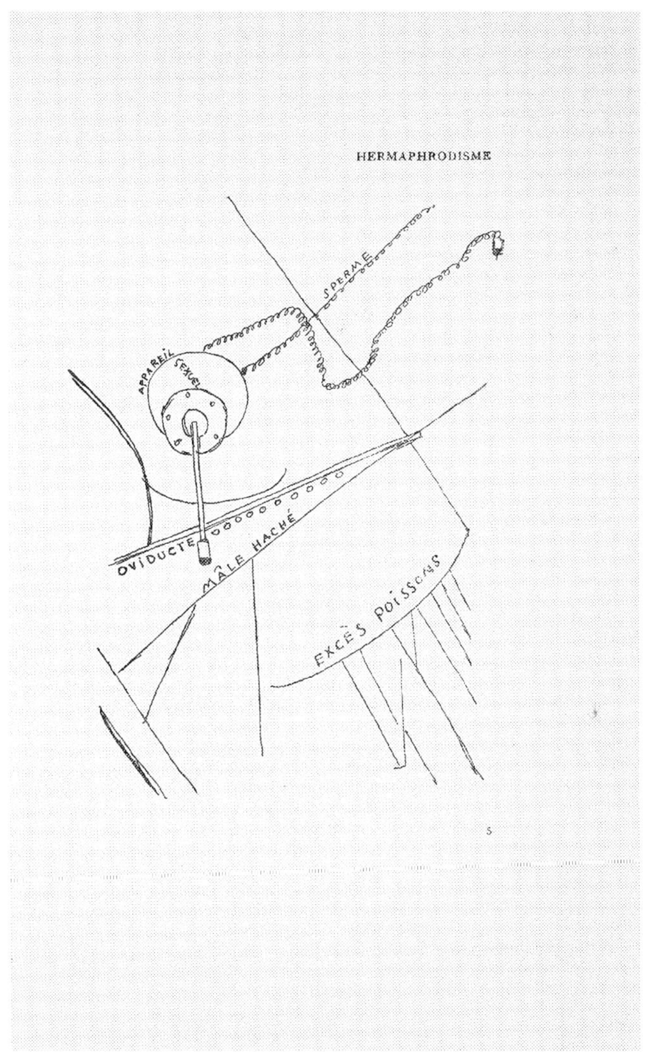

Francis Picabia, *Hermaphrodisme,* 1918. From Picabia, *Poèmes et dessins de la fille née sans mère* (Lausanne: Imprimeries réunies, 1918). Research Library, The Getty Research Institute, Los Angeles. © 2005 Artists Rights Society (ARS), New York/ADAGP, Paris/Estate of Francis Picabia.

My sickness follows my heart
Sealed bud of lost joys
I want to eclipse myself like a rogue in the arms
Of my beautiful mother
Memory of a blue sky
Where I would have been able to cower
One must try to forget everything
The agony of a world gone mad
Of heroes who spin
the hideous waltzes of the war
In an atmosphere enigmatic
And masked.[26]

— and of course, no one has noticed the specificity of Picabia's actions in the *Rastadada Painting*

— Collage. It's a collage. A montage. Why does he call it a painting?

— his specific homage to and singular pastiche of the photomontage activities of the German Dadaists. For here, rather than merely crossing out the actual word "daddy" originally scrawled across his image, Picabia seems specifically to attack that aspect of himself that he evidently took to represent the Father, to obliterate an image that I have previously characterized as the "joyous Father." And Picabia simultaneously achieves a representation of the mutilated self that is the product of this repudiation of the Father, a self still joyous but now evidently full of holes.

— It does not seem to push the connotations of this image too far to read the shoes dancing their wild dance across and around Picabia's body as the agents of this (self-)attack. And these high-heeled, gleaming shoes, of course, are classic representations of the sexual fetish, all shine and stiffened hardness

— Surely not a pair of shoes

— detached in any case, they concern us/look at us, mouth agape, that is, mute, making or letting us chatter on, dumbstruck before those who make them speak . . . and who in reality are made to speak by them. They become as if sensitive to the comic aspect of the thing, sensitive to the point of imperturbably restrained hilarity. Faced with a procedure that is so sure of itself, that cannot in its certainty be dismantled

— the thing, pair or not, laughs.[27]

— What is a fetish? Freud speaks of the fetishism of the shoe.

— Stieglitz photographed a shoe. With a woman's face embedded within it. A woman named "True." Some people call this a Dada photo.

— and a horse. A castrated horse.

— What is a fetish? Is it a substitute? A symbol of the phallus? A defense against castration? And thus a monument to it? A symbol, then, of the vagina? Is it the foot? Or the face? A shine on the nose

— What nose?

— the shoe. This preference, according to Freud, hangs on the fact that in the terrifying experience he has had of what he lives as his mother's "castration," the "boy" looked "from below." Slowly, he raised his eyes. From the ground.[28]

— So the fetish is less an object than a relation. It pertains to a place, to a situation, or rather to a direction, a vector.

— Freud does not say that the foot (or the shoe) replaces what is supposed to be lacking *because of its form* but because of its *directional situation,* the syntax of a movement upwards, from the very-low, the most-low, a system of relationships in the alleged generation of the fetish.[29]

— as if the head now lay rolling, lopped off and at ground level

— or the shoes, floating up into the air, levitating, quite precisely groundless

———

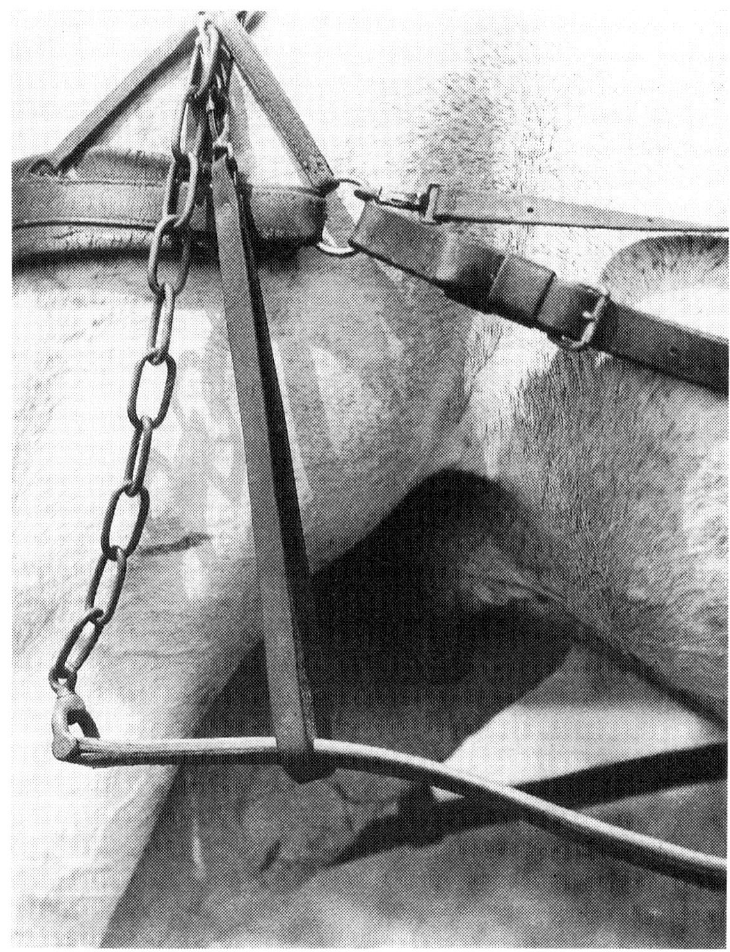

Alfred Stieglitz, *Spiritual America,* 1923. Gelatin silver print. Library of Congress, Prints and Photographs Division, The Alfred Stieglitz Collection. Gift of Georgia O'Keeffe. © 2006 Georgia O'Keeffe Museum, Santa Fe, New Mexico.

— But we are nearing the very ground of masochism. Fetishism, for Deleuze, is the key characteristic of masochism. "There can be no masochism without fetishism in the primary sense," Deleuze writes. Not only does fetishism enter into the accoutrements of the quintessential masochistic sexual scenario, but fetishism, for Deleuze, is the driving motor behind the entire force of masochism—it provides masochism's "logic"—in its operation as a mode of disavowal. "Negation," according to Deleuze, is the key operation of sadism; "disavowal" the major achievement of masochism.

— This theory is ridiculous. You at least have to admit that it has become reasonably controversial. Deleuze's desire to separate out masochism from sadism, to purify submission from the taint of domination, holds no water. It flies in the face of the account of the most eloquent recent theorist of masochism, Leo Bersani, whose own narrative prioritizes the undecidable slippage between sadism and masochism in Freud's work in order to explore the fundamentally masochistic basis of sexuality itself.[30] The erotics of self-dissolution. The erotic *as* self-dissolution.

— So Deleuze is naive

— The Deleuzian separation of masochism from sadism politically sentimentalizes masochism as a resistance to power, thus bypassing the excitement of submitting to power (whether exercised by a man or a woman). By eliminating the sadistic subject from the masochistic scenario, Deleuze's analysis . . . blinds us to sadistic power's most profound appeal (and so to its ineradicability): the promise it contains of masochistic surrender. . . . [T]he rule of the Law (whether presided over by a man or a woman) can hardly be "derided" (as Deleuze argues) as long as that rule continues to be experienced as thrilling.[31]

— Deleuze, rather, is utopian

— Which is what Kaja Silverman has said, as she sees the operations of disavowal acting within the logic of Deleuze's own statements. His is a "utopian" reading of masochism, its "visionary reconfiguration." Masochism has nothing to do with sadism, masochism has nothing to do with the father: we are listening to the very operation of disavowal.

— It is crucial to grasp that although Deleuze does in fact claim that masochism has nothing to do with the father, he obviously knows full well that this is not the case. His account of that libidinal infraction cannot be understood apart from the mechanism of disavowal, which he not only places at the center of *its* organization, but *himself deploys* throughout his study whenever he refuses to acknowledge the place of the father within masochism.[32]

— The place of the Father in masochism is the place of the fetish. This place is disavowed, it is a disavowal. As with the fetish, we are following a vector, traveling from low to high. With the Father, we scurry from death to resurrection. We are creating gods here

— the double-bind of transgression

— "Disavowal," Deleuze writes, consists in "radically contesting the validity of that which is." Disavowal, for Deleuze, creates within masochism the phallic power of the punishing oral mother. Its clearest example, he continues, is Freud's theory of the fetish, here understood most generally as an image or object that substitutes for the female phallus, as the means by which the condition of lack is denied. If, famously, Freud's fetishist is fixated on the last image witnessed before the revelation of sexual difference, Picabia's mutilated image will be surrounded by such images in the series of high-heeled shoes, and it will be debased to the temporal and spatial moment in which Picabia seems to be fixed, like a child dwarfed by the impending approach of the maternal leg. As if the import of these shoes could be missed, Picabia makes their existence as substitutes for the mother, or at least the female, explicit, placing a non-engaged, seemingly distant woman

— detached

— within the body of one of the shoes. And as if the shoes' existence as erect substitutes for the maternal phallus could be ignored, Picabia makes the displaced phallus one of the great stakes of this collage, entering the phallus once more into the scene of representation. Look again at the pipe dangling like a toppled moustache from Picabia's nose.

— Ceci n'est pas une pipe.

— We are well aware, within the language of psychoanalysis and misogynist fantasy alike, of conflations of the female genitals with the hole of the mouth, the mechanisms of displacement and condensation bringing the high down to the level of the low, producing such threatening hybrid figures as the dreaded "vagina dentata."

— A sex and teeth. A sex with teeth. Sounds like the oral mother. She's in the shoes.

— TEETH COME TO THE EYES LIKE TEARS![33]

— But how about the migration of the male penis up to the projecting bump of the nose? What about the movement from low to high? What kind of hybrid figure would this conflation produce?

— René Magritte would try to imagine this. Later.

— But the nose is gone. Don't you see that?

— In Picabia's case, his face seems to sprout a penis-substitute that dangles more than it stiffens, and that ends in a receptacle rather than a penetrating point. Indeed, Picabia's penis/pipe seems itself about to be penetrated by the pointed tip of one of the glistening high-heeled shoes. But perhaps this pipe is not to be understood as attached to Picabia's face and as a projection of *his* phallus—now wildly reconceived as a hole, as an object to allow the penetration of the male subject rather than his penetration of the other in turn. We can just as easily reverse this scenario

— perhaps the reversal is structural here

— and see the pipe as an extension of the fetishized maternal phallus, no longer dangling but sinuously erect, emerging from the tip of the shoe pressed against Picabia's face and ready to penetrate Picabia through the hole of his nose.

— Why should I have a sex, who have no longer a nose?[34]

— The male masochist, in Kaja Silverman's words, "prefers the masquerade of womanliness to the parade of virility."[35] He is a subject full of holes—mouth, nostril, anus, ears, eyes, urethra—but perhaps even these orifices are not necessary for the imagination of male penetration, as we see another shoe assaulting Picabia, another maternal phallus, half-way embedded in Picabia's neck, like a knife on the cusp of completing its bloody duty.

— These are no peasant woman's shoes

— That this image of the male subject, of Picabia, fucked by a fantasized mother through the nose and the neck is pretty hilarious—this should not be passed over in silence. Or at least I find it funny, although perhaps hilarious truly is the better word, connoting mania and wildness in turn. And presumably Picabia saw the humor as well, as we return our stare to the ever-present challenge of that smile, a smile that sets the tone for the whole image, now an attribute of the transgressive Son rather than the prodigal Father. Indeed, for Deleuze, one of the outcomes of a masochistic self-oblation is, not irony (which is the terrain of the sadist), but humor. And masochistic humor is essentially a product of the fact that the Law (of the Father, of castration) which used to forbid the satisfaction of desire under the threat of punishment, now demands punishment up front, as it were, and compels the satisfaction of desire to follow upon the punishment itself.

— Castrate me, the masochist seems to say, and I will be happy; indeed, I will laugh, I will be fulfilled, I will *be able to be filled* by the mother.

— The world is turned upside down; values reversed; and the Law is followed to the letter but proves itself capable of producing the effects it was intended to forestall. This is the hilarity of masochism. The paternal function of applying the Law has been transferred in masochism onto the mother, resulting in these reversals, in the "radical transformation of the law" itself (M, p. 102). It now ordains what it should have forbid; guilt absolves instead of atones; and punishment becomes the fulfillment of what it should have prevented.

— Thus Deleuze:

— The masochistic contract excludes the father and displaces onto the mother the task of exercising and applying the paternal law . . . the same threat which, when experienced as coming from the father and linked to his image, has the effect of preventing incest, has the reverse effect when entrusted to the mother and associated with her image: it then makes incest possible and ensures its success. . . . As a general rule castration acts as a threat preventing incest or a punishment that controls it; it is an obstacle to or a chastisement of incest. But when it is linked with the image of the mother, the castration of the son becomes the very condition of the success of incest: incest is assimilated by this displacement to a second birth which dispenses with the father's role [M, p. 93].

— "A second birth." A resurrection?

— Indeed. The last words of this passage point to one of the major outcomes of the masochistic scenario as Deleuze reads it, a product and twin of its hilarity. The goal of the masochist, in destroying the Father, is the creation of a "new, sexless man"—the masochist's goal, that is, is to give birth to himself, to re-create himself stripped of the Father's power and virility. That Deleuze describes this rebirth as a product of "incest" with the mother is at first deceptive, for the incest connoted here is that of the castrated son with the oral mother, who is invested with the phallus but is actually the disavowal of the (real, Oedipal) mother, and thus a product of the masochistic subject himself. Similarly disavowed by the masochist is the genitality of Oedipalized sex, transformed into this vision of self-creation, with the subject both penetrated and penetrator at once, the orgasmic telos of genitality now transferred to the diffuse ecstasy that creeps across the face of the autochthonous, "devirilized" man.

— One should forget about one's sex organs as one should forget about one's country, and love the abyss, because souls and cows have the same smell[36]

— Such a fantasy of autogenous production was of course a common avant-garde fantasy; it could perhaps be seen as another way of explaining the principles of the bachelor machine, of Picabia's production "without a mother" or a father alike. Unlike Deleuze's vision, this fantasy often existed, in its most extreme and horrible versions, as a destruction of the mother and of female sexuality *tout court* (i.e., Marinetti and the Futurists). I have been trying to distance Picabia and Dada from such a vision, for the endpoint of the Dada scenario—at its best moments— is not the virilization of the male subject, the triumph over (female) lack, but perhaps the opposite: the assumption of lack and utter devirilization, with self-creation reconfigured as a glorious, anti-patriarchal castration, a birth that is al-most indistinguishable from death.[37]

— Look again at Picabia's smile. There is hardly a hint of malice.

— There is a hint of malice

— I am convinced of that by now; as I said, I have been staring at it for a long time. The *Rastadada Painting* was sent to Arp and to Ernst, to Picabia's Dada compatriots in Cologne, as a Christmas greeting. We may doubt that the Dada-ists took such religious celebrations seriously, so perhaps this gift comes as a sur-prise. We may also be surprised at this one sign of a connection between Picabia and Max Ernst. But we may assume, I think, that Picabia took perverse pleasure in inscribing "Christmas" across this image of his masochistic rebirth (death), of his hilarious, ecstatic resurrection (destruction) at the hands of the maternal phal-lus, of this expenditure of the Father-as-general-equivalent and standard, of this proclamation of the birth of the new (Dada) man.

— It is a sacrificial vision, with Picabia as a new Christ.

— Christ?

— The transfigured shoes are in a state of levitation, they are the haloes of themselves. Don't look down any more, toward the low or the very low (the feet, the shoes, the soil, the subsoil) but once more . . . look up, toward the most high, the face facing you, the Face.[38]

— Listen to Deleuze on Christ:

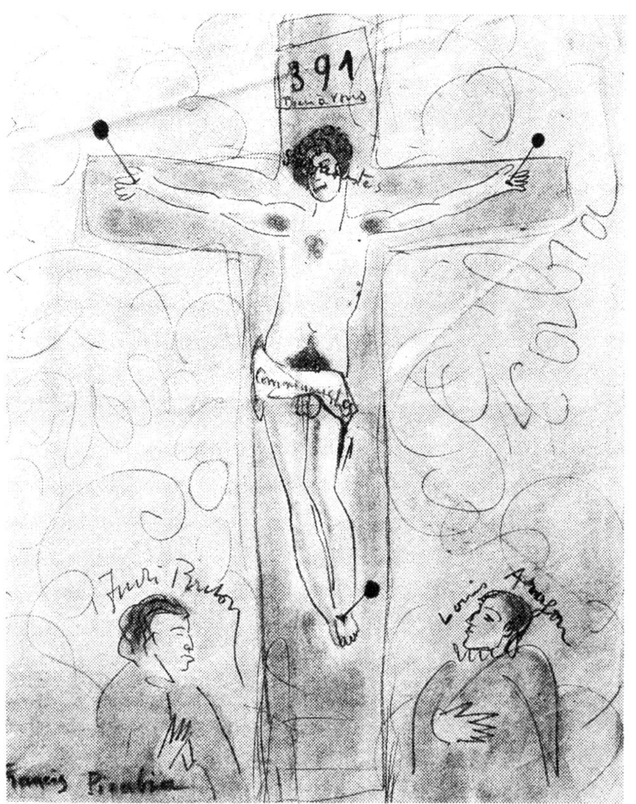

Francis Picabia, *Surrealism Crucified,* c. 1924–25. Ink and watercolor on paper, 31.8 × 25.2 cm. Musée d'Art moderne de la Ville de Paris, donation Henry-Thomas. © 2005 Artists Rights Society (ARS), New York/ADAGP, Paris/Estate of Francis Picabia.

— It is not so much the son who dies so much as God the Father, that is the likeness of the father in the son. The cross represents the maternal image of death, the mirror in which the narcissistic self of Christ . . . apprehends his ideal self (Christ resurrected) [M, pp. 96–97].

— "Dada," as Georges Ribemont-Dessaignes once put it, "is a new Jesus Christ."[39]

— Jesus Christ *rastaquouère*. But it's not a biblical story. It's a modernist story. We have been plumbing the depths of the modernist imaginary

— Picabia's fantasies of the new man were many and various. Perhaps, however, they were never as clearly stated as in this singular Christmas greeting. In his writings, only one passage comes close to this vision. These are Picabia's words

— What I love is to invent, to imagine, to make of myself a new man at every moment, and then to forget him, to forget everything. We must be able to secrete a special gum that would efface as we proceed all our works and their memory. Our brain must be nothing but . . . a mirror in which we would look at ourselves for a second, only to turn our backs on it two moments later. My ambition is to be a man who is sterile for all others.[40]

— Picabia's words? Nothing could be less certain. For actually these were not "Picabia's" words. We don't hear "Picabia" here. Not at all. They were imagined differently. They were included in a text that Picabia entitled "Thank you Francis!" And so they were very much attached to the vision that we see in the *Rastadada Painting,* no matter their separation in time. For such was the gift glimpsed in the broken mirror of the *Rastadada Painting.* It was the gift of a subject without a patronymic.

— *Francis Merci!*

— if only the story ended here

— The story of Dadaism and masochism: we've hardly even told it. I would like to see the two paired around Dada's self-declared war on the general equivalent, on the symbolic economies of Father, Phallus, Language, and Money alike, on the similarly symbiotic terrains of capitalism and patriarchy, of semiotics and sexuality. At its most important moments, Dada enacted its misfires amid the performative self-obliteration of a type of masochistic ecstasy. Think of all the early Paris Dada manifestations, of the repeated offering up of the Dada performers to the violence of the Parisian public. It was a violence that the Dadaists incited, but usually only insofar as it could be directed against themselves.

— Think, for example, of the Dada Festival of 1920, held in May at the Salle Gaveau in Paris. The performances were largely continuations of the various acts from previous Dada manifestations, but there were some significant new attractions. "Unprecedented event," hawked the press release for the Festival:

— All the Dadaists will shave their heads in public.[41]

— And if this promised spectacle of a displaced autocastration was merely smoke and mirrors, only materialized in the bravery of Duchamp's *Tonsure* and the fantasy of Picabia's drawing *Picabia by Francis 1922,* the Festival did commence with the display of *Le sexe de Dada,* Dada's sex (organ), an enormous cylinder of white paper positioned upon two balloons. Presented amid a set design by Picabia, the giant white erection remained on stage for the duration of the evening. But trouble began as the evening wore on, as the assembled crowd became more heated, with the rising temperature of the hall causing the balloons ever so definitely to deflate, precipitating the collapse of the erection itself in time with the final act of the manifestation. According to the recorded memoirs, Tzara began to cry

— The Sex of Dada is deflating!

— with a mixture of horror and joy.[42] Was it intended, a planned event? Separated by the intervening chasm of the years, one can only now hazard an educated guess. At any rate, it was fitting, and it became the detumescent climax of the entire evening.

— BUNCH OF IDIOTS

— And it received a previously unnoticed echo during the earlier performances of the manifestation. For it was at the Festival Dada that André Breton strode onto the stage, covered over in a placard designed by Picabia, transformed into a wandering sandwichman advertising the pleasures of masochism itself. A photograph of Breton dressed up as Picabia's constant proxy exists—for Picabia never himself performed in any of the public Dada events—and this photograph is well known.[43] It shows Breton holding Picabia's board, presenting himself emblazoned with a target to which he points, inscribed with a challenge let loose from the hands of Picabia

— IN ORDER FOR YOU TO LOVE SOMETHING, IT IS NECESSARY FOR YOU TO HAVE SEEN AND UNDERSTOOD IT ALREADY FOR A LONG TIME BUNCH OF IDIOTS FRANCIS PICABIA

— The advertisement did its work. The Dada memoirs again remember this incident, calling Breton a modern "Saint Sebastian" as he impassively faced the shower of objects, from coins to umbrellas, that the audience began to let fly.

— Tears welled up in Tristan Tzara's eyes

— Dada is alive! It's magnificent!

— But the Dada memoirs are a bit untrustworthy. They all claim, for example, that Breton occupied the stage with a target pinned to his "chest."[44] The target was hardly pinned to Breton's "chest." Hung around his neck, the placard instead positioned the target's center at the level of Breton's crotch, a fact Breton's soliciting gesture only seems to underline, like a contemporary, impassible Saint Sebastian calling out for the violent obliteration of his genitals. It is as if Picabia and Breton were here involved in another, repeated presentation of *le sexe de Dada,* but now envisioned in the mode of an unmistakable penile oblation, a replacement of the monumental erection of the Dada Festival's first act with all the metaphorics that one could continue to pile upon the form of the hole. For through Picabia's intervention, Breton as a representative of the new Dada man was made to assume the form of the hole as the form of his own sex, to disavow

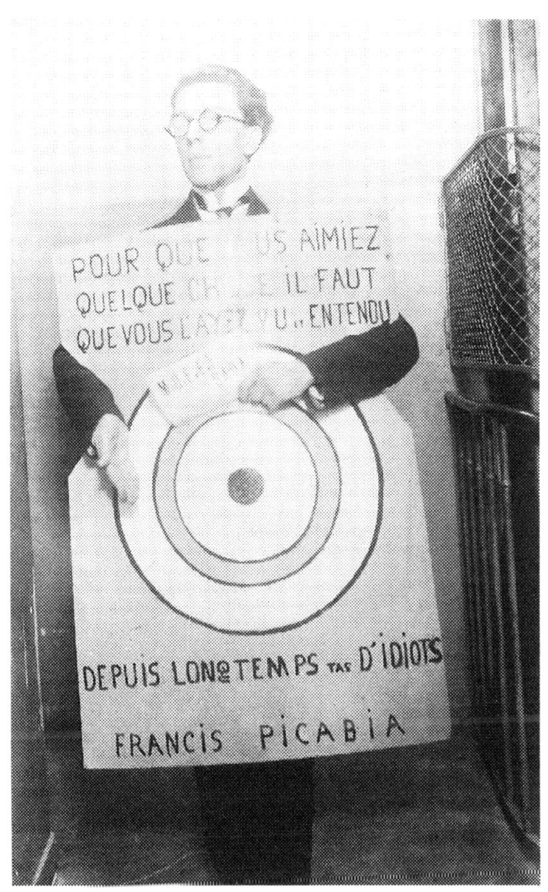

Anonymous, *André Breton at the Festival Dada, Salle Gaveau, May 1920*. Photograph. Collection Timothy Baum, New York.

both penis and Phallus alike in a theatrical, exhibitionist embrace of a form through which Picabia often represented both loss and lack, an embrace that is simultaneously a solicitation of the violent penetration of the male subject.

— Naturally, you are afraid that the wind will lift your skirt and that we will be able to see your sex which is false; your hair too is fake, you have false teeth, you have a glass eye and it's the only one which looks at me sincerely, the other is a counterfeit jewel at 20,000 francs a carat, for imbeciles.

— Sir, first of all I'm leaving, and also I don't wear a skirt since I'm a man!

— Oh! Pants or skirt, it's all the same, it's only the genital that changes. But with you and others like you it can't change, because it's false![45]

— Another manifestation of a constitutive masochism, Breton's performance at the Festival Dada was less a destruction of the Father than a parallel attack upon the Phallus. We see here something like the (masochistic) phenomenon that Kaja Silverman has called "phallic divestiture," a refusal of mastery wherein the dominant and ideological ruse that conflates the privilege of what psychoanalysis calls the Phallus with the actual object that is the male penis can no longer be sustained.[46]

— But something is missing here. The smile, the laughter is gone.

— Instead, Breton holds a piece of the Dada Movement's letterhead, its typography seemingly transforming the French word for "movement" into a misspelling of the word *muette,* or "mute."

— The laughter and the hysteria and the noise are gone. Silence reigns.

— Dadaism and masochism? In Breton's case, the experience seems far less pleasurable than it was made to seem for Picabia, in the wild glee of the *Rastadada Painting* for example. Passive and impassible, Breton's (lack of) expression at the Salle Gaveau points to something different. Perhaps it points to a means to differentiate Dada from what would soon enough (under Breton) become Surrealism, allowing us to differentiate the two movements via their opposed relations to a dynamic of violence and destruction, with Dada's dynamic of masochism in opposition to its presumed opposite and double, a dynamic that has to be aligned with sadism.

— Surrealism . . . still expects nothing save from violence.

— Remember these words? They are from the hand of Breton, six years at least after Dada's demise, in the Second Manifesto of Surrealism.

— The simplest Surrealist act consists of dashing down into the street, pistol in hand, and firing blindly, as fast as you can pull the trigger, into the crowd. Anyone who, at least once in his life, has not dreamed of thus putting an end to the petty system of debasement and cretinization in effect has a well-defined place in that crowd, with his belly at barrel level.[47]

— This is a statement that takes us far afield from the Breton we have just glimpsed standing transfixed at the Salle Gaveau. It is a statement that leaves us deep within the grips of a sadistic redefinition of the avant-garde, at the opposite end of the spectrum, of the spectacle, of Dada's masochistic self-destruction.

And we of course did not have to travel so far into the future to locate such a definitive about-face. For the Breton we can glimpse in action, say, in 1923, at what is by all accounts usually regarded as the last "official" Dada manifestation, Tzara's *Soirée du Coeur à barbe*

— It's easier to shave the head than the heart.

— again utterly reverses the vision of Dada and masochism that we have just presented. There, Breton of course by now refused to participate, situating himself instead within the manifestation's audience. But this did not prevent him, that night, from taking the stage. Early in the evening, Picabia's one-time protégé, Pierre de Massot, emerged on the stage in order to read what Michel Sanouillet has accurately described as a "monotonous litany," a kind of wartime dirge commenting on the present state of the cultural domain:

— André Gide dead on the field of honor

— Pablo Picasso dead on the field of honor

— Francis Picabia dead on the field of honor

— Marcel Duchamp, vanished . . .[48]

— By all accounts, Breton could not contain himself. Taking up the defense, not of Picabia, but of Picasso, Breton charged onto the stage with a cane in hand, accompanied by Robert Desnos and Benjamin Péret, who took it upon themselves to hold de Massot for Breton. Upon de Massot's refusal to step down from the stage, Breton proceeded to beat him with his cane, actually fracturing his left arm. Picabia did not let the event pass unnoticed. In his 1924 novel *Caravansérail,* a novel that remained unpublished but did so much to finalize the irreparable break between Picabia and Breton over the corpse of Dada, Picabia set up its annoying, even cloying, central character, Lareinçay, as a thinly disguised stand-in for Breton, always chasing after the first-person narrator like a younger son after his older father, like, the novel seems to imply, Breton after Picabia. As Maria Lluïsa Borràs has pointed out, "Lareinçay" in French can be read as a pun, as a homophone of the word *la rincée,* namely, a slang term that one could roughly translate as "the drubbing," the "thrashing," or perhaps more awkwardly, the "beating up."

— Yes, I agree with all those historians who see Dada ending on this night, on July 6, 1923, upon the performance of its last "official" manifestation. I agree, but for other reasons.

— Picabia's *Relâche* would be the exception. But this was a dissident's gesture.

— Dada was over in more ways than one.

— The account of masochism that I have embraced here, that of Gilles Deleuze, has been widely dismissed for its "utopianism"—or, less charitably, its "sentimentalism"—for its overzealous attempt to imagine masochism as a perversion in which neither sadism nor the figure of the Father would have a place: an ideal account, then, purified of the stranglehold of Oedipus. If I have accepted that purification here, it is only insofar as Dada too presented itself as a type of utopia, or perhaps dystopia, with all the attendant disavowals.

———

— But it is incorrect to say that Deleuze makes no place for the crossing of sadism and masochism in his account, just as it distorts his vision to claim that his description of masochism banishes the Father once and for all. Deleuze in fact does speculate on the transformation of masochism into sadism, albeit in a manner far different from the Freudian account. "There is a certain sadism in masochism," Deleuze admits. And then he assigns such sadism a temporal position. "However, it is remarkable that . . . the reversal should only occur at the end of the enterprise. [The masochist's] sadism is a culmination; it is as though expiation and the satisfaction of the need to expiate were at last to permit the hero what his punishments were previously intended to deny him." Masochism, upon its completion, upon the "second birth" of the "new, sexless man," can be turned around

— perhaps the reversal is structural here

— It can devolve into a type of sadism. "Once they have been undergone, punishments and suffering allow the exercise of the evil they once prohibited [M, p. 39]."

— And the Father can return as well. Deleuze would not be so idealistic as to imagine that the ruse of masochism could actually *succeed,* that its utopia could be *realized*. Utopias are precisely not real, they are those flash-in-the-pan moments, the ones that cannot be sustained, the ones that allow a glimpse of something different, but just a glimpse, a vision all the more intensely desirable for its rapid fading away.

— Desire fades away if you possess, don't possess anything.[49]

— Deleuze, in fact, actually accepts in his account Lacan's notion of "foreclosure," a mechanism of denial through which Lacan speculated that precisely the object that is expelled from the Symbolic can return, in the modality of what Lacan called the Real. "The Father," Deleuze writes, "though abolished in the symbolic order, nevertheless continues to act in the order of the real, or of experience. There is a fundamental law, first formulated by Jacques Lacan, according to which an object which has been abolished on the symbolic plane resurges

in 'the real' in a hallucinatory form [M, p. 64]." In the wake of masochism's violent expenditure, the Father can return.

— a token?

— The immediate history of the French avant-garde calls out for a closer
account of just such an "aggressive and hallucinatory return of the father in
a world that has symbolically abolished him [M, p. 64]." It is, I think, one way
to understand the collapse of Dada, the turn to Surrealism. It is, surely, one
way to understand the "collapse" of Picabia, to narrate his sudden and absolute
defection from the ranks of the avant-garde in the wake of 1924, the exile of so
many of his future works and writings to the cold, hard land of regression and
pastiche. To a place where gifts from the subject without a patronymic would be
few and far between.

— Is history's signifier the dead father?[50]

— There is another image of Breton that I think should be compared to
the photograph of him at the Salle Gaveau, dressed up by Francis Picabia. It is a
drawing by Max Ernst, created in 1923 as part of the subscription offer for Breton's collection of poems *Clair de terre*.

— The portrait seems an odd image for Ernst, its lines arguably readymade

— they were supposedly appropriated from an image in a medical textbook

— but also deeply engaged with the frigid classicism of the early 1920s in
Paris—like Picasso's Ingresque portraits—as much as with Picabia's increasingly
frequent parodies of such drawings as the 1920s proceeded. To compare the two
images, the drawing and the photograph, and the two rival figurations of Breton
by Picabia and Ernst, is to see Ernst's portrait as a sort of aftermath, perhaps, and
as a definite indication of where the French avant-garde would soon be heading,
and where Surrealism itself would soon be going. It is to see Breton no longer
opened up to his imminent destruction, but bandaged and patched in the mode
of reparation. The Kleinian terms

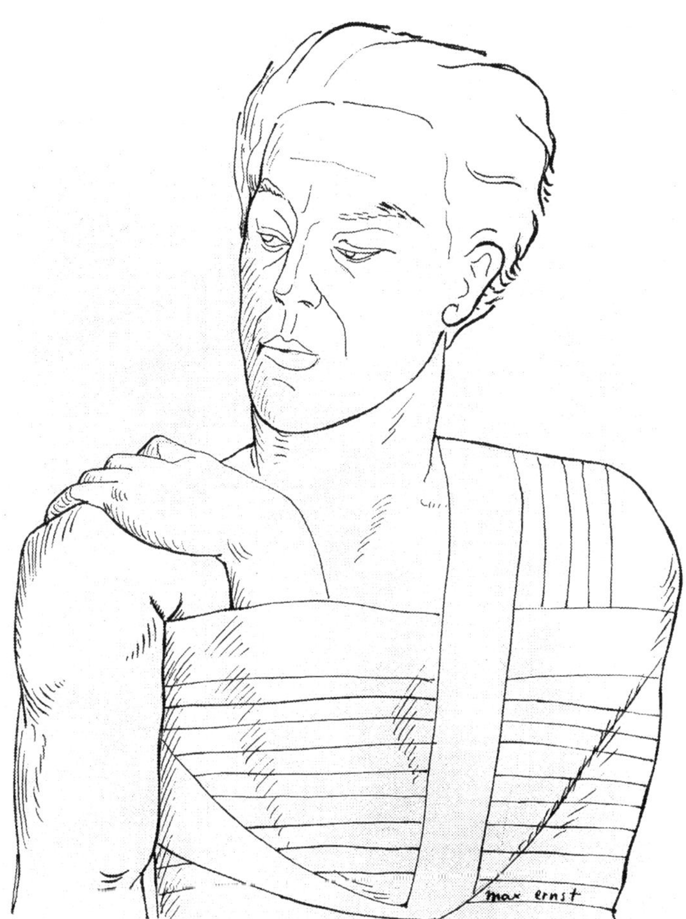

Max Ernst, *André Breton,* 1923. Ink on paperboard, $15^{15}/_{16} \times 12^{1}/_{4}''$. Private collection, Paris. © 2005 Artists Rights Society (ARS), New York/ADAGP, Paris/Estate of Max Ernst.

— A return of the Dead Father? An image of the castrated Son?

— are intended. To compare the two images is to see Breton accepting his wounds in any case, and perhaps making of these wounds a new project, his face expressionless to the end.

— That Picabia was famously hostile to this new project is well known. He would, in effect, be our first "dissident" Surrealist—having already long remained a "dissident" Dadaist—resurrecting the magazine *391,* which had lain dormant since the artist's defection from Dada in 1921, and dedicating it to his own scatological version of "Surrealism" upon the initiation of Breton's new movement in 1924. What is less well known is the extent to which Picabia's dissidence, and even the final break-up of Dada as a movement and thus too of Picabia's Dada work, was staged on the terrain of the loss of Dada's masochistic self-definition, and based on the new importance of the figure of the Father within the aesthetic that would be Bretonian Surrealism.

— With the Father would come the Figure.[51] It was one of the psychic conditions, we could say, of the *retour à l'ordre,* of the general antimodernist reaction.

— Although Picabia had been flirting with a return to figuration since the beginnings of Dada in Paris, the proclamation of this return within his work arrived in the fall of 1922, just before the trip to Barcelona with Breton, with Picabia's submission yet again of a significant pair of works to that year's Salon d'Automne, *La feuille de vigne (Dessin Français)* and *La nuit espagnole.* Created in the spring and summer of 1922, the two paintings were thus developed in tandem with the last "abstract" mechanomorphs that slowly emerged that fall; and as we have seen, these two "projects" at times combined. But this was a stylistic plurality that soon enough began to fade, as Picabia's engagement with a mode of figurative pastiche gained steam throughout 1922, in the repeated black-and-white parodic classicism of his series of magazine covers for the new series of *Littérature,* for example. And it would triumph by May of 1923, in the wake of the "failed" Barcelona exhibition, as Picabia made a big show of repudiating abstraction once and for all, while simultaneously reconciling with his former

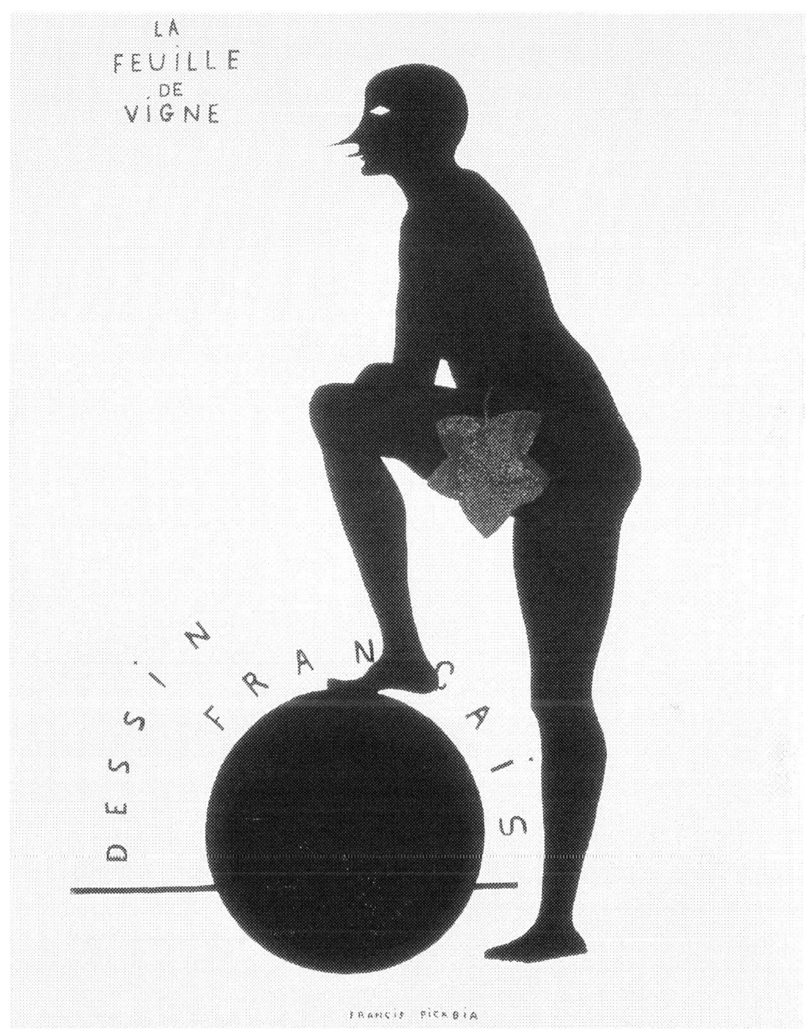

Francis Picabia, *La feuille de vigne (Dessin Français) (The Fig Leaf [French Drawing]),* 1922. Ripolin on canvas, 198 × 158 cm. Tate Gallery, London. Photograph © Tate Gallery, London/Art Resource, New York. © 2005 Artists Rights Society (ARS), New York/ADAGP, Paris/Estate of Francis Picabia.

dealer Danthon with whom he had broken over his conversion to the avant-garde almost fifteen years earlier. At Danthon's gallery, in 1923, Picabia insisted on showing only figurative work. It was like a great gust of wind had blown through the artist's studio, clearing all signs of Dada from the scene.

— At this point, from Picabia, we begin to get statements like this

— There are those who do not like machines. For them I propose Spanish women. And if they don't love Spanish women, I will make them French ones. But if I exhibit, it is also out of a desire for *publicity.* At any rate, I hope that my paintings sell very well.[52]

— Here is one explanation for the disappearance of Dada

— One explanation, you mean, for the reappearance of the figurative. Of history painting, of the Old Master, of the Father.

— a cynical assault on the rising commercialism of art, but only by taking this degradation into oneself, by submission to its rule, by avid assimilation

— it sounds like masochism

— a cynical assault, as well, on the return to tradition in French neo-classicism, by adopting in the mode of parody, as if it were a readymade, all of its outward signs. This was no longer Dada's strategy of the expenditure of the general equivalent. Neither was it an exploration of an alternate symbolic economy, equivalence without measure. It was equivalence following, extremely closely, the measure of the times.

— Our head is round in order to allow thought to change direction.[53]

— It was instead a form of homeopathy. It was a kind of "Dada mime."[54] But its gambit, and its transformation of Picabia's work was aggravated

— Imagine oysters copying out of admiration the false pearls that imitate their own![55]

— intensified, by conditions that had nothing to do, in the end, with the rising conservatism of mainstream French culture. Instead, it had everything to do with transformations occurring within the remnants of the avant-garde, the aftermath of Dada in Paris.

— *La feuille de vigne (The Fig Leaf)* allows us to gauge the distance that had been traveled, and to begin to hazard a series of guesses as to why the former Dada economy collapsed. *La feuille de vigne* takes up many strands within Picabia's Dada work that we are only now in a position to appreciate. It shows the principle of drawing's mechanization leaping forward from the literal cut of a work such as *La jeune fille* to the insistent tracing of a figurative silhouette, couched in the system of black-and-white opposition of the photograph. Self-reflexively proclaiming itself to be in the "second degree," to be a work engaged in covering over a previous image or object (the deletion principle, one could say, implied in the "fig leaf" of the title), Picabia's *La feuille de vigne* actually and literally obliterated a previous, crucial work from his recent Dada past. Beneath *La feuille de vigne* lies Picabia's lost work *Les yeux chauds,* the large-scale mechanomorph that was submitted as the companion piece of *L'oeil cacodylate* to the Salon d'Automne in 1921.

— A fig leaf covers Dada.

— In this sense, Picabia's figurative mode proclaims its eruption into his work by literally obliterating, by covering over and dissimulating, the mechanomorphs that had preceded it. But of course the mechanomorph *Les yeux chauds* is not the only image buried beneath this painterly "fig leaf "; there is the added complication that the retreat from the mechanomorph's appropriation of mechanical diagrams and photographs specifies itself as a retreat into the far distant past, with *La feuille de vigne* turning the powers of its pastiche to the forms of historical painting, to the forms, more precisely, of Ingres and his well-known work, *Oedipus and the Sphinx*.[56]

— Killed his father, slept with his mother.

— And so what we see, in Picabia's *La feuille de vigne,* is an inscription of Oedipus onto the face of Picabia's painting.

— where once he ~~wrote~~ crossed out "Daddy"

— Of course I mean this in more than just the sense that the silhouetted figure in *La feuille de vigne* is a traced version of the actual figure of Oedipus in Ingres's painting, just as I think that this inscription of Oedipus goes far beyond the ramifications that many have seen in this painting's parody of the "return to order" classicism of postwar Parisian art. For what has not been articulated is the extent to which so much of Picabia's Dada work set itself *against* Oedipus, against the entire dynamic which in the language of psychoanalysis Oedipus has come to figure.

— And so this embrace of the Son frozen before the riddle of his (sexual) origins, this inscription of Oedipus onto Picabia's work, becomes suddenly more momentous. It was like an entire set of Dada strategies was in danger of collapse, a transformed symbolic economy abandoned, the equivalent reinstated. It now becomes increasingly obvious how fitting it is that Picabia's stark return to figuration and his turn to a form of recognizable historical pastiche should first be achieved upon the dynamic of a return to Oedipus—a return, in psychoanalytic terms, to the Oedipal laws of the Father and Phallus alike.

— For of course this is another function of the "fig leaf." It is a return of the elision. The general equivalent excluded. Law and Order return.

— This is an investigation that smells of the police.[57]

— The painting literally uses a painted fig leaf to occlude the phallus of Oedipus only to emphasize it, just as the son replaces (murders) the Father only more fully to enact his laws. In terms of the general equivalent, both Father and Phallus will henceforth return to their respective places, transcendent over the scene of representation in their occlusion, and painting now will couch itself in the form of the questing son, foot placed firmly upon the form of a black hole, as if this abstract hole was the enigma that he had faced and evidently mastered.

— The hole will now no longer be inscribed "la jeune fille," nor even "bracelet de la vie." It will instead become "Dessin Français."

— Dessin Francis!

— And both Father and Phallus begin to make their triumphant return within Picabia's paintings, as if he were internalizing the very principles of the oppressive forms that he had initially meant to parody. In opposition to Picabia's earlier embrace of masochism, the forms of sadism return as well. *La feuille de vigne* received a crucial sequel as the years of Dada came to a close, the large-scale 1923 work *Dresseur d'animaux (The Animal Tamer),* submitted to the Salon d'Automne of 1923, the last in which Picabia participated.[58] One sees the same solitary male figure; one witnesses the same reduction of form to the tracing of a figurative silhouette; one senses the same turn back to the language of the distant classical past. Indeed, Maria Lluïsa Borràs has identified at least one of the forms of the painting, the dog standing on its hind legs, as an element borrowed from a well-known classical sculpture group, the struggling *Farnese Bull.* And she has also speculated on the painting's "enigmatic hieraticism," the strange mood of domination and submission that it evokes, the mad slippage of forms that it seems to embrace, from the erect curls of the various dog tails, to the pendant flop of the whip, to the hook of the masked figure's artificial nose. She sees the painting, like the novel *Caravansérail* that Picabia began to compose in its wake, as a veiled reference to and parody of the leadership position that André Breton was preparing to take within the avant-garde.[59]

— André Breton puffs himself up with his hair.[60]

— Picabia, in the words of Borràs, was "obsessed" by the groups constantly forming themselves around Breton at this time. Which is crucial. For if true, this drive to parody Breton in terms of the punishing Father and of sadism allows us to see that Picabia's sudden turn to figuration was not mediated solely by a desire to send up the mainstream French embrace of classicism, and the widespread rupture of the logical progression of modernist styles that this embrace entailed. Picabia's turn to the figure—and thus too the restoration of the Father, of the Phallus, and of sadism—was mediated just as compulsively by the context of emerging Surrealism, and by Picabia's impending break with Breton.

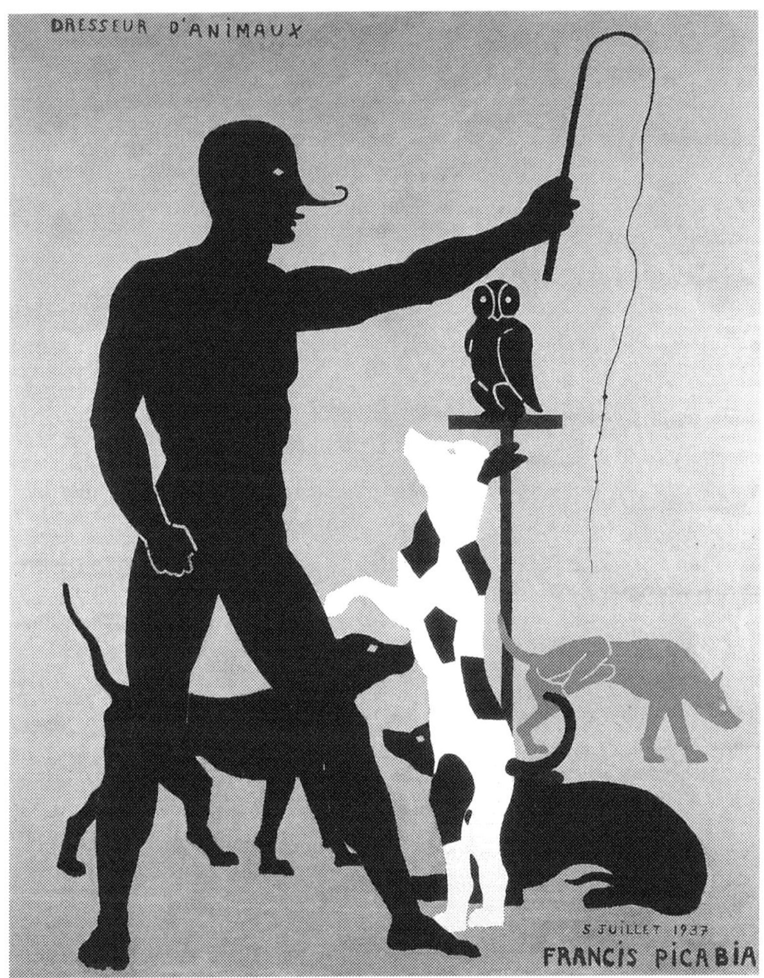

Francis Picabia, *Dresseur d'animaux (Animal Tamer),* 1923. Ripolin on canvas, 250 × 200 cm. Musée National d'Art Moderne, Centre Georges Pompidou. Photo by Jacques Fanjour. Photograph © CNAC/MNAM/Dist. Réunion des Musées Nationaux/Art Resource, New York. © 2005 Artists Rights Society (ARS), New York/ADAGP, Paris/Estate of Francis Picabia.

— For it was in the work of those artists who were soon installed at the core of the Surrealist movement that a perverse relation to the Father and the whole Oedipal dynamic came to occupy the stakes of painterly representation, becoming the motor driving the renewed project of the avant-garde. Indeed, in 1922, at the same time that Picabia inscribes "Oedipus" onto the face of his painting, a painterly relation to the (Dead) Father was becoming increasingly important to the works being churned out by Breton's new, favored artistic "interlocutor," namely Max Ernst. From Ernst's hands, at this moment of Surrealism's emergence, we receive a kind of panorama of sadistic and patriarchal themes, unabashedly Oedipal dynamics, and an almost loving attention given to the terms of castration and the Father.[61]

— I thought you said that we have to love the Father.

— Yes. But it is precisely a question of how one does this. Picabia would begin to take the love (of the Father) and the sadism to their limits, in his typical modality of excess.

— It was in 1922, for example, that Max Ernst completed *Au rendez-vous des amis,* a group portrait of the (post-)Dadaists from which Picabia is conspicuously absent, and in which Ernst is himself depicted seated on the knee of a representation of Dostoevsky, like a child in the lap of his father, with Ernst's brightly colored skin played off the deathly black-and-white pallor of Dostoevsky's painted face. One of the future dissident Surrealists, André Masson, sneered at the time

— Max Ernst is working on a painting, the Dada kids around a photographic Dostoevsky. Limbour finds the figures in it more lifelike than they are in reality.[62]

— and we can imagine Picabia sharing Masson's sneer.

— For if in the *Rastadada Painting* Picabia presented Ernst with a gift, inscribing Ernst's name onto the face of his art for the first and last time, it was a gift whose implications Ernst seems to have ignored. And by 1921, we can assume that any nascent friendship between Picabia and Ernst was beginning to dissolve into rivalry, as we glimpse Breton's glee in telling us that as the Dadaists unpacked Ernst's collages for their first exhibition in Paris in 1921, their revelatory quality for the future Surrealists only made Picabia sick with envy.[63]

— But perhaps Breton was wrong.

— Perhaps Picabia was less envious than filled with disgust. This was the moment, remember, when he first "quit" the Dada movement.

— One particular set of actions by Breton in the summer and fall of 1923 seems to have intensified this rivalry, just as it precipitated the final split between Picabia and Breton.[64] In the late summer of 1923, Picabia's uncle, Maurice Davanne, died, leaving the artist in a state of extreme depression. He composed a poem, "Mon oncle est mort," mailing it off to Breton along with a series of twelve drawings that Breton had requested for the next issue of *Littérature*.[65] But when this issue appeared in the fall, a special double issue (11–12) dedicated to poetry, Picabia's poem was nowhere to be found. Nor were any of his drawings used.

— Instead, Breton chose to print a suite of some forty-five line drawings by Max Ernst.

— He wrote to Picabia, worried, duplicitous, asking for his "confidence," assuring Picabia that Ernst's drawings "did not have the same importance."[66]

— And it was around this same time of personal and professional loss for Picabia that the figure of the Father truly took pride of place in Ernst's endeavors, as the latter completed in 1923 his major painting, a touchstone for the future Surrealist movement, *Pietà or The Revolution by Night*. It was a manifesto painting of sorts, showing not a traditional *pietà,* not the Dead Christ cradled in his loving Mother's arms, but a classicizing male figure usually interpreted as a proxy for Ernst himself, held lifeless in the hands of an older, mustachioed man, another son frozen in the arms of his ghostly father.[67]

— For Picabia, this seems to have been the last straw. Upon hearing, early in 1924, about Breton's plans to launch a new movement that would be christened with Apollinaire's term "Surrealism," Picabia issued a press release, in May, announcing a new series of *391* that would itself be "devoted to Surrealism."[68] Furious, Breton fired off an angry letter to Picabia, which Picabia used to end their association, by simply printing the letter word for word in *391*

— by assimilating it

— under the rubric "A Letter from my Grandfather." Picabia's attachment of the name of the Father to Breton and thus to the Surrealists seems no coincidence in this context, just as his printed response to the letter, with its invocation of waste and expenditure, seems entirely in line with Picabia's past Dada actions:

— When I smoke cigarettes, I am not in the habit of keeping the butts.[69]

— But now Picabia's response to Surrealism in the series of parodic drawings that he published in the last issues of *391* did anything but submit the Father to expenditure. They rather let the Father loose, as if on a rampage, across the surface of Picabia's art. If this rampage has been only dimly perceived, the general critical fog may be due to the fact that it has gone entirely unnoticed that Picabia's parodies can be seen as taking the work of Max Ernst as their target—especially the painting *Pietà or The Revolution by Night*. The possibility that this is so becomes most clear in the drawing published on the back cover of the May 1924 issue of *391,* a nightmarish fantasy usually called *Rimbaud Thermometer*. The form of Picabia's parody of Ernst becomes most obvious in the androgynous muse figure in this drawing, held aloft by a creature half from classical mythology, half from modern life. For the position of this muse, the outlines of its body as well as the curiously and awkwardly bent shape that body holds, can suddenly be explained if it is taken as a pastiche of the "dead" son in *Revolution by Night*. The pastiche is readily apparent too in the face of this figure, as well as in its hair, almost identical to the classicizing lines of Ernst's frozen son. The parody, on the other hand, is there in the transformations Picabia's vision enacts upon Ernst's fantasy. It is there in Ernst's opposition of Father and Son altered into Picabia's opposition of aggressive male and androgynous muse. It is there in Picabia's transformation of Ernst's mustachioed Father into an enigmatic and sightless male, shaved bald, yet evidently all the more phallic for that. It is there in the transmutation of an artistic fantasy of perverse filial surrender into a scene of poetic inspiration crossing the border into rape

— it's a kind of poetic buggering

— the masochism of Ernst's vision flipped over into the sadism of a classical scene of *enlèvement*.

— *Rimbaud Thermometer* is an image that confirms one's worst fears.

— But it's hilarious

— Under the pressure of pastiche, under the rivalry with Ernst via Breton, Picabia's art seemed to lose its connection to the dynamic of sacrifice and expenditure that had sustained it. Instead, brought close to an aesthetic riven by the Dead Father and driven by castration, Picabia's art now spewed forth the Father in all his forms, the Phallus in all its glory—just look at the tail overtaking the entire lower-half of the body of the "Father" in this drawing—as much as it abandoned the former hopes of masochism for the debasement of a spiraling series of visions of sadistic male virility. The turn to parody launches Picabia into an embrace of all that he had once denied.

— And the effects of this embrace ripple through almost all of the other drawings published in the last issues of *391*. Bald aggressors emerge from every corner, their lack of hair no longer embodying the emasculation that for Dada it once evoked. Anal eroticism in *Rimbaud Thermometer* shifts to a scene worthy of Pasolini's *Salò* in *Rimbaud's Chamberpot,* with its initiate forced by an evident caricature of Breton to find inspiration in excrement. The Father begins to return everywhere one looks—"aggressive and hallucinatory," to use Deleuze's words—for instance in the images of Pierre de Massot and Erik Satie published in the June 1924 issue of *391*. Rape becomes de rigueur, the desublimated subtext of all these scenes parodying the passive, automatist inspiration of Surrealism—as well as Surrealism's turn to the celebration of a series of poetic father figures, such as Rimbaud and Lautreamont.[70]

— Our penis should always cast a shadow on our stomach.[71]

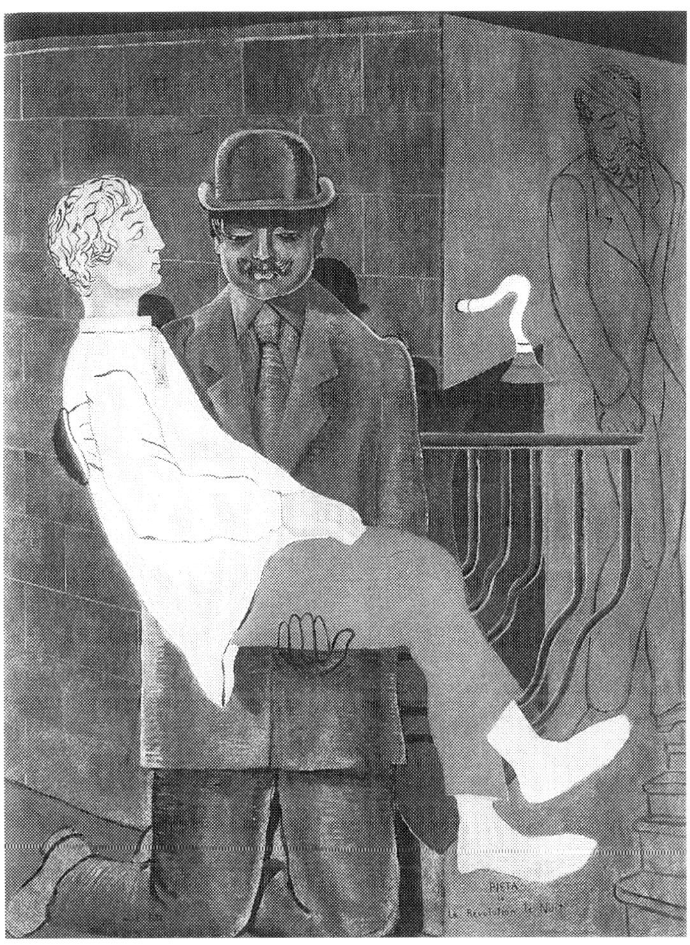

Max Ernst, *Pietà or The Revolution by Night*, 1923. Oil on canvas, 116.2 × 88.9 cm (45³/₄ × 35³/₈″). Tate Gallery, London. © 2005 Artists Rights Society (ARS), New York/ADAGP, Paris/Estate of Max Ernst.

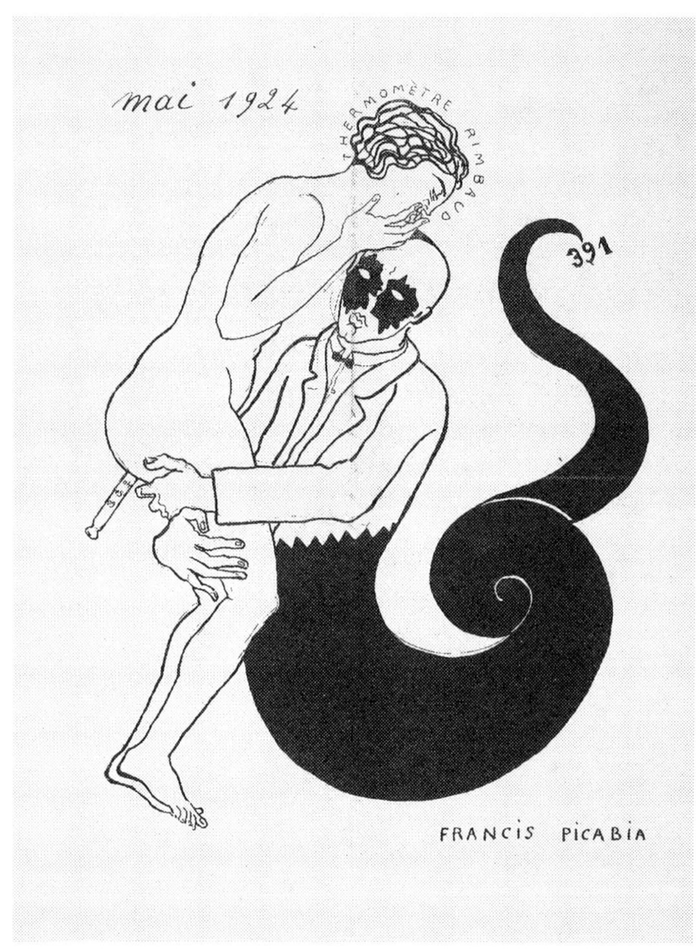

Francis Picabia, *Rimbaud Thermometer,* 1924. Back cover of *391* 16 (May 1924). Research Library, The Getty Research Institute, Los Angeles. © 2005 Artists Rights Society (ARS), New York/ADAGP, Paris/Estate of Francis Picabia.

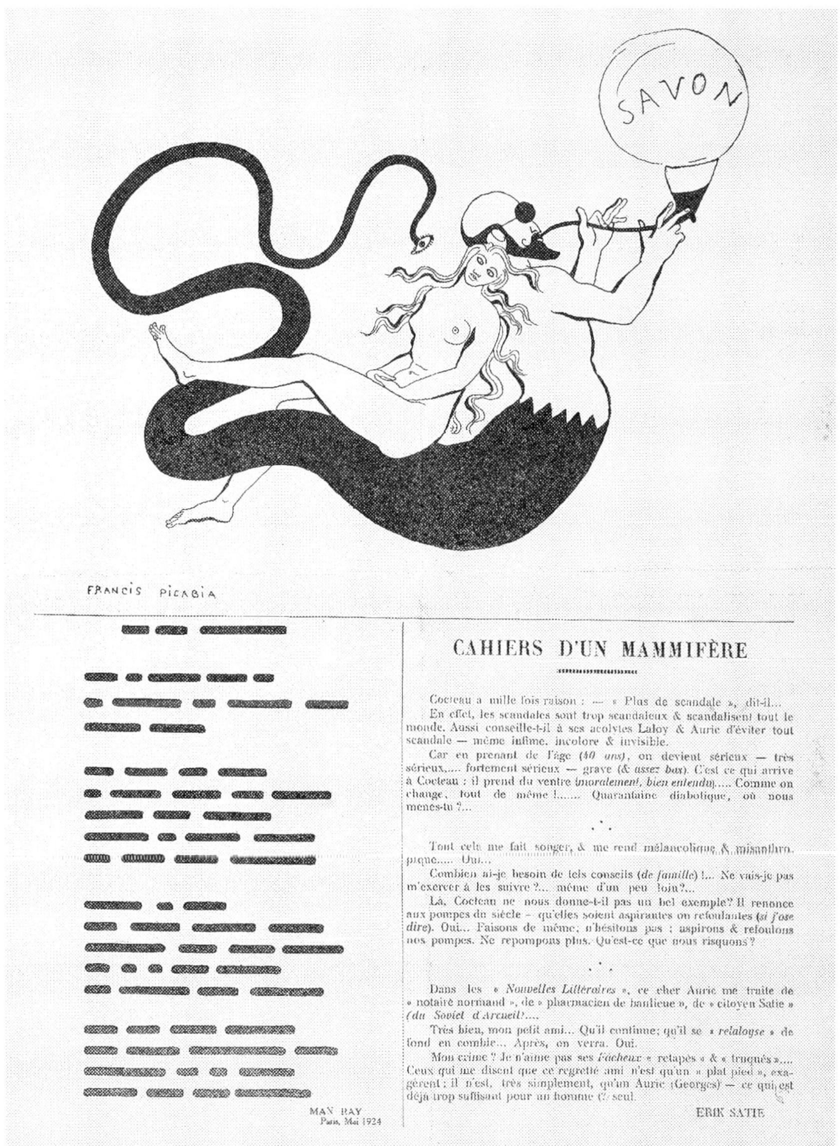

CAHIERS D'UN MAMMIFÈRE

Cocteau a mille fois raison : — « Plus de scandale », dit-il...

En effet, les scandales sont trop scandaleux & scandalisent tout le monde. Aussi conseille-t-il à ses acolytes Laloy & Auric d'éviter tout scandale — même infime, incolore & invisible.

Car en prenant de l'âge (40 ans), on devient sérieux — très sérieux,.... fortement sérieux — grave (& assez bas). C'est ce qui arrive à Cocteau : il prend du ventre (moralement, bien entendu)..... Comme on change, tout de même !...... Quarantaine diabolique, où nous mènes-tu ?...

Tout cela me fait songer, & me rend mélancolique, & misanthro-pique..... Oui...

Combien ai-je besoin de tels conseils (de famille) !... Ne vais-je pas m'exercer à les suivre ?... même d'un peu loin?...

Là, Cocteau ne nous donne-t-il pas un bel exemple? Il renonce aux pompes du siècle — qu'elles soient aspirantes ou refoulantes (si j'ose dire). Oui... Faisons de même; n'hésitons pas ; aspirons & refoulons nos pompes. Ne repompons plus. Qu'est-ce que nous risquons?

Dans les « Nouvelles Littéraires », ce cher Auric me traite de « notaire normand », de « pharmacien de banlieue », de « citoyen Satie » (du Soviet d'Arcueil?)....

Très bien, mon petit ami... Qu'il continue; qu'il se « relaloyse » de fond en comble... Après, on verra. Oui.

Mon crime ? Je n'aime pas ses Fâcheux « retapés » & « truqués ».... Ceux qui me disent que ce regretté ami n'est qu'un « plat pied », exa-gèrent ; il n'est, très simplement, qu'un Auric (Georges) — ce qui est déjà trop suffisant pour un homme (? seul.

ERIK SATIE

Francis Picabia, *Soap,* 1924. Reproduced in *391* 17 (June 1924), p. 3. Research Library, The Getty Research Institute, Los Angeles. © 2005 Artists Rights Society (ARS), New York/ADAGP, Paris/Estate of Francis Picabia.

— And the Phallus returns as well, truly everywhere one looks in the last issues of *391*, from the visually endowed tail of Erik Satie in *Soap,* to his over-sized pipe, to the "bestial" virility of the drawing *Pierre de Massot and His Ostrich.*

— another visually endowed "tail"

— Our phallus should have eyes so that we would be able to believe for a moment that we have seen love from up close[72]

— this one also has a mouth. It can smile.

— or bite

— Such is the compulsive scene of sadistic violence—a scene beholden to Father and Phallus alike—to which Picabia's art will henceforth be devoted. It is as if the underlying logic for the remainder of Picabia's career had suddenly been laid bare, like a nightmare surfacing from the foul depths of repression. The nightmare was never more clear than in a drawing that seemed not to make the cut for the collection of parodies in *391*

— a drawing that was something like an auto-pastiche

— a self-portrait?

— the pornographic *Lever de soleil (Sunrise).* We witness the erect dog from *Dresseur d'animaux,* itself pastiched from a classical sculpture, reappear, an empty (emptied) auto-citation, now perched ludicrously on top of a massive male scrotum

— this drawing has balls[73]

— that is held aloft by another bald patriarch as if it were the round end of a club.

— Picabia and his Ostrich. It is another bestial thing. A sex with eyes, ludicrous false eyelashes

— It is a *queue du chien.* The dog is hardly "perched." This dog is endowed. It is a decoding of the erect dog's stance in *Dresseur d'animaux,* ludicrous excess again

✍✍✍✍✍ L'ÉTOILE AU FRONT ✍✍✍✍✍

Pour avoir consenti à nous dévoiler les baroques mystères de la destinée humaine et, devant une assemblée de la critique parisienne où le talent est à bon marché remis en question la surprenante existence du génie de M. Raymond Roussel n'a pas manqué de dresser contre lui la coalition des Boulevards, des brasseries et des salles de rédaction. Pour ma part je me fais un honneur d'avoir été l'un des rares à applaudir, noyé dans un parterre d'imbéciles et d'incompréhensifs. La destinée humaine est-elle donc si plate que, lorsqu'on l'exprime en légendes charmantes, les gens dits sensés s'indignent et proclament fou l'auteur d'une pièce où les personnages sont tragiquement réduits au rôle de pièces d'échecs soumises à une passion : curiosité, vices, amour...

Nos contemporains sont de plaisants pignoufs qui en sont encore à assigner des bornes au matériel poétique. Lautréamont avait déjà présidé à ces rencontres pathétiques d'objets issus d'univers différents pour des emplois éloignés les uns des autres et destinés en apparence à consommer leur existence matérielle sans emmêler leurs rouages ou heurter leurs énergies hétéroclites. En quoi un garçon de laboratoire faisant fortune grâce à un pied de mammouth congelé et amené à Paris par un professeur curieux d'étudier les putréfactions, une humble servante adaptant son sort avec fatalisme au bon vouloir du calendrier qui la fit naître un jour gris et la fit doter d'un scapulaire d'organdi du fait de superstitions paysannes entourant un sapin vénérable, en quoi la révélation dans un ballon sphérique dominant la guerre de 1870-71 de l'amour d'un évêque pour une infirmière et de l'importance de cette révélation pour le destin d'une bague enfouie dans un puisard féodal, en quoi ces magnifiques épisodes du baccarat humain sont-ils plus scandaleux ou moins touchant que telle aventure survenue à une vierge roumaine dans un cirque ensoleillé en présence de hous nés sous un autre climat, que le choc de deux amours masculins pour la même femme sous un astre habile à découper leurs ombres sur le sable des allées avec la même lumière qui lui fit éclairer, à la même place des fougères arborescentes, des serpents ailés, l'amour nocturne des fourmis rouges ou l'accouchement sans gloire d'une vierge ignorée. En quoi le destin de l'homme est-il moins « dramatique » quand on l'assimile au bizarre équilibre des soleils et des planètes ?

Tout sur terre est baroque. Le bateau n'est pas plus fait pour la mer que pour le ciel ; il est aussi arbitraire de grouper dans un paysage intellectuel une jeune fille et une fleur, que d'unir à des fins d'obscures reproductions la femelle du requin au scorpion mâle.

Ces rencontres imprévues se reproduisent cependant et de l'accoutumance à ces scènes miraculeuses naissent les mythologies. La rapidité avec laquelle le matériel moderne est mis hors d'usage a pour conséquence de nouvelles éditions du Bottin des Dieux et du catalogue de leurs attributs. Du Soleil à Vénus, de Vénus au Christ, du Christ à la guillotine, de la guillotine à la Vénus de Milo, de la Vénus de Milo à l'aéroplane, de l'aéroplane au rayon invisible en passant par les revenants, les volcans et le serpent de mer, s'allonge la liste des geôles poétiques. L'imagination s'épuiserait à les renouveler sans le concours d'esprit comme Raymond Roussel.

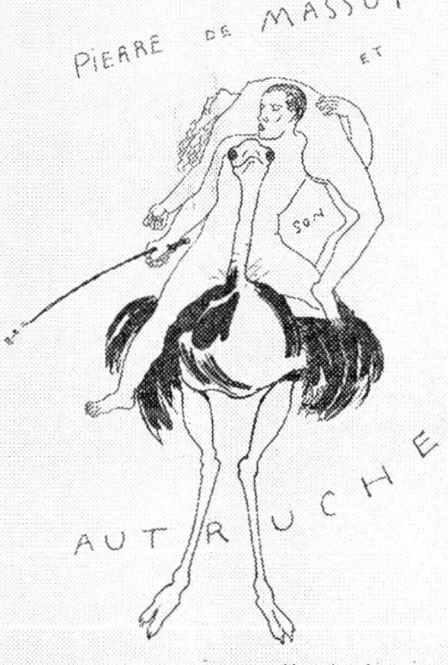

Un critique de peu de valeur et mauvais poète, M. Fernand Gregh constatait l'autre jour (Nouvelles Littéraires) qu'en prenant une à une les histoires de « L'Étoile au « Front en mettant de la sauce autour » en en faisant des volumes de 350 pages, on obtiendrait le plus grand succès du roman contemporain (genre Atlantide !)

Voilà bien où le bât blesse ces ânes.

M. Roussel est trop riche. Il en a déjà constaté lui-même l'inconvénient dans Locus Solus. Il convient de remarquer maintenant que cette constatation n'a pas seulement qu'un sens matériel mais qu'on doit l'entendre également au sens spirituel. Je ne doute pas qu'un jour surgiront des hommes « de talent » qui tireront des romans à succès de l'œuvre de M. Raymond Roussel « homme de génie ». J'ai trop confiance pour ma part en l'auteur d'Impressions d'Afrique pour craindre un instant qu'il succombe à la tentation du tirage à cent mille.

Pour satisfaire ces cent mille lecteurs imbéciles il y a assez de médiocres : Henri Béraud qui délaye Charcot pour les marchands de drap et étale sa tripe pour les concierges, Henri Béraud à qui je ne pardonne pas de m'obliger à prendre parti pour Gide ; André Antoine l'anti-poète et l'introducteur du réalisme conventionnel au théâtre, Antoine dont chaque article est un sottisier, Antoine qui ferait pas mal de retourner à son compteur à gaz ; Courteline roi des crétins ; Anatole France chef avorteur de la Révolution et grand érudit selon le Larousse et combien d'autres !

Mais l'imagination exacte de Raymond Roussel inflige de cinglants démentis à d'autres saligauds : Jean Cocteau qui n'a jamais cessé de plagier Edmond Rostand ; Tristan Tzara faux escroc et premier ennuque du sérail mondain ; Gabory... Marcel Raval éditeur de mes dessins et toute la clique, des capitulateurs et des vulgarisateurs.

La route un instant frayée cesse tout à coup.

La troupe des valets est loin derrière.

Dans la grande plaine poétique, des jeunes filles marchent à Colin-Maillard, vers le nord, plus sûrement guidées par un mystérieux instinct que par la boussole ou l'étoile. Voici la partie vierge de la forêt avec ses lianes, ses serpents, ses trésors, ses femmes adorables et ses dangers merveilleusement mortels. La hache est là. Bientôt nous serons hors de portée des chiens et des fusils.

ROBERT DESNOS

Effets divers : « André Breton fait des effets de torse avec ses cheveux, »

Effets divers : « Georges Auric fait des effets de torse avec son poil dans la main. »

Francis Picabia, *Pierre de Massot and His Ostrich*, 1924. Reproduced in *391* 17 (June 1924), p. 2. Research Library, The Getty Research Institute, Los Angeles. © 2005 Artists Rights Society (ARS), New York/ADAGP, Paris/Estate of Francis Picabia.

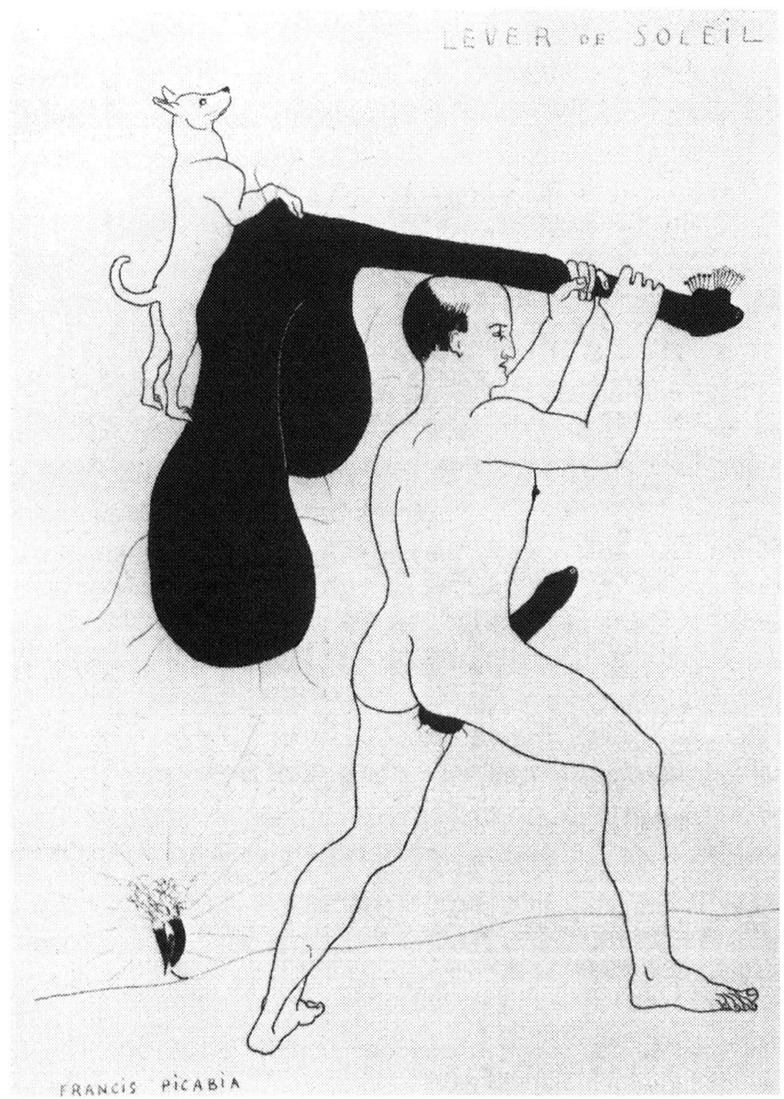

Francis Picabia, *Sunrise,* 1924. India ink on paper, 31.1 × 24 cm. Private collection, Paris. © 2005 Artists Rights Society (ARS), New York/ADAGP, Paris/Estate of Francis Picabia.

— a proclamation of the end? Dada ends in a *queue du chien*?

— *Sunrise* is a mostly pornographic affair, a fantasy revealing a splayed vulva rising into the early morning sky.

— *Vagin brillant*

— Almost Bataillean in its metonymic series of displacements, this sun can be seen producing its radiant effects on the male subject who dominates the foreground of the drawing, priapic in his full arousal, and multiplying that erection by holding the second, giant phallus over his head like a weapon, a stick to beat an other that the drawing fails to show. It is a bald image of domination and aggression, of a sadism without object (except perhaps the self), and thus the sliding of the erect dog from *Dresseur d'animaux* to this drawing becomes entirely appropriate, a product of the sudden equivalence of their identical scenes.

— Upon leaving Paris in 1925, upon abandoning the avant-garde, upon taking up residence on the Côte d'Azur in his beautiful Chateau de Mai, Picabia was asked why he had sought such distance

— My taking distance from Paris stemmed from a great need for the sun.[74]

— *Sunrise* seems deeply engaged with the parodies that Picabia published in *391* in 1924, but was itself never published there. I think the reason for this is clear. For *Sunrise* turns its parody not against Breton, or Ernst, or any of the other future Surrealists; the object of this drawing seems to be Picabia himself. Once again, a parody of the other (Breton, for example, in *Dresseur d'animaux*) has been turned around, converted through a structure of rivalry, its effects now internalized within the self. And now we will see Picabia—another image of Picabia—we will see him erect, sadistic and cruel, succumbing to this sudden equivalence between self and other, as well as embracing the general equivalent, holding it tight, as it were, as if the general equivalent were suddenly necessary for his defense, the depthless key to his salvation.

— to his self-flagellation

— The Sex of Dada is deflating!

— We would do well at this point to remember Tzara's cry, and to imagine it filled with both concern and exuberance. For such had been Dada's relation to the Phallus, its relation to masculinity, to mastery, and to patriarchy. Such had been its relation, that is, to the general equivalent.

— In the horror of Picabia's 1924 parodies, we see instead, everywhere one looks, the return of the general equivalent. It is now as if we stare directly into the blank face of the general equivalent itself, peering deep into the chasm that gapes before the emptiness of the token. We witness Picabia no longer involved in a contestation of the general equivalent, in an unveiling of its baseless and tokenized status, but accepting the passive promiscuity of forms that it will now ordain.

— Universal prostitution returns, in an entirely other key.

— But this is not just a return, a restoration—horrific and irreversible— of the general equivalent in Picabia's work. It is not just the effect of biographical events contributing to a structure of rivalry within Picabia's work—the emergence of parody *as* a self-reflexive structure of rivalry. It perhaps speaks to a *historical* shift, one by which Picabia's work was equally captured. If Picabia's Dada project had always been an incisive negotiation of the status of the general equivalent, an amplification of the economic lessons of the readymade for cultural work, Dada and its strategies had of course been made possible by the epochal shift in the status of the general equivalent itself. For a time, the crisis of the general equivalent within modernity facilitated Dada's symbolic utopia, its redemption of meaning (of the meaningless).

— But that time was over

— But how did we do this? How were we able to drink up the sea? Who gave us the sponge to wipe away the entire horizon? What were we doing when we unchained this earth from its sun? Where is it moving to now? Where are we moving to? Away from all suns? Are we not continually falling? And backwards, sidewards, forwards, in all directions? Is there still an up and a down? Aren't we straying as though through an infinite nothing? Isn't empty space breathing at us?

Hasn't it got colder? Isn't night and more night coming again and again? Don't lanterns have to be lit in the morning?[75]

— The end of Dada in 1924 was also a historical end, the end of a brief moment of possibility. For what we witness in the foul spread of the general equivalent as a kind of empty, vapid lie within Picabia's last parodies in *391*

— parody, an emptying gesture, now levied upon all the avatars of the general equivalent, and then heaped upon the new projects of the avant-garde like so many ruined totems

— was perhaps, instead, the tell-tale sign of a vast consolidation in Western modernity of the general equivalent as token sign, a massive counterinvestment, what Deleuze would call a reterritorialization.

— The token was in control

— But what kind of control exactly? Where once Picabia had brought a kind of hole into the work of art, now the Law returns, but as a hole. Empty. Void. The hole had become the Law.

— and the Law a hole

— From universal prostitution to Surrealism: a return. An entirely different understanding of the French "return to order."

— In this sense, Dada for Picabia had been one great detour.

— a voyage off the tracks

— It had been—to appropriate (paraphrase) the appropriate phrase—an exploration, a testing, of "all that the general equivalent will forbid; and also all that it will permit."

— I thought, after your reading of *Relâche,* that this book would have a happy ending. Strategies full of possibility, the archaeology of forgotten procedures to which radical culture in our own day could still cling. The dawn of the day-still-to-come of transgression.

— Sunrise.

— But this book has two endings. They are utterly opposed.

— No, ambiguously opposed

— How can you have it both ways?

— Dada always did.

— The most beautiful book would be one that would not be possible to consider as a book.[76]

— Is the sky beneath us

— or above us

— if you could see me

— my smile would tell you which[77]

— But just look, for one last moment, at all those smiles.

— Just look, for one last moment, at what was about to be lost. Just look again, before we leave them forever.

— Farewell, farewell.

— It is a photograph of the Dadaists perhaps taken in 1921, arrayed around Picabia, a photograph that always gets identified simply as "Several collaborators of *391*."

— What laughter!

— But it's the same laughter. It's the same image.

— Yes, of course. It occurs to me in staring at this photograph that it must have been this image that served Picabia as the basis for the copying of his face in the portrait *Picabia by Francis 1922,* an image that I have described in terms of the joyous Father as imagined—perhaps in its baldness even as imagined

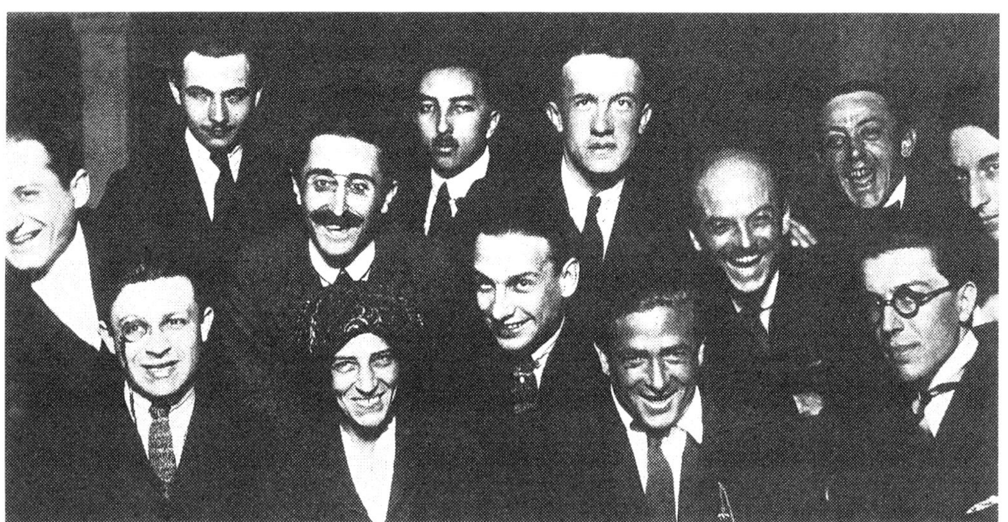

Anonymous, *Several Collaborators of "391,"* 1921. Photograph. Bibliothèque Littéraire Jacques Doucet, Paris.

castrated—by the Son. The expressions are identical, and if for Picabia drawing will always be automated by the photograph, the laughter here is as infectious as the mechanization.

— And what laughter!

— What could it mean

— this is Georges Bataille in the 1930s, thinking aloud about the closeness of his current project to the earlier liberties of Dada

— What could it mean that, for several years, a number of the most talented men have done their utmost to shatter their intelligence, believing that by so doing they explode intelligence itself? Dada is generally considered an inconsequential failure, whereas, for others, it becomes liberating laughter—a revelation transfiguring human beings.[78]

— A liberating laughter. For just a moment. Look again at the photograph. Only a few of Picabia's friends refuse to join in the general hilarity. There is Breton's friend, Théodore Fraenkel, but also, and crucially I think, there is the core trio that would soon be at the heart of the Surrealist movement—Louis Aragon, Paul Éluard, and André Breton, the smiles wiped right off their anxious faces.

— but it's the same laughter

— "The father of Surrealism was Dada," Walter Benjamin once wrote. "Its mother was an arcade."[79]

— Except it wasn't. We have known for a long time the problems with formulations such as this one, with its typical gendering of the arena of culture as masculine, and that of the commodity as feminine: the trope of mass culture as woman.[80] But there are other problems here besides. Dada had little interest in the explicit family romance that this aphorism supplies. Art history has not helped us in this matter, with the implicit familial structures and the patriarchal schemes of its larger apparatus of naming and of labels, of its tracing of the inevitable progression of authors and styles in the infamous family-tree model of modern art. Dada was hardly the "father" of Surrealism. At times, it might have desired to know what it would mean to proclaim that perhaps it was its "mother." It placed its hopes in other aphorisms, different slogans.

— Slogans and smiles? *Mots d'ordre* and laughter? The contradiction seems complete.

— interminable

— *The Father is Dead. Long Live Daddy!*

———

N OTES

I NTRODUCTION :   U NIVERSAL   P ROSTITUTION

1. On Picabia and Apollinaire's voyages together, see Francis Picabia, "Guillaume Apollinaire," *L'esprit nouveau* no. 26 (October 1924), reprinted in Picabia, *Écrits II (1921–1953 et posthumes),* ed. Olivier Revault d'Allonnes with Dominique Bouissou (Paris: Pierre Belfond, 1978), pp. 149–151. On the trip to England and its discussions, see Gabrielle Buffet-Picabia, *Aires abstraites* (Geneva: Pierre Cailler, 1957), pp. 47–57, and for the vacation in the Jura, pp. 58–64. William Camfield's monograph, *Francis Picabia: His Art, Life, and Times* (Princeton: Princeton University Press, 1979), pp. 30–35, contains useful accounts of both trips. For Apollinaire's slogan, see Guillaume Apollinaire, *Méditations esthétiques: Les peintres cubistes* (1913) (Paris: Hermann, 1965), p. 48. For one of the most important accounts of Marcel Duchamp's Munich trip, see Thierry de Duve, *Pictorial Nominalism* (Minneapolis: University of Minnesota Press, 1991). Duchamp wrote four notes relative to the "Jura-Paris Road" project, one of which is in "The Green Box," in *The Writings of Marcel Duchamp,* ed. Michel Sanouillet and Elmer Peterson (New York: Da Capo, 1989), pp. 26–27. The other three can be found in *Marcel Duchamp, Notes,* ed. Paul Matisse (Boston: G. K. Hall, 1983), n.p. (notes 109–111). Because it is the most literal, I have used the Roger Shattuck translation of Apollinaire's "Zone," reprinted in *The Yale Anthology of Twentieth-Century French Poetry,* ed. Mary Ann Caws (New Haven: Yale University Press, 2004), pp. 6–15.

2. Such was the thesis of the most recent major retrospective of Picabia's work, *Francis Picabia: Singulier idéal* (Paris: Musée d'art moderne de la ville de Paris, 2002).

3. Picabia, "Mr. Picabia Breaks with the Dadas [1921]," trans. Matthew S. Witkovsky, *October* 105 (summer 2003), pp. 145–146: "The Dada spirit only really existed from 1913 to 1918."

4. Obviously my implication is that for Dada the readymade overtakes the medium of sculpture; however (or perhaps consequently), the sculptural rears its head in almost every one of the chapters that follows: in the spatial "matrix" of the Dada drawing *La jeune fille* in chapter 1; the relief structure of *Natures mortes* in chapter 2; the translation of theatrical objects into images in chapter 3; and, finally, the reverse of this, the projection of the mechanomorph into physical space and time in chapters 4 and 5 (the set for Picabia's *Relâche,* indeed, long ago made its way into one of the most important, if not the last, histories of modern sculpture, Rosalind Krauss's *Passages in Modern Sculpture* [1977; Cambridge, Mass.: MIT Press, 1993]).

5. For the semiotic reading of Cubism, see Yve-Alain Bois, "Kahnweiler's Lesson," *Painting as Model* (Cambridge, Mass.: MIT Press, 1990), pp. 65–97, and "The Semiology of Cubism," *Picasso and Braque: A Symposium,* ed. Lynn Zelevansky (New York: Museum of Modern Art, 1992), pp. 169–208; Rosalind E. Krauss, "The Motivation of the Sign," *Picasso and Braque: A Symposium,* pp. 261–286, and "The Circulation of the Sign," *The Picasso Papers* (New York: Farrar, Straus and Giroux, 1998), pp. 25–85. As I will make clear in the body of my book, the turn to Goux and symbolic economies occurs first for modernist art history with the work of Krauss in the latter book.

6. This inscription is more ambivalent than its usual translation. As opposed to the more straightforward *Voilà Haviland,* it suggests alternatives: "Stieglitz here!" or "Here, it is here, Stieglitz," the last version distancing the representation from its normative reading as a portrait altogether.

7. Rosalind E. Krauss, "Notes on the Index," *The Originality of the Avant-Garde and Other Modernist Myths* (Cambridge, Mass.: MIT Press, 1985), pp. 196–209.

8. David Joselit, "Dada's Diagrams," *The Dada Seminars,* ed. Leah Dickerman and Matthew S. Witkovsky (Washington, D.C.: National Gallery of Art, 2005), pp. 221–239.

9. On the appropriations contained in Picabia's titles, see chapter 1 and chapter 4.

10. This connection was first made by William Innes Homer, "Picabia's *Jeune fille américaine dans l'état de nudité* and Her Friends," *Art Bulletin* 57 (March 1975), p. 111.

11. Jean-Joseph Goux, "Numismatics: An Essay in Theoretical Numismatics," *Symbolic Economies: After Marx and Freud,* trans. Jennifer Gage (Ithaca: Cornell University Press, 1990), pp. 48–49. Goux is citing Marx from *A Contribution to the Critique of Political Economy,* trans.

N. I. Stone (New York: International Library, 1904), pp. 149–150. Emphasis throughout is by Goux.

12. Metallic paints appear earlier in Picabia's work, most significantly in *Very Rare Painting on This Earth,* usually dated to 1915. A gilt painting with the title *Girl Born without a Mother* also exists (the title was used repeatedly by Picabia); it is usually dated 1916–1917 or even 1918, and I might argue for the later date. *Child Carburetor* is made on wood, which *Very Rare Painting on this Earth* also uses, perhaps connecting them in another way. But this painting on wood also follows Duchamp's instructions in the Jura-Paris Road notes, wherein he concluded that the "headlight child" and its companions should be realized on wood. In contradistinction to these remarks, the appearance of metallic paint on certain hand-tinted covers of *391* or in 1915 mechanomorphic paintings might be narrated as progressing in two stages: from an initial evocation of the aggressive glint of the machine to a slightly later slippage into the gilt appearance of money.

13. Arnauld Pierre, in *Francis Picabia: La peinture sans aura* (Paris: Gallimard, 2002), pp. 148–158, attributes this title (and, convincingly, every other phrase inscribed on the work, as well as several lines from Picabia's contemporaneous poems) to a book by Remy de Gourmont, *Physique de l'amour* (Paris: Mercure de France, 1903). But Marx had used (coined?) the phrase much earlier in a passage from the *Economic and Philosophic Manuscripts of 1844* (New York: International Publishers, 1964), p. 133:

> Finally, this movement of opposing universal private property to private property finds expression in the animal form of opposing to *marriage* (certainly a *form of exclusive private property*) the *community of women,* in which a woman becomes a piece of *communal* and *common* property. It may be said that this idea of the *community of women* gives away the *secret* of this as yet completely crude and thoughtless communism. Just as woman passes from marriage to general prostitution, so the entire world of wealth (that is, of man's objective substance) passes from the relationship of exclusive marriage with the owner of private property to a state of universal prostitution with the community. In negating the *personality* of man in every sphere, this type of communism is really nothing but the logical expression of private property, which is its negation.

CHAPTER 1   *LE SAINT DES SAINTS*: DADA DRAWING

1. Cited in Michel Sanouillet, *Dada à Paris* (1965) (Paris: Flammarion, 1993), p. 233. An original can be found in Picabia's archives in the Bibliothèque Littéraire Jacques Doucet, Paris (cited

hereafter as the Dossiers Picabia), vol. II, p. 242. The Dadaists covered the streets with such slogans as part of the publicity campaign for their initial Parisian activities. Properly untranslatable, Picabia's slogan might be rendered: "Like the designs [*desseins*] of Providence, certain drawings [*dessins*] are impenetrable."

2. A list of Larousse phrases that appear in Picabia paintings was published in the catalog of Picabia's 1976 retrospective at the Grand Palais. See *Francis Picabia,* ed. Jean-Hubert Martin and Hélène Seckel (Paris: Centre Georges Pompidou/Musée Nationale d'Art Moderne, 1976), pp. 47–49. Picabia wrote about the dictionary as a repository of language's commodification and its transformation into a readymade system in "Lutte contre la tuberculose," *Comoedia* (3 August 1921), p. 1, reprinted in *Écrits II,* p. 31.

3. Duchamp's "lesson" was published in the French avant-garde context by André Breton; see Rrose Sélavy, "Litanie des saints," *Littérature,* new series no. 5 (1 October 1922), p. 7.

4. For more on de Zayas's poem and his dialogue with Picabia, see the work of Willard Bohn, "The Abstract Language of Marius de Zayas," *Art Bulletin* 62, no. 3 (September 1980), pp. 434–452, and "Visualizing Women in *291,*" in *Women in Dada,* ed. Naomi Sawelson-Gorse (Cambridge, Mass.: MIT Press, 1999).

5. *Francis Picabia: Exposition Dada* (Paris: Au Sans Pareil, 16–30 April 1920), n.p.

6. See David Hopkins, "Questioning Dada's Potency: Picabia's 'La Sainte Vierge' and the Dialogue with Duchamp," *Art History* 15, no. 3 (September 1992), pp. 325–326.

7. See Francis M. Naumann, *New York Dada, 1915–1923* (New York: Harry N. Abrams, 1994), p. 80, for a different explanation of the *Ridgefield Gazook*'s parodies and signatures. And for an important account of techniques of erasure and deletion within modernism, see Benjamin Buchloh's essay on Marcel Broodthaers, "Open Letters, Industrial Poems," in *Broodthaers: Writings, Interviews, Photographs,* ed. B. Buchloh (Cambridge, Mass.: MIT Press, 1988).

8. In addition to this wordplay, Benjamin Buchloh once pointed out to me that Man Ray's title also strangely prefigures Duchamp's signature "R. Mutt" on the readymade *Fountain* two years later. The best essay on the crossing of the verbal and the visual in Picabia's *La Sainte-Vierge* is Jean-Gérard Lapacherie, "Tache: Écriture? Figuration? À propos de 'La Sainte Vierge' de Francis Picabia," *Mélusine* (special issue: Lisible-Visible), no. 12 (1991), pp. 123–128.

9. I am summarizing some of the positions of, first, William Camfield, in his important monograph *Francis Picabia: His Art, Life, and Times,* pp. 141–142; David Hopkins, "Questioning Dada's Potency," pp. 317–333; and Elizabeth Legge, "Thirteen Ways of Looking at a Virgin: Francis

Picabia's *La Sainte Vierge*," *Word & Image* 12, no. 2 (April–June 1996), pp. 218–242. The characterization of *La Sainte-Vierge* as "incontinent" comes from Legge.

10. Louis Aragon, "À quoi pensez-vous," *Écrits nouveaux* (August–September 1921), p. 150, cited in Michel Sanouillet, *Francis Picabia et 391,* vol. 2 (Paris: Eric Losfeld, 1966), p. 115.

11. Camfield notes the existence in Picabia's archives of an anonymous "series of Rorschach-like ink blots," in *Francis Picabia: His Art, Life, and Times,* p. 142, note 25. The eight ink stains include drips and splatters of ink as well as inscriptions of Picabia's name blurred into indecipherability, and other drawn and written elements blotted by folding the individual paper sheets. Each has been inscribed with a title, like a series of jokes: "Francis Picabia au ciel," "Francis Picabia en enfer," "Francis Picabia en accident d'automobile," "Francis Picabia à la mer," "Francis Picabia en Turquie," "Francis Picabia à voyage," "Francis Picabia aux courses de taureaux," and "Picabia à la montagne." In the summer of 2001, I inquired of librarians in the Doucet about the existence of these ink stains. Looking at them with me, they were able to identify convincingly the handwriting as that of Louis Aragon. I would like to thank Jean-Luc Berthommier of the Doucet and, for his orthography assistance, Yann Sordet of the Réserve of the Bilbiothèque Sainte-Geneviève. Since this (informal) attribution, the director of the Doucet, Yves Peyré, has reproduced one of these ink stains, see "Dada à Doucet," *Les Cahiers du Musée national d'art moderne* 88 (summer 2004), p. 113.

12. Louis Aragon, "Challenge to Painting," in *Surrealists on Art,* ed. Lucy R. Lippard (Englewood Cliffs, N.J.: Prentice-Hall, 1970), p. 42.

13. Tristan Tzara, "Une Nuit d'Échecs Gras," *391* 14 (November 1920), p. 4.

14. That the "inimitable" and the condition of pastiche travel together in Picabia's work as an opposed pair has been indirectly suggested in a different way by Yve-Alain Bois, through a comparison to Joyce's *Ulysses,* in *Picabia* (Paris: Flammarion, 1975), p. 7.

15. To my knowledge, the drawing was rediscovered and published for the first time only with the important exhibition of Picabia's work in Barcelona in 1995 (the paper version is now in the collection of Paul Destribats, Paris). See note 33 below. No one has thought to connect the drawing to the March 1920 distribution of *La Sainte-Vierge.* The major monographs on Picabia's work, those of William Camfield and Maria Lluïsa Borràs (*Francis Picabia* [New York: Rizzoli, 1985]), make no mention of either version of *La jeune fille;* only in Michel Sanouillet's original history of the Paris Dada movement is the work given passing mention, along with Éluard's magazine *Proverbe.* See Sanouillet, *Dada à Paris,* p. 224.

16. Sanouillet, *Francis Picabia et 391,* vol. II, pp. 111–113.

17. Actually, it seems in the end that we can "prove" that *La jeune fille* and *Proverbe* 4 were present at the Maison de l'Oeuvre. In small print on the righthand side of the printed program for the demonstration, we can read a series of announcements for the Dada periodicals that were newly available on March 27, including *Proverbe* 4.

18. This is true of both the reproduction in *Proverbe* and the paper version that once belonged to Tzara. However, when this chapter was first drafted (in 1998), the only reproduction of the latter drawing that existed was photographed on a black ground, which made the work appear to be a drawing of a black circle, not an actual hole such as exists clearly in the magazine version of the work. Again, see note 33 below. This misperception was clarified by the paper version's inclusion in the 2002 retrospective of Picabia's work in Paris, *Francis Picabia: Singulier idéal*.

19. Georges Charbonnier, *Le monologue du peintre* (Paris: Julliard, 1959), p. 136.

20. "Dada philosophe" was published in *Littérature* 13 (May 1920), pp. 5–6. Breton's letter is reprinted in Sanouillet, *Dada à Paris*, pp. 543–544.

21. See Aragon, "Challenge to Painting," p. 49:

> We know that painting vanished so far into his hands that around 1920 the painter contented himself with setting between the framing edge a few threads, which soon seemed to him an exaggerated luxury. The taste for the ephemeral, so contrary to that painter's instinct which makes them brood ignobly over their own products, was so strong in Picabia that he made a picture in chalk on a blackboard expressly *so that* it could be publicly erased.

Aragon, we notice, gets the date of *Danse de Saint-Guy* correct.

22. Georges Ribemont-Dessaignes, "Histoire de Dada," *La Nouvelle Revue Française* 36, no. 213 (June 1931) and 37, no. 214 (July 1931), trans. Ralph Manheim, in *The Dada Painters and Poets* (1951), ed. Robert Motherwell (Cambridge, Mass.: Belknap/Harvard, 1988), p. 120.

23. The following narration of the Dada manifestations of 1920 has been synthesized from various sources, most significantly from the account in Sanouillet, *Dada à Paris*, pp. 148–188. But see too Georges Hugnet, "L'esprit dada dans la peinture," *Cahiers d'Art* (1932 and 1934), trans. Ralph Manheim, in *The Dada Painters and Poets*, pp. 123–196; Hugnet, *L'aventure Dada, 1916–1922* (1957) (Paris: Seghers, 1971), pp. 77–122; Georges Ribemont-Dessaignes, "Histoire de dada," pp. 99–120; Ribemont-Dessaignes, *Déjà jadis ou du mouvement Dada à l'espace abstrait* (Paris: Julliard, 1958); and Germaine Everling, *L'anneau de Saturne* (Paris: Fayard, 1970).

24. Tzara explained the tactic as an ironic answer to his own notoriety: "An attempt was made to give a futuristic interpretation to this act, but all I wanted to convey was simply that my presence on the stage, the sight of my face and my movements, ought to satisfy people's curiosity and that anything I might have said really had no importance." Tristan Tzara, "Memoirs of Dadaism," translated in Edmund Wilson, *Axel's Castle* (1931) (New York: Macmillan, 1991), p. 304.

25. Louis Aragon, "La grande Saison Dada 1921," *Projet d'histoire littéraire contemporaine* (1923) (Paris: Gallimard, 1994), p. 103. Breton made a similar point in the lecture he gave on the night before the opening of Picabia's 1922 Galerie Dalmau exhibition in Barcelona: "It would not be a bad idea to reinstitute the laws of the Terror for things of the mind." See Breton, "Characteristics of the Modern Evolution and What It Consists Of," *The Lost Steps,* trans. Mark Polizzotti (Lincoln and London: University of Nebraska Press, 1996), p. 122. The public announcement for the planned events of Dada's 1921 season had an explicitly Revolutionary tone: "Visites-Salon Dada-Congrès-Commémorations-Opéras-Plébiscites-Réquisitions-Mise en accusation et Jugements"). Aragon tells us that the more parodic elements of the program ("Dada Operas" and a "Salon," for example) came from Tzara; the explicitly political events were the contributions of the Breton-Aragon wing of the movement. It should be noted that Picabia, at least in name, left the movement at this moment, and because of this program. But Aragon's Revolutionary rhetoric—he is writing in 1923, before his Communist politicization at the end of the 1920s—should be preserved as one element of Paris Dada's ambitions.

26. Again, the best account of this manifestation that we retain is Louis Aragon, "Manifestation du Faubourg," *Projet d'histoire littéraire contemporaine,* pp. 81–86.

27. Picabia, "Manifeste cannibale Dada," *Dadaphone* (*Dada* 7, March 1920), p. 3. Translated as "Cannibal Dada Manifesto" in the English reprint of *Dada Almanach,* ed. Richard Huelsenbeck (London: Atlas Press, 1993), pp. 55–56. Translation modified.

28. Georges Charensol, "Manifestation Dada," *Comoedia* (29 March 1920), p. 2. Cited in Sanouillet, *Dada à Paris,* p. 175. Another contemporary description of Picabia's set and costumes exists; see Gustave Geffroy, "Le Mouvement Dada," *France libre* (3 April 1920), cited in Camfield, *Francis Picabia: His Art, Life, and Times,* p. 143. It seems that Picabia published the inscriptions included in the set as, or at least among, a list of aphorisms; see *Cannibale* 1 (25 April 1920), p. 17.

29. See, for example, Hugnet, *L'aventure Dada,* p. 92.

30. See Duchamp's description in Arturo Schwarz, *The Complete Works of Marcel Duchamp* (New York: Harry N. Abrams, 1969), p. 442.

31. In fact, one should note the recurrence of the pun *de saint*—*dessin* in the title of Picabia's string piece, *Danse de Saint-Guy.*

32. By this moment of 1919, for Duchamp to live in "Picabia's" apartment was to live in fact with Gabrielle Buffet, for whom it seems he had long harbored a deep affection. While she was pregnant with Picabia's child at this time, he had already moved into the apartment of Germaine Everling, his partner during the years of Paris Dada (who was herself also pregnant with Picabia's child—the two women would give birth almost simultaneously in early 1920). Picabia always stayed on very good terms with Buffet, and if we cannot imagine Picabia and Duchamp literally living together in the fall of 1919, they remained in close proximity.

33. These comments come from two essays printed in the important Spanish catalog, *Francis Picabia: Máquinas y Españolas* (Valencia: IVAM, 1995). The first belongs to William Camfield; see his essay "Machinomorphic Designs and Dada, 1915–1921," pp. 175–176. We owe the second observation to Jean-Jacques Lebel, "The Picabia Machine," p. 185. This catalog reproduces the paper version of *Jeune fille* originally from the Tzara collection, but not the *Proverbe* version (though it is mentioned). The catalog was where I first learned of the existence of the two forgotten works. However, the situation was still murky enough ten years ago that Camfield describes the Tzara drawing as a black circle on white paper, as opposed to the real hole in *Proverbe* (a mistake provoked by the way the work had been photographed and reproduced), and Lebel, in connecting *La jeune fille* to Picabia's later "target" and "sexual bull's eye" pieces, misdates the drawing to 1922 in the process. I develop this connection of *La jeune fille* to the later 1922 works in chapter 4.

34. The painting was shown in a group exhibition in December 1919 at the Cirque d'Hiver in Paris, where, under pressure, Picabia was forced to change the work's title to *Muscles brillants.* On the episode of the Cirque d'Hiver, see Camfield, *Francis Picabia: His Art, Life, and Times,* p. 132. Picabia reproduced the painting with its original title in *391* 8 (February 1919), p. 7. The title reappeared in 1920 in Picabia's poem *Unique eunuque* (Paris: Éditions Allia, 1992), p. 39, where we read: "Demi-femme demi-chien demi-bière / Pine mate / Et Vagin brillant."

35. This issue has become crucial to recent readings of the work of Marcel Duchamp, especially: Rosalind Krauss, *The Optical Unconscious* (Cambridge, Mass.: MIT Press, 1993), and David Joselit, *Infinite Regress* (Cambridge, Mass.: MIT Press, 1998). Along the model of what Fredric Jameson has termed "cultural revolution," Dada in this respect can perhaps be seen as falling outside a high modernist/capitalist regime of repression, predicting, instead, a later condition—the "late" capitalist dynamic of deterritorialized flow. André Breton, speaking in the 1950s, once commented on this shift in similar terms:

The sickness that the world exhibits today differs from the one it exhibited in the 1920s. In France, for example, the mind was threatened back then with coagulation, whereas today it's threatened with dissolution. All kinds of major fissures, which affect the structure of the globe as well as human consciousness, had not yet appeared (I'm thinking of the implacable antagonism between the two "blocs," of totalitarian methods, of the atomic bomb). It's perfectly obvious that such a situation calls for different reactions from today's youth than the ones provoked in us, in our youth, by *another* situation. (*Conversations: The Autobiography of Surrealism* [New York: Marlowe, 1993], p. 174)

36. The artist Jason Simon was the first to force my attention to the possibility that the inscription on *La jeune fille* in fact could be French slang for a "cock ring." I wish to thank my friend Carl Ghazarossian for his joyous help with all matters of colloquial French.

37. The *Portrait d'une jeune fille américaine dans l'état de nudité* has received an iconographic reading that identifies its subject as Agnes Meyer, a member like de Zayas and Haviland of the *291* group; see William Innes Homer, "Picabia's *Jeune fille américaine dans l'état de nudité* and Her Friends," pp. 110–115. Perceived as too narrow, Homer's reading has recently been challenged by Elizabeth Hutton Turner, "*La jeune fille américaine* and the Dadaist Impulse," in *Women in Dada*, pp. 4–17, which attaches the work to a larger discursive concern in European mass culture of the time with the figure of *la jeune fille américaine*. I would suggest that both readings are too narrow when one sees the entire series of the *fille* within which the work in question functions.

38. This is the reading proposed by Caroline A. Jones, in her excellent essay "The Sex of the Machine: Mechanomorphic Art, New Women, and Francis Picabia's Neurasthenic Cure," in *Picturing Science, Producing Art,* ed. Caroline A. Jones and Peter Galison (New York and London: Routledge, 1998), pp. 145–180. Jones explores the radical ambiguity of Picabia's gender position, both as a "producer" and within the works themselves. It should be noted, as Jones does, that the *fille née sans mère* was Picabia's code word for the machine, a gendered nomination to be sure, but not actually a represented woman at all. See chapter 4 for my own reading of this phrase.

39. Caroline Jones makes this claim in "The Sex of the Machine."

40. Francis Picabia, "Manifeste Dada," *391* 12 (March 1920), p. 1.

41. Paul Dermée, "Premier et dernier rapport du secrétaire de la Section d'Or: Excommuniés," *391* 12, p. 6.

42. Picabia cites and mocks Rosenberg's 1920 *Cubisme et tradition* in *391* 12, p. 2.

---

43. Rosalind Krauss, "In the Name of Picasso," *The Originality of the Avant-Garde and Other Modernist Myths,* p. 38. The modernist readings of collage to which Krauss reacts include the essays of Clement Greenberg, "The Pasted-Paper Revolution" (1958), in *Clement Greenberg: Collected Essays and Criticism,* vol. 4, ed. John O'Brian (Chicago: University of Chicago Press, 1993), pp. 61–66; and "Collage" (1959), *Art and Culture* (Boston: Beacon Press, 1961), pp. 70–83. For an important rereading of the Greenberg texts on collage, see Lisa Florman, "The Flattening of 'Collage,'" *October* 102 (fall 2002), pp. 59–86.

44. I should clarify my use of the term "procedure of loss," and the different inflection that I give it vis-à-vis the reading of collage by Rosalind Krauss. This difference can be summarized by a move that I sense in this historical moment from a Cubist concern with "structure" to a Dada insistence on "process." For Krauss, collage inaugurates, within the heart of the supposed modernist project of perceptual presence, a structural regime of representation—a regime whereby pictorial attributes ("light," "depth," "flatness," "ground") are figured in the face of their literal absence, through arbitrary, differential pictorial signs that can be semiologically compared with the operations of language. My focus on absence and loss is not so much structural as it is procedural, and perhaps even at times phenomenological. Krauss's semiological understanding of absence, however—the absence, in the end, of the referent, the divorce between signifier and signified—depends on the literal, procedural actions on which I focus, and I think that our two accounts are deeply compatible. For an articulation of these terms that argues for an absolute distinction between the critical use of absence and loss, see Dominick LaCapra, "Trauma, Absence, Loss," *Critical Inquiry* 25, no. 4 (summer 1999), pp. 696–727.

45. See, for example, Yve-Alain Bois's gloss on Picabia's famous, insolent statement, published on the cover of *391* 8 (February 1919), "J'ai horreur de la peinture de Cézanne, elle m'embête" (I detest Cézanne's painting, it bores me), which Bois reads as a testament to the artist's fundamental incomprehension of modernist form as it developed from Cézanne through Cubism. Bois, *Picabia,* pp. 22, 73.

46. For readings of Picasso's collage from which I have benefited here, see Christine Poggi, *In Defiance of Painting: Cubism, Futurism, and the Invention of Collage* (New Haven: Yale University Press, 1992), pp. 148–152, and Rosalind Krauss, *The Picasso Papers,* pp. 56–64.

47. I should acknowledge here the methodological and historical parallels between my project and the recent work of Pamela Lee on Gordon Matta-Clark. Lee's exploration of the Conceptualist critique of minimalism parallels the earlier Dada critique of Cubism that I trace here. See Lee, *Object to Be Destroyed: The Work of Gordon Matta-Clark* (Cambridge, Mass.: MIT Press, 2000).

48. Michael Fried, *Three American Painters* (Cambridge, Mass.: Fogg Art Museum, 1965), pp. 10–23.

49. See Fried, *Three American Painters,* pp. 8, 25. Needless to say, Dada falls outside such an understanding of the logic of modernism, a fact about which Fried is explicit at the conclusion of his essay; see p. 47.

50. Walter Benjamin, "The Work of Art in the Age of Mechanical Reproduction," *Illuminations,* trans. Harry Zohn (New York: Schocken Books, 1988), pp. 217–251. For an important analysis of Benjamin's concept of aura in the context of his other essays, see Miriam Hansen, "Benjamin, Cinema, and Experience: 'The Blue Flower in the Land of Technology,'" *New German Critique* 40 (winter 1987), pp. 179–224.

51. On Bataille's interest in Dada, one should consult Denis Hollier, *Against Architecture: The Writings of Georges Bataille* (Cambridge, Mass.: MIT Press, 1989), pp. 77, 183–184, and, for a comparison of the Dada manifestos of Tristan Tzara with Bataille's notion of heterology, pp. 89–91. And if the connection of Bataille and Picabia seems anachronistic at best, tenuous at worst, such a connection can be made intellectually through parallel readings of Nietzsche—Bataille's key philosophical reference point, and, by all accounts, the only thinker who ever meant anything to Picabia. Hélène Seckel briefly compares Bataille and Picabia in her essay "Don Juan Unique Eunuque," in Martin and Seckel, *Francis Picabia.*

52. Georges Bataille, "The Notion of Expenditure," *Visions of Excess: Selected Writings, 1927–1939* (Minneapolis: University of Minnesota Press, 1985), p. 119.

53. Georges Bataille, *The Accursed Share,* vols. 2/3 (New York: Zone Books, 1993), p. 215.

54. On Bataille's reading of Hegel, see especially Jacques Derrida, "From Restricted to General Economy: A Hegelianism without Reserve," *Writing and Difference* (Chicago: University of Chicago Press, 1978). One should also consult Yve-Alain Bois's entry "Dialectic," in Bois and Krauss, *Formless: A User's Guide* (New York: Zone Books, 1997).

55. Michel Foucault indicated as much in the very title of his major essay on Bataille; see "A Preface to Transgression," *Language, Counter-Memory, Practice* (Ithaca: Cornell University Press, 1977), especially p. 33: "Perhaps one day it [the experience of transgression] will seem as decisive for our culture, as much a part of its soil, as the experience of contradiction was at an earlier time for dialectical thought. But in spite of so many scattered signs, the language in which transgression will find its space and the illumination of its being lies almost entirely in the future."

56. Hollier, *Against Architecture,* p. 97. See too Michel Foucault, "Maurice Blanchot: The Thought from Outside," *Foucault/Blanchot* (New York: Zone Books, 1987), and, on the transgression–dialectics divide, Michèle H. Richman, *Reading Georges Bataille: Beyond the Gift* (Baltimore: Johns Hopkins University Press, 1982).

57. The most important recent extension of Bataille's notion of *désoeuvrement* is Jean-Luc Nancy, "La communauté désoeuvrée," trans. Peter Conner, in *The Inoperative Community* (Minneapolis: University of Minnesota Press, 1991).

58. Theodor Adorno, *Minima Moralia: Reflections from Damaged Life* (London: Verso, 1974), p. 151.

59. Roland Barthes, "The Third Meaning," *The Responsibility of Forms* (Berkeley: University of California Press, 1985), p. 58.

60. Picabia cited Ingres's dictum in one of his many attacks on the French postwar "return to order." See Picabia, "Académisme," *Littérature,* new series no. 9 (1 February–1 March 1923), p. 5, reprinted in *Écrits II,* p. 107.

61. Georges Bataille, *Oeuvres Complètes* (Paris: Gallimard, 1971–1988), vol. 2, p. 419, cited in Hollier, *Against Architecture,* pp. 67, 129.

62. Georges Bataille, *Inner Experience,* trans. Leslie A. Boldt (Albany: State University of New York Press, 1988), p. 145.

63. Ibid., p. 16.

64. Georges Ribemont-Dessaignes, "Francis Picabia," *L'esprit nouveau* 1 (October 1920), pp 108–110, cited in Camfield, *Francis Picabia: His Art, Life, and Times,* p. 144.

65. Bataille, *Inner Experience,* p. 68.

66. I refer to the model of Dada's relationship to drawing that has been explored in the work of Molly Nesbit: "Ready-made Originals: The Duchamp Model," *October* 37 (summer 1986), pp. 53–64, and "The Language of Industry," in *The Definitively Unfinished Marcel Duchamp,* ed. Thierry de Duve (Cambridge, Mass.: MIT Press, 1991).

67. See Tristan Tzara, "Préface," in Picabia, *Unique eunuque,* p. 14, translated by Barbara Wright as "Francis Picabia, 'Pensées sans language,' " in Tzara, *Seven Dada Manifestos and Lampisteries* (New York: Calder Publications, 1992). Translation modified.

CHAPTER 2   THE ARTWORK CAUGHT BY THE TAIL: DADA PAINTING

1. Tristan Tzara, "Dada Manifesto 1918," *Dada* 3 (December 1918), in *Seven Dada Manifestoes and Lampisteries,* p. 11.

2. Francis Picabia, "Manifeste Cannibale Dada," *Dadaphone* (*Dada* 7, March 1920), p. 3.

3. Louis Aragon, *Projet d'histoire littéraire contemporain,* p. 105.

4. The Auric photograph is just to the right of the painting's center. The faded, blank Chenal photograph has been attached by a diagrammatic line to her first and last name on either side of the lost image; in this it evokes Picabia's *Chapeau de paille?,* 1921, a work that did concern Chenal, on which see chapter 4. Given its placement, the photograph may be the victim of a gesture that seems to have caused the fading of both Duchamp's inscription and the writer Roland Dorgelès's short poem below it (as well as the additions of lesser-known signers such as the French-Brazilian pianist Magda "Magdadada" Tagliaferro). It seems that liquid—a drink?— was thrown at the painting just left of center. This fading does not seem to be the fault of the ink or paint used, one peculiarity of which is that almost all the male signers wrote in black, and all the female signers in various shades of green, from emerald to aquamarine (the women's inscriptions thus appear lighter in black-and-white reproductions of the work). Picabia signed the work in red, highlighted with black and cream.

5. I mean this term to evoke the description of Georges Bataille and the later *Documents* group as "dissident Surrealists." William Camfield uses the term "dissident Dadaists" to describe the group that coalesced around Picabia in the summer of 1921 with the publication of *Le Pilhaou-Thibaou,* a special issue of *391* (no. 15); see Camfield, *Francis Picabia: His Art, Life, and Times,* p. 165. Picabia alienated more than his fellow Dadaists with this magazine. See for example the reaction of Nicolas Beauduin, editor of *La vie des lettres,* a former ally of Picabia's: "This magazine is abominable. . . . to push forward, yes, but not like these people. . . . It's bad and it's dirty." Cited in Arnauld Pierre, "The 'Confrontation of Modern Values': A Moral History of Dada in Paris," *The Dada Seminars,* pp. 251–252.

6. In a well-known photograph by Man Ray of Duchamp and Joseph Stella, this same photograph hangs directly above Duchamp's close-shaven head, seeming to fuse with Duchamp's visage, though reversed in direction, valence, and gender. If one looks closely at the photograph on *L'oeil cacodylate,* it becomes evident that the anonymous image has been pasted over a prior inscription or signature, beginning in "PE" and ending perhaps with a faded "Y."

7. On the Dorgelès episode of 1910, see David Cottington, *Cubism in the Shadow of War: The Avant-Garde and Politics in Paris 1905–1914* (New Haven: Yale University Press, 1998),

pp. 9–11, and D. Grojnowski, "L'Ane qui peint avec sa queue: Boronali au Salon des Indépendants," *Actes de recherche en sciences sociales* 88 (June 1991), pp. 41–47, cited in Cottington, *Cubism in the Shadow,* p. 198.

8. Louise Norton, "Buddha of the Bathroom," *The Blind Man* 2 (May 1917), p. 5.

9. Man Ray, cited by Margery Rex: "'Dada' Will Get You if You Don't Watch Out: It Is on Its Way Here," *New York Evening Journal* (January 29, 1921), reprinted in *New York Dada,* ed. R. Kuenzli (New York: Willis Locker and Owens, 1986), p. 141.

10. Camfield, *Francis Picabia: His Art, Life, and Times,* p. 143. See too Camfield's account of the display of *Danse de Saint-Guy* in 1922, which may have been intended as part of an assemblage that Picabia then called not a "living painting" but a "living sculpture," including actual mice (perhaps explaining the later change of the work's title to *Tabac-Rat*). See Camfield, *Francis Picabia: His Art, Life, and Times,* p. 173, and Picabia's own account in the essay "L'oeil cacodylate," *Comoedia* (23 November 1921), p. 2, reprinted in *Écrits II,* pp. 37–38.

11. The work is lost, but the actual surface could be cardboard from the surviving image. Picabia often used cardboard—cheap and evidently disposable—as a ground for his work; see for instance *Universal Prostitution* from the Yale University Société Anonyme collection.

12. The reading of these names as "signatures" gains credence through Picabia's strange placement of each name along one of the four borders of the work's surface, this border being the traditional location of the signature in painting, part of the medium's supplementary framing apparatus—and thus it seems no coincidence, too, that the four inscriptions around the monkey in *Natures mortes* form a linguistic instantiation of a visual frame, a frame this piece otherwise lacked. *Natures mortes,* then, insists on what we could call its "discursive frame" rather than a physical one

13. Francis Picabia, *Unique eunuque,* p. 40. English translation: "Germans the detest I / War the during that reason that for is it / Possible as away far as remained I / Now I am going to try and see them from up close / Before like. . . ."

14. Susan Rubin Suleiman, "Feminist Intertextuality and the Laugh of the Mother," *Subversive Intent: Gender, Politics, and the Avant-Garde* (Cambridge, Mass.: Harvard University Press, 1990), p. 152.

15. Ibid., pp. 152–153. Suleiman's brilliant reading of Duchamp's image claims that it confirms, and does not deny, the Oedipal scenario and the Law of the Father. For an anti-Oedipal

reading of Duchamp's project that relies on the work of Gilles Deleuze, see David Joselit, "Marcel Duchamp's *Monte Carlo Bond* Machine," *October* 59 (winter 1992), pp. 8–26, and Joselit's *Infinite Regress*. David Hopkins develops the importance of the Phallic Mother image for Dada in his essay "Men Before the Mirror: Duchamp, Man Ray, and Masculinity," *Art History* 21, no. 3 (September 1998), pp. 303–323; and Caroline Jones considers its specific relevance for Picabia's mechanomorphs in "The Sex of the Machine."

16. If all these potential penises weren't enough, Picabia appended a Dada manifesto to Duchamp's "Tableau Dada" that commenced with the suggestion that the Cubists want to drown Dada by jerking off on it: "Ils veulent vider la neige de leur pipe pour recouvrir Dada." See Picabia, "Manifeste Dada," *391* 12 (March 1920), p. 1. On this manifesto and Duchamp's *L.H.O.O.Q.* as a contestation of the language of the advertisement, see Molly Nesbit, "The Rat's Ass," *October* 56 (spring 1991), pp. 6–20.

17. See Patrick de Haas, "'J'ai résolu de ne jamais m'occuper de cinema,'" *Man Ray, directeur du mauvais movies* (Paris: Éditions du Centre Pompidou, 1997), pp. 10–11, 23, for a full documentation of the trope of shaving and the erasure of hair in Dada.

18. The key section for Goux's reflections is essentially the whole of Part I of *Capital*, entitled "Commodities and Money." See Karl Marx, *Capital*, vol. 1, trans. Samuel Moore and Edward Aveling (New York: International Publishers, 1967), pp. 35–145.

19. Jean-Joseph Goux, "Numismatics: An Essay in Theoretical Numismatics," trans. Jennifer Gage, in *Symbolic Economies: After Marx and Freud* (Ithaca: Cornell University Press, 1990), p. 11. Hereafter cited in the text as "N." First published in 1968, "Numismatics" was collected in Goux's *Freud, Marx: Economie et symbolique* (Paris: Seuil, 1973); the theory was then extended in *Les iconoclastes* (Paris: Seuil, 1978).

20. Marx, *Capital*, vol. 1, p. 63.

21. Ibid., p. 62.

22. These last citations are from Marx, *Capital*, vol. 1, p. 64.

23. The word that Goux uses in the original French text and the word in Duchamp's title *(Trois stoppages étalon)* are the same: *étalon*. At this point in his text, Goux provides an etymology: *étalon* or "standard," as in "gold standard," is derived from the Picard word *estel*, meaning "stake, pole, pale, boundary marker" (N, p. 21). David Joselit's reading of Duchamp's Dada work takes up the issue of the standard in terms of a challenge to measurement, or "mensuration"; see *Infinite Regress*. Measurement is one of the three key roles of the general equivalent that Goux details;

the focus of my book, however, lies more with the second and third of these roles: circulation and the reserve.

24. Denis Hollier, *Against Architecture,* p. 124.

25. For a different account of the relations between the sexual and economic spheres, see Pierre Klossowski, *La monnaie vivante* (1970) (Paris: Éditions Joëlle Losfeld, 1994).

26. See Georges Bataille, "The Notion of Expenditure," *Visions of Excess,* and *The Accursed Share: An Essay on General Economy,* 3 vols. (New York: Zone Books, 1991 and 1993).

27. In proposing this as a Dada strategy, I am following Hollier's characterization of Bataille's later "science" of heterology. See Hollier, *Against Architecture,* pp. 127–129.

28. It might, however, be more accurate to describe Duchamp's fictive check—using a phrase explored most effectively in the work of Rosalind Krauss—as a paradoxical "copy without an original," a simulacrum. *Tzanck Check* exists as a copy for which no model exists, a condition that would, ironically (that is to say, dialectically), render the piece, as Duchamp labels it, an "original." I extend this condition to Picabia's mechanomorphs in chapter 4.

29. Dalia Judovitz, "Art and Economics: From the Urinal to the Bank," *Unpacking Duchamp: Art in Transit* (Berkeley: University of California Press, 1995), p. 168. See also Peter Read, "The *Tzanck Check* and Related Works by Marcel Duchamp," in *Marcel Duchamp: Artist of the Century,* ed. R. Kuenzli and F. Naumann (Cambridge, Mass.: MIT Press, 1989), pp. 95–105, and David Joselit's *Infinite Regress.*

30. Jean Baudrillard, "The Art Auction: Sign Exchange and Sumptuary Value," *For a Critique of the Political Economy of the Sign* (St. Louis: Telos, 1981), pp. 121–122.

31. For biographical information on Tzanck, see Read, pp. 96–99.

32. For the statement to Arensberg, see Read, "The *Tzanck Check,*" p. 100; for Cabanne, see Pierre Cabanne, *Dialogues with Marcel Duchamp* (New York: Da Capo, 1971), p. 63.

33. Given to Daniel Tzanck in gratitude for his dental services, and in lieu of payment, Duchamp's check contains some typical bilingual puns. As Peter Read points out, "The Teeth's Loan and Trust Company" highlights the importance of "trust" to the reciprocity of the structure of the gift; "Teeth" in French, *dents,* homophonically suggests *dons,* or, precisely, "gifts." See Read, "The *Tzanck Check,*" p. 100. On the structure of gift—as opposed to commodity—exchange, see the classic account of Marcel Mauss, *The Gift: The Form and Reason for Exchange in Archaic Societies* (1925) (New York: W. W. Norton, 1990).

34. On Picabia's relation to Ingres and the return to order, see Arnauld Pierre, "Picabia contre le retour à l'ordre," *Francis Picabia: Les Nus et la méthode* (Grenoble: Musée de Grenoble, 1998), pp. 8–19.

35. Picabia, "Trompettes de Jericho," *Comoedia* (19 January 1922), reprinted in *Écrits II,* p. 51.

36. The theory recounted here is developed in Goux, *The Coiners of Language,* trans. Jennifer Gage (Norman: University of Oklahoma Press, 1994). Hereafter cited in the text as "CL." My argument from this point on extends and modifies the use to which Rosalind Krauss puts Goux's general theory in *The Picasso Papers.*

37. The United States placed the phrase "In God We Trust" upon its dollar bills only in the 1950s. See Goux, *The Coiners of Language,* p. 134.

38. Goux, "Figurative Standards: Gold and the Phallus," *Symbolic Economies,* p. 117. Goux has directly addressed the applicability of his theory to pictorial abstraction; see "The Unrepresentable," *Symbolic Economies,* pp. 168–197.

39. If the ascendance of a regime of the token sign requires a "vast investment in the newly enlarged power of the Law," is it indeed the Law that is ultimately *affirmed* in (at least some of) Picabia's practice? Is this a workable definition of his engagement with parody and ultimately pastiche? Must we temper our claims for Dada's engagement with what Bataille would call "expenditure" or transgression, seeing instead the ways in which such transgressions continually affirm the Law that they claim to disrupt? Must we finally see Picabia's parodies as affirming the Law of painting (for he would never cease being a painter)? But what does it mean to affirm a Law that, as Goux puts it, "guarantees value only as *empty value,*" enforces a value that "is at bottom an *absence* of value"? It seems, if anything, that it is this paradoxical Law that Picabia's parodies and pastiches could be seen to affirm.

40. Picabia, "Instantanéisme," *Comoedia* (21 November 1924), p. 4, reprinted in *Écrits II,* p. 159.

41. Duchamp would have been particularly sensitive to the onanistic implications of such an activity, as was Sigmund Freud; see "Dostoevsky and Parricide," *Character and Culture* (New York: Collier Books, 1963), p. 292.

42. Fredric Jameson, "Culture and Finance Capital," *The Cultural Turn: Selected Writings on the Postmodern, 1983–1998* (London: Verso, 1998). I have explored the relevance of the concept of finance capital for recent developments in contemporary art in a book-length essay, *Gerard Byrne: Books, Magazines, and Newspapers* (New York: Lukas & Sternberg Press, 2003).

43. For a different articulation of Duchamp's relation to "finance," see Thierry de Duve, "Marcel Duchamp, or the *Phynancier* of Modern Life," *October* 52 (spring 1990), pp. 61–74.

44. Walter Benjamin, "Some Motifs in Baudelaire," *Charles Baudelaire: A Lyric Poet in the Era of High Capitalism* (London: Verso, 1973), pp. 134–138.

45. See the letters written by Duchamp to Jacques Doucet in *The Writings of Marcel Duchamp,* pp. 187–188.

46. This is the crucial demonstration of David Joselit's *Infinite Regress.*

47. [*The Monte Carlo Bond*], in *The Little Review* 10 (1924–1925), reprinted in Sanouillet and Peterson, *Writings,* p. 185.

48. Baudrillard, "Gesture and Signature: Semiurgy in Contemporary Art," *For a Critique of the Political Economy of the Sign,* p. 105.

49. Picabia, *Le petit bleu* (20 November 1921), reprinted in *Écrits II,* p. 36.

50. Rosalind Krauss, "The Object Caught by the Heel," *Making Mischief: Dada Invades New York* (New York: Whitney Museum of American Art, 1996), p. 250.

51. Ibid.

52. It should be noted that one of the photographs that Krauss brings into her account is the Man Ray image at the center of Picabia's *L'oeil cacodylate*. This photograph also occupies a crucial position in Krauss's initial work on Surrealist photography and Bataille's notion of the *informe*; see "Corpus Delicti," *L'Amour fou: Photography and Surrealism* (New York: Abbeville, 1985).

53. Krauss, "The Object Caught by the Heel," p. 251. Krauss here relies on an essay by Denis Hollier that explores the later critical project of Bataille at the moment of the publication of the review *Documents.* Inasmuch as my book presents a Bataillean reading of Dada, Hollier's argument subtends my reflections here as well. See Hollier, "The Use-Value of the Impossible," *October* 60 (spring 1992).

54. Baudrillard, "Gesture and Signature," p. 102.

55. See Camfield, *Francis Picabia: His Art, Life and Times,* pp. 160–170, for an account of these events. Picabia attributes his absence during the 1921 Dada season to his illness in "Les Dadas visitent Paris," *Comoedia* (14 April 1921), p. 2, reprinted in *Écrits II,* p. 12. He plays allusively on the condition of an illness of the eye in the text "Zona," *La vie des lettres* (July 1921), pp. 512–513, reprinted in *Écrits II,* pp. 20–21.

56. Picabia, "Mr. Picabia Breaks with the Dadas," pp. 145–146. Originally published in *Comoedia* (11 May 1921).

57. See *Littérature* 19 (May 1921), p. 24. Dawn Ades connects the advertisement to the painting in *Dada and Surrealism Reviewed* (London: Arts Council of Great Britain, 1978), pp. 163–164. The full advertisement read: "SONT PRIÉS DE SE PRÉSENTER AU SANS PAREIL: L'anonyme qui écrit NON sur les affiches des emprunts / L'inconnu qui signe Edith Cavell les incriptions des urinoirs / L'artiste qui dessine des compléments aux réclames pour dentifrices / L'auteur de la phrase ON A PRÉFÉRÉ LA GUERRE À L'ESPERANTO / L'auteur de la phrase LA FRANCE JE LA ___ / Les écrivains de bonne volonté désireux de collaborer au supplément mural de LITTÉRATURE. BONNE RÉCOMPENSES."

58. In addition to the opposition of abstraction and the readymade, this transition in Picabia's work from the explosive parody of *Natures mortes* to the sign logic of *L'oeil cacodylate* might be narrated in terms of the linkage explored earlier between "parodic tokens" and "true signs."

59. Picabia, "L'oeil cacodylate," p. 37. My translation; emphasis added.

60. Ibid., pp. 37–38.

61. The complexity inherent in any attempt to "read" the work as a whole approximates the hermetic structures of accumulation characteristic of contemporaneous photomontages by the Berlin Dadaists. This difficulty—a sort of phenomenological opacity—must be included in any account of Picabia's specific deployment of the readymade.

62. This inscription appears on Picabia's *Le double monde (LHOOQ),* 1919, in somewhat reversed order: "Que les malades / Dieu n'a jamais guéri." *Le double monde* was one of the two paintings that Picabia submitted to the Salon des Indépendants of 1921, immediately before beginning "work" on *L'oeil cacodylate.*

63. Jean Cocteau, "La guérison de Picabia," *Le Pilhaou-Thibaou* (July 1921), p. 11. Gabrielle Buffet's text was appended to the end of Cocteau's mocking, anti-Dada tract. Typical of Picabia's dissidence, however, he also appended lines to Cocteau's tract that mocked the poet in turn.

64. In her memoirs, Germaine Everling recounts the story of this eye problem (sometimes described as an attack of shingles), claiming it arose for Picabia in the wake of a visit to Isadora Duncan's home, and that he was unable to paint because of it. She tells the story of the making of *L'oeil cacodylate,* however, *before* detailing the eye problem and fails to link the two events. She does provide, however, a useful portrait of the Sunday salon that coalesced in her apartment around Picabia—which, using a phrase of Pierre de Massot's, she doesn't hesitate to compare

to the famous Tuesday salons of Mallarmé. As almost all of the habitués of this salon appear as signers of *L'oeil cacodylate,* one imagines that the painting was available for signing in 1921 during the course of such weekly gatherings, rather than literally at Picabia's "sickbed." See Everling, "Les 'dimanches' de la rue Émile-Augier," *L'anneau de Saturne,* pp. 114–120.

65. Along these lines, the painting did inspire a New Year's Eve party planned by Picabia with Marthe Chenal at the end of 1921, the Reveillon Cacodylate, where the canvas was again displayed and signed by various guests. The work hung for decades in a Parisian brasserie now off the Champs-Elysées (it was originally closer to the Place de la Concorde), linked to Cocteau and his circle—the Boeuf sur le Toit. The model of collectivity and sociability implicit in this painting, however aristocratic, warrants further exploration, and comparison to other Dada "social spaces" such as Kurt Schwitters' *Merzbau.* On Dada and the loss of collectivity, and its "public display of privateness," see Leah Dickerman, "Dada's Solipsism," *Documents* 19 (fall 2000), pp. 16–19.

66. "Dieu nous aide et fait pousser le caca": Picabia printed this saying on the cover of *391* 14, just above the reproduction of his *Dessin Dada.*

67. Cacodylate also contains the root of the word for "dilate," producing a potential reading close to *caca-dilaté;* and it suggests a further French word used humorously, namely *cacochyme,* which means "doddery" or "doddering."

68. For these comments, see Jean-Jacques Lebel, "The Picabia Machine," p. 177.

69. "Je m'appelle maintenant tu": This is a "Dada proverb" by Tzara, published in 1920 on the front page of *Proverbe* 3 (March 1920), and simultaneously as part of a poem published in *391* 12 (March 1920), p. 2.

70. Some of the signers were indeed rather young, such as Michel Corlin, who signed *Le cuculin*—a play on the words *cul* and *cucul,* or "corny"—Germaine Everling's son by her first marriage.

71. A guide to the identity of the many signers of *L'oeil cacodylate* has been produced; see "Petit Lexique Picabesque '1921,'" in *Francis Picabia: Chapeau de paille?* (Paris: Galerie Louis Carré, 1964). More recently, a passionate and quite lovely "blog" has appeared on this subject, authored by Fabrice Lefaix and entitled "Au temps de *L'Oeil Cacodylate*: Panorama Bio-Icono-Bibliographique des soixante signataires de *L'Oeil Cacodylate* de Francis Picabia (1921)," www.dadaparis.blogspot.com, accessed on July 7, 2006.

72. This could be a forgery, however, and one wonders how many of the signatures on *L'oeil cacodylate* are faked. The Dadaists had proven themselves capable of faking Metzinger's words

before, publishing a mock interview with him on the publication of his friend Albert Gleizes's book on Cubism; see Tzara, "Interview de Jean Metzinger sur le cubisme," *391* 14 (November 1920), p. 8.

73. The form of this inscription can be read as a direct result of Tzara's recent publication, during the summer of 1921, of a theory of Dada's actions upon language. Tzara explicitly defined Dada linguistic innovations as an instantiation of the empty circularity of tautology. See Tzara, "Proverbe Dada," *Proverbe 6/L'Invention* 1 (1 July 1921), n.p.: "Paul Éluard wants to realize a concentration of words, crystallized as if for the people, but void of sense. For example, the definition: '*A proverb is a proverb*' or '*a very proverbial proverb*' [*un proverbe très proverbe*]." Jean Paulhan—whose research on traditional proverbs was the basis for his friend Éluard's decision to call his Dada periodical *Proverbe*—was also important at this moment for a series of essays explicitly developing the theoretical implications of Dada's use of language; see, for example, Paulhan, "Syntaxe," *Proverbe* 1 (1 February 1920), and the three-part essay "Si les mots sont des signes ou Jacob Cow le Pirate," published in *Littérature* 14 (June 1920), 15 (July 1920), and 16 (Sept.–Oct. 1920). A third site of Dada's reflection upon its own linguistic innovations would be Pierre de Massot's forgotten history of avant-garde poetry, *De Mallarmé à 391* (Saint-Raphaël: Bel exemplaire, 1922).

74. Jacques Derrida, "Signature Event Context," *Margins of Philosophy,* trans. Alan Bass (Chicago: University of Chicago Press, 1982), pp. 328–329. See also Rosalind Krauss, "Notes on the Index," pp. 196–209; and her specific theorization of the structure of the index in its form as graffito in *The Optical Unconscious,* pp. 259–266.

75. Krauss, *The Optical Unconscious,* p. 260.

76. The notion of the "ghostwriter," not surprisingly, had a larger resonance within the Paris Dada and early Surrealist context, as collaborative experiments with automatic writing gained importance. Aragon tells us, for example, that the original proposed title for the Dadaist journal *Littérature* was, precisely, *Le Nègre.* See Aragon, *Projet d'histoire littéraire contemporaine,* p. 38.

77. The gesture seems linked to Duchamp's Jura-Paris Road notes of 1912. Long ignored by Dada scholarship, such actions are recuperated for art history by Amelia Jones's work on Dada performance; see "New York Dada: Beyond the Readymade," *The Dada Seminars,* pp. 151–171.

78. *Le Pilhaou-Thibaou* (10 July 1921), p. 6.

79. Much later, after Picabia's death, Duchamp finally completed this pun, inscribing a different version of it on the bottom of a poster for a retrospective exhibit of another key work by Picabia from 1921, the painting *Chapeau de paille? (Straw Hat?).* This painting contained an

inscription that read: *"M. . . . . pour celui qui le regarde!"* Duchamp simply answered Picabia's curse, writing: *". . . et roses pour Fr'en 6 π qu'habillarrose Sélavy."* See Carole Boulbès, *Picabia, le saint masqué* (Paris: Jean-Michel Place, 1998), p. 52.

80. See, for example, Benjamin Buchloh's important distinction between Duchamp's and Picabia's strategies in "Parody and Appropriation in Francis Picabia, Pop, and Sigmar Polke," *Artforum* 20 (March 1982), pp. 28–34.

CHAPTER 3   KEEP SMILING: DADA PHOTOGRAPHY

1. Marcel Duchamp, inscribed in the 1959 exhibition catalog for Man Ray at the ICA London, reprinted in *The Writings of Marcel Duchamp,* p. 165.

2. To decode "Rrose Sélavy" not as *Eros, c'est la vie* but as *Arroser la vie* reduces this difference. "Here's to life," a kind of toast, might be one translation of the latter rendition.

3. The linkage of avant-garde photography with fetishism has long been a part of the literature on Surrealist photography. Rosalind Krauss, for example, sees fetishism as part of the critical project of such images in "Corpus Delicti," pp. 15–114. For a more general linkage of photograph and fetish, see Christian Metz, "Photography and Fetish," in *The Critical Image: Essays on Contemporary Photography,* ed. Carol Squiers (Seattle: Bay Press, 1990), pp. 155–164.

4. See Duchamp's letter to Tristan Tzara (1922?), *The Writings of Marcel Duchamp,* p. 180.

5. Man Ray, *Objets de mon affection* (Paris: Philippe Sers, 1983), p. 20.

6. Man Ray's *New York Dada* has been described as an effort to join forces with Dada in Paris. Indeed, just three months later, by the summer of 1921, Man Ray moved permanently to Paris and had his first one-man exhibition under the auspices of Paris Dada by the end of the year. See, for example, Matthew S. Witkovsky, "Pen Pals," *The Dada Seminars,* p. 272: "Still in New York in 1921, [Man Ray] formalized his ties to Dada in Paris by issuing the journal *New York Dada* with the help of Marcel Duchamp. A letter from Duchamp started the project, a sly request sent to Tzara via Picabia for 'authorization' to use the word Dada in the title; Tzara's pagelong reply then appeared as the journal's centerfold text, surmounted by a racy image that Man Ray boldly called his *Dadaphoto."*

7. Rosalind Krauss speaks of the *Dadaphoto* as articulating the "anthropomorphism" of the readymade in "The Object Caught by the Heel," p. 251.

8. In her recent biography of the Baroness Elsa von Freytag-Loringhoven, Irene Gammel connects the *Dadaphoto* to "male attempts to contain [the Baroness's] body within male parameters." See Gammel, *Baroness Elsa: Gender, Dada, and Everyday Modernity* (Cambridge, Mass.: MIT Press, 2002), pp. 293–294. Gammel's reading builds on the approach to Dada representation offered by Amelia Jones, "'Women' in Dada: Elsa, Rrose, and Charlie," in *Women in Dada*, pp. 142–172.

9. Kaja Silverman, *World Spectators* (Stanford: Stanford University Press, 2000), p. 159, note 40. Hereafter cited in the text as WS.

10. Martin Jay, *Downcast Eyes: The Denigration of the Visual in Twentieth-Century French Thought* (Berkeley: University of California Press, 1993).

11. Kaja Silverman, "Girl Love," *James Coleman* (Ostfildern-Ruit: Hatje Cantz, 2002), reprinted in *October* 104 (spring 2003), pp. 6, 10. Hereafter cited in the text as GL.

12. Ferdinand de Saussure, *Course in General Linguistics,* trans. Wade Baskin (New York: McGraw Hill, 1966), p. 103, cited in Silverman, *World Spectators,* p. 104.

13. Compare the following assertion of Goux on language and the unconscious:

> For the moment let me simply define logocentrism not as the domination of spoken signs over written signs but rather as the reign of linguistic signs (speech or *phonetic* writing) over ordinary (iconic) signs. Logocentrism results from the choice of a very particular type of signs (signs of spoken language) as general equivalents of all other signs, that is, both as their universal measure and ideal principle of evaluation and as the privileged, if not exclusive, vehicle for *the circulation of meaning*. This *logocracy* is thus the reign of the *waking state* over *dream work,* to the extent that—unlike the dream world which, realizing the conditions of polymorphous perversion, has no knowledge of general equivalents—it *enforces* the distinction between linguistic signs and nonlinguistic signs. (N, pp. 42–43)

14. Man Ray, *Self Portrait* (Boston: Little, Brown, 1963), p. 263.

15. Gammel, *Baroness Elsa,* p. 294.

16. Man Ray, *Objets de mon affection,* p. 141.

17. In what follows, I will present a rather utopian reading of the place of the mother in the alternate symbolic economies envisioned by Dada. I actually find it rather problematic that the

Baroness was often referred to within the Dada context as the "Mother of Dada." Although it may seem to support my reading, this appellation was also extended to Beatrice Wood and Gertrude Stein. It is a potentially sexist appellation, and to see it as the literal, iconographic key to the phrase and image presented here by Man Ray would go against the more utopian reading that I think these projects support.

18. In its liberation, this "groundlessness" of signification could also serve as an interesting way to reconceive and in fact transvalue the Dada project of the "destruction" of meaning and sense. My reading of that "destruction" would thus in fact also be an opening of sense, if not a redemption of it, an exploration of long-repressed symbolic economies.

19. Actually, the terms are Silverman's; Freud refers to the negative and the positive Oedipus complexes. Silverman's account of the negative Oedipal mother is heart-wrenching, its loss to the female subject in the wake of the castration crisis leading to a "narcissistic" wounding that produces a "subject no one can love." I point the interested reader to Silverman's texts, as well as to the origins of such reflection on the author's part in *The Acoustic Mirror: The Female Voice in Psychoanalysis and Cinema* (Bloomington and Indianapolis: Indiana University Press, 1988).

20. Krauss, "The Object Caught by the Heel," pp. 248–251.

21. Krauss, "The Photographic Conditions of Surrealism," *The Originality of the Avant-Garde and Other Modernist Myths,* pp. 87–118.

22. Pierre Bourgeade, *Bonsoir, Man Ray* (Paris: Pierre Belfond, 1990), pp. 80–81.

23. Krauss, "Objets de réflexion critique," *Objets de mon affection,* p. 10.

24. In this fusion of object and body, Man Ray's *Portemanteau* operates instead in relation not to the function of the *portemanteau* as object, but to the *portemanteau* as a linguistic concept, a concept, however, that attempts to describe the invention of new forms through otherwise nonsensical combinations of legitimate words, and thus through the subversion of distinct linguistic "articulation" and differentiation. A portmanteau word is a new word formed through the fusion of two established words (e.g., "motel"—or, of course, "Dadaphoto").

25. The account closest to the semiotic conditions that I am tracing can be found in David Joselit's *Infinite Regress.*

26. It could be objected that the violence directed against the object of desire in *Object to Be Destroyed* works to undermine the "maternal" economy that this essay has been exploring, just as the engagement on Man Ray's part with caricature and fetishism—with, then, potential

misogyny—in the *Dadaphoto* militates against any recuperation of the image as incipiently feminist. But if contemporary theory and if philosophies such as poststructuralism have taught us anything, it is that one must engage with the dynamics of the objects that one wishes to critique; to stand apart from them, without ambivalence, is impossible. Indeed, the ambivalence of *Object to Be Destroyed* is so great as to call out for a reading of it in terms of psychoanalyst Melanie Klein's categories of the Good and Bad Mother, and of the Kleinian dynamics of destruction and reparation. See, for example, Mignon Nixon, "Bad Enough Mother," *October* 71 (winter 1995), pp. 70–92.

27. Man Ray, *Self Portrait,* p. 240.

28. Bourgeade, *Bonsoir, Man Ray,* pp. 109–110.

29. This could serve as a description of Carol Armstrong's recent series of essays on woman photographers and their reconfiguration of the medium. Armstrong's project is itself tied closely to a rethinking of Roland Barthes's *Camera Lucida.* See, for example: "Biology, Destiny, Photography: Difference According to Diane Arbus," *October* 66 (fall 1993), pp. 28–54; "Cupid's Pencil of Light: Juliet Margaret Cameron and the Maternalization of Photography," *October* 76 (spring 1996), pp. 114–141; "From Clementina to Kasebier: The Photographic Attainment of the 'Lady Amateur,'" *October* 91 (winter 2000), pp. 101–139; and "This Photography Which Is Not One: In the Grey Zone with Tina Modotti," *October* 101 (summer 2002), pp. 19–52.

30. Rosalind Krauss sees in Man Ray's work a contestation of the Law of Language and (implicitly) the Father in "Objets de réflexion critique," pp. 10–11.

Chapter 4   *Prolem sine matre creatam*: Dada Abstraction

1. Francis Picabia, "Un effet facile," *Littérature,* new series, no. 5 (1 October 1922, special issue devoted to "Rrose Sélavy") pp. 1–2, reprinted in *Écrits II,* p. 88; trans. Rémy Hall, in Francis Picabia, *YesNo* (New York: Hanuman Books, 1990), p. 34. Picabia uses the word *baisse* in the French original; a literal translation would be "Solitude can be compared to a lamp that lowers" or "goes out." Hall conflates *baisse* with the almost-homophone *baise* to arrive at his translation. Both fit my purposes in this chapter.

2. Georges Bataille, "The Solar Anus," *Visions of Excess,* p. 5.

3. All of the Latin headings used in this chapter come from phrases lifted by Picabia from the *Petit Larousse Illustré,* translated into French in his various Dada works.

4. Ulf Linde compares *The Merry Widow* to the *Large Glass* in his essay "Picabia," in Martin and Seckel, *Francis Picabia,* pp. 19–26. For a reading of the *Large Glass* as an allegorical self-portrait, see Rosalind Krauss, "Notes on the Index," pp. 196–209.

5. On several occasions, I have had the pleasure of listening to an as-yet-unpublished lecture by Kaja Silverman on the work of Gerhard Richter entitled "Photography by Other Means." The present chapter thus continues my dialogue with Silverman on photography.

6. The *Portrait of Max Goth* was on the back cover of the first issue of *391* (25 January 1917); *Peigne* served immediately as its sequel, the front cover of the second issue (10 February 1917). "Max Goth" was a pseudonym for Maximilien Gauthier, returning us to the reflection on denominations taken up by *L'oeil cacodylate.*

7. In a gesture that seems allegorical, Picabia painted the Tate Modern's canvas *La feuille de vigne (The Fig Leaf)* over *Les yeux chauds,* parts of which can still be seen through the surface of the present work (the hot pink ground, the large machinic orb/eye once at the top right, etc.).

8. Picabia, open letter, *Le Matin* (10 November 1921), p. 1, reprinted in *Écrits II,* p. 35. Picabia was responding to the anonymous "La turbine et le dada," *Le Matin* (9 November 1921), p. 1. He continued his response in the essay "L'oeil cacodylate," p. 37: "To copy apples, that is comprehensible to everyone, to copy a turbine, that's idiotic. In my opinion, what is even more idiotic is that *Hot Eyes,* which was inadmissible yesterday, now becomes a painting that is perfectly intelligible to everyone by the *fact* that it represents a convention."

9. See Boulbès, *Picabia,* pp. 51–52.

10. David Joselit, "Dada's Diagrams," *The Dada Seminars,* pp. 221–239.

11. After leaving Paris just before the initiation of the Paris Dada manifestations in January 1920, Duchamp returned to the city from New York in June of 1921. He was thus present and participated in the production of Picabia's *L'oeil cacodylate.* Man Ray arrived in France in July of 1921, on Bastille Day. Duchamp returned to New York at the end of January 1922, again just before Picabia's next public enactment of the fruits of their dialogue.

12. For details on the 1922 controversy, spearheaded by the Salon's president, Paul Signac, see Camfield, *Francis Picabia: His Art, Life, and Times,* pp. 172–176. In the great French anti-tradition of the *refusés,* Picabia hung his two rejected works in the "Bar Moysès" —the Boeuf sur le Toit—for the duration of the Independents exhibition. Located originally at 28 rue Boissy-d'Anglas, the brasserie was thus close to the Independents' home in the Grand Palais.

13. In the face of the rejection of *Straw Hat?*, Picabia proposed alternate readings for the inscription such as "*Merci pour celui qui le regarde*" in "On refuse M. Picabia aux Indépendants," *Journal du peuple* (19 January 1922), reprinted in *Écrits II*, p. 48. He proposed inserting Marthe Chenal's name in "Sur les bords de la scène," *Les Potins de Paris* (3 February 1922), reprinted in *Écrits II*, p. 55. Elizabeth Legge has pointed out that *Merde à celui qui le lira* was a common schoolboy graffito in France. See Legge, "Thirteen Ways," p. 238.

14. Francis Picabia, "Histoire de voir," *Littérature*, new series no. 6 (1 November 1922), reprinted in *Écrits II*, p. 94.

15. Francis Picabia, "Dada aux champs," *Le Petit Parisien* (26 November 1922), reprinted in *Écrits II*, pp. 97–98.

16. Francis Picabia, "Souvenirs de voyages: L'Exposition coloniale de Marseille," *Littérature*, new series no. 8 (1 January 1923), pp. 3–4, reprinted in *Écrits II*, pp. 103–104. I have synthesized my account of the 1922 voyage to Barcelona from this and various other sources. See the essays by Jean-Jacques Lebel cited in note 17 below; Mark Polizzotti, *Revolution of the Mind: The Life of André Breton* (New York: Da Capo, 1997), pp. 184–186; Marguerite Bonnet, *André Breton: Naissance de l'aventure surréaliste* (Paris: José Corti, 1988); and Everling, *L'anneau de Saturne*.

17. Jean-Jacques Lebel, "The Picabia Machine," p. 177. See also Lebel, "Picabia, 1922, ready-made empêché," in *Francis Picabia, galerie Dalmau, 1922* (Paris: Éditions du Centre Pompidou, 1996). The IVAM and Pompidou catalogs document the two major recent exhibitions that have reclaimed and examined Picabia's 1922 mechanomorphs.

18. Breton, "Lâchez tout," *Littérature*, new series no. 2 (1 April 1922), translated as "Leave Everything," *The Lost Steps*, p. 79.

19. André Breton, *Conversations*, pp. 44 and 55 respectively.

20. See Borràs, "Spain, The *Mestizo* Ideal," *Francis Picabia: Máquinas y Españolas*, pp. 171–173.

21. William Camfield, *Francis Picabia* (New York: Solomon R. Guggenheim Museum, 1970), p. 34.

22. The full accounting of Picabia's public statements in which he broke with Dada include: "M. Picabia se sépare des Dadas," *Comoedia* (11 May 1921), p. 2, reprinted in *Écrits II*, pp. 14–15; the untitled continuation of this text in *Comoedia* (23 June 1921), p. 1, reprinted in *Écrits II*, p. 16; "Pourquoi nous avons le cafard," *Comoedia* (17 May 1921), p. 4, reprinted in *Écrits II*, pp. 16–18; and "Francis Picabia et Dada," *L'esprit nouveau* 9 (June 1921), pp. 1059–1060,

reprinted in *Écrits II*, pp. 18–19. The latter text concludes with a line by Picabia that I want to remember here: "The bourgeois stands for limitlessness [*l'infini*]. Dada will as well if it lasts too long." But see as well the repudiation of Dada in "Jusqu'à un certain point," *Comoedia* (16 April 1922), p. 1, reprinted in *Écrits II*, pp. 67–69, one of Picabia's first texts to flirt openly with anti-Semitism, however facetiously. On this problem in Picabia's work, which becomes more pressing after his definitive break with the avant-garde and around the late works of the 1940s, see Yve-Alain Bois, "Francis Picabia from Dada to Petain," *October* 30 (fall 1984), pp. 120–127.

23. Both Marcel Duchamp and Gabrielle Buffet related to Jean-Jacques Lebel that they had missed the exhibition but thought it was the most important and the best that Picabia mounted in his lifetime. See Lebel, "The Picabia Machine," p. 178. Everling seems to share this opinion; for her account, see *L'anneau de Saturne*, p. 171.

24. The only positive review of Picabia's exhibit was published on 22 November 1922 in Barcelona. Picabia and Breton triumphantly carried this review back to France, where it was translated and republished in *Littérature*. See M. A. Cassanyes, "À propos de l'Exposition Francis Picabia et de la Conférence d'André Breton," *Littérature*, new series no. 8 (1 January 1923), pp. 22–24.

25. André Breton, "Characteristics of the Modern Evolution and What It Consists Of," *The Lost Steps*, pp. 107–108.

26. Germaine Everling claims that the "Spanish women" were included in the exhibit at the direct request of the gallerist Dalmau, in order to "flatter" his more conservative public. See Everling, *L'anneau de Saturne*, p. 171. Picabia had been producing such figurative "pastiches," however, throughout the moment of the mechanomorphs, surely since the moment in 1917 when he produced the *Portrait of Max Goth* for the first issue of *391*. Their eruption with the most "abstract" of the mechanomorphs hardly seems a coincidence.

27. See Pierre, "The 'Confrontation of Modern Values,'" pp. 241–267.

28. André Breton, "Francis Picabia," *The Lost Steps*, p. 99. This text served as the catalog essay for the Barcelona exhibition.

29. Georges Ribemont-Dessaignes, "Non-seul plaisir," *391* 11 (February 1920), p. 3.

30. This transformation in the relation between title and image was first suggested to me after a reading of John Welchman, *Invisible Colors: A Visual History of Titles* (New Haven: Yale University Press, 1997).

31. Agnès de la Beaumelle suggests that at least one of the last mechanomorphs, *Décaveuse (Fleecer)*, is a pastiche of a specific work by El Lissitzky, his cover for the journal *Ma* 7, no. 8 (August 1922). See "Picabia kaléidoscope, 1922," *Francis Picabia, galerie Dalmau, 1922,* pp. 9–19.

32. Sources for the early mechanomorphs have been proposed by both William Camfield (in *Francis Picabia: His Art, Life, and Times*) and William Innes Homer (in "Picabia's *Jeune fille américaine dans l'état de nudité* and Her Friends"). More recently, Jean-Jacques Lebel claims to have identified a series of scientific books that once belonged to Picabia and contain sources; see the exhibition pamphlet, "Picabia, moteur à toutes tendances," or the reprint of these sources in *Francis Picabia: Máquinas y Españolas,* p. 57. Upon discovering that it was the magazine *La Science et la Vie* that served Picabia for *Les yeux chauds* and that lead to the *Le Matin* exposé, Arnauld Pierre has been able definitively to identify many more. See Pierre, "Sources inédites pour l'oeuvre machiniste de Francis Picabia, 1918–1922," *Société de l'histoire de l'art français* (1991), pp. 255–281; "Le dernier style machiniste de Francis Picabia: nouvelles sources," *Francis Picabia, galerie Dalmau, 1922,* pp. 35–41; the English translation of this essay in *Francis Picabia: Antología* (Lisbon: Centro Cultural de Belém, 1997), which contains additional sources not originally reproduced; "Picabia contre le retour à l'ordre," *Francis Picabia: les Nus et la méthode,* pp. 8–19; and his recent book on Picabia, *Francis Picabia: La peinture sans aura.* Sara Cochran has discovered the sources for many of Picabia's late works; see "La peinture de Francis Picabia pendant la Seconde Guerre mondiale," *Art Press,* no. 222 (March 1997). Carole Boulbès has also proposed new sources in her book *Picabia, le saint masqué.* My work in this chapter would not have been possible without the research of Boulbès and Pierre.

33. Rosalind Krauss has demonstrated these connections between abstraction and photography in text after text. See, for example, Krauss, *The Picasso Papers,* pp. 127–128, or the quite different approach taken in her "Photography and Abstraction," *A Debate on Abstraction* (New York: Hunter College Art Galleries, 1989).

34. See Pierre, "Le dernier style machiniste de Francis Picabia," p. 38. *Shutter (Obturateur)* has been lost, but on the basis of sources culled from the same issue of *La Science et la Vie,* Pierre deduces that the work took its source from an article by Dominique Grasset, "Les objectifs et la photographie," *La Science et la Vie,* no. 45 (June–July 1919), pp. 119–120.

35. I will not illustrate this fact here, but Boulbès has provided such a superimposition for the interested reader. See *Picabia, le saint masqué,* p. 39.

36. My reading here is dependent on Boulbès. See the entirety of her chapter "Le double monde," *Picabia, le saint masqué,* pp. 29–42. See too Fernand Drijkoningen, "Un tableau-manifeste de Picabia: 'Le double monde,'" *Avant-Garde* (special Marcel Duchamp issue) 2 (1989), pp. 97–112.

37. Le Corbusier, "Regulating Lines," *Towards a New Architecture* (New York: Dover, 1986), p. 72.

38. Proclamations of "amnesia" were frequent, even structural within the work of Paris Dada; the pun *M'amenez-y* turns up again in Picabia's *Portrait à l'huile de ricin!* (1919) and was to have served as the title for the proposed Dada review of Céline Arnauld. I am struck, in *Le double monde,* by the fact that the letters of the pun *LHOOQ* are written in different sizes, with the "L" and the "Q"—the beginning and the end, the two letters with a tail—noticeably smaller, so that the central letters seem to jump out at the viewer with an aggressive yell: "HOO." Precisely this same senseless exclamation was adopted in a poem published by Paul Éluard in 1920 that also took amnesia as its subject, and was, we might now imagine, a direct reaction to Picabia's painting: "Hoo! que disions-nous? que disions-nous?/ Nous avons perdu la mémoire./ Hoo! que faisions-nous? que faisions-nous?/ Nous avons perdu la mémoire." See *Proverbe* 4, n.d.

39. On the allegorical dimension of the readymade and Dada montage, see Benjamin Buchloh, "Allegorical Procedures: Appropriation and Montage in Contemporary Art," *Artforum* 21, no. 1 (September 1982), pp. 43–56. On the differentiation between allegorical and symbolic modes of meaning, see Walter Benjamin, *The Origin of German Tragic Drama,* trans. John Osborne (London: New Left Books, 1977).

40. Pierre, "Source inédites . . . ," p. 273.

41. Although it took Benjamin Buchloh to first point this out to me, for which I thank him.

42. The October 1922 issue of *Littérature* dedicated to Rrose Sélavy contained Man Ray's 1920 photograph of the *Large Glass* entitled *Dust Breeding.* The photograph was captioned: "This is the domain of Rrose Sélavy / How arid it is—how fertile it is / how joyous it is—how sad it is—View taken from an aeroplane by Man Ray, 1921." The photograph inserts Duchamp's dual engagement with procedures of transparency and deposit into the Paris Dada context of 1922.

43. Pierre, "Sources inédites . . . ," pp. 258–260.

44. Some of Picabia's mechanomorphic paintings create an effect of overpainting through the application of their pigments; I am thinking primarily of the layering achieved in a work such as *Portrait à l'huile de ricin!.* Marianne Heinz suggests that one read Picabia's largely abstract work of the late 1940s as engaged with the notion of overpainting: "Lines or parts of forms remain visible or shimmer through, as if they had been overpainted, and as if there were a second, a different picture underneath." Heinz, "Francis Picabia: To the Point," *Picabia 1879–1953* (Edinburgh: Scottish National Gallery of Modern Art, 1988), p. 12.

45. Similar rotations occurred to the sources for the drawings *Ventilateur surprise* and *Narcotique;* see the illustrations in Pierre, "Sources inédites . . . ," p. 261.

46. Of course my claims here are informed by Leo Steinberg's notion of the "flatbed picture plane" and the transformations it implies for twentieth-century art. Although he focuses on postwar art, Steinberg sees its initiation in the work of Duchamp, particularly the *Large Glass.* See Steinberg, "Other Criteria," *Other Criteria: Confrontations with Twentieth-Century Art* (Oxford: Oxford University Press, 1972).

47. On the frequent occurrence of titles referring to insects in the mechanomorphs, see the section "Non liquet" below.

48. See Paul Haviland, "We Are Living in the Age of the Machine," *291* 7–8 (September–October 1915), p. 1.

49. See Martin and Seckel, *Francis Picabia,* p. 47. The Larousse definition: *"Prolem sine matre creatam.* Enfant né sans mère. Montesquieu a mis cette épigraphe, tirée d'un vers d'Ovide (*Métamorphoses,* II, 553), en tête de son *Esprit de lois,* pour marquer qu'il n'avait pas eu de modèle." See "Locutions Latines et étrangères," *Nouveau Petit Larousse Illustré* (Paris: Larousse, 1959), p. 1,143.

50. Georges Bataille, "L'art primitif," *Documents* 7 (1930), p. 396.

51. Briony Fer, "*Poussière/Peinture:* Bataille on Painting," *On Abstract Art* (New Haven: Yale University Press, 1997), p. 79. The first text to reintroduce Bataille's notion of alteration into the art historical literature on the avant-garde was Rosalind Krauss, "No More Play," *The Originality of the Avant-Garde and Other Modernist Myths,* pp. 43–85.

52. Bataille, "L'art primitif," p. 397.

53. See Georges Bataille, "The Deviations of Nature," *Visions of Excess,* pp. 53–56.

54. Picabia, "L'oeil cacodylate," p. 37. Emphasis on "deformation" mine.

55. Gilles Deleuze, "Plato and the Simulacrum," *October* 27 (winter 1983), p. 47. See too Hal Foster's remarks on the ramifications of the simulacrum for modernism in "Convulsive Identity," *Compulsive Beauty* (Cambridge, Mass.: MIT Press, 1993), pp. 96–98.

56. André Breton, "Francis Picabia," *The Lost Steps,* p. 99.

57. Ibid., p. 98.

58. Once again, I am leaning here on the words of Denis Hollier, specifically a passage where he explicates Bataille's essay "The Deviations of Nature." See Hollier's revision of his essay, "The Use-Value of the Impossible," in *Absent without Leave: French Literature under the Threat of War* (Cambridge, Mass., and London: Harvard University Press, 1997), p. 140:

> Modern art begins at the precise moment when identical causes cease to produce identical effects. It undoes the reproduction of likeness, the engendering of sameness by sameness, the law of biologico-aesthetic homogeneity. In other words, beauty always results from resemblance, whereas ugliness (like formlessness) resembles nothing whatsoever. That is its definition. Its space is that of abortion, of failures in reproduction. It never succeeds in elevating itself to the stage of the double, the image, the reproduction (the typical and the characteristic). It remains a special case. But the *Documents* aesthetics inverts the value judgments applied to those definitions. We are required to imagine that the reproduction of ugliness is impossible, and that beauty arises out of this failure. Beauty is no longer in any respect triumphant; it is merely the product of a failure, the result or residue of an unsuccessful reproduction of ugliness. For this aesthetics of deviation, which is above all an anti-aesthetics of the untransposable (a resistance to aesthetic transposition), it is of secondary importance that ugliness should be a failure of reproduction (nature's deviations are not the same as nature's failures); what is essential is that beauty itself should be a failure of nonreproduction. A reproduction that has not managed to fail one hundred percent. An expenditure that has not taken place without something held back. Use value has not been wholly used up on the spot. The abortion of an abortion.

59. Francis Picabia, "Dactylocoque," *Littérature,* new series no. 7 (1 December 1922), pp. 10–11, reprinted in *Écrits II,* pp. 98–99.

60. Marcel Duchamp, "The Green Box," *The Writings of Marcel Duchamp,* p. 56.

61. Michel de Certeau, "The Arts of Dying: Celibatory Machines," *Heterologies: Discourse on the Other* (Minneapolis: University of Minnesota Press, 1986), p. 156. Hereafter cited in the text as "CM."

62. Or, as Deleuze and Guattari suggest, the result is a series of "intensive quantities." See their characterization of Michel Carrouges's notion of the bachelor machine in *Anti-Oedipus: Capitalism and Schizophrenia* (Minneapolis: University of Minnesota Press, 1983).

63. Picabia's path toward the production of the mechanomorphs was initiated, it seems, by Duchamp's gift to Picabia of his 1912 painting *The Bride*. On the "bride" as Picabia's principle of abstraction, see "Non liquet" below. Iconographical approaches to the mechanomorphs that isolate each image as a text to be read symbolically have facilitated, it seems to me, the misreading of these works as misogynist, as deeply fraught "images" of woman-as-robot-or-machine, as opposed to procedural enactments of the anti-patriarchal principles of the bachelor machine.

64. Although obscure, references to the sea (*la mer*) do occur in Picabia's mechanomorphs, most crucially in *De Zayas! De Zayas!* (1915), whose Larousse-based title is based on the exclamation *"Thalassa! Thalassa!,"* or "The sea! The sea!" One should remember Man Ray's letter to Tristan Tzara from 1921 in this connection as well.

65. Georges Bataille, *L'expérience intérieure* (Paris: Gallimard, 1954), p. 216. Cited in de Certeau, CM, p. 162. However briefly, Bataille does enter Michel Carrouges's reflections on the bachelor machine; see *Les machines célibataires* (Paris: Chêne, 1976), p. 21.

66. Francis Picabia, "Francis Merci!" *Littérature,* new series no. 8 (1 January 1923), pp. 16–17, reprinted in *Écrits II,* pp. 105–106.

67. Georges Bataille, *The Story of the Eye* (1928), trans. Joachim Neugroschel (San Francisco: City Lights, 1987), p. 48. Translation modified.

68. See William Camfield, "Volucelle," in Martin and Seckel, *Francis Picabia,* pp. 114–117. Camfield suggests the importance of Max Ernst's overpainting *Les pléiades* (1921) to Picabia's work. Dawn Ades takes up Camfield's reading of the painting as referring to constellations, seeing in such an interpretation Picabia's solution to the dialectic of figuration and abstraction that was evidently quite important to him at this moment; see "Between Dada and Surrealism: Painting in the *Mouvement flou,*" *In the Mind's Eye: Dada and Surrealism* (New York: Abbeville Press, 1986). In the wake of the 1995 exhibition that reclaimed the last mechanomorphs, Arturo Schwarz has extended his alchemical reading of Duchamp's work to Picabia, thinking specifically of *Volucelle*; see "Picabia . . . sobre algunos arquetipos alquímicos," *Kalías* 7, no. 14 (1995), pp. 20–31.

69. See Carrouges, *Les machines célibataires,* pp. 32–33, 51.

70. Carrouges suggests that the Milky Way section of the *Glass* be seen as linked to the nocturnal aspect of the moth that he reads in the term *la mariée,* proposing that the shape of this section resembles the body of an insect larva (Carrouges, *Les machines célibataires,* p. 33). I have already mentioned that one of the last mechanomorphs was entitled *Sphinx*; in French, this

term can as well be used to refer to a type of moth. We can now also understand, I think, the prevalence of insect titles among the mechanomorphs of *Poèmes et dessins de la fille née sans mère,* such as *Libellule (Dragonfly)* and *Cantharides (Spanish fly).*

71. André Breton, "Ideas of a Painter," *Littérature* 18 (March 1921), reprinted in *The Lost Steps,* pp. 64–65.

72. Francis Picabia, "Les Ballets Suédois," *Montparnasse* (1 December 1924), reprinted in *Écrits II,* p. 169.

73. Picabia's work has previously received at least one important psychoanalytic reading; see Guy Rosolato, "Picabia, l'exaltation de l'objet bizarre," in *Picabia 1879–1953,* ed. Michel Hoog (Bruxelles: Musée d'ixelles, 1983). Although he refers to the work of Melanie Klein, Rosolato primarily builds on Michel Carrouges's notion of the bachelor machine and its connection to a dynamic of "ritual sacrifice." Here I am building, rather, on the work on the part object that has been done in the context of Duchamp studies and postmodern art; see, for example, chapters 3 and 6 of Rosalind Krauss, *The Optical Unconscious,* and chapters 2 and 7 of *Bachelors* (Cambridge, Mass.: MIT Press, 1999); the entry "Part Object" in Krauss and Yve-Alain Bois, *Formless: A User's Guide*; Annette Michelson, "Where Is Your Rupture? Mass Culture and the *Gesamtkunstwerk,*" *October* 56 (spring 1991); and the work of Mignon Nixon, especially "Posing the Phallus," *October* 92 (spring 2000), pp. 99–127.

74. Mignon Nixon notes the importance of this particular fusion of breast and phallus in the thought of Melanie Klein; see Nixon, "Posing the Phallus," p. 116.

75. Perhaps, using Kleinian terms, one could theorize the shift from Picabia's Dada production to his later Transparencies and other pastiches around a shift from Klein's "paranoid/schizoid" to what she calls the "depressive" position, with an attendant shift from an aggressive logic of destruction to a melancholia of reparation. For one such tracing of a logic where precisely that which is first destroyed then returns via reparation, see my epilogue, "Long Live Daddy."

76. Picabia, "Ils n'en mouraient pas tous . . . ," *Paris-Journal* (23 May 1924), p. 4, reprinted in *Écrits II,* p. 142.

77. Picabia's interest in optical illusion can be traced back, however, to the mechanomorphic drawing *Lampe illusion,* published in *391* 3 (March 1917), p. 7. The scale and disposition of paintings like *Volucelle* tempt the viewer to treat them as potentially anamorphic, like Duchamp's *Tu m'*; the interested viewer should look at *Volucelle* from a radically oblique angle, to the left and right sides of the painting.

78. Such reversals and their connection to photography were shared within Paris Dada, becoming one of the stakes of Man Ray's rayographs, which were initiated at this moment.

79. For the source of *Toton*, see Pierre, "Francis Picabia's last machinist style: new sources," *Francis Picabia: Antologia,* pp. 54–55; for *Jumelle,* see Pierre, "Sources inédites . . . ," p. 273.

80. Georges Bataille, "Sacrificial Mutilation and the Severed Ear of Vincent Van Gogh," *Visions of Excess,* p. 68, 70.

81. Georges Bataille, "Rotten Sun," *Visions of Excess,* p. 57.

82. Ibid.

83. Ibid.

84. Georges Bataille, "Sacrificial Mutilation and the Severed Ear of Vincent Van Gogh," p. 67. For an explication of the place of this essay within Bataille's thought, see Rosalind Krauss, "Anti-Vision," *October* 36 (spring 1986), pp. 147–154.

85. Georges Bataille, "Celestial Bodies," *October* 36 (spring 1986), pp. 75–78.

86. For a reconstruction of the general progression of *Relâche,* see William Camfield, "Dada Experiment: Francis Picabia and the Creation of *Relâche,*" in *Paris Modern: The Swedish Ballet, 1920–1925,* ed. Nancy Van Norman Baer (San Francisco: Fine Arts Museums of San Francisco, 1995); see too Judi Freeman, "*Relâche* and *Entr'acte,*" *Francis Picabia, 1879–1953* (Edinburgh: Scottish National Gallery of Modern Art, 1988). I recapitulate their reconstructions in my next chapter.

87. Picabia, "Les Ballets Suédois," p. 169. Picabia's scenario for *Relâche* utilizes a multitude of male dancers but only one female dancer who at one point in the ballet emerges onto the stage wearing a floral ring that Picabia called a "bridal crown." See the translation of the scenario, "Relâche," in Mel Gordon, ed., *Dada Performance* (New York: PAJ Publications, 1987), pp. 162–163.

88. Interview with Paul Achard, "Picabia m'a dit . . . avant *Cinésketch* au Théâtre des Champs-Elysées," *L'Action* (1 January 1925), p. 4, reprinted in *Écrits II,* p. 175. "Francine" was played by Brogna Perlmutter, the future wife of René Clair. In this interview, Picabia described his project in *Cinésketch* as bringing to the theater "the method and the living rhythms of cinema." The relation then of *Cinésketch* and *Relâche* to vision differs in each case; the former seems to play with the paradoxical ground of the persistence of vision, with a flash followed by darkness that is the flickering condition of cinematic illusion, while *Relâche* enacts a flashing whose relation

to its viewer more closely approximates a photographic model, with both object and viewer immobilized before the camera's artificial light.

89. Francis Picabia, "Ma main tremble," *The Little Review* (autumn 1922), p. 40, reprinted in *Écrits II,* p. 93.

90. Carole Boulbès, *Picabia, le saint masqué,* p. 34.

91. See, for example, Francis Picabia, "À Monsieur Paul Signac, President de la Société des Indépendants," *Comoedia* (23 January 1922), p. 3, reprinted in *Écrits II,* p. 52. Carole Boulbès documents some of the inscriptions in *Picabia, le saint masqué,* p. 46. See too chapter 1 of this volume, note 28.

Chapter 5   Intermission: Dada Cinema

1. Giorgio Agamben, *State of Exception,* trans. Kevin Attell (Chicago and London: University of Chicago Press, 2005), p. 64.

2. James Joyce, *Ulysses* (1922) (New York: Random House, 1986), p. 83.

3. Benjamin, "The Work of Art in the Age of Mechanical Reproduction," p. 238.

4. Ibid.

5. Ibid., pp. 249–250, note 17.

6. Ibid., p. 238.

7. For a close reading of Picabia's writings on the cinema that asserts that by 1922 the artist had already laid out a theory of cinema as distraction, see Annette Michelson, "Painting. Instantaneism. Cinema. America. Ballet. Illumination. Apollinaire," in *Francis Picabia: Máquinas y Españolas,* pp. 67–74, pp. 192–195.

8. On the Stravinsky collaboration, see Camfield, *Francis Picabia: His Art, Life, and Times,* p. 166; on the film (which ultimately, without Picabia, became *L'Inhumaine*), see Borràs, *Picabia,* p. 129, and Freeman, "*Relâche* and *Entr'acte,*" p. 16.

9. Thomas Elsaesser, "Dada/Cinema?" *Dada/Surrealism* 15 (1986), p. 14.

10. Pierre de Massot, letter to Picabia, 22 January 1924, cited in Freeman, "*Relâche* and *Entr'acte,*" p. 16.

11. Before Cendrars's departure, Picabia had already been enlisted only to provide set and costumes for the production. Although Picabia completely transformed the ballet's scenario, it has been argued that the idea for a cinematic intermission also belongs to Cendrars. On Cendrars's contributions, the most meticulous record is Freeman, "*Relâche* and *Entr'acte*," pp. 18–21. Years later, in an unpublished note, Cendrars complained of Picabia's "theft" of his ideas, and, even though the poet only had one arm, he averred that he should have "used his two feet to kick Picabia's ass" (Freeman, "*Relâche* and *Entr'acte*," p. 21).

12. The cover of one of the issues of *391* 18 (July 1924) leading up to the production of *Relâche,* is, significantly, covered over in a veritable collection of scatological sayings and puns, including: "Oh! Do shit again! . . . Oh! douche it again!—Rrose Sélavy," "De la MERDE!," "Collection Caca," "Du dos de la cuillère au cul de la douairière!—Rose [*sic*] Sélavy," and "Où va la peinture moderne? Aux chiottes!—E. P. [Ezra Pound]."

13. Picabia offered his own explanation in "Pourquoi *Relâche* a fait relâche," *Montparnasse* (1 Dec. 1924), reprinted in *Écrits II,* pp. 169–170.

14. Rolf de Maré, cited in Bengt Häger, *Ballets Suédois,* trans. Ruth Sharman (New York: Harry N. Abrams, 1990), p. 52. In an advertisement for the ballet published in *Mouvement accéléré* (November 1924), *Relâche* was described as "neither a ballet, nor an anti-ballet." The ad is reproduced in Martin and Seckel, *Picabia,* p. 124.

15. Auric, in *Les Nouvelles Littéraires* (13 Dec. 1924), in Häger, *Ballets Suédois,* pp. 257–258. For months prior to the premiere of *Relâche,* Satie had been taunting Auric in the pages of *391,* in his column "Cahiers d'un mammifère." See for example *391* 17 (June 1924), p. 3, and *391* 18 (July 1924), p. 2.

16. On Satie's score for *Relâche,* see Robert Orledge, *Satie the Composer* (Cambridge: Cambridge University Press, 1990). On Satie more generally, see Alan M. Gillmor, *Eric Satie* (Boston: Twayne, 1988), and Roger Shattuck, *The Banquet Years* (New York: Vintage, 1968), pp. 113–185. See, as well, Martin Howe, "Erik Satie and His Ballets," *Ballet* 5, no. 8 (Aug.–Sept. 1948), pp. 25–39, 53–54, and *Ballet* 6, no. 1 (Oct. 1948), pp. 25–30.

17. Satie, from the program of *Relâche* (special issue of *La Danse* [Nov. 1924]), cited in Häger, *Ballets Suédois,* p. 251 (French original) and pp. 256–257 (translation).

18. Picabia wrote this requirement directly into his scenario for the ballet. However, one imagines, upon listening to Satie's score, that this alternation was not followed throughout, but occurred periodically during the course of the ballet, and especially at the moment of its start.

19. See Camfield, "Dada Experiment," p. 132; the primary press accounts that Camfield draws on are Jane Catulle-Mendès, *Presse et Patrie* (6 December 1924), cited at length in Häger, *Ballets Suédois,* pp. 53–54; Maurice Bouisson, "*Relâche—Entr'acte* de Picabia et Erik Satie," *L'Evénement* (4 December 1924), p. 2; and Paul Achard, "Soirs de Paris," *Le Siècle* (6 December 1924), p. 4. Picabia's scenario and other documents related to *Relâche* are reprinted in the Grand Palais catalog, Martin and Seckel, pp. 123–133.

20. Camfield doesn't mention the human bridge, but Catulle-Mendès does; see Häger, *Ballets Suédois,* p. 53. One of the six documentary photographs seems to represent it.

21. Camfield, "Dada Experiment," p. 135. Camfield is right, of course, but I think the language is misleading. *Relâche* is "fully expressive of Picabia" only to the extent that this phrase can encompass an artist as set against expression as this one, as dedicated to pastiching the work of others.

22. See Sanouillet, *Francis Picabia et 391,* vol. II, p. 166.

23. Ibid.

24. In a similar gesture that has gone unremarked, Picabia created at this same moment another kind of "correspondence" around a profile drawing, this time of the head of René Clair, in the published program for *Relâche* (see, for example, the reproduction of this program in Häger, *Ballets Suédois,* p. 271). Here, Clair's written statement about the production and *Entr'acte* is made to echo, through typographic layout, the shape of his drawn profile. Picabia's own statement on the collaboration then echoes the form of Clair's words in turn, providing a kind of visual encapsulation of dialogue, and in fact, of the specific dialogue of Picabia and Clair.

25. On the matter of the shared and divergent connotations of the two titles, see Steven Kovács, "Dada Comes In at Intermission: Picabia and René Clair on *Entr'acte,*" *From Enchantment to Rage: The Story of Surrealist Cinema* (London and Toronto: Associated University Presses, 1980), p. 108; and Paul Sandro, "Parodic Narration in *Entr'acte,*" *Film Criticism* 4, no. 1 (1979), p. 44.

26. See Clair, "Picabia, Satie, and the First Night of *Entr'acte,*" *A Nous la Liberté and Entr'acte* (London: Lorimer, 1970), p. 109.

27. Thus, Noël Carroll writes, in "*Entr'acte,* Paris, and Dada," *Interpreting the Moving Image* (Cambridge: Cambridge University Press, 1998), p. 28: "Clair challenges high art by his use of cinematic motifs culled from the most primitive days of early film. His imagery recalls the trick film and the Sennett chase, forms of film-making that belong to the days when film was still a rough proletarian art. What from the high art perspective of the period might be considered the most vulgar forms of entertainment are proffered as an appropriate supplement to that lofti-

est of arts, the ballet." Picabia scholars have brought attention specifically to the similarities between *Entr'acte* and Mack Sennett's film *Heinze's Resurrection* of 1913.

28. Pascale Bonitzer, "It's Only a Movie," *Framework* 14, p. 23, cited in Elsaesser, "Dada/ Cinema?," p. 19: "With the arrival of montage, the close-up, immobile actors, the look (and its corollary—the banishment of histrionics) an entire façade of the cinema seemed to disappear and be lost forever, in a word, all the excrement of vaudeville. . . . The cinema was innocent and dirty, it was to become obsessional and fetishistic."

29. Siegfried Kracauer, *Nature of Film: The Redemption of Physical Reality* (London: Dennis Dobson, 1961), p. 182.

30. Picabia was quoted as saying this in the 1921 *Le Matin* exposé, "La turbine et le dada"; see Jean-Hubert Martin, "Ses tableaux sont peints pour raconter non pour prouver," p. 97.

31. Picabia, "Programme de 'Relâche,'" *La Danse* (November 1924), reprinted in *Écrits II,* p. 167; reproduced in Häger, *Ballets Suédois,* p. 271.

32. Picabia's notorious "scripting" of the film during a meal at Maxim's, jotting down a rapid-fire list of disjointed images for Clair to include in the film, while surely an aristocratic and dandyish gesture, seems aimed too at Surrealist techniques of automatism, techniques that Picabia had prepared with his own earlier poetry of the 1910s and that he witnessed in action during his participation in the "sleeping fits" organized since 1922 by Breton and his friends.

33. Kracauer, *Nature of Film,* p. 182.

34. Sandro, "Parodic Narration in *Entr'acte,*" p. 51.

35. Joyce, *Ulysses,* pp. 77, 80–81.

36. In 1918, Picabia in fact published a volume of poetry to which he gave the title *L'Athlète des pompes funèbres.*

37. Carroll, "*Entr'acte,* Paris, and Dada," pp. 26–33.

39. Mimi White, "Two French Dada Films: *Entr'acte* and *Emak Bakia,*" *Dada/Surrealism* 13 (1984), p. 40.

39. Beyond its play with running the film in literal reverse motion, *Entr'acte* can be seen as full of the operations of reversal, perhaps most infamously in its ballerina seen from below, shifting sex from female to male and back again. In one of his statements on *Relâche* published in the

program (with the words shaped into the form of an upside-down breast), Picabia begins with a list of reversals: "Relâche, rose de feuille—feuille de rose; guêpe de taille—taille de guêpe, cul de lampe, etc. . . ." The reversal cut short by this "etc."—namely *lampe de cul*—might itself be most easily decoded by thinking not only of the part-object "lamps" that range throughout Picabia's Dada mechanomorphs, but also of the transgressive image from *Entr'acte* of the ballerina's "underneaths," lit violently from below. See Picabia, "Programme de 'Relâche,' " p. 166. Picabia's essay "Instantanéisme," p. 159, also begins with a list of phrases chiastically reversed. Chiasmus may be the key figure of *Relâche*.

40. White, "Two French Dada Films," p. 41.

41. Sandro, "Parodic Narration in *Entr'acte*," pp. 44–55. See also Allen Thiher, "From *Entr'acte* to *A Nous la Liberté*: René Clair and the Order of Farce," *The Cinematic Muse* (Columbia: University of Missouri Press, 1979), pp. 64–77.

42. Sandro, "Parodic Narration in *Entr'acte*," p. 53.

43. I have elaborated a very similar reading of an avant-garde film before, a film in fact indebted to the example of *Entr'acte*, namely Robert Smithson's *Spiral Jetty*. My account there of film as open both to processes of analogy and to those of vectorization or the diagrammatic is elaborated in much more detail than I can perform here. See "The Cinema Model," in *Robert Smithson: The Spiral Jetty*, ed. Lynne Cooke and Karen Kelly (New York and Los Angeles: Dia Center for the Arts with the University of California Press, 2005).

44. Walter Benjamin, unpublished letter to Francis Picabia, 22 February 1919, Dossiers Picabia, vol. 1, p. 269. Benjamin mentions in closing this short note that he hopes Richter will see fit to publish his thoughts on the subject of "correspondences."

45. On this point, see Michelson, p. 193

46. Gilles Deleuze, *Cinema 2: The Time-Image,* trans. Hugh Tomlinson and Robert Galeta (Minneapolis: University of Minnesota Press, 1989), p. 57.

47. Ibid., p. 56.

48. Ibid., p. 57.

49. Despite this fact, *Entr'acte* continues to be not just discussed without attention to its musical score, but to be *screened* as a silent film as well (e.g., at the 2006 Dada retrospective at the National Gallery in Washington, D.C.). Pathé International has recently restored the film, including

the musical score in a version approved by Clair, and the Criterion Collection has released this version of the film on DVD (included as an addendum to the title *À Nous la Liberté*). Given this definitive version, the continued severance of music and film seems absolutely gratuitous, and my argument here is in part a plea for it to end. *Entr'acte* should never be screened as a silent film.

50. Satie, cited in Shattuck, *The Banquet Years*, p. 169.

51. The description is from Martin Marks, in "The Well-Furnished Film: Satie's Score for *Entr'acte*," *Canadian University Music Review*, no. 4 (1983), p. 248.

52. On *Vexations*, see Marks, "The Well-Furnished Film," p. 274.

53. See Douglas W. Gallez, "Satie's *Entr'acte*: A Model of Film Music," *Cinema Journal* 16, no. 1 (fall 1976), p. 41. In contradistinction to this point about the orchestra conductor, Gallez points out that the instrumentation of *Entr'acte* lies much closer to that of the music hall; see p. 47 ("trumpet solos over strings, heavy-handed base line, crude use of cymbal and gong, ricky-ticky wood block").

54. Marks, "The Well-Furnished Film," p. 250.

55. Ibid., pp. 261, 255.

56. Ibid., p. 257.

57. Gallez, "Satie's *Entr'acte*," p. 43, writes that "Satie did not slavishly adhere to the illogical visual content of Clair's collage; he wisely concerned himself with changes of rhythm and tempo," and then he cites the description of W. H. Mellers: "Satie realized that *montage* . . . makes the film's rhythm, which the rhythm of the music must reveal." See Mellers, "Film Music: The Musical Problem," in *Grove's Dictionary of Music and Musicians*, 5th ed., ed. Eric Blom (New York: St. Martin's, 1954), vol. 3, p. 103.

58. On this point, see Lynn Garafola, "Dance, Film, and the Ballets Russes," *Dance Research* 16, no. 1 (summer 1998), p. 17.

59. Freeman, "*Relâche* and *Entr'acte*," p. 15.

60. Thomas Elsaesser notes that it was precisely *because* of the ghost of the *Gesamtkunstwerk* that Dada often avoided cinema; see Elsaesser, "Dada/Cinema?," p. 17. Satie was especially known for his hostility to Wagner, whose aesthetic he called "sauerkraut." See Shattuck, *The Banquet Years*, p. 127.

61. See the panoply of positions, especially the essay of Eric Michaud, "Oeuvre d'art totale et totalitarisme," in *L'oeuvre d'art totale,* ed. Jean Galard and Julian Zugazagoitia (Paris: Gallimard, 2003).

62. Beyond the "bearded" ballet dancer, travesty runs throughout *Entr'acte,* although this seems rarely to be noted. Especially during the chase scene, false beards and mustaches and otherwise ludicrous costumes seem the norm, and one of the "New Women" characters, a woman dressed in modern, "flapper"-styled clothes, appears to be in fact a man in drag.

63. A more precise reading would mount a full comparison of *Relâche* with the claims of Jean-Luc Nancy's *Inoperative Community* (see chapter 1). I have explored the usefulness of this text for contemporary art in the essay "The Space of the Stain," *Grey Room* 05 (fall 2001), pp. 5–37. Picabia's work in 1924 also continues to carry through on the claims made by Leah Dickerman in her essay "Dada's Solipsism," although I think Dada's strategies for the "incommensurable" sharing of form significantly revises our understanding of the import of that "solipsism."

64. Picabia, "Instantanéisme," p. 159.

65. Picabia interviewed by Paul Achard, "Picabia m'a dit . . . avant *Cinésketch* au Théâtre des Champs-Elysées," p. 175.

66. Kovács, "Dada Comes In at Intermission," p. 86.

67. Picabia, interviewed by Paul Achard, "Picabia m'a dit . . . ," p. 175. Here is Picabia's full statement on *Cinésketch*:

> Yes, my dear, I, Picabia, have written a review, a sketch to be more precise, to end the year on a happy note, or at least to try to do so. . . I wonder what bit me? But it was very simple; this is how it started: up to now the cinema has been based on the theater; I tried to do the opposite, bringing to the stage the techniques and lively rhythms of cinema. . . I re-create a picture by Cranach, the only painter I can stand at the moment: suddenly in a kitchen you'll see this evocation of Adam and Eve appear. The figures will be completely nude, I want to tell you this right away so there's no misunderstanding. Marcel Duchamp and Francine Picabia, one of my psychic children, will bring this charming painting to life [*feront revivre cette toile charmante*].

68. Something crucial about twentieth-century art remains to be plumbed here. The double (contradictory) choice speaks to a dream unlike that of the dusty, old *Gesamtkunstwerk,* a dream

from which art still has not awoken. Two paths for art in our century part ways in *Cinésketch* by finally coming together, two options bequeathed to us by Dada, emblematized by this image of the "mystical marriage" of Marcel Duchamp and "Francine" Picabia, a celebration of art (n)either murdered or brought back to life. For a reading of Picabia's later work as an attempt at the "reenchantment" of art, see Arnauld Pierre, *Francis Picabia: La peinture sans aura*.

69. Clair, "Picabia, Satie, and the First Night of *Entr'acte*," p. 109.

70. Garafola, "Dance, Film, and the Ballet Russes," p. 17, asserts that the dancing in *Relâche* was deeply concerned with mime, and that this was one of the things in the historical moment that brought cinema and dance together, on which see p. 5:

> Discussing the progressive tendency of modern choreography to "eliminate the artificial dividing line between dancing and mime," the British music critic Edwin Evans insisted in *The Dancing Times* that the "point of intersection" between ballet and cinema lay in the "art of rhythmic movement . . . one and indivisible." Serafima Astafieva, a former Diaghilev dancer, described the connection between the two media even more succinctly. "The cinema *is* mime," she told readers of the magazine in 1917.

Epilogue   Long Live Daddy: A Dada Montage

1. Louis Aragon, *The Adventures of Telemachus* (1922) (Lincoln: University of Nebraska Press, 1988), p. 8.

2. "Enquête," *Littérature* 12 (February 1920), p. 26.

3. Tristan Tzara, "Monsieur Aa L'antiphilosophe nous envoie ce manifeste," *391* 13 (July 1920), p. 3.

4. See *391* 14 (November 1920), p. 6.

5. Picabia, *Jésus-Christ Rastaquouère* (1920) (Paris: Éditions Allia, 1996), p. 36.

6. Joyce, *Ulysses,* p. 171.

7. Marie de la Hire, "Croquis Dada," *391* 14 (November 1920), p. 7.

8. Erwin Panofsky, "Introductory," *Studies in Iconology: Humanistic Themes in the Art of the Renaissance* (New York: Icon, 1972).

9. Michel Foucault, "The Father's 'No,'" *Language, Counter-Memory, Practice,* pp. 81–82. Foucault is of course summarizing here the work of Jacques Lacan.

10. Picabia, *Le Pilhaou-Thibaou (391* 15, 10 July 1921), p. 7.

11. Picabia, untitled aphorisms, *Dadaphone (Dada* 7, March 1920), p. 7.

12. Kaja Silverman, "Masochism and Male Subjectivity," *Male Subjectivity at the Margins* (New York and London: Routledge, 1992), p. 206.

13. For an analysis of the figure of the "prodigal father" and its place within the thought of Georges Bataille, see Denis Hollier, "Bataille's Tomb," *Absent without Leave,* pp. 46–68.

14. Jacques Derrida, "Restitutions," *The Truth in Painting* (Chicago: University of Chicago Press, 1987), p. 360.

15. Ibid., p. 257.

16. Gilles Deleuze, "Coldness and Cruelty," *Masochism* (New York: Zone Books, 1991), pp. 9–138. Hereafter cited in the text as "M."

17. Joyce, *Ulysses,* p. 170.

18. Picabia, "Notre-Dame-de-la-Peinture," *391* 14 (November 1920), p. 5. The image of *Vive Papa* was placed on the page immediately following these words. The line recurs in Picabia's poem "Femmes Fumigations," *Bleu* (autumn 1921), reprinted in *Écrits II,* p. 36. The claim that the shoes in the *Tableau Rastadada* point to Picabia's own real-life preference for wearing high-heeled boots is made in the dissertation of Nancy Ring, "New York Dada and the Crisis of Masculinity: Man Ray, Francis Picabia, and Marcel Duchamp in the United States, 1913–1921" (Ph.D., Northwestern University, 1991).

19. Picabia, "Electrargol," *Littérature,* new series no. 9 (1 February–1 March 1923), p. 14. Published in the midst of the pre-Surrealist "wave of dreams," this text purports to be an account of one of Picabia's dreams, centered completely on a mysterious encounter with pair after pair of shoes. Picabia mentions his boots in a similar manner in the texts "Un effet facile," *Littérature,* new series no. 5 (1 October 1922), pp. 1–2, and "Dactylocoque," *Littérature,* new series no. 7 (1 December 1922), pp. 10–11. Later in the decade, Picabia would compose a text entitled "À propos de bottes," *Le Journal des hivernants* (January 1927), pp. 10–11; although the text was literally concerned with boots once more, this is a phrase that in French also means figuratively "about nothing" or "irreverently."

20. Picabia, "Papa Fais-Moi Peur," *Littérature* 12 (February 1920), p. 2.

21. Joyce, *Ulysses,* p. 170.

22. Anonymous statement [Picabia?], *Bulletin Dada* (*Dada* 6, February 1920), p. 2.

23. Foucault, "The Father's 'No,'" p. 82.

24. Sarah Wilson, however, has noticed the Oedipal dynamics of Picabia's later, figurative work, in her essay on the Transparencies. See Wilson, *Francis Picabia: Accommodations of Desire, Transparencies 1924–1932* (New York: Kent, 1989).

25. The exception here is Caroline Jones; see her analysis of this image in "The Sex of the Machine."

26. Picabia, "Télégraphie sans fils," *Poèmes et dessins de la fille née sans mère* (Paris: Éditions Al-lia, 1992), p. 73. My translation.

27. Derrida, "Restitutions," p. 262.

28. Ibid., p. 267.

29. Ibid., pp. 267–268.

30. See, for example, Leo Bersani, *Baudelaire and Freud* (Berkeley: University of California Press, 1977), and *The Freudian Body* (New York: Columbia University Press, 1986).

31. Leo Bersani, "The Gay Daddy," *Homos* (Cambridge, Mass.: Harvard University Press, 1995), pp. 195–196.

32. Silverman, "Masochism and Male Subjectivity," p. 211.

33. Picabia, *YesNo: Poems and Sayings,* p. 39.

34. Samuel Beckett, *The Unnamable,* in *Three Novels by Samuel Beckett* (New York: Grove, 1965), p. 305.

35. Silverman, "Masochism and Male Subjectivity," pp. 212–213.

36. Picabia, "Un effet facile," pp. 1–2.

37. Denis Hollier has shown the manner in which Georges Bataille also shared such a fantasy of autogenous creation, an operation of "scissiparity" that Hollier dubs "the Caesarean." There are two Caesarean operations, according to Hollier, one that would eradicate the mother as the

principle of difference, and another that would itself become the principle of that difference, an "Icarian" versus a "Dionysiac" Caesarean. See Hollier, *Against Architecture*, pp. 169–170.

38. Derrida, "Restitutions," p. 371.

39. Georges Ribemont-Dessaignes, in an untitled book review of the work of Albert Einstein published in *Littérature*, new series no. 1 (1 March 1922), p. 18.

40. Francis Picabia, "Francis Merci!" *Littérature*, new series no. 8 (1 January 1923), pp. 16–17, reprinted in *Écrits II*, pp. 105–106.

41. Sanouillet, *Dada à Paris*, pp. 182–187.

42. From one of the memoirs of Germaine Everling ("C'était hier: Dada . . . ," *Les Oeuvres Libres* 109 [June 1955], p. 159), cited in Sanouillet, *Dada à Paris*, p. 186.

43. Depending on the source, the photograph is variously identified as part of the Dada event that occurred at either the manifestation at the Maison de l'Oeuvre in March or at the Salle Gaveau in May. Germaine Everling, for example, places the event at the Maison de l'Oeuvre, and claims that Breton was dressed up to read Picabia's "Manifeste Cannibale Dada" presented at that evening. Michel Sanouillet follows her in this identification. But it seems far more likely that Everling simply remembered the events incorrectly, as the manifesto by Picabia read by Breton at the Salle Gaveau, "Festival-Manifeste-Presbyte," actually thematizes an act of violence directed at the performer by the audience, the situation organized by the imagery of Picabia's target sign.

On Picabia's refusal to perform in the Dada manifestations (owing to his "nervous state," his lack of "physical courage"), necessitating Breton's performance of his manifestos, see Georges Ribemont-Dessaignes, *Déjà jadis*, pp. 71, 88.

44 Germaine Everling, *L'anneau de Saturne*, p. 122. This passage also contains the account of Tzara's reaction, and his verbal response.

45. Picabia, "Festival-Manifeste-Presbyte," *Cannibale* 2 (25 May 1920), pp. 17–18. If I am right about Breton's target performance occurring at the Festival Dada, he would have been reading this "manifesto" while holding up his sign.

46. Silverman, "Masochism and Male Subjectivity," p. 160.

47. André Breton, "Second Manifesto of Surrealism [1930]," *Manifestoes of Surrealism* (Ann Arbor: University of Michigan, 1969), p. 125.

---

48. On the *Soirée du Coeur à Barbe,* see Sanouillet, *Dada à Paris,* pp. 392–399.

49. Picabia, in *Cannibale* 1 (25 April 1920), p. 17.

50. Deleuze and Guattari, *Anti-Oedipus: Capitalism and Schizophrenia,* p. 89.

51. This trope was long ago established by Benjamin Buchloh, in his now-canonical essay, "Figures of Authority, Ciphers of Regression," in *Art since Modernism: Rethinking Representation,* ed. Brian Wallis (New York: New Museum of Contemporary Art, 1984), pp. 107–134.

52. Roger Vitrac, "Interview de Francis Picabia," *Les hommes du jour* (May 1923), p. 10, reprinted in *Écrits II,* p. 121.

53. Picabia, in *La Pomme de Pins* (25 February 1922), front cover.

54. On the mimetic as a critical strategy within Dada, see Hal Foster, "Dada Mime," *October* 105 (summer 2003), pp. 166–176.

55. Picabia, "Jesus dit à ces juifs," *La vie moderne* (25 February 1923), p. 1, reprinted in *Écrits II,* p. 112.

56. See Arnauld Pierre, "Picabia contre le retour à l'ordre," pp. 8–19.

57. Derrida, "Restitutions," p. 363.

58. The date inscribed next to Picabia's signature—5 July 1937—is a fantasy on Picabia's part, although the proto-fascist overtones of the work, its muscular male in a dominating salute, its general hypermasculinity (all those erect tails), have in retrospect come to make the date seem almost prophetic.

59. Borràs, *Francis Picabia,* p. 240. Another writer has speculated as well that the figure of Oedipus in *La Feuille de vigne* was meant to evoke Breton; see Jutta Martens, "Das Feigenblatt, Francis Picabia," *Kunst & Antiquitäten* 10 (1994), pp. 16–17.

60. Picabia, aphorism printed alongside the essay by Robert Desnos, "L'étoile au front," in *391* 17 (June 1924), p. 2.

61. The best articulation of this emerging project, characterized as "a subversive association between sexual trauma and artistic representation," is Hal Foster's "Convulsive Identity," *Compulsive Beauty,* pp. 57–98.

62. André Masson cited in Mark Polizzotti, *Revolution of the Mind,* p. 186. On the importance of the Dead Father in Dostoevsky's work, see Sigmund Freud, "Dostoevsky and Parricide," pp. 274–293.

63. On the unpacking of the Ernst collages, which took place at Picabia's house, see Breton's remembrance in "Artistic Genesis and Perspective of Surrealism," *Surrealism and Painting* (New York: Harper and Row, 1972), p. 64.

64. A methodological note is in order, to clarify at least one of the many things this epilogue is trying, in its very form, to achieve. If at times I seem to flirt quite openly with iconography (the reading of the *Tableau rastadada*), I now seem to skirt the biographical as the ground for an art historical shift. Both are misperceptions, perhaps encouraged by the work in question. The first reading I would not call iconographical at all, but keyed to the specific signifiers and their operative assembly within a symbolic economy; and the current shift being narrated in Picabia's project answers to concerns that have to do with a *structure* of rivalry, informed by biography, but not grounded there. Ultimately, I mean my epilogue's narrative to call up the notions of triangular desire and mimetic rivalry in the work of René Girard; see *Deceit, Desire, and the Novel,* trans. Yvonne Freccero (Baltimore: Johns Hopkins, 1965). Rosalind Krauss has harnessed mimetic rivalry for art historical interpretation in her chapter on Jackson Pollock in *The Optical Unconscious,* pp. 243–328. She has harnessed a similar structure directly from the work of Freud on anxiety to theorize pastiche in the moment I am now discussing, namely her account of pastiche as a kind of "reaction formation" in the rivalry between Picasso and Picabia. See Krauss, *The Picasso Papers,* pp. 89–210.

65. As Picabia's mother died when he was seven, Picabia was raised in a household that included his father, his uncle Maurice Davanne, and his grandfather. As cited by Borràs, Picabia was extremely depressed by this event and wrote to Breton: "Dear Breton: I am sending you this little poem. It is three o'clock in the morning, but sleep is impossible with all the hard blows life has been dealing me. This poem will tell you about it. If it gets to you in time, I would like you to publish *Mon oncle est mort* in the next issue of *Littérature.*" Borràs, *Picabia,* p. 239.

66. See the letter from Breton to Picabia dated 19 September 1923, reprinted in Sanouillet, *Dada à Paris,* pp. 575–577.

67. On *The Revolution by Night,* see Malcolm Gee, "Max Ernst, God, and 'The Revolution by Night,'" *Arts Magazine* (March 1981), pp. 85–91; Dawn Ades, "Between Dada and Surrealism: Painting in the 'Mouvement flou,'"; and William Camfield, *Max Ernst: Dada and the Dawn of Surrealism* (Houston: The Menil Collection, 1993).

68. See Camfield, *Max Ernst,* p. 153.

69. "Une lettre de mon grand-père," *391* 17 (June 1924), p. 4.

70. It was in the issue of *Littérature* from which Picabia's drawings were excluded, in the fall of 1923, that Breton had published "Erutarettil," a series of the names of such father figures.

71. Picabia, "391," *391* 17 (June 1924), p. 4.

72. Picabia, *Jésus-Christ Rastaquouère,* p. 27.

73. Picabia writes a passage on artists, men and women, with balls, big and small, in his essay "Premiere Heure," *Le mouvement accéléré* (4 November 1924), p. 1, reprinted in *Écrits II,* p. 157.

74. Picabia, "Réponses à Georges Herbiet," *This Quarter* 1, no. 3 (spring 1927), reprinted in *Écrits II,* p. 188.

75. Friedrich Nietzsche, *The Gay Science,* trans. Josefine Nauckhoff (Cambridge: Cambridge University Press, 2001), p. 120.

76. Picabia, "391," *391* 17 (June 1924), p. 4.

77. Picabia, *OUI NON OUI NON OUI NON* (Alès: P. A. Benoit, 1953), reprinted in *Écrits II,* p. 343.

78. Georges Bataille, "Chronique nietzschéenne," *Acéphale,* nos. 3–4 (July 1937), as cited in Hollier, *Against Architecture,* p. 184.

79. Walter Benjamin, *The Arcades Project* (Cambridge, Mass.: Harvard University Press, 1999), p. 82.

80. Andreas Huyssen, "Mass Culture as Woman: Modernism's Other," *After the Great Divide: Modernism, Mass Culture, Postmodernism* (Bloomington and Indianapolis: Indiana University Press, 1986).

Page numbers in italics indicate illustrations.

Failure (*cont.*)

  of meaning, 179

  and modes of sociability, 146

  of reproduction, 250, 252, 436n58

  treatise on, 345

Fantasy, 5, 310, 344–345, 348, 353, 356, 366, 368–369, 371–372, 390–391, 398

Farewell, 1, 9, 136, 401

Father, 12–13, 111, 116, 133, 154, 165, 178–180, 344, 347–348, 351, 353, 356–358, 365, 367–369, 371–372, 375, 377–379, 383–386, 388–391, 395. *See also* Economy, patriarchal; Equivalent, paternal; Male; Metaphor, paternal

  Dead, 113–114, 117, 160, 179, 348–349, 353, 379, 381, 388, 391, 404

  humiliated, 355

  joyous or prodigal, 344, 347, 351, 361, 367, 401

  loved, 349, 355, 388

  Name of the, 179, 344, 357

  not, 170

  of Surrealism, 403–404

Feasting, excessive, 6, *346*

Fer, Briony, 246

Fetishism, 97, 161, 167, 361–362, 364–366. *See also* Shoes

First World War. *See* World War I

Fish, 336

Fly shit, 75

Fontana, Lucio, 83

Formless, 9, 14, 86, 146

Foucault, Michel, 348, 357

Freud, Sigmund, 13, 114, 168, 170, 176–178, 307, 353, 355, 362, 364–365, 378

Fried, Michael, 83–84

Gesamtkunstwerk, 329–331, 446n68

Ghazarossian, Carl, xvi, 413n36

Gide, André, 376

Gift, 3, 22, 27, 86–87, 121–122, 125, 132, 199, 255, 276, 286, 319, 326, 341, 351, 363, 369, 371, 379, 388, 420n33

Gleizes, Albert, 43, 76

God, 38, 60, 128, 145–146, 289–290, 365, 371

Gold, 24, 26, 111–115, 121, 124–127, 129, 133, 143, 357

Goux, Jean-Joseph, 12–15, 24, 111–118, 125–131, 152, 170, 179, 348. *See also* Economy, symbolic; Equivalent, general; Unrepresentable

Graffiti, 87, 102, 106, 109, 118, 143, 145–148, 150–151, 208, 340

Gravity, 35, 38, 317, 325

Gris, Juan, 76

Ground, 50, 52, 55, 77–78, 80, 82, 88, 98, 128, 154, 229, 238, 262, 264, 274, 351, 362–363

  groundless, 130, 133, 177–178, 195, 206, 228, 244, 257, 268, 286, 295, 362, 428n18 (*see also* Abyss; Hole; Void)

Hausmann, Raoul, 345

Haviland, Paul, 16, 72, 101, 218, 229

Hegel, Georg Wilhelm Friedrich, 84, 86, 415n54

Heterogeneous, 114, 246, 278

Heterology, 86, 278, 415n51

Hole, 14, 35, 48, 50, 58, 66–67, 71, 75–76, 80, 82–83, 89, 109, 149, 190, 254, 260, 263–265, 330, 333, 361, 366–367, 373, 385, 400. *See also* Abyss; Ground, groundless; Void

pictorialization of, 23, 202, 217

reciprocal, 87

Recasting, 11–12, 23, 50, 139, 152–153, 227. *See also* Capital; Exchange; Money

Recoding, 12, 19, 67, 80, 82, 124, 195. *See also* Capital; Exchange; Money

Reification, 86, 101, 136, 238, 265. *See also* Capital; Exchange; Money

Relational, 11–12, 19–20, 22–24, 29, 86, 122, 130, 180, 206, 208–209, 244, 304, 318, 320, 329–330, 355

Renoir, Pierre-Auguste, 40, 99, 102, 111

Repasts, English, 2

Repression, 13, 15, 66, 167, 171, 176, 178, 180–181, 200, 225, 228, 244, 348, 395

Resurrection, 15, 106, 208, 217, 283, 306, 333, 336, 349, 357, 365, 368–369, 371, 381

Return to Order, 9, 122, 341, 381, 385, 400

Reversal, 10, 50, 72, 80, 93, 98–99, 104, 141, 175, 181, 184, 190, 200, 218, 230, 258, 264, 274, 276, 290, 295, 299–300, 308, 310–311, 313, 315, 317–318, 327, 329–333, 335–337, 344, 353, 355–356, 366–367, 376, 378

Ribemont-Dessaignes, Georges, 56, 91, 96, 218, 371

and razor-sharp cheeks, 345

Richter, Hans, 320

Rigaut, Jacques, 96, 151

Rivalry, 12, 112, 348, 379, 389, 391, 398–399, 452n64

Robespierre, Maximilian, 57

Rome, 8

Rorschach image, 38, 409n11

Rosenberg, Léonce, 76

Roussel, Raymond, *Impressions of Africa,* 5, 257

Routchine, Hania, 96, 147

Sadism, 32–33, 50, 246, 353, 358, 364–365, 367, 376–378, 386, 388, 391, 395, 398

Salon d'Automne, 136, 142, 205, 381, 384, 386

Salon des Indépendants, 50, 55, 57, 98, 142, 146, 205–206, 208–209, 225, 260, 283

Sanouillet, Michel, 45, 47, 66, 304, 376

Satie, Erik, 11, 282, 290, 293, 295, 299–300, 308, 329, 336, 391, 395

and furniture music, 324–325

and pornographic music, 295, 298, 304, 306

Vexations, 325

Saussure, Ferdinand de, 126, 169–170, 173, 176–177

Scatology, 35, 146, 175, 294, 381, 441n12

Scorched earth, 13

Secretions, 38, 371

Secrets, 16, 19, 35, 39, 50, 135, 205, 407n13. *See also* Enigma

Sennett, Mack, 306

Sharing of form, 12, 318–319, 325–327, 333, 446n63. *See also* Bersani, Leo; Correspondences; Silverman, Kaja

Shifters, 7, 19–20

Shoes

the abyss of, *354*

dancing, 361

as fetish, 361–362

high-heeled, 161, 299, 351, 361, 365–366

mother in the, 355, 365–366

Printed in the United States
by Baker & Taylor Publisher Services